The Many Faces of L'amour

Macho Mars and voluptuous Venus have woven their spell of love and passion throughout the ages. Their stories are told in the lives of lovers from every time and place, and every tale is as universal as it is unique. What drives us more than this divine, eternal force? How can we begin to understand the ways that it holds us in its power?

Through an astrological look at the many possible combinations of these two planets, *The Mars Venus Affair* lifts the veil and reveals the multitude of shapes and forms love can assume. A simple list tells you what signs apply to you and yours, and vivid descriptions of their effects are illustrated by revealing portraits of famous lovers throughout time.

Although the ways of love will always be a mystery, these ardent planets will at least provide some clues. Prepare to be fascinated, seduced—and enlightened!

About the Authors

Wendell and Linda Perry work and live in Kentucky. Wendell has studied astrology and the influence of the heavenly bodies on interpersonal relationships for twenty-five years. He is a member of the International Society for Astrological Research and has published articles in *Dell's Horoscope* and *The Mountain Astrologer*. Linda Perry is a member of the International Women's Writing Guild.

To Write to the Authors

If you wish to contact the authors or would like more information about this book, please write to the author in care of Llewellyn Worldwide, and we will forward your request. Both the authors and publisher appreciate hearing from you and learning of your enjoyment of this book and how it has helped you. Llewellyn Worldwide cannot guarantee that every letter written to the authors can be answered, but all will be forwarded. Please write to:

Wendell and Linda Perry
℅ Llewellyn Worldwide Ltd.
P.O. Box 64383, Dept. K517-7
St. Paul, MN 55164-0383, U.S.A.

Please enclose a self-addressed, stamped envelope for reply or $1.00 to cover costs.
If outside the U.S.A., enclose international postal reply coupon.

The Mars Venus Affair

Astrology's *Sexiest* Planets

Wendell Perry
Linda Perry

2000
Llewellyn Publications
St. Paul, Minnesota 55164-0383 U.S.A.

FIRST EDITION
First Printing, 2000

Cover design by William Merlin Cannon
Formatting by Karin Simoneau
Interior design and editing by Eila Savela

Library of Congress Cataloging-in-Publication Data
Perry, Wendell.
    The Mars/Venus affair : astrology's sexiest planets / Wendell Perry, Linda Perry.—1st ed.
      p. cm.
    Includes bibliographical references and index.
    ISBN 1–56718–517–7
    1. Astrology and sex. 2. Venus (Planet)—Miscellanea. 3. Mars (Planet)—Miscellanea. I.
    Perry, Linda, 1952– II. Title.
BF1729.S4 P47 2000
133.5'34—dc21
                                                           99-054273
                                                                      CIP

Llewellyn Publications
A Division of Llewellyn Worldwide, Ltd.
P.O. Box 64383, Dept. K517-7
St. Paul, Minnesota, 55164–0383, U.S.A.
www.llewellyn.com

 Printed in the United States of America

Contents

Chapter 2
Mars in Taurus: The Sensualist 35

Chapter 3
Mars in Gemini: The Sexual Technician 71

Chapter 4
Mars in Cancer: The Sentimentalist   101

Chapter 5
Mars in Leo: The Maestro of Love   133

Chapter 6
Mars in Virgo: The Back-to-Basics Lover 167

Chapter 7
Mars in Libra: The Perfect Lover 203

Chapter 8
Mars in Scorpio: The Powerhouse of Passion   237

Chapter 9
Mars in Sagittarius: The Love Child   275

Chapter 10
Mars in Capricorn: The Slave of Love   311

Chapter 11
Mars in Aquarius: The Sexual Liberator   351

Chapter 12
Mars in Pisces: The Love Addict   387

Preface

I've never liked abstractions. When I make a judgement about an issue in astrology, I have to see how it functions in real life. Twenty-five years ago when I wanted to learn about the Sun Sign Leo, I looked at the lives of people born under that sign like Napoleon Bonaparte and Benito Mussolini. When I was curious about Aquarius, I read about Sun Sign Aquarians like Abraham Lincoln and Thomas Edison. This was how I began to learn about astrology even before I picked up my first astrological textbook. Real life is not always the most consistent teacher, but the lessons we discover from it are not easily forgotten.

Because of my aversion to abstractions, the first thing I did when I became serious about astrology was to compile lists. I created all kinds of lists. I made lists of people having the same Sun Signs, the same Rising Signs, the same aspects and house placements, and so on. Today computers are capable of making lists like these in a flash, but twenty-five years ago I had to shuffle through hundreds of horoscopes on paper and patiently pencil each entry into my notebooks. I never interpreted a horoscope without first looking at my lists. As far as I was concerned, they were better than any textbook.

This book began with two of those lists. When I was exploring sexuality within horoscopes, I decided to combine my list of Venus Signs with my list of Mars Signs. I was disturbed to see that I had a lot of blank spaces. While some combinations had several representatives, others had few or none. I might have a lot of people with Venus in Virgo but none with Mars in Gemini and Venus in Virgo. Now, if I were not a compulsive kind of a guy this probably wouldn't have bothered me, but I am a compulsive kind of a guy. So, I went to public libraries and went through their biography sections to look for birth data for people who weren't already on my lists. Of course, I found many people about whom I knew nothing. I had to stop and read their biographies. I then made notes about the sex lives of these individuals. I had worked my way up to Claire Booth Luce, when I decided that the facts gathered could provide valuable information for others to use as examples when searching for answers about sexuality and motivation through astrology.

It was fortunate that I got this idea at a time when I also happened to be married to a woman with exceptional skills as a writer and editor. Of course, I had been married to her for twenty years but, along with being compulsive, I can also be incredibly slow!

In the course of gathering information for this book, I feel that I've made one significant discovery: the typical "scientific" method of categorizing human sexuality only by behavior doesn't work. We are simply missing the point when we assume that people who are aroused by "x" are always "y." The magic of human nature is that people do the same things for very different reasons, and different things for the same reason. If we really want to understand human behavior, sexual and otherwise, we have to look at motivation.

Astrology gives us a unique ability to see and judge that motivation. It allows us to look past an individual's behavior to the emotional quirks and mental intrigue that prodded it into existence. In fact, it is probably only through the study of astrology that we have a chance to observe the infinite variety of ways we humans adapt to any single motivation.

This is why we must avoid believing that any astrological grouping is likely to exhibit, or even have tendencies toward, any particular kind of sexual behavior. People with Mars or Venus in Aries are drawn to extreme behavior but that doesn't mean these individuals are bound to choose, or even desire, the types of extremes favored by the Marquis de Sade or Algernon Swinburne. There are many ways of seeking the quality of extremism that is symbolized by Aries, just as there are many ways of seeking the qualities represented by Aquarius or Sagittarius. Everyone with Venus in Aquarius is not going to be kinky, and your Mars in Sagittarius neighbor is not likely to be a pedophile. It might be convenient or even entertaining to think that an astrological group has certain sexual tendencies, but it is also dangerously misguided.

It's also been my experience that many people assume that astrology is about prediction, and that a clear understanding of a person's horoscope should allow any astrologer to always know what that person "is going to do" or "what will happen" to that person. I've never seen it that way. I'm constantly surprised by the way in which people react to the astrological influences in their chart. They make choices—sometimes good choices, sometimes incredibly stupid choices—based on the motivations provided within their horoscope. I've never been able to make anything more than an educated guess about what those choices might be.

Our book provides 144 examples of individuals with choices presented to them by the "luck" of their birth data along with environmental and genetic influences. We believe you will gain a better understanding of your own sexuality and that of your lovers and friends through the enjoyment of this book.

Wendell Perry

Introduction

You already know your Sun Sign. You know which of the twelve signs of the zodiac (Aries, Taurus, Gemini, etc.) the Sun occupied on the day you were born. You say "I'm a Virgo," and probably think there's not much else to astrology—but there is. There's a whole sky full of objects—planets, the moon, and asteroids—and each one of them has a special place in our astrological make-up.

We're going to tell you about two of these celestial objects: the planets Mars and Venus. Mars and Venus are of particular interest to astrologers because they traditionally symbolize love and sexual energy.

This book is about love, sex, passion, and intimacy. It's about the way we treat, and seek to be treated by, the people we love. Your Sun Sign will tell you part of this story because the Sun is always the most potent symbol in the horoscope.

Mars and Venus will tell us much more about your love life, and perhaps reveal some things that will surprise people who only know you by your Sun Sign. (Your Mars Sign and your Venus Sign will often be different than your Sun Sign.) For example, a Sun Sign Taurus is typically a stable and practical person with strong physical appetites and a conservative outlook. A Sun Sign Taurus with Mars in Sagittarius and Venus in Aries tends to be much more of a risk taker when it comes to romance. Sexually, this person will favor light-hearted fun over heavy sensuality, and variety over stability.

Mars

It might seem odd to be talking about Mars when discussing the gentle arts of love, for the planet Mars is named for the god of war often associated with violence and bloodletting. Yet Mars is an essential player in our sexual make-up. Traditionally, Mars is associated with the "active" or "masculine" side of sex. It symbolizes passion, sexual drive, and lust. Astrologers are sometimes reluctant to talk about the relevance of Mars to sexuality. It brings forth images of brutality and conquest that are anything but politically correct. As rough and raw as Mars may be (particularly in some signs), you can't have a sex drive without it; it is as essential to the sexuality of women as it is to men. Lust is not the province of any one gender, and thankfully so.

Following this introduction, our book is arranged with twelve chapters based on Mars in each of the twelve Sun Signs. We begin each chapter with a description of how Mars generally manifests itself within that sign and then describe how that placement of Mars reacts with each of the twelve Venus Signs. This might give you the impression that we think Mars is more important than Venus. This is not the case. We could have easily reversed this arrangement. We chose Mars because it is the more active element. Individuals use their Mars sign influences when they initiate relationships or sexual contact. Mars also reflects our initial responses to the romantic overtures of other people. In other words, Mars tends to be the primary force in our sexual transactions, while the influence of Venus is more additive and provisional.

Venus

Venus is traditionally associated with the "passive" or "feminine" side of our sexual nature. Its influence is most readily seen in the things that we do to make ourselves more beautiful, pleasant, and appealing to everyone, particularly the people we love. Venus refines the raw energy of Mars and shapes it into a force that attempts to conquer the object of our affection in the truest sense: by making him or her glad to be overcome. Venus also represents our enjoyment of sexual pleasure for its own sake. Through its influence, we are usually able to divert the Martian drive for absolute satisfaction and take the time to savor the wonders of sexual contact, both physically and psychologically.

Just as the energy of Mars is traditionally associated with men, Venus is often thought of as more evident in females. The fact is that men who have been able to separate themselves from the immediate physical demands of survival have always sought to introduce a little Venus into their lives. From the Babylonian princes with their oiled beards, to the Renaissance knight with his brightly colored tights and codpiece, to the modern ensemble of a tight pair of jeans and a torso by Soloflex, men have reveled in their Venus signs, and thankfully so.

Mars and Venus

When it comes to sex, Mars and Venus work as a team. For any individual who is reasonably mature and decently integrated into the world, the act of love is a combination of the "active" and the "passive," of the "feminine" and the "masculine." It doesn't make any difference if it's a passing flirtation or the sex act itself—the energies of Venus and Mars intermingle to the point that any attempt to distinguish one from the other is hopeless. Therefore, the only sensible way to observe how Mars and Venus work in our lives is to consider all twelve Mars signs in combination with all twelve Venus signs. This gives us 144 different types of lovers. This book discusses all of them.

How to Find Your Mars and Venus Signs

This is where things get a little tricky for the novice. The popularity of Sun Sign astrology is partially due to the fact that Earth's path around the Sun is fairly regular. This means that everyone born on July fourth in any given year is going to have Cancer as their Sun Sign. The positions of Mars and Venus relative to Earth are not nearly so neat and predictable. For example: if you were born on July 4, 1965, you have Mars in Libra and Venus in Leo, but if you were born on July 4, 1966, your Mars is in Gemini and so is your Venus.

In order to find your Mars and Venus signs, consult the Mars/Venus chart in the appendix at the back of this book. The chart is divided into two sides within a column: the left side of the column contains the Mars placement during a given year; the right side of the column contains the Venus placement during the same year. So, to find your placement, do the following:

1. Find the year in which you were born within the chart. (Let's use October 1, 1968, as an example.) Read down the chart until you reach 1968 in the left side of the column. Look for the approximate "placement" of October 1.

   The chart lists the dates on which each planet "changed" signs during that year. You can see in the left side of the column that in 1968 Mars passed from Leo to

Virgo on September 21, and from Virgo to Libra on November 9. If you were born on October 1 of that year, you have Mars in Virgo. (October 1 falls between September 21 and November 9 in this example.)

2. To the right of that column, you will see the changes for Venus. You see that Venus moved from Libra to Scorpio on September 26, and from Scorpio to Sagittarius on October 21. With your October 1 birth date this means you have Venus in Scorpio. The chart covers dates ranging from 1920 to 2010.

3. Turn to the corresponding chapter and page number for your Mars/Venus combination listed in the table of contents at the front of the book.

4. Read the information under "General Characteristics" in the chapter associated with your Mars sign. This gives you an overall general description of Mars in that sign.

5. Find your Venus placement within that same chapter and read its description. You'll find the Venus placements under headings like this:

    If you have Mars in Virgo with Venus in Scorpio you are . . .
    the Basically Scandalous Lover

6. Read the case history that follows your particular Mars/Venus combination. A case history is a brief sexual biography of an individual having that same combination of Mars/Venus. Some Mars/Venus combinations list an additional celebrity or celebrities who share that same Mars/Venus combination, though not all of the combinations contain this information.

7. Have some additional fun and look up and read the Mars/Venus combinations for your lover, friends, parents, children, and future offspring!

What do you do if you were born on the actual day either Mars or Venus changed signs? You can do one of two things. You can read both the signs involved to determine which one you think fits you best, or you can have a horoscope charted for yourself. A professional horoscope is drawn for your specific time and place of birth, and it will tell you where all your planets are, including Mars and Venus. This is not nearly as difficult an option as it might sound. In this wonderful age of computers, it takes only a few minutes to make an accurate chart. There are many astrologers ready to provide this service.

Case Histories in This Book

Astrology is a study of potentials. Horoscopes don't tell us what we have to be. They give us a range of choices intermingled with our environment and genetics. It is always our responsibility to make the best of our opportunities. Of course, this is never as easy as it sounds. Nothing brings that difficulty into sharper focus than looking at the life of another person who had choices similar to our own and what he or she did with those opportunities.

That's why we've provided a life example for each of the 144 Mars and Venus types. After you read the general description of your Mars type and the specific section for that Mars sign in combination with your Venus sign, you can examine the love life of someone that had or has the same combination.

Before we go any further we need to say a word about these case histories. Perhaps the most difficult part of compiling the information in this book was finding a representative example for all 144 Mars/Venus types. This was because sex is a private matter. Most of us take precautions to keep it that way. It is usually only through a misfortune that a person's sexuality becomes public knowledge. The most common of these "misfortunes" is fame.

All of our examples are public figures—often people whose lives have been studied top-to-bottom for many years. Of course, even among the very famous there are many people who have managed to keep their sex lives secret. Consequently, many of our examples come from the arts. Poets, artists, writers, and other creative people can hardly escape exposing their attitudes about love, relationships, and sensuality to public view. The works of painters like Gauguin or Rembrandt, or poets like Baudelaire are, in many ways, outright confessions of their attitudes toward sex.

Then there is another group—people who are famous largely, or perhaps only, because of their sex lives. In this group we include individuals like Casanova, Jane Digby, the Marquis de Sade, and Baron Sacher-Masoch—people who had the courage or the self-indulgence to make sex and/or love the primary focus of their lives. The way in which they expressed Mars and Venus is often grossly exaggerated and certainly cannot be considered "typical." There is still much we can learn from them. Whether we approve of their lifestyles or not, we can view these extreme individuals as pioneers whose sexual histories reveal both the joys and the potential errors of their Mar/Venus types to the fullest.

Finally, in choosing these examples we have assumed that all ways of loving are equal. We have made no distinction between heterosexual love, homosexual love, or any other way of loving. No Mars/Venus type is inherently indicative of any kind of sexual preference. There is no need to take offense if you find your example is homosexual while you are heterosexual (or vice versa). If you read carefully, we are sure you will find that your attitude toward sex and love have more in common with the individual in the case history than you might have ever imagined. After all, Mars and Venus in a horoscope also represent the universal need for companionship throughout humanity.

How Close Is This to "Serious" Astrology?

The primary purpose of this book is entertainment. Hopefully you'll also learn a little about astrology while you're having fun reading about your Mars/Venus type and the combinations pertaining to your friends and family. For the serious astrologer, the signs occupied by Mars and Venus are just parts of a multifaceted, multilayered image that is represented by the horoscope. Nothing stands alone in astrology. This means, for example, that your Venus in Taurus could be strongly influenced by the planet Pluto, a factor that would add a touch of Scorpio to its function, or your Mars in Gemini could be closely aspected by Neptune, which would give your Mars a bit of a Piscean flavor.

This is why it's a good idea to keep reading even after you've found your Mars/Venus type. Read all the possible Venus combinations within your Mars chapter. Then read how your Venus placement works within each of the other eleven chapters about Mars. Not only will you learn more about how your particular Mars/Venus combination works, you will also get a chance to observe how a variety of people dealt with the problems, privileges, and opportunities posed by Mars/Venus combinations.

Enjoy!

Chapter 1

Mars in Aries
The Sexual Extremist

General Characteristics

Mars in Aries Lovers often appear to be a bit out of control—that's just the way they like it. They enjoy getting carried away by sex, being swept up in its energy and physical urgency. You can't rankle Mars in Aries Lovers by saying that they don't know what they're doing. "So much the better," they will answer, for nothing takes the thrill out of sex more quickly for these Lovers than knowing where it will end or having everything under control. By their standards, good sex means losing control by creating situations in which his or her partner— and anyone else unlucky enough to get too close to the action—is sent headlong into a maelstrom of trouble and ecstasy.

Given their headlong approach to love, it is not surprising that this Mars type often ends up in troublesome relationships. Once again, the Mars in Aries Lover will answer, "So much the better." This is a Lover who cannot abide being too comfortable. A relationship which has no contention, pain, struggle, or sorrow hardly seems worth pursuing. Thus, these Lovers are frequently found in impossible romantic situations, making one bad choice after another, but loving it.

Why do they love it so? Why is it that they insist on arguments, trouble, and even pain in their sexual relationships? For Mars in Aries Lovers, sex that just feels good is a waste of precious time. Sensation for its own sake means very little to them and the joys of the flesh have only the most minimal allure. Sex must be coupled with strong emotions and extraordinary situations to satisfy these radical Lovers. There has to be drama: a sense of dire need, unstoppable passion, and impending drastic measures in order to lift sex out of the sensual commonplace and transform it into an experience worth remembering.

These are competitive, challenge-oriented Lovers. Typically, they are drawn to the partner who is hardest to get—the one who initially says no or who seems most unlikely to respond. In some cases this competitiveness becomes a major handicap. It compels these Lovers to regard the people they sleep with as trophies and to measure their own ability as lovers solely by the number and variety of their sexual contacts. Sometimes this tendency to see love as a challenge can have happy results. It allows the Mars in Aries Lover to approach relationships with an excitement that is endlessly renewed. As long as the relationship is moving, as long as it is a constantly unfolding process or even an ongoing battle, these Lovers never lose interest.

Mars in Aries individuals can be very desirable and active Lovers due to their fiery passions and endless hunger for excitement. Because their enjoyment of sex is more dependent on psychological factors than physical pleasures, these Lovers are also capable of withdrawing from sex for extended periods of time. It's not that they lose their capacity for passion. It's just that they can't get excited about sex that isn't wrapped in a challenge. Sex without fire is worse than no sex at all for these Lovers. But when the right kind of relationship comes along, it is truly amazing how quickly the fire reignites.

If you have Mars in Aries with Venus in Aries you are . . . the Untamed Extremist

You have no capacity for soft words or gentle persuasion. You win hearts with the explosive force of your ego or not at all. The intensity of your lovemaking, along with your aggressive, sometimes even belligerent approach to relationships, will likely frighten away many prospective partners. But those brave enough to weather the storms will find you a passionate, caring, and fiercely loyal Lover.

The real problem in your sex life is finding a stopping place. You develop intense bonds with your sexual partners but you rarely give yourself a chance to stop and enjoy the fruits of these relationships. You are always moving away from, or struggling against, comfort and complacency. You are a restless and destructively inconsistent Lover who often has difficulty holding on to love, even with all your passion and loyalty.

Case History

Charles Baudelaire (French poet, art critic, and translator noted for his violent and extravagant imagery. Author of Les Fleurs du Mal). *Born April 9, 1821, at 3 P.M. in Paris, France (de Jonge 1976).*

Baudelaire's father was an ex-priest who married late and died when Baudelaire was six. Left to fend for themselves, Baudelaire and his mother developed an extremely strong and affectionate bond. Unfortunately for Baudelaire, his beloved mother remarried. Baudelaire got along poorly with his stepfather and, for the rest of his life, resented his mother's defection.

When he was eighteen, Baudelaire was kicked out of school because of his rebellious attitude. His stepfather sent him away on a voyage to the Far East but this only increased the angry youngster's eccentricity. When he returned, he quickly established himself as a dandy and a libertine. Clothes became his passion and he spent indecent sums of money on fine furniture, art, and the various accouterments of his new lifestyle.

Baudelaire had inherited a small fortune from his natural father but, by the time he was twenty-three, half of his capital was squandered and he was beset by huge debts. His mother and stepfather had the wayward young man declared incompetent and gave control of his fortune to a trustee. This arrangement allowed Baudelaire a small income but did not address his debts. Baudelaire's finances remained a shambles for the remainder of his life. He was constantly harried by creditors and often forced to create new debts in order to keep old creditors at bay.

Early in his career as a dandy, Baudelaire acquired an African mistress named Jeanne Duval. Duval was an actress of sorts who was noted for her sensuous charm. At first Baudelaire was able to keep her in a luxurious apartment but, when he was stripped of his money, he and Duval began living together in much reduced circumstances. Oddly enough, this shocking reversal only strengthened the bond between Duval and Baudelaire. They remained a couple for ten years. Baudelaire continued to give her love and support for the rest of his life.

Duval was not an easygoing woman. She had no appreciation of the writer's new commitment to poetry and literature and she continually badgered him to find a better way of making money. Often Baudelaire had to work while she slept, or he stayed with a friend in order to escape her nagging. Duval also stole from her lover, lied to him, and was constantly unfaithful. However, Baudelaire seemed undeterred by the difficulty of this relationship. He celebrated Duval in his poetry as much for her coldness and cruelty as for her extraordinary sexual charms.

Both Duval and Baudelaire had syphilis. It appears that the poet contracted the disease before he met Duval and possibly infected her. The disease slowly destroyed the health of both lovers, though the toll it took on the once beautiful Duval was perhaps more dramatic. However, it was not the sudden decline in her physical charms that caused Baudelaire to separate from his "black Venus." Rather, at thirty-one, he finally decided that Duval would never give him the peace he needed to work.

Many of his friends observed that although Baudelaire loved to flirt and make sexual challenges to women, he held the sex act itself in contempt. Even though his poetry is filled with images of passionate sexual intercourse, his approach to sex was largely cerebral. He liked to go to the streets where prostitutes met their clients and coolly observe their transactions. Some of his friends went so far as to call Baudelaire a "virgin" poet, but there is ample evidence that, on occasion, the writer did more than just observe prostitutes.

After his break with Duval, Baudelaire began to send anonymous letters and poetry to Apollonie Sabatier, the voluptuous concubine of a man of wealth. His correspondence contained gentle literary declarations of spiritual love, accompanied by a brutal fantasy of sadistic lovemaking. Sabatier was intrigued and, once Baudelaire announced himself, she was anxious to meet him in the flesh. After they met and had sex, the poet suddenly withdrew from the relationship, declaring that he could not continue loving her spiritually as his "white Venus" now that he knew her as a real woman.

Baudelaire had a brief affair with an actress (who became his "green-eyed Venus") and tried once more to set up house with Duval, to no avail. At thirty-six he published *Les Fleurs du Mal*, a book of poetry which he had carefully put together in the hopes of making a literary coupe. Baudelaire planned to shock his audience with his unusual, violently sexual imagery and modernistic themes. Instead, the shock he expected turned into public outrage and Baudelaire was prosecuted as a pornographer.

After the disastrous publication of *Les Fleurs du Mal*, Baudelaire returned to Duval. Her condition was worsening. He saw to it she was admitted to a hospital where her syphilitic paralysis could be treated. He continued to find comfort and a sentimental release in her company even though he could not bear to stay with her very long. When he was forty-one, Baudelaire also became paralyzed by syphilis. He spent his remaining years as an invalid, cared for by his mother. He died at the age of forty-six.

Other Examples

Karen "Isak" Dinesen *(Danish writer whose novel* Out of Africa *recounted her impetuous love affair with a "great white hunter"). Born April 17, 1885 (Encyclopedia Britannica 1997).*

Orson Welles *(actor and maker of the movie* Citizen Kane *who survived a volatile marriage with film star Rita Hayworth). Born May 6, 1915 (Celebrity Birthday Guide, 4th edition, by Axiom Information Services, Ann Arbor, Michigan, 1997).*

If you have Mars in Aries with Venus in Taurus you are . . . the Undercover Extremist

Yours is a difficult combination. A sensualist at heart, you don't really approve of the headlong recklessness of your sexual nature. You would like to slow down and give your senses ample time to drink in each erotic experience. But you find that your Mars in Aries nature runs well only in high gear and the more you try to control it, the more ungainly and muddled you appear. You are among the most practical Mars in Aries Lover but, unfortunately, your actions often give little evidence of this wisdom.

On the positive side, in the right situation and with the right partner, your unique combination of sensual patience and volcanic passion can make you a gifted Lover. And there is a sweetness and soft conventionality about your sexual nature that allows you to get away with sexual extremes that might land other Mars in Aries Lovers in jail. If you can learn from your frustrations and build on your strengths, your capacity for erotic expression is unlimited.

Case History

Edward, Duke of Windsor *(King Edward VIII—British monarch who stunned the world when he gave up his throne to marry an American divorcée). Born June 23, 1894, at 9:55 P.M. in Richmond Park, England (Higham 1988; Zeigler 1991).*

It's probably safe to say that no king in the making has a normal childhood, but Edward's may have been more difficult than necessary. Both of his parents believed that duty came before love and they raised their eldest son accordingly. His father was particularly distant and authoritative.

When Edward was eight his female caretakers were replaced by men in the hope that the constant exposure to manly virtue might cure the boy of his girlish sensitivity and emotionalism. As a result of this ploy, the Prince had little contact with the opposite sex during his early adolescence and remained painfully shy in their presence. As he grew older and developed into a small but handsome young prince, Edward's closeness to his male mentors fueled rumors that he was a homosexual. Actually, Edward showed little interest in sex of any sort until he turned twenty-two.

At that point Edward was in France, serving in the British Army during World War I. Bored and frustrated at the degree to which he was insulated from danger, he looked for diversions. Friends introduced him to an experienced prostitute, who spent a few evenings helping the shy, awkward Prince work through his reserve. After this breakthrough, Edward, who had earlier confessed that he seldom thought of sex, became virtually obsessed with women. He returned to Paris as often as possible to revisit his teacher and to strike up new relationships. The intensity and guilelessness of his ardor often got the better of him. On at least one occasion, a pretty young Parisian blackmailed him after he had written a series of passionate and thoroughly indiscrete love letters to her.

At the same time that Edward was discovering the joys of casual sex in Paris (joys he would often revisit during his life as a bachelor), he was also entering into his first serious love affair. Marion Coke was more than a decade older than the dapper Prince, and she was married. But he found great comfort in her presence and, for a time, he favored her maternal appeal over that of younger, more attractive women.

As inexperienced as Edward was in regard to sex, he was always aware of the advantage that his position in life gave him in relationships. Even though he continually professed love for Marion Coke, he also found time to fall in love with other well-born, young women. Edward's flirtations were, of course, a matter of much concern for both his parents and the press. Everyone wanted to know which of his girl friends might become the next queen. But Edward always seemed most drawn to those women least likely to fulfill the requirements of his rank.

This was particularly true with his next major love affair. Freda Dudley Ward was a small, pretty woman who sometimes gave the impression of being thoughtless and carefree. In reality she was an intelligent and strong-willed woman who controlled the pace of her affair with the prince from the very beginning. She later confessed that she could have made the prince her slave if it had pleased her. There were some things, however, that Ward couldn't change: her common birth, and the fact that she was already married. There was no doubt in either her mind or in Edward's that his parents would never allow them to marry, even though the royal couple came to appreciate the calming influence Ward had on their moody and petulant son.

After four passionate years, Ward tired of the prince's fervent affection. From her point of view the relationship was going nowhere and she sought to withdraw. Edward refused to let the affair end. He clung to his attachment to Ward for several more years despite her cool-ness. He refused to entertain the thought of beginning a new relationship until he met Thelma Furness, another thoroughly unsuitable, married woman.

During these years, thanks to his boyish good looks and stylish wardrobe, Edward became something of an international sex symbol. However, accounts of his sexual prowess were hardly impressive. Not only was he bothered by what he diagnosed as an "inferiority com-plex," but he was also prone to premature ejaculation. His preference for women who were experienced in sexual matters is evidence that he was looking for someone who could take the lead in lovemaking. It wasn't until he met Wallis Simpson at the age of thirty-nine that the prince found a woman who was capable of really taking charge of his sex life.

Simpson was already the veteran of two marriages and several love affairs by the time she met the prince. She was an ambitious American who was intent on using her second hus-band's contacts and moderate fortune to advance socially. When Edward began to show interest in her, she was more than willing to put aside her indulgent husband and join him. What made this relationship different from Edward's earlier flirtations with married women was sex. Simpson's first husband had introduced her to various oriental techniques of pro-longing intercourse and delaying ejaculation. It was rumored she even spent time in a high-class Hong Kong brothel to perfect the art. For the sexually befuddled Prince of Wales, her skills proved to be a godsend.

Although no one knows the exact nature of the sexual relationship between Edward and Simpson, it was immediately obvious that the common-born American dominated the prince in a manner few found appropriate. There were rumors Simpson encouraged Edward's foot fetish and that the couple played games in which the prince dressed himself in a diaper and pretended to be an infant. In the end, the smitten prince was so much under the spell of his new mistress that he was willing to do whatever was necessary in order to keep her by his side.

When Edward was forty-one, he became king when his father died. To the utter dismay of his court, the new monarch immediately made it clear that he intended to make Mrs. Simpson his queen as soon as she divorced her husband. It was quickly evident that there were many powerful people who were intent on blocking this match. Not only was Simpson a commoner, an American, and a divorcée, she also had a rather unsavory past and suspi-cious political contacts with fascist Italy and Germany. Finally, Edward recognized that he would have to choose between marrying Simpson and being king. To the surprise of every-one, he chose the former.

Many regarded Edward's decision to choose love over his throne as the epitome of romance. Others regarded it as a foolish and self-serving act. But for Edward and Wallis, his abdication created a bond between them that nothing could break. They spent the rest of their lives proving to the world that they were right and that love was worth the most painful sacrifice. Edward remained Wallis' dutiful husband until he died at the age of seventy-seven.

Another Example

Walt Whitman (*American poet noted for his celebration of simple beauty and for his homo-erotic imagery). Born May 31, 1819 (Celebrity Birthday Guide).*

If you have Mars in Aries with Venus in Gemini you are . . . the Resourceful Extremist

You are a tricky Mars in Aries Lover. You go through the motions of putting it all on the line and swooping headfirst into love but you still manage to maintain a sense of intellectual distance between yourself and all the crazy things you are doing. To some degree this makes you a supremely enjoyable Lover who blends all-out intensity with plenty of fun. But there is also an element of duplicity in your sexual nature. In your drive for extreme experiences you are prone to promise much more than you intend to deliver.

You may be the most restless and easily distracted of the Mars in Aries Lovers. You have a taste for immediate gratification that often makes you seem less than perfectly loyal. However, physical sex is always a secondary allurement for you. Ideas are what really turn you on. The person who wishes to hold your attention must be prepared to continually fire your imagination.

Case History

Golda Meir (*Golda Maboritz Meyerson—Russian-born, American-educated Jew who capped a lifetime of political accomplishment by becoming Prime Minister of Israel). Born May 3, 1898, in Kyyiv, Russia, now the Ukraine (Martin 1988; Slater 1981).*

After a fearful, poverty-stricken childhood in Russia, Meir fled to Milwaukee with her family when she was eight. She quickly adapted to the freedom of the New World. When she reached fourteen she escaped her domineering mother by joining her elder sister in Denver. When the rigidity of her sister became onerous, the teenage Meir got a job in a factory and began living on her own.

One of the points of contention between Meir and her elder sister was the fact that Meir was not shy about going out with the many young men who called on her. Blessed with a striking figure and sparkling eyes, the self-possessed young Meir had no difficulty attracting men. Many found it an enigma when she chose a puny, balding intellectual named Morris Meyerson as her beau. Meyerson brought a keen mind and a great enthusiasm for the arts to their relationship. For the rest of her life Meir considered him one of her most important teachers. But the two youngsters had little in common as lovers other than their Jewish heritage and their intellectual curiosity.

Meyerson and Meir became engaged when she was seventeen, just before she returned to Milwaukee and her parents. The engagement quickly settled into a long, erudite argument, often conducted through correspondence. Back in Milwaukee Meir discovered her talents as a public speaker and her ability to organize people around a cause. She also discovered Zionism—the notion that the natural home for the Jewish people was Palestine. She became an ardent participant in the movement. Meyerson was not a Zionist and he sharply disagreed with many of Meir's most heartfelt beliefs. Yet their relationship thrived in the midst of these differences. The more Meyerson argued with her, the more convinced Meir became that he was her one true love.

Meir and Meyerson were married when she was nineteen, after Meyerson finally agreed to emigrate to Palestine with her. They spent the next few years saving money for the trip and, when Meir was twenty-three, the couple sailed for the Holy Land. They joined a communal farm in the desert called a kibbutz.

Life on the kibbutz was hard. The climate was brutal, the work was backbreaking and mundane, there was little or no privacy, and the commune members were in constant danger. Meir loved it. Inflamed by her cause, she found no task too great or too lowly. She quickly gained the confidence of her fellow pioneers and became a leader who was frequently asked to speak for the kibbutz in Tel Aviv.

Unfortunately for Meir, her husband was a far less enthusiastic pioneer. He was physically unprepared for the work and found the lack of privacy unbearable. The argument between Meyerson and Meir began anew, though now it was Meyerson who seemed to have the upper hand. Meir wanted children, but Meyerson would not allow her to become pregnant in the kibbutz where child-rearing, like everything else, was a communal effort.

The kibbutz was largely a masculine enterprise. The majority of the members appeared to be young, single men. The rules regarding sexual behavior tended to be liberal, in keeping with the advanced, socialist ideals held by most of the participants. Even though Meir never admitted to being unfaithful to her husband during this period, she certainly had ample opportunity, and rumors circulated.

When Meir was twenty-five, Meyerson suffered a physical breakdown. Doctors advised her that he could not return to the kibbutz. Even though it broke her heart, Meir agreed to join him in Tel Aviv, where they attempted to start a new life. Two children quickly followed but the young couple found it difficult to make a living. Then, at the age of twenty-nine, Meir was recruited to rejoin the Zionist movement.

Meir's new job required her to be away from home, which caused the relationship between Meir and Meyerson to finally reach a breaking point. By now the couple stopped arguing and their time together was typically spent in silence. The Meyersons never divorced, but from this point on their marriage was largely a pretense.

By the time she reached her thirties, Meir was working among the powerful, visionary men who made up the political core of the movement toward a Jewish state. In this largely male preserve, Meir thrived. At first she was valued because of her command of the English language but her political skills soon earned the respect of everyone around her. Meir always considered the cause of feminism as secondary to her service to the Jewish people. This was largely because, in the course of her own career, she had no difficulty being accepted as an equal even by the most egotistical males.

Still young and attractive, Meir's presence among these powerful men (many of whom were noted philanderers) naturally inspired gossip. Some observers went so far as to call Meir "the mattress." These whispers never bothered Meir. Even though she was discreet about her affairs, she refused to be ashamed of them. At the same time, however, she never let any of these sexual contacts interfere with her service to the cause of Zionism.

Early in her career she began an affair with David Remez, the man who had largely sponsored her rise from poverty to power. This affair continued for many years but did not stop Meir from having other lovers. One was a fiery Zionist named Shazar Rubashov. Shazar was noted for his flamboyant style and intellectual range. In some ways he was an assertive, virile version of Meyerson. Later, in her forties, she had an affair with Yaacov Hazan. Hazan was a Zionist but otherwise his politics were quite different from those of Meir. Their romantic relationship continued for many years, even though they were frequently political enemies.

Before the establishment of the State of Israel, Meir was instrumental in raising money in America for the cause. Afterward, she served the government as a diplomat and as foreign minister. When she was seventy she became the head of the Labor Party. At this point Meir wanted to retire but, when she was called to serve as prime minister, she complied. Meir led the Israeli nation for five years, retiring at the age of seventy-six. She died four years later.

Other Examples

Gustav Klimt (*Viennese painter who became famous during the 1890s for his highly decorative and sexually charged murals*). *Klimt's female nudes are often openly erotic and sexually* *voracious. They had a powerful impact on the men in his audience who viewed the increased independence of the "new women" of the age with profound trepidation. In his own sex life, Klimt maintained a long-standing relationship with one of these new women: clothing designer Emilie Flöge. Flöge shared Klimt's revolutionary ideas about sex and had no more use for marriage than he did. However, Klimt was also noted for his sexual adventures with the poor, often starving, young women who modeled for his nude murals. The artist fathered several children by these compliant slum girls and insisted that all the boys be named Gustav. Born July 14, 1862 (Encyclopedia Britannica 1997).*

Mary Wolstonecraft *(British feminist activist and writer). Born April 27, 1759 (Encyclopedia Britannica 1997).*

If you have Mars in Aries with Venus in Cancer you are . . . the Emotional Extremist

You demand more from sex than most Mars in Aries Lovers. You need edgy excitement and far-reaching challenges, but you also need emotional comfort and security. This adds an intense, visceral need to your sexuality that is scary at times. People are drawn to you because of your loyalty and outstanding courage, but they may be put off by your tendency to confuse extreme experiences with extreme love.

Because you take such a radical, all-or-nothing approach to sex and love, the whole operation often becomes terribly inconvenient for all parties concerned. Because of this, you are often happiest when your love life is constrained, by circumstances beyond your control. You are better able to maintain the security you need when there is a social or intellectual buffer between you and the free exercise of your incredible passions. Such constraints also allow you to hide your emotional vulnerability.

Case History

Aldous Huxley *(English author of* Brave New World *who became famous for his sophisticated novels about Britain's "flaming youth" and then moved to California and became a mystic). Born July 26, 1894, at Godalming, Surrey, England (Bedford 1974; Dunaway 1989).*

Huxley's adolescence was marked by three tragedies. When he was fourteen his mother, with whom he was especially close, died suddenly of cancer. A short time later Huxley contracted an eye disease that temporarily blinded him and left him partially blind for the rest of his life. Then Huxley's elder brother, who had failed to meet the family's expectations in his schoolwork and had fallen in love with a working-class girl, killed himself. These sad events caused Huxley to put aside the sciences, in which his family had traditionally excelled, and turn to writing.

In his youth Huxley made a vow with a friend not to kiss any girl of their own class. Even when one of his middle-class girl friends offered herself to him the idealistic Huxley refused. This vow didn't stop Huxley from picking up a working-class girl and having intercourse with her when he was in his early twenties. He was surprised, and apparently pleased, at her aggressiveness.

When he was twenty-two Huxley met a young Belgian woman named Maria Nys. Physically they were an odd pair. Nys was short, petite, and extremely pretty. Huxley had a tall scarecrow's body, a large leonine head, and thick glasses. The attraction between them was apparently instantaneous. Huxley continued to court Nys for three years. They were married when he was twenty-five.

The relationship between Huxley and his wife was unusual. They had a son shortly after the marriage, but this came as a surprise since Maria thought she would be unable to conceive. They had no other children and typically gravitated to people who were unmarried or childless. During much of their marriage the couple did not share a bed and they allowed each other total sexual freedom. Huxley began a long series of casual affairs, while Maria explored her attraction to other women.

Despite their radical ideas about sex, Huxley became deeply dependent upon his wife and she remained devoted to him for thirty-five years. Huxley's vision problems and his peculiar intellect cut him off from everyday life in many ways. Maria became his conduit, caretaker, and protector. She retyped his manuscripts (he wrote on a special typewriter with extra-large letters) and spent long evenings reading to him. Maria carefully guided conversations away from subjects that might upset the writer and skillfully adapted to his periods of dark depression.

But perhaps the most surprising aspect of their relationship was the way in which Maria functioned as a matchmaker for her husband. Too busy and impatient to carry out seductions on his own, Huxley allowed Maria to act as his agent—setting up meetings with likely women, making the reservations, sending the flowers, buying the gifts, and even writing the good-bye letters when the affairs were over.

At this time Huxley and Maria were a part of a sexually liberated group of intellectuals that included D. H. Lawrence, Ottoline Morrell, and Bertrand Russell. In this special crowd their unusual marital arrangement hardly caused a stir. There were plenty of opportunities for both to explore their preferences. Meanwhile, Huxley was becoming famous for his witty and rather cynical novels.

When Huxley was twenty-eight a break occurred in this tidy arrangement. Huxley fell hopelessly in love with Nancy Cunard. Cunard was a poor candidate for true love. She was an heiress who had made a point of living on the edge and defying convention. Her addiction to quick, meaningless sex was well-known. Huxley was undaunted by her coldness. He pursued her obsessively for months, trailing her from nightclub to nightclub like a lost puppy. Cunard found this devotion laughable—when she finally agreed to take Huxley to bed she admitted she found him physically unattractive. Yet Huxley persisted, as if he found pleasure in Cunard's rejection. It was only when he received an ultimatum from Maria and was confronted with the fact that his wife was packed and ready to leave him that the writer came to his senses. Later he seldom spoke of this affair but Cunard became the model of several female characters in his novels.

When Huxley was thirty-eight he published *Brave New World*, a novel set in the distant future, in which the liberated notions of his intellectual friends had become the order of the day. Into the world of free love comes a savage, a man who rejects the hedonism and casual sexuality of the new society. He does all he can to avoid being co-opted by the pleasure-lovers around him. He even lashes himself with a whip in order to stem the tide of his own lust. But in the end the savage participates in an orgy and, afterward, hangs himself because of his shame.

Huxley was embroiled in a personal crisis two years after writing *Brave New World*. Seeking a way to become more involved in the "real" world, he joined a pacifist group and began to speak out against rearmament and war. Unfortunately, this was during the mid-1930s, when war was becoming more inevitable every day. Discouraged by the impending war and anxious to find a climate more conducive to his health, Huxley and his tiny family moved to California.

Huxley landed in Hollywood, where famous writers could find lucrative work writing scripts for movies. He quickly acquired a circle of notable and liberated friends, and resumed the kind of casual, hedonistic sex life he had enjoyed in Europe during the '20s. Maria continued to set him up with "dates" and he had some success on his own with starlets and fans of his novels. Maria joined a group of Hollywood lesbians called the "Sewing Circle." Occasionally she brought one of her girl friends home and shared her with Huxley. People who attended parties at their home sometimes found a nude woman stretched out on a coffee table for the amusement of the guests.

This sensual idyll only served as a temporary diversion from the many problems that beset the Huxleys in Hollywood. Huxley's unwavering pacifism had alienated him from many of his friends in England. He became the target of vicious criticism in the nation of his birth when World War II began. Huxley responded to these attacks by turning to mysticism and meditation. He came to see sexual abstinence as part of the discipline required of someone seeking a spiritual life. He and Maria moved to an isolated farm in the Mojave Desert where he grew vegetables and spent several hours a day meditating.

Maria died when Huxley was fifty-five, and the following year he married a therapist. This new relationship copied that of his first marriage in many ways. Huxley's new wife had a busy life of her own and she remained close to a woman she had lived with for years (a reputed lesbian). Huxley didn't seem to mind. He never sought to make his new wife into the kind of protective mother figure Maria had been. Despite his talk of celibacy, Huxley continued to flirt with attractive women, but these flirtations were considered harmless by all concerned. He died of cancer at the age of sixty-nine.

Another Example

*The **Marquis de Sade** (Donatien Alphonse Francois de Sade) was not the first sadist. The practice of mingling pain and sexual pleasure was already well-established when he made his first forays into the bordellos of Paris during his teens. Contrary to his image, Sade enjoyed being whipped while he was having sex as much as he liked dealing out torture and beatings. His behavior was not that remarkable among the jaded nobility of pre-revolutionary France. What made the Marquis different and dangerous was his angry determination to take his sexual practices and callous disregard of all things sacred to the most self-destructive extremes.*

Sade's one unwavering supporter through all his peccadilloes was his wife. She forgave him everything—even when he ran off with her own sister, a nun, and willingly participated in his bizarre orgies. She remained devoted to him even after he was imprisoned at the age of thirty-eight.

After his release, Sade published the strange writings that had sustained both his sexuality and his anger through the years of his imprisonment. There is little sensuality or real eroticism in works like Justine. *They are rather single-minded studies of the extreme: extreme situations, extreme emotions, and extreme sensations. In Sade's works, sex is only worthwhile when it is joined with pain, cruelty, humiliation, murder, and sacrilege. The new revolutionary government of France quickly put the author back in jail. He died there at the amazingly advanced age of seventy-four. Born June 2, 1740 (Lever 1993).*

If you have Mars in Aries with Venus in Leo you are . . . the Gilded Extremist

You are such a sweet, generous, and exciting Lover that it often goes unnoticed that you are also something of an egotist. This is not to say that you don't care about other people. You are actually a very warm, openhearted individual. But your sexual feelings are so geared toward challenge, so tinged with competitive zeal, that it's difficult for you to separate your need for love from your drive to be the best and also *have* the best.

The greatest problem in your love life is choosing between excitement and control. Unlike most Mars in Aries Lovers, you don't like unpredictability in your sexual adventures. You like to feel you are in control of both your passion and the situation. However, you also love the thrill, the joy, and the heady release of love in flight. So, like it or not, you are always making adjustments: interjecting control into wild situations, and slipping a touch of fire into the predictable.

Case History

Aly Khan (*wealthy Muslim prince who became one of the most noted international playboys of the early twentieth century). Born June 13, 1911, in Turin, Italy (Frischauer 1971).*

Aly Kahn's father, Aga Khan III, was iman of the Nizari Ismailite sect of Shiite Muslims. This made him the spiritual leader of some 20 million people scattered across the Muslim world from India to Africa. Aga Kahn was very active in world affairs. He had once served as head of the League of Nations, but he spent little time among his people. Instead he lived in various European capitals where he accumulated untold wealth and married beautiful women. One of these brides, an Italian ballerina, was Aly's mother.

Raised in this jet-set atmosphere and with little to do but ride his father's famous racehorses and have fun, it was not surprising that Aly Kahn became noted for his romantic exploits at an early age. He reportedly had a longstanding arrangement with an older married woman who taught him much about the care and handling of very rich women. It was also rumored that the young Aly was taught an ancient lovemaking discipline called "imsak" which allowed him to delay ejaculation and maintain an erection almost indefinitely. He added the natural charm and ease of a prince of the blood to this excellent training. Even though he was short and not particularly handsome, women found this dark youngster irresistible.

Because of his success with the opposite sex, many found it surprising (even disconcerting) when Aly suddenly married at the age of twenty-five. His bride was from the highest strata of British society and well equipped to take on the role of "princess," but Aly seems to have made the decision to wed quite impulsively. Even though the marriage quickly produced two sons, Aly's reputation as a womanizer was already so entrenched that few thought the union would last. It came as no surprise that stories of his extramarital adventures surfaced when Aly was thirty, while he distinguished himself as an officer in the British Army.

When he was thirty-two, Aly and his wife agreed to a permanent separation but the marriage remained intact for political reasons. It was the sort of arrangement people in Aly's position often made, but this young prince soon found himself unable to abide by it. Three years after the separation, Aly met the beautiful American film star, Rita Hayworth, and he quickly decided he had to divorce his first wife and marry again.

Hayworth was certainly attractive—a fiery redheaded dancer and actress at the peak of her stardom. If Aly was not already the envy of every man he knew, he certainly was with Rita Hayworth on his arm. But Hayworth was an extremely fragile woman. A tragic childhood had left her an emotional cripple whose sexual and emotional needs were said to be compulsive and insatiable. One Mars in Aries man, Orson Welles, had already married her and fled. Aly apparently felt up to the challenge. Certainly his sexual staying power gave him an advantage—an advantage that Hayworth used to the fullest in the early days of their relationship. He seemed to enjoy her violent rages. It was a novel and exhilarating experience for the heir to the iman to be called names and have ashtrays thrown at his head.

Aly quickly found that satisfying Hayworth's sexual needs was not even half the battle. Her smothering need for attention and emotional comfort soon compelled him to slip out of their mansion at night in search of less complicated assignations. Hayworth, who was monumentally jealous at the best of times, could not bear this. She left him, taking their daughter with her. From this point, the relationship between Aly and his American ex-wife played out in a series of protracted court battles. Their daughter, Princess Yasmin, was a favorite of Aly's father, and he and Aly fought to gain some control of her upbringing. Meanwhile, Hayworth's emotional instability and penchant for bad marriages added to Aly's distress over the welfare of his daughter. For five years the couple battled before Hayworth finally consented to give Aly access to their child. Once this was accomplished, the relationship between the former combatants became quite cordial, even though Aly was no longer interested in Hayworth as a sexual partner.

After his much publicized marriage and breakup with Hayworth, Aly's fame as a lover reached its peak. Women threw themselves at him just for the privilege of sleeping with the best lover in the Western world. There is no evidence that he shied away from this notoriety. A hardened trophy-seeker himself, Aly didn't mind that he was often seen as an erotic trophy. Despite his incredibly active and varied love life, Aly also managed to maintain a long-term relationship with a European model.

In the end, Aly's playboy image cost him dearly. It was probably the chief reason he was unable to inherit the position of iman. His father decreed that the title should go to Aly's son instead. Aly eventually became a diplomat for the new nation of Pakistan. He died in an automobile accident at forty-nine.

Another Example

Monica Lewinsky (famous White House intern). Born July 23, 1973 (Tarriktar, The Mountain Astrologer Magazine, *April–May, 1998).*

If you have Mars in Aries with Venus in Virgo you are . . . the Everyday Extremist

You are a Mars in Aries Lover with a little more common sense than most. There is a quiet circumspection behind your headfirst passion that usually keeps you from making really big mistakes. You typically get your own way in relationships because, no matter how intensely you love, you always give the impression that you can disengage at any moment. This cool-headed practicality makes you a sexual survivor who won't let blind passion get in the way of physical pleasure.

At your worst, this theory of "managed" passion can make you a selfish, uninvolved Lover and a mechanical sex partner. A Mars in Aries Lover who can't be an idealist is not very exciting. However, at your best you can use this down-to-earth approach to channel this high-flying idealism into acts of simple kindness. For you, the inspiration of true love often manifests in performing the most commonplace tasks for your beloved. You are at your most blissfully extreme when you are just being useful.

Case History

David Crosby (singer and musician with The Byrds and Crosby, Stills, Nash and Young). Born August 14, 1941, in Los Angeles, California (Crosby 1988).

A rebellious child from a broken home, Crosby was sent to a private prep school but was asked to leave because of his disruptive behavior. During this period (at the age of sixteen), he won a bet with his school friends for being the first to lose his virginity.

After he turned sixteen, Crosby became increasingly wayward and alienated from his family. He was arrested for burglary and showed little interest in school. He devoted himself to girls and music. Some people who knew him at the time recalled that he was unusually obsessed with sex. But others felt the ardent rebel was "too weird" to be a real ladies' man.

By his late teens Crosby had completely broken with the conventional values of his parents. He lived with his girl friend in Los Angeles while he attempted to start a career as a folk singer. When the girl friend became pregnant, Crosby immediately decided it was an opportune time to leave California and take his act on the road. He let his big brother take the heat from the girl's angry parents.

He eventually went to New York City, where he fell in with a bohemian crowd of folk singers and musicians. These were hard times for the itinerant musician, but not so hard that he couldn't find time for a lot of sex and experimentation with illicit drugs. Marijuana was his drug of choice at this point.

After a few years Crosby was back in Los Angeles. He became part of a musical group, The Byrds, and shifted from folk music to rock-and-roll. Crosby and his friends found themselves becoming well known in the Los Angeles music community where a fan club for them soon developed. The organizer of the club was a teenager named Christine Hinton, who made it known that she would do anything to be Crosby's girl.

Before long, Hinton established herself as an essential element of Crosby's entourage. There was no question about the singer having a monogamous relationship with her. As The Byrds rose to national fame, Crosby lived the rock-and-roll dream of endless and anonymous sex. When he was twenty-six, Crosby had an affair with Joni Mitchell, another folk singer in transition, but this was the exception. Generally, he preferred groupies, waitresses, and other nameless women who were too impressed with his fame and wealth to ask for anything beyond a good time.

Drugs were a big part of Crosby's musical hedonism. He openly used marijuana, LSD, and cocaine. He became known for passing out joints as if they were calling cards. However, he was more secretive about his newest fascination: heroin. He used this drug in private, though seldom alone. He had to have someone else shoot him up because he was afraid of needles.

By the time he was twenty-seven, Crosby had moved from The Byrds to Crosby, Stills, Nash and Young. At this time he recorded the greatest music of his career. He loved sailing and bought a schooner that he filled with beautiful women and recreational drugs. One observer said he lived aboard his pleasure boat like a suntanned sultan, surrounded by naked women, and stoned.

Christine Hinton remained the central figure in this harem, managing Crosby's day-to-day affairs and keeping him supplied with the necessities, including sex and drugs. After a while, Crosby may have felt some compulsion to reward Hinton for her faithfulness. Shortly after Crosby, Stills, Nash, and Young had a triumphant performance at Woodstock, he proposed that he and Hinton move away from the party scene to quiet home in the country. Hinton accepted, but recognizing Crosby's inability to be satisfied with just one lover, arranged for a friend to live with them. For a few short weeks Crosby seemed to become almost domesticated. Tragedy brought this to a sudden end when Hinton was killed in an automobile accident. Crosby was inconsolable.

Hinton's death was the beginning of a long decline for Crosby. Other women came forward to fill her role as primary mistress and party facilitator, but they did not last. One, Debbie Donovan, became pregnant with Crosby's child. Crosby was already enjoying three-somes with women he picked up while the band was touring. When Donovan became obviously pregnant, Crosby refused to sleep with her. She left and one of his "party girls" took her place.

By the time Crosby reached his thirties, drugs and sex were equal factors in his life. By the time he reached thirty-eight and began free-basing cocaine, drugs had become more important. He began a relationship with Jan Dance and introduced her to his newest addiction. After this, they both were junkies, living and dying with the flow of narcotics through their systems. Fortunately, Crosby was still performing and making money, even though large amounts of cocaine and heroin were required to keep him going. Dance traveled with him when he toured—a gaunt, ever-present shadow the roadies named "Death."

Despite their mutual addiction, Crosby and Dance remained remarkably loyal to each other. When people who saw her as a detriment to Crosby's moneymaking potential kidnapped Dance, Crosby shook off his drug-induced stupor and rescued her. When Crosby was put in prison after multiple drug arrests, Dance stood by him. They formed an unbreakable bond through many tortuous years of mutual dependency and rehabilitation. Crosby married Dance when he was forty-five. Eight years later, shortly before he received a liver transplant, she became pregnant with his child.

If you have Mars in Aries with Venus in Libra you are ... the Loving Extremist

You are the Mars in Aries Lover who needs love most and, when it comes to relationships, this puts you in an extremely bad bargaining position. You throw yourself into the pursuit of your beloved, exposing all your weakness and, thus, positioning yourself for every kind of hurt. You idealize the people you love, ignoring their faults, exaggerating their strengths, and giving them your absolute devotion. The energy and sunny optimism with which you enter every relationship is perhaps your most winning trait. Of course, it can also be your most troublesome trait on those frequent occasions when you pursue the wrong person.

Even though you are a very loving individual, you are not always easy to love. You flash between opposite extremes so quickly—love and hate; sexual passion and intellectual coolness; idealization and denigration—that you can try the patience of even the most indulgent of partners. You require someone who can see through your changes in mood and direction to the true warmth and benevolence that pulsate at the core of your sexuality. What you lack in consistency you more than make up for in excitement and devotion.

Case History

e. e. cummings (Edward Estlin Cummings—American poet whose radical approach to punctuation and form changed poetry forever). Born October 14, 1894, in Cambridge, Massachusetts (Kennedy 1979).

Cummings' father was a professor at Harvard University and a Unitarian minister. A large, imposing man, his moralistic attitudes toward sex deeply influenced his son. Cummings was in his late teens before he even thought to complain about these restrictions. At this point Cummings enjoyed chaste infatuations with college girls and titillating joy rides with working-class girls in his father's car. But even in his most rebellious and irreligious moments, the minister's son went no further than slipping a tentative hand up his girl friend's dress.

Cummings had to go all the way to France to lose his virginity. He became friendly with a prostitute who gave him a very pleasurable introduction to the art of lovemaking when he was in Paris during World War I; however, because Cummings was afraid of venereal disease, the couple never had intercourse.

He always spoke highly of this first teacher but he was never capable of applying her lessons in problem-free sex. Back in the United States two years later, he fell in love with the beautiful Elaine Orr who, unfortunately, was the wife of his friend, Scofield Thayer. Cummings had too much respect for Thayer, who was both his friend and his financial benefactor, to seduce his wife. When Elaine Orr made overtures to the poet, Cummings was so shocked that he turned her down. Finally Cummings realized that Thayer and Orr had an "understanding." Cummings began to have sex with Orr even though he was never comfortable with the arrangement.

Eventually Orr became pregnant with Cummings' child. Thayer at first advised an abortion, but he later agreed to accept the child as his own. Meanwhile, their unconventional marriage was wearing thin. They divorced six years after the birth of the child. Cummings immediately sought to legitimize his involvement with Orr and they were married. Orr quickly regretted this decision. Whatever charms that Cummings possessed as a lover, he lacked as a husband. Orr was used to having her men take care of her. Cummings, however, was not only a poor, Bohemian poet, he was an extremely passive husband. He thought only of his poetry and his painting, and left practical affairs to his wife. Orr's dissatisfaction with this arrangement eventually led her into the arms of a wealthy businessman. She divorced Cummings, took their child, and moved to Scotland.

Despite his troubled and frustrated sexual history, Cummings' poetry is full of exuberant sexual references—references which were so plain and streetwise that he had problems publishing some poems. In his poetry Cummings was unconventional. By his early twenties he was already producing the oddly structured poetry, with lines written vertically or at a slant, for which he would eventually become famous. As a poet he had no trouble shaking off his father's influence. As a lover, the older man's idealistic Puritanism haunted him for much of his life.

By the time he was thirty-two Cummings was in love again, this time with a troubled beauty named Anne Barton. Barton had a history of using her beauty to attract the attention and support of wealthy men. Cummings was too sexually infatuated to notice the shady elements of his lover's past. He also chose to ignore, or endure, her irrational tantrums and her unwillingness to put aside her rich husband in order to marry him. At one point he began an affair with another woman to make Barton jealous. Finally, after many struggles, Cummings convinced Barton to become his second wife.

For the first year of their marriage the couple got along quite well, but then the relationship began to sour. Anne verbally abused Cummings so much, calling him "her puny husband," that his friends began to avoid their company. She also slept with other men and made no effort to conceal this from Cummings, who seemed willing to put up with anything to avoid another painful divorce. Finally, Anne put an end to the poet's misery and left him for a doctor.

Even before his divorce from Anne was final, Cummings was exuberantly courting a tall, stately fashion model named Marion Morehouse who was twelve years his junior. His boyish energy and passion deeply impressed Morehouse and, when Cummings was forty, they began to live together. (There is no proof they were actually married although Cummings never failed to refer to her as his lawful wife.) Morehouse was a patient, strong-willed woman who indulged her mercurial husband and protected him. Cummings took a more aggressive role in this marriage. He suffered from a back ailment that caused a great deal of pain and this often made him disagreeable and argumentative. His domestic tyrannies ranged from not allowing Marion to run a vacuum cleaner to forbidding her to drive a car. He also refused to have a child with her. Despite these conflicts, the marriage prospered and lasted until Cummings' death at sixty-seven.

If you have Mars in Aries with Venus in Scorpio you are . . . the Cunning Extremist

You are simultaneously the sexiest and the most conservative of the Mars in Aries Lovers. You enjoy feeling the fire and power of your sexuality but you invariably hold back a large portion of this energy for the sake of propriety and your need to be in control. Instead of leaving you frustrated, this repressed sexual energy and passion held in abeyance only adds to your already tremendous sex appeal.

You can be ruthless when it comes to love. You have a way of going after what you want with a combination of recklessness and high-handed disregard for all the rules; however, even this ruthlessness is typically held in check by your conservative approach to sex. There's a lot that you want to attempt but don't because you don't want to make your desires too obvious. Impulsive love can be fun, but it's the sneaking around that truly holds your interest.

Case History

Gerhart Hauptmann (German realist playwright and winner of the Nobel Prize). Born November 15, 1862, at about noon in Obersalzbrunn, Silesia (present-day Poland) (Weisstein 1954).

The product of a middle-class home, Hauptmann was sent to study sculpture in Breslau when he was eighteen. There the young artist let his hair grow long and spent his nights carousing with a friendly professor. After this he traveled to Greece and the Mediterranean where he observed the dark world of opium dens and child prostitution, an experience that marked him deeply.

Hauptmann's family was not wealthy. At twenty-two, he submitted to his father's wishes and married Marie Thieneman, whose parents were well-to-do. It was a rocky union from the beginning. Hauptmann was a flamboyant advocate of nudism and polygamy (for men only, of course), while his wife was profoundly domestic. Marie allowed her husband to express his radical ideas among his friends, many of them writers, artists, and intellectuals, but she never allowed him to wander far from the conventional lifestyle she favored. Their marriage quickly produced two sons.

The wealth Marie had brought to the union gave her the upper hand early in the marriage. Hauptmann was a spendthrift who hopped from career to career, and he desperately needed his wife's fortune. This situation changed when Hauptmann turned twenty-seven. He wrote a play called *Before Dawn,* based on the socialist and naturalist ideas about which he had been talking for so long. The play was extremely controversial and became a big hit. After this success Hauptmann never had to worry about money.

Hauptmann's interest in young women made itself evident very quickly. As much as Hauptmann wanted to break out of the conventional confines of his marriage, he remained cautious; none of his flirtations were serious until he turned thirty-two. At this time he fell deeply in love with Margurete Marschalk, an eighteen-year-old actress who played the female lead in one of his plays.

Despite his passion for the youthful Marschalk, Hauptmann was still not anxious to give up the security of his marriage. He made a doomed attempt to convince Marie to allow him to keep two households: one with Marschalk and one for her and the children. Marie reacted to this proposal with outrage. She packed up their children and left for a tour of the

United States. Hauptmann became distraught and followed Marie across the Atlantic, leaving his mistress behind. They had a brief reconciliation in the United States but this lasted only until they returned to Germany and Hauptmann was once again within reach of Marschalk.

The final blow came when Marschalk became pregnant with Hauptmann's child. The famous playwright moved in with his lover and began a long estrangement from his wife. When he was forty-two, Marie finally allowed him a divorce and he married Marschalk.

Hauptmann once again became restless two years after his second marriage. He was infatuated with another teenage actress and appeared poised to wreck his second marriage much as he had his first. But Marschalk, his sons, and his friends combined to stop the budding romance. Hauptmann later wrote about the experience with a good deal of bitterness. He spent the rest of his long life living quietly with his second wife. He died at age eighty-three.

Another Example

"Mama" Cass Elliot (singer). Born September 19, 1941 (Celebrity Birthday Guide).

If you have Mars in Aries with Venus in Sagittarius you are … the Hopeful Extremist

You are the most optimistic, open, and altogether positive Lover of this (or any other) Mars type. Your approach to loving is so fresh and free, so brimming with idealism and energy, that sex becomes an act of inspiration for you. You are a very curious Lover, always ready to respond to any sexual challenge. At times you can be foolish and clumsy. You have a disconcerting tendency to place more confidence in your ideals than you do in facts, but these faults typically only add to your charm. You are an exhilarating partner who can make the most mundane sexual situation seem magical.

Physical sex always means less to you than the passion and the ideals that surround it. The relationships that really hold you will be those that are based less on sex and more on intellectual and spiritual affinity. In these situations you can be a very loyal Lover. Otherwise, you will go wherever the next inspiration or wave of passion happens to take you.

Case History

Havelock Ellis (British sexologist famous for his groundbreaking writings on the nature of human sexuality and author of Studies in the Psychology of Sex). *Born February 2, 1859, in Croydon, England (Gollis 1959).*

Ellis had a chance to observe a wide range of sexual attitudes while he was growing up in Australia. Through his father he had contact with the casual and expedient methods of ship-bound sailors. Through his mother and his old-maid aunts he was exposed to the most stringent of Victorian ideals. Ellis developed into an extremely curious, but, at the same time, repressed adolescent who counted the sight of his mother urinating while standing up among his most formative erotic experiences.

When Ellis left Australia and returned to his birthplace, England, he sought a career as a doctor. His troubled feelings toward sex led him to specialize in human sexuality. At the same time he fell in with a liberal group of intellectuals advocating such social changes as birth control and the emancipation of women. Despite his active life, Ellis remained a very shy and introverted young man. He had many female friends but typically backed away when these women attempted to lure him into sexual relationships. One young woman, while in the midst of a philosophical discussion with Ellis, proceeded to prepare for her bath. She emerged naked from her bathroom to seize on a salient issue. To her chagrin, Ellis responded to her discourse but seemingly remained oblivious to her nakedness.

Even when Ellis did slip into a sexual relationship with one of his women friends, the results were not always happy. His relationship with noted feminist Olive Schreiner was cut short by his inability to sustain an erection. Sexual intercourse was apparently a rarity for Ellis. Most of his sexual encounters involved oral and manual stimulation. It is probably for this reason that Ellis became one of the first great advocates of foreplay.

When he was thirty, Ellis married Edith Lees, a woman who shared his feminist and free-thinking approach to sex. Otherwise, Lees was quite unlike the quiet, self-effacing doctor. She was independent and aggressive, a woman very comfortable with lecturing to an audience. She became his voice to the world because Ellis was too shy to speak to groups. She spent much of her time traveling and spreading his ideas of sexual toleration.

The sexual relationship between Ellis and Edith was unconventional. The two of them were seldom together. Throughout their married life they actually lived together only during the winter months and went their separate ways the rest of the year. Edith was also bisexual. Her wild infatuations with young women had been an established pattern in her life even before her marriage. It is apparent that she and Ellis did have sexual relations early in their marriage but this ended after Ellis confessed to his wife that he was having an affair. Ellis later wrote that his marriage prospered in the absence of sexual contact and the two did remain remarkably devoted to each other for twenty-six years, despite his wife's lesbianism and emotional instability.

When he was thirty-eight, Ellis published the first volume of his encyclopedic study of human sexuality, *Studies in the Psychology of Sex*. Using his background as a medical doctor, combined with his amazingly varied knowledge of literature and history, Ellis attempted to make a comprehensive study of man's sexual practices. The publication of this first volume, which dealt with homosexuality, almost landed Ellis in court. It wasn't so much the subject matter that caused Ellis' books to be banned, it was his assumption that all types of human sexual expression are valid.

In fact, toleration was the essential goal of Ellis' expansive research. Unlike his great contemporary, Sigmund Freud, Ellis never brought his ideas together into a cohesive psychological theory. In fact, he later rejected Freud's ideas because of their emphasis on repression and guilt. In Ellis' optimistic and (to some extent) romantic view, sexual health came only from toleration, both of one's self and of others.

Ellis was fifty-six when he met Margaret Sanger, who had achieved notoriety in the United States because of her advocacy of women's rights and birth control. The two crusaders immediately became friends and then lovers. Ellis had apparently enjoyed other extramarital affairs but in his relationship with Sanger, Ellis came close to losing the careful balance of promiscuity and passion that had helped to preserve his unusual marriage. Sanger was more interested in Ellis as a mentor than as a lover. She preferred more virile partners and the sexual side of their relationship slowly withered.

Edith died when Ellis was fifty-six. Ellis began a relationship a year later with a young Frenchwoman named Francoise Cyon. Ellis both surprised and charmed Cyon during their first encounter by ministering to her needs orally, apparently without bringing up his own needs. She was later persuaded to indulge his lifelong fascination with watching women urinate. Even though their relationship was exceptionally close, there were some rocky moments. At one point, when Ellis learned that Cyon was sleeping with a younger man, he lost his toleration and demanded she give up her lover. Their relationship lasted until Ellis' death at eighty.

Another Example

Hermann Göring (Göring was one of the highest-ranking Nazi officials under Hitler). He was head of the Gestapo and German air force—a master of the ruthless infighting that took place in Hitler's government. In his youth, this cold-hearted Machiavellian was actually a dashing romantic. At twenty-seven he won the heart of a Swedish countess who left her wealthy husband and endured the rejection of her family to live with this poverty-stricken war hero. Göring was deeply shaken when she died and mourned her with elaborate display.

Despite his passionate involvement with her, Göring's sex life with his wife was probably quite limited. Shortly after their marriage he was shot in the groin while aiding Hitler in an abortive grasp for power called the "beer-hall putsch." The wound apparently left Göring impotent. It also irrevocably damaged his mental health and left him addicted to drugs.

When he was forty-two and under pressure from Hitler to make his dissolute lifestyle appear more conventional, Göring married his secretary. By all appearances, Göring became quite devoted to his new wife. To the surprise of nearly everyone, the marriage produced a child. Some even hinted that the child was conceived through artificial means or by another man. Göring's Gestapo typically arrested the men who dropped these hints. Göring was captured after World War II and put on trial at Nuremberg. After being sentenced to death, he committed suicide at the age of fifty-two. Born January 12, 1893 (Irving 1989).

If you have Mars in Aries with Venus in Capricorn you are . . . the Earthy Extremist

You are a Mars in Aries Lover who wants to go to extremes and is determined to plan how to get there. For some reason you continually miss the obvious fact that mad abandon and absolute control are mutually exclusive terms. At times this tendency makes you confused and unbalanced—a Lover who is too conservative and calculating to be truly wild, and too impulsive to maintain his or her control for very long.

Given your self-contradicting and often self-defeating approach to sex, it is not surprising that your sex life is frequently troubled. Fortunately, you have two saving graces. The first is your incomparable sexual energy. You are one of the most physical Mars in Aries Lovers and you express your idealism through your body. Your second saving grace is your ability to see your own faults. You have a down-to-earth awareness of your own egotism that allows you to learn from your mistakes, or at least to learn to laugh at them.

Case History

James Agee (American poet, novelist, screenwriter, and critic. Author of Let Us Now Praise Famous Men *and the screenplay for* The African Queen*). Born November 27, 1909, in Knoxville, Tennessee (Bargreen 1984).*

Obsessed with sex from an early age, Agee was also plagued with deep-seated feelings of guilt. He had his first sexual intercourse with a girl by the time he was sixteen. While in a private prep school, he made homosexual advances to one of his friends but was rejected. Then he acquired a steady girl friend; his unwillingness to be separated from her caused him to flaunt the school's curfew. Later, while at Harvard, he found himself falling in love with another woman. He felt so guilty about dumping his old girlfriend that he could not break with her until he had paired her with one of his friends.

When Agee was twenty-three he married Via Saunders, the daughter of a family friend. Agee entered the marriage with distinct reservations. His bride came from a background of Southern gentility similar to his own. He feared that she would lure him into the kind of conventional lifestyle he deplored. Already saddled with a "regular" job as a journalist, he longed to break away and write poetry and novels. When Via had a mild nervous breakdown, however, and left him because of his unwillingness to commit, Agee surrendered and the two were married.

It was an unhappy marriage from the beginning. Agee felt both trapped and inadequate. On the one hand, he hated his wife for forcing compromises on him and, on the other, he hated himself for not giving her the conventional life she wanted. The unhappiness of the situation, along with frustration with his writing, edged Agee closer to alcoholism and suicidal tendencies. He flirted with available women and got even angrier with his wife when she failed to become jealous. He then found himself falling in love with a younger woman named Alma Mailman.

Even though the problems with his marriage were obvious, Agee was surprisingly reluctant to leave his wife. For a while he tried to maintain relationships with both women, convinced that Via would be crushed if he left her and that his waywardness was only a sign of his own brutish lust. He was shocked when, after months of agonizing indecision, he asked for a divorce and Via calmly and instantly agreed.

Agee married Alma Mailman when he was twenty-nine. Agee found the intense sexual relationship that he thought he needed with his second marriage, but he still wasn't content. He decided to experiment and, sensing an attraction between his wife and his best friend, Agee persuaded them to make love while he watched. Instead of finding the experience liberating, as he had expected, Agee began to weep.

A short time later, when Alma was pregnant with his child, James began an affair with a new woman, Mia Fritsch. Again he went through a prolonged period of agonizing indecision, unable to give up either relationship. Shortly after Alma delivered their son he confessed his lapse to her. She immediately offered to put an end to his dilemma by leaving him, but Agee refused to let her go. He used promises, sex, threats of suicide, and even physical violence to keep Alma with him, but he did not stop seeing Mia. Alma managed to escape to Mexico and secure a divorce.

Mia and Agee did not marry immediately because Mia shared Agee's bohemian aversion to convention. They lived together until he was thirty-five. Then, shortly after their first child died at birth, they were inconspicuously wed. Over the next six years they had two more children and settled into what appeared to be a happy marriage. When Agee was forty-one, he went to Hollywood to work on the screenplay for *The African Queen*. With his wife and children thousands of miles away, Agee began an affair with a twenty-two-year-old woman who liked to drink and party as much as he did. Agee immediately began to think of divorce and, once again, he found himself unable to choose between two women. A mild heart attack interrupted this bout of indecision and brought his wife and family to the West Coast to join him.

Agee confessed his infatuation with the younger woman to Mia and she, a true bohemian, acquiesced to the continuation of the affair. But Agee recognized that his relationship with his wife was permanently damaged. His new love affair lasted only a short time. Despite Agee's ardent and somewhat ridiculous pursuit, the young woman rejected him. A despondent Agee returned to his old habits—drinking to excess and chain-smoking Chesterfields. He had another heart attack and died at the age of forty-four.

Another Example

Paul Newman (American actor). Born January 26, 1925 (Celebrity Birthday Guide).

If you have Mars in Aries with Venus in Aquarius you are . . . the Experimental Extremist

You are the coolest of the Mars in Aries Lovers, and for this reason you are often also the most unhappy. You long for over-the-top sexual experiences that will wash away your rational inhibitions but find that no matter how radical you become you just can't lose your capacity for calm, intellectual control. You can be the wildest and most unconventional of all the Mars in Aries types and this makes you a very exciting partner. Until you learn to deal with your frustrations, you will always be restless and discontented.

Sex is always an abstraction for you. The people you love are important because of what they symbolize, not because of who they are. This can make you appear to have a very cold and clinical approach to love, but the fact is you can love a symbol with a steadiness and a purity that will make people jealous. The happiest relationship for you will be one in which sex is a diversion and real love exists in the mind.

Case History

Lou Andreas-Salome (Russian-born essayist and novelist noted for her passionate friendships with famous men). Born February 12, 1861, in St. Petersburg, Russia (Binion 1968).

The only daughter of a wealthy German family living in Russia, Salome developed a passionate identification with her father. As a small child she intentionally misbehaved so that he would have to spank her. A little later she developed an imaginary friend and protector who was an extension of her father and, once again, she earned repeated spankings because of her stubborn allegiance to this fantasy mate.

As a teenager, Salome exchanged her attachment to her father for an infatuation with the family's minister. This middle-aged family man who quoted Goethe as freely as the Bible became Salome's first teacher and, at least in her mind, her first great love. The exact nature of the erudite preacher's feelings for Salome is unknown, but the ardent youngster was quick to find erotic references in nearly everything he said to her. In fact, she became so certain of his secret lust that she finally concluded the minister was just a dirty old man and unworthy of her adoration.

When Salome was eighteen she left St. Petersburg to study at the University of Zurich. Women were not permitted to obtain a degree there but she was allowed to audit classes. She heard lectures on philosophy, theology, and psychology from some of the most learned men in Europe. She immediately attracted attention. Not only was she tall and comely but she was eager to learn and not afraid to make herself known to the professors. She published poetry, joined literary groups, and quickly established herself as a young woman of letters.

Salome was a woman whose sex appeal was perhaps never more evident than when she was under the sway of her passionate intellect. Many of the men who found themselves impressed with her ideas also had designs on her body. Unfortunately for them, the young Salome had already concluded that sexual gratification carried a heavy price for women in her society. During the next several years of her life, Salome flirted relentlessly and inspired the admiration of several men. Some even proposed marriage, but the scholarly Salome stubbornly refused to relinquish both her chastity and her freedom.

When she was twenty-one, Salome met a thirty-two-year-old philosopher named Paul Ree. Like Salome, Ree was in love with ideas and had chosen to renounce sex. They became friends and, in a purely nonphysical way, lovers. Ree was so impressed with Salome that he introduced her to his most esteemed friend, a bombastic philosopher named Friederich Nietzsche. Soon Nietzsche, who was twenty years her senior, was also in love with Salome. For a short time the three philosophers lived together in a chaste ménage à trois. At one point during this relationship Salome was photographed sitting in a mock carriage with a whip as Ree and Nietzsche played the role of draft animals.

It was Nietzsche who finally upset this happy community of three. He made a proposal to Salome in which he expressed a desire to take their relationship to a more physical level. Salome reacted with shock and outrage. For her, the denial of the sex urge was a painful but irreplaceable part of the search for true love. For her idol to suggest otherwise seemed nothing less than a betrayal of her trust.

Salome continued her sexless relationship with Ree after her break with Nietzsche and gracefully fended off the advances of several other ardent (and usually aging) intellectuals. Then, quite suddenly, Salome allowed herself to be caught. The lucky beau was Friedrich Andreas, a noted orientalist and scholar who was several years older than Salome. It is not really clear what set him apart from the other brilliant academics and writers who had proposed to her. Andreas possessed an amazing mind (he mastered over a dozen languages), but he was no genius and his financial and career prospects were rather bleak. Whatever the reason, Salome brought him back to St. Petersburg and there they were married when she was twenty-six.

Salome claimed her marriage to Andreas was predicated on the promise that they would not have sex. Again it is unclear how this agreement was reached or why Andreas, who was eccentric but apparently not sexless, accepted it. Despite these mysteries, the marriage between Salome and Andreas proved to be a strong one. It survived the self-involvement of both parties and lasted thirty-three years, until Andreas' death.

Salome finally came to the conclusion when she was thirty-one that she needed sex, and with characteristic impetuosity, she began an affair with a Russian intellectual. Andreas objected and even feigned illness in order to hold Salome's attention, but his efforts were in vain. After this, most of Salome's passionate intellectual relationships with men were also sexual. From this point forward, instead of attaching herself to elderly father figures, Salome purposely sought out the companionship of younger men.

Salome was an accomplished author by the time she was thirty-six, noted for both her novels and her essays on religion and philosophy. Her work came to the attention of a young poet named Rainer Rilke. The two writers shared many of the same opinions and goals. They met and quickly became both intellectual partners and lovers.

Rilke was fourteen years younger than Salome. He was a man of intense, if sometimes elusive, passions that belied his small frame and frog-like face, and he proved to be a volatile companion. When Salome began spending time with another young man who was helping with a writing project, Rilke became jealous and depressed. He was even less pleased when Andreas, who had apparently learned to live with his wife's adventures, joined them in Germany. Despite the young poet's protests, Salome managed to keep the upper hand in the relationship. When she and Andreas returned to St. Petersburg, Rilke soon followed.

Salome's sexual relationship with Rilke lasted four years before she brought it to an abrupt end. Rilke left Russia, but he and Salome never really parted. He remained her intimate correspondent and friend. For the rest of his life he continued to look to Salome for advice and comfort. Meanwhile, Salome was reunited with one of her old boy friends, a Jewish doctor named Friedrich Pineles, who proved to be a less troublesome lover than Rilke. He also proved useful when Salome became subject to various medical concerns.

It was through Pineles that Salome was introduced to her last and greatest intellectual passion: psychoanalysis. She became a close associate of Sigmund Freud and applied the full weight of her considerable learning and literary reputation to his cause. After a lifetime of sexual repression and intellectual subterfuge, Salome felt right at home in the steamy psychodramas of Freudian thought. Meanwhile her sexual conquests of exciting younger men continued far into her fifties. She died at the age of seventy-five.

Another Example

Gloria Steinem (feminist leader in the United States). Born March 25, 1934 (Celebrity Birthday Guide).

If you have Mars in Aries with Venus in Pisces you are . . . the Delicate Extremist

You may be the most idealistic, volatile, and alluring of all the Mars in Aries Lovers. You combine enormous erotic vitality with a real emotional need for human contact. Unfortunately, this emotional openness also makes you one of the most vulnerable Lovers of this type. The reckless abandon that characterizes the Mars in Aries approach to sex invariably brings you pain and sorrow. It would all be so much easier if you could exercise a little caution in your love life. But what would be the fun in that?

Your attitude toward sex and love changes a great deal as you age. Your sexual energy in youth is so irresistible and your optimism so strong that you rush into relationships. After you've been bumped and bruised a few times, you become more aware of your psychic scars and painful memories than of a sweetheart's potential to make you happy. It is only natural that you will be wary and maybe even a little vindictive. You must be mindful not to make the people who love you in the present suffer for the mistakes of those who failed you in the past.

Case History

Charles Dickens (English novelist noted for his stories about the poor and downtrodden: Oliver Twist, *and* David Copperfield). *Born February 7, 1812, in Portmouth, England (Ackroyd 1990; MacKenzie 1979).*

The events of Dickens' tragic childhood are well known. When his father, a singularly improvident man, was put in a debtor's prison, twelve-year-old Dickens was forced to leave school and work in a factory to support his family. What made this downfall even more painful was the fact that for short periods during his youth when his father's fortunes were on the rise, Dickens had enjoyed all the comforts of a middle-class existence. By the time Dickens was in his late teens he had bettered his position significantly and was making a living as a journalist. However, he never lost his capacity for self-pity. He saw himself as the victim of both his father's financial ineptitude and his mother's cold-heartedness. (She had pushed Dickens to stay at the factory even when he had the opportunity to go back to school.)

Dickens' first love affair began when he was eighteen. It was a pathetic arrangement. He became infatuated with a pretty twenty-year-old named Marie Beadnell. She encouraged his attentions, even though her parents opposed it, but her motives were apparently more playful than passionate. She flirted with Dickens, allowed him to slip her secret correspondence, but never considered him a serious suitor. It took Dickens three years to recognize this and stop pining for her. Like most of the significant episodes of his emotional life, this one left him deeply scarred and wary.

Dickens was probably still a virgin during the years he worshipped Marie Beadnell. This was partly because his work habits left him little time for romantic concerns. He was a journalistic workaholic who seemingly never put down his pen. Also, Dickens' rocky childhood had left him with the highly Victorian notion that physical sex was unsavory and dangerous. It is theorized that he identified sexual promiscuity with the lower classes and, despite his literary defense of these people, he was too ambitious to ever risk returning to their ranks.

When Dickens was twenty-three he began courting Kate Hogarth, the daughter of one of his publishers. She was a plump, slow-moving young woman with a pretty face and a remarkable willingness to be dominated. Dickens' attraction to her is something of a mystery. Even during this courtship his feelings for her had none of the fiery passion that characterized his painful attachment to Marie Beadnell. He criticized her for her slothfulness and treated her as his intellectual inferior. Despite this lack of ardor the couple married when he was twenty-four.

Dicken's lack of sympathy for Kate only increased with matrimony. He was particularly put out by her multiple pregnancies during the early years of their marriage and by the deep depressions that assailed her after every birth. He treated her coldly, criticized her frequently, complained about her to his friends, and rarely took her with him when he made the social rounds expected of a successful young author. Kate responded to this ill treatment by trying harder to please Dickens and by submitting to his domestic tyranny. Unfortunately for her, her passivity only made the author angrier.

There was another side to the relationship between Dickens and his wife. Kate was pregnant fifteen times during the course of their marriage and, even though Dickens liked to pretend these pregnancies had nothing to do with him, they do indicate a degree of physical passion. Kate, for all her shortcomings and despite her depressions and bouts of nervous exhaustion, aroused a sensuality in Dickens that he was always reluctant to acknowledge. This may have been one of the reasons he felt the need to treat her so badly.

The failure of Kate to fulfill his idealized expectations of love caused Dickens to developed intense intellectual infatuations with other women. The first of these involved Kate's younger sister Mary who, as a teenager, often stayed with the Dickenses. She was brighter than Kate, more energetic and had that quality of virginal purity that many Victorian men found so irresistible. She became Dickens' favorite companion and, when they were apart, he wrote her letters that were far longer and more intimate than any he sent his long-suffering wife. Tragically, Mary Hogarth died at the age of eighteen. Dickens was devastated. His infatuation with Mary only intensified after her death. He kept her clothing so that he could hold it and be reminded of her. He insisted that he wanted to be buried not just next to her, but in her grave.

Other such flirtations followed, though none reached the intensity of the relationship between Dickens and Mary. Occasionally Kate became jealous but such was Dickens' control over his wife that nothing came of her complaints. It is unlikely the author had sex with any of the young women who fascinated him. In fact, it was their girlish innocence and lack of sexual pretenses that drew him to them.

Kate's other sister, Georgina, was among Dickens' female admirers. As Kate's emotional state deteriorated, Georgina joined the household and took charge of raising the ten Dickens children. She also became the chief facilitator for the writer's moody whims. Later, when the Dickens' marriage finally collapsed, Georgina chose to stay with Dickens and took his side against her sister. This sparked rumors that she had become the author's mistress and the Hogarth family threatened to take Dickens to court. In order to forgo this, Dickens had Georgina submit to a medical examination that showed her to still be a virgin.

The woman who was really responsible for the end of Dickens' marriage was a pretty and apparently innocent teenage actress by the name of Ellen Ternan. She and her mother had been hired by Dickens to perform in a play. In his later years, after his reputation as a leading novelist was firmly established, Dickens had turned to amateur theater with great enthusiasm. He was a natural actor and felt the need to work with professionals. Ellen came from a theatrical family but it was her youth and virginal charm, rather than her talent, which earned the forty-six-year-old Dickens' rapt attention.

Kate quickly recognized that her husband's attraction to Ellen was dangerous. Dickens responded to Kate's jealousy with outrage and he forced his browbeaten wife to apologized to Ternan. Unfortunately for him, Kate's mother and sister (Helen, the only Hogarth sister immune to the great writer's charm) came to her aid and gave her the strength to demand a separation.

Dickens felt greatly wronged by this turn of events. He fired off correspondence defending his position and placing blame for the dissolution of his marriage solely upon Kate and the Hogarth family. These efforts mitigated the effect the separation had on his reputation and they also made any kind of reconciliation with his wife impossible.

Through all of this Dickens managed to keep his relationship with Ellen Ternan out of the public eye. He continued to see her secretly at every opportunity and to give her family ample financial support. He was obviously very much in love with her but there is no conclusive evidence of a sexual relationship between them. While Dickens' enemies spread rumors of an illegitimate child born while Ellen was in seclusion either in France or the English countryside, his friends and Ternan herself denied it. Meanwhile, Dickens had discovered he could make much more money reading his published works in public rather than writing new ones (money he sorely needed now that he was supporting three households). Although Dickens greatly enjoyed these performances, they left him physically exhausted and caused him to age prematurely. He died, with Ellen Ternan at his bedside, at the age of fifty-six.

Another Example

Sergei Diaghilev *(Russian ballet impresario who guided his lover Nijinski to stardom and then destroyed him). Born March 31, 1872 (Encyclopedia Britannica 1997).*

Chapter 2

Mars in Taurus
The Sensualist

General Characteristics

People with Mars in Taurus have a very simple expectation about sex: they expect it to feel good. Sex is a physical matter for these Lovers and they have no patience for idealism, sentiment, or anything else that might get between them and the absolute enjoyment of their bodies. It's not that the sex drive here is unusually strong. Rather, it is so immediate, physical, and animalistic that it just won't be denied. No matter how much these Lovers try to "control" or "sublimate" their physical need for sex, they will find themselves overwhelmed by the raw, earthy power of Mars in Taurus.

Even though their approach to sex may seem primitive, people with Mars in Taurus are typically very accomplished Lovers. They are gifted with a slow, fulsome sensuality and have few inhibitions—not because they enjoy breaking the rules, but because no opportunity for pleasure should be left untested. They are passionate, but they never let their passions run amok. Mars in Taurus Lovers always follow the calm direction of their own bodies and they always know exactly how to optimize their own pleasure. Thus, they have a pretty good notion about what it takes to bring pleasure to others. Not only are these Lovers inevitably good to themselves, they are good to those they love—or at least to the bodies of those they love.

Despite their deep appreciation of physical pleasure, Mars in Taurus Lovers are very conservative people who prefer to keep their sex lives private and, at least ostensibly, conventional. This can present a problem. Even in the most permissive of societies, their very primitive and earthy approach to sex may be just too much for polite company. The fact is, sometimes these Lovers offend themselves. Consequently, you often find people with Mars in Taurus leading double lives. Sex becomes their "dirty" little secret, an activity relegated to the underground where they can be as bad as they need to be. In some instances, these Lovers do this because of repressive influences in the society in which they live. Sometimes they do it simply to satisfy their own inner censor. They would rather not have to own up to the true extent of their sensual extremes.

The biggest problem for Mars in Taurus Lovers is rooted in the very physicality that makes them such good sex partners. Their single-minded search for sensation means that they often end up in bed with bodies rather than people. They become so involved in their own pleasure that they forget that sex is really about building a loving bond with another individual. This is not to say that these Lovers are unkind. Actually, they are typically quite thoughtful and warm-hearted, but their unshakable assumption that good sex equals a good relationship can make them seem selfish, inflexible, and even cruel to the partner who needs more than an orgasm in order to feel loved.

If you have Mars in Taurus with Venus in Aries you are . . . the Restless Sensualist

You are a competitive Mars in Taurus Lover. Either you are competing for love with someone else or you are competing with yourself—trying to top your last encounter. Even though you have this luscious capacity for physical pleasure, you are never altogether satisfied with your sexuality. No matter what kind of sex you're getting, you find yourself wanting more, or better, or just different. You can't be satisfied with just having more fun than the rest of the population, you also have to find some way to prove it to everyone.

On the positive side, as a Lover you are seldom boring and never lazy, even though you are restless and habitually dissatisfied. You are willing to take chances in your love life and to meet problems head-on. The intensity and even the combativeness of your lovemaking will serve to make you a more interesting and provocative partner—someone who knows that there is more to sex than just sensation. For a person with Mars in Taurus, that's a lot to know.

Case History

Willem De Kooning *(Dutch-born American painter, one of the leaders of the abstract expressionist movement.) Born on April 24, 1904, in Rotterdam, Netherlands (Hall 1993).*

De Kooning's mother was a divorced bartender noted for her violent, domineering nature. He rebelled against her control at an early age. At twelve he was apprenticed to a commercial artist and he began to take night classes at the Rotterdam Academy of Fine Arts. When he was twenty-two, De Kooning left Holland and moved to the United States. He later said he came to America looking for two things: a career as an artist and long-legged American women.

As it turned out, the latter came to him more easily than the former. Long before he had established himself as an artist, the ruggedly handsome and likable De Kooning was known as a ladies' man. None of the many women he slept with during this period seemed to have had much of a hold on him. One friend observed that, for De Kooning, women were more or less interchangeable.

When he was thirty-four, De Kooning met a lively and strong-willed art student named Elaine Fried. At that time Fried was dating another man, but she quickly changed her allegiance when one of her instructors pointed out that De Kooning was considered one of the most important abstract painters in New York. It so happened that her boy friend was also impressed by De Kooning and continued to socialize with the couple. De Kooning was puzzled by this behavior. Full of pride that he had taken the twenty-year-old Fried away from a younger and better-looking rival, De Kooning couldn't understand why her old boy friend didn't just go away.

Partially to conceal their relationship from Elaine's mother, De Kooning became Fried's teacher. His teaching methods were rigorous and staunchly traditional but Fried accepted his discipline with surprising ease. In return, she helped him articulate into English the many passionate ideas he had about art and she added ideas of her own to them. However, the primary force that brought De Kooning and Fried together was sex. Fried was a supremely sensual woman with a taste for experimentation. She responded to De Kooning's powerful libido with a strong physical desire of her own. Soon the artist was totally captivated by Fried.

De Kooning and Fried were married when he was thirty-nine. Many of his friends felt that De Kooning seemed ready to settle into a conventional, monogamous relationship. Elaine had other plans. Even though she professed love for De Kooning, she had no desire to give up her very active and varied sex life. Her flagrant infidelity deeply shook De Kooning. Always prone to periods of sleepless depression, the painter now had more than unfinished paintings to keep him up at night. After a while, De Kooning looked upon his bride's unfaithfulness as a challenge and took lovers himself. What followed was an ugly competition of infidelities, interspersed with public brawls and general drunkenness.

It is uncertain if the women who appear in De Kooning's mature works are based on Elaine, his aggressive mother, or an amalgam of all the women in the artist's life. In choosing to paint them, he alienated many of his supporters who felt any art that was not totally abstract was old-fashioned. For many years De Kooning was unwilling or unable to paint anything else. The images of women he produced are primitive and sexually charged. They loom from the canvas with flashing teeth and wide-open eyes: dangerous, voracious and, in some ways, comical. De Kooning painted these women with violent, slashing strokes of warm, fleshy color as if torn between desire and hatred.

Despite their many conflicts, the De Koonings never divorced. They separated after fifteen years but continued to move among the same social crowd so they saw each other often. Before and after the separation, Elaine tirelessly promoted De Kooning's career. Many of the men she slept with had positions of power in the arts. She used her influence with them to promote her husband's work. Many felt that it was her advocacy, as much as De Kooning's talent, that placed him in the forefront of contemporary American painters.

After the separation, De Kooning had sex with many different women. Though he maintained a reputation as an extremely able lover, most of the women he slept with were "art groupies" who were drawn to him because of his fame. A couple of the relationships became somewhat serious. One woman bore his child, which was a source of great pride to the then fifty-ish painter. And when his friend and competitor Jackson Pollock died, De Kooning quickly acquired his girl friend. Many saw this as De Kooning's way of getting one up on the only abstract expressionist more notable than himself.

No woman, not even Elaine, ever challenged painting for primacy in De Kooning's life, but alcoholism very nearly did. By his late sixties, his drinking binges were notorious and he was suffering blackouts. At this point Elaine De Kooning reestablished herself as De Kooning's wife. She took over every aspect of the aging painter's life, including his estimated $4 million-a-year income. Even after he quit drinking, De Kooning continued to deteriorate mentally. He was eventually diagnosed with Alzheimer's disease, but he continued to paint until shortly before his death at the age of ninety.

Another Example

Pyotr I. Tchaikovsky *(Russian composer, one of the giants of Romanticism in music). Born May 7, 1840 (Celebrity Birthday Guide).*

If you have Mars in Taurus with Venus in Taurus you are … the Complete Sensualist

You are all the best and all the worst of Mars in Taurus. That is to say, you are a Lover totally focused on the sensual experience *and* you are a Lover totally focused on the sensual experience! When it comes to pure eroticism and raw sexual energy you are the tops, but the narrowness of your focus can make you act like a perpetual adolescent—drunk with the power of your own sexuality and unable to see sex as anything other than a means to physical pleasure.

At your worst you can be a very selfish, bossy partner who treats sex like a commodity and has to control every relationship. However, at your best you can be a very caring and practical Lover, every bit as kind as you are sensual. You look after the person you love, solving problems, fixing things, and generally making your affection evident in very real, tangible ways. The only thing you demand in return is the assurance that your partner's love and sex will always be available to you. As long as you are sure you will never go without, then you can be the warmest, gentlest, nicest Lover in the world.

Case History

Charlie Chaplin (comic genius and film legend known for his endearing "Little Tramp" character). Born April 16, 1889, in London, England (Manvell 1974; Milton 1996).

Chaplin was the son of a popular stage performer but he seldom saw his father. Chaplin's mother attempted to provide her two sons with a stable home but these attempts were constantly interrupted by her mental illness, and the boys spent time in foster homes and institutions. Chaplin developed into a quiet, sensitive child who concealed his insecurities behind a natural gift for pantomime. This gift, along with dire necessity, caused him to start his career on the stage at a very tender age.

According to Chaplin, his first romance occurred when, at the age of nineteen, he fell hopelessly in love with a child performer named Hetty Kelly. Chaplin later claimed that sex was not a part of his ardent response to Kelly but, nonetheless, the intensity of his infatuation so alarmed the fifteen-year-old Kelly that she broke off the relationship. A few years later when Chaplin was famous, he had a chance to be reunited with Kelly. Unfortunately, she died of influenza before he could reach her.

Chaplin's early affair with Hetty Kelly established an unfortunate pattern in his love life. He was continually drawn to very young girls by what he claimed was a "pure" appreciation of their feminine beauty. The childlike charm of these girls provided Chaplin with a love that seemed to him to be apart from the raw physical demands of his body. However, Chaplin's sex drive was so strong that he was never able to keep these infatuations "pure" or sexless for very long.

Along with his infatuation for the young and innocent, Chaplin displayed a pronounced attachment to women whose approach to sex was as earthy and direct as his own. He began in his youth by making use of prostitutes as he toured from city to city. After he became famous, he advanced to affairs with celebrities and with rising young actresses. Sometimes the women he slept with were free-thinking intellectuals (a self-educated man, Chaplin enjoyed the company of intelligent people.) But just as often they were star-struck extras or slum girls picked up off the street. His constant and indiscriminate need for women caused some people to compare Chaplin to the animalistic god, Pan.

Perhaps the most thoughtless and tragic aspect of Chaplin's sex life was his aversion to condoms. Sometime during his troubled childhood the comedian developed a phobia about rubber that was so strong he could not abide holding rubber props when he was working. Therefore all his affairs were conducted without the benefit of birth control.

After leaving vaudeville and achieving great success in films, Chaplin had a long-term affair with Edna Purviance, one of his leading ladies. She was a buxom, maternal woman with a problem-free attitude toward sex. She probably would have made a good match for the moody and hyperactive comic; however, even though Chaplin was obviously quite close to Purviance and continued to support her for many years, he had no desire for monogamy.

When he was twenty-nine, Chaplin found himself involved with another teenage lover. Her name was Mildred Harris and she was sixteen when she and Chaplin met. Chaplin later claimed that Harris had victimized him—that she had initiated an affair with him and then blackmailed him into marriage by saying she was pregnant. In reality he was smitten with the youthful actress from the very first and showered her with roses until she agreed to see him. It was only after they had sex together that Chaplin lost interest. By then it was too late—he was forced to marry her when she claimed to be pregnant.

As it turned out, the pregnancy that caused the couple to rush to the altar was a false alarm. A real pregnancy soon followed but the child died shortly after birth. Meanwhile, Chaplin did all he could to make Mildred unhappy. He spent much of his time at the studio (where he was making one of his most famous films, *The Kid*) and when he did see Mildred he typically treated her with open contempt. At one point he created a list for her of all the women he had supposedly slept with since their marriage. After a few months the young bride had no choice but to file for divorce. The result was the first of several messy court battles that would mar Chaplin's career.

When he was thirty-four, Chaplin made another attempt at recreating his youthful love affair with Hetty Kelly. A fifteen-year-old actress by the name of Lita Grey had caught his eye and he hired her as the female lead for *The Gold Rush*. He also began grooming her as his next child bride. The courtship proceeded more slowly than his impulsive infatuation with Mildred Harris. He had time to confess to Grey how his fascination with her childish beauty was consuming his life. Grey later admitted that there was an element of purity in Chaplin's feelings for her. However, this purity soon gave way to lust and, thanks to Chaplin's unwillingness to use birth control, Grey became pregnant. With this accomplished, Chaplin's desire to marry the youngster vanished and he looked for a route of escape. It was only after he was threatened with criminal charges that Chaplin agreed to marry Grey.

Chaplin's marriage to Lita Grey was only slightly more successful than his union with Mildred Harris. The marriage lasted two years and produced two healthy children. Otherwise, it was a torturous experience for both parties. It was during this marriage that Chaplin undertook his most dangerous sexual escapade—an affair with Marion Davies, the mistress of William Randolph Hearst. Hearst was an extremely powerful man who was willing to do anything to guarantee the fidelity of the love of his life. Davies, on the other hand, was a worldly actress with a quick wit who was bored with being the kept woman of the world's most influential publisher. She saw in Chaplin one of the few men powerful enough to give her a means of escape.

Chaplin's second divorce was even more spectacular and gossipy than his first. Lita charged Chaplin with what some would say were cruel and inhuman acts, including the insistence that his wife perform fellatio. Chaplin was once again forced to endure an exposé of his private life and pay a large settlement.

After this second marital disaster Chaplin became involved with Paulette Goddard, a gold digger turned actress who had already done well and had a large bank account to prove it. Her honesty impressed Chaplin, as did her appetite for sex. The relationship prospered for a time and, in order to smooth things over with the press, Chaplin allowed reporters to believe that he and Goddard had secretly married. The story stuck so well that he and Goddard had to get a Mexican divorce when, after six years, they decided to break up.

Goddard was an easy-going, sexually uninhibited woman who, like Purviance, might have made a good match for Chaplin if he had been less self-involved. Chaplin was still unable to tie himself to any one relationship and he continued to dally with a variety of women. One of these paramours was Joan Berry. She had a history of mental instability but the fifty-four-year-old Chaplin was unaware of this. He chose to believe her exaggerated emotional dependency was normal. When Chaplin finally tired of Berry's histrionics, he tried to buy her off. When that didn't work, he had her arrested. Berry responded by filing a paternity suit against him.

In the midst of this disastrous lawsuit, Chaplin married for the fourth time. His bride was the eighteen-year-old Oona O'Neill. Oona entered Chaplin's life at an extremely difficult time. The lawsuit was followed by the withdrawal of Chaplin's visa by federal authorities who disapproved of his private life and were suspicious of his political opinions. Chaplin lived much the remainder of his life as an exile. Despite this turbulent beginning, Chaplin's fourth marriage proved stable. The boyish actor who had always expressed disdain for family life belatedly became an adult. His union with Oona produced eight children and lasted until his death at the age of eighty-seven.

Other Examples

Bertrand Russell *(English mathematician, philosopher, and social activist noted for his many love affairs and four marriages, the last of which began when he was in his eighties). Born May 18, 1872 (Encyclopedia Britannica 1997).*

Paul Verlaine *(French poet as much noted for his tumultuous, bisexual love life as for his verse). Born March 30, 1844 (Encyclopedia Britannica 1997).*

Gustave Courbet *(French painter and leader of the Realist school whose nudes were so openly sexual they were often purchased anonymously). Born June 10, 1819 (Encyclopedia Britannica 1997).*

If you have Mars in Taurus with Venus in Gemini you are . . . the Playful Sensualist

You are a deft, inventive, good-humored Lover who, nonetheless, has plenty of Mars in Taurus earthiness and sexual stamina. The intellectual distance with which you view your sex life makes you a true connoisseur of physical pleasures—a cool, thoughtful sensualist who typically tries to make the most of every sexual opportunity. At times, your tendency to coolly analyze your desires may convince some people that you don't take sex that personally. You know better (and so does anyone who has ever been in bed with you).

What you must avoid is letting your approach to sex become so practical and purely transactional that your sex life is totally divorced from your more civilized needs. You may be the most warm-hearted, loyal companion in the world but, when it comes to sex, you are always drawn to the best deal—the most physical pleasure for the least emotional labor. If you let this tendency get out of hand it will make you seem fickle and opportunistic, when in fact you're just trying to have a good time.

Case History

*Franz Kafka (Czech-born writer whose enigmatic tales—*The Penal Colony *and* The Trial—*made existential angst fashionable). Born July 3, 1883, in Prague, Czechoslovakia (Pawel 1985).*

Kafka was the eldest child of a hard-working Jewish shopkeeper and his devout wife. From the very beginning the sensitive child felt alienated from his parents, both of whom devoted themselves entirely to the business enterprises of the family. For the most part, young Kafka found himself cared for by cold and unenthusiastic servants.

Kafka was a shy, skinny, sexually repressed teenager who was embarrassed by dirty jokes and refused to acknowledge the many prostitutes who plied their trade on Prague's streets. At one point, two of his more worldly friends physically carried him into a brothel where he was given a demonstration of the facts of life. He was greatly disturbed when he confessed this incident to his parents and they responded with sound hygienic advice instead of expressing outrage.

Intellectually, Kafka was a man profoundly at odds with his own body. It was a quality he expressed so well in his story *Metamorphosis* in which a young man wakes up one morning and discovers he has the body of a lowly insect. A sickly man beset with both real and imagined ailments, he saw his physical body as an impediment, a foreign object attached to his soul by some cruel fate. His inhibitions with regard to sex were very much a product of this alienation. He looked upon sex with a kind of horror. In a letter to a friend he summed up his attitude toward sex with, "Coitus is punishment for the happiness of being together" (Pawel, 82).

By the time Kafka reached late adolescence it became evident that it was only within the context of his middle-class background that sex embarrassed him. Whether this was because of a deep Oedipal conflict or his own hypersensitivity is a matter of conjecture. Regardless, when the dour Kafka stepped away from his parent's home and mingled with working-class girls he lost his nervous reserve and could be almost frisky.

Kafka had his first sexual affair with a shop girl when he was twenty. He spotted the girl through the window of his room while he was cramming for an exam and, with sign language, they made arrangements to meet later. The results were "charming, exciting and disgusting" (Pawel, 85). Kafka saw the girl one other time before he and his family left Prague on a holiday. When he came back, he was so burdened by guilt that, when he met the girl again, he could not even bring himself to look at her.

A similar affair followed the next year and, by his mid-twenties, Kafka was a well-known frequenter of brothels and an ardent pursuer of shop girls and barmaids. Among girls of his own class, he was always smitten by the very young, but the lower-class women he preferred were often older and more experienced. Of course, Kafka could still be shy and awkward even among this fun-loving company. On one occasion he made a decision to "keep" a certain waitress, but when he told the woman of his plan she assumed the stiff, evasive Kafka was making a joke and laughed. Kafka was too embarrassed to pursue the arrangement any further.

When he was twenty-nine, Kafka was introduced to Felice Bauer, the woman who would soon become his fiancée. Bauer was a strong-willed, accomplished businesswoman who had little in common with the pretty nymphets who usually caught Kafka's eye. In fact, it seems likely that it was the absence of any sexual feeling that made it possible for Kafka to take the brave step of becoming officially engaged to her. Unfortunately, once the engagement was announced, Kafka immediately felt trapped. It was impossible for Kafka to see the institution of marriage as anything other than the prison of conventionality it was for his parents.

Kafka expressed his reservations to one of Bauer's friends, Grete Bloch. Bloch quickly relayed them to Bauer. Bauer was not a woman to let such matters take care of themselves. Accompanied by her friend, she met Kafka in a hotel room and demanded he explain himself. Kafka refused to even try.

Kafka had other love affairs. One possibly involved Grete Bloch, who later claimed she had given birth to Kafka's child. Another was with Milena Jesenska, a married Czech woman with whom Kafka became passionately involved during his thirties. Unfortunately, she was unwilling to leave her husband for the writer. Kafka's friend and biographer, Max Brod, claimed Kafka stopped visiting brothels and chasing barmaids when he reached his thirties, but Kafka's diaries indicate otherwise. Even after finding a way to enjoy sex with his social and intellectual equals, Kafka apparently still had a need for the expedient sex available to him on the streets.

Kafka's daily life was relentlessly bland. He worked for an insurance company during the day and still lived with his parents. When he wasn't out with Brod or his buddies, he spent his evenings playing cards with his parents or entertaining other relatives. Then he would retire to his room and write the strange stories that would eventually make him famous. Kafka published some of his work during his lifetime and had a circle of literary friends, but his true ambitions remained hidden from the world.

As he grew older, Kafka's health problems became more alarming. He tried many things to gain ascendancy over his body: bodybuilding, a vegetarian diet, and a variety of ascetic regimes, but he only grew weaker and frailer.

At forty Kafka summoned the courage to leave his family home in Prague and take up residence in Berlin. His companion in this adventure was a fervent nineteen-year-old named Dora Diamant. Dora was well-educated, idealistic, and believed strongly in Kafka's work. She was the kind of girl that he might well have married twenty years earlier if he hadn't been so inhibited.

But now Kafka was dying of tuberculosis. Six feet tall, he weighed less than 120 pounds. Not even Diamant's obsessive love could save him. He deteriorated quickly in Berlin and finally returned to Prague, where he died a few weeks short of his forty-first birthday.

Other Examples

John F. Kennedy (*American president*). *Born May 29, 1917 (Celebrity Birthday Guide).*

Catherine the Great (*Russian monarch*). *Born May 2, 1729 (Celebrity Birthday Guide).*

If you have Mars in Taurus with Venus in Cancer you are . . . the Sentimental Sensualist

You have more reasons than most Mars in Taurus Lovers for keeping your sex life private. Sex is doubly important to you. It provides you with a physical release that you cannot live without and a sense of emotional security that makes living worthwhile. Of course, this double importance makes you a doubly sensuous and doubly seductive Lover, attuned to both the physical and the emotional needs of your Beloved. With all this going for you, you can't expect to remain a secret for very long.

Sex is never as simple for you as it is for most Mars in Taurus Lovers. Lust has a way of getting mixed up with emotional dependency in your sex life, and affection can become indistinguishable from sexual attraction. Your sexual desires are so charged with emotion and so deeply felt that they can become almost an addiction, making you a very demanding, even dangerous, lover. All things considered, sex with you is usually more than worth the trouble.

Case History

Liberace (*Walter Liberace—pianist who became one of most popular American entertainers of his day*). *Born May 16, 1919, in Milwaukee, Wisconsin (Thomas 1988; Thorson 1988).*

Liberace's family was poor, but his mother always found money to pay for his piano lessons. By the time he was fourteen, Liberace was making money on his own by playing piano with a band. His mother disapproved of the speakeasies in which he played but she needed his income to support the family after she and Liberace's father divorced.

Liberace became aware of his homosexuality while he was still a boy. Raised in the Catholic Church, he fought against his sexual attraction to men but found it impossible to avoid his desires. At sixteen he had an encounter with another man while he was travelling with the band. After this all his sexual contacts were with men.

It was also as a teenager that Liberace recognized that he had neither the patience nor the inborn talent to be a successful, classical musician. He turned to popular music where his natural gift for showmanship made up for any failings he had as a pianist. As he toured from city to city, he developed a network of homosexual contacts that guaranteed him sexual outlets wherever he went. He still adamantly denied being a homosexual. In his youth he became something of a teen heartthrob and he capitalized heavily on his ability to attract women. He made sure that his courtship and proposals of marriage to several notable women were well-publicized. When a British newspaper dared to accuse him of being a homosexual, he responded with a libel suit and won.

For many, Liberace's act and his flamboyant lifestyle were enough to close the issue of his sexual orientation. His strange combinations of exaggerated sensuality and kitsch—gaudy rings, glimmering jackets, silver candelabra, and bejeweled pianos—soon became more famous than his music. No matter how much he flirted with the ladies during his show or how many dirty jokes he included, Liberace often seemed to be broadcasting his most closely guarded secret from the stage.

This particularly became the case as the 1950s, when Liberace scored his first successes, gave way to the more liberal 1960s and 1970s. When the notion of "camp" reached Middle America, one would have expected that the "campiest" man in show business would come out of the closet. Liberace refused to do so, insisting that the older women who accounted for much of his audience would never accept him as a gay performer. Despite all the wealth and honors he had accumulated, Liberace was still terrorized by the idea that his beloved audience might reject him.

Liberace's lifestyle did change in the 1960s and 1970s. He used his wealth to establish a palatial home that was large enough to keep both his mother and his lovers under one roof without conflict. He surrounded himself with servants and assistants whose loyalty was unquestioned. He trusted them to guard his secret even while he was boldly partaking in the sexual revolution.

When Liberace was fifty-nine he began a relationship with an eighteen-year-old boy named Scott Thorson. In describing his affair with Liberace, Thorson presents himself as a naive young man who was seduced and then discarded. His account shows that, even in middle age, Liberace's sexual demands were substantial. Thorson claimed that he and the pianist had sex at least twice a day during their affair and that Liberace used amyl nitrate to heighten his orgasms. Due to problems with impotency earlier in his life, Liberace had a silicone implant in his penis. He also owned a large collection of homosexual pornography.

Liberace's fondness for pornography was a point of contention with Thorson. Thorson found the images distasteful and thought the musician's forays into porn shops were reckless. Thorson also resisted when Liberace pressed him to experiment with threesomes and other sexual variations. The young man did grant his aging lover one large concession. Thorson agreed to undergo plastic surgery designed to make him look more like Liberace.

This relationship lasted four years before Liberace's interests inevitably moved on to other young men. Thorson was kicked out of Liberace's home and the jilted lover later filed a "palimony" suit. After much publicity, the suit was settled out of court with a cash payment to Thorson. Liberace was certain that this suit would ruin his career; however, it seemed to have the opposite effect. Though he stopped short of making a public disclosure of his homosexuality, Liberace found his audience to be much more tolerant than he had ever thought possible. In the midst of this career surge the pianist began to show signs of physical decline, and it was learned that he had contracted the AIDS virus. He died, still worrying about being considered an old "queen," at the age of sixty-nine.

Another Example

John Derek (*film heartthrob who became better known as the promoter of his beautiful wives: Ursula Andress, Linda Evans, and Bo Derek) Born August 12, 1926 (Celebrity Birthday Guide).*

If you have Mars in Taurus with Venus in Leo you are … the Sensual Show-Off

You are a Lover who is too demonstrative and has too much of an appreciation for drama and display in your love life to ever keep a secret. Typically, you're having too much fun to care. You are a boisterous, fiery Mars in Taurus Lover: warm-hearted, generous, and profoundly sensual. You have a taste for the extreme in your sexual experiences and bragging rights matter as much as sensation.

The conservative side of your sexual nature often shows itself most in your need for control. Sex loses its appeal for you the minute you feel that you are being forced to play by someone else's rules. There is nothing fancy in your need to control your own sex life. You have no taste for psychological manipulation. You just like to be the person who says where, when, and how the relationship is going to progress. If you're not the person in control, you like it understood that you could be. Anyone willing to live by these rules will find you a very willing Lover.

Case History

George Sand (Aurora Dupin Dudevant, the French novelist best known today for her flamboyant lifestyle). Born July 1, 1804, in Paris, France (Barry 1976; Winegarten 1978).

George Sand's father was a gallant French nobleman. Her mother had long been his concubine and he agreed to marry her only shortly before Sand's birth. Her in-laws never accepted Sand's mother because of this and, when Sand's father died suddenly from a fall, her mother fled to Paris. Afterward, Sand saw her mother only occasionally and her paternal grandmother raised her.

By the time Sand was eighteen and had returned home with her convent education, her grandmother was dead. Her mother, aging and bitter, seemed bent on making the restless adolescent miserable. Consequently, when a kindly older man with a secure fortune proposed marriage to her, Sand was more than willing to accept.

Casimer Dudevant, who was nine years older than Sand, had only the most conventional expectations for this marriage. Unfortunately for him, his young wife turned out to be anything but conventional. In the beginning she tried hard to submit to her husband's will and be a good wife. The marriage quickly produced a son. Sand's maternal feelings were quite strong, but so was her need for art, books, and intelligent conversation—things for which her provincial husband had little patience. Soon she rebelled, and at the same time she began to think about other men.

Two years into the marriage Sand became infatuated with a handsome, young intellectual. The affair was not sexual. Sand was not yet ready to step outside the conventional bounds of matrimony. Instead she exulted in the high-minded chastity of the relationship and was deeply offended when her husband objected to it. It was at this point that the overmatched Dudevant began to slowly relinquish control over his headstrong wife.

Sand soon tired of idealistic chastity and sought lovers who could stimulate her physically as well as intellectually. She carefully noted in her diary the influence she had on men and the way she could toy with their affections. When she was twenty-four she had a second child but even she was unsure who the father was. By the time she was twenty-six, Sand was living in Paris, intent on beginning a career as a writer. She chose to write under the name of George Sand. She also became involved in a passionate affair with another writer named Jules Sandeau.

With her indulgent husband slipping further and further into the background (they were officially separated when she was thirty-two), Sand became more open and aggressive in pursuing her affairs. Though she began her career relatively late in life, she quickly surmised that notoriety of any sort could be helpful. Hence, she raised no objection when people called her a female "Don Juan" and she flaunted her independence by occasionally dressing in men's clothing (a decision made for practical, rather than sexual, reasons).

The men Sand preferred were younger, pretty rather than manly, and either physically or emotionally frail. Her most famous and tempestuous affair with the poet Alfred de Musset was typical. Sand was the stronger partner and controlled the pace of the relationship. With motherly patience, she attempted to protect the volatile poet from his own self-destructive habits and delusions.

When she and Musset were traveling in Italy he became ill. Sand found a handsome young physician to tend to him and while her lover languished in bed, Sand and the doctor had their own affair. Musset, who was emotionally unstable under the best of conditions, responded to this infidelity with a wild, jealous rage. Yet, by the time the two writers parted (he on his way to Paris and she on her way to her sexy doctor), they were friends again.

At least one of her lovers attempted to challenge Sand's famous independence. Michel de Bourges was a lawyer and a revolutionary. He looked down on the arts and artists as decorative nuisances. He also had a rather lowly opinion of women in general. Still, this half-mad firebrand fascinated Sand and for two years they were lovers. The letters they exchanged when they were apart are replete with references to clawing and biting—apparently their lovemaking was as full of fire as their political discussions. In due time, Sand tired of her revolutionary's insensitivity and frequent insults and so they separated.

During the period of her most notorious love affairs with men, Sand may have also been enjoying an affair with a woman. She became infatuated with an actress named Marie Dorval and, according to some of Sand's biographers, pursued her until they became lovers. Although opinions about their relationship differ, it is clear that the two women were very close. Sand's letters to Dorval are every bit as passionate as the letters she wrote to her male lovers.

The language that surrounded Sand's many love affairs was sometimes unbelievably florid and extremely romanticized. In fact, she and many of her lovers were significant figures in what came to be called the Romantic movement. But Sand also had a very healthy concern for the physical realities of sex. When she was separated from Michel de Bourges, she complained to him in great detail about her sexual frustration. She once remarked that the notion of love as something separate from its fleshly manifestation seemed ridiculous to her. She considered sex a very important function of life and she never failed to take it seriously.

Her inability to live up to the romantic ideals of her contemporaries, or even of those of her own novels, caused Sand to call herself an "emotional cripple." It was only later in her life, after she had learned to be satisfied with sexual relationships that were more hygienic than passionate, that Sand decided she was not the one at fault. She claimed it was the fact that the men of her era could not love a woman as a friend that made them unable to appreciate her. They were so busy searching for a grand passion that they failed to recognize what a good companion she could be.

In the end, Sand found no enduring love relationship, though she had many important friendships. Nonetheless, by her late sixties Sand reported she was at peace and as chaste in her mind as she was physically. She died at the age of seventy-two.

Another Example

Madonna (American singer and dancer). Born August 16, 1958 (Celebrity Birthday Guide).

If you have Mars in Taurus with Venus in Virgo you are . . . the Naked Sensualist

You may be the most basic and earthy of the Mars in Taurus Lovers. You see sex as a simple bodily function for which all the pretty lies of romance can offer no redemption. Some might find your approach hard and animalistic but, in fact, you are a very kind and civilized Lover. Your purely material approach to love means you measure affection in terms of real acts of generosity and service. You prove your love by what you do for your Beloved every day.

Unfortunately, no matter how nice you try to be, you have a weakness for expediency in your sexual makeup that often gets you into trouble. It's just very difficult for you to pass up any chance for a good time—the quicker and more convenient the better. You are not always proud of this susceptibility to physical pleasure. Sometimes it takes you places you'd really rather not admit you've been. But you'll never get away with denying it. The fact is, the more you try to separate yourself from your lust, the more likely it is to own you.

Case History

Alexandre Dumas, Sr. (French author of The Three Musketeers *and* The Count of Monte Cristo *who attempted to live his own romantic credo to the fullest). Born July 24, 1802, in Villier-Cotterets, France (Schopp 1988).*

Dumas' father was a mulatto, the acknowledged offspring of a wealthy French colonial and an African slave. He was a large, physically aggressive man who prospered in the heady atmosphere of revolutionary France, rose to the rank of general in Napoleon's army, but died of stomach cancer when his son was only three. His heroic exploits overshadowed Dumas' youth and set an example that the author honored all his life.

Unfortunately, the great general left behind little money when he died and Dumas' mother was dependent upon the kindness of her extended family. These arrangements hardly bothered Dumas. An unusually bright and fearless boy, he was the darling of every household he entered and, throughout his youth, never lacked for benefactors. He developed into a tall and striking young man, with a slender frame and exotic features. By the time he was seventeen Dumas had already deflowered one of the local beauties. He claimed her subsequent marriage to a tradesman left him inconsolable; however, by that time he had already been unfaithful to her at least once.

At twenty Dumas moved to Paris. Though he was employed as a clerk in a law office, his clear intention was to make a career for himself in literature and become famous. He applied himself to this goal with amazing energy, not only writing plays, verse, and prose but also using his father's reputation to gain admittance to the best salons where he curried the favor of the rich and titled. Despite his frenetic activity, Dumas also found time for a mistress. Laure Labay was a poor seamstress eight years older than the ambitious writer, but Dumas preferred women who were older and more experienced.

Soon Dumas' irregular union with Labay produced a child. Dumas established the first of several households he would support during the course of his life. Dumas was hardly an attentive husband. With his writing, his job, his socializing, and his mother, he had little time left for his new family. Dumas still seemed pleased to have this little island of conventional domesticity available to him and he never abandoned Labay or his son.

Even while he maintained Labay and their child, Dumas looked for a more affluent mistress who could increase his access to Parisian society. He found her in Melanie Waldor, the lonely wife of an army officer. Unlike most of Dumas' paramours, Waldor was thin and not particularly beautiful, but she was enthusiastic about her young lover's talents. Waldor worked as hard as he did to secure the success they both knew he deserved.

Dumas was twenty-six when he finally achieved his great breakthrough as a playwright. Instantly he was transformed from a poor clerk to a rich literary star—a young revolutionary of letters, and respected, honored, and sought after. However, this transition did little to slow Dumas down. If anything the realization of his dreams of glory only made him work harder.

One reason Dumas had to work so hard was that he had so many people to support. By the time he was thirty, Dumas had two former mistresses with children to maintain, plus his mother, his current lover, and himself. Never a frugal man, even his unbelievably productive pen was unable to keep up with his spending.

One of the most enduring of Dumas' relationships was with an actress named Ida Ferrand. She was a plump, undistinguished woman but Dumas found a welcomed sense of continuity with her. After living with Ferrand for eight years, Dumas surprised everyone by marrying her. It was generally assumed that his creditors had forced the writer into the marriage. The marriage lasted two years before an amicable separation was arranged. At one point during this period, Dumas found Ida in bed with one of his best friends. Too sleepy to fight, he simply joined them and the next morning told his friend that the incident would be forgotten. Jealousy was not one of Dumas' faults.

Of course, the famous author had good reason not to be jealous considering his own innumerable infidelities. Dumas was apparently incapable of letting any opportunity for sensual enjoyment pass him by. Most of his liaisons were with actresses. This was probably because, as a playwright, actresses were always available to him. Generous, expansive, and famous, few women could refuse him. Despite his many mistresses, Dumas also sought out prostitutes. Once a friend walked into the author's room and found Dumas entertaining three of these women at one time. Not known for his modesty, Dumas once claimed that if he ever limited himself to just one woman she'd be dead inside of eight days.

Even though his sexual appetite was obviously substantial, it was probably Dumas' attitude toward sex as much as his activity that gave him a reputation as a satyr. Always mindful of his African heritage, Dumas enjoyed playing the stereotype of the uncouth, animalistic primitive. He became famous for his bawdy asides and total disregard for conventional morality. He bragged that he had sired over 500 illegitimate children. Dumas openly accepted and socialized with his eldest son, who was also named Alexandre Dumas and became an author of note. The younger Dumas took a dim view of his father's philandering. Dumas would hide his girl friends in the closet when his son came to visit, and the son referred to Dumas in public as his "grown-up child."

In one way, Dumas' vitality proved a curse as well as a blessing. It caused him to outlive the age of romanticism in which he had so thrived. The society that came afterward was far less receptive to his literature and tended to judge him only by his lascivious reputation. His last notoriety came to him while he was in his sixties. Dumas unwisely allowed himself to be photographed with a young American performer named Adah Isaacs Mencken, who was better known for her skintight, flesh-colored costume than her acting. Soon pictures of the obese, grinning writer bouncing Mencken on his knee were circulating throughout Paris. This event was extremely embarrassing for many of Dumas' friends and family, but the great man himself remained unrepentant. He died at the age of sixty-eight, surrounded by his numerous illegitimate children and grandchildren.

Other Examples

Edgar Degas (*French painter who blended the styles of impressionism and realism). Born July 19, 1834 (Celebrity Birthday Guide).*

Mick Jagger (*British rock star). Born July 26, 1943 (Celebrity Birthday Guide).*

If you have Mars in Taurus with Venus in Libra you are . . . the Sensual Idealist

Your physical response to sex always hinges on what you think about your partner. You must have a Beloved that you can put on a pedestal and worship. But you must also have someone who can step off that pedestal and love you in a very human, very physical way. Your idealized expectations of what love should be and how a relationship should function will always be very important to you, but never more important than your need for physical pleasure. If forced to choose between the two, you will undoubtedly find some sneaky way to have both.

At heart, you are a conservative Lover but your actions often make this conservatism less than obvious. You expect too much from sex and relationships to be satisfied with the commonplace, and the combination of your intense idealism and your raw sexual energy often push you to extremes in your sex life. You make no apologies for this extremism and, unlike most Mars in Taurus Lovers, you seldom try to conceal it. As far as you're concerned, any sin committed for the sake of love is automatically forgiven.

Case History

Frieda Lawrence (*Frieda von Richthofen Weekley Lawrence, the wife of D. H. Lawrence and the model for Lady Chatterley). Born August 11, 1879, in Metz, France (Lucas 1973; Maddox 1994).*

Frieda was the daughter of a dispossessed Prussian baron and war hero who held a minor government position. She adored her father, not only because he was an indulgent parent, but because of the glamour of his hereditary, if meaningless, title. Unfortunately, Frieda's father was, in fact, a rather weak man whose addiction to gambling played havoc with the family's meager resources.

Frieda married an English university professor named Ernest Weekley when she was twenty. Weekley was a kind, intelligent man. He was also a sexually repressed Victorian and ill-prepared to deal with the sensuous and eager young woman who became his bride. On their wedding night she was disappointed by his formality and alarmed by his apparent fear of the sex act. Afterward, while he slept, she was left seething with anger. She had entered her marriage with the notion that it would provide her with sexual liberation. Instead she found herself in a sexual prison.

Despite her disappointment in their sex life, and the fact that the small college town in which they settled left her stiff with boredom, Frieda's marriage to Weekley was not totally unhappy. It produced three children within five years. Frieda grew to appreciate the security and consistency of married life; however, she never lost her sensual exuberance. Eight years into her marriage, the frustrated housewife was lured by her sister into an extended visit to Germany, where she immediately found herself a lover.

Frieda's lover was Dr. Otto Gross, an early follower of Sigmund Freud who had found in psychoanalysis an excellent excuse for sleeping with his patients. Frieda's sister had previously been Gross' lover. Both Frieda's sister and Gross' wife were pregnant at the same time by the doctor. These two remarkable women quickly impressed their own notions of sexual liberty and feminine autonomy upon Frieda. Frieda responded so wholeheartedly that she too tried, although unsuccessfully, to conceive a child with Gross. Through Gross and her sister, Frieda was introduced to a bohemian milieu quite unlike anything she had known previously. She became familiar with artists, anarchists, and unconventional thinkers of all types. When Frieda returned to her family in England, her outlook was so changed that her children complained that she was not their "old" mother.

Frieda's affair with Otto Gross came to a sad ending. The doctor was a drug addict. After she returned to her family he deteriorated quickly and eventually had to be institutionalized. But his ideas still burned within her and she began to develop strong opinions about personal freedom and sexual expression. These were not notions that she dared to share with Weekley. When she was thirty-two, her husband brought a twenty-six-year-old writer home to dinner who was more than willing to listen to her thoughts and match them with some radical concepts of his own.

The attraction between D. H. Lawrence and Frieda was immediate. The daring Mrs. Weekley proposed they have an affair. But Lawrence was not the sort of man who took sexual matters lightly. Soon it became obvious to Frieda that in order to have a relationship with Lawrence, she would have to give up not only her husband, but also her home and children. Convinced of Lawrence's greatness as a writer and of her own need for freedom, Frieda chose to do so.

The marriage of Frieda and D. H. Lawrence was stormy and strange. Each was strong-willed, opinionated, and prone to preach at the other. One matter of constant contention was Lawrence's theory that the female must defer to the male in a "natural" marriage. Their arguments often became physically violent, with Lawrence swatting and pushing the large-bodied Frieda and Frieda breaking crockery over the novelist's head. Yet, despite their frequent rows, they remained devoted to one another.

Sex was very important to both the Lawrences. D. H. Lawrence's feelings about sex were almost religious. He saw sex as part of the great primitive mystery that modern man was missing. He learned much about the mystery of sex and its practical application from his new wife. The many strong, sexually curious, female characters that populate his novels began with Frieda. There is little that he wrote about concerning the sexual experience that didn't come directly out of his relationship with her. She was both his instructor and his muse.

Although Frieda cherished her husband and the role of "Mrs. D. H. Lawrence," she had not left her family to be tied to any one man. She was determined to sample the sexual liberty about which she had dreamed so long. She had affairs even before she and Lawrence were married and, by at least one report, she had sex with enough men to fill a small telephone book by the time she died. To some extent, Frieda went to bed with other men to punish Lawrence for his psychological bullying and physical abusiveness. It is also evident that she took great pleasure, and found a necessary degree of autonomy, in her surreptitious love life.

Lawrence died when Frieda was fifty. There was no question of her returning to her family. Weekley never forgave her for leaving him, and her children were all grown. She did attempt a reunion with her youngest daughter who was showing symptoms of mental illness. Frieda decided her problems were sexual and hired a male nurse whose duties included having sex with the young woman.

Frieda devoted herself to the propagation and protection of Lawrence's memory. She settled in the artist community of Taos, New Mexico, where Mabel Dodge Luhan, a millionaire avant-garde personality, was her benefactor, her neighbor, and, occasionally, her adversary. She also had a love affair with an Italian named Angelo Ravagli who was fifteen years her junior. When she was sixty-one, they married. Frieda was now something of a cultural icon and she thoroughly enjoyed the role—remaining jolly, defiant, and energetic until her death at the age of seventy-seven.

Another Example

Alma Mahler Werfel (Viennese beauty noted for her string of famous lovers and husbands including painter Gustav Klimt, composer Gustav Mahler, painter Oskar Kokoschka, architect Walter Gropius, and writer Anton Werfel). Born August 31, 1879 (Keegan).

If you have Mars in Taurus with Venus in Scorpio you are . . . the Sensualist of the Soul

You are a plodding, conservative Lover dedicated to the pursuit of pleasure but fully aware of just how much trouble that pursuit can bring. Sex can become a scary proposition in your eyes. That is why you keep everything concerning your sex life under strict control. You recognize, more than any other Mars in Taurus Lover, that sex does not end with sensation, but that it is something sacred—a test of the soul. Even though you are extremely susceptible to the allure of the body's desires, you do not take such tests lightly.

Despite your cautious approach, you are still a very sensual Lover, quite capable of blending the sacred with ample and delicious portions of the profane. You may never be totally comfortable with your blinding passions because you are always mindful that sex is about power as much as it is about pleasure. Yet, with someone you trust, and with all the doors and windows locked tight, you can be the most uninhibited, uncontrollable Lover imaginable.

Case History

Paul Klee *(Swiss-born artist who brought spirituality to expressionism). Born December 18, 1879 in Bern, Switzerland (Di San Lazzaro 1957; Klee 1964).*

The son of a music teacher, Klee was brought up with a deep respect for the arts. His talents ran in many directions. He loved music and was an accomplished violinist. He also wrote poetry and fiction. But at an early age Klee decided to make the visual arts both his profession and his primary passion.

Yet this serious and high-minded youngster was prey to other, less aesthetic passions. At the beginning of his 1898 diary, Klee made a list of childhood memories. Quite a few of these recollections had to do with sex. He recalled dreaming of a woman's genitals at the age of three (he imagined they looked like a cow's udder). He was deeply in love by the time he was seven. When he was eleven, his mother found some of his erotic drawings and was shocked at the boy's imaginative renditions of the female body. At twelve he attempted to force kisses onto a nine-year-old playmate who coyly fought him off. He later lost this juvenile love to another boy.

When Klee was nineteen he was permitted to go to Munich to study art. Given the obvious sensuality of his nature, it is not surprising that once free of the control of his parents, the young student immediately did two things: he fell in love and he acquired a working-class mistress.

The woman he loved was a music teacher named Lily Stumpf. Lily was three years older than Klee and had other suitors. At first she did not take the advances of this penniless art student very seriously. Her offhanded response left Klee frustrated and miserable. As far as he was concerned, they were already engaged to be married though years would pass before he was able to convince Lily to agree with him.

Although we do not know the name of his mistress, Klee gave her the semipoetic name of Evaline in his diaries. Otherwise his references to her are abrupt and straightforward, revealing both the shame and the sexual expediency with which he regarded her presence in his life. She was not a prostitute, but Klee gave her money, particularly after she informed him that she was pregnant with his child. There is little mention of her during the months of her pregnancy and only a single line in the diary to inform us that the child died.

There were other such arrangements. Klee reported an incident at a drawing session in which fellow students took advantage of two female models who became drunk and were passed from lap to lap. Later, when the other men had left, Klee offered to escort the models home. He wrote of his sense of power as he took charge of these two tipsy beauties knowing that he could do with them pretty much whatever he wanted, but he didn't.

He began sleeping with one of these models, who was only sixteen. Because of her youth, he saw her as not yet a part of the "scum." She was also the mistress of one his friends who happened to be out of town. This added a sense of conquest to the affair.

This relationship was short-lived. The girl soon returned to her old boy friend. At the same time Klee broke off his affair with "Evaline." Klee came to the conclusion that he had to apply the deeply moralistic sense of purpose that guided his professional life to his sex life. This meant no more mistresses and complete devotion to his beloved Lily. It helped that about this time Lily Stumpf put aside her other beaus and concentrated her attention on Klee. The engagement that Klee had presumed from the beginning of their relationship became a fact, at least unofficially.

When he was twenty-one Klee traveled to Italy. This proved to be a grave test of his vow of celibacy. Prostitution thrived in cities like Rome and Naples and, as he noted in his diary, Klee always knew where he could find sex for hire. He refused to surrender to this temptation and he avoided the company of young, Italian women in general. He worked diligently on his drawing and attempted to relieve his lust by staring at photographs of classical statuary. Nude models proposed a particularly torturous challenge to his chastity. It was often difficult for him to ignore the feminine charms of the models and concentrate on anatomy. His sleep was restless and his mind unsettled. Later he admitted he might well have taken a mistress again had it not been for the barriers of language and custom that separated his group of Germanic students from the native population. It was only because of these fortunate (or unfortunate) circumstances that he was able to hold onto his precious sense of sexual ethics.

Klee was a new man back in Bern after his six months in Italy. From this point on, his rampant sex drive was completely under his control. Again, the presence of Lily helped immeasurably. At various times he was able to steal away and meet her in Munich where they could hear fine music and spend the night together. Otherwise, Klee concentrated on his studies. It was during this period that he produced his first mature works: a series of satirical etchings such as *Virgin in a Tree* and *Two Men Meet, Each Presuming the Other to Be of Higher Rank*. These highly ironic drawings feature nude human figures carefully and realistically rendered but grotesquely distorted with long, gaunt limbs, and sagging bellies and breasts. Sexual tension pervades these works, as does a sense of frustration and disgust at the human condition.

Klee and Lily Stumpf were married when the artist was twenty-six. The sexual release for Klee must have been overwhelming since, despite his desire to avoid further financial obligations and his typically controlled and orderly lifestyle, Lily became pregnant the first year of their marriage. While Lily supported the family with her music lessons, Klee kept house and cared for their son. It was only after a triumphant exhibit, four years into the marriage, that Klee asked his wife for time off from his chores.

Klee's artistic style went through a remarkable transformation after his marriage. He abandoned the sour irony of his earlier prints, embraced color, and adopted a delightful quality of primitive naiveté. Art historians explain the development of Klee's special brand of sweet and childlike expressionism and abstraction in many ways, but the obvious influence married life had on his consciousness is often ignored. Assured of sex and love, the artist was at last free to explore a far more innocent and cerebral aspect of his art.

Klee was one of the most successful of modern artists. His work was neither strident nor clouded with theories, and it sold well. He was invited to teach at the great school of modernism, the Bauhaus, and when that institution closed he moved to a respectable position at the Dusseldorf Academy. But by this time Hitler was on the rise. When he was fifty-three, Klee was declared a "degenerate artist" by the Nazis and hounded from his job. He fled Germany in fear for his life. All his money in German banks was confiscated. He attempted to renew his Swiss citizenship but his homeland did not want him. About this time he was diagnosed with a degenerative disease. He died in a nursing home with his beloved Lily by his side at the age of sixty.

If you have Mars in Taurus with Venus in Sagittarius you are . . . the Reluctant Sensualist

You are a very sensitive, skittish Lover and you often feel at odds with the raw, unmitigated sensuality of your own sexual feelings. You expect sex to be more than just flesh-on-flesh. You expect it to be an inspiration, a liberation of the spirit as well as the body. Therefore, you are often disappointed, or simply overwhelmed, by sexual experiences you have as a Mars in Taurus Lover. You may try and escape the limitations of physical sex and seek out relationships that are based more on intellectual and spiritual affinity. No matter how much you try to develop the idealistic side of your sexual nature, deep down you will always remain a sensualist.

Even though you are a nervous, occasionally confused Lover who may require some special handling, the impulsive energy of your lovemaking can make you a very desirable partner. You are one of the least conservative Mars in Taurus Lovers and, when the mood is right, you can dazzle your partner with your daring and unpredictability. In your best moments you have the capacity to blend raw sexual energy with childlike innocence and, when this happens, it is worth a little confusion.

Case History

Jackson Pollock (American abstract expressionist painter famous for his "drip" paintings). Born January 28, 1912, in Cody, Wyoming (Naifeh 1989).

Pollock was the youngest of five sons raised in a home dominated by his strong-willed mother. As the smallest, Pollock was pampered and protected during his childhood by his brothers and his mother. He developed into an extremely sensitive, gentle youngster who nonetheless attempted to compete with his big brothers in everything. So, when the older brothers began studying art, Pollock had to join them.

Pollock soon learned to cover his sensitive nature with an often-exaggerated show of masculinity and defiance. Despite this macho exterior and a tendency to brag about his love affairs, Pollock was probably in his mid-twenties before he had sex with a woman. As a student, first in California and then New York City, he watched his friends have great success with female art students and models but somehow never managed to do so himself. He had girl friends but the romances always seemed to wither, mostly because of his lack of interest. His brothers, concerned about his slow development, introduced him to likely partners. One brother even took him on a tour of whorehouses in New Orleans.

During his teens or early twenties, Pollock had some sort of homosexual encounter. He was reluctant to talk about it so there is no way of knowing how often he engaged in homosexual relations during his early years, but it was a source of great concern for him. By his late twenties, Pollock's homosexual encounters were becoming more frequent. He began to hang out in a bar that serviced the homosexual underground in New York. His nocturnal sexual adventures, usually accompanied by heavy drinking, were noted by many. He was also a regular guest at Peggy Guggenheim's home, which had become a refuge for her many homosexual friends. During the period when Pollock was a frequent visitor at the house, homosexual orgies were staged regularly. He also found his way into the homosexual crowd while vacationing in Provincetown on Cape Cod.

It may well have been his shame over this secret life that led Pollock deeper and deeper into alcoholism. It certainly increased his already considerable sexual insecurity with women. Quiet and shy in the presence of women when he was sober, Pollock became openly belligerent when he was drinking—making crude sexual propositions to females he did not know and roundly insulting the ones he did know.

Then when he was thirty, a painter named Lee Krasner came to Pollock's studio. She was a few years older than Pollock, not a pretty woman, but aggressive and worldly enough to fight her way through his sexual ambiguity. She was also perceptive enough to see the talent that was concealed behind Pollock's profound insecurity. Pollock's friends considered Krasner both a masochist and a calculating manipulator. She suffered through his abuse, alcoholism, and sexual turmoil without complaint, always trying to please and protect him. But she also did everything she could to promote his talent and push him toward success, even going so far as to temporarily give up her own painting.

Pollock's attachment to Krasner came as no surprise. She was a woman he could relate to both as a wife and as a mother. He quickly developed a childlike dependency on her. She was also a keenly intelligent painter whose ideas about art fed and stimulated his own. There is evidence that her presence in his life didn't altogether stop his homosexual romps, but they certainly became less frequent, particularly after the couple left the city and moved to a house in Connecticut.

When Pollock was thirty-seven, *Life* magazine did a spread on him that asked its readers whether Pollock was the greatest living painter in the United States. In his thirties, Pollock had cut back on his drinking and dropped his nagging self-doubt long enough to develop an innovative approach to painting. Laying his canvas on the floor of his barn/studio, he dribbled common house paint over the entire surface. The result was a mass of spidery lines that mesmerized the viewer and became the hallmark of the "action" or "all-over" or "abstract expressionist" school of painting. It was quickly noted that Pollock had done more than discover a new technique. He had given birth to a whole new way of thinking about visual art.

The sudden fame that the *Life* article brought to Pollock put a tremendous strain on his marriage with Krasner. Younger, more attractive women were now eager for his company. The sexual conquests that had been so difficult for him in the past now came easily. Soon Pollock had a buxom young girl friend named Ruth Kligman to show off to his buddies at the Cedar Street Tavern. These artists, who respected Pollock's work but never considered him much of a ladies' man, were impressed. Krasner, who knew the degree to which Pollock's alcoholism was interfering with his sexual performance, was not.

By the time he reached forty, Pollock had slipped back into alcoholism. He was proud of his success but deeply uncertain that he could maintain the heroic public image he had been assigned. The situation became so bad that Krasner called in Pollock's mother, a woman with whom she was less than friendly, to help her keep the explosive artist in line. Pollock was still unable to relocate his muse. Krasner, who had been willing to stand by Pollock as he repeatedly fell apart as a man, was unwilling to stand by and watch him fall apart as an artist. Encouraged by her friends, who were alarmed at the viciousness of Pollock's abuse, she began to withdraw from the marriage into therapy and her own painting. Then she left Pollock to take an extended tour of Europe.

Pollock quickly moved Kligman into his home in the country, but his drinking and morose behavior only increased in Krasner's absence. After a few weeks Kligman had enough and left him. Pollock persuaded her to return, but she brought along a female friend. Pollock picked the two young women up at the train station and, drunk as usual, attempted to drive them to his home. He lost control of the car on a narrow country road and crashed into a tree. Both Pollock and Kligman's friend were killed. Pollock was forty-four.

Another Example

Madame Pompadour (*mistress of the French King Louis XV who became his closest friend and advisor). Born December 29, 1721 (Encyclopedia Britannica 1997).*

If you have Mars in Taurus with Venus in Capricorn you are . . . the Disciplined Sensualist

You seek to keep your powerful sexual urges under control more than any Mars in Taurus Lover. It's not that you mistrust your body, but you do mistrust your passion. You recognize the degree to which sexual desire can make you physically dependent upon someone else and this positively scares you. It is this fear of dependency that gives you such a tough, uncompromising attitude about your sexuality. The conditions under which you can truly enjoy sex and let loose your deep, visceral sensuality tend to be very specific and sometimes even impossible.

On the positive side, once you find someone to love in your own special way, you can be one of the most loyal of the Mars in Taurus Lovers, as well as an extremely warm and physically affectionate partner. Your approach to love might best be described as businesslike. For you, love is understood as a system of mutual obligations, and nothing makes you feel more obligated than a good time in bed.

Case History

J. Edgar Hoover (Washington bureaucrat who took a small, scandal-ridden agency called the FBI and made it into a law enforcement legend). Born January 1, 1895, in Washington, D.C. (Demaris 1975; Summers 1993).

Born virtually within the shadow of the Capitol to a family that had long been involved in civil service, Hoover was destined to be a bureaucrat. He was an intent, energetic little boy who was extremely active at school and in his church (following the example of his older brother, whom he idolized). He also worked part-time delivering groceries where his alacrity earned him the nickname "Speed." When he finished high school it came as no surprise that Hoover followed the family tradition and went to work for the government while he attended law school at night. Hoover completed a master's degree in law but never distinguished himself as a lawyer. As a bureaucrat, however, he had no peer.

Hoover worked in the Justice Department, where he earned praise for his single-minded attack on the people the government considered subversive. He was subsequently moved to the Federal Bureau of Investigation where, at the age of twenty-eight, he rose to the rank of director.

During this period Hoover was something of a loner. He lived with his mother in his childhood home (as he would continue to do for the rest of her life). He had no real social life and showed no interest in dating women. Shortly before his appointment as director of the FBI, Hoover made friends with a fellow investigator named Thomas Franklin Baughman. Hoover spent every available moment in the company of Baughman and, when Hoover became director, Baughman was quickly advanced to the number two position in the bureau. Four years after Hoover's appointment, Baughman married. This marriage seems to have had a disastrous effect on Baughman's career. His rank within the bureau began a steep decline and Hoover stopped seeing him socially.

The man who took Baughman's place as Hoover's closest friend was Clyde Tolson. Tolson applied to the FBI when Hoover was thirty-three, but there is some indication that the director knew him before this. Tolson had already proved himself a worthy employee in another agency and was in fact applying for a lower position in the bureau than he already held. It is thought that Tolson did this because he knew that he could expect quick advancement. If so, he was right. Tolson was appointed associate director two years after he was hired at the FBI.

Tolson was certainly not unworthy of the powerful position he held. A keenly intelligent, affable man, he proved to be an extremely able and well-liked administrator. But Hoover's appreciation of his associate director obviously went far beyond his job skills. He and Tolson rode to work together every day; they worked together, ate lunch together, and usually spent their evenings together. During the 1930s, when Hoover was a frequent and very public visitor of nightclubs and horse races, Tolson was typically his companion. Each year the two men took a long vacation together, usually in some sunny locale. During these vacations Hoover took albums full of photographs of his handsome friend. But perhaps the most potent indicator of their intimacy was the fact that Tolson was the only person besides Hoover's immediate family and Thomas Baughman to refer to the director by his childhood nickname, "Speed."

This uncommonly close relationship, and the fact that Hoover remained unmarried and seemingly uninterested in women, naturally led to rumors of homosexuality. Hoover did not take these accusations lightly. He instructed his agents to track down the source of any such rumor and confront the person making the accusation with the full wrath of his bureau. Hoover minced no words in describing his accusers. They were degenerate, sex-obsessed, and vile. He demanded they prove their allegations or retract them, at least during his lifetime. No one ever produced any proof that J. Edgar Hoover was a homosexual, yet the cloud of suspicion never really went away.

The image Hoover tried to project was that of a busy, right-thinking man who was too involved in his work to think about sex. It is also clear that Hoover was not asexual. Agents who chanced to unlock his desk drawer found it bulging with pornographic pictures and literature (all heterosexual, apparently). It was known within the bureau that the director delighted in reading sexually explicit reports. Perhaps the most notable, and notorious, of Hoover's sexual indulgences was the information he kept in a secret file on the sex lives of people in the government. Ostensibly this information was gathered because it was felt that sexual indiscretions (and particularly homosexual indiscretions) made a person vulnerable to blackmail by the "enemy." But Hoover was not above using the information, or the threat of it, for his own purposes. It is apparent that closet homosexuals were made into FBI informants because of the weight of this information. Some people feel that Hoover's secret dossiers also influenced congressmen and even presidents.

During the 1930s Hoover worked hard to establish the FBI as the primary federal law enforcement agency in the mind of the public. He also sought to glamorize the image of his agents. Not everything he did toward this end was honest, or even legal, but Hoover's talent as a bureaucrat was to know exactly which rules he could break with impunity. Hoover also sought to recreate himself in the course of recreating his bureau. He decided he needed to establish himself as a macho crime fighter after years of working wonders from behind a desk. He deftly organized the capture of a nationally known criminal so that he could be the one to make the actual "collar"—secretly surrounded by scores of armed agents, of course.

For all his concern about his image, there was one important change in his lifestyle that Hoover refused to make. He never gave up his close relationship with Tolson. Their cozy routine continued throughout the years of his life despite the rumors and doubts it generated. The only thing that interrupted the pace of their relationship was Tolson's ill health, which became an increasing factor during the final years. But even then the director continued to stop by Tolson's house every day in his chauffeur-driven car to see if the associate director was well enough to be driven to work. This routine was only broken when, at the age of seventy-six, Hoover died alone in his bed.

The questions about Hoover's sexuality did not stop with his death. Although widely admired in conservative circles, Hoover had earned the animosity of many because of his ironclad ideology and highhanded methods. Perhaps the culmination of this dislike and the rumors that buzzed around Hoover during his lifetime was evident by a book written by Anthony Summers called *Official and Confidential: The Secret Life of J. Edgar Hoover.*

Summers introduces testimony from various witnesses, ranging from Mafia figures to the wife of J. Edgar's physician, to show that Hoover was not only a homosexual, but was blackmailed by organized crime. He quotes one woman who claims that she was present at an orgy where J. Edgar Hoover, dressed in a red dress and a feather boa, had sex with two young male prostitutes. Many of the sources in Summers' book are secondhand. His allegations, particularly with regard to the Mafia, have been strongly questioned by both friends and enemies of the director. But true or not, the image that Summers conjures of Hoover in a red cocktail dress rivals the image Hoover tried to create of himself as a manly crime fighter.

Another Example

Belle Starr *(the most famous female outlaw of the Old West). Born February 5, 1848 (Encyclopedia Britannica 1997).*

If you have Mars In Taurus with Venus in Aquarius you are … the Sensualist Without Limits

You are an uninhibited, free-spirited Lover. You bring to your sexual experiences a joy of discovery that is both exciting and infectious. You like to experiment in your sexual play and appreciate variety and openness. Combined with your avid sensuality, this openness often leads you far away from the conservatism typical of Mars in Taurus. But as long as you stay close to your essential earthiness and follow the lead of your body, you can't get into too much trouble.

Typically, the only aspect of your sexuality that causes you problems is your own headstrong idealism. Even though you are the most liberated Mars in Taurus Lover, you are also the least flexible. You have strong opinions about what your sexual experience should be and who it is you must love. Not only does this tendency to intellectualize sensation interfere with your ability to enjoy sex, it also sets up conflict between your mind and body that you may never completely resolve.

Case History

Diane Arbus (Diane Nemerov Arbus, a photographer noted for her probing, often disturbing pictures of people on the fringes of American society). Born March 14, 1923, in New York City (Bosworth 1984).

Diane was the daughter of a well-to-do Jewish family. She was a quiet, daydreaming child, who apparently lacked self-confidence until she turned fourteen and met Allan Arbus. Allan was nineteen and was working in the store owned by Diane's parents while he attended college. His ambition was to become an actor. Diane's parents did not approve of Allan. They did everything they could to discourage the relationship, but the two teenagers would not be denied. They saw each other as much as possible over the next four years.

Under Allan's direction, Diane's sexuality blossomed and with it her confidence and poise. Unlike her friends who hated their bodies during adolescence, she was thoroughly at ease. She liked to tease her unseen neighbors by undressing in front of windows. But the true object of her lust was Allan. Even when her parent's forced her to go out with other boys, she could only think of him. Finally, shortly after she turned eighteen, her persistence won over her parents, and she and Allan were married.

Diane and Allan Arbus were by all accounts an incredibly happy couple. They were poor during the early years of their marriage (despite the wealth of Diane's family) and World War II took Allan away for two years, but they remained devoted to one another despite these trials. When Allan came back from the army, he and Diane started a fashion photography business. Working together only strengthened their cohesiveness. The couple had two daughters and, along with her duties as a photographer, Diane labored to be an ideal mother and homemaker. As far as she was concerned, she had the perfect marriage.

Both Diane and Allan held very liberal opinions and developed a small circle of friends who shared their openness. Among these friends was a man who was very much in love with Diane. An affair didn't develop between them for several years despite a great deal of flirting.

When it did, there was no noticeable strain on the Arbus marriage. Allan seemed content to let his attractive wife roam; however, the friend's marriage was shaken and, because of this, he and Diane stopped having sex.

Diane experimented with other lovers after this affair. Meanwhile, both Allan and Diane were becoming dissatisfied with their careers as fashion photographers. Diane longed to pursue her interest in "street" photography—candid shots of everyday (and some "not-so-everyday") people. Allen dabbled in music and painting until he finally returned to his adolescent dream of becoming an actor. He met and fell in love with a new woman while taking classes in acting.

The gradual dissolution of the Arbus marriage was characteristically calm and civilized. They remained good friends and Allan continued to give Diane financial support that allowed her to develop her singular style of photography. Beneath this polite veneer, Diane was deeply hurt by the transition. Regardless of her casual affairs, Allan remained her ideal— her one true love. Without him and the conventional structure of their remarkable marriage, she developed an almost compulsive dependence on her work.

After the break with her husband, the thirty-six-year-old Arbus embarked on a period of reckless promiscuity that surprised even her most unconventional friends. Not only did she sleep with photographers, writers, and other men she met through her work, Arbus also sought out one-night stands with strangers she picked up at parties or even off the street. Obviously, these adventures exposed her to significant danger, but this only made them more exciting for Arbus.

In many ways, Arbus' sex life followed the same course as her photography. As a photographer Arbus was always drawn to the extraordinary: sideshow freaks, the mentally ill, and people from various extremes. These artistic interests intermingled with her desire to broaden her experience of sex. She attended orgies, both as a photographer and a participant. She talked of having sex with a dwarf. She was interested in sadomasochism and pornography and took her camera into leather bars and porn houses. She was also keenly interested in transvestites and homosexuals. Even though most of her own sexual adventures were with men, she apparently also experimented with lesbianism. She told a friend that she wanted to have sex with as many different kinds of people as possible because she was looking for an authenticity of experience.

Arbus was always extremely forthright about her sexual experiences and about her body. Her haphazard approach to personal hygiene and her tendency to talk openly and often about her menstrual cycle and other bodily functions offended many people, particularly men. Men were also put off by the competitive zeal with which she pursued her career; however, outside her career, Arbus was capable of being very feminine. Many people were surprised at her fragility.

Although several of her love affairs resulted in warm and enduring friendships, Arbus never found a relationship that could replace the one she had with Allan; she continued to secretly mourn the loss of her marriage. Allan experienced some success in his new career (he was a semiregular character on the TV series *M.A.S.H.* playing a psychiatrist). He showed no signs of returning to her. His apparent happiness only exacerbated her own loneliness and misery. The fact that she had been very successful herself since the dissolution of her marriage and was now famous for her photographs did nothing to alleviate Arbus' depression. She resented the expectations placed upon her and the fact that many labeled her as a photographer of freaks. She complained that her work no longer "did it" for her. Without either her work or marriage to support her, Arbus became increasing vulnerable. When she was forty-eight, she committed suicide.

Another Example

Mercedes de Acosta (lesbian writer who liked to sleep with famous women, such as Greta Garbo, or at least liked to brag about sleeping with famous women). Born March 1, 1893 (Vickers).

If you have Mars in Taurus with Venus in Pisces you are . . . the Supreme Sensualist

You are the warmest, most sensuous, and openhearted Lover anyone could ask for. You surrender yourself so sweetly and totally to the act of love that it is as if you were made for nothing else. There is a delicacy, sensitivity, and vulnerability about your sexual nature that is both irresistible and alarming. People feel that you must be protected. But as you well know, you are much tougher than you appear.

For all your passivity and emotional volatility you are, in the end, always a pragmatist. Your sweet surrender to love is only a means of heightening the sensual pleasures to be found there. It is never as complete as it appears and can be duplicated again and again, in the company of many different partners. Yes, you are something of an opportunist, but you are such a loving, gentle, and sexy opportunist that no one really minds!

Case History

Max Ernst (German-born surrealist painter noted for both the breadth and variety of his work and for his many love affairs). Born April 2, 1891, in Bruhl, Germany (Quinn 1976).

After a conventional, middle-class upbringing, Ernst was sent to the university at Bonn to pursue his deep interest in philosophy and psychology. There he studied Freud, Nietzsche, and many other modern thinkers but eventually decided to devote himself to art.

As a college student Ernst evinced a significant sensual appetite and an amazing facility with the local women. He later called these simple Rhineland girls who served as models, as well as bedmates, for his friends and himself "the sources of all good things" (Quinn, 38).

After serving with the German Army during World War I (very much against his will), Ernst returned to Cologne, married, and had a child. Little is known about Ernst's first marriage other than it fell apart soon after Ernst met the poet Paul Eluard and his wife Gala.

Gala was a seductive Russian whose charm was to serve as an inspiration for both Eluard and Ernst (and eventually to her second husband, Salvador Dali.) Ernst and Gala began an affair. Eluard was content to stand aside, at least for a time. He had a high regard for Ernst and was one of the few people to buy his early paintings. Ernst's wife was not so tolerant. Soon Ernst found it more convenient to leave his wife and child and move in with the Eluards.

For a time this ménage à trois prospered. The sexual chemistry between Gala and Ernst was such that Eluard was apparently caught up in it himself. Even when the poet finally grew disenchanted with the arrangement, he took a long trip abroad rather than cause a fight. The sexual magic between Ernst and Gala died without the presence of a wronged husband. They chased Eluard to the Far East, where Ernst formally resigned from the threesome.

Meanwhile, Ernst decided he needed to be in Paris. He had some radical ideas about art that incorporated his early philosophical training. He arrived in France on a forged passport and found his way into the company of a group of artists who would start the movement called surrealism. Surrealism, particularly as Ernst practiced it, made generous use of the irrational, the accidental, and the absurd. The sexual symbolism of Freud, as well as the art of primitive peoples, also influenced the paintings and sculptures that Ernst produced.

For a while Ernst lived the life of an illegal alien, working odd jobs and trying not to draw attention to himself. He soon realized that he needed to be a legal resident of France if he wanted to further his career as an artist. At this point the thirty-two-year-old artist conveniently met Marie-Berthe Aurenche, the seventeen-year-old daughter of a wealthy family with official connections. Using his considerable charm, Ernst quickly made her his mistress. In order to save the honor of their daughter, the family acquiesced to a marriage, solving Ernst's immigration problems.

Predictably, Ernst's second marriage did not last long. After the wedding the teenage bride quickly deserted her avant-garde opinions and turned to the Catholic Church, something the compulsively irreverent Ernst could not abide. It was probably during this period that Ernst developed the practice he called treasure hunting. During a treasure hunt he would roam the streets of Paris, approach attractive women at random and ask them pointblank for sex. It was a practice that might have been embarrassing, even dangerous, for most men. For the handsome and seductive Ernst, the game played out to his favor more often than not.

When Ernst was forty-six he met a dark-haired, English painter named Leonora Carrington. Carrington was an intelligent and sensitive twenty-year-old woman who responded as much to Ernst's rising reputation as an artist as to his notorious charm. The relationship proved to be beneficial to both parties. Carrington learned much from her older lover and Ernst was energized by her presence, producing some of his most memorable works. The advent of World War II brought a painful end to this partnership. Ernst was imprisoned as a German national at the beginning of hostilities. Carrington waited for him to return but fled when she approached both a physical and emotional collapse. When Ernst escaped from jail and returned to their love nest to find Carrington no longer there, he went to Marseilles. Well aware that the Nazis would be much less tolerant of him than the French, he desperately sought passage to the United States.

At this point the art collector Peggy Guggenheim took it upon herself to become Ernst's benefactor. Ernst was not pleased when she bought all the paintings he managed to bring to Marseilles (including many celebrating his affair with Carrington), but he could ill-afford to turn aside her patronage. With Guggenheim's help, he managed to enter the United Sates. When the U.S. also entered the war and Ernst faced internment once again, it was then decided that he and Guggenheim, with whom he was already cohabiting, should marry.

As Guggenheim's paramour, Ernst was at the center of a glittering social whirl which featured millionaires, Hollywood stars, and expatriate artists from all over Europe. Guggenheim was known to have a voracious appetite for sex and the fifty-year-old Ernst was up to the challenge. The millionaire bragged that on their first night together Ernst had intercourse with her three times. Guggenheim wanted more than just sex from this relationship. She was in love with Ernst, or at least in love with the idea of being married to him.

Unfortunately for Guggenheim, Ernst had a different attitude toward their marriage. Not only did he return to treasure hunting, he quickly arranged for a meeting with Carrington, who was recovering from a complete mental collapse. He tried to renew their relationship, but Carrington decided that loving Ernst was too emotionally demanding and she declined.

Meanwhile, Guggenheim was desperately trying to salvage her marriage, first by giving her husband complete freedom and then by tightening the monetary reigns. Nothing she did changed Ernst's determination to find a younger lover. A year into his third marriage he met a painter named Dorothea Tanning who, like Carrington, was young, beautiful, and talented. Like Carrington, Tanning was overwhelmed by the attentions of this accomplished older artist, so much so that she forgot about her husband who was off fighting in the war. Tanning became Ernst's lover.

Helpless to stop the dissolution of her marriage, Guggenheim had to be satisfied with writing unkind things about Ernst and Tanning in her autobiography. By this time Ernst was living with his new wife in Arizona. Later he and Tanning moved to France where Ernst's artistic career continued to thrive (as did Tanning's) until his death on the day before his eighty-fifth birthday.

Another Example

Shirley Maclaine (American actress, author, and channeler). Born April 24, 1934 (Celebrity Birthday Guide).

Chapter 3

Mars in Gemini
The Sexual Technician

General Characteristics

It is curiosity, not desire, that is the source of this Lover's sex drive. Mars in Gemini Lovers regard the urgent demands of the body with intellectual distance and rational coolness. Here sex is less about biology or physical appetite than an excellent excuse to have fun without an emotional connection. These are typically very knowledgeable Lovers who eagerly soak up information about sex. Their mental point of view makes them very adept in the techniques of lovemaking—the art of giving and getting pleasure. True, they may lack the fiery passion or the breathtaking sensuality of other Mars types, but a few hours alone with any Mars in Gemini Lover leaves us all a little better educated.

The key to understanding the Mars in Gemini Lover is to recognize that sex is not essential to this individual. When sex is available they can revel in it without reservation or conscience, but when it isn't or when sex becomes problematic for some reason, this Lover can quite comfortably do without. The Mars in Gemini person sublimates his or her sexuality much more effectively than most. Because sex is essentially an idea for them, their sexual energies are easily redirected. Because sex carries no deep, personal, or emotional baggage for these folks, they can look at it without prejudice or shame. Typically, though by no means always, these Lovers have very liberal, experimental ideas about sex.

The reason that sex is not essential to Mars in Gemini Lovers is that they base their relationships on intellectual compatibility. Shared thinking and ideas are much more important to this person than shared bodily fluids. Sex may serve as a means of attracting a particular person, and it may function as a way of increasing and testing intellectual affinity, but it is always seen as a device. It is quite possible for the Mars in Gemini person to love someone with whom they have never shared sex. It is also quite possible for this Lover to have wonderful sex with people they care nothing about.

It is the latter that most often gets the Mars in Gemini Lover into trouble. Promiscuity comes as easily to them as sublimation. Their sexual playfulness and lack of inhibition make them very desirable and active Lovers. Because sex is not an essential element in their most important relationships, sexual loyalty also tends to mean very little to them. It is often hard for these Lovers not to follow the lead of their incessant curiosity and make love with anyone who happens to interest them at the moment. They may recognize the strain that this kind of behavior places on a relationship, but they typically underestimate the importance of these "irrational" factors. As knowledgeable as these Lovers are about sexual technique, they are often remarkably ignorant about the mechanisms of jealousy and possessiveness.

The Mars in Gemini Lover is often at his or her best when sex in not an issue in the relationship. They are essentially idealists. Their most perfect sexual contacts take place in the mind. Physical sex alone can become boring to these Lovers. Their technical skill, their sexual inventiveness, and curiosity is often merely a means of fending off that boredom. It is only a relationship based on intellectual affinity that will consistently excite and interest them. Since these purely mental relationships typically lack the complexities and emotional vagaries of physical relationships, the Mars in Gemini Lover can have as many partners as they wish and never have to apologize.

If you have Mars in Gemini with Venus in Aries you are . . . the Technician of Hot Love

Your greatest strength is your aggressiveness. You are at your best when you are making a conquest. Some people might find your approach too direct and egocentric. They might even be startled by your bold, unrepentant desire. But when you are motivated to love, you are so charming, so dynamic, and so dazzling that you have a way of making even the most stubborn naysayer forget how to say no.

The problem for you is what comes after the conquest. You are very good at beginning relationships but totally inept at sustaining them. It's not that you're a bad companion. Even at your most listless, you're a witty, inventive Lover. But without the thrill of victory to motivate you, your attention wanders—you become restless and self-absorbed. What you need is a partner who knows how to lose battles without losing the war and who will keep you marching from victory to victory until you're forced to admit that you've been surrounded.

Case History

Gabriele D'Annunzio (Italian poet, novelist, and Fascist hero). Born March 12, 1863, in Pescara, Italy.

The young D'Annunzio had two great passions: poetry and sex. He lost his virginity to a whore in Florence at the age of sixteen after he had hocked his grandfather's watch to pay for the experience. A short time later he wrote a book of poetry celebrating a fiery adolescent affair with the daughter of one of his teachers. The book became a major hit and D'Annunzio traveled to Rome to enjoy the fruits of his new fame. There he quickly forgot about his old lover and looked for new inspiration.

He found it in Maria Hardouin di Gallese, the daughter of the Duke di Gallese. The Duke and the Duchess were not pleased when D'Annunzio paid court to their beautiful daughter. Although D'Annunzio's family had wealth and position in their native Pescara, as far as Roman society was concerned, he was nothing more than a writer of racy verse. Their objections to D'Annunzio only added to his attractiveness as far as Maria was concerned. There was a thwarted elopement and then her parents reluctantly accepted the inevitable. D'Annunzio and Maria were married when he was twenty. Their first child was born six months later. Predictably, D'Annunzio published another book of poetry full of sexual imagery that same year.

Even though the marriage produced two more children over the next three years, it didn't take D'Annunzio long to become bored with married life. He claimed that "the habit of horizontal life" sapped his literary energy, and Maria complained that he spent too much time with his work. Soon D'Annunzio was having affairs with various Roman socialites. Maria found herself more and more excluded from his life, though her money continued to support his flamboyant lifestyle.

D'Annunzio had no problem attracting women. His dynamic personality and endless self-confidence captivated those who were not won over by his sexy poetry, but loving this romantic poet carried a heavy price. One of his lovers went mad, while another became a nun. One of his most persistent amours, Princess Maria Gravina, was convicted in court of committing adultery with D'Annunzio and threatened to kill the illegitimate child she had by him in order to keep his attention.

Yet nothing could hold D'Annunzio once he had tired of a mistress. He changed lovers frequently and without warning. He was not likely to pass up an opportunity for a new conquest even when he was involved in a passionate affair. Although he threw himself totally into the act of love, and was capable of extreme expressions of devotion and sensuality, none of his affairs altered his impenetrable egotism.

In many ways D'Annunzio looked upon his love affairs as research for his poetry and novels. After (or during) a rendezvous with a lover, he would make notes about the way she looked or how he felt about her. One of his most important mistresses, Barbara Leoni, was shocked when he offered to buy back all the letters he had written her during their five-year relationship, not to keep as a memento, but to publish as literature. She also had the mixed blessing of reading his description of her body and their affair in both his poetry and a novel (an experience shared by many of D'Annunzio's women).

D'Annunzio's most famous affair was with the actress Eleonora Duse. Their relationship was a business relationship at first. Duse needed a writer to write plays worthy of her immense talent, and D'Annunzio needed Duse's fame to make his plays profitable. Their mutual sexual infatuation soon overshadowed the more practical implications of their relationship. Their affair continued for nine tempestuous years and predictably, in the end, Duse was the loser. She had been in her mid-thirties when the affair began, but by its end she was too old to hold the interest of the ever-youthful D'Annunzio. The author heartlessly described his rejection of Duse's aging body in his novel about their relationship.

After a lifetime of writing about egocentric heroes and supermen, D'Annunzio got a chance to be a hero himself when Italy entered World War I. The fifty-one-year-old poet distinguished himself as a pilot and as a soldier. His refusal after the war to abide by the Versailles Treaty and give up the city of Fiume made him the darling of the Fascist movement in Italy. Such was his popularity that Mussolini gave D'Annunzio an impressive title and then pushed him into early retirement, far from the public eye.

D'Annunzio spent his last years living well on his family's estate. His long-absent wife returned to him, though she lived in a separate villa. D'Annunzio continued to have lovers far into his old age. His thirst for novelty was such that he sent agents into neighboring villages to find new girls. Although he never gave up sex, the aging D'Annunzio gave up poetry and his late affairs left no literary tracks.

If you have Mars in Gemini with Venus in Taurus you are ... the Technician of Physical Love

You are the most sensual of the Mars in Gemini Lovers. Nowhere are the erotic skills of this type put to better use. Your approach to sex is cool and clear-headed, but you also have a hardy appreciation for the joys of the flesh that makes you a very desirable partner. You are not as adventurous as many Lovers of this type. Even though your own ideas about sex may be wide open, you have a stubborn respect for convention and you don't like breaking the rules.

The problems in your love life are typically caused by laziness. Sometimes you are just too practical and too conservative for your own good. You settle for relationships that satisfy your physical needs but which do not challenge and intrigue you intellectually. You condemn yourself to sexual boredom by sticking to these "safe" relationships. You need partners with whom you have as much intellectual affinity as you do sensual pleasure. These relationships may be a little more risky, but at least you'll be forced to pay attention.

Case History

Libby Holman (American chanteuse who married a tobacco millionaire and was then accused of killing him). Born May 23, 1904, in Cincinnati, Ohio (Bradshaw 1985).

An ambitious girl from a conservative, German-Jewish family, Holman graduated from college and went straight to New York City with hopes of becoming a star. She quickly learned that her sex appeal served her better than her education when it came to getting jobs in the theater. Fortunately, flirting came as easily to Holman as had her studies. She soon found work.

Holman's attitude toward sex was somewhat deceptive. Though she carried herself with a certain sexual daring and had always been popular with the boys, she was still a virgin at twenty-two. She finally seduced an actor who was working with her in a play just to get it over with—a young man she knew would be leaving town the next day. Her interest in sex was provisional even after this turning point. She liked to say sexy things that shocked people, but the men she spent the most time with were homosexuals.

When Holman was twenty-five she met Louisa Carpenter, a wealthy lesbian who invited Holman to her yacht and seduced her there. The affair between Carpenter and Holman became notorious. Holman didn't seem to mind the ribbing she took from her theater friends, but she continued to look for a more conventional relationship.

In the midst of her affair with Carpenter, a young man in the audience of one of Holman's shows became enamored with the sultry singer. He was Zachery Smith Reynolds, heir to the

R. J. Reynolds tobacco fortune. Reynolds had just finished a disastrous marriage. He court-ed Holman obsessively for a year. She was flattered by his impetuous attention and impressed by his wealth. She even slept with him, but Reynold's wouldn't be satisfied with anything other than marriage. Much to the dismay of her friends and his, Holman finally agreed to marry him when she was twenty-seven.

The marriage led some to label Holman a "gold digger," but she had caught no prize in this tobacco heir. Reynolds was a moody, depressed young man with a dangerous fascination for guns and a long history of getting his own way. He was also periodically impotent. Moreover, Reynolds insisted that Holman live with him on his estate in North Carolina after their marriage, far from her New York friends.

Holman was soon unhappy in the marriage—she expressed this by drinking too much and flirting shamelessly with Reynolds' friends. Partly to placate her, and partly to divert his own morose nature, Reynolds threw parties in which his old cronies mixed with Holman's theater friends. After one of these affairs, during which both he and Holman became intox-icated, Reynolds was found dead from a gunshot wound to the head.

At first it was assumed that the death was a suicide, but suspicion began to center on Holman when the locals began to examine the situation more closely. There were many problems with the suicide theory: there were no powder burns around the entry wound; the weapon had been moved after the shot was fired; and the stories of both Holman and Reynolds' best friend, Ab Walker, seemed inconclusive. Holman and Walker were charged with murder, but the Reynolds' family, fearful of scandal, used their considerable influence to make sure there was no trial. Holman was released and, after more legal haggling, won an inheritance for herself and for the son she gave birth to a few months after Reynolds' death.

Although she had been rather cautious about sex prior to her marriage to Reynolds, Holman's attitudes shifted remarkably after his death. She became something of a sexual predator, constantly pouncing on lean young bodies, both male and female. Even though she maintained her relationship with Louisa Carpenter and married a second time to Ralph Holmes when she was thirty-four, Holman recognized no restriction on her sexual appetite. As in the old days, she attracted homosexual men and she even attempted to seduce them. She tended to regard her male lovers, in particular, with a maternal fondness, but when she tired of her lovers or when they crossed her, Holman got rid of them without hesitation. She was as notorious for her cruelty and biting dismissals as she was for her hedonism.

For all her apparent sensuality, Holman found little pleasure in the sex act itself. Her inter-est was in seduction—in making herself desirable to another person. Her performances in bed were clumsy and lackluster, regardless of the gender of her partner. Louisa Carpenter's lesbian friends were fond of contrasting the hot, torchy quality of the songs Holman sang with the coldness of her sexuality.

Holman did not age gracefully. Middle age became a desperate time for this woman who considered twenty-four-year-old men too old for her and who loved flaunting her slender, taut body. She shocked her friends when she was fifty-four by marrying for a third time to a man totally different from the pretty boys and homosexual men she had loved previously. He was Louis Schanker, a brawny, gruff, swaggering artist who captivated Holman with his masculinity and bohemian disregard for good manners. Schanker's dislike for homosexuals alienated many of Holman's friends, and his general offensiveness alienated many others. Holman seemed intent on setting off in a whole new direction in her life, regardless of the cost.

Unfortunately, her new direction did not take her very far. She could not escape the tragedies of her life, nor her alcoholism or depression. Reynolds' death was followed by those of her son and second husband. She committed suicide at the age of sixty-seven.

Other Examples

Thomas Hardy (*English novelist, author of* Tess of the D'Urbervilles *and* Jude the Obscure). Born June 2, 1840 (*Celebrity Birthday Guide*).

Bobby Darin (*American pop singer*). Born May 14, 1936 (*Celebrity Birthday Guide*).

If you have Mars in Gemini with Venus in Gemini you are . . . the Technician of Cool Love

You approach sex like a scientist approaches the laboratory. You just can't wait to see what you will learn. Erotic experiences for you are less a means to sensual pleasure than a way to feed the mind. Sex is a realm of experience that is special because of its intensity, but, in essence, is no different from any other realm of experience. For this reason you can be remarkably free of both shame and restraint. Some may consider you cold and clinical but others will appreciate your openness and indefatigable curiosity.

The one element of sexuality that may scare you just a little is commitment. You have no trouble falling in love, but you find it very difficult to stay that way. Your most important and enduring relationships will always have more to do with ideas than sex. The partner who thinks as you do or, better yet, leaves you free to think the way you want will always be closer to you than the person who just gets you aroused. After all, there is no sexual organ more crucial than the mind.

Case History

Jean-Jacques Rousseau (philosopher and novelist considered one the great figures of the Enlightenment). Born June 28, 1712, in Geneva, Switzerland (Crocker 1973).

Rousseau's mother died shortly after his birth and he was left in the hands of an abusive father and various surrogate parents. Rousseau's curiosity about sex began early in life. By the time he was eleven, he discovered that when one of his caretakers spanked him, he felt sexual pleasure. Rousseau began misbehaving on purpose and the woman, sensing an ulterior motive, stopped using corporal punishment. Rousseau then found a female playmate to take her place. This girl spanked him, fondled him, and treated him "just like a child" until the adults discovered their little game and put a stop to it.

Rousseau fled his native city at sixteen to become a vagabond. His sexual experimentation turned aggressive and he exposed himself to unsuspecting women—exposing his genitals on some occasions and his buttocks on others, perhaps hoping some enterprising girl would take a swat at them.

Rousseau was then taken in by a worldly and well-to-do woman named Francoise-Louise de Warens. Warens was twenty-nine, had recently divorced her husband, and converted to Catholicism. She took an instant liking to the youngster and, in Rousseau's eyes, became both a substitute mother and an object of sexual desire. Their sexual relationship did not begin immediately. It was only after Rousseau turned twenty-one that Warens made him her lover in order to keep the excitable youth out of the clutches of other women. She already had another man installed as the manager of her estate and bedmate, but Rousseau didn't mind the competition. By his own admission he was a poor lover because, by this time, Warens had become such a mother figure to him that sex with her seemed like committing incest.

Warens was not Rousseau's only object of adoration during this period of his life. He was often on the move and he tended to fall in love whenever he was in the company of well-born women. Rousseau's real-life sexual activity never matched his heated imagination. This was because the women he wanted were always from the upper class—women he would not approach because he was too poor and too shy. He could probably have had his way with innumerable servant girls but he never found them attractive. Likewise he found little pleasure with prostitutes, though he did visit them occasionally when he was particularly desperate for sex.

Rousseau's sexual relationship with Warens lasted until his late twenties when she found a younger lover and he began to wean himself from her emotional and financial support. He had some affairs but he remained wary of marriage. Then, at the age of thirty-three, Rousseau became enamored with a poor chambermaid named Therese LeVasseaur in the boarding house in which he was staying. Her simplicity and honesty impressed Rousseau. He made her his lover and promised her two things: that he would never leave her and that he would never marry her.

Rousseau's friends and enemies alike objected to this strange union. Some called LeVasseaur a simpleton and others considered her a devious shrew. It was felt that her influence over Rousseau increased his notorious misanthropy and cut him off from many of his supporters. The fact that LeVasseaur was essentially illiterate, inordinately fond of gossip, and frequently unfaithful to Rousseau only added to her unpopularity with his associates.

Rousseau knew what he wanted. Never a confident man, his insecurity was only increased by daily contact with some of the great minds of Europe. He needed a confidant and ally who could never threaten him intellectually. He also needed a nurse. A urinary tract problem that had plagued him grew worse as he aged. LeVasseaur had to catheterize him and care for him when his bladder problems made it impossible for him to go out. More than anything Rousseau needed a mother. For all her faults, LeVasseaur willingly took the role once played by Warens, if only passively. She even agreed to give all their offspring to orphanages so that Rousseau remained the only child in their household.

Rousseau admitted that his sexual interest in LeVasseaur was minimal. He regarded sex with her as only a supplement to masturbation. Rousseau had always depended on masturbation but he turned to it more in his later years, particularly after his urinary problems increased to the point that intercourse became painful. For Rousseau, imagined sex was always better than the real thing. He never felt secure enough in any of his relationships to ask the woman to repeat the sadomasochistic rites he had learned as a child, but these memories remained a staple of his fantasy life.

Perhaps the most remarkable thing about Rousseau's sex life was how much of it he confessed. At the end of his life Rousseau wrote an autobiography called *Confessions* in which he recounted every embarrassing and ignoble detail of his existence, including his many sexual foibles. The book was not published until after his death at sixty-six, but prior to this he was persuaded to read it aloud at various salons in Paris.

Another Example

Mike Tyson (boxer). Born June 30, 1966 (Celebrity Birthday Guide).

If you have Mars in Gemini with Venus in Cancer you are . . . the Technician of Obsessive Love

You have an intellectual, playful approach to your love life even though you are one of the more emotional Mars in Gemini Lovers. Your heightened sensuality only makes the game more interesting and your ability to tune into the feelings of others only makes you a better player. You know that, with your sex appeal, you have the capacity to manipulate other people both mentally and emotionally, but you only use this ability for recreational purposes. After all, it's about having fun, isn't it?

Of course, it's not only about having fun. It's also about finding shelter for your sensitive and vulnerable emotional self. The fact that you seek this shelter in an idea does not lessen the need. If anything, it makes your obsessive behavior seem strangely calculated and cold-hearted. You are not an easy Lover to understand. You love the things your partner represents more than you love him or her. If they only knew that the person most confused by your contradictory behavior is you.

Case History

Josephine Baker (African-American performer who left the U.S. and went to Paris where she became the darling of Europe). Born June 3, 1906 in St. Louis, Missouri (Haney 1981).

Baker's father was a drummer who had absolutely no taste for family life. After Baker was born, he quickly lost interest in her mother and abandoned her. Baker's mother later married and had other children, but she continued to look upon Josephine as the child who had deprived her of her true love.

Josephine Baker's family was very poor. Her mother typically supported the family by doing laundry. Baker herself was put to work as a housemaid when she was eight. By the time she reached thirteen, Baker was well on her way to a life of drudgery. Consequently, she left her parent's home and began hanging around a local theater doing odd jobs.

Baker did not remain independent for long. Soon after she left home she married Willie Wells. She was ready to settle into domestic bliss until she surmised that Wells was not going to be able to support her. Baker immediately abandoned the marriage and joined a group of dancers performing in the theater where she worked. When the show began a tour, she found a way to go with them.

She married a second time the next year to another performer named Willie Baker. This husband's circumstances were more stable than Wells' had been but, by this time, Baker was too restless to give the marriage much of a chance. She liked the lifestyle she had experienced in the theater and when she saw an opportunity to go to New York, she took it.

Even though she was skinny and underage, Baker managed to get a spot in the chorus line of a black Broadway revue. Her ability as a dancer and a comedienne quickly caused her to be singled out. Soon she was a star. But Baker's opportunities were still very limited as a black star in a segregated system. When a promoter came to her with a plan to take a troupe of African-American musicians and dancers to Paris, the nineteen-year-old Baker simply had to go along for the ride.

In New York, Baker's skin was too dark and she was too flat-chested to be considered sexy. So she was surprised, and a little shocked, when her French producers asked her to dance topless. It took some persuasion, but she finally agreed to disrobe. The result was electric. Bubbling with energy and unbelievably agile, Baker brought a sexual charge to the stage that was both primitive and thoroughly modern. Moments later, she could cross her eyes and strike a pose that would make everyone laugh. Baker's unique ability to combine her sultry sex appeal with endearing comedy earned her immediate success.

Baker found more than just fame and fortune in France. She also found an environment in which the color of her skin was no longer an impediment. The deep racial divisions and oppression that had dominated her life in the United States were no where to be found in France. Suddenly, for the first time in her short life, Baker recognized that she was free. It comes as no surprise, therefore, that the most important and enduring love affair of her life was with France.

Of course, Baker had other love affairs to compliment her infatuation with the French nation. The young Josephine Baker soon became almost as noted for her sexual activity as she was for her singing and dancing. One of her French lovers praised Baker as the only woman who could keep up with his formidable physical demands. Others, on the other hand, noted that she was far more interested in sexual athletics than sensuality. One of her female friends declared that, in fact, Baker had far fewer affairs than either she or the public claimed.

When she was twenty Baker became involved with Pepito Abatino, an Italian-born plasterer who sometimes posed as a count. Abatino was seventeen years older than Baker and many considered him to be an oily appendage bent on cheating the famous youngster out of her fortune. Baker formed a very profitable partnership with the unscrupulous, but affectionate, Abatino. He proved both a crafty manager and a patient, understanding emotional supporter.

Baker and Abatino had their differences, mostly caused by Baker's inability to limit herself to just one man. While she was touring the United States at the age of thirty, Abatino left Baker and returned to France. Baker was unconcerned by his desertion until she learned that he had died suddenly of a misdiagnosed cancer.

Abatino's death made Baker realized just how badly she needed a man like him in her life. She immediately set about looking for a replacement. She found him in a rich Jewish businessman named Jean Lion, whom she married the next year. But Lion proved far too independent and vain in his own right to replace Abatino and the marriage quickly ended.

Baker was thirty-three when World War II ravaged her beloved France and reduced it to a subject state. Without hesitation the pampered performer volunteered her services to the French underground. Using her notoriety as a cover for clandestine spy activity, Baker earned a medal from the French Resistance. She was still able to find time to indulge in some sexual adventures during the war, one of which resulted in a miscarried pregnancy. The treatment of this miscarriage led to an infection which in turn led to several operations that damaged her health to the point that it was rumored that she was dead.

After the war Baker married Jo Bouillon, a French musician and bandleader. Bouillon was well-known in France but he was still willing to defer to the internationally famous Baker in most matters, a fact that made this the most successful of her official marriages.

With Bouillon, Baker attempted to bring to fruition one of her great dreams: a multi-racial family unit with children adopted from all over the world. At first, Baker's makeshift family was to be limited to only four children but soon the sentimental dancer had expanded her aspirations to included twelve orphans of all colors. Bouillon was quite willing to act as the father figure in Baker's dream family and he tried to temper her mercurial methods with some degree of practicality and good sense. After she brought the twelfth child into the financially fragile community, Bouillon threw up his hands and left her.

It is apparent that Baker's appetite for sex had lessened a great deal by the time Bouillon left her. One reason for this was the fact that her aging body had been left badly scarred by the medical problems she had suffered during the war. Another was the degree to which she identified with her new role as the "mother" and protector of a utopian dream. She had occasional encounters with old lovers but mostly devoted herself to her "Rainbow Tribe." Officially retired from the stage, she came back time and again in order to make the money needed to sustain her beloved family.

A new man entered Baker's life when she was sixty-seven. He was Robert Brady, a wealthy artist with surprising business acumen. They began an "imaginary" marriage with the mutual understanding that they would have no sexual contact. He remained her financial advisor and emotional supporter until her death at the age of sixty-nine.

Other Examples

O. J. Simpson (*ex-football hero who was accused, but not convicted in criminal court, of killing his wife). Born July 19, 1947 (Current Biography 1969).*

Zelda Fitzgerald (*writer, painter, and wife of F. Scott Fitzgerald*). *Born July 24, 1900 (Milford 1970).*

If you have Mars in Gemini with Venus in Leo you are . . . the Technician of Dominance

There is never any question about the ground rules of your erotic universe: what best serves your ego, best serves your libido. You have a marvelous capacity for enjoying sex, but your pride and self-possession always come first. Some people might find the egotism of this position offensive, but many others will hardly notice. After all, a Lover as lively, generous, and exciting as you has good reason to be proud.

The control you exercise over your love life does come at a price. Sometimes you lose the sense of play that is so essential to Mars in Gemini, and you take the whole process entirely too seriously. You want sex to be a big event, full of drama and intellectual significance. This is one reason why you often find the idea of love much more appealing than its physical manifestations. The sex in you head is never common or clumsy, and you can always count on great reviews.

Case History

Mary Baker Eddy (*founder and leader of the Church of Christ, Scientist*). *Born July 16, 1821, in Concord, New Hampshire (Thomas 1994).*

Eddy was brought up in a religious home according to strict, Calvinist principles. She was an avid reader, independent, and something of a perfectionist. But the factor that dominated Eddy's youth was her poor health. She was often bedridden and her sister observed that the sickly adolescent seemed cut off from the normal joys of living.

When Eddy was twenty-two she married George Glover, a businessman ten years her senior who had long been a family friend. Eddy entered the marriage with a heavy heart. Glover's business promised to take the couple far away from her family and she dreaded the separation. A greater tragedy occurred seven months after the wedding. Glover died suddenly of yellow fever. The grieving, pregnant widow made her way back to New England on her own. There she bore a son but was so depressed and ill that she could not tend to him. The child was cared for by family members and finally given to foster parents.

Eddy spent the next twenty years of her life suffering through various ailments and desperately seeking a means to health. Even though some of her illnesses may have been largely psychosomatic, this made them no less incapacitating.

Despite the fact that she often appeared desperately ill, Eddy was still an attractive woman. A local dentist named Daniel Patterson paid her court. Eddy later claimed that she accepted Patterson's proposal of marriage only to create a home for her son; however, there was no denying that Patterson was an attractive man. The son did come to live with the newlyweds, but he proved to be unmanageable and was soon returned to foster care.

There was probably very little sex in Eddy's second marriage. Eddy had to be carried to the wedding ceremony and then returned to her sickbed immediately afterward. The marriage produced no children. Soon Patterson was rumored to be having sex with some of his patients. Nine years into the marriage, Confederate forces captured Patterson while he was attempting to transport money to Union sympathizers in Virginia. He spent the next few years as a prisoner of war. Eddy, now forty, was free to pursue her quest for a cure for her ailments.

This quest took her to Phineas Quimby, an older doctor who proposed that spiritual health was the key to physical health. Eddy became a vocal advocate and defender of Quimby's methods and she was allowed to assist him in his "healing" sessions. When Eddy was suffering from "spinal" pain in a distant town, Quimby's spirit allegedly appeared in her bedroom late at night to heal her.

Meanwhile, Patterson was released from prison but their reunion only made the lack of understanding between husband and wife more evident. Patterson returned to his philandering habits and Eddy left. They later divorced.

The turning point in Eddy's life came shortly after Quimby died. Eddy, who was then forty-five, reacted to the death of her mentor with her typical depression and sickness. Then she complicated her psychosomatic pain with a real injury caused by a fall. By reading the Bible and tending to her spiritual health, Eddy was able to bring about a cure and from this triumphant experience she evolved the philosophy that became Christian Science.

Eddy maintained tight control over her movement and her students. She expected them to comply with her opinions without question. Often her most promising converts refused to follow her line. These dissenters—typically men—were regarded as enemies who were capable of mounting spiritual assaults against their former teacher. These assaults, if they caught her unaware, could incapacitate the great lady and bring about the kind of hysterical illness that plagued her early life. Eddy surrounded herself with students absolutely loyal to her. These spiritual storm troopers were expected to step in and "heal" her when she was struck down by a psychic sneak attack.

One of these spiritual shock troops was Asa Gilbert Eddy, known as Gilbert. When Mary was fifty-five, Gilbert rushed in and "healed" her when she had a violent seizure. The cool-headedness and devotion of this younger man struck Mary and she married him a few months later. The marriage did little to raise Gilbert's stock within the movement. He remained a glorified "go-for" until his death five years later.

Shortly after their marriage, Eddy had made it clear that her relationship with Gilbert was not sexual. The body was inconsequential—an illusion—in Eddy's philosophy. Only the spirit mattered. Sex was therefore unimportant, even in the creation of children. She warned parents not to see their children as something they had "made," but as a spiritual manifestation of God. She characterized physical love between a man and a woman as violent and dishonorable, a manifestation of animal lust and hatred. It was her prediction that physical love would eventually be replaced by pure, sexless, spiritual love.

Eddy built Christian Science into a major religious movement and died at the age of eighty-nine.

Another Example

Alan Ladd (*Hollywood star who found success as a leading man after he married his agent*). *Born September 3, 1913 (Celebrity Birthday Guide).*

If you have Mars in Gemini with Venus in Virgo you are . . . the Technician of Real Love

You are one of the sexiest of the Mars in Gemini Lovers. You bring sex down to its most basic level and make no apologies for your direct and earthy approach. This unpretentious practicality has its own charm. You may be the most skilled and resourceful of all Mars in Gemini Lovers. You are also the most manipulative and profane. You just don't take sex seriously enough to watch what you say and do. This often gets you into big trouble.

Like most Mars in Gemini Lovers, you need a relationship that features a meaningful intellectual affinity. And yet because of your earthy appreciation of physical pleasure, sex also has to be a big factor in your choice of partners. Sometimes this makes it very difficult for you to find the right partner. At other times this duality gives you an excellent excuse for restlessly moving from one partner to another. After all, it's not easy to find just the right combination of randiness and idealism.

Case History

Tina Modotti (*actress, model, photographer, and Communist*). *Born August 17, 1896, at 11 A.M. in Udine, Italy (Hooks 1993).*

Modotti came to America at seventeen to join her father who had been working hard to establish a foothold in the New World. She had been forced to work in a factory in Italy, but her luck changed once she arrived in San Francisco. She first found work as an artist's model, and then as an actress in the Italian-speaking theater.

When she was nineteen Modotti met a young artist and poet named Roubaix de l'Abrie Richey. Richey was a striking young man—tall, lean, bohemian, and (despite his French name) thoroughly American. For Modotti he represented exciting new ideas and intellectual liberty, as well as a break from her Italian heritage. He introduced her to a group of artists and idealists. The former factory worker moved with surprising ease within this intellectual group. Meanwhile her theater career prospered to the point that she was offered work in films. She and Richey married when she was twenty-two and moved to Los Angeles.

Modotti, with her curvaceous body and dark, sultry beauty, enjoyed some success in silent films. She made enough money to support herself and her poetic husband. Richey's contribution to the marriage was mainly social. Through him they entered a circle of daring artists and thinkers that included a talented photographer named Edward Weston.

Even though Weston was older, married, and not much to look at, he was a tireless womanizer who made a point of sleeping with every woman who posed for him. When Tina became his model, it was only a matter of time before she became one of his conquests. The affair did not end with this seduction. Weston was soon totally smitten with Modotti, and Modotti found a sexual fulfillment with the emphatically virile Weston that had eluded her in her relationship with the dreamy and irresolute Richey.

Richey was aware of the affair between his wife and his good friend, but he made no move to stop it. He moved to Mexico where he thought the environment would be more conducive to his art. Instead he contracted and died from smallpox when Modotti was twenty-five.

Richey's death only brought Modotti and Weston closer. Leaving a stagnant movie career, she moved to Mexico with Weston, who left his wife to join her. By this time Modotti was no longer content to remain in front of the camera. She was anxious to find a new career and she began to glean all the knowledge she could about the art and the technique of photography from Weston. They set up their own photography studio in Mexico City. Weston held a large exhibit of his work, including several nude photos of Modotti.

Modotti thrived in Mexico. Not only did she advance in a new career, but Weston's photographs also made her an instant sex symbol in Mexico City. She enjoyed the attention, though her relationship with Weston suffered. The two bohemians had agreed on an open arrangement, but Weston quickly learned that he didn't like being the one left home alone. He returned to his wife, leaving Modotti to manage the studio.

During her late twenties Modotti moved through a series of casual affairs. She was more intent on establishing her sexual freedom than finding love, and she once playfully described her profession as "men." She had not forgotten photography and was proving herself a talented practitioner of Weston's style. Modotti had become involved with a group of intellectuals and artists sympathetic with the Communist Party. As she reached her thirties, her work reflected their left-leaning ideology.

By the time Modotti was thirty-two she was a member of the Communist Party and living with a Cuban revolutionary named Julio Antonio Mella. Mella was younger than Modotti, a handsome, romantic figure who inspired both fervent loyalty and hatred. One evening, while he was walking in the street with Modotti, an assassin shot and killed Mella. In a cruel twist of injustice, Modotti was charged with the murder.

Modotti was labeled a "femme fatale" in the trial that followed. Her past sexual history and Weston's nude photographs were brought forth in an effort to defame her. She was eventually acquitted of the charge, but the event solidified her identification with the Communist cause.

Though Modotti continued to have lovers, her friends considered her a "Communist nun." She dispensed with all frivolity (make-up, fine clothes, pretty possessions), and devoted herself to working for the party. Her obedience was so blind that she did not object when her good friend and ex-lover Diego Riveria was dismissed from the party.

Modotti was expelled from Mexico and forcibly shipped to Germany when she was thirty-three. There, she teamed up with another Italian Communist who had been kicked out of Mexico, Vittorio Vidali. She and Vidali made their way to Moscow and put themselves at the disposal of the Soviet government, but they found they were nearly as unwelcome there as they had been in Mexico. Stalin's regime was mistrustful of foreign Communists. Modotti and Vidali were given assignments in Western Europe.

For the next few years Modotti and Vidali worked in France and in Spain for an organization called Red Aid, which gave material support to other Communists. Modotti was deeply involved with the republican forces in Spain and showed remarkable fortitude and courage as the leftist cause collapsed in that country. After the Spanish Civil War she and Vidali were once again deported. Modotti wanted to return to the United States but officials there did not want her. So she ended up back in Mexico.

In Mexico Vidali and Modotti lived as a married couple, but it could hardly have been called a love match. Vidali was habitually unfaithful to Modotti and often abusive. When they fought he brought up the sexual freedom of her youth and called her a "high-class whore." Modotti, her beauty faded and her creative urges stymied, seemed resigned to this unhappy arrangement. She died of a heart attack at forty-six.

Another Example

R. Crumb (Robert Crumb—comic book artist noted for his outrageous sexual images). Born August 30, 1943 (Celebrity Birthday Guide).

If you have Mars in Gemini with Venus in Libra you are . . . the Technician of True Love

You are the most idealistic Mars in Gemini Lover. This idealism provides the potential for both great happiness and absolute misery. The happiness comes from your ability to believe in love. You are a Lover who can't live without a relationship—you need to feel "connected" to another person in order to be complete. Your definition of love doesn't include a lot of sentiment or even a lot of sex. You're looking for a sense of partnership—the perfect blending of two minds.

Misery typically comes from sex. Physical sex has a way of messing up your idealism and muddying your precious mental purity. It takes love out of the domain of the mind where you can operate with breathtaking lightness and skill, and brings it down to the level of the body where you are never quite as comfortable. This is not to say that you can't enjoy physical sex for its own sake. The problem is keeping this frivolity separate from the very serious business of love.

Case History

F. Scott Fitzgerald (American author of This Side of Paradise *and* The Great Gatsby; *uncrowned king of the Jazz Age in America). Born September 24, 1896, in St. Paul, Minnesota (Meyers 1994).*

Despite the fact that he was heralded in the 1920s as one of the leaders of America's rebellious and licentious youth, Fitzgerald was something of a prude. He grew up with a Puritan horror of his own body, particularly his feet, and refused to go with his Princeton friends when they went whoring. It was only after he flunked out of Princeton at the age of twenty-one that the dejected Fitzgerald sought out the comfort of a prostitute. This was probably his first sexual encounter.

What Fitzgerald wanted was a "top girl"—a woman with class, money, and beauty who was universally desired. He had tried to win such a girl while at Princeton and failed. While serving a stint in the army in Montgomery, Alabama, Fitzgerald found another young woman who met all his requirements. This was the eighteen-year-old Zelda Sayre.

Even though Zelda was four years younger than Fitzgerald, she was in many ways more worldly. She obviously liked the handsome and clever young Northerner, but she was used to keeping several beaus on a string. She never let her promise to wait for him limit her social life. During the two years of their courtship Zelda managed to keep both Fitzgerald and her local boy friends guessing about her intentions.

Fitzgerald moved to New York to make his mark in literature. While there he had an affair with an actress and briefly showed signs of sexual adventurism. His sights, however, were set on Zelda and marriage. When he sold his first novel, they finally set a date. He was twenty-five.

As a couple, Fitzgerald and Zelda came to represent the flaming youth of the Jazz Age. Fitzgerald's first novel made a good deal of money, and they spent it all in a mad splurge of exhibitionism and excess. Fitzgerald had probably been an alcoholic even in college, but his drinking now became a part of his persona. Combined with Zelda's exhibitionism, Fitzgerald's college-boy high jinks and general drunkenness made the early years of their marriage seem like one long and outrageous party that was only briefly interrupted by the birth of their only child.

Despite their seemingly perfect partnership, Fitzgerald and Zelda were often at odds. Jealousy was among their more common problems. Fitzgerald liked the idea that men wanted his wife but he reacted with anger when her flirtations violated his sense of propriety. Fitzgerald had very conventional ideas about marriage. He believed in the primacy of the husband and he did not believe in birth control. Because of this, Zelda, who did not want more children, endured several abortions.

As Zelda grew dissatisfied with the marriage, she became more critical of Fitzgerald. She criticized his drinking and his friends. She also criticized his lovemaking and told him his penis was too small. Finally she came to the conclusion that Fitzgerald was having a homosexual affair with his friend Ernest Hemingway. Fitzgerald was shaken by these accusations. He had never been sure of his manliness and admitted that he had a feminine mind. There is no evidence he ever had a homosexual encounter.

While Fitzgerald was struggling with these insecurities and his flagging career, it became obvious that Zelda was assailed by even more powerful demons. When Fitzgerald was thirty-four, his wife was diagnosed as schizophrenic and placed in a mental hospital. Fitzgerald and Zelda saw little of each other for the last ten years of their marriage. Zelda was released from the hospital but her problems quickly returned. She was eventually given over to the care of her mother, though Fitzgerald continued to support her financially and stayed in contact with her through correspondence.

Fitzgerald's sexual relations with Zelda had probably started tapering off long before her breakdown, partly because of her distracted state and partly because of his drinking. For the first two years after her hospitalization, Fitzgerald appeared hopeful of a cure and a chance to resume some semblance of a family life. It was only after the fourth year that he began to have affairs.

Fitzgerald slept with several different women during the last years of his life but he was hardly a libertine. He was obsessively insecure about his penis' size and how he compared as a lover to other men. His attitudes remained staunchly conservative. When one of his lovers revealed to him that she was part African-American, he was shocked and broke off the relationship. Another woman recalled that Fitzgerald was not a passionate man but that he was always "gentle and adequate." He died at forty-four of a heart attack.

Another Example

Sean Connery (British actor who became famous as Agent 007). Born August 25, 1930 (Celebrity Birthday Guide).

If you have Mars in Gemini with Venus in Scorpio you are . . . the Technician of Serious Sex

You are the one Mars in Gemini Lover who has to be careful with sex, because sex simply means too much to you. In the beginning you are only curious, searching for diversion and a little bit of fun. But then you find yourself fascinated by something dark, mysterious, and forbidden—a vision of sex that is awesome, dangerous, and even frightening. You can try being clever and distant in the face of this erotic fascination, but it won't do you any good. You want it too badly to be coy.

Fortunately for you, this dark curiosity is balanced by an equally intense sexual conservatism. Though you may be lured into an occasional safari into the sexual unknown, your greatest strength is your ability to maintain strong relationships in which the intellectual affinity necessary for Mars in Gemini is joined by a powerful erotic understanding.

Case History

Keith Richards (English guitarist who helped create one of the greatest rock-and-roll bands in the world, the Rolling Stones). Born December 18, 1943, in Dartford, England (Booth 1995).

Richards was born the only child of a working-class family, distinguished by their love of music. As a teenager he became entranced by American rhythm and blues. When he met two other youngsters who were equally hooked on this music—Mick Jagger and Brian Jones—they decided to start a band and called themselves the Rolling Stones.

The early days with the band were hard. Richards lived in an unheated apartment with Jones and Jagger. The three of them shared a bed in order to keep warm. When they worked it was often in questionable places for little money. But they slowly established a name for themselves in London and began to travel and play in different parts of England.

Despite their frantic schedule during this period, sex was not a problem for the members of the band. Richards was paired with several different women, though his reputation as a lover always lagged behind that of Jones and Jagger. In his own reminiscence about this time, Richards makes scant mention of sex but instead dwells on the almost evangelical calling he felt to bring blues music to a new audience.

The band succeeded beyond his wildest dreams by the time Richards reached twenty-two. Suddenly they were awash in money. Police on horseback had to hold back screaming fans at their concerts. At this time Richards was introduced to Brian Jones' newest girl friend, an exotically beautiful model named Anita Pallenberg. Richards was so impressed that he mended his failing friendship with Jones and moved into the couple's London home.

Richards had been somewhat intimidated by the sexual exploits of the older, more uninhibited Jones in the past. Now he found himself completely in awe of Pallenberg. Pallenberg was a tough woman who could match Jones in any debauchery and still hold court in what became London's most desirable rock-and-roll "salons." There was nothing easy about her relationship with Jones. When she and Brian were not experimenting with drugs and sex, they were fighting violently. Richards watched all this from the wings, enjoying the show and biding his time.

Two years passed before Pallenberg and Richards had sex for the first time. Jones was in the hospital (a short stopover on his rapidly accelerating spiral downward). Jones joined Pallenberg and Richards in Morocco when he was released. He quickly got into a brawl with Pallenberg and hit her. While some friends distracted Jones, Richards packed Pallenberg into a car and fled. Thus began the liaison that would dominate the next ten years of Richards' life.

Richards claimed that Pallenberg whipped him "into shape." Other people felt that his relationship with her was the beginning of Richards' slide into drug addiction. Certainly heroin and cocaine became the staples of their existence. Richards and Pallenberg were constantly on the move, staying in one swank hotel after another, but they were never far from a connection to the drug market. They were arrested several times over the next few years and forbidden from entering some countries.

In the midst of this drug-taking frenzy, there were moments in Richards' life with Pallenberg that were shockingly domestic. The couple had children. Richards thought nothing of stopping rehearsals with the band to go home and tuck his son into bed. Richards owned a home in a rural part of England where he and his family could go to enjoy quiet time together—until he accidentally burned it down.

By the time Richards reached his mid-thirties, many people felt it was only a matter of time before he became the next dead rock-and-roller. But, seemingly in the nick of time, he managed to turn his life around and wean himself off cocaine and heroin. Part of the reason for his success was the deterioration of his relationship with Pallenberg. Pallenberg, who had gained weight and stopped bathing, was living in a house owned by Richards in New York. She became friendly with the local teens, inviting them into the house and offering them drugs and sex. It was even rumored that she was part of a satanic cult. When one of these teens committed suicide in the house, Richards made his final break with Pallenberg.

Richards was thirty-six when he became involved with another pretty model named Patti Hansen. But Hansen turned out to be quite unlike Pallenberg and their relationship flourished. Richards married Hansen when he was forty. The marriage produced two children and has remained a rock of stability and conventionality in the aging musician's very active life.

If you have Mars in Gemini with Venus in Sagittarius you are . . . the Technician of Joyful Sex

You are a happy, laughing, light-hearted Lover who can be shockingly straightforward and, at the same time, devilishly charming. Despite your adventurous spirit, sex can be problematic for you. You like the energy, fun, and physical activity of lovemaking, but you abhor the emotional mess that comes with it. As a Lover you tend to be aloof and restless, partly because you are anxious to move on to the next sexual experience and partly because you dread being forced to clean up after yourself.

Like most Mars in Gemini Lovers, you are happiest when you can combine your idealism with your sexual needs. For all your erotic energy, sex means very little to you if it is not in the context of shared ideas. Nothing spurs your passion like fighting for a cause in which you believe, and nothing is more likely to hold your interest like good conversation.

Case History

Sir Oswald Mosley (*British politician who made himself head of the Fascist Party in England during the 1930s). Born November 16, 1896, in London, England (Mosley 1991).*

Although he was born with an aristocratic pedigree, Mosley's early home life was less than stable. When Mosley was still a small child his mother became fed up with his father's obsessive womanizing and left. Mosley divided his youth between his mother's family home and that of his father. Mosley maintained a low opinion of his father all his life.

Mosley was a lackluster student and was sent to military school. He joined the R.A.F during World War I and also served in the infantry. Though he saw some action and managed to come home with a minor wound, Mosley's wartime experiences were far less heroic than he would have liked.

At home Mosley was intent on making up for his disappointments on the battlefield with victories in politics and in bed. He was elected to a seat in the House of Commons and had a series of affairs with the wives of his fellow aristocrats. These women were older than Mosley, and they apparently schooled him in the art of seduction as it was practiced in the British upper class. Before long the tall, handsome Mosley, with his square jaw and jaunty mustache, was declared a master.

His political career required a wife. At twenty-four, Mosley found just the girl. Her name was Cynthia Curzon. Her father had been a major player on the political scene a generation before and her mother was a rich American. As a bride, Cynthia not only guaranteed political connections but also ready cash. Mosley applied all his charm to persuading her to marry him.

It was a politically expedient marriage but, in many ways, it turned out to be a happy one. Cynthia had been bred for a political life and Mosley was well equipped to give her one. They shared many of the same ideals and hopes, and often shared the same podium. Cynthia was active on the political front and was elected to her own seat in the House of Commons. The correspondence between Mosley and Cynthia is replete with declarations of love, playful nicknames, and nonsensical baby talk. Cynthia was a warm, surprisingly sexual woman. She made Mosley a better wife than he probably ever expected.

The joys of married life could not sustain Mosley for long and he was soon back to his old tricks. He preferred younger quarry as a married man but, as before, the women he slept with were usually married and always of his own class. Mosley had no interest in the actresses or prostitutes that many of his fellow aristocrats (including his father) favored. That was not the sort of game he wanted to play.

Despite his skill in the art of seduction, Mosley was not an outstanding lover. One woman remarked, "Of course we all slept with him but afterward we felt rather ashamed" (Mosley, 155). It was his gift for talk—his persuasiveness—that made Mosley such a success with women. Appropriately enough, this also became the key to his political success.

Mosley began his political career as a Conservative but his opinions often put him at odds with other members of this party. He switched to the Labor Party. Here Mosley was able to advance, but he soon became frustrated with his inability to institute the kinds of policies he felt the country needed. He attempted to form a "New" Labor Party. When this effort fell flat, his thinking began to slide to the right. Mosley had discovered his gift as a mob orator while a Labor candidate and now he began to imitate Mussolini and Hitler. There had long been Fascist elements in Britain, and Mosley organized them into one group called the British Union of Fascist, complete with black shirts, paramilitary airs, and blind loyalty to their "leader."

His shift to Fascism brought Mosley, then thirty-eight, together with a new mistress, Diana Guinness. Not only was Guinness thoroughly upper class and married, she also had connections to the Nazi regime in Germany. Cynthia, who had chosen to ignore Mosley's infidelities up to this point, objected strenuously to Guinness. Mosley, in an effort to put the affair in context, told his wife about all of his other affairs but his confessions only depressed her further, since all the women he named were her best friends.

After thirteen years of marriage, Cynthia suddenly died. Mosley was shaken and stopped seeing Guinness for a respectable period. His political life was taking up much more of his time and his womanizing, for the most part, ceased. He devoted himself solely to Guinness and, after she had obtained a divorce, secretly married her. Even Diana was part of his political life. She served as a crucial link to Hitler and the German Nazi Party in the years just previous to World War II.

The advent of World War II obliterated Mosley's Fascist dreamland. He and Diana were arrested and spent the next five years in detention. Mosley attempted to retire after the war but his love of political life soon had him out making speeches to his old constituency, though he never gained the following that he had enjoyed during the 1930s. His life with Diana was his one source of happiness. They remained together until his death at eighty-four.

If you have Mars in Gemini with Venus in Capricorn you are ... the Technician of Tough Love

You are one of the earthiest of the Mars in Gemini Lovers and you enjoy sex a great deal. Your reactions to sexual stimuli are very physical and strong; however, this doesn't make your understanding of those experiences any less abstract. Often you feel intellectually removed from your lusts—even from your body—and you regard your own sexual activity with a cool and unsympathetic detachment. Even when you seem to be enjoying sex with unconscious abandon, you refuse to let it have any power over your mind.

Your mistrust of sex will sometimes lead you to the conclusion that any meaningful relationship cannot be sexual. This in turn can lead you to disown your earthy sensuality or to simply give up on the possibility of finding the kind of relationship you need. You assume that if it feels good it can't be love when, in fact, it often can. (You just need to trust your body a little more often.)

Case Histories

Henri de Toulouse-Lautrec (*French artist whose work celebrated the nightlife of Paris in the 1890s). Born November 24, 1864, in Albi, France (Fermigier 1969; Frey 1994).*

The tragic circumstances of Lautrec's youth are well-known. A childhood injury (or perhaps a congenital defect) left him a physically deformed dwarf. His undersized legs were only part of the problem. He was also an ugly man, with thick lips, a prominent nose, and a persistent drool. Lautrec knew he would always have difficulty attracting women from his own privileged and ennobled class. Therefore, he never really tried. Instead, from the age of twenty, he satisfied himself with the whores and other women of easy virtue he found in one of Paris' most degenerate slums, Montmartre.

Lautrec talked a lot about sex but said very little about his own love life. The one great love affair attributed to him—which may, or may not, have occurred—was with the tempestuous and talented Suzanne Valadon. Valadon and Lautrec lived in the same building and may have been lovers. (Valadon was known to sleep with anyone who interested her and Lautrec was nothing if not interesting.) Valadon posed for him and he was one of the few people to know that she had her own artistic ambitions. He referred Valadon to Edgar Degas, who became her mentor. At one point during Lautrec's mid-twenties Valadon reportedly threatened to kill herself if the aristocratic painter didn't marry her. Lautrec was concerned enough to grab a friend and run to Valadon's apartment. There they overheard Valadon talking to her mother and learned that the threat was merely a ploy. The story typically ends with the heartbroken Lautrec separating from Valadon forever. In reality Lautrec and Valadon continued to live in the same place and their relationship doesn't seem to have been greatly changed by this event.

Meanwhile, a real love affair developed between Lautrec and Montmartre, particularly with the women of Montmartre. Lautrec loved the dingy bars and decadent nightlife of the place and he made performers like La Goulue, Jane Avril, and Yvette Guilbert famous with his posters and paintings. By all appearance he was never sexually involved with any of these women, although he counted them among his wide circle of friends. He was a fan, like all the other men who sat in the audience and watched them kick high or sing plaintively of love. It was his giddy enthusiasm for the illusion of sex and glamour they created that fired his art. Had he been intimate with them, perhaps this would have been lost.

For intimacy, or at least a kind of intimacy, Lautrec went to brothels. Lautrec had an easy and extremely familiar relationship with these establishments. Some said he lived in a brothel. In fact, he used these houses as a kind of "headquarters" where he met patrons and entertained friends. The women who worked in these brothels welcomed this dwarfish artist into their world. He was allowed to see and paint aspects of their lives that were off-limits to most men, including lesbianism. Lautrec was fascinated with the notion of sex between two women and depicted it with great tenderness in his work.

Of course, Lautrec did more in brothels than just draw and paint. He was also welcomed because he loved sex and played at it with a sardonic irreverence. Lautrec's physical deformity did not extend to his genitals. In fact, some claimed that nature favored him in this department. Lautrec took an earthy, and even grungy, delight in everything connected to the female body. He loved breasts, armpits, hands, women's hats, stockings, and underwear. He loved older women as much as young nymphets and jaded strumpets as much as (or more than) ladies of fashion. This was why he was so much at ease in the brothels, particularly when he was mingling with the prostitutes during their "off" hours. The fact that he had to pay for this privilege didn't bother Lautrec at all. If anything it made him more comfortable with the whole transaction.

Lautrec's ideas about sex probably differed very little from the opinions of the whores he lived with and painted. He had a cynical disregard for love, which he labeled a farce and, despite his sensuality, he found the sex act itself a matter of comedy. Paying for sex suited him. He knew a paying customer could not be rejected or pitied. The fact that he was unable to form an enduring sexual relationship with any particular woman posed no problem for him. He had his brothels, his work and, of course, his cocktails.

Lautrec's alcoholism was not identified as a problem until his mid-thirties when he was already suffering from hallucinations and tremors. Syphilis and his general disdain of what we might call a healthy lifestyle probably complicated his condition. More aware than anyone that his decline was a direct result of the way he lived, Lautrec refused to change and he remained defiantly upbeat and unrepentant until his untimely death at the age of thirty-seven.

Other Examples

Virginia Woolf (*English writer and central figure of the literary community called the Bloomsbury Group*). *Woolf was a victim of rape and incest when she was a child and this over-shadowed her sexual development. Although her erotic feelings were primarily directed toward women, she may have had only one very limited homosexual affair. Meanwhile, her marriage to Leonard Woolf was essentially an intellectual partnership with only a minimum of sexual involvement. As she grew older, Woolf came to consider herself a "eunuch" because of her inability to respond to sexual intimacy. She committed suicide at the age of fifty-nine. Born January 25, 1882 (DeSalvo 1989).*

Eva Braun (*Hitler's mistress*). *Born February 6, 1912 (Encyclopedia Britannica 1997).*

If you have Mars in Gemini with Venus in Aquarius you are ... the Technician of Transcendent Love

You are the most daring and experimental of the Mars in Gemini Lovers, the one who takes curiosity to the limit. At your best you are a very exciting and inventive partner, someone who knows just how to use ideas to make the raw data of sensory experience into something truly extraordinary and erotic. With your wide-open approach to sexual activity, you make sex better for everyone around you—even those who never have the benefit of sharing your bed.

Unfortunately, the story is quite different when you are not at your best. There is a distant coolness about your sexual nature that often makes you emphasize the experience instead of the person with whom you share it. In fact, since it is the idea of sex that is your true inspiration, sex in its more physical manifestations may bore you. You are a Lover who finds so much pleasure in thinking and talking about sex, that doing it can be a disappointment.

Case History

James Joyce (*Irish author of* Ulysses *and* Finnegans Wake *noted for his modern stream-of-consciousness technique*). *Born February 2, 1882, in Dublin, Ireland (Ellmann).*

The son of an ambitious Irish Catholic family, Joyce entered a Catholic school at an early age. There he distinguished himself both in his lessons and his religious devotion, but adolescence kept him from pursuing a Jesuit calling. He claimed that his first significant sexual experience came when he masturbated in the woods while listening to a woman urinate nearby. When he was fourteen, Joyce picked up a Dublin prostitute and said good-bye to his virginity.

Joyce continued to visit prostitutes when he could afford it and he also masturbated, but he had no serious involvement with women until he met Nora Barnacle at the age of twenty-two. Barnacle was a poor woman from County Galway who had come to Dublin to find work. A relationship developed quickly between the two young people. Joyce, who was living off the good will of his father, had hope of work in Europe. He proposed that Barnacle go with him, though he made no promise to marry her. Barnacle, in love with the cocky young author and desperate for a new start, agreed.

Joyce's common-law marriage with Nora was emphatically sexual in the beginning. Nora, despite her convent education, was earthy and straightforward with regard to sex. She often took the lead in bed, a tendency that delighted Joyce. Even though Joyce's artistic egotism was quite evident by this point, he still enjoyed the idea of being dominated by a woman.

It was an unlikely union in some ways. Nora was by no means stupid, but she had little interest in literature. She did not appreciate Joyce's writing. In the early days she was quite critical of his inability to provide for her and their two children. Firmly convinced of his own genius, Joyce did not require a cheerleader. What he did require was a woman's mind. By constantly questioning Nora about her past, feelings, and dreams, and by watching her closely day by day, Joyce was able to develop one of his most enduring characters: Molly Bloom of *Ulysses*.

Joyce and Nora lived in Trieste, Italy for the first five years of their relationship. Then Joyce traveled back to Dublin on a business venture. Nora agreed to write him erotic letters while he was away, partly to ease the pain of their separation and partly to keep him out of Dublin's whorehouses. Joyce responded in kind and his letters reveal an extremely active sexual imagination. Every possible variety of heterosexual enticements is discussed and lauded, but one topic that turns up continually is Joyce's fascination with anal sex and defecation. Joyce's erotic reveries were not dashed off in lustful haste. Rather they appear to be thoughtfully written out in his clearest hand, as if he wanted to make sure that Nora missed nothing. Interestingly, when Joyce returned from his journey and it came time for the object of his erotic adoration to join him in bed, she found the tireless pornographer sound asleep.

Joyce's interest in sexual experimentation did not last that long. Some experts feel that Joyce's sex life with Nora had ceased, or at least weakened, by the time he turned thirty-five and was deeply involved in writing *Ulysses*. It is possible that Joyce had become bored with Nora and found his sexual fulfillment in the writing of his book. It is also possible that his drinking was interfering with his sexual performance by this point. There are hints in his writing that the author had become impotent.

Joyce was still capable of infatuations. When he was in his late thirties he chanced to see a young woman pulling the chain in a "water closet." Joyce watched this woman for several days before approaching her. His later remark about "exploring the coldest and hottest part of a woman's body" is taken to mean he had anal sex with her (Ellmann, 45).

About this same time, Joyce encouraged Nora to have an affair "to give him something to write about," she claimed (Wallace, 147). Nora was still an attractive woman. Men responded to her but she never was unfaithful to Joyce. Joyce was divided in his attitude toward her loyalty. Although he enjoyed the fact that men found her attractive and he quizzed her closely about her sexual encounters before their meeting, jealousy and feelings of sexual inadequacy often tortured him.

When Joyce was forty-nine he married Nora but this did nothing to renew their sex life. Joyce claimed he was now more interested in women's clothing than their bodies. Nora told her sister that she "hated" sex. As sexless as their union had become, it proved unbreakable and lasted until Joyce's death at the age of fifty-nine.

Another Example

Marion Davies (actress better known as the long-time mistress of newspaper mogul William Randolph Hearst). Born January 3, 1897 (Celebrity Birthday Guide).

If you have Mars in Gemini with Venus in Pisces you are ... the Technician of Enchantment

You are an extremely alluring and sensual Mars in Gemini Lover whose sexuality is an uneven blend of craftiness and innocence. You are very rational about sex and approach it with great clarity of purpose. But even at your most calculating moment, deep emotional needs and feelings of vulnerability cloud your judgements. This makes you one of the most flighty and unreliable Lovers of this type—a partner who can be manipulative and open-hearted at the same time.

At your best moments you are a Lover of extraordinary skill and tenderness. You are a human catalogue of sexual positions with a real, deep-seated emotional need to make the most of them all. At your worst you are a compulsive charmer who wins everyone's love and no one's confidence. In between you are a delightful and infuriating enigma—someone all too easy to love but impossible to hold.

Case History

Eric Gill (English sculptor, engraver, and typographer who sought to integrate craft, art, religion, and sex). Born February 22, 1882, 6:30 A.M. in Brighton, England (MacCarthy 1989).

Gill's father was a Protestant minister. Religion was a matter of serious concern in his child-hood home. Another matter of concern was space; Gill was one of thirteen children. Just as Gill's deep religious feelings were formed by his home life, so was his eroticism influenced by the inevitable domestic familiarity of a large family raised in cramped, lower-middle-class accommodations.

When Gill was in art school at the age of nineteen, he fell in love with Ethel Moore. Moore was two years older than Gill, an intelligent though essentially docile woman. His parent's disproved, but Gill was sure he had found a lifetime mate. The problem was sex. Moore was not inclined to have sex before marriage and Gill knew it would be years before he would be financially ready to take a wife. So he made an extremely unsatisfactory visit to a prostitute. Later he confessed this to Moore and used the incident to persuade her to put aside her Victorian upbringing and sleep with him immediately.

Gill and Moore were married when he was twenty-two. The marriage was a success from the very beginning and quickly produced three daughters. Ethel shared Gill's idealism and his iden-tification with the medieval craftsmen. Gill imagined himself a philosopher as well as an artist. Ethel remained his most devoted supporter through all the dramatic shifts in his thinking.

Despite his marital bliss, it didn't take Gill long to become restless. He had an affair with the family maid three years into the marriage. A short time later he took up with a lively, free-thinking socialist. Ethel was aware of the latter affair and Gill even encouraged her to become friends with his paramour. Ethel refused to see the woman socially but she was determined not to let the liaison disrupt her life with Gill.

A pattern in their marriage was established at this point. Gill maintained a warm, sexual relationship with his wife, but he also exercised an enormous amount of sexual freedom. He had affairs with various women, ranging from feminist intellectuals to servant girls. He cultivated friendships with liberated couples just to see what kind of combinations might develop. He visited prostitutes and collected pornography. More importantly, much of his artistic production centered on sexual themes. Gill felt that the separation of the erotic from "normal" life was one of the gravest errors of modern culture.

Gill's approach to sex had an experimental, even clinical, quality. He made detailed drawing of genitals and his studies of penises were sometimes labeled with measurements or the names of the models. He took smears of his own semen and viewed them under a microscope. His curiosity led him to sample all sorts of sexual experiences including threesomes and fellatio.

One of the many sexually explicit works that Gill created was a relief sculpture of a couple having sex standing up. The people who modeled for this sculpture were his sister Gladys and her husband. When Gill was twenty-eight he began, or perhaps renewed, a sexual relationship with Gladys. He later confessed to his wife that he had sex with two of his sisters. Gill showed no shame regarding his incestuous relationships and, apparently, neither did his sisters. Gill continued to visit Gladys and have sex with her throughout his life.

When Gill was thirty-two he converted to Catholicism and became a vocal advocate of that faith and monastic lifestyle. His religious fervor did nothing to curb his libido. If anything, it made it more obvious. Gill proposed that sex was a sacred act, that it was merely another way of worshiping the divine. His frank enthusiasm for sexual liberty became part of a very public philosophy in which eroticism, God, craftsmanship, art, and an aversion to all things modern were held up as part of the same sacred ideal. Gill even tried to start communities based on his social theories, but they failed. He died at fifty-seven and, for the most part, his philosophy died with him. His design work and his art are still appreciated, though much of his artistic production still cannot be exhibited because of its sexual content.

Another Example

Natacha Rambova (dancer turned designer who married Rudolph Valentino). Some said she created the image that made Valentino famous, but others claimed she manipulated him and lived off his name. In either case, the pressures put on their marriage eventually caused the couple to separate. Born January 19, 1897 (Morris 1991).

Chapter 4

Mars in Cancer
The Sentimentalist

General Characteristics

Mars in Cancer Lovers are a remarkable (and sometimes exasperating) combination of sexual passivity and aggression. On the one hand, they need to be conquered, overwhelmed, and swept away by sex. They long for a complete capitulation of the self in the name of love. On the other hand, they are extremely active Lovers who are rarely content to just sit and wait to be conquered. They work hard to find the kind of sex they need and they are quite capable of taking the initiative in any relationships.

The sensual life and the emotional life are totally intertwined for these Lovers. This doesn't mean that it is impossible for a Mars in Cancer Lover to have sex without emotional commitment. It just means that it is impossible for a Lover of this type to have sex without an emotional price. Here even the most casual sexual contact has a way of getting sloppy and out of control. Their feelings are always on the line, no matter how much they try and deny it; they are easily wounded. For this reason, Mars in Cancer Lovers tend to be happier when they are conservative. Unfortunately, the intensity of their sexual feelings, both on a physical and an emotional level, often makes it difficult for them to be conservative enough.

Here sex is always linked with security. At times Mars in Cancer Lovers can seem like children, desperate for emotional support and protection. At other times they act like nervous mother hens (regardless of gender), compulsively worrying about and hovering over the object of their affection. They need to keep the person they love close in order to be absolutely sure of his or her commitment. Relationships are extremely important to their sexual health. They devote a great deal of energy to maintaining them. When they are secure within a relationship these Lovers can be amazingly sensual and devoted. When they are unsure of their partner, or feel neglected or hurt, their behavior can become exceeding erratic.

Mars in Cancer Lovers are capable of all sorts of messy behavior because their sexual feelings are so loaded with emotion. In some instances they can become obsessively promiscuous in a vain search for emotional sustenance in the transitory passion of physical sex. At other times they can drive people away with their incessant desire for emotional reassurance. Even in the best of circumstances they are susceptible to periods of maudlin self-pity and irrationality.

For all of their whining and apparent passivity, there is a toughness about these Mars in Cancer Lovers that typically sees them through the most difficult of romantic situations. Perhaps the very sensitivity that makes them so vulnerable also gives them this inner resiliency. Perhaps it's just that their need for love is so great that it inspires within them a special kind of tenacity. In any case, these people are emotional survivors who never give up on love.

Change is an essential element in the sex lives of Mars in Cancer individuals. Love is a process for them, and they get nervous when it becomes static. These Lovers never stop tinkering even when they are lucky enough to find the emotionally secure and physically rewarding relationship they need. They like to test their partners, rearrange the rules of their relationships, and otherwise upset the emotional status quo. This restlessness conflicts sharply with the need these Lovers have for security and commitment. But such rational observations are not likely to impress these Lovers. They will always follow their feelings, even when doing so takes them to the edge of disaster.

Why do we put up with these emotionally volatile and thoroughly troublesome Mars in Cancer Lovers? Could it be because, beneath the ebb and flow of their constantly changing passions, they are the most loyal and giving Lovers under the zodiac? Or could it be because they're just so darn sexy? Mars in Cancer Lovers have a sexual allure that transcends age, class, and even downright ugliness. That bubbling caldron of feeling that sits at the core of their sexuality broadcasts need and desire to all. They are very sexual people and, even though their emotionalism sometimes gets in the way of their sensuality, this vaunted sex appeal promises nothing they can't deliver in the flesh. No matter how much trouble these Lovers bring to their partners, they seldom find themselves alone.

If you have Mars in Cancer with Venus in Aries you are . . . the Swaggering Sentimentalist

You would have an easier time as a Lover if you could forget about your ego and just follow your feelings. But you know that those feelings will lead you to a complete capitulation of your pride, your individuality, and your self-esteem for the sake of love. You just don't want to go there. So, you fight against your emotions and try and keep love at bay. For the most part, these struggles only gain you a little time. When you do finally fall in love, you will fall extra hard.

Your erotic life is naturally full of fire, conflict, and crazy extremes. Your feelings are so strong and your passions so compelling that you have no time for either gentleness or good manners. Perhaps more importantly, the contradictions within your sexual nature often cause you to veer wildly between aggression and passivity. One moment you give yourself completely, the next you angrily demand a refund. The person who loves you must be prepared for a challenge, but a sexier and more seductive challenge would be hard to imagine.

Case History

Isadora Duncan (*American dancer who single-handedly established modern dance as a valid art form*). *Born May 17, 1878, in San Francisco, California (Schneider 1969; Seroff 1971).*

Note: This date differs from other published birth dates. It was taken from sources within Duncan's family.

Duncan's origins provided her with little in terms of material support, but her artistic temperament and originality were heartily encouraged. During her early years she applied herself entirely to the task of mastering her novel and provocative style of dance. She failed to find acceptance in America, but in Europe she found audiences enthusiastic for her combination of classical music, graceful and inventive movement, and very little clothing. Despite the sexual impact of her performances, the hard-working Duncan avoided romantic entanglements and remained a virgin until the age of twenty-five.

Her first affair was with a Hungarian actor. It was typical of all her affairs in that she entered into it wholeheartedly and with great physical passion. She fled Budapest to spend several days alone with her partner in a rural love nest. Eventually she returned to her place on the stage and the love affair began to cool. Duncan always maintained that, despite her several lovers, she was monogamous by nature and that she had never given up on any of her relationships. It was only her career and her absolute devotion to her art that limited the level of her commitment.

The next year Duncan was in love once again, this time with stage designer Gordon Craig. She took an abrupt hiatus from her dancing to enjoy her new lover (so abrupt that her manager went to the police because he thought that his star had been abducted). She soon returned to her work, performing even while she was obviously pregnant with Craig's child.

Craig was the son of the famous actress Ellen Terry and he appeared to understand Duncan's ambition. But Duncan soon learned that while she was busy becoming an international celebrity, he was consoling himself with other women. Nonetheless, their affair continued for nearly three tempestuous years. It was finally destroyed—more because of Craig's extraordinary egotism than by Duncan's jealousy.

After Craig, Duncan moved to a much more peaceful arrangement with an American-born millionaire named Paris Singer. Singer proved to be a generous and indulgent lover. The couple had a son to join the daughter she had by Craig. For seven years the relationship seemed quite happy, only to be devastated by an incredible tragedy. The two children were left with their nurse in a parked car that accidentally rolled into the Seine River. All of the occupants of the vehicle drowned.

The death of her children was a tremendous blow to Duncan. Among other things it made clear the limitations of her relationship with Singer. The millionaire was willing to support Duncan financially, but he was not the kind of man who could support her emotionally in her moment of need. Desperate for emotional salvation, she fled to Italy where she had sex with a young Italian sculptor in order to get pregnant again. Singer continued to provide for her during her pregnancy but the child died shortly after birth.

After this, Singer became just another of the several moneyed people Duncan periodically touched for support. She had other affairs, each intense and passionate for a time, but none enduring. Duncan's reputation as an advocate of sexual freedom was enough to draw men to her despite her advancing age. She remained aggressively unconventional in the conduct of her personal life.

When she was forty-four, Duncan married, but it was a marriage designed to be nothing if not revolutionary. Her husband was Sergei Esenin, a twenty-seven-year-old Russian poet. She met Esenin while visiting Moscow at the behest of its new Communist leaders. Duncan and her young husband shared the same socialist politics but little else. Esenin was an emotionally unstable alcoholic who spoke no English, while Duncan knew little Russian. Their marriage collapsed in the midst of her disastrous tour of the United States. Not only did Duncan suffer through the condemnation of the American public but she also had to endure Esenin's half-crazed outbursts. After less than a year of marriage Duncan took Esenin back to Russia and left him there.

Once her career as a performer was over, Duncan was desperate to find a way to support herself and her vast entourage. She contracted with a publisher to write an autobiography. Her first attempts were considered too bland and she was told to add more sex. Despite her revolutionary views, this kind of candor did not come easily to Duncan. She struggled to write a draft that would be titillating enough for her reading public.

Duncan had strong maternal appeal for the younger members of her entourage, including many male and female homosexuals. Her close relationship with the women led to rumors of lesbian affairs. One young woman, Mercedes de Acosta, later claimed she had been Duncan's lover. Given Duncan's long history of heterosexual relationships and Acosta's flair for exaggeration, this seems unlikely. Duncan died at forty-nine.

Other Examples

Arthur Schopenhauer (*German philosopher who proposed that love was just a trick played by nature to assure propagation*). *Despite his avowed hatred for women, Schopenhauer had several passionate affairs and died with syphilis. Born February 22, 1788 (Encyclopedia Britannica, Vol. 10).*

Liza Minnelli (*American singer, dancer, and star of* Cabaret). *Born March 12, 1946 (Celebrity Birthday Guide).*

If you have Mars in Cancer with Venus in Taurus you are . . . the Lazy Sentimentalist

You are less active than most Mars in Cancer types. You are an easygoing Lover who doesn't like to rush and hardly ever feels inclined to scream. You are a hedonist when it comes to sex and for this reason you try to avoid the emotional extremes that plague most Mars in Cancer Lovers. You temper your passions with a strong dose of caution. Typically, you are a rather conservative and secretive Lover.

After the pursuit of pure pleasure, the most important thing to you is security. Unfortunately, you have a tendency to confuse material security with emotional security. After all, material security "feels" good and it is so much easier to control and hold on to than emotional commitments. The combination of your acute sensitivity and practical approach to love makes you wary of emotional bonds and mistrustful of the whole mechanism of falling in love. In the end, the only security that will ever satisfy you is the security that touches your heart.

Case History

Jean Cocteau *(French poet, artist, writer, and filmmaker noted for his various associations with the avant-garde). Born July 5, 1889, in Paris, France (Steegmiller 1970).*

When Cocteau was ten his father committed suicide. The sensitive youngster, who was eight years younger than his nearest sibling, was left in total command of his mother's doting attention. Sex and masturbation became an issue early in his life. In his recollections of his school days, the smell of semen competed with the smell of chalk. Cocteau was apparently aware of his homosexuality even at this early age. The objects of his desire were older, more athletic boys whom he idolized from afar.

Cocteau left his school and staid, middle-class home at fifteen and fled to Marseilles. According to Cocteau's story, his older brothers persuaded their mother that it would be good for her youngest son to be on his own. It was a year before his family came searching for him. In the meantime, Cocteau found his way in the waterfront district of Marseilles, an area in which prostitution, drug use, and other crimes were commonplace. How the slender, effeminate Cocteau survived in this environment is unknown. Cocteau's own accounts of this period were more designed to cloud the issues and reinforce his own legend than to present the facts.

When the teenage Cocteau finally returned to Paris, his adventure had made him a celebrity among the restless young men of his milieu. With his ever-indulgent mother turning a blind eye, Cocteau quickly found his way into a daringly artistic set that had formed under the sponsorship of an aging homosexual actor. This actor paid for Cocteau's debut as a poet. The book of verse drew favorable attention for its exotic imagery, but revealed very little about its author.

Stylish, pretty, and bubbling with nervous energy and new ideas, Cocteau became the darling of Paris society long before he was twenty. Although his homosexuality was assumed, his love life remained private. Cocteau still lived with his mother and, when he tried to secretly keep a "bachelor" apartment, she made him give it up. During this period Cocteau was demonstrative in his infatuations with various female singers and performers. He pursued them ardently and became friendly with some. He occasionally bragged that he had sex with one or another of these women but his boasts were not given much credence.

By the time Cocteau was in his twenties, his infatuations had shifted to the major players of the Paris avant-garde. Vaslav Nijinski, Sergei Diaghilev, Igor Stravinsky, Pablo Picasso, Gertrude Stein, and other notables became the lights of his emotional life. There were often sexual elements in his relationships with these great artists, particularly with Nijinski with whom Cocteau obviously fell in love. The sex was sublimated and made to work for the higher cause of art.

A major shift occurred in Cocteau's sex life at age twenty-eight. With the bloom of youth gone, he now became the protector of younger lovers. The first of these "sons" was a poet named Jean LeRoy, who wrote Cocteau mushy letters from the front during the later years of World War I. Cocteau had many friends in the military and was active in the support of the French war effort himself, but he was particularly concerned for LeRoy and begged friends to protect him.

Cocteau turned to other young men when LeRoy died in the war. He was very devoted to each of his lovers and, typically, his relationships were singular and deeply felt. He overlooked their faults, promoted them in their various careers, and treated them with an affection that was almost maternal.

Cocteau's most notable, and perhaps most beloved, companion was Raymond Radiquet. Radiquet was a teenage poetic phenomenon who had gained the avid attention of the Parisian literary community, much as the young Cocteau had done. But Radiquet was a very different kind of person. Where Cocteau was talkative and always anxious to please, Radiquet was silent and arrogant. He became Cocteau's lover and accepted his support, financial and otherwise, but he often rebelled. He had affairs with women, he went on drinking binges, and disappeared for periods of time. Yet Cocteau was always prepared to forgive him.

This relationship was an emotional roller coaster for Cocteau. Radiquet's cruelty and insolence drove the usually passive Cocteau to unprecedented displays of rage, but his drawings of Radiquet are among the most sensual and revealing artistic gestures Cocteau ever produced. After four years Radiquet was secure enough in his career to break with Cocteau. He became engaged to a young woman. Then, at twenty-one, Radiquet died suddenly of typhoid. Cocteau was inconsolable. It was three years before he devoted himself solely to another lover.

While grieving for Radiquet, Cocteau found refuge from his emotional pain in opium. It also served as a lure for the several handsome young men who became Cocteau's companions in these years. At thirty-six, alarmed at the way opium interfered with his artistic production and sex drive, Cocteau attempted a cure. This period of abstinence, and the several other cures that followed, could not rid him of his addiction.

Cocteau attempted to maintain an air of mystery around his sex life. Without denying his homosexuality, he stopped short of admitting it directly. Even in his later years, he harked back to his supposed affairs with famous singers as proof that he knew the feelings of a heterosexual male. Despite the intensity of his attachments to his various lovers, Cocteau always referred to them as his "adopted sons." Although his erotic feelings for these men is often evident in his artistic production, he was reluctant to own up to it. When Cocteau died at seventy-four he was famous, but some critics felt that his drug addiction and self-indulgence had tragically stunted his artistic development.

Another Example

Wilhelm Reich (a follower of Freud and Marx who believed sexual repression was responsible for social ills). His radical ideas about sexual energy got him chased from several countries and imprisoned in the United States. Within his own marriage, Reich remained a strictly conventional and dominating husband. Born March 24, 1897 (Reich 1969).

If you have Mars in Cancer with Venus in Gemini you are . . . the Smooth-Talking Sentimentalist

Unlike most Mars in Cancer Lovers, you can be reasonable about sex. You are aware of your special sexual allure and your innate sensuality and you are determined to make intelligent use of these gifts. Your approach to sex is less conservative than most Mars in Cancer people and you place a greater emphasis on skill and having fun. For this reason, you may suffer a few more bumps and disappointments than necessary in your love life. But you are flexible and rational enough to recover from these misfortunes with a minimum of self-pity and emotional display.

You still have a deep need for emotional security even with your relatively sane approach to romance. Like all Lovers of this type, relationships are very important to you. A sense of mutual commitment is essential to your enjoyment of sex. When you are apart from the person you love or involved in a relationship that doesn't touch your heart, you can appear to be very clever and in control. But when you get too close you lose those intellectual advantages and you become like all the other Mars in Cancer Lovers—a slave to your feelings.

Case History

Rudolph Valentino (Rudolph Guglielini—Italian-born film star who became the greatest male sex symbol of his day). Born May 6, 1895, in Castellaneta, Italy (Morris 1991; Shulman 1967).

The son of a poor family, Valentino was allowed to emigrate to the United States when he was eighteen because he showed such a stubborn unwillingness to fit into the life of his native village. Once in the United States, he did menial work until he found he could make a living dancing with American women in nightclubs for pay. Tall, handsome, and possessing a natural grace, Valentino became a popular partner and he prospered. Soon he was dancing with women in some of the most exclusive clubs in New York City. It is clear from Valentino's account of this period that many of his female clients wanted more than a dance for their money. Valentino always denied that he was a gigolo during this time but his denials were not always believed.

Valentino's success as a paid dancer helped him to get started as a professional performer. His work with an established female star was less than lucrative, and his partner treated Valentino like hired help, but it was a more respectable job. It served as the beginning of his career in show business. When he was twenty-one, Valentino's life took a dangerous turn. He was accused of involvement in a blackmail ring and put in jail. The actual allegations were vague and the documents that backed them up disappeared from public records after Valentino became a star. The implication was that he allowed himself to be lured into some shady dealing that led, indirectly, to the murder of a wealthy man by his estranged wife. Once he was released from jail, Valentino fled to California.

Valentino found work in Hollywood as an actor and met a lovely young actress named Jean Acker. Valentino proposed marriage after a romantic evening of riding horses in the moonlight. Acker accepted and the marriage was quickly arranged but never consummated. Acker was a lesbian. She had impetuously agreed to marry Valentino because, at the time, she was angry with her female lover. Acker locked the pleading Valentino out of her room on their wedding night and told him she could never be his wife.

It wasn't long before the dejected husband was distracted from his troubles. He met a beautiful dancer turned clothing designer named Natacha Rambova. Rambova was a cool, strong-willed woman who did not immediately respond to the allure of this sexy Italian. But with humor, persistence, and his obvious physical charms, Valentino dispelled her reservations and the young couple was soon involved in a heated sexual relationship—so heated that during one session of lovemaking Rambova passed out and Valentino thought he had killed her.

When Valentino was twenty-seven he married Rambova in Mexico. He knew that technically his divorce from Acker was not yet final, but he and Rambova hoped to evade the law as many couples did at the time. Unfortunately, an ambitious prosecutor decided it might be a good career move to enforce the law to the letter in Valentino's case. The Latin lover was arrested for bigamy. A court battle followed. Rambova and Valentino were ordered to separate for a year. Of course, they defied this order at every opportunity.

Valentino was a major star by this time, idolized by millions of women and despised by many men. Not many people in the movie business were prepared for the kind of sexual attraction Valentino was able to project from the screen. The notion of a male sex symbol was still very new. But Rambova recognized the implications immediately. When the movie studios were unable to give her lover enough work, she arranged for them to take his sexy image on the road to vaudeville theaters across the country with a fiery tango routine.

Rambova maintained a powerful influence over the relatively passive Valentino. She designed his costumes and established his "look." Her opinions about what Valentino should or should not do often differed with the ideas of the studio executives and others involved in his pictures. She pushed her husband toward sexier and, some felt, more effeminate roles. Valentino was torn. He loved his wife dearly and honored her opinions. He also had a head full of Old World notions, and he resented any hint that his wife was controlling him.

The internal and external pressures on Valentino's marriage were tremendous. The couple disagreed over money, his friends, and the Hollywood "crowd" he was so attracted to. Rambova's "high art" pretensions meant little to the essentially lowbrow Valentino, regardless of how anxious he was to please her. Rambova's enemies went so far as to hire a private detective in the hope that they would be able to catch her in a sexual indiscretion. Finally, when Valentino was thirty, Rambova left for a "marital vacation" in Europe. A short time later the couple divorced.

After his break with Rambova, Valentino slept with other women. He established a relationship with an actress named Pola Negri, who made no secret of her determination to be the next Mrs. Valentino. Valentino was not interested in any such commitments, and he continued to wear the platinum slave bracelet that Rambova had given him. A little over a year after their separation, Valentino was operated on for a ruptured ulcer. The infection spread through his body and, to the shock of the world, he died suddenly at the age of thirty-one.

Another Example

William Randolph Hearst (*newspaper magnate who used his tremendous power to support the career of his mistress, Marion Davies, and scare away rivals for her affection*). *Born April 29, 1893 (Celebrity Birthday Guide).*

If you have Mars in Cancer with Venus in Cancer you are . . . the Super Sentimentalist

Sex is a force of nature for you. It can carry you away to unimaginable heights of pleasure and it can also leave you emotionally devastated, all in the same afternoon. The intensity of your sexual feelings and the depth and power of your emotional needs make you an extremely seductive lover. Your gestures, your voice, and your eyes all proclaim a promise that few can resist—a promise of complete surrender to the power of love.

Of course, no one is more aware of the dangers inherent in that promise than you. Because your sexuality is so laden with emotions, it is not unusual for you to view the whole experience with a sense of terror. Your mad compulsion to give all to love makes you a very vulnerable individual. Love can become as addictive to you as a drug, and sexual unhappiness can make you malicious and irrational. You are a person who should always take great care in his or her sexual choices. When you don't—which is often—you will always pay a price.

Case History

Honoré de Balzac (French novelist of The Human Comedy; *as well known for his larger-than-life personality as for his books). Born May 20, 1799, in Tours, France (Gerson 1972).*

The eldest child of a cold and unloving bourgeois mother, Balzac often described his childhood as bleak and devoid of maternal affection. By his teens, however, he had found a way to fill the emotional void in his life. He took money from his indulgent and worldly grandmother to visit prostitutes. He effectively concealed these early sexual adventures, not only from his family, but also from his biographers until long after his death. At one point, when he was about twenty, his grandmother bet the portly youngster that he could not seduce a certain young woman. Balzac won the bet.

When Balzac was twenty-three he began an affair with a woman in her forties named Laure de Berny. An intelligent, sensitive woman of a somewhat higher class than Balzac, Berny found the youngster's ardent courtship alarming at first. But Balzac would not relent and finally Berny allowed herself to accept the fact that this young man loved her. The relationship lasted for ten years. She served not only as his mistress and surrogate mother but also as his literary advisor. She encouraged Balzac to write quality novels and gave him the emotional support he desperately needed in the early days of his career.

Balzac's deep emotional involvement with Berny did not preclude other sexual adventures. He started slowly. A couple of years after he started his affair with Berny, he began sleeping with a wealthy aristocrat who was also in her forties. As his literary reputation expanded so did his sexual appetites. By the time Balzac reached his thirties his promiscuity was unbounded. He had sex with women of all classes, types, and ages: high-born women from Paris' best salons to star-struck, middle-class matrons who wrote the author fan mail inviting him into their bed. Occasionally, he reverted to the secret pleasure of his adolescence and hired prostitutes, sometimes two at a time. At the same time, he maintained sexual relationships with both of his mistresses.

Almost as amazing as Balzac's sexual stamina (particularly in light of his voluminous literary production), was his ability to attract and seduce women with ease. Balzac was short, fat, and ugly as a young man. He gave little attention to either his appearance or personal hygiene. His clothing was typically in disarray and his hair was likely to be both unwashed and uncombed; however, his almost compulsive capacity for chatter, which his male acquaintances often found irritating, mesmerized women. His eyes, large and brimming with emotion, were capable of touching the maternal instinct in even the most hardened feminine heart. Women were not only drawn to him, they typically praised him as a bedmate of the highest caliber.

When Balzac was thirty-three, Berny voluntarily withdrew from her role as his primary mistress. Aging and in failing health, she was no longer able to deal with the author's physical and emotional demands. Balzac was desperate for another companion. At this point Evelina Hanska, the plump, young wife of an aging Russian baron, entered his life. Their love affair was conducted primarily through passionate correspondence, though they managed to meet occasionally for sex. It was an arrangement that well suited Balzac's hectic lifestyle. It allowed him plenty of time to write his books and conduct affairs with numerous other women (at least two of which produced children).

Hanska's husband died when Balzac was forty-two. Hanska had often promised to marry Balzac during their years of correspondence and now Balzac was desperate to formalize their arrangement. Faced with the prospect of Balzac as a husband, Hanska suddenly began to treasure her independence, or at least her purse. The profligate author had an awful capacity for wasting money. Despite his immense success as a writer, he was habitually in debt. Balzac applied all his charm and energy to persuade Hanska to be his wife, but failed. It was only in the last year of his life, when his body began to give way after years of excess and abuse, that Balzac's mistress took pity on him and agreed to marry him. Balzac died five months after the wedding at the age of fifty-one.

Other Examples

Tom Jones (British singer noted for his onstage gyrations). Born June 7, 1940 (Celebrity Birthday Guide).

Nicole Brown Simpson (murder victim). Born May 18, 1959 (Weller 1995).

If you have Mars in Cancer with Venus in Leo you are … the Controlled Sentimentalist

You are basically at odds with your sexuality. The kind of complete surrender to love that is so characteristic of Mars in Cancer scares you to death. You don't want to see your ego dissolved in a sea of feeling. The glorification of the ego is a big part of the pleasure of sex for you. You like being praised, applauded, and made to feel important. The thought of giving all this up, even for true love, is often more than you can bear. So, you love with extreme caution, keeping to the edges of your powerful sexuality and trying never to lose control.

Of course, the chances of you containing this primal passivity forever are slim. Every sexual encounter is, for you, an invitation to give it all up—to capitulate to your sloppy emotions and be taken over by your passions. The good news is that surrendering everything for love isn't nearly as bad as you think it is. You may lose your dignity but what you get in return can make it all worthwhile.

Case History

George Sanders (English actor who made a career in American films by playing cruel, disdainful villains). Born July 3, 1906, in St. Petersburg, Russia (VanDer Beets 1990).

Sanders came from an English family with connections to the Russian upper class, and his early life was exceptionally privileged. But when the Russian Revolution greatly reduced his father's circumstances, the young Sanders had to learn how to earn a living—a turn of events that never ceased to offend him.

After an education in English public schools, Sanders went to South America as an agent for a tobacco company. His sexual history during his early manhood is unknown, but romance was very much a factor in the conclusion of his career as a businessman. The fiancé of a woman Sanders was boarding with accused his intended of sleeping with Sanders. Sanders responded by calling for an impromptu duel that resulted in the jealous man being seriously wounded. Sanders' superiors were not pleased by the peccadillo and they sent the twenty-three-year-old Englishman home.

Tall, good-looking, and gifted with a good singing voice, Sanders drifted into theater work. Although he never showed much enthusiasm for acting as a profession, Sanders was good enough to gain work in Hollywood by the time he was in his late twenties. There he was groomed as a leading man. The studios sought to pair him with various rising starlets for the sake of appearances, but Sanders was unwilling to participate in the ruse. Instead, he had a secret affair with the tempestuous Delores Del Rio.

Sanders cultivated the image of a cad even at this very early point in his career. He appeared to be an unfeeling aristocratic woman-hater who viewed the world with tired contempt. This persona went far beyond the characters he played in films. Sanders was just as haughty off camera. He spent his time between takes reading or napping. After work he rarely socialized with Hollywood types. In the capital of gossip, he kept his private life adamantly private. When he did offer opinions about sex and women, his comments were invariably as barbed and offensive toward women as they were wickedly clever.

Sanders was not nearly as unapproachable as he seemed. When the actor was thirty-two, he secretly courted a young actress named Susan Larson. They were married when he was thirty-four. After the marriage, Larson quit her job and disappeared from public view. She was apparently an unusually quiet and submissive woman who, at least for a time, was content to be treated by Sanders as a domestic servant. The marriage remained a secret for a long time, mostly because Sanders seldom allowed himself to be seen in public with his pretty, new wife. He told his friends that she was boring.

Sanders told a different story later in his life. He claimed that Larson was mentally unstable and compulsively insecure. If this were the case, it suited his needs. The relationship lasted six years and ended only when Larsen displayed a sudden burst of spunk and abruptly packed her things and left. Sanders was surprised and deeply shaken by her defection.

Sanders was not alone for long. By the time his divorce from Larson was final, he was seeing an impulsive Hungarian divorcée named Zsa Zsa Gabor. Gabor was living well from the alimony from her first marriage, but she was willing to give it up for the handsome and courtly Sanders. For two years she pushed the reluctant actor toward marriage until he finally gave in at the age of forty-three.

At first Sanders tried to convert Gabor to his frugal and highly domesticated lifestyle, but Gabor was not content to stay quietly in the kitchen. This resulted in several fights, each of which ended with Sanders leaving the mansion that Gabor had purchased after their marriage and returning to his bachelor flat. The greatest strain on the marriage came from Sanders' refusal to let Gabor accompany him when he worked on location. On one occasion while her husband was away, Gabor accepted an offer to participate as a panelist on an early television show. She was an immediate hit. When Sanders returned from his moviemaking trip he found that Gabor had become a bigger star than he was.

Sanders was extremely unhappy to see his effervescent wife steal the spotlight. He became more distant with her and, with her husband's interest flagging, Gabor fell under the influence of a handsome Latin gigolo named Porfirio Rubirosa. She began an affair with Rubirosa while Sanders was away making a movie. Gabor had none of her husband's knack for secrecy and news of the affair soon reached Sanders. For a long time his only acknowledgement was an occasional snide remark but, as the romance became public knowledge, Sanders had no choice but to take action. After an abortive and silly attempt to catch Gabor and Rubirosa in bed together (during which Sanders tumbled off a ladder, through a window, and into Gabor's bedroom), he filed for divorce.

Gabor and Sanders remained remarkably friendly after the divorce. They continued a sporadic, sexual relationship until his third marriage to Benita Hume Coleman. Coleman was fifty-three, the same age as Sanders, and shared his English background and many of his convictions. They were extraordinarily well matched. The marriage seemed destined to last, but after five happy years, Benita was diagnosed with cancer. She died after much suffering when Sanders was sixty-one.

After the death of his third wife, the emotional insecurity that had long remained concealed behind Sanders' aristocratic disdain became painfully evident. For a long time Sanders had been secretly seeing various psychiatrists. Now he wept openly at the mention of his wife's death and suffered from debilitating stage fright. His psychological ailments were compounded by a mild stroke and by a financial blunder that cost him much of his hard-won, material security.

Sanders wanted Zsa Zsa Gabor to marry him again but, though she cared for Sanders, she was not about to take on such an emotional wreck. She recommended that he marry her older sister instead. Magda Gabor was a wealthy widow who had also suffered a stroke and was seriously handicapped. At first Sanders agreed. Then, shortly after the ceremony, he declared he could not be Magda's husband. The marriage was annulled after a few weeks.

Sanders' last years were spent in the company of a writer named Helga Moray. In contrast to Sanders increasingly morose attitude, Moray was a habitually chipper woman, and she gladly joined him in his slide into alcoholism. She supported his decision to sell the two homes that represented his last attempt to put down roots—an action Sanders immediately regretted. Finally he went to Barcelona, Spain alone and took a room in a hotel. There, at sixty-five, he intentionally consumed a fatal dose of barbiturates and died. In his famous suicide note, Sanders continued to strike the "caddish" pose that had made him famous. He wrote: "Dear World. I am leaving because I am bored" (VanDer Beets, 203).

Another Example

Gerard Manley Hopkins (a Catholic convert who became a Jesuit priest and was recognized as a talented lyric poet only after his death). Although his poetry is filled with beautiful and sensuous imagery, Hopkins constantly chastised himself in his journals for allowing the appreciation of beauty to divert him from the service of God. It is theorized that he was a homosexual who chose to be celibate rather than face his sexual preference, sublimating all his frustrated sexual feeling into his verse. Born July 28, 1844 (Kitchen 1979).

If you have Mars in Cancer with Venus in Virgo you are . . . the Sensible Sentimentalist

There is a practicality about your approach to sex that allows you to make the most of your Mars in Cancer emotionalism. You recognize that your emotional intensity permits you to subtly dominate relationships, and that your sexual allure gives you extra leverage in almost any situation. You can't escape the Mars in Cancer penchant for extreme and obsessive behavior, but you are the one Lover of this type capable of getting exactly what you want even when you seem entirely out of control.

Yet there's always a limit to this romantic efficiency. Sooner or later you open your heart too wide, commit yourself too completely, or touch upon feelings too intense and too compulsive to be ignored. As inconvenient as these missteps may be, they are necessary in order for you to find just the right combination of emotional support and practical cooperation in a relationship. You can't help but lose your heart, but if you're careful, you can certainly lose it to someone who will do you some good.

Case History

Ingrid Bergman (*Swedish-born film star whose films include* Casablanca *and* Notorious, *noted for her cool Nordic sex appeal). Born August 29, 1915, in Stockholm, Sweden (Leamer 1986).*

Bergman's mother died when Ingrid was three, leaving her in the care of her artistic father. Her father was so indulgent that she came to see him more as a big brother than as a parent. When Bergman was eleven, her father died, and her care was given over to a highly religious uncle and aunt. She resented the strict regimen of their home, but quickly found release when, at the age of fifteen, she began her career as an actress.

Even though she was only eighteen, Bergman was already an actress thoroughly devoted to her craft when she met Petter Lindstrom. Lindstrom was a handsome, athletic dentist studying to become a doctor. He was eight years older than Bergman and quite capable of looking after this unworldly young woman, but he was too much in love with Bergman to offer any resistance to her ambitions. After their marriage when Bergman was twenty-one, Lindstrom managed all the couple's practical affairs except his wife's career.

Her long engagement and marriage to Lindstrom served Bergman's career as much as anything she did. It allowed her to forgo the advances of smitten young actors, while providing a stable emotional base for her rise to the top. But by the time she was twenty-five and acting in American movies, Bergman was habitually having affairs. She claimed she couldn't play the female lead unless she was in love with the man playing the hero. Sometimes the leading man wouldn't cooperate and she had to settle for the director. Her lovers—Victor Fleming, Spencer Tracy, Gary Cooper, and others—were always emphatically masculine. The affairs were intense and passionate, but Bergman's life was so compartmentalized that her romances rarely influenced her quiet life at home with her husband and daughter.

Lindstrom, who had become a successful neurosurgeon, remained blissfully ignorant of his wife's infidelities. He seemed oddly content with their marriage, even though Bergman spent much of each year away making movies and Lindstrom was always the odd man out among her Hollywood friends. At one point, two of Bergman's lovers, who were competing for her attention, went to Lindstrom for advice on how to handle his luscious, but fickle, wife. They assumed from Bergman's behavior that her marriage was "open." No longer able to ignore his situation, Lindstrom confronted Bergman. She begged his forgiveness and promised to change.

Shortly after this confrontation when she was thirty-two, Bergman contacted the Italian director Roberto Rossellini about the possibility of making a film with him. Rossellini was a rising star on the international film scene because of the stark realism of his movies. He was also an irresistibly charming womanizer. When Rossellini traveled to the United States to discuss a film project with Bergman, he promised one of his friends that he would be sleeping with the actress within two weeks.

To no one's surprise (except Lindstrom's), Rossellini succeeded in his boast. Bergman was immediately smitten with the director and their business discussion quickly became a romantic rendezvous. To many people Rossellini was a self-important conman, but to Bergman he was a fellow artist and a visionary. His advanced ideas about filmmaking thrilled her, and his smooth, masterful Roman charm quickly made her forget about the promise she had made to her hapless husband.

This love affair was to be different from the rest. Perhaps because she sensed the weakness in her marriage, or perhaps because she needed a dramatic break in her life, Bergman left her husband and child forever and followed Rossellini to Italy. The move cost Bergman a great deal, both personally and professionally. With her reputation now trashed, it would be a long time before Bergman would make movies in Hollywood again. Meanwhile, the movies she made with Rossellini were artistic and financial failures. Bergman bore all this with amazing fortitude, even giving birth to Rossellini's child out of wedlock. She seemed convinced that her new love was the only thing that mattered in her life.

By the time Bergman and Rossellini married when she was thirty-five, Rossellini had already become bored with the arrangement. He had affairs and told his friends that his beautiful wife was cold and a painfully conventional lover. The magic lasted longer for

Bergman but she eventually found the lure of her career too hard to resist. After six years of relative inactivity, she found herself acting again in projects her visionary husband considered unworthy. Her successes in these ventures contrasted too sharply with his failures, and their marriage was brought to the brink. The final blow came when one of Rossellini's love affairs became public. They were divorced when Bergman was forty-two.

Bergman married a Swedish producer named Lars Schmidt a year after the divorce. In many ways, Schmidt resembled Petter Lindstrom and this marriage quickly settled into the same pattern as her first marriage. Schmidt was reserved and egotistical. Bergman was often away working and having affairs, but her marriage to Schmidt was significantly more stable than either her first and second marriages. Unlike Rossellini, Schmidt allowed Bergman complete control over her professional life and was not threatened by her ambition. Unlike Lindstrom, he was involved in show business and therefore could understand and share her trials and victories. Because of this understanding and deep mutual respect, the marriage survived until Bergman's death at the age of sixty-seven.

Other Examples

Natalie Wood (American actress). Born July 20, 1938 (Celebrity Birthday Guide).

Margaret Sanger (American crusader for birth control and women's rights). Born September 14, 1883 (Chester 1992).

If you have Mars in Cancer with Venus in Libra you are . . . the Sentimental Perfectionist

No Lover expects more from love than you do. For you, love is the highest ideal possible and sex is a rapture that exalts your being at every level: mind, body, and soul. This makes you a Lover to be reckoned with—someone who is serious about relationships. The intensity of your approach can make life very difficult for those who love you. You won't stand for halfway measures and you demand a level of commitment that will make many shy away. When you love, you do so with such utter devotion that the brave few who stick with you will have no regrets.

Your love is so intense and so subjective that it has a way of transforming people into the ideals you treasure. The problem is that your partners may not always like this transformation. In fact, very few people are willing to be made over into someone else's sexual ideal. Of course, the wiser ones will have a second objection. They will want to know which it is you really love: the image you have created in your heart and mind or the corporal reality that inspired it. That's a question you probably don't want to answer too quickly.

Case History

D. H. (David Herbert) Lawrence (*English writer whose works include* Lady Chatterley's Lover *and* Sons and Lovers, *noted for his revolutionary ideas about sex). Born September 11, 1885, in Eastwood, Nottinghamshire, England (Maddox 1994).*

Lawrence had a steady girl friend named Jessie Chambers in his late teens, but his bond to his mother was so strong that this relationship could not be sexual. Instead, he spent a lot of time thinking about sex and writing letters to his friends in which he detailed his frustrated desires.

After several flirtations with other women that did not result in sex, Lawrence returned to Chambers. He had a clumsy sexual encounter with her in the woods. Lawrence was exultant about the experience, but Chambers was not. This lack of response caused Lawrence to decide she wasn't the woman for him. When his mother died a short time later, he broke with Chambers and asked another woman to marry him.

This new engagement did nothing to reduce Lawrence's sexual frustration. He and his fiancée were separated as soon as he returned to his teaching job and never had physical relations. He had a single encounter of some sort with a free-thinking suffragette but, if anything, this only whetted his appetite. He was given some condoms as a gift and frantically approached one of his many female friends for sex, but was flatly turned down. When he was twenty-six, Lawrence became seriously ill when he contracted pneumonia. With this as an excuse, he broke his engagement.

Lawrence met Frieda Weekley when he was twenty-seven years old. Sexually, Frieda was exactly what Lawrence needed. She was a supremely sensual woman of the world who was already the veteran of several extramarital affairs. Even though Lawrence had great respect for Weekley's husband, he could not help but respond to her earthy, physical allure. By now this ardent, young, working-class writer had begun to form his elaborate philosophy of sex and he wanted more than just physical release. He wanted a "natural marriage" that was based on a deep spiritual and physical affinity. He told Frieda that she would have to leave her husband and children and begin a whole new life with him. With some hesitation, she agreed.

Lawrence's relationship with Frieda dominated the rest of writer's life. Frieda revealed to Lawrence a whole world of sexual delights including a thoroughly unabashed and unrestrained appreciation of the physical body. Lawrence was a thin man whose health and stamina were always uncertain, but she made him feel like a sexual powerhouse. The ideas that would later emerge in Lawrence's novels, such as the need for people to follow the lead of their bodies and to have complete sexual freedom, owe much to his relationship with the uninhibited Frieda.

Frieda and "Bert" were far less compatible outside the bedroom. Frieda was the daughter of minor German nobility, something she wasn't inclined to let her proletarian husband forget. Moreover, Lawrence's insistence on the "natural" dominance of the male over the female did not sit well with his independent wife. Lawrence also chastised his wife for her lack of domestic skills. He was the one who could be found on his hands and knees scrubbing the kitchen floor or baking bread. The couple fought often and hard. Physical violence and verbal abuse were common, particularly from Lawrence, who had a fiery temper. Lawrence's murderous rages often frightened their friends, but not Frieda. Each new battle only made the couple more devoted to one another.

Even before their marriage began, Lawrence recognized that his free-ranging wife would not remain faithful. Despite his apparent acquiescence to Frieda's promiscuity, it was nonetheless a source of conflict. Lawrence himself probably was guilty of adultery on at least one occasion, but he kept his indiscretion secret. Frieda, on the other hand, flaunted her casual encounters with other men as a way of getting back at Lawrence for his physical and verbal abuse.

Lawrence's writings reveal a fascination with homosexual love and it is possible, though not likely, that he had some sort of homosexual relationship during his thirties while living in Cornwall. Lawrence was friendly with several homosexuals, such as the notorious pederast, Norman Douglas, but he also deplored the lifestyle of such men. Although he was quite comfortable with the notion of men having sexual feelings for one another in his novels, in real life, the concept frightened him.

The Lawrences never stayed in one place for long throughout their marriage. They traveled all over the globe, including the United States and Australia. Lawrence's health slowly deteriorated. By the time he was forty-one, he was apparently impotent due to his illness. He died of tuberculosis at the age of forty-five.

Other Examples

Vivian Leigh (*English actress who played Scarlet O'Hara in* Gone with the Wind *whose insatiable sexual and emotional demands brought an end to her storybook marriage to Laurence Olivier*). *Born November 5, 1913 (Celebrity Birthday Guide).*

Pablo Picasso (*Spanish-born painter noted for his disjointed images of women*). *Born October 25, 1881 (Celebrity Birthday Guide).*

If you have Mars in Cancer with Venus in Scorpio you are ... the Ruthless Sentimentalist

Yours is a powerful sexuality that cannot be taken lightly. You manage to dominate relationships, even though your approach to sex is basically passive. One reason for this is that your incredible emotional intensity can completely overwhelm the unwary. Another is the fact that you are so insightful; you are quick to see other people's weaknesses and figure how they can be useful to you. And of course, there is your extraordinary sex appeal. When all these factors are working together you can become a sexual juggernaut—a Lover who can't help but get your own way.

All this emotional power brings with it a certain degree of messiness. Your feelings and the feelings you inspire in others have a way of getting out of control and disrupting your everyday life. This is particularly disturbing to you because you are essentially a very conservative Lover and like to keep your emotional life as discreet as possible. So, it is not uncommon for you to resort to subterfuge, deception, or even intimidation in order to keep the real story of your inner life from being broadcast to the masses.

Case History

H. G. (Herbert George) Wells (English writer and social theorist whose works include The Time Machine *and* War of the Worlds*). Born September 21, 1866, in Bromley, Kent, England (Smith 1986).*

Wells was brought up at the edge of poverty in a home dominated by his deeply religious mother. He managed to acquire an education and become a teacher by perseverance and luck. Tiring of that profession, he turned to literature.

Wells married his first cousin, Isabel Wells, when he was twenty-five years old. He fell in love with Isabel while they were both still children and became unofficially "engaged" to her when he was eighteen. Even though Wells claimed he was keenly aware of his sex drive from the age of nine, his only sexual experience prior to his marriage was a single unpleasant visit to a prostitute.

The marriage to Isabel was troubled from the start. Even though she and Wells deeply loved one another, Isabel could not respond to her husband sexually. This situation left Wells very frustrated and with no idea of where to turn. One day he found himself alone with one of his wife's friends. He asked this woman to have sex with him and she readily agreed. The event was something of a revelation for the writer. It suddenly became clear to him that there was a world full of women available to him simply for the asking.

Other sexual encounters followed until, at the age of twenty-six, Wells met Catherine "Jane" Robbins. Robbins was one of his students and she shared Wells' intellectual interests—something his nonbookish wife could never do. They began an affair. Isabel learned about the affair and gave Wells an ultimatum. He responded by leaving her and moving in with Robbins. This occurred just as Wells was emerging as a novelist. The result was the first of many sex scandals that would later be associated with his name.

Wells divorced his wife when he was twenty-nine but this in no way concluded his emotional attachment to her. When she remarried nine years later, he went into a jealous rage and destroyed his pictures of her and their correspondence. When Isabel was ill several years later, Wells took her into his home where Jane, now his second wife, nursed her.

In Jane, Wells found a woman well suited to be the wife of an author and compulsive philanderer. She did his typing and edited his many manuscripts. She also attended to all his business affairs. As a sexual partner she was not much more enthusiastic than Isabel had been, but she was indulgent enough to allow the writer the sexual freedom he wanted. Wells began having affairs five years into his second marriage. Some of these affairs were prolonged and passionate, but none seriously threatened his marriage. He had two children with Jane and two other children with two different women. Jane was so accepting of her husband's indiscretions that she even helped buy baby clothes for his illegitimate offspring.

The young women Wells slept with were often rebellious intellectuals from the middle class who were anxious to experiment with their sexual freedom. At least one of these women, Amber Reeves, initiated her affair with Wells. Wells viewed his sexual adventures as part of a broader fight for liberalism in society. He took a degree of pride in his immorality and in his "open" marriage. One of the great inconsistencies in his thought remained the contrast between his advocacy for political equality for women and the predatory lust with which he greeted many of the young women who crossed his path. Wells excused this inconsistency by saying that, when it came to sex, all men thought like fourteen-year-old boys.

One of the most significant of Wells' extramarital affairs was with a young feminist writer named Rebecca West. It began when Wells was forty-six and West was twenty. West was perhaps the most independent of Wells' many paramours. She first drew his attention when she wrote a bad review of one of his books. Even with her critical eye and feminist ideals, West was unable to resist Wells' sexual allure. For a time Wells maintained two households, one with his wife and one with his young lover. After ten tempestuous years West finally tired of Wells' colossal self-involvement and gave up on the relationship.

When Wells wrote about his own love life he always emphasized physiology over emotion; however, physiology could not explain his untiring devotion to Jane or his irrational possessiveness of his first wife. Nor did it explain the spirit of emotional conquest that characterized his seductions or the way in which he used these victories to feed an expansive ego. Despite his apparent candor and rational approach to living, Wells was less than entirely truthful when it came to sex.

When Wells was sixty-one, his beloved Jane died. A few years later he began his last love affair with Moura Budberg, a woman from the Russian aristocracy who had strong ties to the Communist government in Russia. Wells wanted to make Budberg his third wife but she demurred. She remained his mistress until his death at the age of seventy-nine.

Another Example

Pavel Tchelitchew (*Russian surrealist painter*). *Tchelitchew was an active homosexual, but this did not stop his patron, Edith Sitwell, from falling in love with him. Tchelitchew's lifelong exploitation of Sitwell's affection greatly advanced his career. Born September 21, 1898 (Current Biography 1943).*

Marie Antoinette (*queen of France*). *Born November 2, 1755 (Encyclopedia Britannica 1997).*

If you have Mars in Cancer with Venus in Sagittarius you are... the Impatient Sentimentalist

You are an impetuous and unpredictable Lover, constantly pulled between your deep need for affection and an equally powerful need to keep moving. It's not just that you are an incredibly restless Lover. Your extreme sensitivity also makes it difficult for you to stay in one place. Sooner or later even the most cautious and courteous partner is bound to say or do something that simply drives you crazy. Because of this you approach sex with a sense of great urgency, always mindful that you have to get all the emotional sustenance and passion you can before that other part of your erotic nature starts looking for a reason to leave.

You are at your best when you are trying to overcome an obstacle to love. You make a wonderful conquering hero or heroine—courageous, tenacious, and bubbling with optimism and nobility. It's when the obstacles are overcome that you start to get nervous. That's why difficult relationships, relationships in which there is a real or imagined distance between you and your partner, work best for you. That way you can have the emotional anchor you so desperately need without getting too close.

Case History

Lotte Lenya (Karoline Charlotte Blamauer—Austrian singer and actress noted for her performances in The Three-Penny Opera*). Born October 18, 1898, in Vienna, Austria (Spoto 1989).*

Lenya's early life was bleak and overshadowed by poverty and physical abuse. She discovered by the age of eleven that she could obtain both affection and money from men by working as a prostitute. An aunt from better circumstances rescued Lenya from her troubled home and paid for dancing lessons for the wayward girl when Lenya was in her mid-teens. This led to a career on the stage.

By the time she was seventeen Lenya had found her first male patron, a middle-aged playwright who encouraged her to read and helped her find acting parts. Her involvement with this benefactor did not stop her from having younger boy friends. Acquaintances noted that she always had a different beau waiting to take her home after every performance. Even though Lenya was not conventionally pretty, everyone acknowledged her potent sex appeal.

When she was twenty-one Lenya hocked diamonds she acquired from a gentleman friend and moved to Berlin. At that time, Berlin was the most decadent and wide-open city in Europe. Although she failed to find the immediate success as an actress that she had hoped for, Lenya was quickly caught up in the dark hedonism of the city's famous nightlife.

Lenya was twenty-six when she met composer Kurt Weill, the man who became the love of her life. She claimed that he proposed to her in a rowboat just after their first meeting. They were married a year later. Weill was a short, bald, introverted musician from a conservative, middle-class Jewish family. His liaison with the street-smart Lenya shocked his family and surprised their friends. Weill's fascination with Lenya was such that he paid no heed to his family's objections. For her part, Lenya found great comfort in Weill's gentle devotion and emotional support, and she sincerely believed in his talents as a composer.

The relationship between Lenya and her husband was anything but conventional. Weill made it clear at the beginning that his music came first. He spent much of his time alone working on his compositions. Lenya consoled herself with a wide array of male and female lovers. At first the arrangement seemed amicable enough but as time passed the complexities of two separate careers and two separate sex lives took their toll on the marriage. She divorced Weill when she was thirty-five.

At the time of the divorce Lenya had just finished a passionate affair with an actor, and was in the midst of a scandalous interlude with a beautiful actress. In the wings waiting to become her next lover was the noted artist and ladies' man, Max Ernst. Despite these distractions, Lenya immediately regretted her decision to divorce Weill. She attempted to slash her wrists in a moment of despondency. Then she worked with her friends to reestablish her relationship with the composer. It took perseverance, but by the time she was thirty-seven she and Weill were a couple again. It was also at this time that they were forced to flee Europe because of the rise of the Nazis.

Lenya and Weill reestablished their careers and their unusual marriage in America. Lenya continued to depend upon her husband for emotional support and on other men for sex. None of this bothered Weill. His career prospered in the United States and he was kept busy. The transition was more difficult for Lenya, but she too found work as a performer.

When Lenya was fifty-one, Weill's health suddenly deteriorated due to hypertension and heart disease and he died. Lenya was left in a state of emotional collapse. Suddenly her compulsive infidelity to Weill (even though it was always with his knowledge) haunted her and she was beset by deep feelings of guilt. Desperate for emotional support, Lenya turned to an old friend named George Davis, an editor and noted wit.

She and Davis were soon married. Davis was younger than Lenya and a brilliant conversationalist, but he brought little else to the marriage. He was chronically unemployed and depended upon the wealth Lenya and Weill had built over the years. He was also an alcoholic and a self-destructive homosexual with an unhealthy taste for "rough trade." He often returned from nocturnal forays into the city, bruised and badly beaten. Not only was it impossible for Lenya to have a sex life with her new husband, but she frequently had to nurse him back to health after his drunken adventures.

Lenya assumed this new maternal role with surprising ease. It was as if she was exorcising herself for her years of unfaithfulness to Weill by becoming the emotional anchor for this pathetically unstable man. When Davis died six years later, Lenya married a third time to another alcoholic homosexual. This husband also died young and, when she was seventy-one, Lenya married a fourth time, again to a younger man who never lived with her. Meanwhile she kept busy with work on the stage and small parts in movies. She also labored incessantly to extend and maintain Weill's reputation as a composer. Lenya died at eighty-one.

If you have Mars in Cancer with Venus in Capricorn you are . . . the Hard-Nosed Sentimentalist

You present a double challenge to anyone who hopes to love you. On one hand, you are a delicate bundle of soft and vulnerable emotions that desperately needs to be loved and protected. On the other, you're an uncompromising realist who feels that love is like a business deal: an equal exchange of labor where the most important thing is not to be cheated.

In order to find a compromise between these two points of view, you often try to quantify love. You express your feelings through objects, gifts and services, and other tokens of material support for the people you love. But no matter how much you keep score and no matter how carefully you watch your emotional expenditures, you will always be at a disadvantage in this business of love. The bottom line is that no matter how tough you seem, you always need love and sex much more that just about anyone you know—in the end you'll pay whatever they ask.

Case History

Gypsy Rose Lee (Rose Louise Hovick—probably the most famous striptease dancer of all time, as well as a successful author, playwright, and businesswoman). Born January 9, 1914, in Washington State (Priminger 1984).

Lee began her stage career when she was a child in a vaudeville act managed by her mother. At about the same time Lee outgrew her little girl costumes, the vaudeville theaters she had toured for years were being converted into burlesque houses. Responding to the mood of the times, Lee became a stripper. Her routine remained essentially the same throughout the next two decades. The sexiness of Gypsy Rose Lee's striptease was always in the anticipation, rather than the reality, of her nudity. She maintained complete control of her audience at all times, not just with the calculated removal of her clothing but also with her witty banter. Lee did not strip to her g-string until the very last instant so that the viewers never got more than a glimpse of what they had paid their hard-earned money to see. Yet, she quickly became the biggest star in burlesque.

Lee's sex life began when an older vaudevillian, known as a womanizer, seduced Lee when she was still a teen. A little later, after she emerged as a burlesque star, Lee gained the sponsorship of a wealthy married man. Lee claimed that the unknown patron was planning to rewrite his will in her favor but that he died before this was accomplished. When she was twenty-three, Lee married a businessman who wanted her to give up her act. Even though Lee was always proud of her domestic skills, she had no desire to become a housewife. They were divorced a short time later.

At twenty-six, Lee came into contact with the high-powered impresario, Michael Todd. Todd had started in show business as a manager of strippers and made his fortune by bringing striptease into high-class venues on Broadway. In terms of their business goals, he and Lee were natural partners. Together they managed to make a good deal of money. Their love affair did not come until later but, when it did, Lee was thoroughly smitten.

Lee's emotional and business involvement with Todd continued to the point that, when he was desperate for financial backers, Lee came up with several hundred thousand dollars to produce their show. Lee made it clear she wanted something in return for her money. She expected Todd to divorce his wife and marry her. Todd was not happy in his marriage, but neither was he anxious to marry his business partner.

The situation came to a head when Lee announced she intended to marry William Kirkland, an actor who had long been infatuated with her. She hoped this action would force Todd to commit to her, but her bluff failed. Todd made no effort to stop her marriage to Kirkland. Out of pride, Lee was compelled to go through with the wedding. Lee was devastated when Todd later married another woman after his wife died. And yet despite their romantic difficulties, Lee and Todd remained profitable business partners.

Lee's marriage to Kirkland was predictably troubled. On her wedding night she smeared herself with Vicks and feigned a bad cold. She later claimed that she made an effort to be a good wife, but she and Kirkland separated after only three months.

Lee had an encounter with the director Otto Preminger around the same time as her break with Todd and her marriage. The affair was so fleeting that Preminger did not know until years later that Lee had become pregnant with his son. When the child was born, Kirkland was assumed to be his father but Lee made certain that she was the only parent. Even when Preminger found out about the boy and offered Lee financial aid, she refused to take it.

Lee's third marriage was to a Spanish-born painter named Julio de Diego. Diego was a handsome, singularly seductive man with whom Lee enjoyed a good sex life. Although he held an Old World attitude toward a woman's role in the home, Diego did not interfere with Lee's career aspirations, which now included writing mystery novels and plays. For a time she achieved a comfortable balance in her life. She enjoyed periods of quiet domesticity with Diego without renouncing her role as a hard-driving businesswoman. Unfortunately, the marriage only lasted seven years, ending when Lee was forty-one.

After her divorce from Diego, Lee lost interest in sex—at least according to her son. It was this son, Erik, who was now her most constant male companion. He had been "trouping" with her since he was an infant. Now Erik had become her "dresser" and general assistant. Their close relationship continued for several years until Erik found her controlling maternity too oppressive. It was only when Erik was an adult, and Lee was near the end of her life, that she revealed to him the true identity of his father. Lee died at the age of sixty-six.

Another Example

John Kennedy, Jr. (president's son and magazine publisher). Born November 25, 1960 (Celebrity Birthday Guide).

If you have Mars in Cancer with Venus in Aquarius you are . . . the Intelligent Sentimentalist

You are the most imaginative and the least conservative of the Mars in Cancer Lovers. Conversation and the exchange of ideas are just as important to your emotional well-being as snuggling, and you have the capacity to analyze and even laugh at your obsessive sexual nature. In some ways, you are the sanest Lover of this type. No matter how much emotional abuse you suffer, you never lose your balance or your hopeful, idealistic notions about love.

This very nice package comes with a price. Your emotional needs are so mixed and so varied that you never seem quite sure what you want. You demand a great deal of warmth and nurturing but, at the same time, you insist that your partner keep his or her emotional and physical distance. You like cool, intellectual camaraderie, but you also want to be overwhelmed by intense feelings. These contrasting needs often make it difficult for you to find a completely satisfying relationship.

Case History

William Burroughs (American author noted for his frank autobiographical novels, such as Naked Lunch, Junky, *and* Queer). *Born February 5, 1914, in St. Louis, Missouri (Morgan 1988).*

Burroughs recalled that his first sexual experience occurred when he was a small child. His beloved nanny enticed him to take her boy friend's penis into his mouth. According to Burroughs, he promptly bit it. Burroughs also insisted that he was a homosexual at birth and that this traumatic incident had nothing to do with his later sexual development.

While a schoolboy, Burroughs suffered through two unconsummated infatuations with classmates. His abject subservience to these boys made him the target of much abuse and caused him to drop out of one school. It was the beginning of a pattern that would dominate much of Burroughs' sexual history. He tended to fall in love with young men, many of them hustlers, who were primarily heterosexual. These men were only attracted to Burroughs when he had money and/or drugs. Though he had many male lovers, none of these relationships came close to meeting his emotional or physical needs. Even his prolonged pursuit of his homosexual friend Allen Ginsberg proved unsuccessful. Ginsberg had great admiration for Burroughs as a writer and as a person but was put off by the extreme passivity of Burroughs' response to sex.

Burroughs was brought up in a straight-laced, WASPish home. He remained painfully ignorant and frustrated about sex until his college days at Harvard. One of his early sexual encounters came while in St. Louis on a summer break. It was with a woman—a busty whore he visited frequently that summer. His first adult homosexual encounter did not come for another year and it was also with a prostitute.

Even this breakthrough did not end Burroughs' profound inhibitions. He contracted syphilis from the male prostitute. The shock of contracting this infection and the resulting cure (with arsenic) cast a forbidding shadow over his sexuality for another two years. Burroughs still managed to stumble into matrimony when he was twenty-four, but it was a marriage of convenience that allowed a German woman he knew to gain passage to the United States during the rise of Hitler.

When Burroughs was thirty-two, he began an affair with Joan Vollmer. He was living in New York amid the literary coterie that would later make him famous: Allen Ginsberg, Jack Kerouac, and the so-called "Beat" poets and writers. He was also beginning his exploration of the dark world of heroin addiction. Vollmer was a friend of both Kerouac and Ginsberg. She was a keenly intelligent and sexually aggressive woman who enjoyed the company of these iconoclastic intellectuals. She was also a drug addict, though she preferred Benzedrine to heroin.

Burroughs eventually married Vollmer. Their relationship was often very warm and sexual. Vollmer was aware that her husband was a homosexual but she found his capacities as a heterosexual lover more than adequate. At one point Burroughs and Vollmer were nearly arrested when they stopped their car at the side of a country road to have sex. This marriage produced one child, born while the couple was living in Texas.

When Burroughs was thirty-five, after an abortive attempt to make a living as a farmer, he moved his little family to Mexico City where both drugs and boys were cheap. Burroughs enjoyed Mexico City because he felt it still had the flavor of an Old West town. Vollmer liked it less because it was difficult to get the Benzedrine she needed and she was forced to switch her addiction to alcohol.

It was in Mexico that one of the defining events of Burroughs' life occurred. He always had a fascination for guns and one day he decided to sell one of his many pistols. While sitting around the house discussing the deal, Burroughs wanted to demonstrate the pistol's accuracy by shooting a drinking glass off the top of Vollmer's head. Vollmer fearlessly agreed, knowing that her husband was an excellent shot; however, on this particular day, Burroughs' exceptional eye failed him. His shot was a few inches too low and Vollmer was killed instantly.

After the death was ruled accidental by the court, Burroughs fled Mexico City. He settled for a time in Tangiers where the prohibitions against homosexuality and drug abuse were lax enough to accommodate his lifestyle. The death of Vollmer was the end of Burroughs' heterosexual experiment. He kept to boys from this point on, starting with youngsters that he found on the streets in Tangiers. These relationships were often intense but, almost by definition, not enduring.

Later, as his reputation as a writer grew, Burroughs left Tangiers and lived throughout Europe and the United States. The times had changed enough that he no longer had to hide his homosexuality. His boy friends were more often young men who admired him for his work and for his uncompromising rebellion against conventionality. It was one of these young men who lured Burroughs to Lawrence, Kansas, where he lived alone with his cats and guns until his death at the age of eighty-three.

Another Example

Wolfgang Amadeus Mozart (composer). Mozart was a failure at almost every aspect of life except for his music and his marriage. His union with the musically ignorant, but warm-hearted Constanze Weber was a model of sexual compatibility and enduring affection. Born January 17, 1756 (Encyclopedia Britannica, Vol. 8).

If you have Mars in Cancer with Venus in Pisces you are . . . the Irresistible Sentimentalist

If there can be a creature of pure sexual passion on this earthly plane, you are it. And for this very reason, your love life tends to get complicated. You are too susceptible to your feelings to pay much attention to either propriety or good sense. To others, you appear to make sex too big an issue in your life, devoting an inordinate amount of your time and energy to matters of love and romance. But if these people only knew the intensity of your feelings, they would also understand just how moderate you really are.

Your main problem is learning how to focus your ultraintense sexual feelings. Too often you get caught up in the elemental force of your sexuality and lose sight of the fact that one good partner is always preferable to a hundred bad ones. Maybe it's because people fall in love with you so easily. Or maybe it's just that you have so much trouble saying no to that love. In any case, you often end up with many more demands upon your affection than you can possibly fulfill.

Case History

Lord Byron (George Gordon Byron—one of the preeminent poets of his time, he made his life his greatest and most shocking work of art.) Born January 22, 1788, in London, England (Maurois 1930).

Although he was a fat little boy with a deformed foot and an overbearing mother, Byron nonetheless began his career as a lover very early. When he was a small boy his nurse introduced him to the mysteries of sex, first by fondling him while he was in bed, and then by allowing Byron to watch while she had sex with her boy friend. In public school he found satisfaction in casual homosexual relations with other aristocratic boys and, when he went off to college, he brought along a mistress dressed like a boy.

By the time Byron burst on the English literary scene at the age of twenty-four with the publication of *Childe Harold*, he was already a jaded libertine. Now he was also a romantic hero. Not his clubfoot, his tendency toward corpulence, or even his nasty reputation could stop women everywhere from wanting to sleep with him. His power over women was now so evident that it occasionally embarrassed him and, of course, it often got him into trouble.

The foremost of his admirers was Lady Caroline Lamb, an impetuous and headstrong twenty-seven year-old woman who was not about to let her marriage to a lord stop her from having sex with the most romantic figure of the age. Lamb had the androgyne type of figure that Byron preferred, and a passionate disposition few men could resist. Byron did not remain Lamb's lover for long. She was too aggressive and too unpredictable for his taste. Unfortunately for him, Lamb later took her revenge by enlarging on the rumors already current in London society as to Byron's perversities, in particular his bisexuality.

After his break with Lamb, Byron retreated into the embrace of an older woman for a time. Then he was reunited with his half-sister, Augusta. He and Augusta shared the same father but had been reared in separate houses. She was just as strikingly beautiful as Byron, but of a much more docile disposition. She was no more able to resist the spell of her flamboyant brother than any other woman and Byron made her his next mistress.

In many ways Byron's affair with his half-sister seemed calculated to take him over the edge of public acceptance. He made scant effort to hide it or to hide the fact that the child Augusta soon bore was his. At the same time, he felt enough remorse over the relationship to make a desperate attempt to settle into a stable marriage. The woman he chose was a "country cousin" of Caroline Lamb named Annabella Milbanke, a woman every bit as conventional as Lamb was eccentric. They were married when he was twenty-seven.

The marriage was anything but happy and Byron's behavior became more and more erratic. He was plagued by nightmares and at times refused to let his wife touch him. He abused Annabella constantly, brutally filling her unworldly ears with tales of his past debaucheries. The final blow came when Byron moved his half-sister into their house and forced Annabella to listen while Augusta read aloud from the scandalous love letters he had written his sibling.

Mercifully, Byron left Annabella immediately after the birth of their only child. This break only precipitated the public airing of the scandal that now surrounded him. No longer was

Byron the wicked boy everyone wanted to know. Now he was regarded as an unsightly pervert who had to be avoided. By the time he was twenty-eight, Byron was forced to flee to the continent, though not before having one last English affair with a brazen young woman named Claire Clairmount.

Byron eventually settled in Venice where he resumed the debaucheries of his youth. It was only at the age of thirty-one that he began to settle down. He eased into a relationship with Teresa Guiccioli, a young Viennese woman of wealth. He became her "official" lover with the full endorsement of her elderly husband—at least until the husband was alerted to the fact that Teresa had actually fallen in love with Byron. Then the angry husband demanded a separation. After this Byron lived with Teresa in as close to a monogamous arrangement as he ever managed.

When Byron was thirty-five, he broke with Teresa, who was persuaded to return to her forgiving husband. It was not debauchery that lured the restless Byron this time, but war. He joined the fight for Greek independence from the Turks. While engaged in this crusade Byron wrote his last love poems to a young Greek soldier. He died soon afterward at the age of thirty-six.

Chapter 5

Mars in Leo
The Maestro of Love

General Characteristics

The first thing you need to know about Mars in Leo Lovers is that sex is never just an avenue to pleasure for them, it is also an art form. They approach every encounter as if it were a masterpiece—even if it later turns out to be simply a three-minute sketch. They cultivate sexual pleasure with aesthetic flair and a singular sense of purpose. These are high-energy Lovers—their joyous enthusiasm for love and their creative approach makes them irrepressible, breathtaking partners. They bring a wholehearted belief in the power, the glory, and the higher value of love to every sexual encounter.

The second thing to keep in mind about these Lovers is that they must be in control. They are usually nice about it. They are so charming and so loving that their partners may not even notice how the Mars in Leo Lover completely dominates the proceedings. But the fact remains that the most desirable position for the Mars in Leo Lover is always on top; if not physically, then certainly psychologically. This doesn't mean that everyone with Mars in Leo will have a dominant personality. They may, in fact, be rather meek or passive in other areas of their lives. When it comes to sex, however, Mars in Leo Lovers always seek relationships that allow them some measure of command. They will always be most attracted to the partner they can most easily control.

The third thing to remember about these Lovers is that their sexual exuberance, childlike wonder, and warm, laughing playfulness ends the moment the game stops being played their way. It's not that these Lovers are selfish per se. Rather they simply cannot sustain an interest in sex that does not, in some way, center on their needs, desires, and egos. They may attempt to be good sports and let someone else be the boss for a while, but these moments of generosity don't last long. A Mars in Leo Lover will gladly choose celibacy over sex on someone else's terms.

Why would anyone put up with such an egocentric attitude toward sex? Why would anyone submit to such autocratic control? Well, as we have said, Mars in Leo people are very good Lovers. Their warmth, enthusiasm, and artistic approach to lovemaking compensate for a whole lot of egotism. Also, Mars in Leo Lovers have a way of making their partners feel privileged. No matter how bossy they may be in private, these status-conscious Lovers tend to treat their partners like royalty in public. They typically become the unabashed advocates of everything their partners do; they have no sense of reserve when it comes to showering their partners with praise and reinforcement. As far as they're concerned, if you're good enough to have a Mars in Leo Lover, then you have to be someone very special.

The last thing one needs to know about this type is that there can be no secrets. It isn't simply that Mars in Leo Lovers are flamboyant and love drawing attention to themselves. These Lovers look upon sex as an important, even sacred, activity. Sex is, after all, an extension of their ego and it would be an offense to nature to keep it under wraps. Mars in Leo Lovers always reserve the right to brag. There are times, of course, when this noisiness about sex conflicts with the essential conservatism of this type. While these people love attention, they dread ridicule and embarrassment. This is why no one should take the bragging of a Mars in Leo Lover too literally. Pride always rules over truth in the stories they tell.

If you have Mars in Leo with Venus in Aries you are . . . the Maestro of Extreme Love

You have the zest for love, the irrepressible sexual energy, and the fresh, almost juvenile charm of a complete egotist. There's nothing to worry about, however. Your supreme and perhaps less than realistic self-confidence is the key to your warm and exciting sexual nature. If you weren't totally infatuated with yourself you'd have no capacity for loving anyone else. In fact, the worst thing that can happen to your erotic life is for someone to convince you that you are less than the best.

You are drawn to extreme sensations and situations when it comes to sex. Peace and contentment have no place among your priorities. You must be challenged in your love life, pushed to the brink physically, mentally, and emotionally. This extremism often means that you have to sacrifice at least some of the control which most Mars in Leo Lovers find necessary. You fight for control, but the real fun won't start until you lose that fight.

Case History

Algernon Swinburne (one of the most renowned poets of his era, noted for the fleshly eroticism of his verse). Born April 5, 1837, in London, England (Fuller 1971).

Born to a family firmly ensconced in the British upper class, young Swinburne attended Eton, England's most elite public school. It would be the defining feature of his adult life, though not in the way his parents imagined. At Eton, Swinburne learned the pleasures of flagellation. A fiery but woefully undersized youngster, Swinburne found a sexual thrill on "the block" where he was spanked for a variety of small (and sometimes intentional) offenses that would haunt him the rest of his life. Long after Swinburne had left school, a friend sent him a photograph of the infamous "block" as a present. Swinburne responded by requesting a photo of a boy actually being whipped on the apparatus, "say the tenth cut or so" (Wilson, 146).

Swinburne evinced a peculiar pride concerning his sexual perversion. Even though he never directly declared himself a flagellant, he conducted lively and unabashed correspondence with like-minded men, and he was an avid collector of the works of the Marquis de Sade. The poetry that made Swinburne one of the most famous and controversial literary figures of his time contained exaggerated imagery that was definitely tinged with sadism. He secretly wrote other works, some of them published anonymously as pornography, that openly described the joys of the rod.

It didn't take the young poet long to discover a brothel in Victorian London that catered to his special needs. He became a regular visitor and talked about being "the powerless victim of the furious rage of a beautiful woman" (Wallace, 207). But Swinburne was only willing to be a "powerless victim" as long as he was in control. When he discovered that the whores were trying to cheat him out of money, he became enraged and took his business elsewhere.

Even though the imagery of his poetry was emphatically heterosexual, Swinburne never had a normal sexual relationship with a woman. His closest female companion was a cousin, Mary Gordon, with whom he played "swishing" games when he was a small boy. When Swinburne was twenty-five he apparently wanted to marry this woman but, since they were double first cousins, both their families considered the marriage unwise. Later in life, after the cousin had married and had several children, she and Swinburne renewed their friendship. She showed a surprising interest in his secret flogging literature.

When Swinburne was thirty, his good friend Dante Rossetti intervened in his companion's errant sex life. Rossetti hired Adah Isaacs Menken, a well-known actress and prostitute, to sleep with Swinburne. The woman made a concerted effort for several nights running to have intercourse with Swinburne. She finally returned her fee to Rossetti in disgust, confessing that she had been unable to convince his high-strung pal that "biting was no use" (Wallace, 207).

In all probability there was another side to Swinburne's sexuality about which he was less inclined to brag. It was assumed by many of his contemporaries that this bizarre and effeminate poet was also a homosexual. He often associated, and even lived, with men who were known to be homosexuals. His playful interactions with these men, though never overt, gave rise to rumors. But even in his most intimate correspondence, Swinburne was mute about his relations with other men. He went out of his way to poke fun at "sodomites," just as he went out of his way to lie about his sexual conquests with women.

Never a strong man, Swinburne's explosive temperament and heavy drinking had seriously undermined his health by the time he was in his forties. At this point another writer named Walter Theodore Watt-Dunton took charge of the ailing poet. He took Swinburne into his home and became his companion and guardian for the next thirty years. Swinburne was able to live to a relatively calm old age under Watts-Dunton's maternal care, though his subsequent writings had none of the fiery sexual energy that had made his early poems so popular. He died at the age of seventy-two.

Other Examples

Jim Jones (demented evangelist who led his follows to the promised land and then to death). Born May 13, 1931 (Rodden 1980).

Dennis Rodman (basketball star). Born May 13, 1961 (Current Biography 1996).

If you have Mars in Leo with Venus in Taurus you are . . . the Maestro of Pleasure

Your sexuality is a wonderful combination of sensuality and basic laziness. You allow yourself be carried along by your pleasure-seeking instincts. You greet every new experience eagerly, but take the time to fully experience the joys that each encounter offers. This easygoing approach to sex not only makes for good technique, it also conceals the egocentric strength and stubbornness that is at the core of your erotic nature. People don't realize that you are always in control beneath your passive hedonism.

You are a conservative Lover for whom appearances are always important. There may be occasions when your sensuality will lure you into indiscretions, but you seldom venture far from convention. Your supremely practical sexual nature serves as a handy antidote for your egotism. Even though you are loaded with self-confidence and heady sexual exuberance, you never forget your limitations.

Case History

Gary Cooper (soft-spoken Westerner who became one of the most enduring male sex symbols in American movies). Born May 7, 1901, in Helena, Montana (Swindell 1980; Wayne 1988).

Though born in the American West, Cooper's parents were both English. His mother intermingled her son's cowboy childhood with exposure to the finer things. Cooper probably had some sexual experiences while in college, but it wasn't until he reached Hollywood in his early twenties that his reputation as a lover blossomed. He immediately began to work his way through the extensive population of script girls, secretaries, and other female employees of the studios. His encounters often served to open doors for him in the studio system, and these women appeared to welcome the opportunity to be used by him.

Cooper's reputation as a supremely skillful lover began at this point, long before he became a leading man. He came to be known for his charm, his gentleness, and his physical prowess. More than one of the many women he slept with during this period remarked on the size of his member and his sexual stamina. But it was his casual "ah shucks" approach that was the key to his appeal. His reputation as a nontalker grew with his reputation as a ladies' man.

When Cooper was twenty-five, he became the paramour of Clara Bow, one of the reigning sex symbols of the time. Despite her star status, Bow was still a common young woman from the streets. She tended to be very forthright about her sexual needs; her directness, along with her sizable libido, shocked the quiet and reserved Cooper. A year after the liaison began Cooper was excited enough to propose marriage. Then their relationship began to cool. Bow's compulsive sex drive was very much linked to her emotional instability and Cooper apparently recognized she was not the kind of girl he could bring home to his parents. He started to see another beautiful actress who was far less talkative than Bow, but he and Bow continued to meet occasionally for sex.

Cooper began a rather noisy affair with the Argentina-born actress Lupe Velez when he was twenty-seven. Like Bow, Velez was loud and boisterous—she liked to talk about her love affair with the handsome Cooper. Velez had a fiery Latin temper and was extremely possessive. Because of this their relationship often became violent. Cooper sometimes reported to the set with bruises that had to be hidden with makeup. Velez claimed that Cooper was equally violent with her. At one point, as Cooper tried to disengage himself from the affair, Velez fired a pistol at his head.

Cooper's high-profile love affairs helped his early career in two ways. His important girl friends helped him to get good parts, and they kept him in the public eye. It was generally acknowledged that Cooper was an opportunist in his relationships with women, but Cooper's charm was such that the women he wronged could not think ill of him. Even the stormy Velez remained friendly with Cooper after their affair ended.

When Cooper was thirty, he became involved with the Countess di Frasso, a wealthy American woman in her fifties. Cooper came dangerously close to becoming a gigolo with this relationship. The Countess supplemented his education in the finer things in life, such as wine and gourmet cooking, and used him as a handsome arm piece during her lavish parties. Her husband was typically absent on these occasions. For a time Cooper seemed to enjoy the sophisticated lifestyle the Countess offered him, but when she tried to force him to break his contract with Paramount and stay in Italy with her, di Frasso found her passive actor suddenly adamant. Soon Cooper was back in Hollywood making pictures and the Countess was mending her broken heart in seclusion.

At thirty-two, Cooper was firmly established as a star and he began looking for a wife. He selected a pretty but level-headed young actress named Veronica Balfe and he started a single-minded courtship. When the two married, many who knew Cooper as a party boy predicted a quick divorce, but Cooper was quite ready to put his wild bachelorhood behind him. He and Rocky (as he called his wife) settled into a domestic bliss that surprised everyone.

Although Cooper was quite happy with his wife and the daughter the marriage produced, he continued to have affairs. For the most part, his extramarital flings were tied to movie making. He slept with attractive young women, usually his leading ladies, while he was away from home on location. The affairs promptly ended when the shooting was done. Rocky was aware of her husband's infidelity but she remained confident of her position.

This situation held until Cooper turned forty-four and had an affair with his costar, Patricia Neal. He discovered that he could not walk away from her at the end of the picture. Rocky sensed that Cooper's infatuation with Neal was something different and, discreetly, Cooper moved out of their home. Rocky began to date other men while Cooper continued to see Neal, but the relationship with Neal eventually ran its course and she married another man. Cooper and Rocky continued their separation, with sporadic reunions at various places around the globe. When Cooper was fifty-three, he and his wife finally made amends. During his last years their marriage was remarkably happy. Cooper died of cancer at the age of sixty.

Other Examples

Imelda Marcos (wife of the former president of the Philippines, noted for her bulletproof bra and collection of shoes). Born July 2, 1929 (Ellison 1988).

James Taylor (American musician and singer). Born March 12, 1948 (Celebrity Birthday Guide).

Paul McCartney (British musician, former Beatle). Born June 18, 1942 (Celebrity Birthday Guide).

If you have Mars in Leo with Venus in Gemini you are ... the Maestro of Amusement

Your attitude toward sex is uncomplicated, playful, and far less serious than the typical Mars in Leo Lover. You are an inventive Lover who enjoys surprises and a spirit of discovery in your sex play. This frolicsome nature sometimes conflicts with your need for control. It's hard to constantly introduce new elements into a sexual situation without losing a degree of mastery. But you don't spend much time worrying about this kind of problem. You're too busy looking for adventure and having a good time.

Your approach to sex is essentially cerebral. It is ideas, not sensations or emotions, that make sex exciting for you. What you think about your partner is always more crucial than what your feel. This is quite all right as long as your ideas are fresh and lively, but when your thinking becomes stale and exhausted so does your sexuality. Without new ideas to inspire your desire, you can simple lose interest in sex or at least lose your capacity to make sex interesting.

Case History

Paul Gauguin (French post-impressionist painter noted for his flat, colorful depictions of the South Seas). Born June 7, 1848, in Paris, France (Anderson 1971; Hanson 1954).

Gauguin's family moved to South America when he was a child and his prolonged exposure to non-European culture greatly influenced his later development. Art was not his first ambition. At seventeen he became a sailor, and in his early twenties he began a career as a stockbroker. He did well until the stock market crashed when he was thirty-five years old. At this point he decided to pursue a career as a painter.

Gauguin was introduced to the joys of the flesh when he was a small boy. The family's African maid slept with him in the nude and he later bragged that he had tried to rape one of his cousins when he was only seven. He enjoyed boasting about his varied sexual experiences as a cocky young sailor. At twenty-five, shortly after he became a stockbroker, Gauguin put aside the waywardness of his youth and married a sheltered but canny Danish woman named Mette Sophie Gad. The marriage produced five children over a ten-year period. Gauguin's loyalty to both his wife and his family was apparently quite genuine.

While prospering as a stockbroker, Gauguin sought out a new hobby. He became a "Sunday painter" and soon was taking instruction from that patriarch of the impressionist movement, Camille Pissarro. Pissarro not only taught Gauguin how to paint, he also presented the businessman with the notion of art as a higher calling. At this time, impressionist painters like Pissarro were regarded as revolutionaries of the art world and, under Pissarro's tutelage, Gauguin learned that artists were people of vision who defied social convention. Gauguin, who had always pictured himself as an outsider, was quick to align himself with these rebels.

When Gauguin quit his job at the brokerage and chose to become a full-time painter, he was not just changing careers, he was joining a cause. Gauguin was probably always an egotist, but as an artist his egotism was matched with a mission. Mette could not understand this change in her husband. She retreated to her family in Copenhagen along with their children. Gauguin accompanied her there for a time and seemed intent on making his marriage work on his new terms. But the unrelenting disapproval of his wife and his in-laws finally drove him back to Paris.

Even in flight Gauguin was reluctant to give up his role as a family man. He took one of his sons with him to Paris where the boy was forced to share his father's severe poverty. For a long time Gauguin's correspondence with Mette remained intense, affectionate, and predicated on the fact that their separation was only temporary. Gauguin was too poor and too harried to have a mistress or even visit a prostitute during this period. It was only after they had been separated for three years that Gauguin's frequent claims of sexual loyalty to his wife became hollow. This was when he made his first attempt to escape civilization with a short voyage to Panama and Martinque.

When Gauguin was forty-three, he left France for Tahiti. He landed in the port town of Papeete hoping to find a primitive paradise. Instead he found a French colony in which the natives had already taken on Western ways. In particular he was disappointed in his first Tahitian girl friend who was hopelessly contaminated by civilization. Gauguin had to go deep into the countryside to find a bride primitive enough to please him. He called her Tehura. She was thirteen years old, pretty, docile, superstitious, and totally inscrutable to her love-smitten French husband. He considered the year or so that he lived with her to be the brightest of his life.

At forty-five, Gauguin returned to France to exhibit his new paintings and with hopes of collecting an inheritance. He relationship with Mette had deteriorated into a sputtering, long-distance quarrel over money. Gauguin didn't even bother to visit his family. Instead he found a girl of mixed Indian and Malay heritage and he called her Annah the Javanese. Annah was his favorite age, thirteen, but she was already used to being kept by European men. Gauguin painted her and enjoyed showing her off. Unfortunately, the locals were noticeably intolerant of his "colored" girl friend when he traveled from Paris to the more provincial Brittany with Annah. Some children insulted her and a friend of Gauguin's tried to box their ears. When the parents of the offending children attacked Gauguin's friend, the artist jumped into the fray and ended up with a broken leg. While Gauguin was recovering in a hospital, Annah returned to his Paris apartment and stole everything she could carry except his paintings.

When Gauguin made his second trip to Tahiti two years later he was a profoundly disappointed man. Not only had his Tahitian paintings not made the splash he had anticipated, but his hopes of a windfall inheritance had proved unfounded. When he arrived in Papeete he called Tehura to join him. She had since married another man but such was Gauguin's attraction and the sexual mores of Tahiti that she came to him; however, when Tehura discovered her Frenchman's genitals were covered with syphilitic lesions, she quickly retreated to her village. Gauguin had to be satisfied with more civilized girl friends.

Gauguin was gifted with a marvelous physical resiliency. He survived malnutrition, malaria, syphilis, and even a suicide attempt with arsenic. His sex drive was equally indestructible. Despite depression and many physical ailments, he continued to have sex with the native women at a pace that became more and more frenetic as the years passed. It was a joyless, animalistic kind of sex that provided only a momentary respite from his physical suffering and growing sense of failure, but he kept at it right up to his death at the age of fifty-four.

Another Example

Cher (Cherilyn Sarkisian—singer and actress). Born May 20, 1946 (Celebrity Birthday Guide).

If you have Mars in Leo with Venus in Cancer you are . . . the Maestro of Emotion

You are one of the most alluring and passionate Mars in Leo Lovers. Not only are you a very sexy Lover, you are driven by deep and powerful emotions that few people can resist. You like to dramatize your emotions, your relationships, and your partners. In fact, your love life often resembles a somewhat overwrought play in which everyone, even those who don't realize that they have a part, performs as expected.

You are a sensitive Mars in Leo Lover with a remarkable capacity for anticipating the needs of your partner. This insight gives you an incredible amount of control in relationships that is only as apparent as you want it to be. This control can be a wonderful thing for all concerned, as long as it serves your need to be loved. When it starts serving your ego and pride, then you have a problem.

Case History

Mata Hari (Margaretha Geertruida Zelle MacLeod—dancer, courtesan, and accused spy who was executed by the French at the end of World War I). Born August 7, 1876, in Leeuwarden, Holland (Howe 1986).

As a child Margaretha was the favorite daughter of a prosperous hatter. But when she was in her early teens her father went bankrupt and he and her mother were separated. When she was fifteen her mother died, leaving Margaretha practically orphaned and with few options. Even though she was notably pretty, her relatives recognized it was going to be difficult to find a husband for Margaretha. Not only did she lack a dowry, but she was taller than most of the Dutchmen of her time and extremely flat chested.

In desperation, Margaretha turned to the equivalent of today's "personal ads." She saw a newspaper item stating that a colonial officer named John MacLeod was seeking a wife. Actually the ad had been placed as a joke by one of MacLeod's friends, but the photograph Margaretha sent him intrigued the thirty-nine-year-old military man and a courtship ensued. When Margaretha was nineteen she married Captain MacLeod.

The marriage produced two children, but otherwise turned out to be a disaster for Margaretha. Her husband had spent all his adult life in the army and he was used to the easy fornication of a rootless soldier. Only a short time after the wedding he was visiting brothels. The situation only got worse when he returned with Margaretha to his assignment in Indonesia. The couple fought constantly and a servant poisoned one of their children. Once Macleod retired and the family had returned to Holland, he deserted Margaretha and took their daughter with him. Margaretha made a halfhearted attempt to fight her husband in the courts but gave up. She fled to Paris to seek her fortune.

Margaretha arrived in Paris at twenty-six with a lot of dreams and no marketable skills. At first her prospects were bleak, but she soon acquired a wealthy lover named Henry de Marguerie who was a playboy diplomat. With his help she created the persona of Mata Hari.

She began to perform what she passed off as traditional dances from the Indies in fashionable Parisian salons. As Mata Hari, she was the daughter of an English nobleman and an Indian woman who had been brought up in a Hindu temple. In reality she had only a passing knowledge of the culture of the Far East and no training at all as a dancer. She made up for these deficiencies with a natural grace and a remarkable gift for deceit.

There was one deficiency that no amount of fibbing could conceal. Mata Hari, the exotic beauty from the East, was still the flat-chested Margaretha Zelle. Only now, after two children and several years, her tiny breasts had begun to sag. Since Mata Hari's act was always a mixture of ethnological hype and striptease, her reluctance to reveal her breasts posed a problem. Mata Hari met this challenge by designing her own costumes and making sure they accented her long, shapely limbs and torso while covering and augmenting her bosom. Later, as her fame increased and questions began to be asked, she spread a rumor that one of her nipples had been bitten off by her husband, a story that not only excused her from showing her breasts but also added to her exotic legend.

By the time Mata Hari was thirty-two, her career as a dancer had long since peaked. She worked infrequently and depended on the support of wealthy men for her lavish upkeep. Even though she was quite capable of having sex with men for the fun of it, she had by now decided that the chief purpose for sexual desire was to give women power over men. The money she obtained from various lovers was sufficient for Mata Hari to live in the most expensive hotels and to wear the finest jewels and clothing. Yet, as skilled as she was in the arts of seduction, she was never able to find a benefactor who could give her sustained protection. Some went broke, some she put aside for better prospects, and some simply bored her.

Despite her luxurious (if somewhat uncertain) lifestyle, Mata Hari had not forgotten about the daughter she had been forced to leave behind. During this period she made several unsuccessful attempts to communicate with the girl. She even went so far as to send her loyal maid to Holland to kidnap the child, but the plan failed. Meanwhile, the advent of World War I was having a particularly disruptive impact on her livelihood as an international courtesan. After being kept for a time by a German officer in Holland, Mata Hari returned to her beloved Paris and made a feeble attempt to revive her career as a dancer.

When Mata Hari was forty, she fell in love for what was apparently the first time with a twenty-one-year-old Russian captain named Vadim de Masloff. Masloff was part of an elite Russian unit that had been sent to fight with the French. At the time he met Mata Hari he was recovering from wounds suffered at the front. Mata Hari was so infatuated with her young lover that she searched for a way to make money so she could stop sleeping with other men. When a member of the French intelligence service proposed that she help the war effort by spying, Mata Hari leaped at the opportunity. What she didn't know was that at the time this offer was made to her, she was already suspected of being an agent for the Germans.

The legend Mata Hari created for herself became her worse enemy at this point. The evidence indicates Mata Hari was not a German agent. It appears she even made some ineffective efforts to spy for the French; however, it was impossible for the men who ran the French intelligence unit to see this exotic-looking woman with a shady past as anything but an enemy. At her trial one of her former lovers acted as her lawyer, and another testified on her behalf. But many others turned their back on her. Even Vadim de Masloff, whom she still loved desperately, shrugged off their affair as a passing fling. Mata Hari was executed by a firing squad at forty-one.

Another Example

Thomas Eakins (one of the greatest American painters of all time who was fired from the Philadelphia Institute of Art when he displayed a nude male model to a class of female art students). Born July 25, 1844 (Encyclopedia Britannica).

If you have Mars in Leo with Venus in Leo you are . . . the Divine Maestro of Love

You are the divinely anointed autocrat of sex. No one tells you what to do and nothing can limit the expression of your sexuality. You break rules, not because you are rebellious, but because your sexual needs supercede all man-made laws (and even some natural ones). Of course, you'll probably deny that you've ever had notions like this and chuckle over the implications. That's okay. The divinely anointed autocrat of sex shouldn't be forced to admit to anything.

The one skill missing from your erotic arsenal is compromise. It's not that you'll ever have problems getting people to do what you want. If your effervescent charm doesn't get them then your commanding self-confidence surely will. But life is seldom as cooperative as your partners are prepared to be. If you can't learn how to fit your exorbitant demands into the context of reality then you'll never be happy, no matter how many hearts you manage to conquer.

Case History

Wallis Warfield Spencer Simpson (Duchess of Windsor—American divorcée who cost England a king). Born June 19, 1895, in Baltimore, Maryland (Higham 1988).

Note: This date differs from other published data.

Conceived during an indiscretion between two young members of Baltimore's high society, Wallis was born out of wedlock. (Her birth year was typically reported as 1896 to conceal this fact.) Her parents were married soon after her birth, but her father died of tuberculosis when Wallis was two. She spent her childhood dependent upon her rich relatives for financial support. Her pedigree allowed Wallis into the highest circle of Baltimore society, but she always lived on the fringes of real wealth and power.

Wallis developed into a thin, angular woman who was never really pretty. Yet she knew how to dress and flirt and had no problem attracting the attention of eligible men. When she was twenty, a naval officer named Win Spencer became smitten with her and proposed. Wallis had a weakness for men in uniform, and for cocky, handsome, young men in general. The fact that he came from a wealthy Midwestern family also pleased her. They were married when she was twenty-one.

It was only after the wedding that Wallis discovered that her glorious hunk of a husband was also a violent alcoholic with bisexual tendencies. Wallis begged her family to allow her to divorce him but she was ordered to persevere. She did so, in keeping with the custom of her class, by having affairs. Left alone in Washington D.C. while her husband was away in China, Wallis began an affair with an Italian Fascist. Then she boldly embarked on the seduction of one of the most desirable men in the city. Unfortunately, Wallis was unable (or unwilling) to keep her affairs private. When she lost her handsome boy friend, she found herself the object of derision among the capital's gossips. Deeply embarrassed, the twenty-nine-year-old Wallis decided to join her husband overseas.

Wallis went to China with the notion of repairing her broken marriage. Spencer seemed agreeable at first. According to some sources, he introduced Wallis to the most refined brothels of Hong Kong and, apparently at his direction, she learned exotic sexual techniques while there. But Wallis was given little time to apply this education toward the regeneration of her relationship with Spencer. He was soon sharing an apartment with another man and she was on her own. After this point there are many, often conflicting, stories about Mrs. Spencer's activities. She was accused by some of being a spy, by others of running drugs, and by still others of being a "kept woman." Undoubtedly she had multiple affairs. One resulted in an unwanted pregnancy. The child was aborted and the operation apparently left Wallis sterile.

Wallis returned to the states at the age of thirty and obtained a divorce from Spencer. By the time the ink was dry she had already found his replacement—a successful businessman named Ernest Simpson. Simpson had the same easy self-confidence that had attracted her to Spencer. Educated in the United States, he was a British citizen with high-level contacts on both sides of the Atlantic. Unfortunately, he was also married, but Wallis was not about to let that stand in her way. She broke with Simpson for a period of time and resumed the affair when his wife became ill. It was the wife who filed for divorce. As soon as Simpson was free he married the thirty-three-year-old Wallis.

Wallis had one thing in common with her new husband—both were anxious to advance socially. Wallis received a crash course in the manners and habits of the English upper class but she needed little direction when it came to playing social games. Wallis was a bright, witty woman who always mixed just the right amount of sex and gossip into her lively conversation. Soon it was evident that their plan for social advancement was succeeding beyond their wildest dreams. Unfortunately for Ernest Simpson, Wallis was now already well on her way to making her greatest conquest.

By the time Wallis was thirty-seven she was the mistress of Edward, Prince of Wales. The Prince was regarded as one of the most eligible bachelors in the world. He had several secret love affairs but, nonetheless, questions about his virility persisted. There were rumors that he dressed himself as an infant and rode in a baby carriage, and that he was a repressed homosexual. It was also reported he suffered from premature ejaculations. Whatever the Prince's tastes or problems were, Wallis proved up to the challenge. Moreover, Wallis knew how to flatter the insecure Prince and how to bend him to her will. Very soon, the Prince of Wales was thoroughly in love with Wallis Simpson.

When Wallis was forty, Edward became Edward VIII, King of England. He wanted Wallis to be his queen, but it quickly became apparent that this could not happen without a fight. She was a twice-divorced American with only the most flimsy of royal connections. The result of her marriage to the king would be a tremendous scandal and many powerful people decided they were not going to let it happen. Wallis saw this long before Edward, but abdication fit too well into Edward's romantic dreams of self-destruction. To the shock of the world, he chose to give up his throne for Wallis.

Wallis argued against the abdication. Thoroughly rattled by the public outcry, she still hoped a compromise could be worked out, but once the decision was made and she found herself with the singular distinction of being the woman for whom a king had sacrificed his throne, Wallis quickly warmed to the role. They were married shortly before her forty-second birthday.

Wallis continued to dominate the relationship, but this posed no problem. The passive duke was quite happy to have a strong-willed woman organize his life and tell him what to do. Through her marriage, Wallis attained the kind of wealth she had always dreamed of and she enjoyed it to the hilt. She dragged her increasingly depressive husband through an endless array of parties and social events. They were the most famous romantic couple of the age. The marriage lasted almost thirty-five years, until Edward's death. Wallis died thirteen years later, at the age of ninety.

Other Examples

Thomas Wolfe (*American author noted for his long autobiographical novels*). *Born October 3, 1900 (Celebrity Birthday Guide).*

If you have Mars in Leo with Venus in Virgo you are . . . the Mundane Maestro of Love

There are no humble Mars in Leo Lovers, but there is a quiet, self-effacing charm about your sexual nature that comes pretty close to humility. You have a way of winning the sexual game without trying, of being devastatingly sexy while holding yourself aloof from the heat of the moment. It's not that you can't be passionate. It's just that you prefer to express your affection discreetly and practically in mundane acts of service and real physical intimacy.

Your sex life tends to be divided between "little sex" and "big sex." "Little sex" is sex that is easily available and purely physical. It's fun but you can't be very proud of it. "Big sex" is sex that is larger than life, in which you can fully express your pride and your idealism. Of course, "big sex" doesn't come around very often and when it does it requires a lot of effort, both emotionally and spiritually. That's why, whether you like it or not, you are constantly drawn back to "little sex." It fills the gaps between your grand passions.

Case History

Christopher Isherwood (*English writer whose stories about Berlin during the 1930s were made into the play and movie* Cabaret). *Born August 26, 1904, in Wyberslegh, Cheshire, England (Finney 1979).*

Isherwood was born into an upper middle-class home where he and his brother were raised by nannies. His parents were distant, almost mythic figures. His father was killed in World War I when Isherwood was ten. Isherwood's rebellion against his father's soldierly heroism later made him a confirmed pacifist. His rebellion against his strong-willed mother's unbending conventionalism, according to Isherwood, made him a homosexual.

Isherwood claimed he was aware of his attraction to his own sex from the time he was a small boy; however, he waited quite a while before doing anything about it. He was a dead-serious and rather prim youngster, who found his vocation as a writer early in life. He channeled all his energy into perfecting his craft. He was at Cambridge when he had his first sexual experience, and then only because another young man was willing to make the first move. Finally, when he was twenty-four, Isherwood moved to Berlin where his real sex life began.

The "boy bars" and other venues for anonymous sex that thrived in Berlin in the 1920s fascinated Isherwood, but he was seeking a monogamous relationship. Since the boys he chose were working-class hustlers who turned to homosexuality for money, these relationships were a source of great disappointment for the romantic Englishman. Still, he did not tire of them.

There was conjecture, even on Isherwood's part, that he chose to be a homosexual as a means of setting himself apart from the staid, bourgeois lifestyle that his mother had planned for him. His homosexuality also served as a link between him and a circle of young English writers at odds with the older generation. During his early days in Berlin, Isherwood also had sex with a woman. He described the experience as "workable" but concluded that he could only fall in love with boys.

At twenty-seven, Isherwood formed a relationship with a seventeen-year-old boy he called Heinz. In Heinz, Isherwood found the kind of relationship he was looking for: a companion who was essentially pleasant, basically loyal, and always available for sex. The fact that the uneducated Heinz could not relate to him intellectually did not bother Isherwood. Even though he sometimes appeared bored with the boy's company outside the bedroom, the author remained devoted to his young lover. Isherwood took charge of Heinz's life, whisking him away from Germany during the rise of Hitler, and rescuing the lad from various scrapes.

Once back in London, Isherwood discovered he could make money by writing dialogue for movies. From this point on, screenwriting would be his primary means of earning a living. Isherwood's main concern during this period was saving his boy friend from conscription into the German army. To this end Isherwood obtained visas, provided money for bribes and lawyers, and moved with Heinz from country to country. For four years they scurried around Europe but, in the end, Heinz fell into German hands and was sentenced to a year in prison for draft evasion. He eventually survived the war, married, and had a family.

Isherwood reacted to this loss by diving into his work and by entering into a period of uncharacteristic promiscuity. Although he was regarded by many as the most important English novelist of his generation, Isherwood was so distraught over the rise of Hitler's war machine and what he saw as the inevitability of war that he could not enjoy his success. Then Isherwood suddenly found himself travelling to the states with an American boy friend.

Once in the United States, Isherwood returned to writing movies scripts and moved to California. Isherwood adjusted quickly to his new lifestyle. He soon acquired a new semi-permanent boy friend, a young Kentuckian named William Caskey. Isherwood made an effort to make Caskey a more independent lover than Heinz had been. The young man had some skill with a camera and Isherwood tried to launch him as a professional photographer. Unfortunately, it was as a drinker that Caskey really excelled. Like an indulgent father, Isherwood dutifully bailed his lover out of jail and paid his fines. After five years Caskey joined the merchant marines and his visits with Isherwood were only occasional.

Isherwood had a longstanding interest in Eastern religion and philosophy. In California he found his way to a Buddhist monastery and for a time he devoted himself to a swami. Isherwood made an attempt at celibacy during this period but it was short lived. After years of practice, it was too easy for him to find casual sex.

When Isherwood was forty-nine he formed what became the most enduring sexual relationship of his life with a high school student named Don Bachardy. The two not only became lovers but Isherwood paid Bachardy's way through college. They later collaborated on various writing projects for movies and television. Despite the discrepancy in their ages, the relationship lasted until Isherwood's death at the age of eighty-one.

Much of Isherwood's early writings were autobiographical but they made no mention of his homosexuality. As Isherwood entered his fifties he regretted this self-censorship and resolved to become more open about his preferences. His ideas about the homosexual's place in society gained militancy. He expressed the opinion that homosexuals were an embattled minority who needed to fight for their rights. When he was in his seventies Isherwood published *Christopher and his Kind*, an account of his own sexual history written in the third person. Isherwood felt that love, not sex, was the acid test of a person's sexual nature.

Other Examples

Brigitte Bardot (French film star who became a teenage sex symbol). Born September 28, 1934 (Celebrity Birthday Guide).

Wilt Chamberlain (African-American basketball star). Born August 21, 1936 (Celebrity Birthday Guide).

If you have Mars in Leo with Venus in Libra you are . . . the Maestro of Higher Love

There is a sweetness and a delicate artistry about your sexuality that makes you an extraordinary Lover with no time for the commonplace. You have to take sex to a higher level and infuse it with a sense of physical, emotional, and spiritual perfection. This erotic idealism touches every area of your life and makes you a very demanding Lover. But the partner who learns how to meet these egocentric and sometimes quirky demands of yours will be rewarded with devotion and ardor fit for royalty.

You are an exceedingly warm and passionate person, so it is a tragedy when your sexual perfectionism makes you appear cold and controlling. Yet there are times when your sexual expectations become so unrealistic and so festooned with idealistic conditions that no partner can hope to satisfy you. You must recognize that perfect love means nothing if all it gets you is frustration.

Case History

Edith Sitwell (English poet, critic, and patron known for her allegiance to the new, and disdain for the mediocre). Born September 7, 1887, Scarborough, Yorkshire, England (Glendinning 1981).

Sitwell's father was a scholar more interested in the medieval past than his own family. Her mother was an undisciplined and erratic character who was once imprisoned for a bad debt. Neither parent paid much heed to their oldest child and, though she was brought up in a home steeped in privilege and family pride, Sitwell found very little affection there.

Sitwell grew into an odd-looking adolescent: tall, thin, and hooknosed. Concerned about a possible curvature of her spine, a doctor persuaded the awkward girl's parents to put her in a metal body brace. If this were not enough, the doctor also contrived a brace for her face to take the hook out of her nose. It is uncertain how long Sitwell was forced to wear these contraptions, but it is unlikely this treatment did either her bone structure or her self-confidence any good.

Despite the situation with her parents, Sitwell lived with her family until she was twenty-five. Without a vocation or marriage proposals she had nowhere else to go. She spent this extended childhood reading, studying, and developing her own poetry. With few friends outside her home, the bond between Sitwell and her two brothers, Osbert and Sacheverell, became unusually strong. They formed an artistic triumvirate that would last their whole lives. Even when they were adults, outsiders tended to see the three Sitwells as a unit, a fact that often angered them individually.

Even though Sitwell's youth appeared sheltered, intellectually she was anything but a prude. She read widely both in fiction and nonfiction, and had to know a great deal about sex, or at least about sex as it appeared on the printed page. As a young woman her favorite poet was Algernon Swinburne, noted for his passionate, fleshly verse. She also read Baudelaire's scandalous *Les Fleurs du Mal*. But in her personal life, sex was a subject that simply was not approached. Although she had a keen ear for gossip, Sitwell had no interest in the prurient.

When Sitwell left her home at twenty-five, she was well prepared to burst onto the London literary scene both as a poet and as a formidable advocate for other young poets. Rather than trying to conceal her eccentric appearance, she accentuated it with strange, avant-garde clothing; she achieved a visual impact and a personal style that her artistic competitors could only envy. Her prim, unassailable virginity, though never stated outright, was always a subtle part of Sitwell's unforgettable persona.

By the time Sitwell was twenty-eight she had fallen in love for the first time with an intemperate and bisexual Chilean painter. The painter was equally fascinated by Sitwell, but the affair never became physical. He was not the only man drawn to Sitwell. Even with her odd appearance, her intelligence, strength, and unabashed yen for the modern won her many admirers. Moreover, all this occurred during the "roaring '20s" when sexual experimentation was the order of the day. Even though free love seemed to be in the very air she breathed, Sitwell remained stubbornly aloof and chaste, saving all her passion for her work and friendships.

During this time, and for much of her life, Sitwell shared her apartment with Helen Rootham, the woman who had once been her nanny. Rootham shared her artistic ambitions and zeal for beauty. This relationship, and Sitwell's coolness toward sex with men, caused some to whisper that she was a lesbian. But there is no evidence of passion in the attachment between Sitwell and Rootham. When Rootham became ill in her later years, Sitwell seemed more bothered than grief-stricken, and she began to slowly disengage herself from the friendship.

The defining moment in Sitwell's sex life did not come until she was forty and met the twenty-eight-year-old Pavel Tchelitchew. Tchelitchew was a Russian (Sitwell called him her "boyar") who fled the Communist revolution. He was also a painter, a set designer, and a brilliant and untiring self-promoter. Shortly after his arrival in Paris, Tchelitchew attached himself to Gertrude Stein. Stein soon tired of the Russian's flamboyant egotism and, at least according to Stein's story, she gave the artist to Sitwell. Tchelitchew was a homosexual and was living with a male lover named Allen Tanner, but this did not stop Sitwell from falling completely in love with him.

For the next thirty years Sitwell remained devoted to Tchelitchew. She appears to have decided at the very beginning that their relationship would not be physical, but the artist always insisted on the presence of a chaperone when he visited her because he feared she might "rape" him. There was certainly an element of opportunism in Tchelitchew's relationship with Sitwell, but he seems to have also been quite genuine in claiming her as a muse. He painted her and drew her face almost compulsively, always as the exceedingly plain woman she was. Yet Sitwell adored the portraits.

Five years after they met, the relationship between Tchelitchew and Sitwell reached a turning point. Tchelitchew began an affair with a strikingly pretty American novelist named Charles Henri Ford. Sitwell hated Ford and considered his novel about homosexual life obscene. She begged Tanner to stay with Tchelitchew. Despite Tchelitchew's increasing unkindness toward him, Tanner tried desperately to hold on to his lover. But neither Sitwell's disapproval nor Tanner's self-sacrifice was enough to keep Tchelitchew and Ford apart.

At Ford's behest, Tchelitchew moved to New York City but this did not end his relationship with Sitwell. He corresponded with her and looked to her for emotional support and patronage. They had a reunion in New York when Sitwell was sixty-one but this fell flat when Sitwell reacted with noncommittal silence to the painting Tchelitchew regarded as his masterpiece. The fact that her American tour was a rousing triumph and made Sitwell an international figure probably only added to her boyar's ire. By the time that Tchelitchew died, when Sitwell was seventy, their relationship had grown distant, though it is likely Sitwell never fell out of love with him. She survived him by seven years.

Another Example

Margaret Mitchell (*author of* Gone with the Wind *and creator of the character Scarlet O'Hara*). *Born November 8, 1900 (Celebrity Birthday Guide).*

If you have Mars in Leo with Venus in Scorpio you are . . . the Maestro of Mystery

You are one of the most controlling of all the Mars in Leo Lovers, but that's not a problem. There are always people willing to be controlled and the sexual payoff you provide allows for few complaints. You are very serious about sex. There is a depth to your sensuality—a quality of dark, compelling passion that makes you a thoroughly captivating Lover. Sex is seldom all that you are looking for in a relationship. Making another person bend to your will is always more thrilling for you than any kind of physical pleasure.

There is a devilish quality to your sexuality. You have a knack for bombast and display, and you love upsetting people who are prudish or complacent. And yet for all your iconoclastic passion, you are a sexual conservative at heart. One of the chief conflicts in your sexual history will be your attempts to balance your penchant for bad behavior with your appreciation for conventional comfort.

Case History

Benjamin Disraeli (*English novelist and politician who twice served as prime minister*). *Born December 21, 1804, at 5:30 A.M. in Bloomsbury, England (Bradford 1982).*

Disraeli's father was a literary scholar and a Jew. When Disraeli was thirteen, his father had a falling out with the local synagogue. As a result, he had all his children baptized Christians.

Disraeli remained proud of his Jewish heritage all his life but he also took full advantage of the social and political opportunities that his conversion to Christianity opened for him.

As a youth Disraeli was more interested in money and fame than in sex, but he wasted no time in learning how to manipulate women. His first victim was an older, married woman who was a family friend named Sara Austen. Disraeli and Austen were probably in love for a time but it is unlikely that they had sex. Instead Disraeli persuaded Austen to help him write his first novel, a daring exposé of the upper class (of which he knew next to nothing). Austen helped her twenty-one-year-old protégé get the novel published. The book drew a lot of attention because many of the characters were thinly disguised representation of public figures, but this attention quickly dissipated when it was revealed that the author was an inexperienced law clerk.

Despised and ill at twenty-seven, and deeply in debt after other failures in both business and literature, Disraeli traveled to Greece and Jerusalem. It was on this tour that he probably lost his virginity. Far away from his loving but watchful middle-class family, the convalescing author sampled some of the local prostitutes and picked up a case of venereal disease for his trouble.

Back in England, a rejuvenated Disraeli made his first unsuccessful bid for public office. In the midst of this defeat, however, he managed to take a few steps up the social ladder. Disraeli had always identified himself with Lord Byron. Now he played the role of the dandified romantic to the hilt. He curled his hair into ringlets and dyed them the deepest black so as to accent his pale skin. He dressed himself in outrageous ensembles of velvet and lace. These changes in his appearance, along with his outstanding wit, got him noticed even though he remained poor.

At this time, Sara Austen, who was woefully middle class, lost her place in Disraeli's heart to the more socially mobile Clara Bolton. Bolton was the wife of the writer's physician and their friendship had begun even before his trip to the East. Now they were lovers and Bolton, a woman who took pride in her social connections, managed Disraeli's entry into "society." She even tried to find a wealthy wife for her young lover, but Disraeli disapproved of her choice. Instead he turned to another married woman, Henrietta Sykes.

By the time Disraeli was twenty-eight, he and Sykes were passionately involved. Sykes was richer than Bolton; her husband was a lord. Moreover, Sykes had a different attitude toward sex. She was more interested in passion than in power and manipulation. With Sykes's husband perpetually out of town, Disraeli became uncharacteristically impetuous. For a time the young lovers lived like a married couple. Then they realized that they had an enemy—the jilted Mrs. Bolton.

Bolton conspired with Sykes' husband to "ruin" the pair but, in the process, she and Mr. Sykes became lovers themselves. Henrietta Sykes discovered the affair and thus put a stop to any argument Mr. Sykes might have raised about her and Disraeli.

It was through Mrs. Sykes that Disraeli was able to gain the favor of one of the most powerful men in Britain's Conservative Party, Baron Lyndhurst. With this man's support, Disraeli, who had failed repeatedly to win an election as an independent candidate, was able to run for a seat in Parliament with the party's support. The price he had to pay, however, was his mistress. Lyndhurst, though aging, had a weakness for beautiful women and Sykes capitalized on that weakness to assure the support of Disraeli. Even though only a season before Disraeli had been utterly infatuated with Sykes, he now stood by and allowed her to prostitute herself for his benefit.

Predictably, by the time Disraeli won his first election, his relationship with Sykes had cooled. Disraeli turned his romantic attentions to a rich widow named Mary Ann Lewis. She was a middle-class woman who had married up but kept her bourgeois practicality. She was forty-five, twelve years older than Disraeli, but her wealth attracted several suitors. Even though Disraeli was her favorite, Mary Ann enjoyed being courted too much to rush into a decision. Disraeli became so angry at her procrastination that he gave her an ultimatum: marry him or else. Mary Ann chose marriage.

In his ultimatum Disraeli admitted that he had first been attracted to Mary Ann because of her wealth but that later he had come to love her. By all indications this appears to have been the truth. Disraeli treated his wife with utmost affection and respect, deferred to her eccentricities (which became more and more uproarious as she aged) and never spoke ill of her. There were problems in the marriage. Mary Ann, who was anything but an intellectual, was extremely jealous of the close relationship her husband had with his erudite sister, Sarah. Disraeli's wife also kept a tight hold on the purse strings so that, even though he was one of the most influential men in England, Disraeli was still plagued by creditors. Yet these problems never interfered with the affection Disraeli felt for his wife.

Mary Ann and Disraeli began to have sex shortly before their engagement and, despite the difference in their ages, there were no problems in their sex life—at least during the first few years. But by the time Disraeli was in his forties (and his wife was nearing sixty), it is evident that he was sleeping with other women. These affairs were so smothered in secrecy that present-day biographers only have hints as to the circumstances.

Mary Ann died when Disraeli was sixty-eight. She left her aging and sickly husband with specific permission to remarry. Surprisingly, Disraeli was ready to comply. At seventy he became hopelessly infatuated with a socialite named Lady Bradford. In accordance with the pattern established in his youth, the woman was already married. Disraeli died at seventy-six.

Other Examples

Arthur Miller (American playwright and husband of Marilyn Monroe). Born October 17, 1915 (Celebrity Birthday Guide).

Bob Guccione (publisher of Penthouse magazine). Born December 17, 1930 (Celebrity Birthday Guide).

Hillary Rodham Clinton (First Lady). Born October 26, 1947 (Celebrity Birthday Guide).

If you have Mars in Leo with Venus in Sagittarius you are ... the Maestro of Excitement

You are a sexual idealist, a daring Lover who refuses to acknowledge any limitations. Your enthusiasm and confidence are such that people often fail to notice that your ideal of unlimited love does not include a sense of responsibility. You are so intent on sexual freedom that you often forget other people might be hurt or offended by your liberty. You need to cultivate the ability to say "no," particularly to yourself. As awful as it may sound, a little frustration can actually do you some good.

On the positive side, you manage to have as much fun with sex as is humanly possible. Your approach to the erotic is always fresh and wondrous. You never allow yourself to be pulled down by the mundane. At times there is an almost spiritual quality to your lovemaking. You always aim for the best in your sex life and with your rambunctious enthusiasm and emphatic charm, more often than not you get it.

Case History

Artie Mitchell (pornographer and sex industry mogul who, with his brother, produced the film Behind the Green Door). Born December 17, 1945, in Lodi, California (Hubner 1992; McCumber 1992).

Mitchell's parents were "Okies" who went to California during the Depression in search of a better life. They found it, though not in the typical way. Artie's father was a cardsharp. His skill was such that he could afford to settle his family into a middle-class neighborhood not far from San Francisco. The Mitchell brothers grew up during the 1950s. They sported crew cuts, cruised for girls, and got into the normal mischief expected of teenagers at the time.

The Mitchell brothers entered their early twenties with no particular ambition. Jim liked to take pictures and was adept at convincing the liberated young women he found in San

Francisco to pose topless or in the nude. He soon discovered that there was a booming market for these photos and he began to sell them to tourists. After Artie finished a hitch in the army, the Mitchell brothers joined forces. Soon they were in the pornography business. They found their performers among the free-loving youngsters who flocked to the San Francisco "hippie" culture. They showed their films in a rundown theater called the O'Farrell. Before long they had a thriving business.

One reason for the Mitchell brothers' success was that they did not act like pornographers. They showed their hard-core fare without shame. When the law intervened, they fought the charges in court and won. Advocates of freedom of speech celebrated these victories, but the Mitchell boys saw these victories only as an excuse to have more fun. They ran their business like an extended party. They surrounded themselves with army and high school buddies with whom they drank, caroused, and even worked when it was convenient. When they weren't showing "dirty" movies at the O'Farrell, they showed classic black-and-white comedies and invited anyone with a sense of fun to come in and enjoy. Despite their profession, they maintained a clean, all-American front that made their most outrageous acts of defiance seem like playful mischief.

Behind this fun-loving facade, Jim and Artie Mitchell were very shrewd businessmen. First, they beat the distribution system that would have kept them from showing their X-rated films in other large cities. Then they exploited the expanding market for hard-core fare with the 1972 release of *Behind the Green Door*, a high-budget skin flick that starred a professional actress and model named Marilyn Chambers. Later, they anticipated the video cassette market for pornography and profited from it immensely. Since this new trend emptied theaters like the O'Farrell, the brothers made the old movie house into a "state-of-the-art" sex club that featured nude dancers and the most daring live sex performances that the law would (and in some case would not) allow. In this new incarnation, the O'Farrell not only continued to earn tremendous profits, it became a San Francisco institution.

The brothers had worked as a team during the early days of their daring enterprise. Even though they often argued, there was no strict division of labor; however, as the business prospered it became clear that Jim was the business head and that Artie provided the venture with its edgy vitality. This distinction was crucial because, as the years passed, Jim grew up. He settled down and began to act like a member of the establishment. Artie refused to change. He remained a little boy in constant rebellion against authority. Nowhere was this refusal to grow up more evident than in his relationship with women.

Early in his career Artie fell in love with Meredith Bradford, a flower child who had come to San Francisco to escape her wealthy New England family. Bradford was a brainy, strong-willed woman who was accepted into the loose, mostly male circle of friends with whom the

Mitchell's made their movies. They all became partners in what seemed to be the perfect antiestablishment prank. Within this aura of impish collusion, Artie and Meredith developed a special closeness. When Artie was twenty-four, he and Meredith married.

Once they were married, the brash and rebellious Artie Mitchell suddenly revealed the conservative side of his nature. He wanted all the trappings of the middle-class American dream: a house in the suburbs, backyard barbecues on the weekends, and even a company softball team. This meant Meredith could no longer be part of the business. She had to retire to their suburban home and look after the three children the marriage quickly produced.

It didn't take long before Meredith recognized that her relationship with Artie was always going to be secondary to the relationship he had with his brother and his work. Artie spent most of his time making movies and frolicking at the O'Farrell. The fact that he was enjoying a great deal of casual sex during these long nights bothered Meredith less that the realization that, as his wife and the mother of his children, she was forever separated from the true center of his life. She was the one who had to be responsible while he had all the fun.

Seven years into their marriage Meredith told Mitchell she wanted a separation. He was outraged. Sure he had behaved badly, but he failed to see how that had any bearing on his marriage. As far as he was concerned, he was still a family man.

Shortly after separating from Meredith, Mitchell began another relationship with a young businesswoman named Karen Hassall. Three years later they were married. In many ways this marriage mimicked Mitchell's first. Karen was ensconced in suburban splendor and the house immediately began to fill with children. By this time, Mitchell's misbehavior became more violent and Karen bore the brunt of it. Driven by an insane jealousy and cocaine, Mitchell threatened her with a gun, beat her, and repeatedly humiliated her. All the while he spent more and more of his time cavorting with the dancers at the O'Farrell. Before long Artie's second marriage also ended in a bitter divorce.

Early in their careers the Mitchell brothers gained a reputation for treating the people who performed in their films fairly and with respect. At the same time both brothers stayed clear of actually performing sex in front of the camera and they shared a quiet contempt for the people who did. This contempt now became quite evident in Artie's behavior toward the female performers at the O'Farrell. He treated the club as if it was his private sexual reserve. Any woman who worked there was expected to submit to his advances. Those who didn't were subjected to intimidation or violence, or they were simply fired.

Yet there were many women who loved Artie Mitchell. After his second divorce Mitchell divided his time among a string of beautiful girl friends, most of whom were dancers at the O'Farrell or porn stars. These women described him as an extraordinary lover with a fun-loving spirit that was absolutely infectious. With Artie, every night was a party without limits.

The only rule was to have as much fun as humanly possible. Some of these women were so infatuated with Mitchell that they spent months by the phone waiting for this bald little madman to call and invite them back to the festivities.

Of course, the key ingredient to all this fun was the fact that Mitchell was in control. Whether he was showing off his naked girl friend to a bar full of men, or commanding one of his women to dress up in a gorilla suit and make love to another woman, Mitchell called the shots. He enjoyed manipulating the women who loved him, playing the affections of one off another, and generally treating them as if they were his sex slaves. It was all part of the game to him. Such was his egotism that he assumed that all would be forgiven as long as they occasionally got to sleep with him.

Surprisingly enough, it was not one of his women who put an end to Artie Mitchell's party, nor was it the law. It was his brother, Jim. Confrontation had always been a part of the working life of the Mitchell brothers. They were constantly bickering; however, as Artie got wilder and Jim more conventional, the fights became more serious. Finally, when Artie was forty-five, one of these mean-spirited arguments got out of control, and Jim shot and killed his brother.

Other Examples

George Eliot *(Mary Ann Evans—British novelist who wrote* Silas Marner*). Eliot was as remarkable for her ugliness as for her talent and independence. One contemporary called her "a fungus of pendulous shape." This didn't stop Eliot from enjoying a long, though unofficial, union with fellow writer George Henry Lewes, as well as passionate attachments to at least two women. While Eliot was naturally circumspect about her lesbian relationships, she was quite outspoken about her enjoyment of sex with Lewes. Born November 22, 1819 (Wallace 1981).*

Ezra Pound *(American poet and Fascist convert). Born October 30, 1885 (Celebrity Birthday Guide).*

If you have Mars in Leo with Venus in Capricorn you are . . . the Maestro of Pain

You are one of the sexiest Lovers of this type—an exceptionally physical Lover with a simple, down-to-earth approach to the erotic. Even though you are a very controlling Lover, you never let your need to be the boss get in the way of your equally strong need for earthly pleasure. To some degree you are more calculating and less exuberant than the typical Mars in Leo Lover, but this reserve only serves to increase your sexual artistry and maximize your passion.

Despite your earthy enjoyment of sex, there is often a self-destructive quality about your love life. All Mars in Leo Lovers are thespians of one sort or another—you are a tragedian. You tend to dramatize your most negative feelings and your least desirable traits. You are also instinctively drawn to situations that will humiliate you and lay bare all your weaknesses. The funny thing is that no matter how sad you appear to be, you have no trouble finding partners. You publicize your misery so well that people line up to take care of you.

Case History

Edith Piaf (Edith Gassion—French singer who became enormously popular for her sad songs of love and betrayal). Born December 19, 1915, at 3:00 A.M. in Paris, France (Crosland 1985).

Even though Piaf's life story went through several edits as her fame grew, the basic facts are still strikingly tragic. Her mother was a "street singer" who deserted Piaf soon after she was born. Her father, a traveling acrobat, left the child in the care of his mother, who was a cook in a brothel. When Piaf was old enough, she traveled with her father, singing and passing the hat while he performed on the streets. By the time Piaf was sixteen and left her father to move in with a lover, she was already well acquainted with adversity and sex.

This first union lasted long enough to produce a child, but Piaf soon tired of her boy friend who was apparently too gentle and easygoing for her taste. A year later the child died. Piaf made a living with various jobs and by singing in the streets. She fell in with thieves and pimps, but she rather liked these dangerous men. She might have become a streetwalker if she had not been so small and plain; however, she could make more money singing for handouts.

Piaf's life was suddenly turned around shortly before her twentieth birthday. The owner of an important nightclub heard her singing in the street and invited her to sing in his club. This man soon died and her career then fell into the able hands of a songwriter who not only wrote songs specially crafted for her voice and style, but also worked incessantly to get Piaf before the public. This man, Raymond Asso, also became Piaf's lover and apparently managed to hold her to three years of relative fidelity—something few, if any, of her subsequent lovers could claim.

By the time Piaf broke with Asso she was already an established star. Not even the advent of World War II and the fall of France could stop her rise to fame and fortune. By all appearances Piaf enjoyed her success immensely. She thrived on the adulation of her audience and she spent the money that adulation earned her with thoughtless indiscretion, often on gifts for her many lovers. Her success and wealth gave Piaf the upper hand in her sexual relationships; this was something she could appreciate.

Piaf was a passionate and difficult lover. She claimed she had to love a man in order to sleep with him, but she fell in love so often and quickly that this in no way limited her bed-mates. Her most significant relationships were with men she could mold. Piaf wanted her men to be successful in their various fields, but under her direction. She bought them clothes, guided them in their careers, and used her influence to make them famous. One such young man was Yves Montrand, who became her lover when she was thirty and he was just beginning as a singer. She dressed him, instructed him, and made him a star. Then she moved on to someone new.

Despite her generosity, Piaf was hard on her partners. Tragically insecure, she needed con-stant attention. Sex satisfied only part of this need. She also needed violence in her relation-ships. She often goaded her lovers to fight with her, even to hit her. As she grew older she despaired that this kind of "primitive" man—a man who would forcefully express his jeal-ousy—was so hard to find. At the same time, her infidelity was legendary. No matter how much she loved a man it was rarely enough to prevent her from falling in love with someone new.

The exception to this rule was possibly Marcel Cerdan, the French middleweight boxer. Cerdan was one of the few men in Piaf's life whose fame equaled her own. Already the European champion, he was regarded as a hero in France. He was also married, but both he and Piaf chose to ignore this detail as they eagerly pursued their secret affair. Piaf even had herself smuggled into Cerdan's training camp. She reorganized his life and was instrumental in the replacement of his long-time trainer. Her efforts did not make Piaf popular with either Cerdan's friends or his wife, but the boxer was thoroughly enamored. A year after the affair began, Cerdan was killed in a plane crash. He was flying to New York City to join Piaf; she had begged him to come to her because she was lonely. She reacted to his death with a wild mixture of grief and guilt. For a time it was feared she would commit suicide.

When Piaf was thirty-six she married a singer-songwriter named Jacques Pills. As always, she seemed totally infatuated with her new spouse and singing partner in the beginning, but quickly tired of him. It seemed Pills' most outstanding qualification was the fact that she could easily dominate him. However, it was during her five-year marriage to Pills that Piaf made the first attempts to fight the drug addiction and alcoholism that were slowly ruining her health.

After her divorce, Piaf went through many men, most of them significantly younger than herself, and she continued her drinking and drug abuse. She married for the second time at the age of forty-six to a twenty-six-year-old Greek hairdresser named Theo Sarapo. True to form, she trained her young lover to be a singer and he was forced to endure her particularly dictatorial style of instruction. But Sarapo remained devoted to his wife and teacher until her death a year after the wedding.

Other Examples

James Dean (*American film legend noted for his sexy screen persona and self-destructive lifestyle*). *Born February 8, 1931 (Celebrity Birthday Guide).*

Frank Sinatra (*American singer*). *Born December 12, 1915 (Celebrity Birthday Guide).*

If you have Mars in Leo with Venus in Aquarius you are . . . the Maestro of Enlightenment

You take the playfulness of Mars in Leo and add to it a mischievous edge and a yen for experimentation and discovery. Even though you take sex seriously, you always look at your passions from an intellectual distance that allows you to have a great deal of fun with relatively little emotional display. Some people may find you cold and manipulative and it is true you are quite skilled at playing with other people's minds, but there is never any malice in your manipulations, only curiosity.

There is a formidable idealism within your sexual nature that will likely be responsible for both your best and worst erotic moments. At best, this idealism allows you to leap over the fears and insecurities that limit the sex lives of most people and achieve an almost visionary sense of sexual joy. At worst, it makes you preachy, stubborn, and insensitive to some very real emotional and moral concerns.

Case History

William H. Masters (*American doctor and expert on human sexuality who attempted to study human sex as it happened*). *Born December 27, 1915, in Cleveland, Ohio (Masters 1966; Moritz 1968).*

Masters had a very conventional, upper middle-class upbringing. He attended good schools where he excelled in his studies and in athletics. He pursued a career in medicine, though early on he knew he was more interested in research than dealing with patients. He postponed marriage until the year before he obtained his M.D., marrying Elisabeth Ellis at the age of twenty-seven. The only thing that was the least unusual about Masters was his decision to devote his career to the study of human sexuality.

In his preface to *Human Sexual Response* Masters gives a hint as to his motivation for pursuing this controversial subject. Before Masters and Johnson published this and other works in the early 1960s, there was little actual research into human sexuality. Although much had been written about the psychology of sex and the philosophy of sex, researchers had long shied away from the scientific examination of the physiology of sex. By choosing to specialize in sex, Masters was entering unexplored territory.

Still, Masters approached his ambitions with a reasonable amount of circumspection. When he asked an older colleague for advice, he was told to first establish his credentials in a related field, and to wait until he was forty to begin his work. Masters entered the fields of obstetrics and gynecology, where he soon distinguished himself. He also joined the faculty of the University of Washington Medical School. Then, hedging a bit, he began his research into human sexuality at the age of thirty-eight.

Masters' aim was to study sex under controlled conditions in the laboratory. This not only meant that the subjects of his research had to have sex while other people watched, they had to have sex while every part and function of their bodies, from blood pressure to rectal contractions, were measured and scrutinized. Masters anticipated he would have difficulty finding willing subjects, so in the beginning he hired prostitutes. As word of his project spread, the doctor found he could persuade ordinary people to participate in his work. These anonymous subjects were not just good sports. Some married couples reported that the clinically controlled sex they had in the laboratory actually helped them to improve their sex lives at home.

Shortly after he began his research, Masters hired Virginia Johnson, a psychologist, to help him screen subjects. She became the coauthor of *Human Sexual Response* and the codirector of the Reproductive Biology Research Foundation that Masters founded in St. Louis. When Masters was fifty-five, Johnson became his second wife.

Masters was fifty when *Human Sexual Response* was published. Criticism of his work began even before the book was out. Some of the criticism was based on moral grounds. Others felt that the cold, clinical approach Masters favored dehumanized human sex and discounted psychological and spiritual factors. Still, regardless of the fact that the book was written in dry and highly technical language, *Human Sexual Response* immediately became a bestseller.

Masters responded to the outrage that his studies inspired among moralists and traditionalists with ill-concealed contempt. As a scientist, he told his critics, he had to be concerned with truth and not with morality; however, whether intentionally or not, Masters and Johnson did take a moral stand in their book. Just the fact that the object of their research was the facilitation of pleasure in sex and that they treated masturbation and homosexual relations in the same context as heterosexual coitus was significant to many. In debunking many of the prohibitive myths surrounding sex, they made it easier for their readers to experiment and gain a sense of sexual freedom. *Human Sexual Response* quickly became one of the cornerstones of what was to be called the "sexual revolution."

Masters and Johnson continued their research at the Reproductive Biology Research Foundation through the 1970s and 1980s. They coauthored several books and published many articles in popular magazines, always advocating a free discussion of all aspects of human sexuality. In the mid-80s they created a new controversy with a book about the AIDS crisis in which they overestimated (according to some critics) the danger the disease posed to heterosexuals. Shortly after this, Masters and Johnson were divorced. Masters closed his research facility in St. Louis when he was seventy-nine.

Another Example

Vanessa Williams (*American singer and actress*). *Born March 18, 1963 (Celebrity Birthday Guide).*

If you have Mars in Leo with Venus in Pisces you are . . . the Maestro of Dreams

You are the most optimistic and generous of all the Mars in Leo Lovers. Perhaps you are just the most unrealistic. To you, sex is the ultimate affirmation of life. It is a grand ideal that shines a kind and forgiving light on even the most tawdry and unsavory human practices. Your extraordinary sexual idealism can, at times, make you seem unworldly and even unapproachable, but it also is your great gift to all the people who love you.

You typically appear less controlling than most Lovers of this type but, of course, that's not all together true. As far as real life is concerned, you are pretty easygoing. You accept people as they are and you take your pleasure where you find it. This is only because in your fantasies—in the world of your sexual ideals—you enjoy a control that is absolute and unquestioned. This is one reason why this world of fantasy is so precious to you. It is also why only the most privileged and beloved are permitted to join you there.

Case History

Vladimir Nabokov (*Russian poet and novelist, author of* Lolita). *Born April 23, 1899, in St. Petersburg, Russia (Field 1972).*

Nabokov was born into a rich and illustrious Russian family. His father was strict, but Nabokov was his mother's favorite and was pampered accordingly. The Russian Revolution put an end to the privileged life that Nabokov had known in his youth. He and his family were forced to flee to Germany. His father was an important official in the "White" Russian government, but the younger Nabokov stayed clear of politics and concentrated on developing himself as a poet.

Nabokov had his first love affair in Russia when he was seventeen with a girl who lived on a neighboring estate. When Nabokov's father attempted to explain the facts of life to his son, he was shocked to learn the boy had already learned most of them by rolling in the grass with this young lady. The couple continued their outdoor romps for several months until the weather intervened.

As a refugee Nabokov continued his erotic adventures. During his family's leisurely flight through Greece he managed to have affairs with three different women. Later he was sent to Cambridge University, where he found plenty of time for both local girls from the lower classes and fellow Russian emigrants. When Nabokov rejoined his family in Berlin he quickly became engaged to a young Russian woman from a good family. The engagement was suddenly called off when Nabokov kissed his fiancée in a manner her parents thought indecent. Nabokov was not too upset by this turn of events. He distracted himself with other women, including a noted German film star.

What is perhaps most amazing about young Nabokov's love life is the fact that, at the time he was enjoying himself with a seemingly endless parade of women, he and his family were suffering through a series of disasters. Separated from their means of financial and social support, his parents and extended family struggled for survival. For a while they waited for the Bolshevik government to fall. When this didn't happen they spread out across Western Europe and tried to adjust to the hard times that had befallen them. Nabokov's father was assassinated and his mother lived in intense poverty. Nabokov, though well educated and well dressed, was barely able to support himself by giving language lessons and publishing poetry and stories in small, Russian-language publications.

When Nabokov was twenty-six he married Vera Evseevna Slonim, a Russian emigrant like himself. Vera was a brilliant young woman from a wealthy Jewish family who had lost everything in their flight to Germany. She was a proud, rather imperious woman who had once plotted to assassinate Trotsky. Many were surprised by her marriage to the apolitical Nabokov, but the marriage proved to be a happy one. Nabokov continued to give lessons, and Vera took on the role as the primary breadwinner so that he could concentrate on his work. Later, when the couple had a son, it was Nabokov who stayed home and cared for the child. The former aristocrat liked to joke about his skill at washing diapers.

In order to promote his writings Nabokov had to travel for public readings of his work. These periodic separations from his wife gave him the opportunity to sleep with other women. These encounters apparently meant little to the author; however, when he was thirty-eight,

Nabokov fell in love with a Russian poet living in Paris. Vera, who later joined her husband in Paris, learned of the affair from an anonymous letter. The marriage was deeply shaken.

Nabokov and Vera withdrew to the south of France, somehow reaching an agreement not to talk about the affair. Nabokov continued to correspond with the other woman on the sly, claiming it was only his attachment to his son that kept him from leaving Vera. Then, suddenly, Nabokov changed his mind. He wrote the woman and requested that she return all his letters; when she attempted to see him, he rebuffed her. A short time later Nabokov and his family left France for the United States. Nabokov obtained employment as a teacher at a college for women where he enjoyed flirting with his students, but apparently never again strayed from his marriage.

Vera's overriding influence in Nabokov's life continued even after he came to be regarded as one of the leading writers of his time. An intensely private woman herself, she attempted to control the information her husband gave out to interviewers. She refused to allow Nabokov to accept a copy of *The Story of O* when it was offered to him as a gift and she tried, without much success, to control his drinking. Nabokov endured her control with a mixture of mischievous rebellion and humorous acquiescence. The marriage lasted until Nabokov's death at seventy-eight.

Although actual sex scenes are rare in his work, sex and sex as fantasy was often a central theme in Nabobov's writing. Even in his earliest stories and novels, his heroes tend to have sexual issues: premature ejaculation, impotence, homosexual tendencies, and pedophilia. Nabokov was always quick to separate his own sexuality from those depicted in his literature, maintaining that he was not Humbert Humbert (the child abuser from *Lolita*), or any of the less-than-admirable characters he created. By his account, the source of his knowledge of sexual dysfunction was the work of Havelock Ellis, the only authority on sex accepted by Nabokov.

Another Example

Hans Christian Andersen (Danish author of children's stories, such as The Little Mermaid, *and lifelong virgin). As a young man he quit a job in a carpenter shop because he could not stand the coarse language of his companions. Even after he became a famous author Anderson avoided sexual entanglements with women. He fell in love with several women but the relationships never became physical. When he was twenty-nine, Andersen was assailed by what amounted to a fit of frustrated sexual desire. But this episode only strengthened his determination to resist what he regarded as his sinful physical urges. Born April 2, 1805 (Stirling 1965).*

Chapter 6

Mars in Virgo
The Back-to-Basics Lover

General Characteristics

Sex comes with no frills when Mars is in Virgo. These Lovers see sex as a means to physical pleasure. Their approach is simple, direct, and uncomplicated by considerations of decorum or idealism. Needless to say there's nothing virginal about this placement. Mars in Virgo Lovers enjoy sex a lot. They usually have it whenever and however it is expedient for them to do so. When other people complain that this attitude is immoral or primitive, these practical Lovers are seldom impressed. It's not that they object to morality or idealism. It's just that they can't see what any of those fine qualities have to do with sex.

Despite their straightforward approach, Mars in Virgo Lovers tend to be rather reserved and circumspect when it comes to sex. They don't like drawing attention to their love lives and prefer to keep these matters quiet and low-key. In fact, one reason they are so direct and plainspoken about sex is that they just don't see it as being all that important. It's a simple bodily function and nothing more. Why all the hoopla? If someone attempts to deny them sex or to make them feel ashamed of it, however, these Lovers will definitely make themselves heard.

Since Mars in Virgo Lovers are so clear-headed and rational about sex, one might guess that they always make wise decisions in this area. Unfortunately, this is not true. These pragmatic Lovers trust little beyond their own senses. They have a tendency to discount any rules, traditions, or even good advice that appears tainted with romantic or unrealistic notions. Thus, they are often left with only the school of experience to teach them all the perils of love and sex. These Lovers often develop slowly and they are inclined to make egregious errors in judgement early in life.

One thing that their analytical approach does guarantee is that these Lovers learn from their mistakes. Perhaps the best quality of Mars in Virgo people is their resourcefulness and ability to adapt their sexuality to all sorts of situations. Guided by experience, common sense, and a very healthy sex drive, these folks always find a way to have the best sex they can possibly have under any set of circumstances. They are sexual opportunists—always ready to adapt or change direction for the sake of a good time.

Of course, this opportunistic approach to sexual happiness has its drawbacks. Mars in Virgo Lovers are often too quick to settle for easy sex—sex that doesn't require struggle or emotional strain. At times this tendency induces them to stay in bad relationships simply because those relationships satisfy their physical needs. In other instances it can cause them to choose sex that is mechanical and anonymous over the complexities and inconveniences of sex with someone they love. There is always a potential for cynicism with this Mars placement. Since these lovers don't need romance, idealism, or emotional bonds in order to enjoy sex, they sometimes allow themselves to be convinced that they don't need these things at all.

Anyone who thinks that Mars in Virgo Lovers are too cool and clinical for love needs to think again. For these Lovers, bonds of affection are built with the most mundane acts of kindness. They seek to be useful to the people they care about and they go out of their way to simply be of service. Of course, there is usually a degree of reciprocity in this arrangement. It's rare for a Mars in Virgo Lover to fall in love with anyone who is not in some way useful to him or her. This may sound calculating but, in fact, it is an excellent basis for a relationship. Love that is defined in terms of common interests, common goals, and material interdependence cannot be threatened by flagging passions or the vicissitudes of feeling. Relationships formed by Mars in Virgo Lovers can be exceptionally warm, physical, and enduring.

If you have Mars in Virgo with Venus in Aries you are . . . the Basically Bold Lover

You are an eager and aggressive Lover who makes more noise and is more prone to brag than the typical Mars in Virgo individual. You are also more inclined to get caught up in your passions. In your case, cool-headed analysis is employed only after the lovemaking is over and, quite often, after the mistake has been made. This makes you a more spirited Mars in Virgo Lover but not always a wiser one.

You are the most energetic Lover of this type and the least likely to settle for less than the best. You are constantly looking for challenges in your love life and expect more from your relationships than mere physical gratification. You need to be proud of your partners—to see them and yourself as strong and heroic. This sexual egotism does not make you any less expeditious in your approach to sex. Of all the Mars in Virgo Lovers, you may be the most unabashed proponent of the "quickie," but with you, it becomes a quickie of heroic proportions.

Case History

Jayne Mansfield (Jayne Palmer Mansfield Hargitay Cimber—busty actress who endures as a sex symbol even though few remember her movies). Born April 19, 1933, in Bryn Mawr, Pennsylvania (Saxton 1975).

Jayne Mansfield became pregnant while she was still in high school. The father of the child was a handsome college boy named Paul Mansfield who completely swept the inexperienced Jayne off her feet. He quickly did the "right thing" and married her. This came as a shock for Jayne's middle-class Texan parents. Jayne's natural father had died when she was young, but her stepfather cared deeply for her and her mother absolutely doted on her daughter. The pregnancy and early marriage was particularly disturbing to her mother because it appeared to put an end to the dream they both had shared that Jayne would someday be a movie star.

Oddly enough, it was only after her marriage and the birth of her first child that Mansfield's sex appeal became truly apparent. When she joined her husband at college she found she could turn heads even while pushing a baby carriage. When Paul was drafted and she accompanied him to an army camp in Georgia, she was regarded as a scenic wonder by his fellow soldiers. Mansfield began doing some amateur acting and quickly came to the conclusion that she had to go to Hollywood. When her husband returned from a tour in Korea she persuaded him to move the family to Los Angeles. She was twenty-one.

Paul Mansfield did not last long in Hollywood. He was unable to deal with his wife's all-consuming drive to succeed. Jayne went directly to Paramount Studio and told them she wanted to be a star. When this approach failed, she looked for any kind of film work and publicity. Soon after Paul left her, Mansfield joined forces with a young publicist named Jim Byron. Mansfield and Byron shared an approach to public relations that was both bombastic and opportunistic. Together they started an all-out media blitz that continued for the rest of Mansfield's life.

Under Byron's direction Mansfield sought any type of endorsement, recognition, or excuse to be in front of a crowd or a camera in a bathing suit. From the very beginning Mansfield felt that the key to her success would be her forty-inch bust, her platinum-dyed hair, and "dumb blond" giggle. Many of the situations Byron set up for her were tasteless, lowbrow, and even ridiculous, but this did not deter Mansfield. She had no problem laughing at her unusual proportions or the influence they had on men. She seemed to thoroughly enjoy exhibiting herself, just as she seemed to revel in the exhausting, almost frantic pace of her new life.

During the time they worked together, Byron and Mansfield became lovers but their sexual relationship was simply an extension of their professional life. Mansfield had other affairs during this period but always in the context of her career. She used sex as a form of persuasion or as a reward for a job well done. The men who had sex with her described her as voracious, but not sensual.

Mansfield's greatest publicity coup came at a poolside photo session. It had been designed to promote a movie starring Jane Russell until the top of Mansfield's bikini artfully came off in the water and every lens focused on her. This led to an offer to star in a Broadway play. The play was a satire on Hollywood. Mansfield played a caricature of the "blond bombshell" that she was trying to become, but this didn't bother Jayne. She found her skills at self-promotion worked just as well in New York City as in California, and the play was a tremendous hit.

About this time Mansfield chanced to see Mickey Hargitay in a Mae West "beefcake" revue. She quickly rescued the brawny former Mr. Universe from West and made him her own. They were married when Mansfield was twenty-four. They performed together in a nightclub act and in several very bad movies. She distanced herself from Byron and her early advisers. Hargitay acted as her manager, though it was really Mansfield who made the decisions. Her career and her marriage became as one. From their pink palace with its heart-shaped pool, to the birth of their three children, to their several messy break-ups and reconciliations, every aspect of Mansfield's relationship with Hargitay became part of her endless publicity campaign.

By the time Mansfield was twenty-nine she was frustrated with her stagnant career and her passive husband. She began to have affairs. For a while she preferred Latin men and the possibilities of passion and romance they represented. Yet it was no Latin lover who won Mansfield away from her stalwart husband. Instead it was a tough, hard-driving director named Matt Cimber. At first Mansfield found Cimber's take-charge attitude refreshing and she encouraged him to manage her career; however, Mansfield was too used to her independence to be bullied for long. The marriage produced one child and broke up after a year.

At this point a mysterious ex-carnival performer named Anton LaVey entered Mansfield's life. He was the head of the so-called "Church of Satan" based in California. He had already drawn several celebrities into his fold with a flashy mixture of irreverence, mysticism, and cheap sex. Mansfield came to LaVey when she was fighting Cimber in the courts for custody of their child. LaVey cast a spell and she won her case. A short time later a lion accidentally mauled another of Mansfield's children and she sought LaVey's magical intervention to save the child's life.

Mansfield was probably drawn to the satanist less for his magic than for his showmanship. In a sense they were kindred spirits. Both understood how to use the repressed sexual yearning of the masses for fun and profit. She probably also felt that the cult's philosophy, which was a variation of Aleister Crowley's "Do what thou wilt," summed up her own approach to life. Mansfield joined the cult and advanced to the rank of "high priestess." The other show business personalities who participated in LaVey's rites tended to avoid publicity. Mansfield displayed no such shame. She even allowed herself to be photographed taking the "unholy communion" from LaVey.

Mansfield's newest boyfriend, Sam Brody, was not so impressed with LaVey. Brody was a lawyer (litigation was a dominate theme in Mansfield's later years), and he was extremely possessive toward his favorite client and lover. A row erupted between LaVey and Brody and the satanist put a hex on the jealous attorney. Mansfield was warned to stay away from Brody, who was now regarded by the adherents of the "church" as a condemned man, but Mansfield apparently did not take the threat seriously.

Mansfield never gave up her frenetic work schedule. She refused to relax, even though she had accumulated a substantial amount of money and she refused to give up her dream of becoming a major Hollywood star. She was hurrying from a nightclub engagement in Biloxi, Mississippi, to an interview in New Orleans when she and Brody were killed in an automobile accident. Mansfield was thirty-four.

Another Example

Robert Downey, Jr. (American actor). Born April 4, 1965 (Celebrity Birthday Guide).

If you have Mars in Virgo with Venus in Taurus you are … the Basically Beautiful Lover

Your sexuality is built for comfort. You are a slow, fulsome Lover with a sense of grace and a concern for aesthetics that might just pass for romanticism in some instances. But no one should be fooled. It is sensation, not sentiment, that is your real concern. Romance means nothing to you unless it has a physical payoff.

You are the most conservative of the Mars in Virgo Lovers and this often places you in a very difficult position. How do you satisfy your enormous appetite for pleasure without breaking the rules or at least drawing unwanted attention to your sensual self? There is no easy answer to this question because there will always be someone who finds your direct and thoroughly earthy approach to sex offensive, no matter how polite and circumspect you try to be.

Case History

Lady Ellenborough (Jane Digby Law von Venningen Theotoky Sitt Mesrab—Victorian beauty who defied every convention in an international search for "Mr. Right"). Born April 3, 1807, in Dorset, England (Schmidt 1976).

When Jane Digby debuted into London society at the age of seventeen she immediately became the hit of the social season. Everyone wanted to know which bachelor would claim this stunning, blue-blooded beauty. There was some surprise when the winner was a widower, Edward Law, Earl of Ellenborough. He was nearing middle age but still good looking and vain. He was also a man of considerable wealth and power, and a dynamic force on the political scene. When he proposed, both Jane and her parents eagerly accepted.

The marriage floundered from the very beginning. Lord Ellenborough turned out to be a cold and distant husband who devoted his time to his career and reserved his sexual passion for women other than his wife. For two years the naive young bride waited for her husband to give her the attention she needed. Then she began to see other men. The first was her cousin to whom she had been strongly attracted even before her marriage. When she bore a child four years into the marriage, the gossips wondered who the father was. Ellenborough, however, had no doubts the child was his.

Immediately after the birth of the child, at Jane's request, Lord and Lady Ellenborough slept in separate rooms. At the same time, Jane fell in love with a dark and dashing Austrian diplomat, Prince Felix Schwarzenberg. The two began an affair. Had Jane played by the rules of her class and her time, this indiscretion would have hardly been noticed. Jane was unable to do this. She and her handsome prince were constantly in each other's company and they never missed an opportunity to steal away for sex. Soon her all-consuming passion for Schwarzenberg was the talk of London.

Lord Ellenborough, still entangled in parliamentary politics, ignored the situation for a long time. He was forced to act when Jane became pregnant with the Austrian's child. He filed for divorce and, at twenty-three, Jane left England in disgrace. The divorce, which took place in her absence, was made into a public spectacle by Ellenborough's many political enemies. By the time Lady Ellenborough settled in Paris she had become one of the most notorious women in Europe.

Jane and her prince continued their affair in Paris but Schwarzenberg's devotion was beginning to flag. He was a man unaccustomed to monogamous relationships and even Lady Ellenborough's world-famous sacrifice was not enough to hold him. As the affair cooled, Jane bore him another child. Then there was a dramatic break, the direct cause of which is unclear, though there were accusations of infidelity on both sides.

Lady Ellenborough moved to Munich where she caught the eye of King Ludwig of Bavaria. Ludwig had a weakness for pretty women and collected them in the same way he collected art. He may have slept with Jane, but their relationship was more a friendship than a love affair. The king showed great interest in the ebb and flow of Jane's relations with other men, particularly in her efforts to win back her Austrian prince and in her response to a Bavarian baron named Venningen.

According to the gossip mills of the time, King Ludwig had paired Jane with Venningen to conceal his own liaison with the infamous Englishwoman. The truth was more complex. Jane and Venningen had an affair that resulted in her third illegitimate child. Then, when she was twenty-six, they married. Venningen was completely infatuated with his new bride, but Jane was never more than fond of the agreeable baron.

The marriage was only two years old when Jane's weakness for dark-eyed noblemen reasserted itself. This time it was a Greek, Count Spiridion Theotoky. Jane's easy romance with King Ludwig suddenly ceased as she surrendered herself to the advances of this fiery count. When Venningen caught them together he demanded a duel and won, leaving the Greek wounded, but even though he had won the duel, the baron had to concede the girl. Jane left with Count Theotoky, had her fourth illegitimate child by him, and then married him after a divorce was secured from Venningen.

This third marriage, which began when she was thirty-six, was almost idyllic for the first two years. Then the Theotokys joined the court of the King of Greece in Athens and Theotoky began to have affairs. This breech of faith, along with the death of their son, killed the relationship from Jane's point of view. At forty-five, Jane found a new sexual fascination. She left her privileged home to live with the leader of a tribe of Albanian brigands.

The union of the noble Lady Ellenborough and this rough, unprincipled prince of thieves at first seemed unlikely, but Jane apparently found something refreshing and sexy in her earthy new beau. Never a fragile woman, she had no difficulty adjusting to the primitive accommodations of his mountain stronghold. She seemed ready to marry him; however, the decision was abandoned when she learned the bandit had attempted to rape one of her female servants. Instead of marrying, Jane went to Syria to buy horses.

It was during the journey, at the age of forty-six, that Jane met the final love of her life, a Bedouin sheik, twenty years her junior, named Medjuel el Mesrab. He was so impressed by this Englishwoman's beauty and her skill with horses that he gave up his three wives in order to marry her. Jane spent the rest of her long life with her sheik, and her diaries reveal that she was sexually active right up to her death at the age of seventy-four.

Other Examples

Princess Diana (*Princess of Wales*). *Born July 1, 1961* (*Celebrity Birthday Guide*).

Willie Nelson (*country singer and Farm-Aid activist*). *Born April 30, 1933* (*Celebrity Birthday Guide*).

If you have Mars in Virgo with Venus in Gemini you are . . . the Basically Brilliant Lover

You are the most skillful of all the Mars in Virgo Lovers. The techniques of sex and the mechanics of courtship and love never cease to fascinate you. Despite this fascination and your very serious appreciation for the physical joys of the erotic, your approach to sex remains cool, lighthearted, and sometimes even perfunctory. Anyone who feels they can keep you fascinated by just giving you a good time will be profoundly disappointed.

For you, relationships have to be based on mutual self-interest and on intellectual affinity. You're not the sort who waits around for love. As far as you're concerned, if you genuinely like a person there's no reason why you shouldn't also sleep with him or her. This attitude may seem cold and unromantic to the sentimentalists of the world, but you know that it is impossible to be a good Lover unless you can first be a good friend.

Case History

Henry VIII (*King of England—monarch remembered for his many wives*). *Born June 28, 1491, in London, England* (*Erickson 1980*).

At the age of seventeen Henry VIII married Katherine of Aragon (his brother's widow) to whom Henry had been engaged since he was thirteen. Even though Katherine had been living in England, the two saw little of each other. After the death of Henry's older brother his father had kept his new heir in virtual seclusion while he gave him a crash course in politics. The older Henry was an unrelenting taskmaster, plagued by paranoia and bouts of uncontrollable rage. When the old king's death finally freed Henry of his confinement, he entered his new role with a terrific thirst for fun. He did not have to marry Katherine, who was older than he and no great beauty, but the young monarch was not about to wait any longer to enjoy the privileges of adulthood.

From the very beginning Henry's sex life was complicated by the overwhelming political necessity that he produce a male heir. Even though in most ways Katherine was an exemplary spouse—devout, courageous, and well schooled in the responsibilities of her position—the fact that she was unable to bear him a son produced a rift in the marriage that could not easily be healed. Henry began his first extramarital affair two years into the marriage and he reacted with great anger when Katherine attempted to interfere. After that he had several mistresses; one bore Henry an illegitimate son. The long-suffering Katherine and her sole surviving daughter, Mary, were pushed further and further into the background of the king's very active life.

Henry never had to work very hard for his mistresses. The court was full of ambitious women, or ambitious men with wives and daughters, who were anxious to please him. Henry was, of course, wise to the game and he typically made sure that both his mistresses and their male sponsors were generously rewarded. One man who profited greatly from the king's weakness for willing young women was a commoner named Thomas Boleyn. While his eldest daughter Mary was Henry's primary mistress, Boleyn was made ambassador to France and given many other lucrative honors. When the king tired of Mary, Boleyn brought forth his second daughter, Anne.

Anne Boleyn was worldly, keenly intelligent, and much more interested in power than pleasure. More importantly, she was not afraid to gamble. When the thirty-five-year-old king first approached her, Anne refused him. At another time Henry might have moved on to a more docile woman, but Henry was ripe for a major change of direction. Katherine was now in her forties and she had entered menopause. The king was looking for a way out of the marriage and the haughty, beautiful, and (by all appearances) fertile Anne Boleyn came to represent his chance at a fresh start.

It was not uncommon for a noble of this era to have his or her marriage annulled by the pope. Henry's own sister had done so, as had some of his friends. Plus, Henry had the Bible on his side: a verse from Leviticus stated that a man should not marry the widow of his brother; however, Pope Clement VII, who was at the time fleeing German soldiers, found it politically expedient to refuse Henry's petition. Although negotiations continued it was soon apparent that the only way Henry would be able to put aside Katherine and marry Anne was to separate the Catholic Church in England from the authority of the pope in Rome. It was a drastic measure, certain to produce political and social upheaval, but Henry did it anyway.

Early in their relationship the willful Anne manipulated the king with an ease that shocked everyone. Her imperious nature had also alienated many people in the court, including her own relatives. The tables were turned after the marriage. Henry was quick to remind his new wife that she was a commoner whom he had raised up for one purpose: to give him a son. Even before the birth of their first child he was dallying with other women in the court. When this child turned out to be a girl, Henry withdrew from Anne just as he had withdrawn from Katherine.

When Anne's second pregnancy resulted in a miscarriage, her many enemies in the court went to work. The queen was accused of adultery and four men, one of who confessed under torture, were brought forth as her lovers. All were executed for treason. Henry remained surprisingly aloof from these events. He diverted himself with gay celebrations and coyly sought the sympathy of the pretty ladies of his court. One of these pretty young women had already caught his eye. Her name was Jane Seymour. She was demure and docile but, like Anne Boleyn, she at first refused to have sex with her amorous king. A few days after Anne's death, Henry married Jane.

Henry's short marriage to Jane Seymour gave him the son and heir he had wanted for so long. The king ordered a massive celebration of the event and, in the midst of the revelry, Jane died of an infection. Whatever grief Henry felt for her was masked by the happiness he found in his new son.

Henry was forty-six when Jane died and he was already feeling old and decrepit. He was in no hurry to marry again but he allowed his courtiers to bother themselves with various plans for a politically valuable, dynastic marriage. The only thing the king insisted on was that he would have a chance to see the prospective bride before the papers were signed. Henry still had an eye for pretty women.

Of course, not all the nominees were able to submit to Henry's personal inspection and, as was often done in those days before photography, the court painter was sometimes sent to record the likeness of a candidate. Thus, the court painter was sent to the little Germanic duchy of Cleves to paint a likeness of the duke of Cleves' sister, Anne. Unfortunately for Henry, his court painter was Hans Holbein, who was a great artist but not much of a reporter. Moreover, Holbein was German and liked the Duke and his sister. He used his talents to make the astoundingly plain Anne seem almost comely. Henry agreed to the marriage.

When Anne was shipped to England for the wedding, Henry immediately realized his misjudgment. She was so ugly and unappealing to the aging king that he found himself unable to consummate the marriage. However, Anne was a very practical woman. She agreed to an annulment of the marriage as long as she was given a house in England and an income. Henry found the businesslike approach to the impasse much to his liking and the arrangements were made.

Even before he had relieved himself of Anne of Cleves, Henry was considering a plump but fetching young woman named Catherine Howard. They were soon married and, for a time, Henry's youthful vigor returned. Henry quickly broke off their relationship when he learned that the skill Catherine displayed in his bed had been learned from a lover she had before their marriage. Then he had her tried for treason and executed when he learned that Catherine had seduced another man after their marriage.

Henry's last marriage came when he was fifty-two. His bride was the thirty-one-year-old Catherine Parr. Of all Henry's brides, Parr was the only one who shared his intellectual curiosity and deep interest in theological questions. She was also kind, patient, and attentive to the king's three children. Even with this wife Henry grew restive. He bemoaned the fact that she proved unable to conceive and her Protestant theology worried both the king and the conservative elements in his court. At one point Parr was on the verge of being arrested, but at the last minute she persuaded the king not to abandon her to her enemies. She was still the queen when Henry died at the age of fifty-five.

Other Examples

Charles Laughton (*English character actor who starred in the* The Hunchback of Notre Dame *and countless other films*). *Laughton was married to Elsa Lanchester, who was also a noted thespian. Their relationship seemed completely successful to the outside world. Not only did the two share career interests, but they collected art together, enjoyed literature, and were part of a glittering social circle; however, Laughton was a homosexual and though he had sexual relations with his wife early in the marriage, all his later contacts were with males. The marriage survived this problem because Laughton and Lanchester remained such close friends. When he reached his forties, Laughton went through a phase his wife termed a "change of life" and he began to fall in love with his male paramours. He had one relationship that lasted seven years—but he never gave up his marriage. Laughton died at the age of sixty-three. Born July 1, 1899 (Callow 1987).*

Joan Collins (*British actress*). *Born May 23, 1933 (Celebrity Birthday Guide).*

If you have Mars in Virgo with Venus in Cancer you are . . . the Basically Bewitching Lover

You are one Mars in Virgo Lover who needs more from sex than just a physical release. Feelings mean something to you and you are always looking for emotional security and reassurance. This sensitivity generally makes you one of the better Lovers of this type. Your love-making never stops with just the simple mechanics of sex. There is always intensity, commitment, and vulnerability to add spice and substance to your physical expertise.

No matter how serious about sex and love you appear to be, there is always part of you that finds all the sentiment rather laughable. You have very real emotional needs but you abhor being forced to admit to them. This conflict makes you a very unpredictable Lover—someone who changes from warm and cuddly to cool and critical without warning. It can also make you appear both ungrateful and insincere to the people about whom you care the most.

Case History

Amedeo Modigliani (Italian painter whose evocative nudes were deemed too sexy even for Paris). Born July 12, 1884, in Livorno, Italy (Rose 1991).

Modigliani was born into a wealthy and cultured Jewish family. They lived in one of the few cities in Europe where anti-Semitism was all but unheard of; however, this good fortune was not to last. While Amedeo was a small boy, several financial reverses ruined the Modigliani fortune. The youngster still managed to get an education and to inherit many of the patrician tastes of his ancestors, but he lived all his life under serious financial constraints.

Even as a teenager, Modigliani evinced a remarkable ability to attract women. Handsome and doe-eyed, he apparently never lacked for feminine companionship as a student, though none of his adolescent affairs have been documented. His most significant seduction had nothing to do with sex. After he had completed his artistic education in Italy, Amedeo wanted to go to Paris. Using all his charm, he persuaded his formidable mother to put aside both her monetary concerns and desire to hold on to her favorite son and give Amedeo the money he needed to travel to France.

Modigliani reached Paris at twenty-one. He quickly made the acquaintance of several of the rising young artists who lived in Montmatre, including Picasso. But Modigliani was not a joiner and stayed clear of the groups, styles, and "isms" that dominated art of the time. This independence in no way helped his sales and the young painter was soon reduced to extreme poverty. He lived in rundown shacks and cheap hotel rooms and sold his drawings in cafes for whatever he could get. Modigliani's situation was further endangered by his taste for various intoxicants including wine, absinthe, and hashish.

Even Modigliani's dire poverty and frequent drunkenness were not enough to curtail his love life. His ability to find women to pose and sleep with him for free amazed his fellow artists. As the years passed, the handsome Italian built an impressive reputation as a lover of women and as the consummate bohemian.

Modigliani became the subject of many anecdotes. He was a genuine admirer of women, and a sensitive, courteous, yet wildly sensual companion. One woman reported how she watched in bemused admiration as Modigliani and his girl friend of the moment danced naked beneath a full moon in the middle of the city. In another anecdote, Modigliani's lover turned out to be under the protection of a wealthy lawyer. When the attorney learned he was sharing a mistress with a penniless painter he demanded a confrontation. The two men met in a cafe but, instead of coming to blows, Modigliani insisted his competitor join him in toasting the considerable charms of their mutual paramour. By the end of the evening, the jealous protector had purchased one of the artist's nude portraits of the woman.

Other stories reveal another side of the artist's nature—his addiction to alcohol and drugs. Sober Modigliani was a quiet, even shy, man who read philosophy and recited Dante from memory. When he was intoxicated, however, Modigliani was loud, obnoxious, and often crude. He could be the life of the party or he could also ruin an evening with his belligerent arrogance. Beatrice Hastings summed up Modigliani's unpredictable nature by saying he was both "a pig and a pearl."

Modigliani was thirty when he began his affair with Hastings. She was a journalist and a self-consciously modern woman who prided herself on both her sexual freedom and her independence. Of all the women Modigliani loved, she was probably the one who best matched him intellectually, but intellectual interests did not play a large role in their relationship. Sex and a mutual fascination with art and the nightlife of Paris did.

One overriding factor doomed Modigliani's relationship with Hastings from the start: he needed a woman who would mother him and she had not an ounce of maternal feeling. After three stormy years, the love affair was over and Modigliani began looking for a quieter companion. He quickly found one in a seventeen-year-old named Jeanne Hebuterne.

Hebuterne was a talented art student when she met the notorious Modigliani. She fell in love with him immediately, much to the displeasure of her bourgeois family. She was a beautiful woman, but so quiet and passive that many men did not notice her. Modigliani did, and by the time he turned thirty-three, he and the teenage beauty had set up housekeeping.

For friends who knew Modigliani as the great bohemian, this new domesticated Modigliani was a shock. Most were glad to see that the painter had acquired a mistress who would come to the cafes and carry him home after one of his frequent drunks. Modigliani's behavior when he was intoxicated had not improved. If anything, he became more violent and abusive as he got older. Hebuterne bore this, their poverty, and many other trials with motherly patience. She took care of the drunken artist and (perhaps more importantly) she posed for him.

Not long after he began his relationship with Hebuterne, Modigliani had an important exhibition of his nudes and portraits. The model for most of the nudes was Jeanne and the dealer was so impressed with them that he hung one of the paintings in the window of the shop. Unfortunately, when the police saw the picture they felt compelled to shut down the exhibition. It was claimed that the paintings were deemed indecent because Modigliani painted his nudes with pubic hair. The raw sensuality of these paintings goes far beyond this one detail. His paintings of Jeanne are among the most erotic depictions of the female body in the history of art.

Meanwhile, Modigliani's health was beginning to fail. His friends were now less alarmed at his drinking than by the amount of blood he coughed up and by his refusal to seek medical help. Hebuterne gave birth to a daughter. Even though the child had to be placed in foster care, Modigliani was very proud of her. During the winter of his thirty-fifth year, the painter's condition deteriorated rapidly and he died of tuberculosis. Jeanne Hebuterne, pregnant with Modigliani's second child, committed suicide a few days later.

Other Examples

Ernest Hemingway (*macho American writer who mastered every manly enterprise except the art of living with a woman). Born July 21, 1899 (Celebrity Birthday Guide).*

Napoleon Bonaparte (*French military leader and emperor who has been alternately accused of being oversexed and undersexed). Born August 15, 1769 (Encyclopedia Britannica 1997, Vol. 8).*

If you have Mars in Virgo with Venus in Leo you are … the Basically Exuberant Lover

You are a dreamer—a sexual perfectionist always searching for a better and more powerful erotic experience. This doesn't mean you can't have quick, expedient sex. You approach each sexual encounter with such optimism that even the most insignificant erotic moment can have the potential for greatness. Your enthusiasm for sex is quite infectious. You typically have little trouble finding people willing to accompany you on your quest for the ultimate pleasure. But no matter how grand your ideals become, you never lose your essential earthiness.

Control is also very important to you and, even though you're always very polite about it, you typically dominate relationships. It's not so much that you need to be the boss. You just have a clearer vision of where the relationship is going and what needs to be done. You take charge because that's what's in the best interest of your partner. How can you hope to make them perfectly happy if they don't follow your direction?

Case History

Marie Bonaparte (*princess who became a psychoanalyst in order to cure her own frigidity*).
Born July 2, 1882, in Paris, France (Bertin 1982).

Shortly after Marie Bonaparte's birth, her mother died, leaving the infant a great fortune. This
money was of little interest to Marie's father, a self-involved intellectual who paid as little heed
to practical affairs as he did to his daughter. It did matter a great deal to his mother. Marie
later described her grandmother, who dominated the girl's childhood, as a "phallic" woman.

Marie's childhood was exceptionally sheltered, partly because of the royal pretensions of
her family and partly because her Bonaparte relatives wanted control of her wealth. By the
time she was sixteen, Marie was a thoroughly frustrated and insecure girl who suffered from
various illnesses (some of them psychosomatic). At this point an older man, her father's secretary, seduced her. The inexperienced and eager Marie was completely captivated by his
apparent passion for her. It didn't even bother her that the man's wife seemed ready to facilitate the affair. Marie wrote passionate letters to him and sent him a lock of her hair with an
amorous declaration attached. Then, when it was far too late, she realized that the man and
his wife intended to use these items to blackmail her.

Between the ages of eighteen to twenty-one, Marie sent this man money borrowed from
an understanding uncle in order to keep the matter a secret. Then, when she obtained full
control of her inheritance, the greedy blackmailer upped the ante. There was no choice but
to bring her father and lawyers into the affair. A reasonable payoff was arranged but Marie,
deeply shaken and stripped of her self-esteem, fell completely under the power of her distant
father and crafty grandmother.

The issue at this point in her life was to find a suitable husband. For the next four years,
suitors were brought to the Bonaparte's home, but Marie, convinced that she was unattractive, assumed that these men were only interested in her money. Then, when she was twenty-
five, a young man who obviously had no need for her fortune asked for Marie's hand. He was
Prince George, second son of King George I of Greece. He was tall, blond, and connected by
blood to the ruling families of England, Russia, and Germany. Marie immediately liked him
and they were married.

Prince George was a man who took his duty to his family and his country very seriously. Unfortunately, Marie was to learn on her wedding night that it was that devotion to duty
and not sexual attraction that brought him to her bed. After they had sex he told her it had
been as awful for him as he was sure it had been for her. The marriage produced two children and Marie maintained a deep respect and affection for her husband, but their sex life
was minimal.

Shortly after the birth of her first child when she was twenty-six, Bonaparte began to have affairs. At first these affairs were with various underlings. They were conducted with extreme secrecy, since she had no wish to embarrass her esteemed husband, but the sex remained cordial and uncomplicated. When she was thirty-one, Bonaparte fell in love with Aristide Briand, a powerful political figure in France. Briand was an older man who was well acquainted with the joys of clandestine love, but his affection for Marie was of a different order. The couple did not have sex for the first two years of their liaison. Bonaparte felt that having sex with a man she loved would be a true betrayal of her husband. For sex, she continued her relationship with one of her palace boyfriends.

The love affair of Bonaparte and Briand was conducted in the midst of the most distracting circumstances imaginable. World War I was raging and Briand was Prime Minister of France. The fact that he was in love with the wife of a Greek prince at a time when Greece was leaning toward an alliance with France's enemies was a matter of great concern. The first time they attempted to have sex, Briand was impotent. Bonaparte immediately assumed that it was an indication of her lack of sexual allure, forgetting the position in which her lover had been placed. Later attempts prove more successful but the political turmoil of the period continued to bother the couple.

Oddly enough, after the war was over, Briand's interest in Bonaparte began to wane. The heated and dangerous love affair was slowly reduced to a sexual friendship. By the time she was forty, Bonaparte had moved on to a new lover—a friend of the family whose identity she kept secret. Bonaparte referred to him as the "friend." Their relationship had a casual, unforced quality; however, Bonaparte was enamored enough with her new love to be jealous of his sexual relationship with his wife. She objected when her "friend" tried to control the relationship and she called him a sadist. But despite their differences and the constraint under which their met, Bonaparte and her secret lover remained devoted to each other for many years.

One important link between Bonaparte and her lover was the fact that she could talk openly to him about her inability to obtain an orgasm during sex. In the course of seeking a medical solution for this problem, she discovered Sigmund Freud and psychoanalysis. Bonaparte became an enthusiastic supporter of the new science. She went through analysis with Freud himself and became a close friend to the aging doctor. Soon Bonaparte, who had wanted to become a doctor since childhood, was a practicing psychoanalyst and writing papers on psychological problems. In particular, she was interested in female sexuality.

After spending a lifetime conducting her sex life in secret, Bonaparte embraced the sexual frankness of psychoanalysis with great enthusiasm. She immediately accepted Freud's diagnosis that she was a latent homosexual and his theory that she had witnessed her servants having sex while she was a small child. After a time she began to develop her own ideas about female sexuality. She felt that it was the masculine component in a woman's nature that facilitated her enjoyment of sex. Her minor disagreements with Freud's theories in no way damaged their relationship. Bonaparte and her money were instrumental in rescuing Freud from the Nazis.

Despite Bonaparte's enthusiasm for Freud's methods, they never cured her frigidity. She concluded that her problems were physical rather than psychological and submitted to three operations to correct the problem. None of them worked. Meanwhile, during her forties and fifties, Bonaparte continued to see her "friend" and she also enjoyed affairs with other (usually much younger) psychoanalysts. Her inability to have orgasms never seemed to limit her ability to enjoy sex.

By the time she reached her sixties, however, the "friend" had died. Bonaparte reluctantly relinquished her personal sex life, even while she was beginning to write extensively about the sex lives of others. Still, like a good Freudian, she continued to record her sexual dreams right up until her death at eighty.

Another Example

Sylvester Stallone (movie star). Born July 6, 1946 (Celebrity Birthday Guide).

If you have Mars in Virgo with Venus in Virgo you are . . . the Most Basic Lover

There is a clarity and directness about your sexuality that is unique and, at your best moments, utterly charming. You always know exactly what you want from sex and you will waste no time or ceremony in getting it. Occasionally your straightforward approach makes you seem brusque and calculating. But you can also be a very warm and gentle Lover capable of the most amazing acts of kindness and service.

The main problem in your sexual makeup is your lack of ambition. You like convenience in your sexual diet. All too often this causes you to pass up quality in loving for the sake of accessibility. It's not that you lack the energy. Your physical drives are quite impressive. You just need to find the sense of purpose and the imagination necessary to push past a prepackaged, microwaved sex life and move on to the gourmet fare you deserve.

Case History

Mae West (sultry screen star whose uninhibited approach to sex made her the bane of all censors). Born August 17, 1893, in Brooklyn, New York (Eells 1982; Hamilton 1995).

From the moment she first stepped on stage at the age of seven and demanded her spotlight, Mae West made no excuses and offered no apologies for her essential egotism. The child of poor immigrant parents, she never doubted she was destined to succeed.

West had her first sexual experience at the age of twelve but this precocious beginning in no way traumatized her. West never saw sex as anything but pure (and occasionally profitable) fun. Even within the rootless show business community of vaudeville, her teenage antics became the object of derision and alarm. The other players, particularly those from middle-class backgrounds, found Mae's blatant sexual adventurism and working-class vulgarity crude and unseemly. This disapproval only made West bolder and more uninhibited.

When West was eighteen, she allowed herself to be talked into marriage in a rare moment of weakness. An older actress convinced her that a marriage of convenience to her stage partner Frank Wallace would at least allow West a measure of respectability. Immediately after the wedding West decided that even a hint of respectability was too much for her. She locked her unfortunate hubby in their hotel room and went out for a night on the town alone. Later West returned to her parent's home and made Wallace swear to keep the wedding a secret. She never gave another thought to her abortive marriage until twenty-five years later when Wallace attempted to make some money from the affair and sued her for support. Only then did West acknowledge her wedding long enough to obtain a divorce.

During her early twenties West forged a career in vaudeville using suggestive dancing, bawdy songs, and naughty banter. The act was sufficient to gain her some attention, but it never fared well with the critics and never brought her the stardom she craved. Vaudeville at the time was aspiring to be "clean" family entertainment and West's swinging hips and thoroughly adult asides were not in keeping with the trend. By the time she was twenty-four West ceased to tour the vaudeville circuits. For a time, despite her later denial, she probably performed in burlesque houses. Here she would have found a sympathetic audience for her unrefined eroticism but neither the prestige nor the money she wanted.

West was hardly finished. When she was thirty-three she obtained money from two male backers to stage a play on Broadway, a play written by Mae West for Mae West. Titled *Sex*, the show centered on the activities of a prostitute played by West. It featured plenty of sexy jokes and a fairly realistic depiction of the criminal underworld. The critics not only panned it, they universally declared the play a moral outrage. This didn't keep people out of the theater, however, and *Sex* became the hit of the season.

West followed *Sex* with another raunchy comedy featuring female impersonators. This show got her jailed as a pornographer. Then West succeeded again with a more subdued melodrama set in the 1890s. It soon became obvious that despite the best efforts of the law and theater critics, West's sensational and sexually daring shows were going to make money.

It took the crash of the stock market in 1929 to put an end to West's golden run on Broadway, but by this time she had turned her attention to Hollywood.

An old acquaintance named George Raft recommended West for a small part in one of his movies. No one expected much out of the thirty-nine-year-old vamp, but West rewrote her part of the script and proceeded to steal the show. Over the next two years she made two immensely popular movies that firmly established her as a major star. The Hollywood censors, even though they had certainly been forewarned, were totally unable to deal with West's skill at slipping sexual innuendo into every line she delivered and every gesture she made.

The more successful West became, the more determined the censors were to clean up her movies. West was forced to compromise, to stop playing prostitutes and abandon the low-life underworld settings that had always been a key element in her shows. The result was a series of bad movies and a sudden fall from grace. When West was forty-five her contract with Paramount Studios was dropped and she appeared in only two films during the next five years. After that she was abandoned by Hollywood altogether.

It was not just Mae West's sexiness that ran afoul of the prudes of her day, it was also her unrefined earthiness and working-class directness. In her youth West had used her uncomplicated, physical approach to sex to shock people who might have thought themselves better than she. As an adult she used the same tactic to shock and tantalize her audience. West was not a reformer or a crusader. She pushed the moral restrictions of her day because they got in her way and because doing so made her very rich.

Despite her flamboyant public life, Mae West's private life was private. She never dated public figures or famous actors. When people asked her personal questions she hardly ever answered with the truth. After her short-lived marriage to Wallace, West had a long series of boyfriends. These men were typically chosen for their looks and physical prowess. She liked men with broad muscular bodies and rugged masculine faces—boxers and wrestlers. These various "managers" and "bodyguards" looked after the increasingly affluent West, and she looked after them. Sometimes the only indication of a man's rise to favored boyfriend was the sudden upgrade of his wardrobe.

Even though she was generally very kind to her men friends, West felt no need to be faithful. West liked variety and throughout her life she was prone to proposition any man who happened to catch her eye. Not every man responded to this direct approach, but rejections never deterred her from trying again. West insisted on having sex with somebody at least once a day and continued insisting on this at least into her sixties. At this point a bodybuilder named Paul Novak became the primary man in West's life. He held that position longer than anyone, remaining her devoted companion until she died at the age of eighty-six.

Another Example

Guy de Maupassant (French writer who was probably as well known in his own time for his erotic adventures as for his novels and short stories). Handsome and athletic, Maupassant was sexually active by the time he was sixteen and was a hardened womanizer long before he rose to fame as a writer. His physical prowess in bed and his insatiable appetite for sex became a matter of legend. He had many affairs with women of his own class but never lost his fondness for prostitutes and girls from the streets. A vocal opponent of marriage, he enjoyed making disparaging remarks about wives and women in general; however, Maupassant portrayed women with great sympathy and showed an intimate understanding of both the psychological and physical needs of the female sex in his fiction. At twenty-eight, Maupassant was diagnosed with syphilis, but the diagnosis only made him more profligate instead of curtailing his sexual activity. By his late thirties, he was going mad. He died in a mental institution at forty-one. Born August 5, 1850 (Wallace 1981).

If you have Mars in Virgo with Venus in Libra you are . . . the Basically Sociable Lover

You differ from most Mars in Virgo Lovers because you are just as interested in courtship as you are in the sex act itself. You enjoy the romantic games and flirtatious jousts that go along with sexual arousal. You like to watch the way that people react in sexual situations—the way desire muddles thinking and alters behavior (sometimes even your own.) Unlike most Mars in Virgo Lovers, you tend to avoid approaching sex directly. You are one of the few Lovers of this type who can actually be embarrassed by the erotic.

Your appreciation for sex as social play makes you one of the most agreeable Mars in Virgo Lovers—a sensual and earthy Lover who is willing to wait. There is one problem with you and this sexual game playing: you're too good at it. The cool practicality of Mars in Virgo allows you to play these games and go through all the motions of love and romance without ever surrendering yourself to passion. Since that surrender is what these games are about, winning in this way is the same thing as losing.

Case History

Georgia O'Keeffe (American modernist painter noted for her organic, abstraction-based images from the American Southwest). Born November 15, 1887, in Sun Prairie, Wisconsin (Robinson 1989; Hogrefe 1992).

During O'Keeffe's childhood her father owned a prosperous dairy farm. She was sent to private schools where she received her first education in art. As she grew older, her father's mismanagement brought a steady decline in the family fortunes, and she had to support herself through teaching in her adulthood.

Apparently, O'Keeffe was slow to develop sexually. At eighteen she found the nude male models in her drawing class extremely distressing. She had her first beau at twenty while studying in New York City, but the relationship was apparently not sexual. By all appearances her first sexual experience came when she was twenty-eight and teaching in South Carolina. A boyfriend came to visit her over the Thanksgiving break and it appears that they slept together.

It is difficult to know exactly when O'Keeffe lost her virginity because, despite her plainspoken directness in other areas on her life, she tended to equivocate with regard to sex. She avoided any reference to sexual activity in her correspondence. She seems to have used "kissing" as a euphemism for more intimate action. Even later in life O'Keeffe was known to bristle when critics saw penises and vaginas in her abstract paintings. O'Keeffe was not a prude. In certain contexts she spoke about sex with brazen authority. In other contexts, however, it embarrassed her.

At about the same time as her first sexual experience, O'Keeffe began to create abstract drawing replete with phallic eroticism. A friend in New York showed these drawings to the noted photographer, gallery owner, and advocate of modern art, Alfred Stieglitz. Stieglitz was so impressed that he exhibited the works. A short time later, when O'Keeffe came to New York to protest the exhibition, Stieglitz became both her agent and lover.

The necessity of making a living meant that O'Keeffe could not remain in New York for long. She found another teaching job in Texas. Stieglitz continued to exhibit her work but his relationship with O'Keeffe was still ambiguous. For one thing, while she was still in New York, O'Keeffe began an affair with Stieglitz's protégé, Paul Strand. Concerned about her health and career, Stieglitz sent Strand to Texas to look after O'Keeffe. Strand, who was very much in love with the painter, was surprised to find O'Keeffe intimately involved with another woman when he arrived. This lesbian affair may not have been O'Keeffe's only conquest in Texas. She shocked the matrons of her school by boldly taking a brawny student up to her room.

By the time she was thirty, O'Keeffe was back in New York and completely under the thrall of Stieglitz. Stieglitz was twenty-three years older than O'Keeffe. He was a confident and accomplished man, though none of his accomplishments, either in photography or art, had netted him much worldly success. Stieglitz was also married, and over the next several months O'Keeffe calmly watched as he struggled with his conflicting obligations.

Thanks to Stieglitz, O'Keeffe no longer had to worry about earning a living and could concentrate solely on her work. In exchange for this support O'Keeffe became Stieglitz's chief model. He took a long series of portraits and nudes of her that are ample evidence of the degree of his sexual infatuation. When Stieglitz exhibited these photographs, many of which were frankly erotic, O'Keeffe was demonstratively uncomfortable with the exposure of her body and her sexuality, but she did nothing to stop the exhibition.

Due to the difficulty Stieglitz had in leaving his first marriage, he was not ready to marry O'Keeffe until she was thirty-seven and he was sixty. O'Keeffe agreed to the ceremony reluctantly, seeing little advantage in sanctifying their arrangement. She had already had at least one affair (with novelist Jean Toomer), and Steiglitz's sexual fascination had since moved to other women. About a year after their marriage, a twenty-one-year-old woman named Dorothy Norman entered Stieglitz's life. She adored the aging photographer with an unqualified zeal and soon became his assistant and lover. O'Keeffe was unhappy with this turn of events but she had other options and patrons. A wealthy advocate of modernism named Mabel Dodge Luhan had offered her a studio in Taos, New Mexico.

O'Keeffe was forty when she went to New Mexico and realized that she had found a home. Not only was she drawn to the stark landscape and the harsh light but, at least at first, she thrived in the atmosphere of sexual tension and intrigue that surrounded Mabel Dodge Luhan. O'Keeffe traveled to Taos with Beck Strand, who had succeeded her as the primary model of Stieglitz's erotic photographs. Beck was also the wife of O'Keeffe past lover, Paul Strand. While in Taos the two women enjoyed sunbathing and swimming in the nude together and apparently became lovers. At the same time, O'Keeffe was drawing close to the Mabel, who made a hobby of collecting talented people.

The plot thickened when Mabel became ill and returned to New York for an operation. Mabel was extremely protective of her Native American husband Tony Luhan. Luhan was a large, soulful man who was very much attached to his flamboyant wife. O'Keeffe began to keep company with Tony and wrote letters to Mabel telling her what a fine man her husband was and that she had no business being so selfish with his charms. It is unlikely the ailing Mabel found any comfort in these cruel and divisive missives.

O'Keeffe's relationship with Stieglitz was not over, even though they no longer were lovers. She continued to spend time at his family's summer home in Maine and he continued to exhibit and sell her paintings. O'Keeffe made no secret of how strongly she disapproved of the elderly photographer's dependency upon Dorothy Norman. But by the time O'Keeffe was fifty-eight and Stieglitz died, she had established an almost identical relationship with a young female photographer who acted as her personal attendant in Taos.

After Stieglitz's death, the increasingly wealthy and irascible O'Keeffe had several relationships. She often found herself surrounded by people who were overwhelmed by her fame and her talent. She treated them accordingly, and even referred to these people as her slaves. She was more generous with people who had no concept of her fame. She became the protector of various young toughs who hung around her ranch. Then, when she was in her eighties, O'Keeffe took in a wandering potter named Juan Hamilton. Some saw Hamilton as an interloper and an opportunist, but he remained with O'Keeffe until she died at ninety-eight.

Another Example

Mary Shelley *(author of* Frankenstein *and wife of the poet Percy Shelley). Born August 30, 1797 (Walling 1972)*

Will Smith *(American actor and singer). Born September 25, 1968 (Celebrity Birthday Guide).*

If you have Mars in Virgo with Venus in Scorpio you are … the Basically Scandalous Lover

You are the sexiest Mars in Virgo Lover, one who knows that proper lovemaking is much more than just technique. Your sensuality runs deep; it touches the psychological roots of pleasure as well as the nerve endings. You are always alert to your partner's feelings and moods. You have a capacity for slow seduction that is rare in this type; however, it is not how good you are that makes you such a desirable partner—it's how bad you can be.

Sex is never quite as simple for you as it is for most Mars in Virgo Lovers because when you break down sex to its most elemental parts what you find is power. You don't have to have power over your partner in order to enjoy sex but, with your irresistible sexual allure and your cool-headed approach to passion, it's almost too easy for you to get that kind of physical power and emotional control. The only thing that is open to question is: how are you going to use it?

Case History

Norman Douglas *(British writer famous for his breezy novels and shameless hedonism). Born around midnight on December 8, 1868, in Falkenhorst, Austria (Holloway 1976).*

Douglas's father was an Englishman who had inherited a large manufacturing concern in Austria. He died in a mountaineering accident when Douglas was a small child. With his mother distracted by a love affair with a local artist, Douglas grew up with very little discipline. When his strict Scottish grandmother tried to impose her will over him, he attacked her with a stick.

Douglas was an intelligent youth. With the backing of his wealthy family he avidly pursued his interest in several branches of natural science while attending schools in England and Germany. At the age of twenty-three he entered the British Foreign Service and was given a diplomatic post in Russia. After two years he left this post and turned his active mind toward literature.

At the same time that he was assembling this wide-ranging resumé, Douglas was also gathering a great deal of experience as a lover of women. Tall, handsome, and totally uninhibited, he began having affairs in his teens. His paramours ranged from women of his own class to working-class girls to prostitutes. Douglas used brothels during his student days but later he engaged the services of professional procurers to assure a steady supply of cheap sex.

When he recounted these affairs later in life, Douglas tended to emphasize his own emotional aloofness. He claimed that whenever he felt himself getting serious about a woman, he promptly "put a slice of sea" between himself and the object of his desire until his ardor for her passed. This technique worked nicely until he reached St. Petersburg. Here, while he was serving in the British Embassy, he reached the climax of his heterosexual life. He was juggling affairs with two highborn Russian women when one of them became pregnant. The woman's rank was such that Douglas feared that his life would be in immediate danger once their affair became known. He resigned his post and fled Russia at top speed.

Douglas had developed a love for Italy during his youth, so he retreated to Naples where he bought a house. He had vague plans of working with a zoologist in the area, but Douglas' primary aim was to have fun. He quickly became familiar with the local procurer who kept Douglas supplied with virgins. (Douglas feared venereal disease after being infected once in his early twenties.) One of these virgins had a mischievous brother that Douglas found even more attractive than the girl. This boy became Douglas' first homosexual lover.

Shortly after this incident, Douglas married his first cousin, Elsa FitzGibbon. Douglas later claimed he married only because he was bored with sex. He also claimed that once he learned the joys of sex with boys, he no longer cared for women. Despite these claims, Elsa was pregnant when she and Douglas eloped. She later bore the author a second child.

Early in the marriage Douglas treated his wife with great affection but the relationship quickly deteriorated, particularly after Douglas settled his family in Naples and explored a new interest in pederasty. The only surprise was that it was Elsa's admission of adultery that proved to be the grounds for their divorce. Meanwhile, Douglas published his first book of stories and determined to establish himself as a writer. He also discovered the island of Capri, which would be his home for the next ten years and the place most often associated with his name.

Capri had long been a haven for homosexuals and other northern European outcasts but, in order to keep the moral advantage during his protracted divorce, Douglas was at first forced to maintain a degree of discretion. During his early days on Capri he even had his two sons with him. Douglas was nearly forty by the time the divorce was final and he felt truly free to live as he wanted. He began openly cohabiting with a "laughing" local boy named Amitrano, who was the first in a long series of youthful paramours who would share his life.

At various times during his fifties, Douglas kept company with other male homosexuals, first a writer named Maurice Magnus and then an Italian publisher named Pino Orioli. These men were not so much his lovers as they were hunting partners. With one of these gentlemen, Douglas searched for boys in the towns and countryside of Italy. Once he and Orioli purchased a gross of cheap metal noisemakers which they passed out to droves of eager children.

Meanwhile, Douglas was becoming a popular author noted for his easy, conversational prose and his evocative descriptions of the warm, sunny places he loved so well. He also published a book of scandalous limericks and books on aphrodisiacs which, though far less popular, established Douglas' reputation as a world-class hedonist. Despite his seemingly single-minded search for pleasure, Douglas' life was often quite miserable. His success as a writer never gave him the income his lifestyle required. During the last half of his life Douglas was often on the edge of starvation and suffered bitterly from various health problems.

Old age and poor health never lessened Douglas' appetite for pleasure. Even though he complained of being "all but impotent," the old writer was still pursuing boys even in his last years. When he was eighty-three and beset by constant pain, Douglas committed his final act of hedonism. He took an intentional overdose of painkillers and died.

Other Examples

Charles Manson (mass murderer). Born November 12, 1934 (Bugliosi 1974).

Brad Pitt (American actor). Born December 18, 1964 (Celebrity Birthday Guide).

If you have Mars in Virgo with Venus in Sagittarius you are … the Basically Bountiful Lover

You are an impulsive Lover whose approach to sex is so straightforward and optimistic that you often find yourself misunderstood. People take you for an irrepressible bundle of pure animal passion and proceed to hide the breakables when you get in the mood for love. In reality you are one of the most idealistic Mars in Virgo Lovers. You believe sex has a higher, more spiritual purpose. It's just that these higher regions of loving can only be reached after a very energetic exploration of the more basic levels.

Your sexual idealism can be either a great strength or a great weakness, depending on how you use it. On the positive side, it can help you see beyond the immediacy of your physical drives and allows you to apply your energies toward establishing an enduring and satisfying relationship. On the negative side, this same idealism can cause you to segregate sex from love, and force you into the disastrous assumption that the person who satisfies your physical needs cannot answer your need for love.

Case History

Auguste Rodin *(French sculptor whose sensuous realism revolutionized the art of sculpture in the late nineteenth and early twentieth centuries). Born November 12, 1840, in Paris, France (Grunfeld 1987).*

The Rodin family had been a family of weavers for generations but Auguste was to take a different direction. He wanted to be a sculptor. His family could only afford to send him to a trade school for decorative sculptors. This school was separate from the more esteemed school that trained the fine artists. Still, the youngster harbored dreams of making statues like those of Michelangelo. He was encouraged in these ambitions by his older sister, Maria, with whom he was particularly close. Maria became a nun. When Rodin was twenty-two, she suddenly died. Rodin was overcome with grief.

While Rodin continued to honor the memory of his sister, he shied away from relationships with other women. He later admitted that he held women in contempt at this point in his life. At the age of twenty-four his attitude changed when he hired a young woman of peasant stock named Rose Beuret to model for him and help in his studio. He and Rose soon became lovers. They remained companions for the rest of their lives.

When describing Beuret years later, Rodin claimed he was attracted by her "physical vigor" and by her "lovely, frank, decisive, masculine charm." He made use of her lovely body in countless sculptures since, in these early years, she was the only model he could afford. He made use of her physical vigor in many ways as well: keeping his clay models damp in dry weather, cooking and cleaning for him, and lugging his ornamental stone sculptures around the city to prospective patrons. There was little evidence of warmth or affection in the relationship. Some of Rodin's friends felt the sculptor only keep Beuret around for sex and as a model. He apparently gave no thought to marrying Beuret even when she became pregnant with his son. Rodin supported the child but refused to be officially declared his father.

Early in their relationship Rodin apparently made some effort to dominate Beuret. She later jokingly reminded him of how he had once called her a "slut" and demanded she submit to him. Such outbursts seem to have been rare and rather unnecessary. The docile Beuret remained absolutely devoted to Rodin even though he often treated her more like a servant than a mistress. For his part, Rodin appears to have remained faithful to Beuret, at least for the first eighteen years of their relationship. Of course, during much of this period, Rodin was working fifteen hours a day, making ornamental sculptures during the day for money and working on his own artwork at night. Such a physically taxing schedule left little energy for sexual adventures.

But by the time Rodin was forty-two he was becoming recognized for his supreme skill and originality as an artist. At this point he met a beautiful young artist named Camille Claudel. Claudel was nothing like Beuret. She was bright and educated, aggressive and self-confident. She came to Rodin as a student, but quickly advanced to become both his assistant and lover. It is apparent that Rodin saw her as something more than a sex partner. She had a fiery idealism about art that no doubt reminded him of the dreams of his own youth. It is also possible that Rodin saw in Claudel a reflection of his beloved sister with whom he had once shared those dreams.

Even though she was twenty years younger than the great sculptor, in many ways Claudel dominated their relationship. Such was his determination not to lose her that Rodin was often reduced to the role of a stumbling suitor. His physical fascination for her quickly became evident in the writhing, highly erotic figures he was sculpting for the work that would become known as the *Gates of Hell*. Despite the hold Claudel had over her middle-aged lover, she was still unable to get him to give up Beuret. Perhaps more importantly, she was unable to stop him from dallying with other young admirers who wandered into his studio. The fifteen-hour days were a thing of the past. Now Rodin had plenty of time and energy to devote to these women.

After several years of struggling to hold on to Rodin, the proud Claudel finally surrendered. She shut her mentor completely out of her life and pursued her own career. Meanwhile, Rodin continued to develop his reputation as an irrepressible satyr—a sexual "force of nature." Even his libertine friends were shocked by the artist's seemingly uncontrollable lusts, mostly because Rodin never bothered with the flirtatious games of a typical womanizer. When he wanted a woman, he approached her directly. Either he stared at her until she responded (or fled), or he simply reached out and grabbed the object of his desire. Often women who posed for him were shocked when the nearsighted artist shifted his ever-moving, ever-caressing hands from the clay to their flesh.

The truest expression of Rodin's sensuality remained his sculpture. He gave a sense of being touched and molded to his sculptures. Even when cast in bronze, their surfaces have the quality of flesh. His erotically posed figures remained highly controversial long after he had risen to almost godlike stature among the artists of his day. Many critics considered Rodin a maudlin sensualist with an unhealthy fixation on sex and spread-eagled women. Rodin offered no apologies for his preference for nudes, and his figures only became more daring and sexual as he aged.

Rodin's constant womanizing changed his relationship with Beuret. Her jealous rages humbled Rodin and caused him to treat her with a degree of sweetness and caution. She remained his dutiful servant who got up at 5:30 each morning to fix his breakfast and warm his smock, but more than once the tables were turned and it was Rodin who was on his knees before Beuret, begging her not to leave him. Despite his rampant infidelity, Rodin seems to have truly needed Beuret's presence in his life.

In his sixties Rodin became involved with an English painter in her twenties named Gwen John, another artistic idealist who occasionally had one of her girl friends join them in bed. Later an American socialite tried to bully her way into primacy in the old artist's life. Despite these women and many more, Rodin held on to Beuret. When Beuret was sick and near death, Rodin finally married her. A few months later he died at the age of seventy-seven.

If you have Mars in Virgo with Venus in Capricorn you are . . . the Basically Prudent Lover

You like sex to serve a purpose. It's not that you can't appreciate physical pleasure for its own sake. The fact is that you are a very sensual Lover. You are not likely to resist anything that makes your body feel better, but your level of excitement always goes up a notch when your sex play fits into a larger, nonsexual context. You want something out of sex you can use, something to make that expenditure of energy worthwhile.

At times, your search for sex with a payoff makes you seem hard and self-serving. Your judgement can be harsh of people and relationships that are not useful to you. But once you find a relationship that serves your overall needs, you are willing to labor long and hard to maintain it. Your approach to sex may lack much in terms of romance, but you can more than make up the difference with your impressive work ethic.

Case History

Clark Gable (film star who was considered the epitome of masculine charm by a whole genera-
tion of American women). Born February 1, 1901, in Meadville, Pennsylvania (Tornabene
1976).

Gable's father worked in the oil fields. A hard-drinking, hard-living man, he pushed his son to be masculine and tough. Gable's mother died when he was a year old. He was raised by his stepmother, whom he regarded with a lot of affection but who never took the place of his real mother.

By his late teens Gable had dropped out of school and lived on his own. His father's lessons in toughness and self-reliance had taken all too well. Tall and brawny, the young man had no problem finding work, but the kind of labor he found most congenial had nothing to do with the sweaty, he-man example his father had set. Gable developed a fascination for the theater and whenever he could he worked as an actor.

His determination to become an actor led Gable to break with his father by the time he was twenty-one. It also led him to his first love—an actress named Franz Dorfler. At first this young woman was unimpressed with Gable, both as an actor and a suitor. But he was so persistent and sincere that she finally persuaded the man in charge of the troupe she was to tour with to hire Gable as well. Soon they were engaged and Dorfler encouraged Gable to see an acting coach. This proved to be valuable advice for him, but unfortunate for their relationship.

The teacher was Josephine Dillon. She was seventeen years older than Gable and the guiding passion of her life was acting. Dillon saw a spark of talent in the clumsy, overeager youngster that had eluded everyone else. She set about developing that potential. Her confidence in her new protégé was such that, when Gable was twenty-three, she agreed to marry him. It is apparent that neither Dillon nor Gable expected the union to be a typical marriage, but Dillon quickly found that she was far more encumbered than Gable. While she labored to get him parts and attention, her young husband was unfaithful to her at nearly every opportunity.

Even as their marriage was falling apart, Josephine continued to be Gable's advocate. She landed him the male lead in a Broadway play but, by the time the play opened, he had cut her completely out of his life. His new love interest was Ria Langham, a wealthy, utterly refined woman who gave the rough-hewn Gable a glimpse into another way of life. It was a glimpse that proved all too enticing. At twenty-eight, he divorced Josephine and married Ria Langham. Ria was also seventeen years his senior.

About the same time as his second marriage, Gable starred in a play in Los Angeles that won him the attention of the film industry. Over the next few years Gable surrendered himself to

MGM, allowing MGM to portray him as a working-class Don Juan—a sexual brute with a winning smile. It was an image that found an immediate response among female moviegoers. MGM capitalized on that response by working their new star almost constantly.

Gable's busy schedule strained his ties to Ria, as did his incessant womanizing. As Hollywood's new sex symbol, he was expected to sleep with any available woman. Gable was determined to meet those expectations, but it was his dissatisfaction with the direction his career was moving that killed his marriage. Gable felt he was no longer called upon to act. He complained that he had become a personality—a professional idol. Ria, who saw only Gable's success and the money he was making, had little sympathy for this artistic angst. So Gable turned to alcohol and away from his wife.

By the time he was thirty-five Gable's marriage to Ria was over. He quickly found a new companion who shared his earthy approach to life and sex, and was well acquainted with Hollywood's fame games. Carole Lombard was as noted for her outrageously foul mouth as for her bleached-blond beauty. She enjoyed announcing that Gable was "the worst lay in town," but she was jealously protective of her relationship with him.

Ria's reluctance to grant Gable a divorce forced him to keep his affair with Lombard a secret for several years. They were not married until he was thirty-nine. In many ways, Lombard was the perfect match for Gable; she could share his work and also blend in the outdoorsy, all-male recreation he favored. Even with Lombard as his wife, Gable felt the need to have other women. It was rumored that he was with another woman when Lombard died in a plane crash two years into the marriage.

Lombard's death deeply affected Gable. He did not attempt a serious relationship for a long time. During a stint in the army his companions were shocked at the ugly women he chose to sleep with. It was as if nothing mattered to him but the sex. When he was forty-eight Gable married an Englishwoman, but the marriage lasted less than two years. He had a stable of girl friends in various cities around the country, plus an endless procession of eager starlets to grant him sexual gratification on demand.

Gable made his last marriage in his late fifties to an actress in her thirties named Kathleen Williams. Even though he was still ruggedly handsome, Gable's health was deteriorating due to his drinking and a heart condition he refused to acknowledge. Nonetheless, his marriage to Williams was noticeably passionate and produced one child. The child was born shortly after Gable's death at fifty-nine.

Another Example

Indira Gandhi *(prime minister of India). Born November 19, 1917 (Celebrity Birthday Guide).*

If you have Mars in Virgo with Venus in Aquarius you are . . . the Basically Rebellious Lover

There is an intellectual quality about your sexuality. You like to examine your erotic feelings. You view sexual behavior, both your own and that of others, with a cool, almost clinical objectivity. This intellectual distance in no way decreases your susceptibility to physical desire. If anything it makes you more open, inventive, and unconventional in your pursuit of earthy delights. Of all the Mars in Virgo Lovers, you are the most independent and the most uninhibited.

This free-and-easy, anything-goes approach to sex may make you appear as though you are uninterested in commitment, but this is not true. Actually, what you want more than anything in your sex life is a sense of permanence and finality. You are looking for an ideal, quintessential love that will satisfy both your curiosity and your physical needs. All your intellectualizing about sex and experimentation is not about having fun. It's about finding a place to stop.

Case History

Oskar Kokoschka (*Austrian expressionist painter noted for his lush palette and nervous brushwork). Born March 1, 1886, in Pochlarn, Austria (Hodin 1966; Whitford 1986).*

Kokoschka's father was a goldsmith who was put out of work by mechanization. His mother was a peasant. He was brought up in a poor, but loving and proud, home in which his artistic ambitions were encouraged from the very beginning. All his life Kokoschka remained close to his family, and he found ways to send his aging parents money even when he was starving.

Kokoschka wasted no time establishing himself as a rebellious force in the Viennese art scene. His primitive yet brutally realistic paintings and sculptures shocked the public, as did his poetry and plays. The plays were particularly indicative of Kokoschka's intense, yet confused and rather misogynistic, approach to sex. One, titled *Murderer, the Hope of Woman*, ends with a man killing a woman.

During this period Kokoschka was involved with a Swedish girl he called Lilith. He eventually broke off the relationship because he felt she was sapping his creative powers. When he was twenty-two Kokoschka was kicked out of art school because of his radical ideas. Even though Kokoschka had a patron, Adolph Loos, who bought his work and steered him toward other buyers, his life was a struggle.

When he was twenty-six Kokoschka fell in love with the beautiful widow of the composer Gustav Mahler. Alma Schindler Mahler was a sensitive and keenly intelligent woman from a privileged, extremely artistic background. She was also a very sensual woman, but her marriage to Mahler had done little to satisfy those needs. So, at thirty-three, Alma was ready to be swept away by a romantic and virile young man like Kokoschka, even though his poverty and coarseness put her off at first.

The couple found themselves to be exceptionally compatible sexually. This was enough to make the raw and somewhat immature Kokoschka push for marriage, but Alma was reluctant. She may have been thinking about the differences in their ages and backgrounds. She may have also wondered what the improvident young artist and his poor family would do to her comfortable income. The excuse she gave Kokoschka, however, was the fact that he had not yet completed his masterpiece.

Responding to this challenge Kokoschka made a painting of Alma and himself called *The Tempest* which is still considered one of his signature pieces. But it was not enough to make Alma marry him. The beginning of World War I gave the couple an excuse to separate. Alma encouraged Kokoschka to enlist, as did some of his friends who did not approve of the distracting influence the relationship had on the young painter. Kokoschka continued to write Alma after he joined the army, not knowing she had already found a new lover. Then, when he was twenty-nine, Kokoschka's short career as a soldier came to a violent end when he was shot in the head and bayoneted through the chest.

After he recovered from these wounds, Kokoschka's sex life took an outrageous turn. While convalescing in Dresden he had a dressmaker create a life-sized and anatomically correct female doll. Kokoschka claimed that the doll was designed to serve him both as a model and a mistress, thus eliminating the necessity of emotional entanglements. Some people believed that this new "girl friend" was Kokoschka's way of getting back at Alma. If so, he took the vindictive hoax to the farthest extreme. He bought his manufactured girl friend the finest clothes, borrowed his landlord's maid to wait on her, and proudly escorted the doll to the theater and other occasions.

Kokoschka's "affair" with the doll proved to be a turning point in his relations with women. The artist continued to be surrounded by women and he had sex with many of them, but none of his affairs seem to have been remarkable. He remained the most confirmed of bachelors. At one point while he was living in Dresden, he invited twelve women he had, or was having, affairs with to the theater on the same night. He coolly watched their interactions from a safe distance and then left with a new girl friend.

It was only after the death of his mother that Kokoschka seriously looked for a wife. The woman he chose was a tall, intellectual law professor he met at the University of Prague named Olda Palkovska. They were married when he was forty. The efficient young woman quickly took charge of Kokoschka's rather messy life.

By the time Hitler began his rise to power, Kokoschka had become one of the leading figures of the expressionist movement, both in painting and as a playwright. He topped the list of what the Nazis called "degenerate artists"—artists who were inspired by primitive, non-European cultures. At first Kokoschka seemed determined to meet this challenge head-on. He even painted a self-portrait titled *Portrait of a Degenerate Artist.* But soon it became apparent that he would have to flee or die.

Kokoschka was still reluctant to leave his life's work and his home. It was up to Olda to get the artist out of Europe in the nick of time. Then she helped him reestablish his career in England. By all accounts Kokoschka was as good of a husband to Olga as she was a good wife to him. The relationship lasted until his death at ninety-three.

Another Example

Yoko Ono *(Japanese-born performance artist who married John Lennon). Born February 18, 1933 (Celebrity Birthday Guide).*

If you have Mars in Virgo with Venus in Pisces you are … the Basically Vulnerable Lover

You are the Mars in Virgo Lover most susceptible to the joys of the flesh. This is because, for you, sex represents both a necessary physical and an emotional release. It is very easy for you to get so caught up in your pursuit of pleasure that you completely forget more practical concerns. You are the kindest and most gentle of all the Mars in Virgo Lovers, but you are also the one most likely to overindulge, overstep, and underestimate the consequences of your actions.

What makes this tendency so dangerous, both to yourself and to others, is the fact that you are so easy to love. You are a very sensual and sensitive Lover. You always give the impression that you are just as interested in the person you are with as you are in the act you are performing. You seem so agreeable and so sexy that your partners fail to see that you are only in it for the thrill. Sometimes even you forget—at least for a while.

Case History

Friedrich Alfred "Fritz" Krupp *(German industrialist who turned a grotto in Capri into his very own sexual theme park). Born February 17, 1854, in Essen, Germany (Batty 1966; Manchester 1968).*

Fritz Krupp was the sole heir of one of the greatest fortunes in Europe: an empire of steel, munitions, and battleships. He was a sickly youngster. During his childhood he was kept from the company of other children and shuttled by his slightly demented mother from one spa to another. When he turned twenty his father, Alfred Krupp, decided that it was time for his heir to learn the business and he took charge of young Fritz with a vengeance.

Alfred Krupp was an egocentric, capricious, and dictatorial man. Fritz's business education consisted of following his father everywhere and writing everything the older Krupp said into notebooks. The young Fritz became skilled in judging his father's moods and remained completely submissive in the face of Alfred's pedagogic furor. One of the few matters of contention between father and son was Fritz's desire to marry the daughter of a Prussian government official that Alfred thought beneath him.

Margarethe von Ende, Fritz's intended, was an idealistic, even rebellious young woman who worked as a governess in order to be independent of her family. It is likely that Fritz's independent mother recommended Margarethe to him, and she agitated most strenuously for the marriage. It was only when Fritz's mother threatened to move out of the house that Alfred gave in and permitted Fritz and Margarethe to be wed. Fritz was twenty-eight.

When Fritz was thirty-three both his father and mother died. This shy, circumspect man took up the task of leading the Krupp empire with an alacrity that surprised many. But Fritz's rise to power seemed to have had a negative influence on his marriage. Margarethe had given birth to their first child the year before and was pregnant with a second when Alfred Krupp died. The marriage produced no other children. After a few years it was apparent that Fritz and Margarethe were living separate lives.

The reasons for this estrangement between Krupp and his wife became clear as he entered his forties. Krupp's business often took him to Berlin. He and Margarethe always stayed in separate hotels when there. Krupp had asked the management of the hotel he favored to hire some young Italian men as waiters and bellboys. Krupp even agreed to pay the salaries of these young men—a good thing since they were not very good workers. Whenever Krupp came to Berlin his young Italians crowded into the rich man's suite. It didn't take long for the staff to realize that Krupp was staging homosexual orgies with his young protégés. As the frolics became more and more boisterous, the manager of the hotel feared he might be criminally liable. He decided to go to the police himself.

The manager's complaint probably did not surprise the Berlin police. They had long established a policy of observing and recording the activities of the many homosexual men who secretly inhabited the higher echelons of German society. Homosexuality was against the law in Germany, but men such as Krupp were never in jeopardy of arrest. The police were more concerned about the blackmailers and other opportunists who sought to take advantage of such behavior.

When he found no help forthcoming from the police, the hotel manager decided to tell Krupp to take his business and his friends elsewhere. This only escalated Krupp's degeneration. Since childhood he had harbored an intense interest in marine biology. Now, after years of sacrificing himself for his parents and his company, Krupp decided to pursue his ambition to become a scientist. He outfitted a ship for such purposes and established a research base on the island of Capri, a place noted for its tolerance of illicit pleasure.

Krupp purchased an almost inaccessible grotto on the island and set it up as his own private playground. Soon it was apparent that Krupp was after more than rare sea creatures. Keys to his hideaway were passed out to the prettier and more compliant of the island's young men and boys. Once inside the grotto, these young guests found themselves in a theater of sex presided over by the aging, overweight, but nonetheless exhilarated Krupp. Intoxicated by his newfound freedom, Krupp became flamboyant. Skyrockets accompanied ejaculations and, in remembrance of the grotto's history as a haven for religious ascetics, a man dressed like a monk acted as the gatekeeper. Krupp even allowed himself to be photographed while having sex with his boyfriends. These photographs revealed that many of them were seriously underage.

Krupp's extravagant party continued for four years. Then the Italian government began to secretly pressure the intemperate German to leave Capri. Meanwhile stories about the orgies staged in his grotto and even some of the photographs taken during the parties began to surface in the Italian press. Within a few months the German press began to drop hints. Margarethe panicked when she learned of the scandal and went directly to the kaiser, who was a personal friend of Krupp's. Krupp, however, was not worried. He seemed confident that the scandal would blow over if he remained quiet. He was so upset with his wife's response that he had her locked in a mental institution. Krupp's confidence proved ill-founded. Soon the story was front page news in the German newspapers as well.

There is no doubt that Krupp had the money to buy his way out of this difficulty, but he could never buy back his reputation, or the reputation of the House of Krupp. A man steeped in family pride, Fritz could hardly allow himself to be publicly humiliated. On the day on which Krupp was to have a personal interview with the kaiser in regard to the Capri affair, the forty-eight-year-old industrialist was found dead in his mansion in Essen. Family physicians and local officials made every effort to declare it a natural death, but the timing and circumstance left little doubt that the industrialist had killed himself.

Another Example

William Holden (*William Beedle, Jr.—film actor who was known for his all-American looks and unpretentious appeal). Although he was married for twenty-four years, Holden had many love affairs, the most notable of which was with Audrey Hepburn. It was after his break with her that Holden vowed to make love to at least one woman in every country he visited in his extensive travels around the world. After his marriage finally broke up, Holden became involved with actress Stefanie Powers, but this relationship was brought to an end because of his growing alcoholism. He died as a result of alcohol abuse at the age of sixty-three. Born April 17, 1918 (Thomas 1983).*

Chapter 7

Mars in Libra
The Perfect Lover

General Characteristics

The sexuality of people with Mars in Libra hinges on the eternal but always elusive concept of the "other." For most of us the "other" is just the person we happen to love: that individual who is willing to put up with our imperfections and stand by us through the good and bad times. People with Mars in Libra see the "other" as something much more abstract and larger than life. For them the "other" is an ideal. More importantly, it is a necessary ideal without which life has no meaning. In many ways the Mars in Libra Lover lives for this ideal, or at least for the process of relating; it is this thirst for companionship, the search for the truly significant other, that is the primary fire within this person's sexuality. Physical desire comes in a weak second.

This being said, it should not be assumed that Mars in Libra Lovers are sexually deprived. Just because physical sex is not that important to these individuals doesn't mean they can't have a lot of fun with it. Typically, Mars in Libra Lovers follow the sexual attitudes and mores of their own social group. They can quietly and happily sublimate their physical desires in the company of celibates, but they will definitely be the life of the party if they are in a community of swingers. What is different about sexually active Mars in Libra Lovers is that they always maintain a strict divide between what they perceive as frivolous sex (sex with anyone who is not their significant other) and sex with that special partner. The former simply doesn't matter, no matter how much energy they put into it. The latter matters tremendously, not because of the quality of the sex, but because it takes place in a zone of perfect love.

Mars in Libra Lovers approach sex with their special partners as if it were a fantasy. They seek to create a zone of perfect beauty, balance, and grace around the objects of their affection. Often they will inundate that person with physical manifestations of their ideal conception of love: gifts, flowers, and gestures of respect and idealized affection. Anything that seems tawdry or harsh to them is banished from the scene. It may seem that they are putting the person they love on a pedestal, or that they are making sex into a highly mannered ritual in which consummation matters very little. Always remember that it is the ideal of the relationship and the "other" that this Lover is really worshipping, not the person who happens to be standing on the pedestal.

There is probably no more privileged position imaginable than to be the object of a Mars in Libra Lover's sexual adoration. These Lovers make the person they love feel as if the universe is centered on their relationship. But despite all this devotion, the Mars in Libra zone of perfect love can be a rather cold and unforgiving place. The perfectionism that makes these Lovers so anxious to please their partners also makes them extremely judgmental of people who can't live up to the fantasy.

Since these Lovers need relationships so desperately and spend so much of their time thinking about their relationships, it is not surprising that they are innately adept at the social maneuvering and posturing that go along with the human mating ritual. No Lover knows better how to play the games of romance, how to flirt and be flirted with, and how to make love with just the right mixture of delicacy and emphasis. This gives them a very special kind of sexual allure. They are Lovers who always know what to do. They have an uncanny understanding of what it takes to move smoothly from the most staid and conventional social situation right into the bedroom.

Their constant awareness of love and relationships also makes these Lovers natural-born experts in the field of romance. They are astute observers of the sexual games people play and the need we all have to find the right mate. Moreover, they like talking about sex and love. They are equally eager to hear the opinions and experiences of others on the subject. So, no matter how sexually active or inactive they are, Mars in Libra Lovers always tend to be very knowledgeable about sex. When one of them offers advice on any aspect of the human search for love, it's always a good idea to listen closely.

If you have Mars in Libra with Venus in Aries you are . . . the Perfect Lover in Pursuit

The best part of sex for you is the anticipation. You enjoy the excitement of the chase, the gentle swordplay of meaningful flirtation, and the thrill of impending conquest. This is not to say that you are uninterested in the act itself; however, the physical finality of orgasm has only a limited charm for you because of your restless, idealistic, and essentially intellectual approach to sex.

You are the most adventurous of the Mars in Libra Lovers. You like a hint of danger, challenge, or even conflict in your relationships. You are much more willing than most Lovers of this type to go against convention and seek out controversy. This taste for audacity and fire in your sex life can cause you problems. Just as you often prefer flirtations to intercourse, you also have a tendency to get so involved in the conflict in your sex life that you actually dread resolution.

Case History

Sigmund Freud (founder of the psychoanalytic movement and one of the foremost explorers of human sexuality). Born May 6, 1856, at 6:30 P.M. in Freiburg, Germany (Gay 1988).

We know a lot about Freud's earliest sexual feelings. He wanted to sleep with his mother. She was a confidant and imposing woman who showered her first and favorite son with unqualified affection; he hated his father for intruding on their relationship. The fact that Freud was the first to categorize and name this age-old family conflict is ample indication of how meaningful it was for him. His mother continued to be a potent force in his emotional life far into his adulthood.

Freud's sex life becomes something of a mystery between the time of his toilet training to his marriage. He admitted to no sexual contacts before his marriage at age thirty. Considering his later frankness about these matters, it is likely that he had none. Regardless of his radical ideas, Freud was essentially an extremely conservative bourgeois and he never ceased to conduct himself as such.

The frustration of his bachelorhood was particularly evident when he was twenty-six and became engaged to Martha Bernays. It was an impetuous affair by the standards of their class. Freud proposed only two months after they met, despite his lack of financial prospects and the disapproval of Martha's mother. The couple was separated most of the time during the long engagement that followed because they lived in different cities. Freud's poverty was such that he could only occasionally visit his intended. When he did, their interaction was strictly regulated. Freud struggled to contain his ardor. It is very possible that his opinions about the power and dangers of pent-up sexual energy were born during this period of his life.

The sexual infatuation Freud felt for Martha Bernays only lasted a few years into their marriage. Martha was pregnant six times during the first nine years of the marriage. Freud sympathized with his wife's physical burdens but he refused to use birth control. He felt condoms could cause neurosis. Meanwhile, Martha became a stout and thoroughly competent housewife. In his late thirties, by his own reports, Freud's sexual relationship with Martha began to wane. Their last child was born when he was thirty-nine. He recorded a sexual dream at fifty-nine that he theorized had been influenced by "successful" coitus the night before. The emphasis on "successful" would indicate that "unsuccessful" coitus was not uncommon for him.

One year after his marriage Freud began another significant relationship which, according to his own theories, was fraught with sexual undercurrents. He corresponded with a Berlin doctor named Wilhelm Fliess. Freud and Fliess were brought together by a shared fascinated with ideas that were then considered outrageous. Freud's theories about the unconscious and infantile sexuality would later be vindicated. Fliess' notion that the nose was the dominant organ of the body never caught on. But for a time these two theorists gave each other valuable support and encouragement, and their relationship prospered.

After his rigorous self-analysis, Freud admitted that his feelings for Fliess were "feminine" and that their relationship was latently homosexual. It is obvious that only a Freudian would have found anything erotic in the chaste and thoroughly conventional communication that took place between Freud and Fliess. Yet the significance of the relationship cannot be denied.

Freud's "affair" with Fliess set up a pattern that was repeated with his primary disciples. First Alfred Adler and then Carl Jung became exceedingly close to Freud and were dubbed his intellectual successors. Then they each developed their own ideas and broke with the master. Freud viewed these breaks and the intellectual battles that brought them about as personal betrayals. On the other hand, Freud tended to hold his more subservient followers at a distance. He showed a preference for people with strong, forceful personalities even though his relationships with these people were often fraught with conflict.

Freud's circle also included some independent and sexually active women who might have entertained the notion of having an affair with the great man. Freud showed no sexual interest in any of these women even though he appreciated their company. It was rumored that Freud had an affair with his sister-in-law, who lived in his household for a time. She was more intellectually curious than Martha, but there is no factual evidence to support this accusation. All in all it appears that, for a man who spent so much of his later years thinking and talking about sex, Freud was shockingly uninterested in its physical manifestations. In fact, though he began his research with the notion that the repressive mores of his society were causing psychological damage to his contemporaries, he congratulated himself for being among the minority who could remain sane in such a sexually barren environment.

In his later years Freud became increasingly dependent upon his youngest daughter, Anna, who was a leading figure in psychoanalysis. When Anna was nineteen, Freud steered her away from a marriage to an older man and it is likely that his overpowering influence on her life was the primary reason his favorite daughter never married. Freud remained strangely blind to this facet of their relationship. On the one hand, he expressed the hope that Anna would one day marry and, on the other, he denied that she had any sexual feelings.

While he was courting Martha and suffering through intense sexual frustration, Freud remarked that a man needed to smoke cigars when there was no one to kiss. He continued to smoke after his marriage and for the rest of his life, often at a level even he found excessive. This addiction finally led to the cancer that brought a painful end to his life when he was eighty-three.

Another Example

Jimmy Swaggart (American evangelist who was almost driven from his pulpit after it was revealed he may have hired a prostitute to pose nude for him). Born March 15, 1935 (Celebrity Birthday Guide).

If you have Mars in Libra with Venus in Taurus you are . . . the Perfect Lover in the Flesh

You are an earthy romantic—an idealist who can still keep both feet firmly planted on the ground. This usually means you are a wiser Mars in Libra Lover whose judgements are based on real facts, not just idealistic illusions. This also makes you one of the more sensual Lovers of this type. You still have dreams of perfect love but now they include some perfectly rousing, physical sex.

Of course, there are problems with being both an idealist and a realist. You have a tendency to expect real sexual experiences to match your intellectualized ideal and, of course, this never happens. You also have a tendency to expect your partners to be more than human. So, it's not surprising that you are often disappointed in your sex life. The sex of your dreams always seems to be just beyond your finger tips, which, of course, is an excellent excuse to keep having more.

Case History

Ottoline Morrell (English socialite noted for her ability to attract people of genius as both friends and lovers). Born June 16, 1873, in London, England (Seymour 1992).

Ottoline was the product of an illustrious gene pool. She grew up in England ever mindful of both the privilege and the responsibility of her rank. Her father died when she was five but she cherished affectionate memories of him. Her mother was a sickly woman. It fell upon Ottoline, the youngest child and only daughter, to nurse her. When she turned nineteen and her mother died, Ottoline began to quietly assert her independence.

Due, in part, to her sheltered early life and her remarkable religious fervor, Ottoline reached sexual maturity rather late. She was strangely attractive: tall and willowy, with a strong hatchet-like face, and a shy, but thoroughly aristocratic, manner. Older men were particularly ready to respond to her. Early in her life, Ottoline was eager for the approval of surrogate father figures.

Her first affair occurred when she was twenty-four and touring Italy and Capri. Her lover was a forty-year-old doctor and writer named Axel Munthe. The degree to which Ottoline surrendered herself to this man's worldly ways surprised her prim companions. Munthe was apparently impressed enough with Ottoline's charms to consider marriage, but he found her deep religious convictions inconvenient and he moved on.

Ottoline consoled herself with a brief flirtation with a lesbian literary group in Rome, and with a more physical relationship with an older politician in England named Herbert Asquith. Her family discussed the prospects of her marriage, but Ottoline remain cool to the idea. Despite her weakness for strong, individualistic personalities, she recognized that being married to one would curtail her own independence.

The answer to her dilemma came when a young lawyer named Phillip Morrell paid her court. Morrell was beneath her both in class and income. He was a handsome but rather passive man who lacked ambition, intellectual or otherwise. At first Ottoline was reluctant to respond to Morrell because she felt none of the physical desire that had characterized her attraction to Munthe. However, after several proposals, she changed her mind and they were married when she was twenty-nine.

The marriage was a sexual failure. During the honeymoon it became apparent that Morrell was as physically unimpressed with Ottoline as she was with him. Their sex life was sporadic and unsatisfying, producing only one child. Otherwise Morrell and Ottoline developed a remarkably strong bond. Ottoline felt protective toward her diffident husband and quietly undertook the redirection of his career. She used her family connections and wide circle of friends to launch Morrell into politics. Meanwhile she established herself as a champion of liberal causes and as the cordial hostess of one of the most influential salons in London.

Along with clothes and religion, Ottoline's great passion was culture. She had an unqualified respect for writers and artists combined with an unerring instinct for picking the best. Some of the most creative people of her time entered her circle of friends. Many of them were helped by her tireless advocacy. It was her fascination with the arts that led Ottoline, then thirty-five, to pose for the scandalously bohemian society painter, Augustus John. By the time the portrait of her was finished, he had become her lover.

The affair was doomed to be short-lived, considering John's reputation as a womanizing egotist, and the fact that his long-time mistress was soon to join him in London. Nonetheless, Ottoline held nothing back. She stole away with her lover at every opportunity. She showered him with patronage and expensive tokens of her affection. She was profoundly disappointed when, after several months, John began to withdraw. Fortunately, she soon found herself distracted by another artist who was just as charming as John but much younger.

Unlike John, Henry Lamb accepted Ottoline's adoration and boundless generosity without reserve or embarrassment. He encouraged her to be reckless in her passion, just as he openly invited her financial support. Even the docile Morrell might have objected to his wife's none-too-secret adultery had he not been having affairs of his own. But Ottoline soon tired of her mercurial paramour, particularly after she found a man closer to her own age and background to love.

Bertrand Russell was a man in transition. He had already made his reputation as a mathematician—now he was ready to embark on a career as a social reformer. He was also in flight from a bad marriage. He was an egotist and he needed to be saved—an irresistible combination for Ottoline. The affair began when she was thirty-seven and continued for several years. Russell was a physically demanding lover and Ottoline apparently had difficulty meeting his need for sex. At one point in the relationship she even proposed he sleep with another woman. To her chagrin, she became jealous when he did.

Even though her attachment to Russell was intense, Ottoline resisted when he begged her to divorce Morrell and marry him. She excused herself by saying that her husband could not live without her. It is also possible that she recognized what kind of husband Russell would make.

Despite her obvious attraction for highly sexed men, Ottoline's attitude toward sex was somewhat coy. She never made direct references to coitus in even her most personal journals and correspondence, and she couldn't help but disapprove of writers who did. Even D. H. Lawrence, at one time her close friend, met with her disfavor because of his frankness about sex. She was often criticized and lampooned for her overly refined and artificial way of speaking and acting. People close to her thought she was not "natural." Ottoline, on the other hand, felt she was always just being herself.

Ottoline's affair with Russell was winding down by the time she reached forty. She had one last love affair at the age of forty-three with a young man who worked on her estate. For a while Ottoline was certain that she had found her romantic ideal in this uneducated youth. Tragically, he died less than two years after the affair began.

The death of her Tiger (as she called her last boy friend) apparently put an end to Ottoline's sexual adventures. She continued to have passionate friendships with exciting people, and she took great interest in the mating games of her many friends and associates, but she remained an observer. Meanwhile Morrell's extramarital affairs (far less well-managed than Ottoline's) had resulted in a scandal that ended his political career. Ottoline found herself playing the wronged but forgiving wife and quickly warmed to the role. She remained devoted to Morrell until her death at the age of sixty-four.

Another Example

Richard Chamberlain (*TV and motion picture star*). *Born March 31, 1935 (Celebrity Birthday Guide).*

If you have Mars in Libra with Venus in Gemini you are . . . the Perfect Lover at Play

You are forever choosing between your idealistic dreams of a perfect relationship and the tantalizing prospect of a new experience. At heart you are an exceedingly loyal Lover who will do anything to make his or her partner happy. But you also have a weakness for expediency in your sex life and a highly developed sense of fun. So, though no one can fault your intentions, you are not likely to be known for your consistency.

Of course, this lack of consistency won't always be a bad thing. It adds a quality of energy and playful unpredictability to your sexual nature. You are the eternal optimist of love who is always starting fresh and always looking for a new beginning (even within the same relationship). You are the Mars in Libra Lover who knows how to love meaningfully and still not take it all too seriously. That's a good thing to know.

Case History

Ingmar Bergman (*Swedish film maker noted for his intense studies of women, death, and the human condition in such films as* The Seventh Seal, *and* Fanny and Alexander). *Born July 14, 1918, in Uppsala, Sweden (Cowie 1982; Gado 1986).*

Bergman's father was a highly respected Lutheran minister whose ironclad notions of duty and sin had a devastating impression on his sensitive second son. Bergman grew into a shy, skinny, stammering adolescent burdened with guilt over his growing awareness of sex and his inability to stop masturbating. His guilt was somehow relieved when he found a female classmate to join him in his sexual exploration. The girl was fat, unattractive, and as unpopular as he was but this did not deter Bergman. If anything it made their adolescent affair less subject to notice.

By his late teens Bergman was in a state of open rebellion against the restrictive regime of his parents. He attended college for a couple of years but his ambitions centered on theatrical work. Finally, Bergman left home altogether after slugging both his father and mother, and went out on his own. (Actually, a third party brought him food from his father's house.) He worked as a director, a playwright, and an actor with local theater companies. He distinguished himself both for his exacting standards and his dour bohemian personality.

During this period Bergman lived with a daring young poet whose wanton promiscuity continued to fascinate his imagination long after he had broken off their affair. Then, when he was twenty-four he met and married the dancer and choreographer Elsa Fisher. Oddly enough, the scruffy young rebel submitted to a full-blown church wedding with all the romantic trimmings. He even chose the hymns. Not long after the marriage a child was born and Fisher was diagnosed with tuberculosis. While she was in a sanitarium in Stockholm, Bergman was hired to direct a theater company in another city. Bergman met another dancer there named Ellen Lundstrom. He coolly informed Fisher that he wanted a divorce and when he was twenty-seven, he entered into his second marriage.

This marriage produced four children and material for a whole series of movies dealing with dysfunctional couples. The scenarios of Bergman's work indicate that he placed the blame for the collapse of his marriage squarely on himself. The power he enjoyed as the director of a theater and then as a rising filmmaker gave him ample access to women. He was unable to resist them. Bergman claimed that "deep down" he was a faithful man, though he expected no one would believe it. He said that he sought "an exchange of souls" when he was with a woman, and that he rarely had sex with a woman just for the sake of physical release.

Bergman's third marriage came when he was thirty-two. This wife was a journalist, Gun Hagberg, who had come to Bergman to interview him and ended up becoming his lover. The marriage produced one child before Bergman was distracted by an affair with a young actress. His fourth marriage came when he was thirty-eight. He married a noted pianist from Estonia named Kabi Laretei. This marriage lasted longer than his first three, but it too was shattered when he cohabited with one of his actress girl friends.

When Bergman was fifty-three his fourth wife was killed in a car accident. A few months later he married for the fifth time. His bride was Ingrid Karlebo Von Rosen who had just recently divorced a count. She was forty-one.

Bergman's marriages were not just destroyed by his affairs with actresses, in many ways they were overshadowed by them. Bergman slept with many of the women he used in his movies: Harriett Anderson, Bibi Andersson, Liv Ullmann, and others. These women were beautiful and significantly younger than Bergman. (Harriett Anderson was still in her teens and Bergman was thirty-four when they began living together.) They were also extremely talented. This talent allowed Bergman to make insightful and complex films about women. Many of his films centered on female characters, and often more than one of his past paramours shared the screen. It might be said that each of these women became a part of his creative palette and that he used them, or at least their personae, as a painter uses his paints.

If you have Mars in Libra with Venus in Cancer you are . . . the Perfectly Contrary Lover

You are the most emotional of the Mars in Cancer Lovers and this adds a quality of urgency to your perfectionism. Relationships are more than a necessary ideal for you—they are essential to your emotional well being. This makes you an intense Lover who always struggles and strains to get more out of relationships. You need a lot of love, but, of course, you are prepared to give a lot in return.

Sex can be an explosive commodity for you because you take relationships so seriously. You react to sex with both a deeply felt emotional release and a cool, intellectual appraisal. You see it as everything and as nothing—all at the same time. The sex act often brings out the worst in you by exaggerating your essential confusion. You might contemplate skipping it altogether, but you are much too sensual a person to do that and not regret it later.

Case History

Sara Teasdale (lyric poet whose poetry won the favor of both traditionalist and the avant-garde). Born August 8, 1884, in St. Louis, Missouri (Drake 1997; Carpenter 1979).

Teasdale had a privileged and serenely sheltered childhood. Her parents were well-to-do and extremely conservative. They pampered their youngest daughter and made sure that she knew nothing of the harsh realities of life. From this environment Teasdale developed into a highly romantic but extremely delicate woman who was subject to many ailments, both real and imagined. She remained thoroughly dependent upon her parents far into adulthood.

Teasdale read a great deal as a teenager and developed a fascination for poetry. During her youth she was subject to typical schoolgirl crushes on her female classmates. She became infatuated with girls who were more beautiful and confident than she was.

Teasdale was a published poet by her early twenties, even though she still lived in her parents' house and rarely went anywhere outside of their company. She corresponded with a young man who shared her enthusiasm for the ancient Greek poet Sappho. During the course of their long correspondence the man sent Teasdale verse hinting at a more intimate and passionate connection between them; however, when Teasdale finally met her distant beau she realized that his invitation was not serious.

Despite her limited experience, Teasdale became well known for her poems about love. She wrote of a desire to be overwhelmed by love and of the sadness of a woman waiting for love to come her way. She remained curious about sex and, along with her bouts of illness and depression, she suffered a state she called "imeros" or periods of intense sexual frustration. At the same time, she maintained an extremely puritanical outlook on sexual matters. When she was introduced to the notion that her poetic heroine Sappho was actually the lover of other women, she primly chose to ignore these "erotic rumors."

In her late twenties Teasdale engaged in correspondence with another poetic suitor and traveled to New York City regularly to visit him. For several months Teasdale waited for this man to boldly declare himself and sweep her away into a new life, but it never happened. Teasdale started to believe that she was bound to become an old maid.

By this time in her life Teasdale was spending more time on her own in New York City, where she had an array of literary contacts and admirers. She became familiar with poets and writers who lived outright bohemian lives, with no regard for the conventional mores regarding sex. Even though Teasdale had a high regard for the work of some of these people, she could not condone their lifestyle. She showed no desire to shed her staid Baptist upbringing and join the party.

Teasdale's bad luck in love suddenly changed as she prepared to turn thirty. Her long-time friend and correspondent, Vachel Lindsay, decided he wanted to marry her. Lindsay and Teasdale had sparred over poetic issues via letters for years. Lindsay felt that only a return to the land and to the people could revitalize American culture. Teasdale still clung to European models. Now the impulsive farmland poet came to New York City with vague notions of making his literary nemesis his wife.

At the same time a businessman named Ernst Filsinger, who had long admired both Teasdale and her work, made a play for her. He inundated Teasdale with flowers and declarations of love from his home in St. Louis. Suddenly the shy poet who had always doubted her ability to attract men was forced to choose between two desirable prospects.

The choice was not difficult. As close as she felt to Lindsay, she knew she could never share his vagabond lifestyle. A woman who rarely traveled without her maid or nurse, and who loved to shop for pretty clothes, wasn't about to surrender the sweet comfort she had grown to expect from life for the pursuit of art. Filsinger, though not rich, could sustain the kind of lifestyle she had known since childhood. Moreover, he was a born romantic who loved her without reserve and had the highest respect for her work.

They were married when Teasdale was thirty. Both parties were always careful to speak of their union in only the most glowing terms; however, the truth of the matter was quite different. The honeymoon period had been a fiasco. Then Teasdale became ill with a bladder infection that lasted for months and finally put her in a hospital. Perhaps more importantly, soon after the marriage Teasdale recognized that she was never going to realize her dream of a love that would completely engulf her and completely take charge of her life. Instead, she found herself feeling as independent and isolated as she did when she was a spinster.

Filsinger responded to the troubled relationship by devoting himself to his work. His involvement in international trade meant he was often out of the country. At first Teasdale traveled with her husband, but her delicate health and career obligations made this difficult. The couple continued to express the utmost devotion to one another. Teasdale was intensely jealous whenever she felt Filsinger might be vulnerable to the attractions of another woman, but the marriage was slowly coming apart.

The turning point probably occurred when Teasdale became pregnant and, convinced that bearing a child would damage her health and creativity, had an abortion. This direct denial of her religious faith and her expectations of herself apparently convinced Teasdale that she could not remain a married woman. She waited until Filsinger was halfway around the world and filed for divorce. Filsinger was shocked.

After the divorce, Teasdale was beset with financial and health concerns. Both were largely imagined but, nonetheless, these were sufficient to keep her in a state of nervous anxiety. A simple bump on the head became a prolonged, physical hardship. She became obsessed with the notion that she was going to die with a stroke. At the age of forty-eight, four years after her divorce, Teasdale took an overdose of sleeping pills and died in her bathtub.

Another Example

Leona Helmsley (*American real estate agent noted for her advantageous marriage and poor labor relations*). *Born July 4, 1920 (Pierson 1989).*

If you have Mars in Libra with Venus in Leo you are . . . the Perfect Lover on Display

You are but a poor player and romance is your stage. You delight, amaze, shock, and befuddle as your partner watches with rapt attention. Basically, you can play any role he or she may require of you. The only catch is that you have to control the performances. You say when they start and when they end. No one, not even the person you love the most, is allowed to peek behind the curtain. Not only would that compromise your control, it would also spoil the illusion.

Even though you are one of the warmest and most charming of all the Mars in Libra Lovers, you can also be one of the most illusive. You don't want your partners to get too close or know you too well. For this reason you tend to be a little shy about sex although, if you are guaranteed complete control, you can even play the role of a sex machine with gusto. The only part of the play that's apt to give you trouble is intimacy. Unfortunately, until you learn this role, the grateful applause you earn elsewhere will be of no consequence.

Case History

George Bernard Shaw (Irish-born playwright who, by means of his startling wit and impish satire, became one of the most notable cultural figures of his time). Born July 26, 1856, in Dublin, Ireland (Peters 1980; Du-Cann 1963).

Shaw's mother was a strong-willed, cool-headed woman who left her drunken husband and fled to London where she managed to earn a living for herself and her two grown children. Thanks to his mother's example, and the example of his equally independent sister, Shaw developed an attitude toward woman that was unusual for his time. He tended to treat the women he met as fully developed human beings who were not too different from himself.

Young Shaw was not much to look at. He was tall, pale, somewhat effeminate, and typically ill-clothed, but women responded to his wit and his way with words. (His mother's work as a music teacher brought many single women into his life.) He designated mythological code names in his early diaries for his various women friends and slyly tracked the ebb and flow of each affair. He loved flirtation and the process of falling in love. As keen as he was on fascinating women, Shaw remained a virgin.

Shaw held on to his virginity by choice. He enjoyed many other activities with his female companions: high-minded and heated conversations, playing music, and attending plays and exhibitions. But sex was too vulgar, common, and too much like commitment for

Shaw's sensibilities. He tried to maintain his relationships at just the level where both sex and actual commitment could be expected, but not demanded.

Jenny Patterson was the woman who finally broke through Shaw's crafty reserve. She was fifteen years older than he was, somewhat experienced in the ways of the world, and just sensual enough to quickly tire of his flirtatious teasing. Shaw later claimed she raped him when he was twenty-nine. It is probably more to the point to say that he was caught in the web of his own intrigue, and remained so for a period of eight years.

Shaw's relationship with Patterson served him in several ways. Despite her aggressive sexuality, Patterson was passive enough emotionally to put up with Shaw's egotism and peevish self-involvement. Their affair existed almost totally on Shaw's terms. He came and went as he wanted and he maintained his freedom to keep company with any other woman that pleased him. Patterson reacted to Shaw's waywardness with intense jealousy, but this also served Shaw's purposes. His relationship with Patterson kept his relationships with other women in a state of romantic limbo, just the way he liked it.

About the same time as Shaw lost his virginity, he began his involvement in socialist politics with the progressive group called the Fabians. He also earned a living for the first time as a music and theater critic for various publications. Both these activities allowed him access to numerous women. Shaw went through a series of heady infatuations with women ranging from social reformers to actresses.

These affairs were all equally intense and, apparently, equally sexless. Often he chose married women—women who could entertain his intellectual passion but who were beyond his reach physically. Other times the women involved were as uninterested in sex as he. In general, despite his active (if chaste) philandering, the tone of Shaw's affairs remained light and sociable. Shaw moved from woman to woman with a minimum of hard feelings. It was only Jenny Patterson who railed and threatened.

Shaw's success as a playwright did not come until he was forty. About the same time he met Charlotte Payne-Townshend, the woman who would become his wife. He described her as "a large, graceful woman." She shared his intellectual interests and his uncertainty about the value of sex. The couple had intercourse early in their relationship when Shaw deduced that Charlotte's enforced celibacy was making her ill. Later, however, he was disgusted at the notion that he had been used as a tonic to cure a nervous woman.

Shaw and Charlotte were married when he was forty-two. She became both his nurse and his secretary, and often behaved more like his mother than his wife. Despite their premarital experiment, the couple apparently abstained from sexual relations after the wedding by mutual consent. Shaw, of course, continued his flirtations with various actresses and female admirers, but now he had a wife to chase these women away when their attentions struck him as onerous.

Shaw wrote an account of his sex life in his old age to his friend and noted philanderer, Frank Harris. He told Harris that he had never been the aggressor in his love affairs, that women had pursued him. He didn't condemn sex. He approved of "its amazing power of producing a celestial flood of emotion or exaltation of existence" (Ducan, 279). In this account Shaw indicated that he had experimented with partners other than Patterson and his wife. His conclusion was that sex was a poor basis for a relationship.

Shaw's apparently sexless union with Charlotte continued for many years, until she died when Shaw was eighty-seven. Shaw continued with his ambiguous love affairs and turned down the offer of one of his lady friends to move in with him. There are hints he had a sexual relationship with this woman that lasted into his nineties. He died at the age of ninety-four.

Other Examples

Alfred Hitchcock (*British film maker considered the master of suspense and also noted for his fascination with blond actresses). Born August 13, 1899 (Celebrity Birthday Guide).*

Percy Bysshe Shelley (*English poet of the Romantic era). Born August 4, 1792 (Celebrity Birthday Guide).*

If you have Mars in Libra with Venus in Virgo you are . . . the Perfectly Practical Lover

You want sex to be real, tangible, and easily accessible. For this reason you are prone to divide your sexual contacts between those that serve your physical needs and those that involve your search for the perfect relationship. Your approach to the former will be practical and matter-of-fact, while you will look to the latter with dreamy fascination. This dual approach can be quite confusing to others. They may consider you insincere or perhaps just schizophrenic.

Your attitude toward sex is essentially passive. Whether you are looking for love or just a good time you are easily led, emotionally lazy, and careful to avoid relationships that might require hard work or struggle. You are essentially an opportunist capable of making the best of any sexual situation. You are such a charming opportunist that you typically manage to get exactly what you want from relationships, both in terms of sexual gratification and your romantic ideal.

Case History

John Lennon (*pop musician, singer, songwriter, and cultural icon*). *Born October 9, 1940, in Liverpool, England* (*Goldman 1988*).

Lennon was the only child of a couple ill-suited for parenthood. His father was a sailor who was often away at sea during Lennon's infancy. During these absences Lennon's mother left her child unattended at home while she went out with other men. By the time he was five, his mother and father were divorced. Lennon was raised by his maternal aunt in whose home he found some stability.

He developed into a pompadoured rebel with an interest in art and music but an even keener interest in fun. Lennon's sexual initiation came when he was fifteen. His girl friend was more experienced and very sexy; she found Lennon to be a romantic lover. Yet expediency was often more important to him than romance at this point in his life. He and his lover once shared a bed with Lennon's best friend and his girl friend when more civilized accommodations proved unavailable.

Three years later, during an abortive stint in art school, Lennon met Cynthia Powell. Powell was a shy, conservative girl who was at first frightened by the angry man who habitually swiped her art supplies. Soon she found herself overwhelmed by the force of his personality, and she became Lennon's lover. Powell's passive conventionality meant that she received the brunt of the rage Lennon felt toward his mother (who had recently died) and the rest of the world. Yet Powell gladly suffered Lennon's cruelty and arrogance for the privilege of being his girl.

Powell's position in Lennon's life may have been special, but it was hardly exclusive. Lennon soon gave up on art school and devoted his attention to his band, which had recently recruited Paul McCartney. Lennon had many opportunities for casual sex as this group, which finally settled on the name the Beatles, slowly moved up the Liverpool music scene. When the Beatles began playing in Frankfurt, Germany, those opportunities multiplied. Lennon and his friends would return to the single room that they shared to find the darkened apartment full of female fans waiting to have sex with them. The group was so popular that the local prostitutes took them on for free.

This period of Lennon's life was not just an orgy of sex. There was also a good deal of violence. Even though he was not really from the streets, Lennon liked to play the part of the tough. He and a friend once attempted to roll a drunken sailor who fought back and foiled their plans. Apparently this incident was not just a lark. Later in his life Lennon told a confidant that he thought he might have killed a man in Frankfurt during another mugging.

When Lennon was twenty-two, Brian Epstein became the manager of the Beatles and he set about changing the image of the group from that of a leather-clad bar band to the stylish but innocent mop-tops who would soon capture the imagination of the world. Just at the point when they were on the brink of breaking into the big time, Cynthia Powell announced to Lennon that she was pregnant. The singer was by no means happy about this turn of events, but he felt compelled to marry his long-suffering companion. A quiet, civil ceremony was arranged and the marriage was kept from the public in the interest of the group's image.

Despite his thoughtless infidelity to her, it is apparent that Lennon felt an affection for Cynthia that made her different than the countless other women he bedded; however, marriage did nothing to bolster this relationship. Lennon acted as if he were as ignorant of his married state as were his fans. When the child was born, he deliberately contrived to be somewhere else.

At this same time Lennon was developing a sexual relationship with Brian Epstein. Epstein was a self-destructive homosexual. From the very beginning it was thought by many that his interest in the band had less to do with business than with sex. Lennon's relationship with Epstein was to some degree a willful experiment. Epstein introduced Lennon to a subculture he had never known. There was also a hint of opportunism in Lennon's seduction of the group's crafty manager. It gave him the upper hand over the one man who most controlled the fate of the Beatles.

The turning point in Lennon's sex life came when he met Yoko Ono at the age of twenty-seven. Ono was very different from Cynthia. She was an aggressive rebel with a hardened ambition to become a famous artist. She applied herself toward this goal, not by making art, but by cultivating connections. It is evident that, at first, she saw Lennon as just such a contact and she pursued him relentlessly. Her manager-husband, Tony Cox, encouraged her to get money from Lennon by whatever means necessary. Unfortunately for Cox, the means turned out to be divorcing him and marrying Lennon.

In many ways Lennon and Ono were a natural combination. They turned their marriage into a continuous piece of performance art. Many saw her as a controlling interloper, but the objections of other people to the relationship only made Lennon more devoted. Under Ono's influence, the violent young man who had often shocked people with his cruelty and arrogance became passive and selfless. For her part, Ono put aside her artistic ambitions. Lennon became her life's work.

When he was thirty-three Lennon suddenly bolted from his marriage to Ono. Ono, who wanted to have an affair of her own, may have orchestrated even this event. For a short time Lennon traveled with May Pang, a young woman who was just as pliant and eager to please him as Cynthia Powell had once been. He responded to this passivity by becoming violently abusive. In contrast, another woman who slept with him during this period called Lennon a wimp who had little interest in intercourse and only wanted to be mothered.

Despite his apparent defection, Ono never really lost her control over Lennon. After a madcap debauch of drugs, liquor, and sex, the singer meekly returned to his wife. A short time later Ono was pregnant. Lennon had long wanted to have a child with Ono and he was delighted. Lennon withdrew from the public eye to devote himself to raising his son and being a "house-husband." Yet, at the same time, he was sinking deeper and deeper into drug addiction, reclusive paranoia, and childlike dependence on Ono. As he neared forty Lennon managed to rally himself enough to produce a final, triumphant album featuring music by both Ono and himself. A short time later he was assassinated.

Another Example

Roman Polanski (*Polish filmmaker who was forced to flee the United States after he was charged with having sex with an underaged girl*). *Born August 18, 1933 (Celebrity Birthday Guide).*

If you have Mars in Libra with Venus in Libra you are . . . the More Than Perfect Lover

You are a lover to whom total devotion and selfless affection come easily. You are a natural born romantic with extremely idealistic notions about love and sex. Your search for romantic perfection may not always be appreciated. For some people, your hearts-and-flowers approach to loving seems shallow and false. For others, your intense idealism about these issues will be intimidating. But the person who does respond to your special and undeniable need for true love will be rewarded with a love that is beyond perfection.

Your big problem is sex. The physical realities of sex don't often fit comfortably within your unique and somewhat precious concept of love. Oh, there will be moments when it all comes together (wonderful, breathtaking moments, for certain), but there will also be moments when sex seems to lose all connection with love. This extraneous lust is never very important to you but it can still get you into trouble. If you choose to ignore it, you will seem cold and lacking in passion. If you choose to enjoy it, you run the risk of seeming duplicitous and unfaithful.

Case History

Annette Funicello (*Mouseketeer who went on to become a teenage film and singing star*). *Born October 22, 1942, in Utica, New York (Funicello 1994).*

Funicello was brought up in a conservative Catholic home. Her parents impulsively moved from New York to sunny California when she was a small child. She was a shy kid, even though she was surrounded by an adoring extended family. She found release from this shyness when she discovered music and dance in school.

When Funicello was twelve, a representative from Disney Studios asked her to audition after seeing her in a school play. Through this break she became a Mouseketeer, one of several children who donned a mouse-eared cap and starred in a television show called *The Mickey Mouse Club*. Unlike many other child stars, Funicello reported only pleasant memories of this period. She always remained close to Walt Disney and people at Disney Studios.

Funicello projected such a bright and happy innocence on TV that she became one of the most popular Mouseketeers. As the years passed, these qualities, combined with an increasingly voluptuous figure, set her career off in a new direction. She starred in a series of "beach blanket" movies that established her as a sexy but wholesome all-American sweetheart. She also established a career as a singer.

During this period Funicello had contact with many of the top male teenage "heart-throbs" of the 1950s. She costarred with Frankie Avalon, who became a close friend, and she dated Paul Anka, for whom she had a serious teenage crush. Despite her fame and the fact that she regularly rubbed elbows with some of the most desirable young men of her generation, Funicello remained completely and happily under the control of her parents. Even when Funicello decided to tour to promote her record career, her mother went with her. The other members of the tour were warned to behave themselves and watch their language around the teenaged star.

As Funicello grew older and her audience tired of naive beach movies, an effort was made to put her in more adult roles that were more explicitly sexual. These attempts fell flat. Despite her beauty and perfect figure, Funicello could not be blatantly sexy. By the time she reached twenty-one her career outlook was uncertain.

Funicello had other matters on her mind. When Funicello was twenty-two she married her agent, Jack Gilardi. Gilardi was hardly a teen idol. He was twelve years older than Funicello. Early in the marriage, his interaction with her seems to have been almost parental. Funicello had always been reluctant to leave the absolute security she had felt in her parent's home and she found her husband's fatherly attitude a comfort.

The marriage lasted twelve years and produced three children, but it was apparently troubled from the beginning. The nature of his work meant that Gilardi had to be an extrovert; constantly out among the movers and shakers in Hollywood. Funicello, on the other hand, was a homebody. After the birth of their first child she decided she could find fulfillment in her role as a mother.

Two years after the birth of her third child, the strife in her marriage became so bad that Funicello asked for a divorce. It was not a step she took lightly. She saw it as a personal failure and was terrified at the prospect of being alone. As a woman who had been sheltered from many of life's dirty realities, first by her parents and then by her husband, Funicello found the challenges of single motherhood quite intimidating.

Some people felt that Funicello, once the sweetheart of millions, would be flooded with marriage proposals after her divorce. As it turned out, she remained alone for a long time. Nine years later she married Glen Holt, a rugged horse breeder twelve years her senior who she described as a romantic. This marriage proved much more successful than her first. A short time after her second marriage, Funicello was diagnosed with multiple sclerosis.

Other Examples

Jawaharlal Nehru (leader of India and successor of Gandhi). Even though he was educated in England, Nehru submitted to the customs of his class and married a girl chosen for him by his parents. It turned out to be a remarkably good marriage. The couple remained devoted to one another despite frequent separations caused by Nehru's political involvement and his wife's illness. The marriage produced two children.

When his wife died after twenty years of marriage Nehru continued to honor her memory and always kept her ashes with him; however, the handsome and powerful Nehru was not yet ready to forswear sex. During the remainder of his life he was known to keep company with unattached and intelligent women. Even though these affairs were carried out with the utmost discretion, they nonetheless caused alarm among some of his more conservative associates. They saw Nehru's mistresses as a sign of Western decadence. These objections made no impression on the very popular prime minister of India. Born November 14, 1889 (Akbar 1988).

Althea Flynt (stripper noted for devotion to her troubled husband, Larry Flynt). Born November 6, 1953 (Rodden).

William Jefferson Clinton (American president). Born August 19, 1946 (Celebrity Birthday Guide).

If you have Mars in Libra with Venus in Scorpio you are . . . the Dangerously Perfect Lover

You are the most seductive of the Mars in Libra Lovers. Your interest in sex is almost as keen as your need to find the perfect partner. Moreover, you are just as savvy about sex as you are about social maneuvering. Yet this sexiness does not make you any less of an idealist. You are still looking for an ideal love. It's just that this bond must take place on an emotional level as well as in the mind.

Your idealism often falters over the issue of trust. You are always more comfortable and secure in a relationship when you have some sort of advantage over your partner—when you feel you know more about what is going on in the relationship than he or she does. There is a ruthlessness about your perfectionism. You are willing to do whatever it takes to have just the right balance of sexuality and companionship.

Case History

George S. Kaufman (*playwright and director noted for his long string of Broadway hits and his collaboration with the Marx Brothers on such film comedies as* A Night at the Opera). *Born November 16, 1889, in Pittsburgh, Pennsylvania (Goldstein 1979; Meredith 1974).*

Kaufman came from a well-to-do family of German Jews. Despite his father's frequent business failures and relocations, he grew up with all the middle-class comforts. He first began to write plays when he was a teen. After honing his literary skills as a journalist and a theater critic for the *New York Times*, he began seriously writing for the stage in his late twenties. Kaufman typically worked with a collaborator, but he was so amazingly prolific that no single partner could possibly keep up with him.

About the time that Kaufman was making his first advances as a playwright, he met Beatrice Bakrow, a bright young woman whose background was very similar to his own. The two were brought together on a blind date and hit it off immediately. Beatrice was a large woman, by no means pretty, but attractive and decidedly sensual. She had recently been kicked out of Wellesley College due to failing grades and what the school regarded as improper conduct with young men.

Despite Beatrice's college highjinks, she was a virgin when she and Kaufman married, as was the twenty-eight-year-old Kaufman. Beatrice later hinted that their mutual ignorance was the root of their marital difficulties. In any case, the couple enjoyed a very brief sex life. Beatrice became pregnant within the first year of the marriage and gave birth to a stillborn child. Kaufman was so disturbed by this tragedy that he was unable to maintain an erection with Beatrice ever again.

This development would have spelled disaster for most marriages, but it presented only a passing difficulty for the Kaufmans. They were too compatible in every other aspect of life to allow sex to drive them apart. The marriage continued with both parties looking to other people for sexual release. Beatrice tended to favor ambitious young men who reminded her of Kaufman. Kaufman preferred women who were quite different from his wife—women who were petite, noticeably pretty, and non-Jewish.

Throughout his life Kaufman was an extremely prim and private man, whose conversation was remarkably free of dirty words or bawdy stories. The playwright's squeaky-clean persona was often a point of fun for his more earthy friends, such as the members of the "Algonquin" group or his many Hollywood contacts. Despite this apparent prudishness, the tall, gangly Kaufman enjoyed a very active sex life. One rumor spread about Kaufman was that he had an arrangement with a "madam" who sent girls to a prearranged locale to be picked up by Kaufman. Kaufman would invite the prostitutes to the apartment he kept for his extramarital affairs and go though all the motions of seduction. At the end of the month he was billed. If this is true it must have occurred early in his career because by the time he reached his thirties, Kaufman was far too skilled in the ways of romance to require such services.

Kaufman's ability to charm and bed women came as a surprise to his many friends and associates. He did not look or act like a womanizer, nor did he brag about his sexual accomplishments. Yet there he was with a different beauty on his arm, sometimes every night. The women who slept with him were almost unanimous in singing his praises. They found him to be a courteous, gentle, and highly skilled lover with a strong sex drive and an even stronger sense of style and decorum. There is no counting the number of hearts Kaufman broke in his lovemaking career, but none of the women he left behind held a grudge against him.

It wasn't until Kaufman was forty-three that the monumental discretion with which he had conducted his sex life was shattered. One of his paramours, a gorgeous actress named Mary Astor, became involved in a custody battle with her ex-husband. In the course of the trial her diaries were opened for public inspection and her florid description of the love-making techniques of a certain "George" sparked particular excitement. In one passage Astor declares, "twenty—count them, diary twenty—I don't see how he does it" (Wallace, 151). It is quite likely the number cited refers to something other than orgasms (Kaufman's twenty Broadway hits, for example), but the public was not interested in such esoteric interpretations. When the press learned that "George" was George Kaufman, he was dubbed "public lover number one." For months reporters followed his every moment.

This incident was no less embarrassing for Beatrice than it was for Kaufman. The marriage was obviously shaken but it did not break. The couple remained close until Beatrice died suddenly of a cerebral hemorrhage when Kaufman was fifty-five. Grief-stricken, the playwright withdrew from his very active social life. When he gradually began to resume his old habits, his friends assumed that they would once again witness a whimsical parade of pretty girl friends. To their surprise, Kaufman instead decided to remarry when he was fifty-nine.

Kaufman's bride was a thirty-five-year-old actress named Leueen MacGrath. The couple immediately became professional partners. Kaufman wrote plays for Leueen and they collaborated on various writing projects; however, the relationship never developed into the kind of easy partnership that had characterized his relationship with Beatrice. As Kaufman's health failed he encouraged Leueen to have affairs. The couple divorced when he was sixty-seven. Leueen remained a good friend and was with Kaufman when he died at the age of seventy-one.

If you have Mars in Libra with Venus in Sagittarius you are . . . the Perfectly Adorable Lover

There is a quality of lightness, optimism, and an almost childlike innocence about your sexuality that makes you one of the most charming of the Mars in Libra Lovers. At your best you can be an adventurous and extremely playful Lover, someone who absolutely glories in sexual fun. But you are also a very skittish Lover who reacts strongly to any hint of disapproval or distress. The emotional and psychological extremes of romance often leave you startled and ill at ease.

The problems in your love life come when you are forced to choose between your need for a strong committed relationship and your equally strong desire for freedom. This choice is so difficult for you that you will resort to almost anything to postpone it—making promises you can't keep, manipulating people you love, or even celibacy. But sooner or later you will have to choose. Your need for love is such that you will almost always pick commitment, even though you'll never stop missing your freedom.

Case History

Federico Fellini (Italian filmmaker who first established his reputation as a realist but then proved himself to be a master of the fantastic). Born in the evening of January 20, 1920, in Rimini, Italy (Alpert 1986; Chandler 1995).

Fellini enjoyed a middle-class and relatively trouble-free childhood in the midst of Fascist Italy. His sexual development would probably not seem unusual had he not romanticized it so much in his films and writings. Rimini was a resort town that blond northerners liked to visit in the summer to sunbathe by the sea. As a boy Fellini enjoyed spying on these leggy foreigners from a distance. He also entertained an infatuation with a stylishly dressed local seamstress who had an impressive physique. One day he followed her into a movie theater and attempted a furtive grope at her leg. Years later the woman didn't even remember the incident, but for Fellini it was a defining experience.

When Fellini was eighteen he left his home and traveled to Rome. He was supposed to be studying law but supplemented the allowance sent to him by his parents by drawing caricatures and writing humorous pieces for magazines. Soon his writing career expanded to scripts for radio.

Fellini was a virgin when he arrived in Rome. He had avoided pressing any advantage with his teenage girl friends out of fear of pregnancy and an early marriage. Once free of his family, Fellini rectified this deficiency by visiting a bordello. He had a pleasant experience with a pretty girl at the bordello, though he had to admit he was too eager and naive to notice the less pleasant aspects of the place. He even promised to return, but he never did.

Fellini had little to say about his sex life after this initiation. He mentions that he was occasionally forced to move because his landladies made advances on him. There are only vague references to a girl friend during this period. His sexual experience was apparently still fairly limited when he married at the age of twenty-three.

His bride was Giulietta Masina. She was twenty-two, from a musical family, and studying for a degree in the classics. At the same time she was having some success as an actress. The couple first met while they were working together on a radio show. Within a short time they were engaged, despite the reservations of Masina's parents. Fellini was a tall, rather slovenly young man whose career aspirations were as yet too diverse to impress his prospective in-laws, but World War II was raging around Rome and survival was much more the issue. Fellini and Masina were married as Rome waited to be liberated by the Allies.

Fellini's career in film began almost immediately after the war. An up-and-coming director named Roberto Rossellini asked him to persuade one of his actor friends to perform in a Rossellini movie. Later Rossellini asked Fellini to help write a script. From this beginning, Fellini became Rossellini's assistant and formed an unshakable determination to become a filmmaker in his own right.

During Fellini's long apprenticeship in the film industry, his marriage to Masina prospered. Masina was capable of playing the role of housewife when called upon, but she was also a skilled actress. She performed in several of her husband's movies and in other films as well. She also wrote for magazines, and starred in an Italian television series that, for a time, made her more famous than Fellini within their own country. Fellini considered Masina his partner, and he used her as an advisor and a critic. She was always the first to see his scripts. He valued her opinions about the business and creative aspects of moviemaking.

The physical contrast between Masina and Fellini was sharp. Masina was a small, rather impish woman, closer to cute than beautiful, while Fellini was tall and managed to look large and expansive even in his youth, though he was extremely thin. Early in their marriage Masina became pregnant but miscarried. After this the marriage produced no children.

Fellini expressed no great remorse for this, perhaps because he never stopped thinking of himself as a child.

Despite what appeared to be an idyllic relationship, Fellini's marriage had its problems, all of them stemming from his infidelity. It was a failing to which Fellini freely admitted. He was a man with an almost obsessive interest in sex. The process of filmmaking stimulated his lust rather than distracted him from it. Sex is typically a large part of the appeal of his films. At least three of his movies, 8½, City of Women, and Casanova, deal with the trials and disappointments of a confirmed womanizer. Fellini, particularly in his maturity, had a remarkable ability to fascinate women. He liked to surround himself with female admirers, among whom he divided his rather avuncular attention as equally as possible.

There are no specifics concerning Fellini's affairs. He names no names and only drops hints in his films as to what actually happened between him and his women. When the Italian press tried to link him with a particular young actress, Fellini sued and Masina came forward to say her husband and the young lady were "just friends." The only thing that can be said with certainty about Fellini's extramarital sex life is that, as trying as it often was for Masina, it never seriously threatened their marriage. Fellini maintained a clear distinction between the sex he had for fun and his relationship with the woman he regarded as his one true love.

Fellini's treatment of women in his movies has always been controversial. His tendency to portray women as symbols, either of wantonness, sensuality, or motherhood, had raised the ire of many critics. His use of fat women, inordinately top-heavy women, and women who might even be called freaks caused others to consider his movies "antiwoman." Fellini made no apologies for his obsessions or his tastes. When critics labeled his sexuality as "adolescent," he replied that in reality it was "preadolescent" images of women that appear in his films. These images stem from the sexual feelings of his early childhood.

As important as sex is to many of Fellini's movies, it is never presented in an obvious fashion. He was a firm believer that the best sex takes place in the imagination. When filming an orgy scene for his first major hit, La Dolce Vita, Fellini surveyed his friends to find out what actually happened at an orgy. When this research proved futile, he resorted to directing his actors to more or less fend for themselves. Later, working in collaboration with a younger director, Fellini objected to the blatant representation of intercourse. He maintained that the sight of other people having sex could only be funny.

Just as Fellini's fascination with women sustained him throughout his long filmmaking career, his fascination with Masina also never wavered. He claimed his wife still mystified him even after nearly fifty years of marriage. Fellini died of a stroke at the age of seventy-three. Giulietta Masina died the next year.

Another Example

Louise Brooks (Ziegfeld girl who became a silent screen vamp and later wrote a book detailing her bisexual romps through Hollywood, noting that sex was an excellent way to kill time). Born November 14, 1906 (Celebrity Birthday Guide).

If you have Mars in Libra with Venus in Capricorn you are . . . the Damned-Well-Better-Be Perfect Lover

You are the most devoted of the Mars in Libra Lovers. You honor your commitments not just because you need a relationship to feel whole, but also because you feel the essence of love is living up to your obligations. Your standards are high. Love is a serious matter and only the best need apply. Physical attractiveness will be judged as strenuously as mental, moral and emotional attributes. However, when you find the right person, he or she becomes the object of affection so endless that it will almost pass for worship.

Your sex life is full of rules and regulations, mostly of your own design. But the one overriding concern is always your strong physical need for sex. It is very easy for you to play the Mars in Libra game of dividing sex into the kind that matters and the kind that doesn't. The problem is that you tend to be more dogmatic about this intellectual division than you need to be, and this can seriously limit your ability to enjoy either kind of sex.

Case History

Elvis Presley (the "King" of rock-and-roll). Born January 8, 1935, in Tupolo, Mississippi (Goldman 1981).

Presley's childhood was dominated by his indulgent mother with whom he shared a bed throughout his childhood. It was only when he was sixteen, a few years after the family had moved to Memphis, that the pampered mama's boy showed some signs of rebelling. He went to a women's hairdresser and had his hair arranged in a defiant pompadour. Then he began wearing "tough guy" clothes. About the same time this shy outsider discovered that he could gain the acceptance of his classmates with his singing.

During the early days of his performing career Presley was surprised and put off by the aggressive sexual response his music elicited from female fans. Still, as much as the antics of these young women may have offended his Southern sense of propriety, it wasn't long before he was gearing his performances toward exciting their passions even further. He began wearing eye shadow to accent his girlish beauty and perfected the characteristic snarl and "bad boy" swagger that made his fans swoon. The suggestive movement of his hips and his dancing came naturally. He quickly learned how to use them to keep his audience enthralled.

Presley also adapted his private life to make the most of his sexy image. In those days he was an irrepressible flirt, coming on to any and all women who crossed his path. He haunted the streets at night looking for pickups, sometime taking as many as four girls in succession back to his motel room. Presley divided the world into "bad girls" and "good girls." He was a sexual animal with the bad girls who came to his motel room at night, while he remained the perfect gentleman who did not curse, drink, or press for sex with the good girls he dated back in Memphis.

Presley's period of reckless promiscuity did not last long. By the time he moved from rock-and-roll star to movie star he had been stuck with at least one paternity suit. His approach to sex grew more and more circumspect. He appeared hopelessly repressed to the girls he met in Hollywood and Las Vegas. He treated them like "nice" girls even when they expected something else entirely. He even took some of them back to Memphis to meet his beloved mother. Marriage was definitely on his mind at this time but he never found a girl old-fashioned enough to please him.

Meanwhile, back in Memphis, Presley persuaded the parents of three girls in their early teens to allow their daughters to spend long evenings with him at Graceland. These slumber parties were by all accounts perfectly innocent. Presley loved to play with toys, usually big, expensive toys, and these children became his playmates. Occasionally the play sessions resulted in wrestling matches in which Presley would become sexually excited, but he was easily turned away. The girls would be brought back to their respective homes, pure and unmolested.

There were other parties staged by Presley later in his career that were not nearly so innocent. These affairs mostly took place in his home in Bel Air. The guests included his coterie of loyal henchmen and as many women as could be crowded into the house. After choosing two or three of the women, Presley would take them to his bedroom, leaving the rest for the pleasure of his friends.

Presley's version of an orgy was unusual. He would ask the girls to strip to their panties and wrestle with each other while he watched. Always somewhat fearful of women, it bothered him if a woman took off all her clothing in his presence. He was also reluctant to remove his own underpants, doing so only when absolutely necessary. He typically did not penetrate his sex partners, particularly if they were strangers to him. He was fearful of another paternity suit. So he often resorted to "dry humping" or being masturbated by one of his girl friends.

When he did not have the time or the energy for one of his parties, Presley sent his cronies out to buy pornographic magazines. He also collected pornographic movies. His favorites where the relatively soft-core films it which nude women wrestled. His taste for voyeurism extended to spying on members of his male entourage while they made love to women in a special room equipped with a two-way mirror.

At twenty-three, while serving in the army (a reluctant draftee), Presley met Priscilla Beaulieu, who was fourteen at the time. Presley quickly developed a relationship with her that was similar to that he had enjoyed with his slumber-party mates back in Memphis. Later, when he was in the states, Presley arranged for Priscilla to stay with him at Graceland. He spent the next six years grooming her to be his bride—picking her clothing, her makeup, and her hairstyle. When he finally married her, she became pregnant immediately. At that point their relationship quickly faltered. Presley did not like the idea of having sex with a woman who had borne a child, even his own. So, he diverted himself with his parties and with other girl friends, leaving his beautiful young wife to her own devises.

It didn't take long for Priscella Presley to tire of being a fantasy bride. She left Elvis two years after the birth of their child. Presley was deeply shaken by the loss of his "perfect" marriage. Even though Presley's self-indulgent lifestyle was already very much out of control, it is theorized that his decline into total drug dependency was triggered by this event.

Presley found other women to console his battered ego. One was an ex-beauty queen with whom he had been sleeping even before the divorce. After he broke with this woman he became enamored with a twenty-year-old girl and talked seriously of marrying her. By this time, Presley's sex drive was overwhelmed by his misuse of drugs, and the young girl became more his friend than his mistress. Presley died at the age of forty-two.

Another Example

Frank Harris (Irish-born writer and publisher). Harris became so famous for the sexual adventures described in his scandalous autobiography that it was almost embarrassing for him to admit that he still loved his wife. Born February 14, 1856 (Encyclopedia Brittanica, Vol. 5).

If you have Mars in Libra with Venus in Aquarius you are . . . the Universally Perfect Lover

You are the most idealistic Mars in Libra Lover—an uncompromising dreamer whose fantasies of love sometime require an "out-of-body" experience. This is not to say you don't appreciate physical sex. What you can't appreciate, and find difficult to overlook, are the mundane bits of ugliness, awkwardness, and inanity that naturally go along with sexual intercourse. You expect sex to be as perfect, pristine, and effortless as it is in your dreams. Real-life sex, which is flawed and not always sweet smelling, typically leaves you very disappointed.

Fortunately, in most cases you are tolerant enough to deal with these disappointments, and your idealism in no way limits your ability to love. In fact, at your best your intellectual approach to love adds a breadth and a high-minded sense of purpose to your affection. Even though you never lose your need for partnership, you are also capable of expanding your ideal of perfect love to include the causes in which you believe and the people who fight for them. No matter how much human nature offends you, you never lose your love for humanity.

Case Study

Paul Cadmus (American realist painter noted for his homosexual themes). Born December 17, 1904, in New York City, New York (Kirstein 1984; Weinberg 1992).

Few American painters came to their craft as naturally as Paul Cadmus. Both his mother and father were artists. He was raised to follow in their footsteps, and began his professional training at age fourteen. He quickly distinguished himself; he had his first one-man exhibit at twenty-two. Cadmus first worked as a commercial illustrator. When he was twenty-six he took the money he had saved from his commercial work and went to Europe with his friend and fellow artist, Jared French. When he was twenty-nine he returned to the United States and joined the WPA program for artists. At this point during the Depression, the government paid artists to create art. Cadmus submitted a painting called *The Fleet's In* to a government sponsored exhibition.

The Fleet's In is an excellent example of Cadmus' mature style—merging exacting realism with bawdy satire. In the painting a group of drunken sailors are depicted on the prowl for sex. Some are accosting women, some are being accosted. Everyone in the painting looks at least a little foolish and besotted with lust. The head of the Department of the Navy disapproved of the painting and other top navy officials were outraged at what they saw as a slur against honest American sailors. Through their efforts Cadmus' painting was taken out of the exhibit. The removal of Cadmus' painting from the exhibit created a firestorm of controversy between the forces of free speech and artistic integrity, and those of patriotism and decency. Oddly enough, the one element of the painting that was probably the most offensive to the latter group was hardly mentioned in the resulting battle of words. One of the obviously available individuals seeking the attention of the lusty sailors was a man.

By the time Cadmus made this notorious painting he was apparently already aware that he was a homosexual. He made no public declarations of this fact, and the press of the period only dropped the gentlest hints. He was termed an "unsocial" bachelor in the 1942 *Current Biography*. His preference for male nudes (often depicted in sexually charged poses) continued to make his public commissions controversial, even as his skill and adherence to the values of the "old masters" caused him to be considered one of the most important artists of his generation.

When Cadmus was in his forties, American art shifted to abstraction. His carefully rendered realism was left in the dust. His standing in the art world went into decline but Cadmus was untouched by this loss of prestige. He continued to make paintings in the slow, exacting medium of egg tempera and showed no interest in the fashions of his time. He could afford to do this because there was still an assured market for his realist paintings. His gallery had buyers waiting for his work. The only problem he had was parceling out the paintings so as not to anger any of his eager collectors. What attracted at least some of these collectors were the homosexual themes and sensual male nudes that are featured in most of his paintings.

Cadmus was not always kind to the homosexual community. His depictions of the homosexual lifestyle often expose its seamiest aspects, including sleazy pickups and the bathroom rendezvous. During the 1930s and 1940s, when homosexuals were essentially an unseen minority, Cadmus showed the secret signals and social exchanges that were the currency of sex on the sly. At times he openly ridiculed homosexual men, particularly unattractive gays desiring or gossiping about the ever-elusive perfect male specimen. Perhaps more importantly, as the times changed and more gay men publicly aligned themselves with "Gay Liberation," Cadmus remained silent. He was content to let his artwork speak for him on this issue. Even people who have written about Cadmus' art were reluctant to discuss his sexuality, perhaps fearing such revelations would alienate the artist from the mainstream.

Even though Cadmus remained shy about talking publicly about his sexual preferences, he was never shy about displaying his complete fascination with the male body. Few artists have painted or drawn the male nude with such erotic power as Cadmus. His sexy men always represent a youthful, broad-shouldered, hard-bodied physical ideal—an ideal often emphasized by the juxtaposition of many flabby bodies (usually women or feminine homosexuals).

Two paintings define Cadmus' attitude toward life and sex. One, entitled *What I Believe,* was painted when he was forty-four. It contrasts one group of nudes, enjoying nature and themselves with a dignified and cerebral moderation, with another group immersed in excess and abuse. Cadmus sits with the former group with a male companion at his side, intently observing and drawing the latter.

The second was painted almost fifteen years later and is titled *Study for David and Goliath.* It is a clever allusion to a much older masterpiece by Caravaggio. In that seventeenth-century painting, the youthful David holds up the severed head of Goliath—whose face is that of the artist—a ruthless, brutal homosexual. In Cadmus' adaptation of the theme, his long-time companion, Jon Anderson, is the muscular David. Cadmus' head takes the place of Goliath's. Whereas Caravaggio portrayed himself as miserable and defeated, Cadmus' expression is emphatically happy.

Jon Anderson began to appear in Cadmus' work in the 1960s. He was probably the artist's favorite model and companion. One observer wrote that their life together seemed the model of idyllic domesticity. Happily, Cadmus lived long enough to see artistic fashions shift to the point that he is once again considered a major American painter.

Another Example

Gennifer Flowers *(alleged paramour of an Arkansas governor). Born January 24, 1950 (Flowers 1995).*

If you have Mars in Libra with Venus in Pisces you are . . . the Deceptively Perfect Lover

No Lover believes in love the way that you do. No Lover infuses the sex act with such cosmic implications. You are looking for more from love and sex than a bond to another human being. You are looking for salvation—an emotional catharsis that will totally overwhelm your soul. It is for this reason that you can be one of the sexiest and most alluring of the Mars in Libra Lovers. For the same reason, you can also be the most fearful Lover of this type. Sex can be pretty intimidating when it goes cosmic.

The key to understanding your sexual nature is that your real sex life takes place in your dreams. The sex you have in your bedroom (or anywhere else) is nothing but a faint and illusive shadow. You can get a lot of joy from this shadow. At times, you might even confuse it with your dream love life, but not for long. This makes you a very self-sufficient Lover, despite all your deep emotional needs. No matter how good your real life partner may be, he or she is only a corporeal placeholder for your ideal.

Case History

Anaïs Nin (multinational writer noted for her voluminous diaries). Born February 21, 1903, in Paris, France (Bair 1995).

Nin's Cuban-born father was a pianist. He was also a womanizer and an egotist. He married Nin's mother, who was ten years older than him and the daughter of a wealthy Dane doing business in Cuba, for her money. The marriage was troubled from the very beginning, even though it produced three children.

When Nin's father lost his temper, he would beat both his wife and his children. His abuse also became sexual with Nin. Nin's father was an amateur photographer and he forced her to pose for him in the nude. Even as he was caressing her and taking her picture, Nin remembered her father telling her over and over what an ugly girl she was.

When Nin was twelve her parent's marriage finally broke up. Her mother took the children to America where she struggled to make a living. Nin developed into a romantic adolescent with a slim body and a delicately beautiful face. She evinced little sexual curiosity during these years. At eighteen she worked as an artist's model but she still managed to fend off all assaults on her virtue. She remained a virgin until her marriage at the age of twenty.

Nin married Hugh Parker Guiler, a dutiful banker with a keenness for the arts. His family was wealthy, but they disapproved of the marriage and Guiler had to make his own way. He did so rather nicely, moving his wife to France where he became so successful that his talented wife had nothing to do but work on her writing.

The sexual side of the Guiler marriage got off to rocky start. The actual consummation of the union did not occur until six months after the wedding. Part of the problem was the ignorance of both parties, and Guiler's exaggerated sense of propriety around his beautiful but fragile wife. There was also a basic physical incompatibility. Nin felt Guiler's penis was too large, and intercourse with her husband was often painful.

Early in the marriage Guiler tried to spice up their failing sex life by bringing home pornographic pictures and sex manuals, but Nin was repelled by these efforts. By the time she reached her mid-twenties, the shy wife had found her own way to bring excitement into her sex life. She flirted with other men. For the first few years these flirtations were harmless, but this changed radically when Guiler brought home a starving writer named Henry Miller.

Miller was a man for whom sex was always serious fun, and her flirtation with him quickly turned into a full-blown love affair. The situation became infinitely hotter when Miller's enigmatic wife, June, joined the writer in Paris. Nin was fascinated by June even while the two women were competing for the attention of Miller. June and Nin had their own flirtation in which they kissed and caressed but never went any further. Soon it was Miller who was the jealous third party.

Meanwhile, Nin had not forgotten her beloved husband. She instigated a trip to a bordello for the two of them where they saw a live sex show and a demonstration of lesbian intercourse. This stimulated Guiler's sexual interest in Nin just when her affair with Miller was at its height. Nin enjoyed playing Miller against her husband; she recognized that she had the upper hand in both relationships. She knew Guiler would not discover her infidelities because he wanted so badly to believe she was still his shy little bride. Miller, despite his threats to the contrary, accepted the role of second-string lover because he was too dependent on the money Nin gave him.

After June returned to the United States, Nin felt the need for more intrigues, or "treacheries," as she called them. She began an affair with the poet Antonin Artaud, and another with her analyst, Rene Allendy. Neither affair was tremendously sexual. Artaud was impotent, and Allendy could only sustain an erection while he was spanking her with a whip. Nin was too fascinated by the poet to care. Her relationship with Allendy, who had become something of a father figure to her, was just a dry run for what was to come next.

Nin was twenty-nine when she began her sexual adventures with Miller. The next year she took the adventure to another level. She went to see her father for the first time since he had left her mother. Father and daughter found themselves quite compatible. Both loved art and beauty, and both were flamboyantly narcissistic. The elder Nin was confined to his bed because of a bad back but this didn't stop the younger Nin from joining him there and having sex with him repeatedly during her visit.

What all of these relationship had in common for Nin was the fact that she recorded them in her diaries, first briefly reporting the incident and then, later, returning to expound in great detail about each seduction or affair. Often it seemed that the sex she had only became real when she reported it in her journal. When Allendy spanked her she found it humorous, but went along partly because she thought of what fun she would have writing about the experience. Then, while she was writing, she suddenly began to find the lingering sting of his whip very erotic.

More than one of her lovers objected to, or belittled, her keeping a diary. Her father was particularly upset at the notion that she had recorded their mutual sin. Otto Rank, a noted psychoanalyst who became her doctor and lover after Allendy, told Nin that her only hope for a "cure" was to put aside her diaries. Nin tried but was drawn back to recording her thoughts by an almost physical compulsion. Nin's diary was her confessor, her mirror, and (in her own words) her "best friend." Through more than sixty volumes, they represented the most perfect relationship of her life—the one that overshadowed both her marriage and all her love affairs.

Nin continued her sexual game playing through her thirties and into her forties. She experimented further with lesbianism and orgies but found her preference was for one-on-one seductions of men. In her forties, these men were often much younger. Her marriage to Guiler continued, as did her relationship with Miller, though by this time it was mostly about money, for Nin was tired of these "old" men. She arbitrarily lopped ten years off her own age and, at least for a time, she had the looks and the energy to convince many people she was telling the truth.

Nin stopped keeping her diaries about the same time she met Rubert Pole. He was a handsome man of twenty-eight who looked remarkably like Hugh Guiler. Nin was forty-four. This relationship became her last sustained love affair, and perhaps most enduring "treachery" of her life. Until her death, Nin maintained two homes: one with Guiler in New York, and one with Pole in California. Pole eventually found out about the deception, but Guiler remained unaware until Nin died at the age of seventy-three.

Another Example

Edgar Allan Poe (American writer noted for his fascination with death and the macabre). Born January 19, 1809 (Celebrity Birthday Guide).

Chapter 8

Mars in Scorpio
The Powerhouse of Passion

General Characteristics

Sex is an all-consuming fascination for people with Mars in Scorpio. Strictly speaking, they are the sexiest Lovers in the Zodiac—or at least the Lovers for whom sex has the deepest significance. They tend to be very conservative, cautious people who conduct their sex lives with weighty deliberation, like a general planning an important campaign. They treat sex with great deference, and with a respect that borders on awe. It is as if they know something that everyone else has somehow missed—something a little scary.

For Mars in Scorpio Lovers, sex has a significance that goes far beyond the personal. They recognize that sex is the key that unlocks the most elemental forces of nature and allows us to touch the infinite. In this sense, copulation becomes a spiritual act and every aspect of sexual excitement becomes a sacrament. This cosmic approach to sex means that these Lovers are seldom able to limit sex to just one area of their lives. Sex is everywhere as far as they are concerned, though the omnipresent sexuality has less to do with titillation than it does with power.

Sex and power are often interchangeable for these Lovers. This, of course, makes control the salient issue in their love lives. This doesn't necessarily mean that the Mars in Scorpio Lover needs to be in control of his or her partner. On the contrary, their interest in the partner is always secondary. What these people need to control is sex itself. They need to know sex at its deepest and most primitive level. They need to touch it, see it, consume it and, in some cases, be consumed by it.

This need to understand the power of sex means that even the most conventional of these Lovers will have an active interest in the darker aspects of sexual expression. If nothing else, they find validation for their own concept of sex as a powerful and dangerous force, while observing the bizarre things sex makes other people do. Of course, some Mars in Scorpio Lovers take this interest further than others. It is often difficult for these Lovers to balance their essential conservatism against their incessant curiosity. Sometimes they take a tumble into the extreme. Sex has an almost addictive quality to these Lovers, and it can consume the lives of those who are not watchful.

Mars in Scorpio Lovers often exert a strong sexual presence. They have an allure that is mysterious, seductive, and tinged with danger. Power also plays a role in this attraction. The notion of using sex as a means to gain power over another person comes easily to these Lovers. Mars in Scorpio Lovers can be very subtle, almost insidious, in their domination of a relationship; they can also be shockingly cruel and duplicitous. There is always more going on than meets the eye in the Mars in Scorpio universe. This is what makes these Lovers so dangerously exciting.

Yet there are many Mars in Scorpio Lovers who look upon this kind of manipulation of sex with horror. They are too respectful, or perhaps too fearful, of their sexuality to ever use sex in such a calculated manner. These Lovers show their singular attitude toward sex in ways that are more conventional, such as an overwhelming sexual fascination with their spouses. Their deep awareness of the power and the danger of sex only makes them more conservative and evasive. For these "other" Mars in Scorpio Lovers, the full power and glory of sex is something that can be revealed only in their most intimate moments, when its awesome significance can be truly appreciated.

If you have Mars in Scorpio with Venus in Aries you are . . . the Pushy Powerhouse of Passion

The bad news first: you are one of the least subtle of the Mars in Scorpio Lovers. Your attempts at using your sexual power are likely to be clumsy, bombastic, and, in the end, ineffective. Your biggest problem is a lack of patience. The true Mars in Scorpio experience of sex requires time, nurturing, and emotional resonance. You are just too impulsive and too hungry to wait on this process.

Now the good news: you are one of the most active Lovers of this type. You are not content to just sit back and observe passion. You go out, find it, and make it your own. You like challenges in your relationships—new experiences, aggressive partners, and the spice of a good fight. This keeps your sexual instincts sharp and helps you resist the temptation to sink into redundant sensuality. In a nutshell, you are the most alert, dynamic, and energetic of all the Mars in Scorpio Lovers. So, who cares if you're a little impatient?

Case History

Enrico Caruso (probably the most famous operatic singer of all time and a pioneer recording star). Born February 25, 1873, in Naples, Italy (Jackson 1972).

Caruso was born into dire poverty in the dismal slums of Naples. He quickly surmised that his remarkable voice might be his ticket to a better life. He was scoffed at by his irascible father, but encouraged by his beloved mother who died when he was fifteen. By this time the determined youngster had already begun his career as a professional singer.

Sex often got Caruso into trouble. This first occurred when he was in his early twenties. Engaged to the very proper daughter of a theater manager, Caruso suddenly bolted from that overly chaperoned arrangement to run off with a ballerina (who happened to be the mistress of an influential conductor). For a few days the passionate youngsters were sure that they were in love but, when their money ran out, the girl left Caruso and he was forced to go back to work. Of course, his new boss turned out to be the very conductor whose girlfriend he had stolen.

Fortunately for Caruso, he became involved with a dark-eyed, voluptuous singer named Ada Giachetti only a short time after this peccadillo. Giachetti was ten years older than Caruso and a veteran performer, even though she had never risen to the top ranks. She held on to her own career aspirations for a while after she took Caruso for a lover. But once his career skyrocketed, and he could afford to keep her in a manner that was well worth growing accustomed to, she retired from the stage.

For the intensely oedipal Caruso, the relationship with Giachetti was well augured. She was a sex partner who was old enough and strong enough to mother him. She was separated but still married early in their relationship and, therefore, could not become his wife. Nonetheless, their relationship produced two sons and several unsuccessful pregnancies.

Caruso spent much of his time traveling from city to city and continent to continent. He was often separated from Giachetti. During these separations he was known as a flirt, but for the most part his flirtations were innocent. The glamorous divas with whom he sang typically characterized the tenor as uncouth and juvenile—a likable lout who was entirely too addicted to practical jokes to be of romantic interest. He had better luck with the female fans that crowded around his dressing room door. With them he would steal a kiss here and there or make ostentatious displays of generosity. But such was Caruso's fascination with (or fear of) the jealous Giachetti that he was incapable of letting these situations go any further.

By the time Caruso reached his early thirties he had achieved a sizable reputation both as a singer and as a flirt. His reputation landed him in jail when he was accused of pinching a woman's behind in the monkey house of the Central Park Zoo in New York. Caruso denied the allegation, but this episode would not have been out of character for a Latin male of his time. The "pinchee" refused to testify, but Caruso was convicted and fined. Despite his embarrassment, the incident did not interfere with his popularity with New York audiences.

Worse times were on the way. Caruso discovered that Giachetti had taken a younger lover a short time after the "Monkey-House Incident." After she confessed, he forgave her and left for another foreign tour. This proved to be the wrong thing to do; when he arrived at his first port of call, Caruso found a letter from Giachetti waiting for him. She had left him to live with her virile young chauffeur. Caruso suffered a breakdown so severe that it even compromised his remarkable voice. Some felt that this event was the beginning of a downward trend in his abilities as a singer.

After this betrayal, Caruso began womanizing in earnest. Starting with Giachetti's sister, he bedded a series of women and quickly managed to equal all the rumors that had once been spread about his Mediterranean libido. These impetuous affairs were no doubt pleasant but, for the most part, they served merely to assuage his wounded pride. His attention was still centered on Giachetti, though now hatred, vengeance, and recriminations characterized the bond between them. They battled in the courts and in the popular press for many years, each angling for a real or imagined advantage over the other. Meanwhile, Caruso continued to send her a monthly stipend. ("For the mother of my children," he told his accountant.) (Jackson, 204).

When Caruso was forty-five his sex life took another surprising turn. He began seeing an American woman named Dorothy Benjamin, who was a member of one of New England's oldest and most illustrious families. She was not an opera lover, nor was she anything like the loud and lusty Giachetti. Yet when Caruso impulsively asked her to marry him, she accepted. When her family disapproved, citing differences in their ages and cultures, and the fact that Caruso had often bragged that he would never marry, Benjamin ignored them and married him anyway.

Not many of Caruso's associates gave the relationship much of a chance. Wouldn't the sexy singer be too much for a prim descendant of Puritans? These critics were proven wrong. The marriage gave Caruso the stability he needed during the few remaining years of his life, and the couple became genuinely close. The marriage produced one daughter, and endured until Caruso's death at the age of forty-eight.

Other Examples

Auguste Renoir (*impressionist painter noted for his fluffy female nudes*). *Born February 25, 1841 (Celebrity Birthday Guide).*

Marilyn Chambers (*star of* Behind the Green Door, *a host of other X-rated movies, and the model in an Ivory Snow ad*). *Born April 22, 1952 (Hunter 1992).*

If you have Mars in Scorpio with Venus in Taurus you are . . . the Voluptuous Powerhouse of Passion

You are gifted with a lush sensuality and a quiet, unhurried eroticism that tends to get noticed whether you want it to or not. You are very straightforward in your approach to sex. You make no excuses for your substantial physical desires. In some ways you are one of the most conservative Mars in Scorpio Lovers. But this only means you will do everything in your power to keep your private life private and avoid noise or scandal—everything except deprive yourself of sex.

Because your response to sex is so physical, it is easy for you to think of your sexual needs in purely physical terms. Nothing could be further from the truth. For you sex always involves deep and complex psychological issues like power, security, and control. These complexities don't necessarily detract from your concern for sensation, but they will make it more difficult for you to manage your sex life in the neat, practical fashion that you prefer. Emotions get you in trouble. Of course, emotions also make it all worthwhile.

Case History

Lillian Hellman (*American playwright and political activist noted for her provocative dramas,* Little Foxes *and* The Children's Hour). *Born June 20, 1905, in New Orleans, Louisiana (Mellen 1996; Wright 1986).*

Hellman grew up in a house divided. Her Jewish mother came from a family with deep roots in the South. Her father's background was far less genteel and more intellectual. Hellman emphatically aligned herself with her father and his values, even though she secretly felt betrayed by the elder Hellman's frequent infidelities to her mother.

In her own account of her early years Hellman presented herself as an earthy, liberated woman thoroughly in control of her sex life. The events, however, tell a different story. Hired against all odds as an editor for a prestigious publishing house at the age of twenty, she almost immediately became pregnant by one of the other editors. After an abortion, she married the man and quit her job.

Hellman's husband, Arthur Kober, was a short, funny, affable man who shared her own vague ambitions of becoming a writer. Early in the relationship his easygoing manner was a nice compliment to Hellman's more aggressive style. People thought them the perfect couple; however, during a long, low-budget tour of Europe, Hellman's fascination with Kober waned. She began to have affairs. By the time the marriage was five years old, its main advantages to Hellman were that Kober gave her monetary support and plenty of freedom to do what she wanted.

Unfortunately for Hellman, she had almost no notion what she wanted to do at this point in her life. The couple drifted to California when Kober landed a job as a screenwriter. She frittered away her time reading, gambling, and working in a dead-end job. This all changed when she met Dashiell Hammett, the famed creator of Sam Spade. Hammett was a striking man—tall, handsome, and soft-spoken—with the laconic yet forthright manner of the best American hero. He was also a famous writer who was the darling of the literary world and Hollywood, despite his ill-concealed contempt for both these institutions. That Hellman immediately fell in love with him was no surprise. And yet the relationship that developed between Hellman and Hammett proved to be quite remarkable.

Hellman's relationship with Kober had been a loose union of equals in which she typically had the upper hand. When Hellman became "Hammett's girl," she surrendered herself both professionally and sexually to his exacting standards. Professionally, Hammett nurtured Hellman's thus-far untapped talent and gave direction to her extraordinary ambition and energy. Through him she became familiar with some of the greatest literary figures of the time. She was introduced to an approach to literature that was stern and demanding. It was Hammett who gave Hellman the theme for her first play, *The Children's Hour*, and his patient coaching and criticism spurred her to make it into a hit.

It was Hammett's sexual domination that really changed Hellman's life. Hammett was an inveterate womanizer with an irresistible sex appeal and a taste for cheap women. He immediately placed Hellman in a category apart from the whores and starlets with whom he filled his nights, but this was little comfort to Hellman. Forgetting her own freewheeling past, she was constantly jealous. She knew that she was not a pretty woman and she felt profoundly insecure when she saw Hammett flirting with various Hollywood beauties. Early in the relationship she tried to appease him by agreeing to threesomes. These were probably the only lesbian encounters Hellman had, though she liked to hint at others. She claimed that she refused to continue this practice because she was afraid she might come to enjoy it. It would have been unthinkable for her to admit that she was just too conservative for that kind of sex play.

Yet there was an even darker side of Hammitt's sexuality that never ceased to fascinate her. Long before he and Hellman met, Hammett had been known as a nasty drunk who was capable of offhanded cruelty and even violence when he was properly oiled. He was a man who expected women to do as they were told or stay out of his way when he was drinking. Hellman refused to do either and Hammett often beat her because of this. Those who knew Hellman as an aggressive and independent woman were surprised that she endured this treatment, but the punches, the threats, and the very physical sense of fear Hammett inspired in her only added to his inescapable sexual allure.

Hellman decided to have affairs of her own when she saw that her jealous rages were not going to stop Hammett's infidelity. She later admitted that she took lovers as an act of revenge. Too proud to be a passive victim in her relationship and too much in love to abandon it, she took charge of the situation the only way she knew how. Hammett was not pleased by this turn of events but he was too consumed by his own problems and too desperate to hold on to Hellman to complain. The only thing that bothered him was that Hellman often lied to him about other men and to the other men about him. Since he honored brutal honesty, Hammett could not understand Hellman's duplicity.

When he became aware of Hellman's sexual adventures, Hammett accused her of taking on his hard-hearted personality, and of becoming a "she-Hammett." Hellman often surprised men with her aggressiveness and by being as direct and unsentimental about sex as they were. At other times she could also play the coquette, full of feminine wiles and greatly appreciative of fine silks and expensive gifts. Many of the men she bedded found her to be an extremely passionate lover and heartily regretted that she would never break her bond to Hammett. Others found her physically unappealing or were unable to match her demands for sex.

Both Hammett and Hellman needed solitude when they wrote. Their need for solitude, their globetrotting lifestyle, and Hammett's alcoholic binges meant that the two writers were frequently apart. During their thirty-year relationship they shared quarters only sporadically, even though they owned the various properties jointly. During one period they didn't even speak. Yet they never ceased to be a couple. During the last years of their relationship Hammett's improvident lifestyle and failing health made him totally dependent on Hellman. He spent much of the last three years of his life bedfast in her apartment, listening to her greet her many friends on the floor below with loud complaints about the invalid upstairs. He died when Hellman was fifty-five.

Hellman continued to have affairs during Hammett's long illness, but her sex life drew to a close with his death. She occupied herself writing her memoirs. Each new volume created a literary stir quite equal to her first hit play. She was accused, with some justification apparently, of being less than truthful in her autobiography. Though quite open about her attitude toward sex, she left many of her love affairs out of her account and perhaps invented others. She remained controversial and belligerent until her death at the age of seventy-nine.

Other Examples

Jean-Paul Sartre *(French writer and existential philosopher). Born June 21, 1905 (Celebrity Birthday Guide).*

Grace Jones *(American singer). Born May 19, 1952 (Celebrity Birthday Guide).*

If you have Mars in Scorpio with Venus in Gemini you are ... the Impish Powerhouse of Passion

You have two options. Since you are the coolest and the most rational of all the Mars in Scorpio Lovers, you can become a world-class manipulator of sex—someone who combines wit and sex appeal to take the advantage in every sexual situation. This allows you to have a great deal of fun without giving anyone an even break. It also makes it very difficult for you to trust another person or be trusted by anyone else. Without trust, love is not possible.

Your second option is to concentrate on having a good time and forget about being in control. Of course, you never give up lusting for control even when you are in a poor position to hold on to it. This option will always leave you feeling a little frustrated and vulnerable. But it also makes it very easy for people to fall in love with you. If you have someone who truly loves you, that's all the power you really need.

Case History

Rembrandt Van Rijn *(Dutch painter noted for his dramatic use of light and his ability to convey poignant humanity). Born July 15, 1606, in Leyden, Holland (Mondadori 1977).*

As the son of a miller, it was only his precocious talent and his persistent demands to study art that caused the young Rembrandt to be apprenticed to a local painter. He quickly proved himself and was allowed to travel to Amsterdam to study further. When he was only nineteen he returned to his hometown to set up a studio with another painter. The business thrived, and Rembrandt became a local celebrity.

Nothing is known of Rembrandt's early sex life. But it is not likely he would have maintained the favor of the staunchly conservative citizens of Leyden had he not been, at the very least, exceedingly discreet. When he was twenty-five he returned to Amsterdam and began courting his future wife, Saskia van Uylenburch. They were engaged when he was twenty-seven and married the next year.

There can be no doubt that Rembrandt loved his wife. He painted her over and over with unvarying affection and sexual fascination. Not only did she sit for numerous portraits, but she also posed, often in the nude, for countless biblical and classical figures. Unlike other artists who used their loved ones as models, Rembrandt did not do this out of financial necessity. This period was the most prosperous of his artistic life, and Saskia herself brought to the marriage a sizable dowry. Rembrandt thought nothing of splurging on expensive costumes and props for his paintings, but he wanted no model but Saskia, whether he was painting a chaste Susanna concealing her nakedness from the elders, or a lascivious Danae waiting for Zeus to invade her bed as a shower of gold.

As much as he loved Saskia, Rembrandt never sought to idealize her in his paintings. Regardless of how exotic or dramatic her guise, she is presented as a rather common-looking Dutch woman: her round face and rounder belly, bulbous nose, and short legs are all strikingly evident. Of course, to some extent Rembrandt was reflecting a standard of beauty that was much more fleshy and natural than that of the present day, but his obsession with Saskia's body is very specific. It seems he could imagine no woman more alluring than his wife.

Rembrandt's wife was more than just a patient model. She was also a very astute judge of her husband's character. She knew that Rembrandt was a spendthrift who was so undisciplined with his money that he had made and wasted a fortune by the time he was thirty-five. In that same year Saskia bore him their fourth and only surviving child. The delivery shattered her health, and she prepared a will leaving her personal wealth to their child. All that Rembrandt could count on was the interest from her holdings. A few months after making these arrangements, Saskia died.

Unfortunately, what Saskia couldn't have known was that the Dutch economy, which had thrived for so long, would begin to fail. This problem was compounded by the fact that shortly before Saskia's death Rembrandt had "botched" a large portrait commission. The painting, which is commonly known as the *The Night Watch* is now one of Rembrandt's most famous works, but the men who had paid for it found it unsatisfactory. As money became tight in Amsterdam, Rembrandt found that he was categorized as a painter who was too avant-garde to be trusted.

Rembrandt's reputation was further damaged two years after his wife's death. A woman he had hired as wet nurse for his son filed suit against the artist, claiming he had taken advantage of her and had promised to marry her. Rembrandt was forced to pay this woman a yearly annuity—something he could ill-afford in the face of his monumental indebtedness and shrinking income.

When Rembrandt was thirty-nine he began an affair with his housemaid, a young woman of twenty-three named Hendrickje Stoffels. This situation eventually resulted in yet another scandal in Rembrandt's life. Stoffels was hauled before an ecclesiastical court and excluded from the rights of her church because of their illicit arrangement. Rembrandt was unable to marry Stoffels because a clause in his wife's will provided that he would be deprived of the interest on his son's trust if he remarried. He desperately needed this income as his financial situation continued to worsen.

Rembrandt's sexual infatuation for Saskia was quite naturally transferred to Stoffels. Like Saskia, Stoffels found herself cast in a variety of glamorous roles for which she was physically an unlikely candidate. If anything, Rembrandt's portrayal of Stoffels was sexier than that of his wife, perhaps because of the unofficial nature of the union or because she had "ruined" herself in the eyes of the citizens of Amsterdam for him.

Stoffels' devotion to Rembrandt is unquestionable. She supported him despite public censure and through a long decline in his fortunes. When he was fifty-one he declared bankruptcy. His house, his artwork, and all the costly baubles he had purchased during his prosperous youth were sold at a public auction. Even after this Rembrandt was in debt. Stoffels and Rembrandt's son formed a company to handle the artist's affairs and protect him from his persistent creditors.

When Rembrandt was fifty-six, Stoffels died. It was a shattering blow. After this he devoted more of his time to his introspective self-portraits. He died at the age of sixty-three.

Another Example

Alfred, Lord Tennyson (*English poet during the Victorian era*). *Born August 6, 1809 (Celebrity Birthday Guide).*

If you have Mars in Scorpio with Venus in Cancer you are . . . the Profound Powerhouse of Passion

The word that describes your sexuality is formidable. You come at your partner with so much sexual energy and depth of feeling that even the most casual contact can be breathtaking. You take up an enormous amount of emotional space in relationships. You need lots of love, lots of attention, and lots and lots of sex. For people with plenty of room in their hearts and sufficient physical stamina, your boundless capacity for devotion will make you a challenge well met.

There are times when this emotional power can get out of hand. Your awareness of relationships is so subjective and so much an extension of your own sexual needs that you sometimes lose track of both your partner and reality. Driven as you are by your own powerful emotions, you have a bad habit of forgetting or minimizing the emotional needs of others. No one will deny that you are a wonderfully intense and committed Lover, but you are often a kinder and more pleasant Lover when you are not taking it all so seriously.

Case History

William Makepeace Thackeray (*British novelist, author of* Vanity Fair). *Born July 18, 1811, in Calcutta, India (Forster 1979).*

Very much a child of the Victorian era, Thackeray was born in one of the farthest bastions of the British Empire, where his father worked for the British East India Company. When Thackeray was five his father died. He was sent back to England alone where he was shuffled from one dreary school to another. Thackeray was reunited with his mother when he was nine, but the separation made a deep impression on him.

As a teenager Thackeray entered Cambridge with no real mission except to pass time while he waited to come of age and collect his inheritance. He fell into the usual vices available to well-to-do Victorian youngsters, including whoring. His particular downfall was gambling. A large part of Thackeray's patrimony would be lost at the gaming tables or through speculation in the years that followed.

Thackeray had little opportunity to court women of his own class until he traveled to Europe when he was twenty-one. He spent time in Weimar where he fell in love with a couple of young women, and showed himself quite capable of romantic flights of fancy. None of his adolescent infatuations breached the limits of propriety.

Having left the university without a degree and with no professional aspirations to speak of, Thackeray found himself placed as a clerk in a London law office. Thackeray so hated this job that he applied himself to writing and soon began to publish articles and reviews. He talked his stepfather into buying a small publication so he could become an editor. But despite his interest in journalism, Thackeray's career goals were still in flux. By the time he was twenty-four he was in Paris studying to be an artist.

Thackeray had run through most of his inheritance, and his financial situation was growing desperate. He could have solved his problems with a prudent marriage to a likable heiress. Instead he fell in love with a young woman named Isabella Shawe who was even poorer than he was.

Shawe was only a teenager when she met Thackeray. She lived very much under the thumb of her domineering mother. She was shy, petite, and sexually undemonstrative; and yet Thackeray was thoroughly charmed by her demure demeanor. He began a courtship so passionate and resolute that even the imperious Mrs. Shawe had to give way. Thackeray and Isabella were married when he was twenty-five.

The first year of Thackeray's marriage was essentially a long honeymoon. The young couple lived cheaply in Paris on the money Thackeray made as a correspondent for a London magazine. They spent the bulk of their time simply enjoying one another. This blissful situation ended when their first child was born and the little family returned to England. Mindful of his new responsibilities and with poverty breathing down his neck, Thackeray applied himself to his journalistic labors with real vigor for the first time in his life. His long days were often followed by long nights at his "club" where he enjoyed the exclusively male company of his fellow members and made necessary business connections.

At first Isabella quietly accepted her new role as the wife of a busy, sometimes dictatorial, literary man. When her second child died shortly after birth, Thackeray's sensitive wife fell into a deep depression. Thackeray, much to his later regret, assumed that another pregnancy would be the cure. It proved to have just the opposite outcome. After the birth of her third child, Isabella's behavior became startlingly erratic. Although it took some time for Thackeray to realize that Isabella was slowly going insane.

The situation came to a head when Thackeray was twenty-nine. Fearful of leaving Isabella alone, he took her with him on a ship sailing for Ireland. Late at night, Isabella slipped out of bed and jumped off the ship. She was rescued but, from this point on, she required constant supervision. Thackeray spent the next several years seeking a cure for his deranged wife. At first she had periods of normality during which she was particularly passionate toward her husband. These remissions became increasingly rare and, in the end, she failed to recognize him at all.

When he was thirty-five, Thackeray lodged Isabella with a permanent caretaker. He was in the midst of writing *Vanity Fair*, the work that would make him a rich man. The novel contrasts the progress of two women: one an amoral adventuress, the other a paragon of goodness. Thackeray claimed the second character, perfect beyond the belief of some critics, was modeled on his adored wife.

The publication of *Vanity Fair* when Thackeray was thirty-six established him as a major literary figure. At the same time he began a relationship with William and Jane Brookfield. William was an old friend of Thackeray's. He was apparently pleased when the writer began spending nearly all his evenings at the Brookfield residence. It didn't occur to William Brookfield that the sexually frustrated Thackeray had fallen in love with his wife.

Thackeray's infatuation with Jane Brookfield was, to say the least, unwise. Even though Jane may have been flattered by the author's attention, an affair between them was impossible. Jane was a passive and dutiful young woman who thoroughly enjoyed the domestic bliss she shared with her husband. It was just this tranquil domesticity that attracted Thackeray. He saw in Jane the wife Isabella could have been and, against all reason, he wanted her for his own. His silent obsession was so intense that, when Jane became pregnant, Thackeray fell desperately ill.

After the birth of the Brookfields' child, Thackeray renewed his platonic admiration for Jane. Motherhood only made her more attractive to him. By this time William Brookfield began to have suspicions. Either gossip had reached his ears or he saw something he didn't like in his wife's behavior. With Jane sitting silently beside him, he accused Thackeray of making him a cuckold. The ensuing argument put a sad end to Thackeray's hopeless courtship, though his infatuation with Jane Brookfield lasted for many more years.

Thackeray was a large, emotional man with a lusty fondness for good food and wine and a rather shocking penchant for "bawdy" talk and vulgar puns. By all accounts he was a poor candidate for celibacy. But with the exception of a few isolated remarks in his correspondence, in which he claims the desire for sex is often on his mind, we have little information about Thackeray's sex life after his separation from Isabella. When Thackeray died his journals and letters were heavily edited by friends and family anxious to preserve his image as the perfect Victorian gentleman. So, beyond a few hints and rumors, the outstanding feature of Thackeray's later sex life remains his lifelong devotion and respect for the wife who no longer remembered his name. He was still officially married to Isabella when he died at the age of fifty-two.

If you have Mars in Scorpio with Venus in Leo you are . . . the Royal Powerhouse of Passion

You are the Mars in Scorpio Lover most likely to talk about your love life, though you'd be the first to admit that there's no guarantee that what you're saying is the truth. You are always unsure about how much you want to reveal about yourself. On the one hand, you are a secretive person who is very serious about sex. On the other, you hate that your best moments on the planet all occur behind closed doors. So, you hide your secrets behind a theatrical display of frankness and hope everyone still gets the message.

You are also one of the most controlling Lovers of this type, though you can be exceptionally charming and gentle in the way you apply this control. Typically, you are more apt to get your way through passive stubbornness than by pushing people around. Of course, you are an extremely sexy Lover with an all-out commitment to pleasure and a wonderful capacity for pure fun. This also helps take the bite out of your otherwise imperial, sexual nature.

Case History

Jacqueline Susann (novelist noted for her racy books such as Valley of the Dolls, *about starlets, drug addicts, and poodles). Born August 20, 1918, in Philadelphia, Pennsylvania (Seaman 1987).*

Susann's father was a flamboyant society painter. She was introduced to sex at the age of four when she interrupted him while he was making love to one of his models. After this, Susann was unusually preoccupied with sex. She alarmed her mother, a conservative schoolteacher, by making all her dolls anatomically correct.

By the time she had finished high school Susann had already decided she was going to be a star of stage and screen. She lacked a perfect face and figure, but learned how to use clothes and make-up to conceal her deficiencies. Susann got a chance to audition in New York City by winning a local beauty contest. She spent several months making the rounds with various agents and producers looking for a break. She got nowhere; however, when men tried to take advantage of the stage-struck youngster they also got nowhere.

After about a year of struggling for parts on Broadway, she met a publicist named Irving Mansfield. Mansfield was ten years older than Susann and was already somewhat successful in his field. They shared a Jewish background (though Susann's family was much more affluent than Mansfield's), and an unqualified infatuation with show business. When Susann was twenty, she and Mansfield were married.

Susann was very fond of Mansfield and probably loved him after a fashion, but he did not satisfy her sexually. The pain that she felt when she lost her virginity with him was apparently the most outstanding feature of their sex life. At the time Susann's sexual interests were centered on a comedian named Joe E. Lewis. He was a veteran performer whose wit, energy, and "star quality" captivated Susann even though she had never actually met him.

Shortly after her marriage, Susann focused her attention on Eddie Cantor, another comedian. Her husband was trying to get him as a client, and Susann decided to help. She not only persuaded Cantor to hire Mansfield as his press agent, but she got herself a small part in his new Broadway show. At the same time she and Cantor started an affair. She proudly recalled later that this was her first adultery. Unfortunately, their indiscretion came to a disastrous end when one of Cantor's daughters spied on them while they were making love. Cantor was forced to close his show and flee to Florida with his outraged wife.

Mansfield was drafted into the army in the midst of this uproar and Susann joined the road production of a play. While in Chicago she finally got the opportunity to sleep with Joe E. Lewis. She immediately wrote Mansfield a "Dear John" letter and began making plans to live with Lewis. Even though Lewis found Susann a fantastic sex partner, he was alarmed at her intimations of a permanent relationship. He was a forty-year-old bachelor who had no intentions of changing his ways. As soon as Susann abandoned her husband, Lewis abandoned Susann.

Susann went on a sexual spree in New York after this disappointment. She had excused her affairs with the physically unimpressive Cantor and Lewis by saying she had a weakness for Jewish comedians. Now she surrendered herself completely to this strange erotic fascination and she slept with a series of them.

After a while, however, she began to use her sexual liberation in a manner that better served her career. At the beginning of her career, Susann had forcefully avoided using sex to get parts. Now she sought such opportunities with zest and surprising cunning. At the same time, she began a habit of abusing both amphetamines and barbiturates that would haunt her for the rest of her life.

At least according to some of her lovers, Susann was not particularly interested in orgasms. She preferred fellatio to intercourse and considered semen a health drink. Her skill and eagerness for oral sex became something of a legend within her circle. Her female friends observed that Susann preferred power to physical perfection. Susann was attracted to successful, charismatic men in all walks of life, and she slept with them regardless of their age or appearance.

Only one affair during this period had special meaning to Susann. When Susann was twenty-six she had a lesbian affair with a beautiful actress named Carole Landis. This brief encounter struck a chord with Susann. Later she used her experiences with Landis in her books. Susann had at least one other lesbian infatuation several years later with singer Ethel Merman, whom she pursued with shameless abandon until Merman rebuffed her. This affair was more in the character of her encounters with men. Merman was just a female personification of the rough "star quality" she idolized.

By the time Susann was twenty-nine, she and Mansfield were reunited. Susann sought the reconciliation, partly because she needed the conventionality and emotional security Mansfield represented, and partly because the two of them made an unbeatable team. Mansfield used Susann's brassy sex appeal to attract clients, and Susann used Mansfield's skill as a deal maker to sustain her career on the stage and, later, on television. The renewal of her marriage, however, did not interfere with Susann's sexual adventures with powerful men.

Mansfield and Susann did make a good team, but not good enough to make Susann a star. Although she had many roles ranging from sexy "straight woman" to television interviewer, she never achieved the kind of audience appeal enjoyed by people like Cantor or Merman. Other problems compounded her career worries. A son born shortly after her return to Mansfield was autistic and had to be institutionalized and Susann's dependency on alcohol and pills reached a dangerous, even self-destructive, level.

Susann developed breast cancer when she was forty-four. At first she refused to have a mastectomy. After living for sex for so many years, she viewed the loss of her breast as a fate not much better than death. But Mansfield insisted she have the operation and he supported her as much as possible. Even with this support, Susann fell into a deep depression afterward. She was saved from this despair when she learned that her first book would soon be published.

Susann and Mansfield teamed up once again, this time to promote Susann as an author. Together they made her one of the most visible, literary figures of the period. Deprived of sex (or at least of her extramarital affairs), Susann turned all her amphetamine-driven energy toward writing her flashy novels and making them bestsellers. Finally, she was a star and she remained one until her death at the age of fifty-six.

Another Example

Hilda Doolittle *(pen name was H. D.—American poet who moved among the intellectually and socially privileged of Europe during the 1920s and 1930s). Her first marriage broke up because her fears of pregnancy limited her sex life. She later took up with a wealthy lesbian writer known as Bryher. When she was forty-two she found another male lover but decided it would be inconvenient to marry him. Bryher married him instead. Born September 10, 1886 (Guest 1984).*

If you have Mars in Scorpio with Venus in Virgo you are . . . the Picky Powerhouse of Passion

You are an extremely physical Lover, but you spend so much time analyzing lust that you barely have time to enjoy it. It is your goal to understand the mysterious core of your sexual feelings, and your conviction is that you can't really start having fun until you figure it all out. At some point you have to realize that there's no way you can ever arrive at a rational understanding of this cosmic force. The only reasonable course of action is to just lay back and let it take you where it will.

Of all the Mars in Scorpio Lovers you are the one least capable of using sex as a means to power. The deep emotional issues that both exalt and torment these transactions are just more than you can handle. You would like sex to be simpler and more direct, but your efforts to find this kind of expedient gratification have a way of becoming convoluted and laden with dark implications and emotional mysteries. Like all Mars in Scorpio Lovers, you can't resist a secret even if you don't entirely understand what it means.

Case History

Lawrence of Arabia (T. E. Lawrence—hero of World War I who united Arab tribes against the Turks and helped changed the face of the Middle East). Born August 16, 1888, in Tremadoc, Wales (James 1993).

Lawrence was the illegitimate son of an Irish baron who left his estate and his wife for a penniless, Scottish servant girl—Lawrence's mother. Later in her life Lawrence's mother was plagued by feelings of guilt over her actions. She expressed these feelings by beating Lawrence and his brothers for even the most insignificant infractions. Lawrence was by far her most unruly child. His sins included failure to practice his piano lessons and acts of "beastliness" committed with another boy.

Despite his early bullheadedness, Lawrence grew up to be very much his mother's child, sharing her austerity and her spiritual aspirations. He showed a pronounced interest early on in antiquarian studies and romantic literature. Even though he was an unusual boy who held himself apart, he was nonetheless popular with his schoolmates. With a head full of dreams of knighthood, he was the kind of youngster who gladly put himself at risk in order to protect the underdog.

Lawrence showed little interest in women. Like smoking and drinking, sex was a subject about which he proudly proclaimed ignorance. At the same time he was surprisingly tolerant of homosexuals. While at college he became interested in a group that produced mildly homoerotic verse, and he counted some known homosexuals among his friends. But at this point in his life, Lawrence's interest in male bonding was purely aesthetic.

After college Lawrence traveled to the Middle East where he pursued his interest in antiquity and adventure. The familiarity he gained of the Arab culture and language put him in a special position when War World I began. The British wanted to instigate a rebellion within the Arab population against their Turkish rulers. He was recruited by the British Intelligence Service and commissioned as a second lieutenant. Lawrence not only instigated a movement toward Arab nationalism, he became an enthusiastic and daring leader of that movement.

Lawrence found a tolerance toward homosexuality with which he quite agreed in the culture of Arabia. It thrilled him that his soldiers preferred the expediency of sex with each other over the unhygienic embrace of local prostitutes. He developed close relationships with the men who fought beside him and he kept one handsome youngster as his personal servant. However, Lawrence's own sex life during this period remains a matter of conjecture.

In his book *The Seven Pillars of Wisdom*, Lawrence describes a sexual experience that was to become a focal point of his life. He tells of going to the town of Deraa as a spy and being captured by the Turks. The Turkish commander attempted to fondle Lawrence. Lawrence resisted. Insulted, the Bey ordered his men to lay the Englishman face down on a wooden plank and beat him with whips. Lawrence describes this beating in lavish detail, even speaking of a feeling of sexual "fullness" that came upon him in the midst of the pain. As it is written, Lawrence's confession is stunning. What is even more amazing is the fact that scholars now believe Lawrence's story of torture and rape was a total fabrication.

It is unknown whether Lawrence's "Deraa story" was a diversion to cover up other more embarrassing sexual encounters, or whether it was just an elaborate masturbatory fantasy. Lawrence seemed to have at least convinced himself of the veracity of his tale. He referred to the Deraa event as fact repeatedly during his life. The only thing about the event that is certain is that, imagined or real, this incident had an overwhelming influence on Lawrence's sex life.

The outcome of the war left Lawrence deeply disappointed. His glorious cause of Arab unity and liberation was lost to politics and tribal feuding. He quietly returned to the role of a likable but stubbornly independent outsider. He continued his intellectual interests and some of the most talented and influential people in Britain were his friends, but Lawrence eschewed the trappings and the luxury usually due a hero. He rejoined the military as an enlisted man—a common "ranker" and lived in barracks with other working-class soldiers.

There was another side to Lawrence's Spartan existence. Not long after the war ended, he sought out places in the London underworld where he could indulge his desire to be whipped. His activities became a problem when one of the organizers of these events threatened to reveal Lawrence's involvement. The hero secretly called upon his important friends to have the bothersome man removed from England.

Lawrence developed a more discreet and far more intricate procedure after this brush with disaster. He concocted an imaginary uncle and he convinced a young soldier that this uncle was prepared to pay someone to spank and otherwise torture Lawrence. The soldier would get detailed instructions from the uncle, who would list Lawrence's various crimes and the punishments that were to be given for each. Afterward the soldier had to report back to the uncle (aka Lawrence) with a vivid description of the beating. The soldier then received more instructions and technical hints about meting out pain. Lawrence himself played the role of passive victim in this ruse.

This elaborate ritual of deception and delight continued for over ten years. During the same period there were apparently other men, perhaps responding to other ruses, who performed the same service for Lawrence. Meanwhile, Lawrence became a legendary figure to the people of England. His writings kept him in the public mind, and his unconventional modesty and self-denial only increased his prestige. This noble and pristine public image made it possible for Lawrence to keep his bizarre sex life a secret until long after he died in a motorcycle accident at the age of forty-six.

Other Examples

Pee Wee Herman (comedian whose career took a dive when he was caught in the wrong kind of fun house). Born August 27, 1952 (Celebrity Birthday Guide).

Eleanor Roosevelt (first lady). Born October 11, 1884 (Celebrity Birthday Guide).

If you have Mars in Scorpio with Venus in Libra you are . . . the Polite Powerhouse of Passion

You are the most romantic Lover of this type. You like sex but also like the niceties and the delicate intrigue of courtship. This makes you a Mars in Scorpio Lover for all seasons. The simplest flirtation or domestic conflict can become a source of endless erotic fascination for you. You dole out your sexual wonder in discreet packages, a little at a time, and this makes you appear to be a much safer and less intimidating Mars in Scorpio Lover. Of course, appearances can be very deceiving.

The problems in your sexual make-up typically have to do with how you deal with power. Part of you is just too polite to use sex as a means to power but, at the same time, another part of you finds any juxtaposition of sex and power intensely erotic. You sexual feelings are often torn between a desire to play nice and a deeper desire to play very dirty. Of course, regardless of which way you decide to play, sex with you will still be amazing!

Case History

Grace Kelly (American movie star who lived the fairy tale and married the Prince of Monaco). Born November 12, 1929, in Philadelphia, Pennsylvania (Lacey 1994).

The child of well-to-do and highly accomplished parents, Kelly was sent to a convent school and brought up according to conservative Catholic traditions. This didn't stop her from having her first sexual encounter before she was out of high school. The man was the husband of a family friend; his relationship with Kelly never went beyond a single stolen afternoon. However, it was enough to show the sheltered youngster the kind of power her perfect face and figure could exert over the opposite sex.

When Kelly traveled to New York City to study acting when she was eighteen, her sex life went into high gear. Her boy friends were typically shocked at how quickly this cool, elegant, and seemingly aloof young girl could transform herself into a sexually voracious temptress. The combination of her beauty and intense passion was enough to keep several men thoroughly enamored.

Kelly applied her remarkable sex drive to a wide range of partners. At acting school she maintained a steady boy friend her own age, but she had affairs with several older men. One was an aging actor who, in his day, had been a swashbuckling, romantic lead. Another was one of her teachers who, impoverished by a divorce, shared happy evenings with her in his low-budget flat. Later she moved into the high life and had affairs with international play-boys, such as the Shah of Iran and Aly Khan. Kelly never consciously used her sex appeal to advance her career, but her penchant for hopping from man to man convinced some (women, for the most part) that she was a heartless man-trap. The men, on the other hand, hardly ever complained.

Success came as easily to Kelly as men. She gained acceptance to the prestigious American Academy of Drama through the influence of her uncle, a noted playwright. Then she moved effortlessly into a modeling career that allowed her to earn enough money to finance her schooling and live independently of her parents. After school, she quickly found success in films, and was recognized as one of Hollywood's most promising actresses by the time she was twenty-four. The apparent ease of her accomplishment did not diminish Kelly's work ethic. From the beginning she was quite serious about her career and she allowed nothing, including her sex life, to interfere with her professionalism.

The double life Kelly had developed in New York continued in Hollywood. On camera she presented the image of well-bred purity, worldly yet untouchable. When the cameras were off, Kelly quickly resumed her sexual adventuring. At least two or three men fell in love with her on every movie set she worked and she relished the power. Her pursuit of older stars was nothing short of trophy hunting. She showed little concern about the marital state of her lovers. One affair, with the very much-married Ray Milland, threatened to blow the cover off her dual existence. Kelly's mother had to go to Hollywood in order to rescue her daughter from the edge of scandal.

Throughout her years as a single woman, Kelly continually brought her favorite men home to meet her parents. These visits were always disastrous. Invariably, these men were older, non-Catholic, and either married or divorced. Kelly's parents greeted each with cold disdain. Kelly was a remarkably independent and fearless young woman away from her parents, but immediately lost her nerve in their presence. She stood by quietly as her parents criticized or snubbed each of her beaus, refusing to speak up in their defense. None of her early relationships survived these nightmare visits.

Kelly had one suitor who passed her parents' muster: Bing Crosby. He was twice Kelly's age but a widower and Catholic. Perhaps because he had her parent's approval, Kelly could sustain no interest in the famous crooner. When he proposed she turned him down. Later rumors that she and Crosby had slept together profoundly irritated her.

Despite her rebellious approach to the problem, Kelly really did want to get married. She recognized, even at twenty-six, that her days as one of Hollywood's top beauties were numbered. She did not want to spend her childbearing years pursuing a dream that was bound to self-destruct, but she could not bring herself to marry without the approval of her parents. Finally, she brought home a suitor that even her parents could not intimidate—a man wealthy enough, conservative enough and Catholic enough to warm their hearts (and he was a prince).

The attraction between Prince Rainier of Monaco and Kelly developed rather quickly, despite the difference in their backgrounds. From a publicist's point of view it was, of course, a natural: Hollywood's classiest star and Europe's most eligible royal. The lovers corresponded extensively during their long engagement. These letters formed the basis of a very strong bond. Kelly entered the marriage fully accepting the fact that she was not just marrying but was changing careers.

Kelly's marriage to Rainier produce three children and was relatively happy, considering it was one of the most intensely observed marriages of all time. Kelly brought the same cool professionalism to the role of princess as she had to her acting career. There were problems: Rainier was a man raised to be a monarch and he had the egotism and willfulness to prove it; Kelly, on the other hand, remained an outsider. By the time she was in her forties, the relationship was growing distant. In her fifties, Kelly took a separate residence in Paris where she kept company with several significantly younger men.

Despite these troubles, there is no indication that Kelly ever thought of ending her marriage. Always a devout Catholic, even during her most promiscuous period, she considered matrimony a commitment that ended only with death. Kelly died in a car crash at the age of fifty-two.

Other Examples

Joseph Goebbels (*Hitler's clubfooted minister of propaganda*). *Goebbels used his power over the German film industry to bed beautiful movie stars. He could be a helpless romantic, showering the objects of his lust with flowers and gifts, but he also saw to it that those who refused him lived to regret it. Born October 29, 1897 (Meissner 1980).*

k. d. lang (*Canadian-born pop singer*). *Born November 2, 1961 (Celebrity Birthday Guide).*

If you have Mars in Scorpio with Venus in Scorpio you are . . . the Ultimate Powerhouse of Passion

You and sex have a special relationship. Sometimes your sexuality is your greatest adversary. You struggle with it night and day. It gets the best of you as often as you get the best of it, but winning and losing is less important than the struggle. At times your sexuality is your greatest friend. It provides you with a phenomenal, almost supernatural, store of physical energy and psychological intensity that cannot be confined to your sex life. Lovemaking represents only a small part of your sexual power, though it may well be your favorite part.

Sex is such an overwhelming issue in your life that it is sometimes difficult for you to focus all that power on any one partner. In some instances, the partner may even become superfluous because you are so busy wrestling with your own inner demons. At your worst, this self-involvement masks the true warmth and sensuality of your sexual nature and makes you seem cold and ruthless. At your best, it makes you a stronger Lover—able to reach out to the people you love with confidence and spiritual purpose.

Case History

Betty Pack (*Amy Elizabeth Thorpe Pack—American-born spy who slept her way to some of Nazi Germany's most valuable secrets). Born November 22, 1910, in Minneapolis, Minnesota (Lovell 1992).*

Betty married a British diplomat named Arthur Pack at the age of twenty. Arthur was nearly forty and a conservative man despite his interest in music and younger women. He had an eye on Betty from the moment he first saw her. A bright, lively, and extremely beautiful debutante, she was turning many heads that season. Yet, nothing could have surprised him more than when he returned to his room one evening and found the pretty youngster waiting naked in his bed.

What Arthur didn't know, and what Pack probably didn't know, was that she was pregnant by another man even as the seduction took place. When he was told, Arthur was not pleased but he was too smitten with Pack to give up the notion of marrying her. The date of the wedding was moved up and when the child was born he was given to foster parents.

From the beginning of their marriage, both Pack and her husband recognized that they were ill-matched sexually. Even though the marriage produced another child whose parentage was not in doubt, Pack was unfaithful to her husband from the very beginning. Soon an understanding developed between the staid diplomat and his restless wife. Arthur turned a blind eye to Pack's sexual ramblings, and she conducted herself with appropriate discretion. In this way the couple remained friends even though they stopped being lovers.

When Arthur was stationed in Madrid, Pack began one of her most ardent attachments with a married Spanish aristocrat. Pack's extramarital relationships were always intense and yet her passionate devotion to "Carlos" (as she called her Spanish lover) did not stop Pack from also conducting an impromptu affair with her priest. The young and handsome priest was hiding from the Loyalist forces during the early days of the Spanish Civil War. His plight, along with his highly conflicted, forbidden lust made him too romantic and dangerous of a figure for Pack to resist.

Not long after her affair with the priest, Loyalist forces captured Carlos. He, like most of Pack's Spanish friends, had chosen to fight on the side of Franco. While agitating for his release, Pack fell in love with one of her husband's coworkers, an older man who shared her taste for adventure. The diplomat wanted Pack to choose between him and Carlos before he helped her rescue her former lover. In the end, Pack chose neither. Carlos was saved, she enjoyed a heated, sexual affair with the diplomat, and then she left both to join her husband at his new post in Poland.

Pack's activities during this period, both in the interest of Carlos and otherwise, revealed her to be a remarkably courageous woman who thrived in dangerous situations. Members of the British secret service had taken appreciative notice of her adventures. At some point shortly after she left Spain, Pack was approached by this organization and enlisted as a spy.

One reason the British secret service was interested in Pack was her easy contact with the higher echelons of the Polish government. During the years just prior to World War II there were elements within the fragile Polish state who knew more about spying on the Germans than anyone in Europe. These Poles had information that the British would need, including the key to the German coding device called "Enigma." The most important coup of Pack's early career as a spy occurred when she managed to acquire key elements of this cipher for her British controller.

At the time Pack was not totally conscious of the importance of the information she was gathering. Instead, she relished the power sex gave her over men. In the languid afterglow of sex, these competent, accomplished men seemed prepared to tell her anything, even to betray their countries. Pack was given great latitude in her work. She picked her own "targets" and approached them on her own terms. She claimed she always enjoyed the sex she had for the purpose of spying and looked upon these seductions as love affairs rather than as work. Even when her target turned out to be an overweight, impotent old man, Pack maintained a warm, loving relationship in concert with her purposeful snooping.

A short time before the invasion of Poland by Germany, Arthur Pack was reassigned to Chile. This put a stop to Pack's spying, but not for long. With the world at war, Pack could not sit idle. She did some "freelance" intelligence gathering in Lima. She then left her husband and moved to Washington, D.C., where she went to work for the Americans. Pack first proved her worth by acquiring Italian secret codes. Then she went to work on the French.

By this time France was a German conquest. The French Vichy government was a puppet controlled by the Nazis. This created mixed loyalties in the French embassy that Pack hoped to use to her advantage. First she attracted the attention of the embassy's press attaché, Charles Brousse. Brousse was a rich and worldly man who was highly trusted by the Vichy government, but he secretly harbored deep reservations about its validity. Pack gave him the opportunity to act on those reservations. She also gave him the opportunity to become her lover, an invitation he answered with impressive gusto.

From the first time she made love to Brousse, Pack was aware that her feeling for this newest target was much deeper than anything she had ever felt. However, this realization did nothing to deter her mission. If anything it intensified her purpose, which was to obtain copies of the Vichy government cipher. The two lovers met secretly as often as possible for sex and brainstorming. Neither Brousse's inside information or Pack's wiles offered a means of gaining access to the codes.

It was at this time that Pack suffered her first defeat on the sexual battlefield. Independent of both Brousse and her bosses, she decided to approach a young man who worked with the codes. Her plan was to use the man's patriotism rather than sex as a means of winning him over. But once she revealed that she was a spy and offered him a chance to strike a blow against Hitler, the young man quickly turned the tables. Brushing aside her offer, the official made one of his own. Either she had sex with him or he would "blow her cover." Pack, for once powerless, had to comply. This was the only sexual intercourse Pack had during her spy career that she considered base and disgusting.

Pack had her revenge, however. Brousse convinced a guard at the embassy that he was using his office there for late-night assignations with a young lover. Pack had taken a crash course in safecracking. Once inside the embassy, she liberated the codebooks, passed them out a window to be photographed, and then returned them to the safe. Brousse and Pack performed this operation with most of their clothing removed so they could pretend to be making love if they happened to be interrupted by the guard.

Brousse divorced his wife after the war and married Pack who was already divorced. The two ex-spies lived well in Brousse's ancient mansion in southern France and remained devoted to one another. Brousse was somewhat older than Pack, and by the time she reached her fifties he was already an old man. At this time one of their old comrades from the intelligence community visited. Pack and this man had sex while Brousse napped. This was her last fling. A short time later she was diagnosed with cancer. Pack died at fifty-three.

Other Examples

Mohandas Gandhi (*political activist who used nonviolent protest to liberate India.*) *Mohandas Gandhi was married at the age of thirteen. Despite his youth and the fact that he was still living very much under the power of his own father, Gandhi was not shy about asserting his dictatorial rights as a husband in Indian society, including sex on demand. When Gandhi was sixteen his father became gravely ill. One night Gandhi left his father's sick bed and went to his own rooms where he demanded intercourse from his young wife. His wife resisted because she was in the later months of pregnancy, but Gandhi would not be stopped. While he was engaging in this matrimonial rape, Gandhi's father died. Feeling of guilt over this incident haunted Gandhi the rest of his life.*

Gandhi renounced sex when he was thirty-seven. He decided that absolute chastity was an essential part of self-mastery and the search for inner peace. Not only did Gandhi cease to have sexual intercourse, he also sought to rid himself of all sexual thoughts and fantasies. It was not an easy task, he admitted. He wrestled with it throughout his life. When he was in his sixties and recuperating from an illness he had an involuntary ejaculation. He was greatly disturbed by this incident.

By the time Gandhi reached his seventies, he apparently felt he had finally conquered his sexual feelings. To test himself, he invited women to sleep with him. At first the women just shared his room but then he moved them into his bed where Gandhi and the women slept together in the nude. Some of Gandhi's supporters were shocked by this behavior and begged their idol to put aside his "experiments." But Gandhi was apparently so delighted at his mastery of his sexual instinct that he kept testing himself over and over again. Born October 2, 1869.

Larry Flynt (*publisher of* Hustler *magazine*). *Born November 1, 1942 (Celebrity Birthday Guide).*

If you have Mars in Scorpio with Venus in Sagittarius you are … the Curious Powerhouse of Passion

You are the most adventurous of the Mars in Scorpio Lovers. You are bound to explore all the facets of your sexuality, and no amount of personal restraint or social restriction will stop you. Sometimes this will be a psychological process that will, for the most part, take place in your head and in your soul. Other times your explorations demand a public arena, in which case you are capable of all sorts of sexual high jinks and extreme behavior. Either way you will carry out your exploration with an almost childlike eagerness and wonder.

You are often rather blunt when you are talking about your sex life. You are one of the few Mars in Scorpio Lovers who has trouble keeping a secret. Some people might find this lack of reserve offensive. Others might balk at your willingness to accept even the darkest secrets of the human mind with blissful toleration. These people don't interest you. You treasure the opinions of people that share your fascinations and curiosity.

Case History

Robert Mapplethorpe (photographer who dazzled the art world with his classically beautiful photos of nudes and flowers). Born November 4, 1946, in Queens, New York (Fritscher 1994; Morrisroe 1995).

Born into a fervently Catholic, middle-class family, Mapplethorpe grew up trapped between his perfectionist father, whom he could never please, and his all-American older brother, whom he could never equal. Mapplethorpe was aware of homosexual feelings in his early adolescence, but was determined to avoid them. In college he joined an elite unit in his ROTC class in an attempt to live up to the masculine ideal set by his father and brother. And yet despite his tenacity, he remained an outsider.

Mapplethorpe changed his major in college from advertising to fine art. He joined the counterculture and became known for his odd behavior and for the satanic imagery in his artwork. Still, even though he wore love beads and let his hair grow long, Mapplethorpe remained determinedly conventional in his sex life.

When he was twenty, Mapplethorpe met Patti Smith, a semipsychotic artist whose androgyne appearance offered a way out of his sexual dilemma. Mapplethorpe found a soul mate in Smith, someone who shared his grungy esthetics and his dreams of artistic success. The two became so inseparable that Mapplethorpe was able to convince his mother that he and Smith were married. Smith and Mapplethorpe shared an apartment for a year before Smith became dissatisfied with the sexual side of their relationship and found a new boy friend. Mapplethorpe was deeply shaken when she told him that she was leaving. He pleaded with her, "If you go, I'll become gay" (Morrisroe, 57).

After Smith left him, Mapplethorpe decided it was time to come to terms with his homosexuality. Even in adopting a gay lifestyle, he still could not accept his sexuality in a positive way. He began by renting himself out as a "call-boy." He found the experience disgusting, but repeated it several times. He had been secretly collecting homosexual pornography for some time; now those images joined the satanic emblems in his collages and assemblages. When he began living with a male lover, Mapplethorpe flaunted the relationship in front of Smith.

Soon Smith and Mapplethorpe were back together. Mapplethorpe was so ill with an infection that Smith had to carry him into the Chelsea Hotel, where she badgered the manager into giving them a room in exchange for artwork. There, broke and desperate, the two artists began to rebuild their lives. At the Chelsea, which had long been a haven for artists, they began networking with people in the New York art community.

Even though Smith and Mapplethorpe lived together and pooled their resources to make the contacts they needed, they were not lovers. During this time, Mapplethorpe found his way into that segment of the homosexual community that favored leather, bondage, and sadomasochism. Mapplethorpe claimed he had found "his kind of sex" in this strange sexual ghetto. As far as he was concerned, this was sex at its most daring, dangerous, and all-consuming.

Mapplethorpe was an orderly person despite his extreme lifestyle; he managed to keep his various sex lives separate. First he had his relationship with Smith, which wasn't sexual but provided continuity and emotional support. Then he had his life in the leather bars. Finally he had his protectors who were usually also his lovers. At first these benefactors had little more money than Mapplethorpe, but by the time he was twenty-five Mapplethorpe had come to the attention of Sam Wagstaff, a wealthy homosexual art collector who was "looking for someone to spoil" (Morrisroe, 111).

Under Wagstaff's guidance, Mapplethorpe gave up his other artistic endeavors and concentrated on photography. With Wagstaff's connections he was able to get those photographs seen by the right people and obtain commissions for portraits. Smith went off on her own career track and Wagstaff took over her role as Mapplethorpe's adviser and confidant. Wagstaff was an extremely indulgent benefactor. Not only did he deny his protégé nothing in terms of material comforts, he also allowed Mapplethorpe the freedom to continue his exploration of the gay, sadomasochistic wilderness. The sexual relationship between Mapplethorpe and Wagstaff waned after a few years, but Wagstaff remained the artist's "father figure" for much longer.

Mapplethorpe considered himself a "sex addict" who had to have sex at least once a day. He typically took the aggressive role in the leather culture, but he was adventurous enough to allow himself to be subjected to pain as well. In his mid-thirties, Mapplethorpe moved away from the sadomasochistic bars and focused his erotic energies on African-American males. These encounters were also exercises in dominance and submission in which Mapplethorpe played the aggressor. Mapplethorpe attempted to establish relationships with a few of his black boy friends but without success.

Shortly before Mapplethorpe died of AIDS at the age of forty-two, a major exhibit of his photographs toured the country. The exhibit consisted of two parts, reflective of the way Mapplethorpe himself had segregated his work during his rise to art stardom. One part featured the portraits, nudes, and flower pictures in which Mapplethorpe's sexuality was tempered by a lush and classical aesthetic. The other part of the exhibit consisted of his homoerotic and sadomasochistic works. These pictures showed Mapplethorpe and other men involved in various sexual acts and strange, sadomasochistic rites. Many people, even people sympathetic to Mapplethorpe's conventional work, found the latter photographs superfluous and offensive. But to Mapplethorpe, these sexual pictures were just as important as the work that had made him famous.

Other Examples

Barbara Hutton (*Woolworth heiress noted for her many marriages*). *Born November 14, 1912 (Celebrity Birthday Guide).*

Jimi Hendrix (*rock-and-roll guitarist*). *Born November 27, 1942 (Celebrity Birthday Guide).*

Bela Lugosi (*actor famous for his portrayal of Count Dracula*). *Born October 20, 1882 (Celebrity Birthday Guide).*

If you have Mars in Scorpio with Venus in Capricorn you are … the Earnest Powerhouse of Passion

You are probably the most insatiable of all the Mars in Scorpio Lovers and the one most prone to channel all your imposing, emotional energy directly into physical sex. You are not always an easy Lover. You demand a lot from your partner, both physically and emotionally, and you can be brutally critical if that person falls short of your expectations. This is only because you take your relationships seriously and do not want to be bothered by people who aren't prepared to do likewise.

One odd feature of your sexuality is your tendency to mix physical pleasure with misery. It is as if you can't really appreciate the good stuff unless there is some impediment, some problem, or some painful element to put your pleasurable moments in perspective. For this reason you are prone to have partners who bring hard luck stories and various troubles into the relationship. There is nothing altruistic in your sexual nature. As long as the misery of your partner heightens your own sexual response you are interested. After that, you stop listening.

Case History

Henry Miller (American writer whose bold, autobiographical books were banned in the United States for a generation). Born December 26, 1891, in Brooklyn, New York (Ferguson 1991).

Miller wrote incessantly about his sex life, but much of what he said was false. He happily portrayed himself as a crude, egocentric sex machine who took his pleasure where it could be found with no second thoughts or regrets. In fact, Miller was surprisingly romantic. His sexuality was far more conflicted and passive than he ever cared to admit.

Miller's first confessed love affair was an adolescent infatuation with a girl from his own working-class, German immigrant neighborhood. He was totally preoccupied with thoughts of her and made a ritual of riding his bike past her home every evening. Yet he was too shy and certain of rejection to approach her. Instead he made her into his personal idol of frustrated, sexual desire and worshipped this mental image of her far into his old age.

Miller began an affair when he was eighteen with a woman in her thirties named Pauline Chouteau. It was Pauline who initiated the sexual relationship and Miller responded with enthusiasm. Miller felt a strong, physical attraction to this woman but he was also drawn to her by pity. Pauline had lived a sad, trouble-filled life and had an invalid son. Miller became so caught up in her problems he went into debt in order to give her financial assistance.

Soon Miller began to feel confined by this relationship. Pauline was uneducated and unable to share in his enjoyment of books. He was increasingly bothered by the difference in their ages and ashamed to be seen with her. His pity for her and the promise of easy sex paralyzed Miller and made it impossible for him to tell this simple, guileless woman that he did not love her. The relationship continued until he was twenty-four. In the end, he lied and told her he was leaving town.

By the time Miller concocted this story he was already seeing another woman, Beatrice Wickens, who was his age and shared some of his interests in music and literature. Beatrice apparently felt a strong physical attraction to Miller but she lacked Pauline's easy sexuality. And yet something about Beatrice's neurotic puritanism appealed to him. Her resistance and remorse only served to make the sex more interesting from Miller's point of view—so interesting that, when he was twenty-six, he married Beatrice.

Whatever bohemian trappings Beatrice possessed before the marriage were quickly replaced by a staunch and vociferous conventionality. The marriage was in trouble almost from the beginning and, at least according to his own account, Miller did little to save it. He confessed to beating Beatrice, being constantly unfaithful to her, and generally regarding her as an impediment to be avoided by any means possible.

It is almost certain that Miller exaggerated his misdeeds as a husband, and that he made at least some effort to preserve the marriage. At Beatrice's insistence, Miller put aside his literary aspirations and took his first "real" job as a personnel manager for Western Union. Despite their obvious incompatibility and constant bickering, their marriage lasted five years and produced one daughter.

When Miller left Beatrice, it was for a bewitching young woman named June Mansfield Smith, who offered to support him while he pursued his dream of becoming a writer. It was only after they were married that Miller surmised that the support June provided him came from prostitution. This awareness tortured Miller. Not only was he jealous of June's other lovers, but he felt that the money she made was tainted. The problem was compounded when June insisted on moving her lesbian lover into their apartment. Soon Miller realized that living his bohemian fantasy had become just as unbearable as living a conventional family life with Beatrice. As miserable as he was, the writer could not bring himself to break with the beautiful and indomitable June.

When he was thirty-nine, June proposed that Miller go to Paris alone to write. She planned to send him money from New York. In Paris, Miller worked on a vast analysis of D. H. Lawrence, a project he eventually put aside in order to write bawdy novels. While doing so he met Anaïs Nin, who became both his lover and a much more predictable source of financial support than June. When June made a trip to Paris, a strange three-sided relationship developed between her, Nin, and Miller—a liaison that resulted in some marvelous literature and the end of Miller's second marriage.

Miller's relations with Nin dominated the next several years of his life. Nin was married and Miller wanted her to leave her husband and live with him. But Nin had an agenda of her own and it did not include starving to death with an impoverished writer. She enjoyed sex with Miller, but she also enjoyed the comforts of her marriage. No matter how much Miller protested she knew that he was far too dependent on her money to ever end their relationship.

Nin and Miller formed an artistic team. Both were talented and original. They helped each other with advice, criticism, and emotional support. Even though they never lived together, Miller's relationship with Nin may have been his most successful. Yet he was still haunted by memories of June and laboring over a book describing their relationship.

When Miller was fifty-three he married for the third time to Janina Lepska, a twenty-one-year-old Polish-American. By this time he was a famous author, not rich but widely known and sought after. He settled in California with his new wife, living primitively in a place called Big Sur. Two children were born. It seemed that Miller might be ready to settle down; however, his young wife found Miller to be a distant, self-involved husband who preferred to spend his time with his male cronies or literary fans. Apparently, Miller had used up his capacity for real emotional rapport and romantic rapture in his earlier relationships. In his later affairs and marriages Miller was quite content, or perhaps compelled, to be the heartless scalawag he had always pretended to be in his books.

Miller had two more failed marriages and several affairs during his sixties and seventies, always with much younger women. By his eighties his health, which had always been phenomenally good, began to deteriorate. From this point on, his erotic life was for the most part limited to sexy correspondence with female admirers. Of course, he still enjoyed playing the hypersexed rogue for the media. He happily allowed himself to be photographed surrounded by beautiful women. He died at the age of eighty-six.

Other Examples

Beatrice Potter Webb (*English social reformer and leader of the socialist group called the Fabians). Webb recognized early that her rampant sexual needs would be an impediment to her deep desire to be useful to society. Therefore she worked to curtail her "indecent" thoughts and devoted herself to working with the poor. When she was twenty-five a powerful politician asked her to marry him but, even though she found the man physically attractive and was tempted, Webb rejected him because his ideals were quite different than her own. Beatrice continued her uneasy celibacy, about which she strongly complained, until she married Sidney Webb, a young man who shared her liberal ideas and reformist zeal. Even though Sidney was not her physical ideal, the marriage prospered and together Beatrice and Sidney became a potent force for change in British politics. Born January 22, 1858 (Muggeridge 1967).*

Rock Hudson (*American film star). Born November 17 1925 (Celebrity Birthday Guide).*

If you have Mars in Scorpio with Venus in Aquarius you are … the Extraordinary Powerhouse of Passion

You are the most idealistic of the Mars in Scorpio Lovers and in some way this doubles your sexual power. The mingling of sex and big ideas gives you a sex appeal that goes beyond the personal and adds breath and objectivity to your desires. You are a challenging and inspirational Lover who brings out the best of the people who love you. Of course, you can also be a judgmental Lover. Your treatment of those who fail to meet your standards or satisfy your needs can be quite ruthless.

You are often torn between the power of sex and the power of ideas. You need the physical and emotional charge that you get from sex but you also find it overly subjective, irrational, and just plain messy. It's so hard to fit your very elemental Mars in Scorpio sex drive into a rational concept. Yet you always feel more comfortable about your sexuality when it is matched with an ideal, cause, or creation.

Case History

Mao Tse-Tung (Mao Zedong—bookish peasant who became the leader of the Chinese Communist Party and the man who made China a world power). Born December 26, 1893, in Shaoshan, Hunan Province, China (Salisbury 1992; Terrill 1980).

Mao was the son of an ambitious peasant farmer who, through hard work, cunning, and extreme frugality, managed to become a minor power within his own community. Mao and his father often clashed, particularly over Mao's love of books. Mao's mother, on the other hand, was a pious, caring person who often gave food to the needy when her hardhearted husband wasn't looking.

When Mao was fourteen, his father decided he could better control his stubborn son if the boy was saddled with a wife. He arranged for Mao to marry an older girl. Mao submitted to the traditional marriage ceremony but he refused to live with his new wife or have sex with her. His father was apparently so impressed by Mao's abstention that he allowed the teenager to pursue his education.

Once away from his native province, Mao quickly discovered both the joys of learning and radical politics. He excelled as a student of classical Chinese philosophy but he also became one of the founding members of the Chinese Communist Party. During this period Mao claimed he was too busy and too inflamed with ideas to think about sex. He enjoyed an apparently chaste infatuation with a Communist girl friend. He even shared her bed; however, their relationship never went beyond their impassioned belief in a common cause.

When Mao was twenty-six he began living with Yang K'ai-hui, the daughter of one of his most influential teachers. They were later married. Yang was an attractive young woman but, more importantly, she shared Mao's dangerous political ideals. The new Communist party was beginning to battle with more conservative factions for control of the unstable Chinese government. Seven years into their relationship, the intense fighting caused Mao to leave his wife and their two children in what he thought was a safe haven. A short time later the enemy took this town and imprisoned Yang. Yang refused to denounce her husband and, when Mao was thirty-six, she was executed. Mao later confessed that he honored her memory and felt a deep sense of guilt over his inability to save her life.

This sense of guilt may have been caused by the fact that, even while his wife was in prison on his account, Mao was enjoying an affair with a pretty eighteen-year-old revolutionary.

The girl, Ho Tzu-chen, was also enthusiastic about Communism. Soon she began bearing Mao's children. They were officially married soon after Yang's execution.

During the four years that followed the wedding, the fortunes of the Chinese Communist army plummeted. They were forced to retreat to the western part of the country. Before this retreat, which became known as the "long march," Mao had fallen from grace among the party leaders. But during the march his organizational skills and ability to inspire his people propelled him to the forefront. Mao was the acknowledged leader of the movement by the end of the "long march."

Unfortunately for Mao, the same event that launched his career destroyed his marriage. Ho Tzu-chen was pregnant at the beginning of the march and she suffered serious shrapnel wounds during the ten-month ordeal. The combination of these trials and her husband's complete involvement in the task of saving his army and creating the image of himself as the inspired and infallible party leader thoroughly embittered their relationship. Afterward, her animosity toward Mao and her increasing mental derangement were evident to any careful observer.

How much Mao was bothered by his wife's disaffection is unknown. By this time he was powerful enough that he had no problem finding willing mistresses. Yet Mao still had a deeply ingrained appreciation for conventional, committed relationships. Many of the new policies Mao's Communist Party implemented in the part of China it controlled were quite radical and forward-looking. And yet the policy Mao favored with regard to marriage betrayed a rather old-fashioned traditionalism. When it came to sex, Mao was something of a countrified reactionary.

By the time Mao was in his forties, Ho Tzu-chen had been sent to Moscow where she languished in a mental institution. Mao announced his plans to marry an actress named Lan P'ing. Her shadowy past and married status mattered little to Mao; however, it mattered a great deal within the gossipy inner circle of the Chinese Communist Party. They couldn't stop their leader from putting aside Ho Tzu-chen and marrying this woman whom many of them regarded as little more than a harlot, but they did make Mao promise that Jiang Qing (the name she took after the marriage) would not participate in any political activity.

Mao married Jiang Qing when he was forty-five. Apparently his sexual fascination with her did not last long. Unhappy with her domestic prison, Qing suffered from a variety of unspecified ailments and was often a nuisance to her husband. Yet Mao never abandoned her and, after nearly twenty years of nagging, he finally agreed to give her small jobs within the government. At first the tasks were meaningless but the compulsive energy she brought to them was such that Mao couldn't help giving her more "useful" roles. Soon Jiang Qing became a force within the Communist Party.

By the time he reached his sixties, Mao did not need a wife to satisfy his sexual needs. He had people working for him whose main function was to provide him with sexually explicit literature and art (he built a collection that rivaled those of the lascivious Chinese emperors who preceded him) and sex partners. His bed, in fact his entire bedroom, was often filled with young women recruited for his pleasure. Mao remained remarkably physically fit far into his old age. During these years he more than made up for the idealistic celibacy of his youth.

Even though Mao was probably the most erudite and poetic dictator of the twentieth century, he always remained a peasant at heart. His lack of pride or posturing was both refreshing and, at times, perfectly disgusting. He cared little about personal hygiene. Once he dropped his pants in the presence of foreign dignitaries because he got too warm. These qualities were also reflected in his taste in concubines. Some of his followers attempted to pair him with an attractive and well-educated young woman with an upper-class background, but Mao showed little interest in her. He preferred sex partners whose tastes were closer to his peasant roots.

Meanwhile his relationship with his wife became a matter of much concern. As Mao neared seventy, his country was ripped apart by what was called a "Cultural Revolution." Young people who idolized Mao took his ideas to their most radical extremes. They enforced their will on the older generation by destroying books and objects of art, and compelling figures of authority to submit to unbelievable humiliations. Jiang Qing rode this wave of madness toward absolute power. Mao watched from a safe and inscrutable distance, content to give the movement his quiet endorsement and stand by as the men who had helped him mold modern China scrambled for survival. How close he felt to his wife at this point is unknown, though it is apparent he was impressed with her skill as a revolutionary.

During the last years of his life, Mao finally reined in Jiang Qing and her hot-headed followers, and encouraged the rise of more conservative elements in his regime. Aware of his failing health, the leader had apparently decided he didn't want perpetual revolution to be his legacy. He died at the age of eighty-two.

Other Examples

Boris Pasternak (*Russian poet and novelist, author of* Dr. Zhivago). *Born February 10, 1890 (Encyclopedia Britannica).*

Oprah Winfrey (*talk show host*). *Born June 29, 1954 (Celebrity Birthday Guide).*

If you have Mars in Scorpio with Venus in Pisces you are . . . the Pulsating Powerhouse of Passion

Your sexuality is so powerful that it has a way of changing reality—of remaking the world in the image of your desires. It's not just you that can be led around by your strong emotions. The influence of these powerful feelings is bound to spread to all who love you, and many who don't. Now this is not necessarily bad. Those who are willing to submit to your subtle, psychological bullying are so amply rewarded with love and sex that they seldom complain. But you have to be mindful of the power you possess and use it wisely.

Because your feelings are so strong and so personal there is little middle ground in your emotional life. You tend to love and hate with the same extreme prejudice. Sometimes it even becomes difficult for you to distinguish between these two strong emotions, and you begin to enjoy the hatred as much as you delight in the love. In the world of dark sexual extremes that is Mars in Scorpio, the difference between these two emotions is not so great.

Case History

Ayn Rand (Alissa Rosenbaum O'Connor–Russian-born author of The Fountainhead *and* Atlas Shrugged, *noted for her fervent anticommunism). Born February 2, 1905, in St. Petersburg, Russia (Branden 1986).*

From the time she was twelve, Rand and Communism were at war. Her father was a prosperous pharmacist, but the Russian Revolution stripped him of his shop and Rand's family became starving refugees. Rand and her family lived in the Crimea for a time, but when this area fell to the Red Army they returned to St. Petersburg, where they lived on the margins of starvation. The only benefit of the new Communist state was that, poor as they were, Rand was still able to attend the university.

Even as a child Rand was passionately interested in books and ideas. She regarded the typical concerns of girls her age with surly disdain and had trouble making friends. It came as a great surprise when, at the age of seventeen, she fell deeply in love with a good-looking university student. Her fascination for him was so intense that she forgot her distaste for ordinary life and actually dated him. The relationship did not last long. Plain and undernourished, she was no match for the other girls vying for the young man's attentions. Separation did nothing to diminish Rand's ardor. Her memories of this chaste courtship remained a compelling force in her life for several years.

When she was twenty-one, Rand was able to leave the Soviet Union to go to the United States. A distant relative helped her to obtain a visa. She traveled to California where she was certain she could become a successful screenwriter within a year. While she was working toward this goal, she met a young actor named Frank O'Connor, whose perfect profile and passive disposition she found irresistible. They became lovers and, when she was twenty-four, they married. Rand confessed that she married O'Connor for his looks. It is thought O'Connor allowed himself to be persuaded to marry Rand because her visa was due to expire and she needed an American husband to remain in the United States.

The next several years were hard for the couple. O'Connor had some work as an actor but he lacked the drive and ambition to be a real success in such a competitive field. Rand, on the other hand, was bubbling over with ambition. She continued her writing while she worked at various jobs at the movie studios. She managed to sell some movie scripts, which gave her the free time to work on the first of her bulky novels. It was published and achieved just enough success to set her to working on a second.

This second novel was *The Fountainhead*, in which she proclaimed much of her anticommunist, pro-individual philosophy. In the central character of this novel, she sought to lay out her own conception of a "perfect man"—a positive egotist who was driven only by his own ideas and desires, and untouched by social pressure or the opinions of others. In one scene of this novel, Rand's rugged individualist rapes the leading female character. This scene caused some controversy. Rand admitted that it was the product of her personal sexual fantasies.

Rand made an effort to portray her relationship with O'Connor as a "typical" marriage. She cooked for her husband, even though the meals were prepared around her late-night writing schedule, and she made a great show of deferring to his decisions. But when ideas were being discussed, and this was the only kind of talk she would endure, Rand stepped into the dominant role. It was O'Connor who sat quietly or went to fetch the drinks. For most of their marriage, it was her income that supported them and it was her career that was their primary concern. Rand decided she would not have children, and so the marriage remained childless.

For the most part O'Connor was happy to defer to his strong-willed and charismatic wife. The force of her personality was just too overwhelming. It only became stronger after *The Fountainhead* rose to great success and made her a rich woman. As the years went by, O'Connor found himself left with little to do except light Rand's cigarettes. He began to drink in secret. At about the same time, Rand began to look outside their relationship for sexual gratification.

By the time Rand was in her fifties she was surrounded by a group of admiring young people who found an ideological counter to Socialist and Communist thought in her writings. One of these youthful admirers was Nathaniel Branden. He was won over to Rand's point of view when he was a college student and later formed an institute to spread her ideas. The lecture series of the Nathaniel Branden Institute became a great success. The series gave Rand both a forum for the systematic presentation of her philosophy, and a place to accept the adulation of her many fans and followers.

Rand's interest in Branden was intense. She had always liked discussing her opinions with good-looking men, and Branden was both handsome and brilliant. Rand witnessed Branden's wedding and left her home in California (which O'Connor had loved) to join the young couple in New York City. There her relationship with her young protégé took an unexpected turn.

At this time, Rand called a meeting with O'Connor, Branden, and Mrs. Branden. She announced that she and Mr. Branden, who was over twenty years her junior, had fallen in love and that henceforth would spend one evening a week alone together. O'Connor and Branden's wife, who was also a great worshipper of Rand, both condoned this arrangement. For the next two years O'Connor would "go for a walk" one or two evenings a week while Branden and Rand had sex. Their relationship was not just limited to these scheduled meetings. When the couples were together, which they often were, Rand openly displayed her affection for Branden. As she had with O'Connor, Rand pretended to defer to Branden's judgement in all things, while at the same time remaining in complete control of him, his wife, and O'Connor.

After the completion of *Atlas Shrugged*, Rand recognized she had said all she had to say as a novelist. She went into a period of depression that temporarily put a stop to her sexual affair with Branden. Branden then became her counselor and helped her fight her way through this bleak period. By the time she was fifty-nine Rand felt well enough to begin having sex with Branden again but, to her amazement, her young lover was unwilling. He had found another younger woman and respectfully explained that the sexual side of his relationship with Rand could not go on.

Branden's rejection sent Rand into a rage that no amount of rational explanation could cool. She demanded that Branden leave the institute he had started and make a public announcement that he had failed to live up to its standards. Branden did this, but it was not enough. At Rand's insistence, his former associates, none of whom knew about the love affair, shunned Branden. For the next several months Rand talked constantly about her ex-lover's immorality and treachery. Years later, when Branden tried to publish some of his own philosophy, Rand did everything in her power to stop him. She maintained a violent animosity toward Branden for the rest of her life.

Meanwhile, Rand's marriage to O'Connor continued. She remained emotionally attached to her husband and, as his health declined, her devotion seemed to grow. When Rand was seventy-four, O'Connor died and she mourned him profoundly. She died three years later.

Another Example

Helen Gurley Brown *(publisher of* Cosmopolitan *magazine and author of* Sex and the Single Girl*). Born February 18, 1922 (Celebrity Birthday Guide).*

Chapter 9

Mars in Sagittarius
The Love Child

General Characteristics

Sex must be natural for the Mars in Sagittarius Lover. It must be a seamless extension of life and the natural world—spontaneous, unplanned, and brimming with animalistic verve. These high-energy Lovers don't make a big deal out of sex. They don't put it on a pedestal to be worshipped, nor do they grind it into the dirt. They want sex to be simple, direct, and unfettered by social constraints or emotional baggage. These are not the sort of Lovers who want to fight for sex, nor do they want to work for sex. They just want to open their front door and find it waiting for them with a big "Howdy, partner!" grin plastered on its face.

Sexual enjoyment comes naturally to these eager and carefree Lovers, but responsibility requires some effort. These are typically very generous Lovers, who are anxious to please and full of high-minded principles. They tend to be quite impulsive in matters of love and quick to commit themselves. Yet in those crucial moments when the decision is made whether to go or stay, these Lovers have a bad habit of forgetting their commitments and principles, and remembering only their tremendous fear of confinement. It's very hard to pin down Mars in Sagittarius Lovers. Even when they seem restful and content you suspect that somewhere in the house there's a suitcase already packed and ready in case—perhaps at the next commercial—they get the urge to bolt.

If you do manage to get your hands on one of these elusive Lovers, even temporarily, it can be a truly joyous experience. Mars in Sagittarius Lovers are the least controlling and demanding Lovers in the zodiac. They are always fun, straightforward, and typically very agreeable. They treat their sex partners like good friends, and build relationships on the very simple basis of trust and mutual respect. Some people might find this approach lacking in emotional depth and sincerity, but for the Mars in Sagittarius Lover, this simple, spontaneous friendliness can be the foundation of a life-long commitment.

Because these Lovers are so spontaneous and restless, they often appear to be sexual adventurers. They are, insofar as they love change and are always hungry for new experiences; however, their sexual adventurism generally stops short of any real risk taking. True, a tendency to thoughtlessly respond to their sexual impulses does get them into some incredible jams and their flexibility and open-mindedness mean that there are few things they won't try just once. But they are not the sort of Lovers who wish to make a battleground out of their sex lives. Typically, they avoid confrontations and defer to authority. Their sexual passions may inspire them to some pretty wild and rebellious behavior, but they are usually contrite and ready with a good excuse if they happen to get caught.

There is often a skittish quality about these Lovers. They get nervous when they're forced to stop and think about their romantic high jinks. They tend to be very sensitive to the situations that surround a sexual experience; they are alert to stimuli ranging from changes in hairstyle to changes in the weather. Almost anything can get them out of the mood. Their superheated passion can be extinguished in a heartbeat by the wrong word, the wrong gesture, or even the wrong kind of music.

The keystone of Mars in Sagittarius sexuality is innocence. There is often a childlike quality to their approach to sex—a thoroughly charming combination of clumsy eagerness and wide-eyed wonder. Much of this springs from the optimism which these Lovers have in limitless supply. These Lovers also have a fascination with the simplicity, the directness, and the unquestioned trust of childish love. Often their ideal relationship is modeled on this kind of juvenile attachment, in which such "adult themes" as control, emotional manipulation, and competitiveness are not an issue. As far as the Mars in Sagittarius Lover is concerned, nothing spoils love or sex as quickly as being too mature.

If you have Mars in Sagittarius with Venus in Aries you are... the Daring Love Child

You are a charming, effervescent Lover, so full of life and optimism that no one can resist you for long. Of course, your approach to love is so reckless, direct, thoughtless, and impulsive that you need every bit of that charm, plus a fair amount of luck, just to survive the often calamitous consequences of your actions. From your point of view, good sex is a matter of creating as much excitement as you can tolerate.

It's not just thrills that you're seeking in your sex life. You're also looking for experiences that will feed your ego and leave you feeling empowered. Sensation for its own sake holds little interest for you. Sexual relationships that offer only basic gratification are essentially useless to you. You often push your relationships and the people you love to the edge because you want them to love you for the challenge. Pleasure is just a fringe benefit.

Case History

Vita Sackville-West (English writer best known for her unconventional lifestyle and friendship with Virginia Woolf). Born March 9, 1892, at Knole (her family's estate) in Kent, England (Glendinning 1983).

A rough-and-tumble tomboy despite her illustrious pedigree and privileged upbringing, Vita often cried when she was forced to wear girl's clothes. As a teen she was tall, clumsy, and plain. She did well in school and was already thinking of herself as a writer.

Vita met Harold Nicolson when she was eighteen and he was twenty-three. He was clever, charming, and just sophisticated enough to hold her attention. The attraction between them was immediate, even though Vita confessed there was nothing sexual in her feelings for Nicolson. She thought of him as a wonderful playmate, lively and full of fun. For a while it bothered her that he did not talk of love or make sexual advances, but when he abruptly asked her to marry him, Vita promptly accepted.

While Nicolson was courting her, Vita was developing another important friendship with a young woman named Rosamund Grosvenor. Grosvenor had been brought to the Sackville-West estate to be a companion for the solitary Vita. Instead she became Vita's lover. This sexual relationship for Vita was neither shameful nor unnatural, even though she was careful to keep it a secret from both her mother and Nicolson. She confessed that her attachment to Grosvenor was strictly physical. As a companion, she found the other girl dull and unimaginative—nothing like her brilliant fiancé.

Nicolson and Sackville-West married when she was twenty-one. Vita entered the marriage with mixed feelings. Apparently she never really got over her revulsion of heterosexual sex, even though she claimed Nicolson was the only man who brought out the feminine side of her sexuality. Still, the early years of the marriage were happy. Vita, whose interest in Grosvenor was beginning to wane, seemed ready to be a conventional wife and mother.

Then Nicolson came to his young wife with a confession. He told her he was a homosexual, and that he had been unfaithful to her with men. Vita was not put off by the fact that her husband had homosexual tendencies, but she was shocked by his infidelity. Nicolson, who was a member the British Foreign Office, was often out of the country. Vita had traveled with him early in their marriage, but now she decided to establish a life separate from her husband.

A young woman named Violet Keppel reentered her life at this very vulnerable moment. The two had been childhood friends and there had been a hint of sexual attraction. Violet was an attractive, feminine woman who understood Vita's sexual needs much better than Vita herself. One night when they were alone together at Knole, Violet seduced Vita—or at least gave the more masculine Vita an invitation she couldn't refuse. Their affair became a passion that overwhelmed both their lives.

Violet brought out Vita's masculine side in a way the writer had never thought possible. While the two women were in Paris, Vita took to dressing like a man and calling herself "Julian." She and Violet went out on the town and "Julian" flirted liberally with other women. Vita apparently found a great release in her ability to literally play a male role, but she rarely repeated the experiment outside of Violet's influence.

Meanwhile, Violet had her own problems. A young man named Denys Trefusis had proposed to her. Violet, pressured by her mother, had accepted. Violet begged Vita to save her from the marriage. But even though she loved Violet deeply, Vita was unwilling to leave the security of her marriage and commit herself to a totally unconventional lifestyle with her lover. Violet married, but she extracted a promise from her husband to forego sex so that she could remain true to Vita.

Vita was infuriated at the thought of her lover living with a man, even though she had not stood in the way of the wedding. She went to Violet during the Trefusis' honeymoon and, by her own account, "took her." The bizarre situation came to a head when Vita and Violet fled to Paris, and the two husbands joined forces and traveled together to fetch them. At this point Vita began to suspect that Violet and her husband were not honoring their vow of chastity. Her infatuation with the other woman began to sputter.

After this trying and not particularly private crisis, Vita was careful to conduct her sex life in a more civilized fashion. When she was thirty-one she had a brief encounter with a younger man, but her primary sexual interests were lesbian. Meanwhile, her marriage to Nicolson continued. With their mutual duplicity a thing of the past, it became a model of trust, affection, and intellectual compatibility.

By the time Vita entered her thirties she was an extremely prolific best-selling author. At this time she became involved with another literary lioness of the time, Virginia Woolf. Vita's confidence and brisk masculinity astounded Woolf, who was much more hesitant about her lesbian tendencies; however, it was Woolf who made the first move toward making their friendship a love affair.

The sexual affair between the two writers did not last long. Vita was too highly sexed and Woolf too distracted by her own inner demons. Nicolson, who was out of the country at the time, wrote his wife with some alarm when he learned of the affair. Woolf had a history of emotional problems, and he sensed trouble. Vita reassured him that she was not going to get overly involved with Woolf because she feared her unstable personality. After a while Vita moved on to more passionate partners, though the two women remained good friends until Woolf's suicide.

Woolf became one of many women who had their hearts broken by the elusive Vita. With Vita, every love affair began with an explosion of deliciously illicit passion. Vita was typically the aggressor though, and as one of her lovers put it, she has "two strings in her lute" and could take on a more feminine role. Repeatedly the women who fell in love with her confessed that they were willing to do anything she asked. But no amount of subservience or adoration could keep Vita from tiring with the affair and seeking a new explosion of passion. Even though she remained friendly with all her lovers and was, after a fashion, fiercely loyal, Vita was not in the market for a sustained relationship.

When she was forty-five, Vita was reunited with Violet Trefusis. It was not a passionate reunion. By this time Violet had become a conservative and rather prickly matron, anxious to forget about her lesbian past. Vita had her own misgivings about renewing the relationship even though she was obviously still deeply in love with Violet. The two women visited each other often during the last years of their lives, but Vita found little joy and much frustration in their chaste friendship.

Meanwhile, Vita and Nicolson remained the "perfect" couple. They raised their two sons and supported one another impeccably through a variety of trials. Although their unusual arrangement was well known within their circle, both were careful to keep their private indiscretions out of the public eye. Even in their correspondence they referred to homosexual activity with the code word "back stairs" or "b. s." The marriage lasted until Vita's death at seventy. Nicolson died six years later.

Another Example

Jack Nicholson (actor). Born April 22, 1937 (Celebrity Birthday Guide).

If you have Mars in Sagittarius with Venus in Taurus you are … the Lusty Love Child

You are the most sensual of the Mars in Sagittarius Lovers. Your sensuality gives you the ability to turn all that nervous energy into a really good time. You can be a very adept and sensuous Lover who combines innocence with a slow appreciation of sensation if you can get past your inherent mistrust of your body. You are not always at ease with the gritty earthiness of your own sexual feelings, and this skittishness is bound to disrupt many a pleasant moment.

You enter into commitments impulsively, like all Mars in Sagittarius Lovers. What makes you different is the fact that you frequently seek to forge these off-the-cuff decisions into life-long obligations. You are more conservative than most Lovers of this type. You appreciate consistency and continuity in your relationships. Of course, this doesn't make you any less protective of your independence or any less likely to dash off on some mad tangent now and again. Your partner just has to understand that even though you love stability, there's only so much of it that you can take.

Case History

Henrik Ibsen (Norwegian-born playwright noted for his realism and controversial themes in plays such as A Doll's House and Ghosts). Born March 20, 1828, in Skien, Norway (Heiberg 1967).

Ibsen's father was a prosperous merchant who suffered serious financial reverses while Ibsen was growing up. The family was reduced to near bankruptcy and Ibsen, who apparently never felt a strong bond to his large family, was apprenticed to an apothecary in another town when he was sixteen.

Ibsen's life as an apprentice was bleak. He worked for room and board and his impoverished employer could barely provide him with that. Ibsen slept in a room above the apothecary. The maid slept in an unheated room next door. The door to her room was left open in the winter so she could get heat from Ibsen's room. At some point when Ibsen was eighteen, he and the maid decided to ward off the Norwegian cold by sleeping in the same bed. It must have seemed a natural solution to more than one pressing problem. Ibsen was alone in his new home and had no other sexual outlets. Unfortunately, the solution had an equally natural outcome. The maid became pregnant with Ibsen's child. Ibsen had to pay child support for the next fourteen years.

When Ibsen was twenty-two he left the apothecary and published his first play. He traveled to the university town of Kristiania, where he earned a precarious living from his writing. Then he was hired to manage a theater in the city of Bergen. The job required Ibsen to write plays, but the plays he produced were seldom successful. He proved inept as both a business manager and as a director, but Ibsen learned the skills necessary to make a good drama from all his failures.

Ibsen's feelings about sex during this period are unclear. He was too poor to marry and he felt some misgivings about casual affairs after his misfortune with the maid. Instead the young playwright courted a girl who had not yet reached puberty. The courtship was filled with romantic gestures and professions of love, but when Ibsen asked her father for the girl's hand, the outraged parent told him to leave his daughter alone. Later, when the father once again caught them together, he threatened Ibsen with a beating. The frightened writer made a hasty retreat.

Ibsen scored one of his rare successes as a young playwright when he was twenty-seven. A local patron of the arts subsequently invited him to dinner. This woman had a nineteen-year-old stepdaughter named Suzannah Thoresen who attracted the attention of the love-starved Ibsen. He proposed immediately and she accepted. Her parents conceded to the marriage but insisted it be postponed until Ibsen was thirty and had better financial prospects.

Ibsen considered his marriage to Suzannah to be a turning point in his life. She was not a great beauty, nor did she possess the kind of incisive intellect her husband might have appreciated. Yet, according to Ibsen, Suzannah had "a broad-minded way of thinking and a hatred of pettiness" which greatly appealed to him (Heiberg, 79). He was also pleased that she was a strong-willed, independent woman.

Suzannah had a child about a year after the wedding. The birth must have been difficult, because she later insisted that she did not want any more children. It is unknown how Ibsen reacted to this announcement. He was beset with a multitude of problems in his theater at the time and was generally depressed. It is also unclear what influence Suzannah's ironclad determination had on their sex life. It is possible her decision curtailed all sexual relations between them, or it may have just placed those relations under a restraint that Ibsen found unpleasant.

When Ibsen was thirty-six his theater closed. Suddenly he was an unemployed playwright. Disgusted with the narrow-mindedness of his Norwegian audiences, Ibsen traveled abroad and wrote plays to please only himself. He produced all of his most important works in this way. His new plays were too controversial to find a large audience, but they did find an audience among the intellectual elite. He soon developed a devoted following. At the same time, his work was constantly decried by conservative critics who considered his brand of realism nothing short of a message from the devil.

Regardless of the state of their sex life, Ibsen and Suzannah remained very much a couple. She supported him during his trials and nursed him during his bouts of depression. As strong as the marriage seemed, many were struck by the lack of closeness that characterized the relationship. One observer described Ibsen and his wife as a pair of "solitaries" occupying the same house.

Many of Ibsen's plays, in particular *A Doll's House*, feature strong, freethinking women taking charge of their own lives and challenging convention. These "feminist" characters were controversial. But for a generation of intelligent women, Ibsen's bold, female characters were an inspiration. These women often gravitated to Ibsen in his later years. Suzannah was not so distant from her husband as not to notice the advances made by these youngsters. Ibsen deflected her objections by pointing out that he couldn't write about these lovely creatures without at least talking to them.

When Ibsen was sixty-one one of these flirtations almost got out of hand. A young woman named Emilie Bardach, who had a particularly strong tendency toward hero worship, managed to get the elderly writer to fall in love with her. The relationship apparently never became physical, but Ibsen seems to have entertained the notion of leaving Suzannah and running off with the young and impetuous Bardach. The infatuation quickly passed. Ibsen remained with his wife until his death at seventy-eight.

Another Example

Warrren Beatty (actor and noted ladies' man). Born March 30, 1937 (Celebrity Birthday Guide).

If you have Mars in Sagittarius with Venus in Gemini you are . . . the Lighthearted Love Child

You are the Mars in Sagittarius Lover who never wants to settle down. It's not that you don't love with fiery enthusiasm. It's just that you can't maintain that intensity for very long and, without the intensity, you quickly forget the point. You are an adventurous, uninhibited Lover, endlessly curious about sex and always eager for new experiences. You are very flexible and can find a way to have flirtatious fun in almost any situation. In fact, the only thing that is sure to dampen your irrepressible desire is any hint that you might have to be responsible for your actions.

You are a Lover who often loves best without sex. Sex complicates love and sometimes makes it difficult for you to be the warm, imaginative, energizing companion that you are. Your best approach to sex is offhand and casual. When sex is not the aim of the relationship—when it comes to you unbidden, perhaps even by surprise—you are not only more likely to enjoy it but you are also more likely to find a reason to stick around afterward.

Case History

Katherine Anne Porter (American short story writer and novelist noted for her strikingly good looks as well as her rich characterizations). Born May 15, 1890, in Indian Creek, Texas (Givner 1982).

Porter's family had once been a part of the white, Southern aristocracy but their circumstances had been greatly reduced by the time she was born. He parents were well-educated but poor. These problems were compounded when, shortly after Porter's birth, her mother died. Her father's mother, a strong-willed and puritanical woman, stepped into the breach but she died when Porter was eleven. This left the future of the family totally in the hands of Porter's devoted, but aimless, father.

The instability and sadness of her early years made Porter anxious to leave her family. Even though she voiced ambitions of becoming an actress, Porter married when she was sixteen. Her husband was John Henry Koontz, a quiet young man from a prosperous family who had a steady job and little imagination.

Porter's later accounts of this marriage were horrific but, in reality, it wasn't so bad. Her in-laws claimed that Porter's effusive affection for Koontz early in the marriage left them embarrassed. It was only later that the couple began to argue. Part of the reason was probably Porter's inability to either conceive a child or have an orgasm with her husband. But for the most part, it was Porter's restlessness and dissatisfaction with her husband's conservative ways and complacent family that made the marriage so painful for her. When she was twenty-three, she abruptly left her husband while he was out of town on business.

Porter went to Chicago, where she hoped to find work in the budding film industry. She found employment as an extra, but the job was so taxing that soon she was back in Texas in a hospital. There she met a young woman who was working as a journalist. This profession appealed to Porter. She followed her friend's example, and eventually landed a job on a newspaper in Denver. She worked hard there and saved her money for the day when she would escape to New York City and become a "real" writer.

That day came when she was twenty-nine. Porter had acquired a fiancé in Denver, but she left him behind. She established herself in Greenwich Village, where radical politics and free love were very much in vogue. It soon became apparent that Porter was just as interested in these activities as she was anxious to develop herself as a writer. She breezed her way through several love affairs and acquired many friends who were later crucial in the advancement of her career.

Among the men Porter slept with during this period were exotic bohemians, dedicated revolutionaries, and fascinating intellectuals. Several of the relationships sparkled with passion for a time and Porter seemed ready to marry again. But when she did finally remarry at the age of thirty-four, the man she picked was neither exotic nor exciting. He was a handsome Englishman with no real ambition and ten years her junior. The couple moved to a farm outside the city, but Porter soon found herself stifled in her new marriage. Early one morning while her husband was sleeping, Porter hitched a ride on a milk truck and escaped.

Back in her bohemian haunts, Porter became involved in still more tempestuous love affairs with men who could not, or would not, marry her. When she was forty, Porter went to Bermuda, where she hoped to recover her health and concentrate on her work. She met a writer named Eugene Pressly who was twenty-five (most of Porter's lovers, and all but one of her husbands, were significantly younger than she) and totally fascinated by her. Porter was apparently less impressed by Pressly, but she found it agreeable to move in with him and settle into an uneasy monogamy.

Porter found it difficult to concentrate on her creative work throughout her life. She was, by all accounts, lazy and easily distracted. The onerous task of making a living and the revolving door of her personal life also cut sharply into her productivity. Her time with Pressly proved to be the exception to this rule. Pressly provided enough financial support and emotional stability to allow Porter to work in relative peace.

Porter was far from happy with Pressly. His passive devotion was as much a source of irritation as pleasure for her. Pressly drank too much and lacked her gregarious temperament. But as miserable as she was when Pressly was with her and as much as they bickered, she was even more miserable when they were separated. She wrote Pressly long letters and cried a lot when they were apart.

Porter eventually married Pressly. By that time the relationship had already weakened. Porter was becoming a respected and honored author by her mid-forties and she had less need for the security and reassurance of her fawning husband. She and Pressly separated six years after they wed.

Shortly after her break with Pressly, Porter became involved with a college professor named Albert Erskine. The couple spent little time together but they courted through correspondence. Soon Erskine proposed and Porter accepted. Unfortunately, Erskine was shocked to learn on their wedding day that his bride was not forty as he had judged but was actually pushing fifty years old. Erskine, who was twenty-six at the time, found this age discrepancy more than he could handle. The marriage was over before it began.

Porter's pride was deeply wounded by her failed union with Erskine, but this didn't stop the glamorous writer from seeking the company of other young admirers. She maintained an active love life through her sixties and she enjoyed shocking her relatives and friends with tales of her sexual exploits. She still had a boy friend when she was seventy, but she admitted that their relationship was platonic.

Porter always felt that she was in love with the men she slept with. She described the experience as like being struck by lightning. She was so proud of her sexual freedom that she even sent nude photographs of herself, all taken by her husbands or boy friends, to her conservative relatives back in Texas. But Porter could also be a puritan. Even though she fought to stop the censorship of writers like D. H. Lawrence and Henry Miller, privately she hated the direct approach to sexual subject matter championed by these men. Her opinions on sex and her love life remained contradictory and clouded by her own stubborn egotism until her death at the age of ninety.

If you have Mars in Sagittarius with Venus in Cancer you are . . . the Temperamental Love Child

You have an obsessive approach to love that makes you both a Lover to be desired and a Lover to be dreaded. On the one hand, you are very warm and sexy. You understand people better than most Mars in Sagittarius Lovers and you know how to make them feel loved. On the other hand, you are a wild and unrestrained Lover who is doubly hungry for experience and possessed by a curiosity that has no bounds. At times you are so intent on charging from relationship to relationship that you are unmindful of the damage that you cause.

Of course, the big secret here is that, beneath this brash aggressiveness, you are really a very sensitive and vulnerable individual who feels every psychic cut with ten-fold intensity. This is one reason you're often on the move—it keeps you from dwelling on the pain. It is also the reason you get away with so much. People respond to your emotional vulnerability and feel a need to protect and nurture you. You'll stop charging around and become surprising sedate when you find a relationship that gives you the security and protection you need.

Case History

Egon Schiele (*Austrian artist whose highly erotic renderings of the human figure eventually landed him in jail*). *Born June 12, 1890, near Vienna, Austria (Comini 1974; Whitford 1981*).

From an early age Schiele showed an unusual interest in his younger sister, Gerti. The two children were inseparable. When he was sixteen and Gerti was twelve, they ran away together to the city where their parents had spent their honeymoon, staying overnight in the same hotel in which mom and dad had slept. The uncommon closeness of these two siblings naturally roused some nasty suspicions. Schiele's father once broke down a locked door to see what his two offspring were up to. On that particular day their activities were quite innocent. Schiele later wrote, "Have adults forgotten how . . . sexually stimulated and excited they were themselves as children?" (Whitford, 29).

By the time he was sixteen, Schiele had already been admitted to the prestigious Vienna Academy of Fine Arts. The portfolio of artwork he presented with his application contained several nude drawings of Gerti as well as nude sketches of his older sister. Gerti remained his chief model for the next few years. Then he used his undeniable charm to recruit youngsters from the slums to pose for him. Schiele depicted their thin, immature bodies with a line so stark and true that even the most brazenly sexual of the images seemed edgy and devoid of sensuality.

Schiele left the academy at nineteen. He had long since divorced himself from his bourgeois family. His father died when he was fifteen and he felt little affection for his mother. Even at this early age, Schiele already saw himself as a great artist, the heir of Vienna's then-reigning "art star," Gustav Klimt. Klimt had once shocked Vienna with his vampish female nudes, but soon Schiele was drawing attention with his own brand of eroticism. Among his most notorious works was a series of nude self-portraits in which he depicted himself masturbating.

It didn't take long for this brash young painter to find patrons, though some of them were less interested in the quality of his work than in its erotic content. Pornography was already a thriving business in Vienna, and Schiele did not mind making his own contribution. In fact, he treated his sexually explicit works as a simple extension of his more conventional art and never sought to segregate or hide them.

When Schiele was twenty-two Gustav Klimt introduced him to a new model. She was a tall, lanky redhead named Valerie Neuzal but more commonly referred to as "Wallie." Schiele immediately fell in love with this sensual and warm-hearted young woman. He celebrated her long, angular body in many sexually-charged works. Never happy with city life, Schiele decided to move with his new model to a small town outside Vienna. Their irregular lifestyle drew the disapproval of the villagers. Schiele made matters worse by inviting the local children into his studio to pose and by leaving his erotic drawings out for them to see.

The officials in the province saw Schiele's open disregard for "normal" morality as an arrogant challenge to their authority. They responded by jailing the artist. He was held without bond for twenty-four days before he was tried and given a token punishment. Schiele reacted to this event with outrage and a highly exaggerated sense of persecution. But despite his bitter resentment of the punishment, it had a chilling influence on the eroticism of his art. It would be several years before he would once again concentrate on the nude in his artwork.

When he was twenty-four and living in Vienna again, Schiele suddenly decided to marry. At the same time he concluded that Wallie could not be his bride. Despite his radical pretensions, Schiele remained a man of his time and chose to marry a woman from his own class.

To this end he courted two teenage sisters who lived in a conventional, bourgeois home across the street from his studio. He courted both for a time, with Wallie acting as a chaperone, and then settled on the younger sister, Edith Harms. Edith was young but no fool. Although thrilled by Schiele's proposal, she made it clear that if the artist wanted their relationship to go forward, Wallie would have to be dismissed.

The exchange of partners was surprisingly civilized. Schiele made a rather ill-mannered attempt to persuade Wallie to join him for a "vacation" after the wedding, but the model calmly refused. (She later became a nurse with the Red Cross and died while working in an army hospital.)

At the beginning of their relationship Schiele found his virginal fiancée sexually inadequate and he was flagrantly unfaithful to her. But with Wallie out of the picture, Harms proved remarkably indulgent, even when her own sister became one of Schiele's erotic conquests. Her patience had its rewards. After a rocky beginning Schiele grew more and more devoted to his new wife, and showed signs of becoming a family man.

Meanwhile World War I was raging. Schiele was drafted into the Austrian army only a few days after his wedding. At first he suffered greatly but by constantly complaining and harping on his artistic reputation (which had been rising steadily for several years) he was assigned to light duty near Vienna. This allowed him to both advance his artistic career and continue his close relationship with Edith.

During his last years Schiele returned to depicting himself in the nude but now the context of the drawings and painting was very different. Edith appears with him in many of these pictures. One picture even shows the couple with a child that was yet unborn. The strident narcissism that had characterized his early works was replaced by a warm and almost wholesome sense of emotional interdependence and physical vulnerability. Schiele and his wife survived the war, but both were taken in the influenza epidemic that followed. Schiele was twenty-eight when he died.

Another Example

Judy Garland (actress and singer). Garland's youth was essentially stolen from her by the professional ambitions of her mother and the dictatorial control of the bosses at MGM (who fed her amphetamines to keep her thin and extend her working hours). To escape this control and her image as a childish innocent, she rushed into her first marriage. Four other marriages followed, all equally unwise. Garland had a frenetic curiosity about sex, and pursued it with all sorts of partners, in the most casual of circumstances. These encounters, like her drug addiction, provided only temporary respite from her insecurity and emotional fragility. Born June 10, 1922 (Shipman 1993).

If you have Mars in Sagittarius with Venus in Leo you are … the Proud Love Child

You are always trying to stay one step ahead of your own sexuality—no mean feat considering how dynamic that sexuality is. It's not that you're opposed to having fun, but your sexual enjoyment is so tied to your ability to maintain control that the surging, uninhibited energy of your Mars in Sagittarius can't help but make you nervous. You have to have just the right situation before you can fully release your ferocious sexual nature. Your determination to wait for such a situation can make you seem cold and aloof at times.

What happens when you find that special set of circumstances is the real story of your erotic nature. At such times you become one with your instincts—a true child of nature unmindful of obstacles or convention. You are not a sensualist. You are less interested in pleasure than experience, but you pursue that experience with single-minded glee and a burning sense of glorious purpose. In fact, it's probably a good thing you have to wait for just the right time to release your sexual energy. If it were a round-the-clock phenomena, you'd probably hurt somebody.

Case History

Greta Garbo (Greta Gustafson—Swedish film star who became a Hollywood icon). Born September 18, 1905, in Stockholm, Sweden (Paris 1995; Vickers 1994).

The child of a poor, working-class family, Garbo was deeply influenced by the death of her father when she was fourteen. Yet she kept her grief to herself and chastised her family for making a display of their feelings.

Garbo grew into a tall, plump teenager who, despite her apparent shyness, was determined to become an actress. Her first efforts were undistinguished. She was forced to go to work selling hats in a department store. There, at the age of sixteen, she probably had her first love affair with a wealthy playboy. Her romantic good fortune in no way lessened Garbo's ambition. When a director of comic films offered her a part she immediately quit both her job and her boy friend.

Garbo's "big break" came when the noted director Mauritz Stiller took her under his wing. Stiller was an explosive egotist who first insisted Garbo lose twenty pounds. He kept his protégée guessing, alternately showering her with high praise and biting criticism. But the eighteen-year-old Garbo was too aware of what the great director had to teach her to complain.

As Stiller's favorite leading lady, it was assumed by many that she was also his mistress. But Stiller was secretly homosexual, so the sexual aspect of their relationship was probably quite limited. What was most important from Stiller's point of view was the opportunity he had to mold this insecure, adolescent girl into the cinematic woman of his dreams. It is likely that this was the most important aspect of the relationship from Garbo's point of view as well.

Stiller and Garbo were offered work in Hollywood very quickly. There the relationship between the image maker and the image was shattered. Garbo prospered unbelievably in America while Hollywood largely ignored Stiller. At the same time Garbo began to entertain the attentions of other men, most prominent among them a fiery film star named John Gilbert.

For a short while Gilbert and Garbo seemed serious about one another, or at least that's how the gossip columnists saw it. Their relationship was definitely sexual; they lived together for a time. Garbo never bothered to tell Gilbert about Stiller's homosexuality, allowing the overemotional actor to assume that she refused to marry him because she was still in love with the by-then-distant director. Some observers thought that Garbo just used Gilbert to further her career and cover her less conventional love affairs. Later in life Garbo claimed she had loved John Gilbert but couldn't marry him because she "had to be the boss" (Vickers, 240).

When Garbo was twenty-three, Stiller was dead and her affair with Gilbert was cooling. By this time, she had attracted the attention of a lesbian clique within Hollywood's inner circle. Garbo apparently had affairs with at least two of these women, Lilyan Tashman and Fifi D'Orsay. But neither Tashman, who was an aggressive lesbian fond of cornering young women in the washroom, nor the empty-headed and talkative D'Orsay was discreet enough for Garbo. The relationships were extremely short-lived.

Another woman who lusted after Garbo was Mercedes de Acosta. According to Acosta, she and Garbo spent six weeks in the actress's isolated, mountain cabin. She even had snapshots of the bare-breasted Garbo posing amid the evergreens as proof of the intimacy they shared. It is likely Garbo and Acosta had a sexual affair, but Acosta was known for her tendency to exaggerate her sexual conquests. This casts doubt on the depth of their relationship. Garbo may have been impressed by the aristocratic screenwriter's worshipful devotion at first, but she later disassociated herself from Acosta. Garbo was deeply disturbed when the writer wrote a book revealing their affair.

Another international personality in love with Garbo was the bisexual photographer, Cecil Beaton. Beaton began pursuing her when she was twenty-eight and continued to do so, against all odds, for the next twelve years. He also reported carefree jaunts during which Garbo swam and hiked in the nude. They had sex, according to his account, but always on Garbo's terms. This meant she picked the time and there were few preliminaries. Garbo's relationship with Beaton lasted long after they stopped being lovers, though the aging actress was embarrassed when Beaton proclaimed his enduring love for her on his deathbed.

When Beaton was making his alleged conquest of Garbo, the actress was already a film legend without a film career. Garbo had tired of the film industry and Hollywood had tired of her controlling personality and astronomical salaries by the time she reached her mid-thirties. For the last half of her life Garbo was a jet-set recluse, often in the company of tremendously wealthy people but always wary of the press.

Garbo did not talk about sex because she considered such talk vulgar. For this reason, all reports of her love affairs are emphatically one-sided. It is possible, in fact, that she had no love affairs at all or, at least, that she never fell in love. The dominating emotion of her life seems to have truly been her oft-repeated desire to be alone. To a large degree, she got what she wanted.

During her last years Garbo kept company with George Schlee, a married millionaire, and Cecile de Rothschild, a wealthy collector of art. Both these relationships were intimate but not necessarily sexual. Garbo died at the age of eighty-four.

Another Example

Louis XIV (French monarch known as the "Sun King"). Born September 5, 1638 (Encyclopedia Britannica, Vol. 7).

If you have Mars in Sagittarius with Venus in Virgo you are . . . the Uncertain Love Child

You are the most skittish and inconsistent of all the Mars in Sagittarius Lovers. Sometimes you run away from sex, love, and commitment liked a scared puppy. Other times you go charging at all three with rapacious abandon. You possess a very strong and physical sex drive, but you are often too nervous to put it to good use. At your worst you will favor expedience over quality in your sexual experience, and you are all too likely to rush through the proceedings with at least one eye closed.

This is not always the case. You are also a very resourceful and alert Lover and seldom repeat your mistakes. If you are given time to sit back and analyze the sexual comedy, you can overcome your nervousness and become a very skilled and eager Lover. If you are lucky, you may be able to find a strong partner who understands both your earthy needs and your idealistic reserve. In the right hands you can be the best kind of Lover—someone physical enough to please the body and innocent enough to replenish the soul.

Case History

Stephen Crane (*American journalist and novelist, author of* The Red Badge of Courage). *Born November 1, 1871, in Newark, New Jersey (Benfey 1992).*

Crane's father was a proud and conservative Methodist minister, and his mother was an activist in the temperance movement. But the religious fervor of his parents had little influence on Crane. At a young age he was determined to go his own way. The early death of both of his parents gave him the freedom to do so without conflict.

Crane showed an unusual interest in criminals while a student at Princeton. He haunted the local police courts to learn more about their ways. After his mother died, Crane moved to New York City to work as a freelance journalist. He settled in one of the worst slums in the city called the "Tenderloin" to find the subjects for his writing. It is likely he already had the theme of his first novel in mind, but his experiences in his new home further fueled the writer's imagination.

Cranes' first novel was called *Maggie, a Girl of the Streets.* It was a rather maudlin tale of a young girl from the slums who becomes a prostitute. Published at his expense, the book came out when Crane was twenty. The novel is interesting because it was conceived and written at a time when Crane knew little of prostitutes. He had been carefully shielded from such evil endeavors during his youth and his exposure to life in the big city had begun only a few months before the book was issued. Apparently, much of what Crane put into his realist novel of New York slum life was imagined. It is not even known if the intrepid writer had included a visit to a prostitute in his research. Despite his avowed determination to get close to his subjects, Crane always managed to keep them at a distance.

Crane's next experiment in imaginary realism was his soon-to-be-famous war novel, *The Red Badge of Courage.* Crane knew even less about war than he did about prostitution, but this didn't stop him from producing what is still regarded as a remarkably "true" presentation of a soldier's experience. *The Red Badge of Courage* was an instant success and launched Crane's career both as a journalist and as a writer of fiction.

After the completion of his second novel, the twenty-two-year-old Crane settled in a tenement occupied by artists. Crane liked the genteel poverty and casual morality of the place. The familiarity between these painters and their models, and the models' free and shameless nudity fascinated Crane, and helped to establish the subject for his third novel. There is no evidence that Crane actually slept with any of the women who happily posed for his friends. Despite the fact that he had long left his Methodist upbringing behind him, Crane may have still been a virgin at this point.

When Crane was nearly twenty-four he entered upon his first real courtship. *The Red Badge of Courage* had been published, and he was celebrated as an important young writer. This gave Crane the courage he needed to approach a woman of his own class. Even then he conducted his courtship primarily through correspondence. Unfortunately, the young woman he selected was not to be won by fine writing. She announced she preferred strong, confident men of fashion. Crane gave up the chase.

After his failure as a swain, Crane returned to New York's Tenderloin region. The reserve that had characterized his earlier foray in the world of crime and sex for hire had by now completely worn away. Crane lived more or less openly with a female journalist named Amy Leslie for about six months. He also managed to make contacts with a whole range of people involved in the criminal justice system, from prostitutes to Theodore Roosevelt, who was then New York City's police commissioner.

One night Crane found a woman of his acquaintance (who was a known prostitute) was about to be arrested by a zealous officer. Crane interceded and tried to save the woman. Through his efforts the case against the young woman was thrown out of court. When the woman filed suit against the officer, the resulting testimony cast a tawdry light on Crane's reputation and convinced the writer he could no longer remain in New York.

Crane traveled to Florida to cover the rebellion of Cuban peasants against the Spanish. He was still corresponding with Leslie but he quickly found himself drawn to another woman. By this time Crane had developed a real-life familiarity with prostitutes, though his approach to them remained oddly chivalrous. This interest led him to the Hotel de Dream, a "nightclub" which doubled as a classy bordello. It was the proprietress of this establishment, Cora Taylor, who captured Crane's attention.

Cora, born in Boston, was the daughter of an artist. She was educated and cultured enough to know Crane's writing and to spend the evening with him discussing books. By the time Crane met Cora she had already survived two failed marriages and was making her own way in the world. This worldliness and the fact that she was six years older than Crane may have been the key reasons Crane found Cora attractive. She was an educated woman from his own class who had an easy familiarity with sex comparable to the women he met in the Tenderloin.

About this time Crane was shipwrecked while attempting to sail to Cuba. His story *The Open Boat* became one of his first "real life" literary triumphs. When Crane was back in Florida he made Cora his mistress and his journalistic partner. They traveled to Greece together as war correspondents.

Male journalists, who had long known Crane, found Cora an unimpressive partner. Her age, her disreputable past, and her bleached hair all rated scathing criticism. But Crane could find no such fault with his new mistress. Cora's last husband had neglected to give her a divorce, so Crane had a mock wedding staged. Now they could claim to be man and wife. It was probably out of consideration for Cora that Crane settled in England when he was twenty-five. Cora's past sins were unknown in England, and her proven skills as a hostess could be put to good use.

Very quickly the home of Stephen and Cora Crane became a meeting place for some of the most prominent literary people of the age, Joseph Conrad and H. G. Wells among them. Crane still felt the call to adventure. When the United States entered the Cuban war, Crane rushed to cover the action even though this meant he would be away from Cora for nine months.

Crane's health was broken when he returned from Cuba. He had shown signs of tuberculosis since childhood, and now it was slowly killing him. Despite his bad health, Crane kept up a rigorous schedule, producing both fine literature and hack writing to pay his bills and entertain his many friends. He died at the age of twenty-eight.

Another Example

Jerry Lee Lewis (rock-and-roller whose career took a tumble when it was revealed he had wed his underaged first cousin). Born September 29, 1935 (Celebrity Birthday Guide).

If you have Mars in Sagittarius with Venus in Libra you are … the Starry-eyed Love Child

You take love to a higher level. You harness all the Mars in Sagittarius energy and fire and combine it with a romantic dream of perfect love. This optimism makes you a gloriously enthusiastic Lover who looks for something sacred and beautiful in every act of love. But that same faith in love can also make you behave in ways that are wildly reckless and unwise. Even when you look before you leap, you never see anything but the good stuff.

You are perhaps the one Lover of this type who values companionship over freedom. You need one partner—someone toward whom you can channel all your warmth, dreams, and grandiloquent hopes for love. Often this singular approach to love requires you to compromise the freedom and independence you treasure so much. You are frequently willing to make this sacrifice for the sake of your perfect love. Unfortunately, sooner or later, someone is going to pay a price for this betrayal of your basic sexual nature. All too often it's you.

Case History

Rita Hayworth (Margarita Cansino—redheaded dancer and actress who became the leading sex symbol of the 1940s). Born October 17, 1918, in Brooklyn New York (Leaming 1989).

Hayworth's father was a flamenco dancer. He enjoyed great success in vaudeville during his youth but his career as a dancer was in decline by the time Hayworth turned twelve. At this point her father took Hayworth as his partner. She was removed from school, isolated from children her age, and forced to perform in various low-class clubs. Her father was careful to keep her out of the hands of the drunken patrons who assumed she was a prostitute. But his watchfulness was apparently more a matter of jealousy than paternal concern. Along with bullying her, physically abusing her, and forcing an adult role onto her for which she was not prepared, Hayworth's father also regularly committed incest with his daughter.

When she was sixteen, Hayworth's parents turned their attention to Hollywood. They promoted their beautiful, talented daughter to various people in the film industry. Unfortunately for them, their eagerness for success and Hayworth's youthful beauty drew the attention of con man Eddie Judson. Judson claimed that he had contacts with Hollywood power brokers. His contacts proved to be a sham, but this did not become obvious until after he had seduced Hayworth. Even though he was twice her age, Hayworth agreed to make Judson both her manager and her husband.

Judson quickly assumed complete control over Hayworth's life. He directed her career, controlled her income and, when it was necessary, instructed her to sleep with powerful men. Because of these activities, Judson was widely considered a pimp and Hayworth his whore. Nonetheless, his methods and Hayworth's natural talent eventually made Hayworth a star.

By the time she was twenty-three, Hayworth felt secure enough in her career to stop sleeping with her bosses, even though Judson was still pressuring her to do so. Judson threatened her with violence and disfigurement when he saw that she was gaining confidence. Fortunately for Hayworth, she found another man who gave her the moral support she needed to break with Judson, even if only on Judson's terms. Judson kept virtually all the money she had made during their marriage. All that Hayworth gained was her freedom.

The man who had facilitated Hayworth's divorce was not able to marry her, but she quickly fell into the arms of another suitor, a charismatic and aggressive young filmmaker named Orson Welles. Welles had developed an erotic fascination for Hayworth even before he met her. As soon as he learned she was free he began a determined courtship of the woman he saw as the greatest prize in Hollywood. For the emotionally bruised Hayworth, his ardent pursuit was the ultimate flattery. They were married when she was twenty-five.

Both Welles and Hayworth entered the marriage with great passion, but that passion was quickly tempered by the recognition of some harsh realities. Hayworth's traumatic past meant she needed almost constant attention and emotional support. She was insanely jealous, prone to irrational rages, and sexually insatiable. Perhaps no one was less capable of meeting her emotional needs than the egotistic, career-driven man she had married. Even though Welles continued to profess deep affection for Hayworth, he took every opportunity to escape his troubled marriage.

Hayworth and Welles were divorced when she was twenty-nine. The breakup had lasted almost as long as the marriage, because Welles was distracted by business concerns and Hayworth continued to maintain hope that she could get her wayward husband back. Even when the divorce decree was granted, Hayworth was still not willing to give up. After a secretive encounter with Howard Hughes that resulted in a pregnancy and a hurried abortion, Hayworth traveled to France with the notion of tracking down Welles. Instead Hayworth became the prey of the notorious womanizer Aly Khan.

Like Welles, Aly won Hayworth with an extravagant and resolute courtship. Unlike Welles, he was a man who was quite capable of devoting himself to love. Aly was an internationally famous lover noted for his exotic lovemaking techniques. He seemed the perfect choice to meet Hayworth's incessant sexual demands. But Aly was also a man used to variety in his sexual diet and he wasn't about to devote himself entirely to one affection-starved woman. The marriage began to fall apart when Hayworth discovered his infidelities. One day she took her two children, one daughter by Welles and one by Aly, and sailed for the United States.

Hayworth's fourth marriage to singer Dick Haymes strongly resembled her first. Haymes used Hayworth's money to pay his debts and her star status to revive his sinking career. For two years she suffered through a bizarre series of legal struggles and public humiliations as she silently submitted to Haymes' unsteady direction. Then after receiving one punch too many, Hayworth slipped away from her domineering husband and later filed for divorce.

Hayworth made one last stab at marriage at the age of forty. Once again she found herself with a husband intent on running her life. By the time this relationship ended two years later, she was already showing signs of the Alzheimer's disease that eventually reduced her to an invalid. She died at the age of seventy.

Other Examples

Oscar Wilde (*English playwright and poet*). *Born October 16, 1854 (Ellmann 1988).*

Prince Charles (*Prince of Wales*). *Born November 14, 1948 (Celebrity Birthday Guide).*

If you have Mars in Sagittarius with Venus in Scorpio you are ... the Naughty Love Child

You are the least optimistic Mars in Sagittarius Lover. You expect no cleansing grace from the thrill of sexual experience. You expect trouble and guilt, and all the sticky emotional complexities that are the inevitable outcome of human entanglements. Yet, oddly enough, this touch of wisdom (or, in some cases, cynicism) makes you no less eager for adventure. You will tackle love at any opportunity, no matter how many times it kicks you in the face.

Unlike most Mars in Sagittarius Lovers, sex is not just an ideal for you. It is a physical and emotional necessity. This can make you one of the most daring Lovers of this type, an essentially shy person who nonetheless feels compelled to nibble at the darkest extremes of sex. It can also make you the Mars in Sagittarius Lover most susceptible to commitment—a pretty dangerous and extreme measure in itself, when you think about it.

Case History

Katherine Mansfield (*Katherine Beauchamp—New Zealand-born writer noted for her impeccably crafted short stories and liberated lifestyle*). *Born October 14, 1888, in Wellington, New Zealand (Alpers 1980; Tomalin 1988).*

Mansfield's father was a prosperous banker, as proud of his English heritage as he was of his business acumen. Her mother was also proud, but somewhat distant. But even the combination of these two strong-willed parents was not sufficient to subdue young Katherine.

From an early age Mansfield displayed a keen distaste for the values of her parents and a remarkable sexual curiosity. Her first sexual experience may have come before the age of fifteen with a beautiful Maori girl. Between the ages of fifteen and eighteen she attended school in England. She developed what became a lifelong friendship with the adoring and submissive Ida Baker. Back in New Zealand at eighteen, Mansfield trifled with some male suitors, but eventually sought out the companionship of an older woman—a placid, attractive painter with whom she shared her parent's beach house.

How "far" these early affairs went in the physical sense is unclear. What was more important to Mansfield was that she identified the caresses and kisses she exchanged with these women as intensely sexual. In them she found an eroticism that completely outstripped anything she had ever known with men. Mansfield described her lesbian tendencies as fits of madness, but it was a madness she was never able to escape.

By the time she was twenty, Mansfield had made her way back to England. She was engaged in a more conventional love affair with a young musician named Garnet Trowell. Trowell was also a native of New Zealand and his family was friendly with Mansfield's. He was a sensitive, passive man who was quite content to let Mansfield take charge of their relationship. He was apparently even unalarmed when she talked of marriage, though he was still far too dependent on his parents to consider it. The relationship ran into trouble, though, when Mansfield frankly announced to his parents that she and Trowell were having sex. They were outraged and banned her from their home.

Katherine responded by accepting the proposal of another man, George Bowden, a thoroughly conventional music teacher who was several years her senior. She forced herself to go through the ceremony, but told her husband that she was unable to consummate the marriage. Then she ran away to join Trowell, who was touring with a musical show. Unfortunately, by this time she was pregnant. Her imperious mother arrived from New Zealand to take Katherine in hand. She quickly got Mansfield to a spa in Germany, out of sight of their English friends, where the pregnancy ended in a miscarriage.

Left by her mother to convalesce in Germany, Mansfield had an affair with a Polish translator through which she gained knowledge of the Russian writer, Anton Chekhov, and a case of gonorrhea. Meanwhile, back in England, her family and Bowden decided that it was Mansfield's unhealthy attachment to Ida Baker that had caused the failure of her marriage. Baker's parents were informed and they sent their daughter away on a cruise. Undaunted, the ever-loyal Baker found her way to Bavaria where she joined Mansfield.

A short time later Mansfield arrived at Bowden's home and demanded to be accepted as his wife. No sexual relations took place, but Mansfield did use Bowden's contacts in the publishing world to sell some of her short stories. After this she deserted her husband for a second time and began her life as a writer in earnest.

Feeling utterly free of the conventional bonds of her parents' world, Mansfield eagerly picked up the free-love morality of her new, literary coterie. She enjoyed playing games with her affairs, taking a man away from another woman and then playing him against another lover. Mansfield was always the aggressor in her romantic encounters. She gravitated toward weak, compliant men. When she became involved in a magazine venture with a young writer named John Middleton Murry, who had a pronounced appreciation for strong-minded women, the results were inevitable.

A first both parties were reluctant to become lovers. They felt sex would ruin their friendship and journalistic partnership. After a time the attraction between them became too intense. Mansfield began to pressure Murry to make her his mistress. Murry continued to resist for a while, but Mansfield was not to be denied.

Murry and Mansfield began their affair when she was twenty-three. By this time they were very much involved in the literary scene of their day and were familiar with many important writers and artists. Murry published their work and Mansfield used their influence to make herself a better writer. Despite their obvious intellectual compatibility and their shared ambitions, the sexual side of their union was far from successful. Mansfield described their sexual relationship as childlike. Murry claimed he never found any sexual fulfillment with Mansfield.

This lack of sexual compatibility never destroyed the friendship that existed between Mansfield and Murry. She remained loyal to him even though she felt free to take other lovers. At one point she slipped away to meet a soldier who was stationed near the front during World War I. Yet her account of this adventure makes it clear that she was more interested in the thrill of the assignation than the sex. Overall, even though he disappointed her in many ways, Murry remained her closest companion.

Both Murry and Mansfield enjoyed a close relationship with D. H. and Frieda Lawrence for a period of time. Lawrence influenced Mansfield's writing and advised Murry to be more assertive in his marital relations. Mansfield was never converted to Lawrence's ideas about the sacredness and importance of sex. Despite her fondness of using sex to shock and annoy the conventional, Mansfield quickly tired of the Lawrences' constant talk of sexual symbols and the omnipresence of sex in the natural world. She was shocked and disgusted by their intense and often violent arguments.

Mansfield never lost the adoration of Ida Baker. Baker would not permit it. She followed Mansfield like an obedient and uncomplaining servant, whenever Mansfield permitted her to do so. On occasion Mansfield used Baker shamefully, referring to her in jest as her slave. At times Baker's passivity irritated Mansfield, and she subjected her friend to vicious verbal attacks. Again it is unclear how physical this lesbian infatuation became. Mansfield did go so far as to call Baker her "wife" and Baker always reacted with jealousy to Mansfield's relationships with men, even Murry.

Murry married Mansfield when she was twenty-nine. By this time she had been diagnosed with tuberculosis and her health was in deep decline. During the years that followed they were often separated as she roamed Europe to seek a cure and he sought employment. Murry managed to be with Mansfield when she died at the age of thirty-four.

Another Example

Montgomery Clift (film star). Born October 17, 1920 (Celebrity Birthday Guide).

If you have Mars in Sagittarius with Venus in Sagittarius you are ... the Natural Love Child

You are the most innocent of all the Mars in Sagittarius Lovers and are often the most unrealistic. Sex has to be a seamless, shameless extension of your own joyous life force or it just can't work for you. It has to be something you don't think about, something that just happens. At times you can be so protective of this erotic purity that you seem shy and standoffish. Even under the best of conditions this search for sex as simple, animal energy will always make you a very difficult Lover to please.

So, what's your best-case scenario? Well, to keep on looking, of course. Your frustrated search for innocence may often leave you incomplete, but it will also make you an inspired, hopeful, and humane Lover who is full of playful energy and warm affection. If you give up on this search for purity in an impure world, you stop being a Lover of any sort. You become just another cynical observer.

Case History

Charles Dodgson (Lewis Carroll—Oxford don and mathematician who also wrote the children's classics Alice in Wonderland *and* Through the Looking Glass*). Born January 27, 1832, in Cheshire, England (Gattegno 1974).*

The son of a respected churchman, Dodgson decided early in his life to remain a bachelor. At the beginning of his academic career at Oxford, where he was first a student and then an instructor of mathematics, marriage would have been a hindrance. Later he indicated he lacked the financial means. But the fact that Dodgson never showed a sexual interest in a mature woman was probably the most important impediment.

At twenty-four Dodgson met Alice Liddell, the first and most famous of his "child-friends." She was four years old. Dodgson spent much of his free time with Alice and her sisters, inventing games, telling stories, and generally enjoying their childish company. Alice's mother was a bit suspicious at first but soon put aside her reservations. The childlike joy Dodgson found in the company of her girls, and their affection for him, was enough to calm her fears. During his friendship with Alice, Dodgson composed his most famous stories, *Alice in Wonderland* and *Through the Looking Glass*. His relationship with the Liddells and with

Alice in particular stopped suddenly when Alice was eleven. It was rumored that Dodgson approached Alice's father about the possibility of marrying Alice and this brought about the breach. Dodgson quickly moved on to other friendships, all of which followed the pattern he had established with Alice.

Dodgson was always on the lookout for attractive children. He was sure to have toys and other lures in his pockets when he was on holiday or in a situation where he might meet children. The fact that he was the writer of famous children's books also served as a respectable introduction, especially to the parents. Dodgson approached both boys and girls, but his special friends were always girls. Dodgson had no trouble winning the acceptance of children. He was warm and confident in their presence and always knew how to please them.

Parents rarely objected to the attention that Dodgson paid their children, even when he asked for unchaperoned visits or kissed the girls on the lips. After all, he was an ordained deacon and a man of the most austere habits. His attitude toward sex was typically Victorian. A great fan of the theater, he would walk out on any play in which sex was even mentioned. So, the parents of the children Dodgson courted could be assured of his exemplary chastity. What they didn't know was that, despite his unimpeachable lifestyle, Dodgson was plagued by feelings of guilt.

Dodgson's diaries are full of references to his sinfulness and evil thoughts. He never elaborates on the nature of these thoughts, but given his sheltered and upright lifestyle, it can be surmised they involved sex and possibly masturbation. It is also probably significant that these distressed references began to appear in his diary during his relationship with the Liddell children.

Dodgson was an avid photographer. His "girl friends" were his favorite subjects. He liked to dress the children in costumes or, if a child were agreeable, he photographed her in the nude. Typically, he had no trouble gaining the approval of the parents even for this activity. There is no evidence that Dodgson ever did or said anything overtly sexual with any of his child-friends. He was always delighted when he found a child who would pose nude for him, but he never forced the issue. He promptly withdrew if the parents of the girls showed any mistrust of his motives.

Dodgson typically lost interest in his child-friends when they neared puberty. In Dodgson's opinion, the contaminating influence of sexual awareness robbed these children of the innocence, the brilliance, and lack of self-awareness that so fascinated and reassured him. Even his ideal, Alice Liddell, seemed dull to him when he met her later in her life.

Many people around him were concerned about Dodgson's relationships with children. Even his sister warned him of the implications. But Dodgson, a staid conformist in every other aspect of his life, defied these conventional opinions. He maintained that there was nothing "impure" in his relations, and that his conscience was quite clear (despite what he was writing in his diaries). He continued to pursue the company of children until his death at sixty-five.

Other Examples

Joe Dimaggio (*American baseball hero and husband of Marilyn Monroe*). *Born November 25, 1914* (*Encyclopedia Britannica, Vol. 4*).

Samuel Clemens (*Mark Twain—American writer*). *Born November 30, 1835* (*Celebrity Birthday Guide*).

George Burns (*comedian who rose to fame as the straight man for his talented wife, Gracie Allen*). *Born January 20, 1896* (*Celebrity Birthday Guide*).

If you have Mars in Sagittarius with Venus in Capricorn you are … the Conscientious Love Child

You are a serious dreamer who can't be satisfied with just thinking pretty thoughts—you have to live them. You require concrete fulfillment of your childlike idealism more than any Mars in Sagittarius Lover. Often this means sex that encompasses a cause or includes an important sacrifice—sex that gives you the chance to play at being a hero or savior of someone less fortunate. But for all your emphasis on obligation and noble self-sacrifice, you are practical enough to always take care of yourself first.

You are one of the most physical and calculating of all the Mars in Sagittarius Lovers. You adore innocence but do what you have to do to get laid. For this reason you are prone to segregate your carnal desires from your high-minded concepts of love. This plan may work in some instances, but it is fraught with potential problems. In the end, dividing your love life only makes it all that more complex and Mars in Sagittarius Lovers always suffer when love gets too complex.

Case History

Andre Gide (*Nobel prize-winning French novelist, author of* The Immoralist *and* The Counterfeiters). *Born November 22, 1869, in Paris, France* (*Painter 1968*).

Gide fell irretrievably in love with his first cousin, Madeleine Rondeaux, at the age of twelve. It was a time of tragedy for both youngsters. Gide's father had died the year before, and

Madeleine had just discovered that her mother was unfaithful to her father. When Gide found Madeleine praying and crying at her bedside he immediately decided that his "mystic orientation" was to love and protect her. He clung to this dream through his adolescence. When he was twenty-one, after the publication of his first novel, Gide proposed to Madeleine. Unfortunately, Madeleine had already renounced sexual pleasure because of what she saw as her mother's treachery, and she rejected her cousin.

Gide had an intense interest in religious and moral issues during his childhood and adolescence. He studied the Bible and philosophy. He adopted the lifestyle of an ascetic; he bathed in cold water and slept on boards. By the time the young writer had reached his early twenties, however, he had grown tired of this physical mortification. At this point he met Oscar Wilde, who was at the height of his fame. Wilde's disregard for conventional morality stirred Gide's imagination and made him renounce his "prison of morality."

A friend persuaded Gide to sleep with one of the local girls when he was twenty-three and traveling in North Africa. Gide found the experience unrewarding. A short time later in Algeria, Gide chanced to meet Oscar Wilde and Alfred Douglas again. The two Englishmen were intent on cruising for dark-skinned boys. After some hesitation, Gide was persuaded to join them. It was at this time that Gide recognized he was a homosexual.

Back in France, Gide's mother died, leaving her son a young man of considerable means and no visible restraints. Gide had resumed his courtship of Madeleine with renewed vigor. He convinced his virginal cousin that even if they were married he would not pressure her for sex. What he didn't tell her was why. They were wed when he was twenty-five.

Even though Gide's marriage was never consummated, it was nonetheless a very real marriage. In many ways, the childish infatuation Gide had developed for his sad playmate persisted throughout his life. Madeleine remained the "mystical" center of his existence. He respected her chaste devoutness, nursed her through her various illnesses, and traveled with her whenever her health allowed. The couple recognized the singularity of their relationship. They never referred to each other as husband and wife, but as brother and sister.

Meanwhile, anonymous encounters with young men and boys remained Gide's only sexual outlet. Most of these sex partners were found during his many travels, particularly in North Africa. They were typically poor hustlers more interested in the rich Frenchman's purse than in his personality. This was something Gide understood—even expected. Despite an occasional flight of passion, he did not allow these passing, sexual attachments to interfere with his sexless adoration of Madeleine.

The problem was that the sheltered and conventional Madeleine was totally incapable of understanding her husband's sexual preference. The necessity of keeping his sex life a secret from the person he loved caused Gide a great deal of anxiety or, as he called it, "inquietude."

When he was thirty-three, Gide wrote *The Immoralist*, which recounts the story of a cold, cruel young man who marries for the sake of appearances and devotes himself to unabashed hedonism. Even though the experiences of his hero approximated his own, Gide was no immoralist. He was deeply concerned with moral issues raised by his lifestyle. These unresolved questions haunted his thoughts and his writings.

When Gide was forty-seven Madeleine chanced to read a letter meant for her husband, in which an old friend chronicled the homosexual sprees he and Gide enjoyed. Mrs. Gide, who had somehow contrived to remain ignorant of her husband's secret life, was shocked. The rift created by this incident only widened when, the next year, Gide fell in love with a fifteen-year-old French boy named Marc Allegret. This relationship was unlike any of his other homosexual relationships. Immediately both Gide and Madeleine recognized that the delicate balance of their marriage had been damaged beyond repair.

The problems in his love life inspired Gide to return to a work that he had begun some time before called *Corydon*. In this book Gide undertook an itemized defense of homosexuality, attempting to prove that it was historically, medically, and morally a "natural" phenomena. Gide read most of his other books aloud to Madeleine for her approval. He tried to read *Corydon* to her, but it proved too painful for both of them and he could not finish.

In the midst of his marital crisis and his affair with Marc Allegret, Gide also began the most unusual relationship of his life. He met a young woman named Elisabeth van Rysselberghe and teasingly told her he wanted to father a child with her. The relationship continued to develop through a mutual interest in books and poetry. When Gide was fifty-two, Rysselberghe bore him his first and only child.

Madeleine died when Gide was sixty-eight. During the ten years before her death, she and Gide had once again grown close, even though Madeleine continued to see her husband as a pitiful sinner. She prayed for him every night and always felt his morality could be restored if he would accept a religious conversion. Madeleine's hopes proved to be false, however. Although Gide never stopped being concerned about questions of morality, he died unrepentant at the age of eighty-one.

Another Example

Magda Friedander Goebbels *(wife of Nazi propaganda minister Joseph Goebbels). At twenty-nine, Magda was a beautiful and wealthy divorcée. Although she had previously been apolitical, she was won over to the Nazi cause after hearing Joseph Goebbels, Hitler's silver-tongued propaganda minister, speak. Goebbels, who was known as a ladies' man, responded immediately to his new fan. Magda was so impressed with his cause that she was content to ignore his clubfoot and lack of physical appeal. They were married with the stipulation that Magda would not object if*

Goebbels were guilty of an occasional infidelity. She soon learned that her husband's appetite for extramarital sex was far from occasional. After several years of living with Goebbels philandering, Magda finally went to Hitler himself to ask permission for a divorce. Hitler refused her request. Magda continued in the marriage, which produced six children, even though her hatred for her husband was now quite obvious. Yet, despite her distaste for her husband, Magda made no attempt to divorce herself from his radical ideas. When Hitler's empire fell, Magda followed her husband's lead by poisoning herself and her six children. Born November 11, 1901 (Meissner 1980).

If you have Mars in Sagittarius with Venus in Aquarius you are … the Wild Love Child

You are the most adventurous of all the Mars in Sagittarius Lovers—a liberated and liberating Lover with an enthusiasm for sex that is both thrilling and infectious. There are few things you won't try and virtually nothing about sex that makes you nervous, with the exception of commitment. You tend to be an unconventional Lover and you have some pretty strong opinions when it comes to sexual issues. Because of this, and your unwillingness to compromise your freedom, it is difficult for you to hold on to relationships. To like you is easy. To love you can be a trial.

Despite all the frenetic energy you bring to it, physical sex is not all that important to you. You use sex mostly as a way to know people, or simply to get their attention. Occasionally, you also use it just for fun; but you do not use sex as the basis for a relationship. Relationships must be based on matters far more intellectual and spiritual, as far as you are concerned. They have to represent a blending of energy and purpose. Sex can be a part of this, or it may not. You can be happy either way.

Case History

Janis Joplin (singer who fused blues with rock-and-roll). Born January 19, 1943, in Port Arthur, Texas (Amburn 1992).

Joplin was brought up in a stable, conservative, middle-class home. From puberty on, she rebelled against the values of her parents in every way possible. At fourteen she was making out with boys after church choir practice. Then she dropped out of church altogether and became a provincial beatnik. Joplin idolized people like Jack Kerouac and Neil Cassidy. The images of independent, hard-living men like these would remain sacred to her all her life. She called them her "mythic men."

When she entered high school Joplin had probably already lost her virginity. Her offhand approach to sex, along with her liberal ideas, foul mouth, and penchant for outrageous behavior thoroughly alienated her from most of the other kids at her school. She did manage to make friends with three boys who were more sensitive and intelligent than most, and were willing to accept her as an equal. Joplin, who wore no makeup and dressed like a boy, proved herself as smart and as tough as any of her compatriots. And she turned out to be everyone's equal when it came to the consumption of alcohol. Joplin was already well on her way to alcoholism by the time she was sixteen.

Joplin was a pudgy, acne-faced teenager who possessed little in the way of sex appeal. This deficiency apparently only made her more determined to sleep with as many men as possible. She had sex casually with each of her three friends and, during their forays to the redneck bars outside of Port Arthur, she flirted aggressively with strangers. Her actions placed her and her friends in very real danger, but this risk only added to the thrill for Joplin.

After high school, Joplin made an attempt at attending a local college, but quickly bolted to Houston and then to California. She had her first lesbian lover while still in high school, but it was during her first sojourn to California that Joplin began her lifelong pattern of moving easily between male and female lovers. Joplin's bisexuality was remarkable in that she was equally drawn and responsive to both her male and female partners.

Joplin found California to be a disappointment and quickly returned to Texas. At nineteen she was in Austin where she found a community of "beats" and rebels around the University of Texas. Here Joplin found a free-loving, hard-drinking, idealistic environment in which she could thrive. In Austin she drew attention because of her singing. She gave up her previous ambition to be a graphic artist to concentrate on music. But at this point Joplin's ability to concentrate on anything other than having a good time was limited.

Joplin made friends in Austin with a young man named Chet Helms with whom she hitchhiked to San Francisco. With Helms' encouragement and promotion she managed to make a little money singing. Joplin came close to being "discovered" more than once during the next few months in the fecund music scene of San Francisco, but bad luck and her rowdy lifestyle got in the way.

Her sex life was frenetic. Earthy by nature and uninhibited as a matter of principle, Joplin took on all comers, men and women. Never shy about sex, Joplin developed the aggressive "macho" sexuality for which she later became famous. Still, she was capable of a variety of "poses" with her sexual partners. She could be very feminine and passive with some, adventurous and exuberant with others.

Regardless of the great display Joplin made of her gargantuan sexual appetite, it was drugs that became the central issue of her life. She was injecting both methamphetamine and heroin by this time, and using copious amounts of marijuana, LSD, and alcohol. Still a chubby teenage when she arrived in San Francisco, Joplin quickly took on the gaunt look of an addict. Even her wild friends, most of them also heavy drug users, became alarmed. Then Joplin somehow acquired a fiancé. A party was held to give her enough money to leave San Francisco and join him in Seattle. This groom never made an appearance and the wedding was cancelled.

At twenty-two Joplin was a beaten rebel back in her hometown. With her family's support she entered therapy for her drug and alcohol addiction, began to dress like a "normal" young lady, and embarked on a course of study at a local college designed to give her solid secretarial skills. She was, by all accounts, miserable. After a while she looked for singing gigs on the side. Through one of these jobs she found that Travis Rivers, another friend from her Austin days, was looking for her.

Back in San Francisco some people she knew had formed a band called Big Brother and the Holding Company. They had scored some successes locally and were looking for a "chick" singer to help them out. Joplin's name had immediately come up, but her unstable history had made the band members hesitate. Finally, Rivers was dispatched to Texas to lure her back for an audition. Rivers was one of those people who had been concerned for Joplin's health during her last days in San Francisco. He was reluctant to approach her when he found she had dried out and was in therapy; however, once Joplin learned what was up there was no holding her back.

Joplin's second assault on San Francisco was very like the first. She quickly put aside her recovery and resumed her relentless schedule of drugs, booze, and sex. But now there was a new element added: rock-and-roll. Even before she landed the job with Big Brother, Joplin seemed to know this would be her big chance. She applied herself to her work as never before despite her almost constant state of intoxication and incredibly active sex life.

Joplin cemented her union with the members of her band by sleeping with all of them at one time or another, even the ones who were married. She had several other lovers but Travis Rivers remained especially close to her. He was a burly philosopher; unconventional, affectionate, and virile—the epitome of the type Joplin called her "mythic men." When he proposed marriage to Joplin she refused him, claiming that marriage would hurt her career and limit her options just at the point when she could have any man she wanted.

Another important relationship that Joplin developed during this period was with Peggy Caserta. Joplin was more secretive about her lesbian affairs than her heterosexual adventures, and her girl friends were far less numerous that her boy friends. Her relationship with Caserta became one of her most sustained sexual affairs. This did not necessarily make it any more meaningful.

In fact, it is debatable whether any of Joplin's relationships were meaningful, particularly during and after her rise to fame and fortune. Her fame gave her access to a variety of "mythic men" including Jimi Hendrix, Jim Morrison, and Kris Kristofferson. Yet, none of these affairs endured. She was left to console herself with male groupies and other hangers-on. Sex became a way of filling her amphetamine-charged time.

By the time she was twenty-five, Joplin had broken with Big Brother and the Holding Company. It was a bad decision both for her career and for her emotional stability. She never found a band as capable and she completely lost the sense of camaraderie that had characterized her first years with that group. But Joplin still had her voice and that was enough to keep her career moving forward.

During her last few months Joplin became engaged to marry a handsome junkie with a shady past named Seth Morgan. Even this relationship was not monogamous. She had invited Caserta to join Morgan and her for a threesome one night when she was twenty-seven. Neither Morgan nor Caserta showed up. Meanwhile Joplin had acquired some heroin that was of a much higher purity than she expected. She injected it and died of an overdose a short time later.

Another Example

Ruth St. Denis (*American dancer, considered one of the great pioneers of modern dance*). *St. Denis claimed to be a virgin until she was married at the age of thirty-five. After this, St. Denis dallied with various young men, but probably had only a limited sex life with her bisexual husband, who preferred men. By her own account, it wasn't until she was fifty-five and took up with a thirty-eight-year-old Chinese poet that she had her first "complete" sexual experience. Born January 20, 1879 (Shelton 1981).*

If you have Mars in Sagittarius with Venus in Pisces you are . . . the Luscious Love Child

Your sexual nature is almost too fragile for real life. You are so sensitive and emotionally vulnerable that almost everything you do in your love life has the potential of leaving you deeply hurt and uncertain. For this reason you often avoid making decisions about your sexuality and gravitate toward partners whose opinions and direction with regard to sex are strong enough to make yours unnecessary. You may be an independent and willful person in other areas of your life, but when it comes to sex, you are always most secure and happy when you are following someone else's lead.

Even though you are passive, you are not always easy to control. You are one of the most passionate Mars in Sagittarius Lovers. Your natural taste for adventure is augmented by an undeniable sexual allure. Even when you are too shy to go looking for trouble, it has a way of finding you. So, even though you are one of the most loyal and devoted Lovers of this type, your affection can never be taken for granted.

Case History

Edith Wharton *(Edith Jones Wharton—American writer noted for her quiet novels and stories about private heroism). Born January 24, 1862, in New York City, New York (Lewis 1975).*

Wharton was born into the most exclusive social set in the United States, a group of powerful families whose wealth predated the Revolution. Her father was a handsome, affable man with whom Wharton shared an intense interest in history and art. She felt very close to him and was deeply affected when he died when she was nineteen. It was Wharton's mother who controlled her life. A stern, uncompromising woman who apparently valued nothing more than social grace and propriety, she thoroughly indoctrinated Wharton in the ways and the duties of her class.

Wharton was not a very sociable child. She preferred her books to parties, and horseback riding to dancing. Her determination to be a writer developed early and she published a short story and finished her first novel by the time she was sixteen. This precocious intellectual activity alarmed her mother so much that she insisted that Wharton be "brought out" a year earlier than the traditional age of eighteen.

As her mother expected, the whirl of social engagements and male admirers temporarily distracted Wharton from her writing. At nineteen she was engaged to a particularly good-looking and popular young man. But as susceptible as she was to the glamour of her new life, Wharton proved totally inept in the social maneuvering and game playing that might have allowed a not-so-pretty young heiress to reel in a husband. The engagement was off by the time she was twenty-one.

Wharton quickly met a new man, Walter Berry, who shared her sensitive appreciation of art and literature. She was on the verge of falling in love with him, but Berry mysteriously withdrew. A true representative of his class, he apparently was unable to conceive of a woman as both a friend and as a sex object. Wharton remained his friend for years but, for sex, he preferred women whose conversation was lighter and less intimidating.

Shortly after her letdown with Berry, Wharton met a lazy but strikingly handsome thirty-three-year-old man name Teddy Wharton. Teddy had no intellectual pretensions, but his good looks and good humor attracted Wharton nonetheless. Besides, as her mother very likely told her, she was getting too old to be picky. Wharton and Teddy were married when she was twenty-three.

In her early teens Wharton had asked her mother about the strange "feelings" she was having when she read certain books or rode her horse. Mrs. Jones angrily told her it was not nice to ask such questions. Before her marriage Wharton once again went to her mother asking for advice. Once again she was brusquely turned away. Ignorant, shy, and extremely sensitive, Wharton found the sexual side of her marriage a brutal disappointment.

Wharton and her husband settled in Newport, Rhode Island, where they hobnobbed with the Astors and the Vanderbilts. Wharton, following her mother's example, devoted herself to the onerous business of running her house and being a socialite. For a woman of Wharton's intelligence and ambition, it was a painfully empty existence. Her marriage offered her little respite. She and Teddy shared an interest in horses and dogs but little else. Their sex life had apparently ceased altogether shortly after their honeymoon (the marriage produced no children). She found herself increasingly irritated by his company. By the time Wharton reached her thirties, she was subject to a series of "breakdowns" and "nervous disorders" for which she sought various ineffective treatments.

Despite her troubles, Wharton continued to write, first poetry and short stories and then novels. During her thirties, she gathered people around her who shared her deep, intellectual interests. Berry reentered her life and she became friendly with many writers, including Henry James, who was a major influence on her work. This cerebral coterie of friends helped divert Wharton from her marital problems and depressions. But none of these relationships answered her need for physical love.

When Wharton was forty-four she met an American journalist living in Paris named Morton Fullerton. Like Walter Berry and Teddy Wharton, Fullerton was notably handsome and masculine. Unlike any of the other men in Wharton's life, he was also experienced enough as a philanderer to sense Wharton's sexual needs and bold enough to make the first move. What ensued was a tremendously passionate, sexual relationship. Wharton's belated introduction into what she called "real life" only made her more anxious to taste all its joys. Fullerton, who was in an excellent position to make such comparisons, considered Wharton to be a supremely sensuous and adventurous lover.

Wharton's relationship with Fullerton was hardly idyllic. Wharton worried about keeping the affair a secret and was tormented by feelings of guilt. Also, Fullerton was a man with a history. At one point Wharton had to give him money so he could buy back incriminating letters from an old girl friend. Despite the blistering heat of its beginning, Wharton soon realized that her affair with Fullerton would not last forever.

Meanwhile, Teddy decided he too had had enough of his sexless marriage. Wharton was apparently aware of infidelities on the part of her husband even before she met Fullerton. Now Teddy began making a display of his sexual liberation—allowing himself to be seen in public with various women and registering his paramour of the evening as "Mrs. Wharton" in the best hotels. It is not clear whether it was the sense of betrayal or the breach of propriety that convinced Wharton to petition for a divorce. In either case, the marriage ended when she was fifty-one.

After the end of her affair with Fullerton and her separation from Teddy, Wharton finally turned to her old friend, Walter Berry, as a lover. This change in their relationship came at a price. Wharton, who had dominated her sexless marriage with the easy-going Teddy, treated Berry with surprising deference, allowing him to rule her actions to a degree that surprised and disturbed many of her friends. When Berry died, the sixty-five-year-old Wharton grieved for him as a wife might grieve for her husband. She died ten years later.

Other Examples

Lucrezia Borgia *(illegitimate daughter of Pope Alexander VI noted for the bad luck that she brought her husbands). Lucrezia's first marriage was arranged when she was twelve. By the time she was seventeen her father and brothers decided that this arrangement was politically unworkable and they ran her husband out of Rome. Later, this unfortunate duke was forced to agree to an annulment of the marriage. At eighteen Lucrezia married a second time but changes in the political climate soon made this marriage obsolete as well. Lucrezia's fiery brother, Cesare Borgia, ended it in the most expedient way possible—he killed the husband. Meanwhile, all the excesses of violence and sensuality of which the Borgia clan were capable were attributed to the beautiful and seductive Lucrezia. She was accused of a variety of crimes, ranging from incest with both her father and her brother to murder by poison. Yet there is no hard evidence she was guilty of anything except the extreme docility with which she surrendered her body to the ambitions of her conniving family. Fortunately for Lucrezia her third marriage, another nakedly political arrangement, took her out of Rome and away from these scandals. In her later years she became known as a patron of the arts (mostly of male poets who were a little in love with her) and for her political astuteness. Lucrezia died at the age of thirty-nine. Born April 18, 1480 (Fusero 1972).*

John Travolta *(American actor). Born February 18, 1954 (Celebrity Birthday Guide).*

Chapter 10

Mars in Capricorn
The Slave of Love

General Characteristics

Sex should be a simple matter for Mars in Capricorn Lovers. They are among the earthiest Lovers of the zodiac—people who identify the joy of sex directly with the body and make no apologies for their strong, erotic drives. These are practical, sometimes calculating, Lovers who go after physical satisfaction with an unbeatable combination of relentlessness and raw lust. But despite this apparent simplicity, the sexuality of Mars in Capricorn Lovers is complex.

One of the most remarkable aspects of these Lovers is their aversion to happiness, or at least to any happiness that has not been tempered and purified by intense misery. Mars in Capricorn Lovers need adversity in their love lives. They are unable to really appreciate their considerable sensuality until guilt, responsibility, or dire circumstance has somehow hobbled their sex drive. Hardship brings out the best in Mars in Capricorn Lovers. Their real capacity for loyalty and devotion is often only apparent in the proximity of pain.

Mars in Capricorn Lovers are typically very conservative. They are most comfortable when they can keep their sexual activity well within the limits proscribed by their own social milieu, and they tend to avoid the company of people who can't. This conventionality brings up another complex issue in the sexuality of this type. Their physical drives are so elemental, and they pursue them with such dogged determination, that it's almost impossible for these Lovers not to break the rules now and again. When they do, they are so incapable of seeing themselves as rebels that they often turn the situation on its head. They look at their own activity as normal, no matter how unusual it may be, and wonder why the rest of the world doesn't agree. For this reason, Mars in Capricorn Lovers—who usually have little tolerance for sexual risk taking—can sometimes become the most outlandish of sexual revolutionaries.

Control is another issue in which the complexity of this type becomes evident. Mars in Capricorn Lovers are typically very controlling Lovers who can't really relax in a sexual situation unless they think they can physically, emotionally, or mentally "manage" a partner. They are often drawn to relationships with people over whom they have some sort of advantage; however, it is rare that these Lovers are able to enjoy being the boss. For the Mars in Capricorn Lover, control is measured in terms of obligations and responsibilities. It becomes just another means of self-sacrifice or, in many cases, self-sacrifice becomes a means of control.

The final complexity of the Mars in Capricorn sexuality has to do with romanticism. These Lovers seem full of old-fashioned chivalry and sweet, romantic notions because they honor self-sacrifice and the obligations that come with relationships. But while it is true that these Lovers do tend to be old-fashioned, it is typically old-fashioned lust that is their real motivation. For all their determination to "love till it hurts," Mars in Capricorn Lovers tend to be very practical when it comes to forming relationships. They seek relationships that are grounded in material interdependence and sexual capability. Of course, they feel guilty for it afterward.

If you have Mars in Capricorn with Venus in Aries you are . . . the Combative Slave of Love

You are a Mars in Capricorn Lover who knows exactly what you want from sex. Unfortunately, you seldom let yourself have it. Even though your approach to love is forthright to the extreme, your energies are often misdirected and your efforts self-defeating. Love is often like a punishment for you. The good news is that's the way you like it.

The really odd thing about your sexuality is your optimism. No matter how much trouble love brings, you never lose your confidence or your taste for sexual adventure. You are among the most energetic and demonstrative of the Mars in Capricorn Lovers. You tend to be competitive and sometimes a little pushy where sex is concerned. You are not afraid to go after a challenging relationship. It is this ability to shake off the past and believe in love all over again that is your most charming quality. Of course, some might call it your most foolish quality.

Case History

Jean Harlow (Harlean Carpenter—film star labeled "the blond bombshell"). Born March 3, 1911, in Kansas City, Missouri (Golden 1991; Stenn 1993).

Harlow's mother (also named Jean Harlow) was a great beauty who had her own notions of stardom until she was forced by her domineering father to marry a well-to-do dentist. Frustrated and thoroughly self-involved, Harlow's mother projected all her dreams onto her only child. When Harlow was ten her parents divorced, and her mother took her to Hollywood.

The elder Jean Harlow was already too old to break into pictures but she immediately began to groom her daughter. Harlow was sent to an exclusive girl's school where her play-mates were the daughters of high-powered, movie-industry executives. Unfortunately, this plan was thwarted when Harlow's grandfather threatened to cut off his support to the mother and daughter if they did not return to Kansas City.

By this time Harlow had developed into a ravishing adolescent whose sex appeal was obvious to everyone. At fourteen while at a summer camp, she lost her virginity when she brazenly offered herself to a counselor for whom she had a yen. Meanwhile, her mother had found a new beau: an Italian-born gigolo named Marino Bello. Bello became Harlow's stepfather when she was sixteen. A short time later Harlow herself eloped with Charles McGrew, a young man she had met in school.

Harlow and her new husband moved to Hollywood where, despite McGrew's substantial income, the new bride began looking for work. Harlow later claimed it was blind luck that got her started in pictures, but her registration as an extra under her mother's name indicates she was consciously fulfilling the older woman's long-postponed dream. Of course, as soon as "Mother Jean" learned that Harlow had become a movie actress she came to Los Angeles with Bello to manage her daughter's career. McGrew was quickly pushed out of Harlow's life. The child she had conceived with him was aborted.

Harlow remained ambiguous about her acting career until, with the breakup of her marriage, she became the sole support of herself, her mother, and her perpetually unemployed stepfather. Then she applied herself with admirable diligence. With no acting skills to speak of, Harlow (and her mother) counted on her looks to give her an advantage. She apparently wasn't above a little exhibitionism to further her cause. When doing a bit with comedians Laurel and Hardy in which her dress was to be accidentally ripped off, Harlow shocked the film crew by "forgetting" to wear tights under her clothing.

Harlow's big break developed when Howard Hughes hired her to play the female lead in an extravaganza called *Hell's Angels*. She was eighteen years old. She played a cynical, man-eating tramp and, at least according to the critics, did it badly. However, the audience thought otherwise (thanks partially to Hughes' publicity blitz), and Harlow became an instant star. Her platinum blond hair started a fashion craze. The public demanded to see her in more movies, always playing the same sexually aggressive bad girl.

By all accounts, Harlow's off-the-screen personality was not nearly so brassy. She was down-to-earth and completely lacking in pretension. Many felt she was unaware of her considerable sex appeal, or that it was just part of the role she played for the public. And yet, even after her career was established, Harlow was capable of using that sex appeal very aggressively. She enjoyed flashing the "boys" on the set, sometimes met visitors to her home in the nude, and had a calculated aversion to underwear—all indicating that she was very aware of the unsettling effect her body had on men.

Harlow managed to have affairs despite her mother's watchfulness. Her sexual appetites were rather straightforward. She slept with male friends, usually men unconcerned with commitment, who could satisfy her physical needs and help her in her career. She showed no taste for either romantic intrigue or passionate fireworks.

In fact, the man she saw most often during this period, a studio executive named Paul Bern, had never made a pass at her. She respected him for that. Harlow's relationship with Bern has been the subject of much conjecture. Bern was a sensitive, intelligent man who was known for his ability to get close to troubled, young actresses. He was not known to have had sex with any of them. The fact that he became Harlow's confidant and advisor surprised no one; however, many people were surprised and concerned when they learned he had asked the likable twenty-one-year-old actress to marry him.

To say that Bern was a poor candidate for matrimony would be an understatement. He was a physically undersexed man with an abnormally small penis and a womanish body. He was also secretly married to a woman he had met in his youth and left in New York in an insane asylum. Although the precise nature of Bern's problems was not known, rumors about his various deficiencies abounded. Harlow had heard them all, but she was still determined to go through with the wedding. She liked Bern because he was intelligent and encouraged her to read and follow her girlhood ambition to write stories. He also represented a replacement for the father figure she had lost with her parent's divorce. Harlow indicated later that she had accepted the notion that sex was not going to be the most important thing in her life. How long she would have continued to accept this is unknown. Bern killed himself two months after the wedding.

Bern's death left Harlow badly shaken, but she chose to return to work rather than surrender to her grief. She also returned to her habit of having casual affairs. She slept with Victor Fleming, a director who was quite experienced in bedding his leading ladies, and boxer Max Baer. When Baer's wife learned of the affair, she threatened Baer with a messy divorce. This may be why Harlow suddenly proposed marriage to a veteran cameraman named Hal Rosson.

Like Bern, Rosson was older than Harlow and had long been her close friend. Also, like Bern, he tried to separate Harlow from the control of "Mother Jean" and Bello. Unfortunately, Harlow became ill shortly after their marriage and she returned to her mother to be nursed back to health. At this point Rosson knew the marriage was doomed.

The quick dissolution of her third marriage left Harlow feeling depressed and insecure. She longed for a husband and children. When she was twenty-three she began seeing a forty-one-year-old actor named William Powell. He was suave, cool, handsome, and strong-willed enough to compete with "Mother Jean." Harlow immediately fell in love with him.

Harlow's affair with Powell dragged on for the next four years. There were rumors of an engagement, but to Harlow's dismay, no marriage. Powell had already been married to one blond bombshell, Carole Lombard, and he had apparently found the experience sexually intimidating. As much as he enjoyed Harlow's company and her earthy, good humor, he was determined to keep their arrangement unofficial.

Powell's prolonged influence in Harlow's life had at least one positive result. He uncovered that Bello had long been stealing Harlow's money. He convinced "Mother Jean" to file for divorce. But even he was unable to release the famous actress from the control of her mother. Harlow used gin to drown her frustrations with her mother and Powell and her health was becoming a constant problem. She was actually suffering from kidney disease but the condition was misdiagnosed until it was far too late to save her. Harlow died at twenty-seven.

Another Example

Laurence Olivier (English actor and beleaguered husband of Vivien Leigh). Born May 22, 1907 (*Celebrity Birthday Guide*).

If you have Mars in Capricorn with Venus in Taurus you are … the Stubborn Slave of Love

Self-control is always an important concern for you because you are the most conservative *and* the most sensual Mars in Capricorn Lover. This completely physical approach to sex means that your body is uniquely responsive to erotic stimuli. If you just let nature take its course, you can become a slave to pleasure—or at least you think so. Thus you work hard to keep your powerful physical urges under control and strictly within the bounds of convention.

At your worst you can be an inflexible and narrow-minded Lover, who is all too quick to condemn the indiscretions of others while turning a blind eye to your own sensual extremes. At your best you combine a hardheaded practical approach to sex with a pervasive sweetness. You are usually very solicitous with regard to your partner. You are willing to make dramatic sacrifices on his or her behalf, even though you always find a way to also look after yourself.

Case History

John Wayne (*Marion Morrison—all-American film star*). *Born on May 26, 1907, in Winterset, Iowa* (*Wayne 1987; Zolotow 1974*).

When Wayne was a small child his family moved to a farm in California after his father was diagnosed with tuberculosis. The move impoverished the family and increased the tension that already existed between Wayne's weak-willed father and aggressive mother. These tensions made Wayne a rather neurotic child, but in high school he managed to bury his insecurities in athletics and became a football star.

Despite his status as a sports hero, Wayne did not date in high school and in college he observed the strict prohibitions of his coach against sex. Because his family was poor, Wayne had to augment his football scholarship and he found a job working in a movie studio. There he met John Ford, who would become both his friend and mentor.

Wayne's football career ended at age nineteen when he injured his shoulder. At the same time he fell hopelessly in love with Josephine Saenz. Saenz was the daughter of a wealthy, Spanish businessman who had settled in Los Angeles. Saenz's parents disapproved of the relationship with good reason. She was a beauty from the highest level of society, and he was a lovesick ex-football player with minimal prospects. They came from different cultures, different religions, and possessed very different personalities, but these obstacles only made Wayne more determined to make Saenz his wife.

Saenz also cared for Wayne, but she was a devout Catholic. She refused to have sex with him during their courtship. The courtship went on for the next six years. During this time Wayne worked his way up from a "gaffer" to a stuntman and then to an actor in cheap Western movies. He also developed lasting friendships with a small group of men in the motion picture business. He began to favor such "all-boy" pastimes as hunting, playing poker, and drinking. He apparently stayed clear of other women. He was, according to his friends, a one-woman man.

When the marriage finally occurred, it turned out to be as mismatched as many had predicted. Josephine was a society woman, active in her church and charity functions, and used to rubbing elbows with refined, well-to-do people. Wayne had become a man's man who played at being a cowboy during the day and spent his nights drinking with his macho friends. Josephine felt her husband's career was an embarrassment, and Wayne had no sympathy for her allegiance to the Roman Catholic Church. The most important problem in the marriage was sex. After waiting for six years, Wayne found his wife to be cold and unresponsive. Wayne was probably exaggerating when he said he had sex four times with his wife during ten years of marriage, once for each of their four children, but it was obvious the two of them were as incompatible sexually as they were in every other way.

By the time Wayne was thirty-three he moved out of what had become his wife's home. He had finally broken out of "B" pictures and was on his way to becoming a star. Wayne also began to have affairs, always discreetly and always with women with foreign accents. Wayne had a weakness for non-American women. His first girl friend was Swedish-born. Later he moved on to the very German and very sexy Marlene Dietrich. Wayne's penchant for foreign-born women seems rather odd considering his all-American image, but he made no apologies for it. During a trip to Mexico he told an interviewer that he liked Latin women because of their appreciation of family life and their "respect" for their husbands.

When Wayne made this statement he had already fallen under the spell of a beautiful and daring Mexican actress named Esperanza "Chata" Baur. Baur was fourteen years younger than Wayne. She had a rather shady past, and his more worldly friends warned him that she would be trouble. But once again Wayne was determined. He began consorting with Baur so openly that Josephine, who had thus far resisted the prospect of divorce for religious reasons, finally agreed to end their marriage. Wayne immediately wed Esperanza.

Wayne's second wife was as fiery and common as his first wife had been cool and elitist. Esperanza matched the hard-drinking Wayne bottle for bottle. Since he discouraged her from continuing her acting career, she had little to do after their marriage except drink and worry about the possibility that her famous husband was sleeping with other women. Wayne did not help matters by continuing to devote more time to his work and his poker-playing cronies than to his wife. Nor did Esperanza help the situation by bringing her volatile mother up from Mexico to live with them or by having affairs. Despite their loud and often violent disputes, Wayne remained sexually fascinated by his explosive wife. Their drunken brawls often ended in passionate sex.

Due to his continuing sexual attraction for Esperanza, and his unwillingness to suffer through another divorce, Wayne's second marriage lasted until he was forty-six. Then it ended in a messy and very public court battle. Wayne's bachelor friends encouraged him to give up on marriage, but the middle-aged actor had little taste for casual affairs. He was looking for another wife. True to form, he found her in another country.

Pilar Palette Weldy was a young Peruvian stewardess from a wealthy family who had dramatic aspirations. She had just ended a marriage to an older man who found her too independent. This man happened to be an acquaintance of Wayne's. He told the actor all about his problems with Pilar. Nonetheless, Wayne developed an instant, erotic infatuation with the lithe young woman when he saw her dancing on a movie set. Smitten, he soon proposed and began his third marriage.

Despite the discrepancy in their ages, this marriage proved to be Wayne's best. It produced three children and provided Wayne with the warm family environment he had always craved. Pilar endured his drinking and his obsessive involvement with his work. She also supported him through his first bout with lung cancer when he was fifty-seven. But even this marriage had a breaking point. When Pilar began to show some of the independence that had so alarmed her first husband, Wayne was unable to accept it. After eighteen years of married life they separated. Six years later Wayne died of lung cancer.

Another Example

Doris Day *(American film star known for her squeaky-clean persona). Born April 3, 1924 (Celebrity Birthday Guide).*

If you have Mars in Capricorn with Venus in Gemini you are … the Sly Slave of Love

You are the cleverest of the Mars in Capricorn Lovers. This allows you to control both your strong sex drive and your relationships with apparently little effort. Of course, it's never as easy as it looks. You have to be both smart and tough to keep the emotional distance you require in your love life and satisfy your enormous appetite for physical pleasure. Sometimes you even hurt people, but your charm is such that you typically get away with it.

Unfortunately, too much control can be just as bad as not enough control for a Mars in Capricorn Lover. If you organize your love life so well that there is no need for sacrifice and you never have to face the kind of adversity which typically brings out the best in a Mars in Capricorn Lover, you will soon find yourself becoming bored. If nothing else, you almost have to let yourself slip now and again so you can be reminded of the pain that makes love worthwhile.

Case History

Frida Kahlo (Mexican painter noted for the highly personal images she drew from her own tragic life). Born July 6, 1907, at 8:30 A.M. in Coyoacan, Mexico (Herrera 1983).

Kahlo's father was a German Jew who went to Mexico to seek his fortune. He found it as a photographer. He married a pretty, young Mexican woman who became Kahlo's mother. Kahlo grew up amid political upheaval that often jeopardized her family's middle-class lifestyle. Nonetheless, Kahlo remained a vocal advocate of revolution all her life.

As a child Kahlo suffered through a bout with polio, but this did not diminish her thirst for experience. At seventeen she actively flirted with an older boy noted for both his intellect and his good looks. They apparently had a sexual relationship, which was quite in keeping with the revolutionary morality Kahlo was already espousing. At eighteen she was seduced by one of her female teachers. Even though she was shocked at first, a relationship ensued that had to be squelched by her parents. Then, she had a casual affair with her boss while serving as an apprenticeship with a printer.

When Kahlo was eighteen her life was shattered when a bus in which she was riding collided with a trolley car. A metal rod from one of the bus' seats plunged into Kahlo's back. It exited through her vagina. For the rest of her life Kahlo lived with the results of this horrible injury. She suffered through scores of operations and had to wear a back brace much of the time. In many ways she was an invalid, but she refused to let the world know this.

Kahlo's boy friend was with her on the bus and he helped pull the metal rod from her naked body. (The force of the impact had somehow stripped away her clothing.) He was unable to resume their relationship, and by the time Kahlo was nearing twenty they had broken off their relationship. At this same time Kahlo attracted the attention of a man she found infinitely more desirable: Diego Rivera.

Kahlo's infatuation with the great Mexican mural painter began many years earlier when she was still a schoolgirl. One day she wandered into a building where the artist was painting a mural and asked to watch. Rivera's mistress, Lupe Marin, was also present. This fiery, often violent, woman did everything she could to frighten the twelve-year-old Frida away. Frida ignored her and continued to gaze intently at the master. Now, eight years later, Lupe had left Rivera, and Frida was determined to take her place.

Diego Rivera was not a physically attractive man. He had a huge, frog-like head, a massive belly, and legs that seemed entirely too long for his ungainly form. Yet he possessed amazing vitality and a charming egotism tempered by gentleness and childlike candor. He had always attracted women. Rivera had a penchant for difficult relationships. Pistol shots, broken crockery, and several dramatic showdowns had characterized his long affair with Lupe.

When he began to see Kahlo, her father took the painter aside and warned him that his daughter was a "devil," not knowing that this description would only make her more attractive to Rivera.

Diego Rivera and Frida Kahlo were married when she was twenty-two. They made a strange-looking couple—an ugly giant of a man and a delicate china doll of a woman—but they were professionally and intellectually well matched. Kahlo had studied art before her accident and she was already developing a distinctive style of painting that Rivera wholeheartedly supported. She, of course, was quite proud of her new husband's artistic accomplishments. They shared political affiliations as well; both were ardent Communists. They also shared an enthusiasm for indigenous Mexican art and culture, and a deep love for their homeland.

Despite this apparent compatibility, there were problems in the marriage almost from the beginning. Rivera was famous for casual infidelities. He claimed his waywardness was the product of his strong sex drive and his naturalistic view of human sexuality. He also used his affairs to maintain the upper hand in his more permanent relationships. Thus, when Kahlo felt depressed and incomplete as a woman after she lost the first child she had conceived with Rivera, Rivera had an affair with a model. Later he seduced the one woman Kahlo would have considered absolutely off-limits—her own sister. Kahlo had no doubt been prepared for Rivera's unfaithfulness. She tried to pretend as if it didn't matter, but over and over her husband intentionally slept with just the right woman at just the right time to provoke her to jealousy.

Kahlo no doubt suffered because of Rivera's compulsive infidelity, but his efforts to control their relationship were never completely successful. At an emotional level, it was Kahlo who held the reigns. Rivera's dependence on her approval and support was quite complete. Even after she granted him a divorce ten years into the marriage, he begged her to marry him again after only a few months. In one of her paintings Kahlo painted herself in the arms of Mother Earth holding an infant-like Rivera in her maternal arms. In many ways her relationship with her husband, who remained boyish despite his years, was that of a mother and her mischievous son.

Of course, Kahlo was capable of her own mischief. While Rivera was distracted with his girl friends, she had girl friends of her own. She found ample opportunity to explore her lesbian tendencies in the freewheeling, bohemian circles in which they moved. Rivera was aware of this and even teased her about her lesbianism. He was less aware of her heterosexual affairs. Kahlo kept these a secret, knowing that even the liberated Rivera, who openly acknowledged his wife's strong sex drive, would not allow himself to be made a cuckold without a fight.

The pain Kahlo constantly suffered and her frequent ill-health had little influence on her sexual activity. Her lovers were surprised at how freely she used her battered body. One of her affairs, with a man ten years her junior, began while she was in a hospital bed. Some of these affairs became serious, but Kahlo always returned her devotion to Rivera.

During her life with Rivera, his reputation as an artist completely overshadowed Kahlo's career. While he painted giant murals about larger-than-life issues, she painted small pictures about her life. Nonetheless, the originality of these images and their enigmatic, often gory, personal references won respect. She presented a view of life that was distinctly feminine. Her work aptly expressed the suffering, both physical and emotional, which life had brought her. In one of her many self-portraits, the face of Rivera appears like a brand in the middle of her forehead.

Kahlo and Rivera were often apart during the latter years of their marriage. Even when they were home together they lived in separate wings of the same house. Yet in many ways their marriage was stronger at this time than ever before. Their mutual devotion grew without the struggle of power that had marred their marriage for so long. Meanwhile Kahlo's health continued to decline. There were more operations and more pain. It was said that Kahlo should have died at the time of the accident. It was only her phenomenal strength of will that allowed her to survive until she was forty-seven.

Another Example

Mary Pickford (pixyish star of silent films who was proclaimed "America's sweetheart" and later became one of the most powerful women in Hollywood). Born April 8, 1892 (Eyman 1990).

If you have Mars in Capricorn with Venus in Cancer you are . . . the Moody Slave of Love

Your sexual nature often seems out of balance and prone to extreme contradictions. On the one hand, you are a very practical and physical Lover who seeks to control every relationship. On the other, you are a profoundly emotional and essentially passive Lover who needs to give up everything for the sake of love. There's no possibility of compromise. Conflicting desires and wild inconsistencies are just things you have to get used to in your sex life. Of course, the people who love you have to be willing to get used to them, too.

Despite the contradictions in your sexuality, you are a very desirable Lover. First of all, you are gifted with an irresistible sexual allure—a combination of emotional vulnerability and tough, down-home sexiness. Secondly, you are a person who is utterly serious about love. It may take time and a great deal of trouble to find someone who answers your intense and divergent needs, but once you do, you are theirs forever.

Case History

Dante Gabriel Rossetti (British poet, painter and leader of the Pre-Raphaelite Brotherhood). Born May 12, 1828, in London, England (Daly 1989).

Rossetti came from a remarkable home. His father was an Italian revolutionary who fled to England where he was employed as a teacher. His mother was a stern, deeply religious woman, who nonetheless had a lively intellect and respect for learning. Between them, Rossetti and his three siblings grew up steeped in both morality and the arts.

Rossetti was a restless art student at twenty, who composed poetry when he felt too lazy to paint. He expounded revolutionary ideas about art and its relationship with society. His ideas struck a responsive cord with the idealistic young men who gathered around him. They proposed a style of painting based on exacting observation of nature and on the highest moral principles. They took the painters of the Italian Renaissance before Raphael as their models, thus the name Pre-Raphaelites.

These young men came from highly conservative, middle-class backgrounds and they felt themselves to be moralists as well as painters. They considered chastity a primary virtue. Sex is often portrayed as something wicked and destructive in their work. Even though he shared their moralistic viewpoint, Rossetti differed somewhat with his Pre-Raphaelite Brothers on this issue. Early in his career he showed a distressing, though distant, fascination with prostitutes.

When Rossetti was twenty-two he met Lizzie Siddal. Siddal was from a poor, but educated, family. She worked in a shop until one of Rossetti's friends persuaded her to pose for him. She was such a beauty—a tall, stately, young woman with thick, reddish hair and a striking, angelic face—that the painter couldn't help but brag about her to Rossetti and the rest of the Pre-Raphaelite Brothers. In short order, they were all in love with her; however, it was the charismatic Rossetti who won Siddal's devotion. Soon she was posing only for him.

At this point in his life Rossetti was completely entangled in the Victorian myth that true love could not be sexual. The fact that Siddal was not only pretty but also intelligent and talented increased his dilemma. His respect for her was such that he stretched his own minimal means to free her from her job and allow her time to write poetry and draw. But the more he honored and loved Siddal, the more terrible Rossetti felt about his equally strong desire to take her to bed.

The relationship between Rossetti and Siddal was two years old before he made sexual overtures to her. Siddal, a practical woman despite her romantic looks, recognized that her special allure would be dead once she had sex with the enamored painter. So, she refused him. Rossetti responded in a way that was quite conventional for his time; he allowed Siddal to remain his pure true love and took his physical needs to prostitutes. After a while he established a more or less permanent arrangement with a prostitute-turned-model named Fanny Cornforth.

Rossetti's infidelities angered and embarrassed Siddal. She was beset by a series of unspecified illnesses (some theorize that she was anorexic) that confined her to her bed or required her to travel in search of a cure. When they were together they had violent arguments that shocked their middle-class friends. Both Siddal and Rossetti recognized her hold on him was weakening. Yet, the painter fell in love with Siddal all over again every time he saw her suffering in bed, and would make yet another promise to marry her some day.

Finally, after ten years, Rossetti made good on his promises. He and Siddal were married. By this time his beautiful model was not only ill but also addicted to laudanum. The next year Siddal was pregnant. Unfortunately, the child was delivered dead. She was left emotionally and physically drained. Meanwhile, Rossetti returned to the embrace of his buxom mistress. Siddal grew depressed and took an overdose of laudanum. She died despite Rossetti's desperate efforts to revive her.

Siddal's death was a great psychological blow to Rossetti. Consumed by his loss and by guilt, Rossetti impulsively placed a notebook containing his youthful poetry in Siddal's casket. Years later, when his artistic production was drying up and his publishers pressured him for more work, Rossetti secretly had the coffin exhumed and retrieved the notebook. This act of ghoulish pragmatism only increased his deep sense of contrition.

Rossetti lived with his mother for some time after Siddal's death because he was unable to return to the home he had shared with Lizzie. When he reestablished his own residence, he was joined by Fanny Cornforth, who became both his housekeeper and his live-in lover. Cornforth was a fat, earthy woman, full of good humor and commonplace charm. Rossetti called her "Elephant" and she called him "Rhinoceros." Yet Rossetti had not lost his taste for ethereal beauty; when he was forty he began an affair with Jane Morris, the unhappy wife of his friend and colleague, William Morris.

Like Lizzie Siddal, Jane Morris was a poor girl who had been hired to pose for the Pre-Raphaelite artists because she approximated their ideal of feminine beauty. Naturally, the two women were similar in appearance. This similarity both added to Rossetti's delight and to his pain. He could have sex with Cornforth, who was very much a creature of the real world, without dishonoring the memory of Lizzie Siddal. By sleeping with the divine Jane

Morris, Rossetti became a vile betrayer of both her living husband and his dead wife. Yet, neither Rossetti nor Jane seemed able to end the affair.

Rossetti's mental state began to deteriorate. He had bouts of paranoia and was tortured by hallucinations. When Rossetti was forty-four he attempted to imitate his beloved Lizzie and took an overdose of laudanum. He was saved by his friends, but remained an emotional wreck.

During his last years Rossetti's male friends and family closed ranks around him, determined to shelter the now-famous poet and painter from nervous strain and women. Jane Morris tried to nurse him, but was banned as a dangerous influence. Even the loyal Fanny Cornforth, considered coarse and unworthy by those who thought Rossetti a romantic hero, was shut out of his life. Oddly enough, however, it was Cornforth's name that was on Rossetti's lips when he died at the age of fifty-four.

Another Example

Barbara Stanwyck (American actress noted for her "tough broad" roles, who was actually an abused wife in her personal life). Born July 16, 1907 (Celebrity Birthday Guide).

If you have Mars in Capricorn with Venus in Leo you are . . . the Noble Slave of Love

You are not always clear about what you want from sex. Like all Mars in Capricorn Lovers, you have a rather grungy and low-down appreciation of raw, physical sex. But you also view your sexuality with a great deal of pride and you long for a more refined and aesthetically measured means of expressing your sexual feelings. This creates a gap between what you really want and the way in which you want it presented that can be very confusing to anyone trying to love you.

Control is an important issue in your love life, and you are often tempted to get it by any means possible. Fortunately, this ruthlessness is tempered by an equally strong need to be adored and to be thought of as generous, noble, and kind. Taking absolute control of sexual situations without making anyone mad is a tricky game. You will not always be successful. If you're smart, you'll learn to settle for a little bit of control offset by a sizeable amount of adoration.

Case History

*Leo **Tolstoy** (Russian novelist, reformer, and moralist—author of* War and Peace *and* Anna Karenina*). Born September 9, 1828, at his family estate south of Moscow (De Courcel 1980; Shiver 1994).*

Tolstoy was raised by indulgent relatives in an atmosphere that combined the bucolic pleasures of a great landowner with a very civilized appreciation of art and literature. Debauchery was considered to be his birthright. Tolstoy was fourteen when his brother took him to a brothel to be introduced to sex. By the time he reached twenty, the young count was well acquainted with this kind of sex and the venereal diseases it spread. Along with his fervent womanizing, Tolstoy was also a compulsive gambler and showed little talent for anything other than having a good time. And yet no one raised any moral objections to his lifestyle—no one except Tolstoy himself.

Tolstoy had a profoundly divided attitude toward sex. On the one hand, he had a very earthy appreciation for physical pleasure and a strong sex drive. On the other, he felt that sexual intercourse, at least for a bachelor, was an inherently evil and exploitive venture. He supposedly wept after his first encounter with a prostitute. Yet he couldn't stop himself from returning to brothels again and again. When he took over the administration of his estate a safe distance from the fleshpots of Moscow, he immediately began to seduce peasant girls and servants. Tolstoy followed his brother in the military in the hopes of finding some discipline. Instead he found hardy Cossack women and more prostitutes. The intense young writer elaborated on his carnal failings repeatedly in his journals and swore to redouble his efforts toward self-control, but repeatedly he failed.

Eventually, Tolstoy's near-mania for self-examination and criticism led to his first literary triumph in an autobiographical account called *Childhood*. The aimless young man now had a vocation, but he continued his unequal struggle with his body and he continued to search for an outlet for his idealistic yearning. His appreciation for family life led him to spend a great deal of time with the Behrs family. Mr. Behrs was a physician for the royal family, and Mrs. Behrs had been one of Tolstoy's playmates during childhood. He had even been in love with her during this time, and had once pushed her down a flight of stairs when he thought she was not paying enough attention to him. Now it was the Behrs' daughters that held Tolstoy's attention, in particular Sofya or Sonya Behrs. In the midst of her bright and happy family, this intelligent young girl seemed like a beacon of purity and domestic tranquility to the troubled writer.

Leo Tolstoy and Sonya Behrs were married when he was thirty-four and she was eighteen. By this time Tolstoy already felt like an old man and he was anxious to escape the sexual hell of lust and guilt that had been his bachelorhood. He saw his young bride as someone he could educate and mold. Not only was she young and inexperienced, but Sonya was also beneath him in terms of class. When they moved to his vast estate (which was now somewhat less vast than it had been thanks to Tolstoy's gambling losses), she was quite overwhelmed by her new position as a countess with absolute power over hundreds of peasants.

The Tolstoys began their marriage by opening their journals to one another. It was not an auspicious beginning. Sonya was shocked by what she read of Tolstoy's tortured, but nonetheless voluminous, sexual history. What disturbed her most was his account of a long-term affair he had begun with a peasant girl six years before the marriage. This woman still lived on the estate where Tolstoy could see her every day and she had a son who looked far too much like the master. It was almost more than Sonya could bear. Meanwhile, Tolstoy was no more pleased with what he read in Sonya's diaries. Her innocent, teenage crushes made him burn with jealousy. But despite the pain it caused both of them, the Tolstoys continued the practice of reading each other's journals throughout their long marriage.

Sonya was extremely proud of her husband's literary accomplishments. She began the marriage with the notion that they would become intellectual partners. But it didn't take long for her to see that her famous husband had other ideas. Although he was happy to let Sonya function as his secretary (she transcribed *War and Peace* three times), Tolstoy shared little of his intellectual and spiritual pondering with his wife. Soon Sonya was complaining in her journals that her husband wanted nothing from her but sex, and that he wanted it entirely too often for her taste.

When Tolstoy read Sonya's complaints, they caused him "pain like a toothache" but did not lessen his physical demands. Of course, Tolstoy had his own complaints about the marriage. As Sonya grew older she proved to be far less malleable than anticipated. This became particularly evident when the author converted to socialism and pacifism, and began to adopt the ways and values of the peasants he had once ruled. Sonya refused to join her husband as he embraced "the people," and she was profoundly disturbed by his desire to renounce all their wealth and live in poverty. Her stubborn opposition to his idealism infuriated Tolstoy and it caused him to regard Sonya and women in general with great bitterness.

The situation deteriorated further when the author reached his sixties and began preaching sexual abstinence, even in marriage. He laid out his theories in a short novel called *The Kreutzer Sonata*. Many people, particularly conservatives, responded favorably to Tolstoy's radical notion of absolute chastity, but not Sonya. At the time she was pregnant with their thirteenth child. She saw her husband's advocacy of abstinence as nothing short of hypocrisy. Despite what he wrote and preached, Tolstoy continued to have an active sex life with Sonya. He excused himself by saying that chastity was an ideal and not a requirement.

In a sense, Tolstoy's attitudes toward sex were just as divided in his old age as they had been during his adolescence. He still regarded every sexual event as a fall from grace, and he saw women as the instrument of his spiritual destruction. When he spoke of sexual issues his listeners were often shocked at his gutter language and flagrant misogyny. His proven inability to control his carnal passions had made Tolstoy a bitter old man. The writer took refuge in relationships with other men; he saw his affections with men as pure and intellectual. One of these friendships became so intense that Sonya accused Tolstoy of being a homosexual. But she was probably more upset at the notion that her husband's young friend was helping him to change his will so as to exclude her and their children.

The relationship between Tolstoy and Sonya did have its bright spots. Sonya never lost her fascination with Tolstoy, both as a writer and as a man, and there are entries in her journals that reveal that she enjoyed her husband's sexual advances much more than she sometimes pretended. For Tolstoy, misery was an essential ingredient for sexual happiness. He generally behaved like a very happily married man. And yet when Tolstoy was eighty-two, he decided that he had had enough. He stole away in the middle of the night, leaving both his wife and his ancestral home. Sonya was so distraught when she couldn't find him that she attempted to drown herself in a frozen pond, but was rescued. A few weeks later, weakened by the rigors of his daring escape, Tolstoy died in a train station.

If you have Mars in Capricorn with Venus in Virgo you are . . . the Analytic Slave of Love

You are a Lover so concerned with managing sex that you often appear shy and inhibited when, in fact, you are just examining all the options. Your physical drives are very strong, but you are too much of a pragmatist to let them run free. You cultivate your sexuality and avoid emotional entanglement. In the process, you become very knowledgeable in the ways of love.

Unfortunately, your caution and resourcefulness can't save you from the Mars in Capricorn penchant for misery. You will always be drawn to relationships that demand self-sacrifice. Even when you are too practical to answer that allure, it will never release its hold on your heart. You are a very sensible and level-headed Lover who secretly longs to be foolish for the sake of love.

Case History

Johann Wolfgang von Goethe (German poet, playwright, and novelist; author of The Sorrows of Young Werther *and* Faust*). Born August 28, 1749, at noon in Frankfurt am Main, Germany (Friedenthal 1963; Van Abbe 1972).*

Goethe's grandfather was a lowly tailor but he managed to make a fortune sufficient to establish both his son and his grandson as gentlemen. Goethe's father was a disciplinarian, and young Goethe was not particularly close to his mother. It was his younger sister who became his primary playmate and confidante during his childhood. Perhaps for this reason, he often looked for "sisterly" affection from many of the women he later loved.

There was a strong contrast between the reality of Goethe's love life and what he later wrote about it in his letters, journals, novels, and poetry. His writings make him seem an irrepressible romantic who was completely girl-crazy from the dawn of puberty until his old age. In reality his conduct in matters of romance was far more circumspect.

Certainly he started early enough. At fourteen he ran with a group of older boys for whom he wrote love poems which they, in turn, used to impress their girl friends. Among the girls with whom they flirted was a young bar maid. She became the first woman immortalized in Goethe's verse. Despite his poetic enthusiasm for this girl, their relationship appears quite chaste. Even when he dared to take a stroll with her, he was careful to wear a disguise.

While a student in Leipzig, Goethe chased women both below and above his station, but his various infatuations apparently never went very far. At the age of twenty he fell in love with the daughter of a country parson. This relationship may have actually resulted in intercourse, since Goethe wrote a friend he was troubled by guilt over his behavior with the girl. This turn of events probably had more to do with the country girl's lack of inhibitions than Goethe's ardor.

Goethe retreated to a somewhat safer infatuation after this. The object of his affection was already engaged to marry another man and considered Goethe to be only a friend. The young poet pined for this young woman in secret. Even though he was often in her house, neither she nor her fiancé suspected the writer's motive. Goethe and the fiancé even became friends. There were no violent scenes or emotional declarations of love. Goethe simply left, and the couple later married. The next year Goethe published his most famous novel, *The Sorrows of Young Werther.*

Goethe channeled all the emotions and drama that he had been too practical to express in real life into this novel. A young man falls in love with a beautiful young woman who has been promised to an older man. Forced to choose between the romantic young suitor and a secure marriage, the woman chooses the later. The dejected hero then commits suicide. Goethe's tragic novel captured the imagination of his generation. Women longed for lovers like Werther, and men imitated his manner and his dress. Some even went so far as to follow his example and shoot themselves. The movement called Romanticism was born.

Goethe made one attempt at what might have seemed a conventional relationship. At twenty-five he began courting Lili Schonemann, the teenage daughter of a wealthy banker.

Goethe later called this his "only" true love. It was true that, unlike most of his other romances, Lili was available for marriage, but her brothers hoped that she would find a richer husband than Goethe.

For a time it seemed Goethe was up to this challenge. What could be more romantic than a not-so-rich writer winning the heart of a patrician beauty over the objections of her family? But Goethe lost his nerve at a crucial juncture in the relationship and left town on a long journey. His absence gave the brothers ample time to find other suitors. Meanwhile, Goethe, thanks to his growing literary reputation, managed to find a place in the court of the Duke of Weimar.

At Weimar Goethe fell under the influence of Charlotte Von Stein, a lady-in-waiting to the Duchess. Von Stein was a woman of remarkable intelligence. She not only instructed Goethe in the ways of the court, but also provided guidance and direction to Goethe at a time when he seemed likely to rest upon his laurels. It is unknown if the two were lovers. Von Stein was seven years older than the writer, married, and had already had seven pregnancies, most of which resulted in miscarriages; however, Goethe's relationship with Von Stein was as intense as any love affair. It was more prolonged than almost all of his other relationships with women.

Some experts on Goethe propose that he had a horror of sexual intercourse and, though he reveled in the preliminaries of love and used the feeling these flirtations stirred for his writings, he purposely avoided the conclusive act. If this is true, it appears that the poet found a cure for his phobia in his late thirties. At this time he left Weimar and traveled to Italy where he took an Italian woman as his mistress. He must have found the experience rewarding because, once he was back in Weimar, he began cohabiting with a chubby, blond working-class girl who had once asked him for a handout.

Goethe's relationship with this live-in lover (Christiane Vulpius) was problematic to those who had identified the writer with his romantic heroes. But Goethe apparently found her simplicity and loyalty convenient. He remained with her for the rest of his life. She bore him a child when he was forty, and he married Vulpius when he was fifty-seven. It is unlikely he was faithful to her. He wrote a friend that, even when he was away from Weimar (and Vulpius), he seldom slept alone. In his old age Goethe was prone to poetic infatuations with younger women. When he was eighty-one, he had to fend off the attack of a woman intent on bearing his child. He died at eighty-two.

Another Example

Fay Wray (American actress most remembered as the girl friend of King Kong). Born September 15, 1907 (Celebrity Birthday Guide).

If you have Mars in Capricorn with Venus in Libra you are . . . the Idealistic Slave of Love

There is an intellectual fury about the way you approach love and sex that can be hard to take. You expect a lot out of your partners because you expect a lot out of sex. Not only do you have very strong, physical drives but you are also a sexual idealist. You have a conception of perfect love that embraces the mind as well as the body. No one can seriously contend for your affection unless they are prepared to meet all your standards. Those who try and fail are dismissed without notice.

This intellectual intensity doesn't stop you from being a very warm and charming Lover. You value relationships a great deal, and this makes you one of the most gregarious and open of the Mars in Capricorn Lovers. Of course, when you find a partner who meets your high standards you tend to be very loyal to that person and treat him or her with the highest regard. The unfortunate thing is that your idealistic standards are never really fixed. As you change, so do they. This presents a difficult problem for the person who has just gone through hell and back to meet the old standards.

Case History

Aleister Crowley (Edward Alexander Crowley—British occultist who was considered, by himself as well as many others, to be the most evil man in the world). Born October 12, 1875, between 11 P.M. and midnight in Leamington, England (Symonds 1951).

Crowley was the son of a wealthy tradesman and his devoted wife. Both parents were members of a fundamentalist Protestant sect. They tried to impart their beliefs to their only surviving child. But from an early age Crowley rebelled against their doctrine. His resistance to Christian virtue was so intense that his mother referred to him as the "Beast" of Revelations. For the rest of his life Crowley did his best to live up to this biblical appellation.

Crowley's sex life began when he accosted his mother's maid in his early teens. A short time later he caught a venereal disease from a prostitute. He favored prostitutes for the rest of his life, particularly ugly ones who looked depraved or pathetic. There are also hints of homosexual tendencies during these early years. He fantasized as a child about being tortured and dominated by other males. He was ejected from his first school for "corrupting" another boy.

When he was twenty-three Crowley completed his first book of poetry. It was self-published, as were the majority of his early works, and it earned him nothing. The poetry was of sufficient quality for the young man to be considered a legitimate, if derivative, artist. For many years after this, Crowley was known to the outside world as a poet and a mountaineer.

It was the occult that ultimately proved to be Crowley's true vocation. Crowley joined the Order of Golden Dawn when he was twenty-three. The Order had been formed around an occultist name MacGregor Mathers who claimed he had decoded a manuscript in which ancient, magical laws had been handed down through the ages. The group's activities featured a free and unequal mixture of a sincere truth-seeking and gaudy charlatanism. It proved to be a natural environment for Crowley. He rose through the ranks of the Order. When the other members rebelled against Mathers' dictatorial policies, Crowley aligned himself with the master. Mathers set up new headquarters in Paris. Crowley, as his representative, attempted to physically take possession of the London temple. Another member of the group, the noted Irish poet W. B. Yeats, foiled his effort.

Meanwhile, Crowley acquired a few acres of land and a house in Scotland and with a commoner's love of titles, he called himself the "Laird of Boleskine." He practiced some magical rites there, and brought prostitutes in from larger towns for entertainment. Then he traveled to Mexico where he did some mountaineering. This led to an invitation to join an assault on one of the giant peaks of the Himalayas. The climb was a failure, but it gave Crowley the opportunity to add some Eastern ideas and techniques to his occult arsenal.

Crowley gained a reputation as a braggart and a cad through all these adventures. In some instances, Crowley's arrogance and lack of concern for the welfare of others was almost psychopathic. Yet he managed to maintain a few sincere friendships, and he developed a knack for making even educated, intelligent women fall in love with him. These conquests, along with an endless string of prostitutes, help stem what he admitted was an unrelenting, physical need for sex.

Back in Scotland, one of Crowley's friends, Gerald Kelly, introduced the twenty-seven-year-old magician to his sister, Rose. Rose was a confused young widow who had recently accepted marriage proposals from two men who were coming to Scotland to marry her. Impulsively Crowley made his own proposal. Rose could marry him and then she wouldn't have to worry about the two other suitors. At first Crowley indicated that he and Rose would each go their own way after the wedding. Once he was married to this pretty and passive woman, Crowley suddenly found that he was also in love with her. He immediately brought her to live with him at Boleskine.

There is no doubt that, early in their relationship, the bond between Crowley and Rose was very strong. During a honeymoon trip to India, Rose exhibited occult tendencies. By the time the couple journeyed to Cairo she had become her husband's psychic guide. In a trance, she instructed Crowley on how to contact Aiwass, his guardian angel. It was also in Cairo that voices from "beyond" dictated to Crowley the text that would become *The Book of Law*. From this volume Crowley would devise what he described as a new religion, the axioms of which were "Do What Thou Wilt" and "Love is the Law, Love under Will." He and Rose also began to experiment with sexual magic.

Sex magic, as described by Crowley, was a matter of intellectually directing the emotional and psychic energy engendered by the sex act toward a nonsexual goal. For example, in order to conjure up money, Crowley would envision his room filling with gold as he was having sex and maintained that vision through his orgasm. Crowley could perform sex magic alone or with a partner. The primary focus of his life was often finding partners who could accept his version of "magick" without giggling. It might be added that Crowley's magical practices appear to have made him proficient at postponing ejaculation and prolonging intercourse.

Crowley was in no rush to become a full-time magician. When he got a chance to lead another expedition in the Himalayas, he put aside *The Book of Law* and returned to being an English adventurer. The expedition was a disaster, and several men died. Crowley's incompetence as a leader was blamed. To make matters worse, Crowley apparently fled rather than help the wounded and recover the bodies of the dead. He rushed down the mountain and filled the newspapers with his own account of the tragedy. This ploy only postponed his expulsion from mountaineering circles.

When he rejoined Rose in India, the twenty-nine-year-old Crowley was a broken man. The fortune he had inherited as a child was nearly spent, and his reputation was in shreds. He returned to his habit of using prostitutes and began serious experimentation with opium. To add to the misery, his daughter died while traveling with Rose in Asia. The couple returned to Scotland. A second child was born, but the marriage was doomed.

By the time Rose divorced Crowley six years after their wedding, she was a hopeless alcoholic. She died in an asylum three years later. Crowley moved on to other women and men in his search for a material benefactor and a compliant partner for his sex magic. With the onset of World War I, he went to the United States. He made a tenuous living by writing for a pro-German newspaper (even though he claimed he was a patriotic Englishman) and by giving lectures on magic to generally unimpressed American audiences. He also had numerous affairs as he searched for the sexual partner who would become his definitive "Scarlet Woman." When he was forty-two, he found her in Leah Faesi.

Faesi was a thin, flat-chested woman in her thirties who often looked as if she were about to cry. She was not pretty and had no money, but she had a keen mind and a sexuality that readily lent itself to sex magic. The "Ape of Thoth," as Crowley called her, signed a pact by which she agreed to submit to all manner of carnal depravity for the sake of Crowley's "magick." Crowley brought his new love back to Europe where, along with the child she bore him, another mistress and her two children, Crowley set up shop in a deserted Sicilian church he called Thelema.

At the Sacred Abbey of Thelema, Crowley attempted to develop a cult around the teachings of *The Book of Law*. It was not easy. His two mistresses fought constantly. Faesi's child died (a death that greatly disturbed the supposedly hardhearted "Beast"), and another was miscarried. A few believers took interest in their strange rites and sex magick, but money was a constant problem. To make matters worse, both Crowley and Faesi were addicted to heroin and used a range of other drugs. Their drug habit played havoc with their physical and emotional health. At one point Crowley wrote a novel called *Diary of a Drug Fiend* in an attempt to raise money. Its publication only provided more ammunition for his numerous enemies.

When Crowley was forty-seven, a young Englishman died while visiting Thelema with his wife. A short time later, Crowley was expelled from Sicily by the Italian dictator, Mussolini. Crowley was so desperate he even thought of taking a regular job. Instead he found a new "Scarlet Woman." Faesi quietly stepped aside while Crowley traveled to Africa with his new lover and her money. Cast aside with Faesi was Norman Mudd, one of several servile homosexuals that Crowley attracted. Mudd, who had once been Crowley's chief lieutenant, committed suicide six years later. Faesi, however, managed to break with the "Beast" without permanently losing her sanity, making her the exception to the rule among his paramours.

The next few years were Crowley's best. A mysterious benefactor called the "Man from the West" supported him and paid for the publication of several of his books. The "Beast" had become world famous, mostly because of shocking newspaper stories. He was sought by both occultists and curious intellectuals. Despite his success, Crowley found that being the "most evil man in the world" was not that lucrative. Booksellers were afraid to stock his books, and the police harassed him wherever he went. He had followers but they were neither rich nor numerous enough to support his flamboyant lifestyle. Crowley was once again reduced to poverty when the "Man from the West" cut off his support.

"Scarlet Women" came and went during the later part of Crowley's life. His sex drive was unabated, and he never lost his faith in sex magick. Even though he seems to have genuinely wanted to hold on to some of these relationships, his own abusive behavior and the emotional instability of the women he attracted made this impossible. At one point he married one of these partners because that was the only way he could get her into England. The marriage was over in less than a year, and the woman entered a mental institution. Even as his fortunes entered a rapid decline, Crowley was still able to find women to do his bidding. Among his last liaisons was a woman he called Sister Tzaba. She was a brilliant artist who illustrated his last book, a work on the tarot. Sister Tzaba was with Crowley when he died at the age of seventy-two.

Another Example

Woody Allen (filmmaker and actor). Born December 1, 1935 (Celebrity Birthday Guide).

If you have Mars in Capricorn with Venus in Scorpio you are . . . the Salacious Slave of Love

You are the Mars in Capricorn Lover who has the most difficulty keeping his or her sex life under control. This is unfortunate, since you are also the Mars in Capricorn Lover to whom this control is most crucial. It's not that you don't try to hold to your essential conservatism, but with your devastating sexual allure, the temptation to do otherwise is sometimes just too great. Once you lower your guard and all that erotic madness is let loose, it's hard to go back to being careful again.

Of course, in the final analysis, you are never quite as out of control as you seem to be. You have a way of controlling relationships without appearing to be in control. Typically, you need only the subtlest of means to assert your dominance, but are not above using sexual and emotional leverage in order to get your way. Even when your attempts at managing your sex life don't work and you are utterly defeated by love, you have a way of coming back stronger, wiser, and sexier than before.

Case History

Eleonora Duse (Italian actress and international star generally considered one of the greatest actresses of all time). Born October 3, 1858, at 2 A.M. in Vigevano, Italy (Weaver 1984; Winwar 1956).

The daughter of an actor and an actress, Duse was born into the theater. She began performing on stage when she was still a child. Duse's mother died when she was seventeen, and her father soon relied on his talented daughter to be the family's major breadwinner. Duse applied herself diligently to her craft, while her father also took the time to educate her. Duse's strengths as an actress included her intelligence and awareness of fine literature.

This dutiful and bookish youngster did not mix well with most other thespians. For this reason, young Duse's knowledge of sex and romance was limited to parts she played on the stage. When she was twenty-one, a dapper journalist named Martino Cafiero became her first lover and shattered this innocence. Cafiero was something of a playboy and did not take the affair seriously. Duse was in love and she fully expected her older lover to marry her when she became pregnant. It was quickly revealed that Cafiero had no such intentions and Duse fled to a small resort town where the child was born and died the next day.

Although this tragic affair left Duse with emotional scars, it did not interfere with her career. She became a "prima donna," or primary female actress of her troupe. Duse introduced a new style of acting to Italian audiences that favored naturalism and subtlety over the highly stylized techniques of the past. In some instances, audiences were unwilling to accept her innovations. But gradually, her singular talent and evocative power as an actress were universally recognized.

When Duse was twenty-two she married Tebaldo Checchi, an esteemed character actor in his thirties. Checchi represented security to Duse, and he was a good husband by all accounts. The marriage produced one child. But problems developed as Duse's fame increased. Checchi may have felt less than comfortable with Duse's notoriety, and his attempts at managing her career were not always appreciated by Duse. Three years into the marriage the troupe went on a tour of South America. Duse began to pay attention to her handsome leading man, Flavio Ando. Apparently, the jealous husband gave Duse a choice and when the tour was through, Checchi remained in South America while Duse and her boy friend returned to Italy. Duse had little contact with her husband after that.

The affair with Ando, who was good-looking but empty-headed, did not last long. But the twenty-five-year-old actress had plenty to keep her busy. Her reputation was such that she could start her own acting troupe. This required her to function both as an actress and as a manager. As the manager of her own group she chose the plays, hired and fired the actors and actresses, and oversaw all aspects of stage management. It was a challenging position, but one that gave her complete control over her own career.

At the same time Duse became friendly with Arrigo Boito, a writer and musician. Boito was a brilliant man with all the qualities of a confirmed bachelor. He was regular and austere in his habits, immaculate in his dress, and fervently independent. He was also a very busy man whose work as librettist for such composers as Verdi required much travel. Duse also traveled a great deal and had little time for herself. Yet, these two busy people conceived a passion for one another that transcended all obstacles.

The affair between Duse and Boito was conducted in secret. Duse was still technically a married woman. Even though such scandals were not unexpected from theater folk, she sought to avoid detection at all cost. The two lovers met in hotels and various other places as their hectic schedules allowed. Marriage may have been discussed. Duse's notes to Boito refer to her fond desire for "three heads in a window"—a happy family setting with herself, her daughter, and Boito but this couldn't happen as long as Duse continued with her career. Even though she talked about saving money and retiring, her devotion to her work was too intense.

By the time Duse was thirty-five her enthusiasm for this clandestine affair with Boito began to wane. She begged him to be more open and emotional with her. She expressed a concern that he no longer found her sexually attractive. At the same time she developed a relationship with a fiery poet named Gabriele D'Annunzio. At first this relationship was strictly a matter of business. Duse felt confined with her repertoire of plays, often poorly translated French and English works, and she wanted plays written for her in Italian. D'Annunzio, who had already scored successes as a poet and novelist, was anxious to try his hand at drama. Duse knew D'Annunzio's work and considered him a great writer. D'Annunzio knew that Duse's name would make a success of any play he wrote.

Duse and D'Annunzio became lovers in the midst of these business negotiations. Those who knew the poet were not surprised, since he was an inveterate womanizer. Duse's motivation is less clear. Apparently feeling distant from Boito and conscious of her age, she was flattered by the approaches of this highly romantic man who was a few years younger than she. It is also likely that she saw her liaison with D'Annunzio as a way of uniting her working life with her love life. Now that she was legally separated from Checchi and her daughter was nearly grown, she could afford to be a little reckless.

However, loving D'Annunzio was a much more reckless venture than she ever imagined. The affair had hardly began when D'Annunzio sold his first play, supposedly written for Duse, to her French rival, Sarah Bernhardt. Duse forgave him and went on to perform his next plays even though they were hardly the masterpieces he promised her. Meanwhile, the poet continued to divide his attentions between Duse and his many other lovers. Although she was often tortured by jealousy, Duse continued to forgive her inconstant lover. But perhaps the unkindest thing D'Annunzio did was the most predictable. Long known for transcribing love affairs into his poems and fiction, D'Annunzio published a novel about an affair between a young man and an older woman. In the novel there were references to the woman's aging body that Duse could not have found reassuring.

Even this did not stop Duse from loving D'Annunzio. His insults and infidelities only seemed to increase her mad devotion. When she was forty-four, D'Annunzio maneuvered a younger actress into the lead role of his latest play. By this time he had another long-term affair underway. Duse wrote his new girl friend a letter in which she claimed that she would never stop loving D'Annunzio and asked the newcomer if she were prepared to make the same sacrifice. But after many hopeless letters and telegrams, Duse did stop loving D'Annunzio, or at least she buried that love in her work.

By the time she was fifty, Duse had earned enough money to retire from the stage; however, she never gave up her intense interest in the theater and returned to acting later in her life. She even made an attempt at directing and acting in a silent film. She also divided her time among her female friends, her daughter, and various charitable interests. She showed no further inclination toward romance. An immensely popular and honored public figure, she died at the age of sixty-five.

Another Example

Franz Liszt (Hungarian-born pianist and composer and one of the great sex symbols of his age). Born October 22, 1811 (Encyclopedia Britannica, Vol. 7).

If you have Mars in Capricorn with Venus in Sagittarius you are … the Saucy Slave of Love

You are the most impulsive Lover of this type and the one most likely to forget practicality and follow your instincts. This spontaneity, when combined with your strong physical drives, makes you a tremendously exciting, adventurous, and unpredictable sex partner. It also gets you into more than your share of trouble. But acting in haste and repenting in leisure is not a problem for you. Like all Mars in Capricorn Lovers, you rather like repenting.

What is lacking in your sexual nature is subtlety. Your restlessness and inconsistency make it difficult for you to manage your relationships as most Mars in Capricorn Lovers do. This often forces you to resort to means that are overly direct, blatant, or just plain rude in order to keep control of your love life. The problem isn't that these techniques are crude and clumsy. (You are so charming and effusive with your affection that you could be forgiven for that.) It's just that they very rarely work.

Case History

Christina Onassis (heiress to one of the great shipping fortunes of modern times whose life became an object lesson in the things that money can't buy). Born December 11, 1950, in New York City, New York (Wright 1991).

Onassis was brought up on one her father's (Aristotle Onassis) yachts, where she and her brother seldom saw playmates their own age. Their father had little to do with the youngsters, though he was careful to see that they had the best of everything. Their mother, a great beauty somewhat younger than her husband, was too involved in herself and her socializing to give much attention to her children.

Onassis was not a pretty child. Her prominent nose and raccoon eyes were a stark contrast to her mother's perfect features. If this were not enough to make her insecure, her father assured her that the only reason men would like her was because of her money. In her late teens Onassis had plastic surgery that reshaped her nose and removed the dark circles around her eyes. The surgery left her with a sultry kind of beauty when augmented by the best clothes and make-up. Nonetheless, Onassis maintained deep misgivings about her ability to attract a man.

By the time Onassis was eighteen her father was already negotiating her marriage to an equally wealthy Greek shipping heir. Onassis dated the young man and liked him. Yet she found the fact that she was completely excluded from the marriage negotiations too much to bear, and bolted from the relationship. Instead, she became friendly with a well-to-do American boy. She became pregnant with his child and wanted to marry him despite her father's angry disapproval.

As happened many times in Onassis's life, her personal drama was overwhelmed by a larger drama within her extended family. Her mother's sister, who was married to the shipping tycoon Stavros Niarchos, suddenly and mysteriously died. Many, Onassis and her father chief among them, felt that Niarchos had killed her. The trauma of this event so belittled Onassis's romantic rebellion that she had an abortion and left her American beau.

Onassis had other affairs. Some were with men who were "beneath her," such as a professional polo player named Luis Basualdo, and others were her financial equals. None of these men sought to marry her, and this only increased her insecurity. Finally, when she was twenty, Onassis met a California businessman named Joseph Bolker. Bolker was in his forties, slim, handsome, and very successful (though hardly up to the standards of Aristotle Onassis). Onassis was immediately attracted to him and, as was her way, approached him directly. They had a brief affair in Europe and Bolker returned to California. To his surprise, Onassis followed.

Bolker, who had recently divorced, confessed to Onassis that he had no desire to remarry, particularly to a youngster the same age as one of his own daughters. Onassis became distraught and took an overdose of pills. After reviving his impetuous lover, Bolker reassessed his position. He decided it couldn't be that bad to be married to a pretty, young billionaire. He acquiesced, and they became man and wife.

Onassis and Bolker had anticipated some disapproval from her father, but they were unprepared for the all-out war Aristotle Onassis waged against his daughter's first marriage. He had everyone connected with the Onassis family call his rebellious daughter and beg her to give up her marriage. Then he did everything in his power to blacken Bolker's reputation and destroy his business. Finally, he threatened to withdraw the trust fund that Onassis was due to inherit. Onassis loved Bolker and rather enjoyed playing at being a housewife, but the thought of living for a substantial period of time on her husband's income gave her pause.

Once again a family disaster spurred Onassis to make a difficult decision. Her mother, who had divorced Aristotle some time before, married Stavros Niarchos, the ex-husband and suspected murderer of her own sister. This emotionally wrenching event completely distracted Onassis from her matrimonial rebellion. She decided that it was not fair to Bolker to expose him to her father's destructive wrath and asked him for a divorce.

When Onassis was twenty-two her life was redirected by another family tragedy. Her older brother was killed in a plane crash. Aristotle Onassis, who had previously regarded his daughter as merely a pawn to be married off to the highest bidder, was now forced to regard her as his only heir. Onassis was given a crash course in running a multimillion-dollar shipping business and proved an apt pupil. Perhaps more importantly, for the first time in her life, she felt that she was earning her father's respect.

With the weight of the family business on her shoulder, Onassis was now willing to submit to an arranged marriage. Despite some active scheming on her father's part, no such union came about. Then, when Onassis was twenty-four, Aristotle Onassis died. A few months later, an aunt steered Onassis into a relationship with the son of another Greek shipping magnate, Alexander Andreadis. They were soon married.

Onassis may have wondered why her father had not proposed a marriage to the very eligible Andreadis. She soon found out. The Andreadis family fortune was on a downward slide. They were looking for large infusions of cash—Onassis cash—to save them. Once Onassis determined that she had been married for her money, she lost all interest in the arrangement. She left her husband and went to Paris, intent on pursuing both business and pleasure.

The business had to do with making a deal with the Russians to ship oil but, as it turned out, this venture also became pleasure. The Russian she worked with in Paris was Sergei Kausov, a short, fun-loving man who found Onassis extremely sexy. They saw each other in secret. Onassis reported that he was the best lover she had ever had. But it proved impossible to keep the relationship a secret from the KGB, and Kausov was sent back to Russia. After a frantic search, Onassis found him there and plans were made for a marriage.

This time it was the Russian government that made Onassis's love life an obstacle course. The couple could marry, but they would have to live in Russia, sharing a small apartment with Kausov's mother. Meanwhile, the international business community was abuzz with legal concerns and rumors of political intrigue. Onassis ignored all this and went ahead with the wedding. She made an attempt to live with Kausov in his tiny apartment and she tried to share the hardships of a typical Russian citizen, but the Russian winter proved more than she could bear. Within a few months she had escaped from the marriage and was soaking up the sun in Greece. She remained friendly with Kausov. She made him a very rich Russian, even though they were divorced when she was thirty.

During her late twenties and early thirties Onassis spent much of her time on her private island, Skorpios. She played with a constantly shifting entourage of wealthy friends and hangers-on, and become increasingly dependent on amphetamines and barbiturates. Her old boy friend, Luis Basualdo, was paid an exorbitant salary to live with her and provide her with companionship. Otherwise, her love affairs were varied, ranging from a poor student she carried off to Skorpios in a helicopter to a seventy-year-old jeweler for whom she developed a very short-lived infatuation. In all these arrangements, however, she was the one in complete control.

When she was thirty-four Onassis developed a relationship with Thierry Roussel. Roussel had been her lover several years earlier, but his attachment to his mistress proved too strong for the relationship to prosper. Now he claimed that relationship was behind him. His family was wealthy, and he seemed more serious than most of her other jet-set friends. He was also very confident and extremely good-looking.

Shortly after they were married and Onassis was pregnant with his child, she learned that much of what she thought she knew about Roussel was false. He had not given up a long-time mistress. In fact, she was also having his baby and he was seeing her frequently. Moreover, his family fortune was failing. Like Andreadis before him, he had apparently married Onassis because of her vast supply of ready cash. But this time Onassis was determined to hold on to her marriage, no matter how much it cost her in money and pride. She made no effort to interfere with the relationship between Roussel and his mistress. She even became friendly with the woman in an effort to make the woman and her children by Roussel an extension of their family. She gave Roussel millions of dollars. The only thing she denied her husband was control of her company.

Even after Roussel divorced Onassis, her struggle to hold on to the relationship continued. Onassis was obsessed with the happiness of her daughter and Roussel's presence, albeit occasional, was extremely important to her. By the time Onassis was thirty-seven Roussel was making noises about marrying his mistress. Onassis could see that her hold on him was slipping. She had moved on to a relationship with an older Greek living in Argentina that promised to be less stressful. She was visiting this man when, shortly before her thirty-eighth birthday, she died. At first is was assumed to be a suicide, but medical records indicate that she may well have died of a heart attack brought on by years of drug abuse.

Other Examples

Diego Rivera *(Mexican painter and muralist noted for his massive sexual appetites and his turbulent marriage to Frida Kahlo). Born December 8, 1886 (Celebrity Birthday Guide).*

Roger Vadim *(French filmmaker noted for his beautiful, famous wives and paramours). Born January 26, 1928 (Celebrity Birthday Guide).*

If you have Mars in Capricorn with Venus in Capricorn you are ... the Secretive Slave of Love

You are the earthiest Lover of this very earthy type. Sex is an elemental force in your life—so visceral and so primitive that at times it overwhelms you. Of course, very few people know this because you are such a conservative Lover and are so good at concealing your true feelings. This sexual reserve and distaste for display makes it very difficult for you to find a partner who shares your very physical kind of sexuality.

Control is the central sexual issue for you. Unlike other Lovers of this type, you are more concerned with controlling yourself than your partner. Your mistrust of your powerful sex drive is such that you are willing to use any means, even submitting yourself to the control of others, in order to keep your desires in check. Other people may wonder why you appear so scared of your own sexuality. If they had a chance to see your rampant libido at work, they'd probably be a little apprehensive themselves.

Case History

John Ruskin *(British writer noted for his influential art commentary and his visionary social criticism). Born February 8, 1819, in London, England (Hunt 1982).*

Ruskin was the product of an extremely sheltered and devout upbringing. His parents shared strict, evangelical Christian beliefs, and an equally deep conviction that their only child was going to live the life of a gentleman. His father was a prosperous businessman who applied himself to work with unremitting dedication. Ruskin's mother taught her son at home when he was small and carefully guarded him against physical harm and questionable influences. Even when Ruskin went to college at Cambridge, his mother went with him in order to guard his delicate health.

Not surprisingly, young Ruskin was an oddity—precocious in his intellectual development but hopelessly underdeveloped socially. This became woefully evident when he was seventeen. His father's French business partner sent his fifteen-year-old daughter, Adele Domecq, to stay with the Ruskins. Ruskin immediately fell in love with her. He flirted with her clumsily for a time and she seemed to be amused. Then she went home. It apparently never occurred to Ruskin that their relationship had essentially ended at that point. His infatuation only grew in her absence. Even though he was too shy to declare his feelings, he continued to believe that Adele would someday be his wife.

With his mother in tow, Ruskin did well at Cambridge. He won prizes for his poetry and excelled in natural history. He was ready to graduate with honors when disaster struck. Ruskin learned that Adele Domecq was engaged to marry another man. He was devastated. The disappointed lover suffered a nervous breakdown and was forced to withdraw from school without taking his final examinations.

To help him recuperate, Ruskin's parents took him on a prolonged holiday on the European continent. Ruskin was not a man to be idle for long. He found his vocation amid the artistic and architectural triumphs of the ages. He began to study, sketch, and write. Soon he put together the first of a series of books that would establish him as the most respected authority on art in England. The first volume of *Modern Painters* was released anonymously a few years after his breakdown. It was so well received that he published the second volume under his own name. Consequently, Ruskin was a famous man by the time he was in his mid-twenties.

His confidence renewed and feeling pressure from his parents to start a family of his own, Ruskin began to court two women when he was twenty-seven. The one he proposed to, Effie Gray, was a teenager he had first met when she was fifteen. Effie was pretty, sociable, and sufficiently impressed with the author of *Modern Painters* to ignore the difference in their temperaments. Ruskin was in such a hurry to marry her that he rankled when matters of propriety threatened to postpone the wedding day. In the end, he had his way and they were married when he was twenty-nine.

Because of later tragedies, the events of Ruskin's wedding night are a matter of public record, even though they are still not clearly understood. Some theorize that, after years of looking at marble statues, Ruskin was unprepared for the sight of Effie's pubic hair. Another theory was that, due to a misfortune in timing, the honeymoon coincided with Effie's menstrual period, and this shattered Ruskin's illusions of feminine perfection. In any case, the consummation of the marriage was postponed. As the marriage continued, Effie became aware that her husband was masturbating before he came to bed in order to perpetuate that postponement.

Ruskin and Effie were by no means the perfect couple even without these sexual problems. Effie was a young woman who liked to have fun and be with people. Ruskin preferred his books and studies, and had only a limited taste for social life. Perhaps more importantly, Ruskin remained extremely close to his parents. Effie found herself unable to compete with their longstanding influence. These problems, combined with her sexual frustration and the growing recognition that her marriage was not "normal," slowly changed the lighthearted teenager Ruskin had married into a bitter and deeply unhappy woman.

Meanwhile Ruskin's concern for art caused him to champion a group of young painters who called themselves Pre-Raphaelites. They shared an affinity for the Middle Ages with him and a deep, though occasionally saccharine, romanticism. One Pre-Raphaelite in particular caught Ruskin's attention: John Everett Millais. Millais was a child prodigy in art. He came from a good family and, like Ruskin, had received the wholehearted support of his parents in his artistic endeavors. He was handsome, serious, single, and very close to Effie's age.

As his friendship with Millais developed, Ruskin proposed that the painter travel with the couple to a wild area of Scotland that he favored. Ruskin planned to spend his days examining the local plant life (another of his passions), while Effie posed for Millais. The likely result of this arrangement should have been obvious even to Ruskin. It is possible that he had some subconscious desire to set his wife free. Unfortunately, this subconscious wish proved very costly. In order to end her marriage to Ruskin and marry Millais, Effie had to tell the court that her marriage of seven years had never been consummated. Ruskin's reputation would remain sullied by this admission for the rest of his life.

Once again Ruskin escaped his problems by burying himself in work. He always acted as if he were on a mission. Now his mission began to change. He spent less time working on issues related to art and more time on social problems. He became openly critical of the British "laissez-faire" economic system and the hardship it created for the working class. He was one of the founders of the Working Men's College, a night school where poor people could gain access to higher education for free. About this time Ruskin also became involved in another educational venture. He began to give lessons at a girl's school. It was not a paid position but Ruskin was not looking for money. He did it because he enjoyed the company of prepubescent girls.

Rosie LaTouche was such a girl. She was thirteen when Ruskin met her. Her keen intellect and unshakable religious convictions were already evident. As with Adele Domecq and Effie Gray, Ruskin courted her by first becoming her teacher. She proved very receptive to his romantic notions about art and beauty and his deep moral convictions. Before long the forty-one-year-old Ruskin was in love.

In many ways, Rosie LaTouche was even more troubled by her sexuality than Ruskin. She was frequently ill, and later became the first documented case of anorexia. It is theorized that she starved herself to postpone or retard menstruation because she feared sexual maturity.

Ruskin was unaware of LaTouche's problems, but he knew he felt a profound affinity with her. When she turned eighteen he proposed.

Over the next few years LaTouche and her family contrived to put off the amorous philosopher. Then, when Ruskin was fifty, Rosie seemed to warm to the idea of marriage. She decided to contact Effie, now Effie Millais, about the true circumstances of her divorce from Ruskin. When she learned that Ruskin had maintained his chastity by masturbation, LaTouche was shocked. She refused Ruskin's proposal.

Ruskin and LaTouche continued to see each other and to correspond. The troubled girl still found comfort in the advice and support offered by her older friend. LaTouche died when Ruskin was fifty-six. Ruskin was at her bedside and never quite recovered from the loss. Shortly after her death he began showing signs of mental illness. These symptoms gradually became more and more alarming, until he had to be confined to his home. Ruskin continued in this pitiful state until his death at the age of eighty-one.

Other Examples

Greg Louganis (*American diver*). *Born January 29, 1960* (*Celebrity Birthday Guide*).

Humphrey Bogart (*movie star noted for his "tough guy" persona*). *Born December 25, 1899* (*Celebrity Birthday Guide*).

If you have Mars in Capricorn with Venus in Aquarius you are . . . the Visionary Slave of Love

You are the most unconventional Mars in Capricorn Lover. You are willing to follow your down-to-earth attitude toward sex and strong need for physical fulfillment wherever it leads you. This does not mean that you are out of control. Quite the contrary. The absence of conventional restrictions only strengthens your own personal standards of behavior and sense of purpose. No matter how wild and shocking your actions, your rebellions are always carefully calculated to fit into a larger plan.

There is always an element of idealism in your sex life. This tends to raise the sacrifices and suffering you endure to a higher level. Of course, you first need a partner who is a proper target for all this visionary affection. Sometimes you find one, and sometimes you just have to invent one. In the latter instance, your partner may rankle at the pressure you put on him or her to be worthy of your dreams, but if that person can see how lucky he or she is to have you, there's no telling what you can accomplish together.

Case History

Cosima Wagner (daughter of composer Franz Liszt and wife of composer Richard Wagner). Born December 24, 1837, in Como, Italy (Skelton 1982; Sokoloff 1969).

Cosima was the product of a remarkable love affair. Her mother, Marie d'Agoult, (considered one the great beauties of the age) left her husband and two children to live with Franz Liszt who was then considered the greatest pianist in Europe. The relationship between these two independent and accomplished individuals was always stormy and ended after ten years. At this point both parents found reason to separate themselves from the children created by their union. Franz Liszt's mother raised Cosima and her siblings.

Even though they were mostly absent, these two remarkable parents still managed to exert an influence on their children, and Cosima idolized her father from a distance. She was overjoyed when, at seventeen, she was given the chance to join him in Germany. Even at this late date in his daughter's life, Liszt did not want to get too close to her. He boarded Cosima in the home of a good friend. There she met a young musician named Hans Bulow. Bulow was also a great admirer of her father, and love bloomed out of their mutual hero worship.

The news that her middle daughter was getting married did not please Marie d'Agoult. After her affair with Liszt, d'Agoult had grown to mistrust love and the institution of marriage. For her, men were insignificant drones to be used and discarded. She did what she could to impart this hardhearted doctrine on her daughter, but Cosima refused to surrender her romantic notions. After a long engagement, Cosima and Bulow were married when she was nineteen.

Bulow was a highly strung man prone to periods of deep depression and nervous prostration. Though he could be a fiery advocate for the men he admired, he lacked confidence in himself. When Cosima accompanied him to meet the composer Richard Wagner, whom Bulow admired even more than Liszt, she was shocked at how her husband's personality was overshadowed by that of his idol. She felt that Bulow could become a great composer. She encouraged him to work on his own music and develop his own approach. She made sure her husband took time each day to work on his compositions. She organized her household both to accommodate his moodiness and his work. She even cowrote the libretto for an opera he was trying to compose.

As Cosima was doing this, it may have dawned on her that Bulow could never be made into a genius. Meanwhile, she found herself falling under the spell of Bulow's hero, the visionary and egocentric Wagner. A year after her wedding Cosima had a breakdown during which she expressed the desire to kill herself. What brought her to this point is unknown, but it was a highly unusual lapse for a woman whose mental health, both before and after this incident, served as a shining example to less-secure souls.

At the moment the most prominent of these less-secure souls was that of her husband, whose black moods and irrational outbursts challenged even Cosima's resolute devotion. What upset her the most was that the libretto she had helped write for him in secret and presented to him as a Christmas gift lay unused on his desk, while he labored over the arrangements of part of Wagner's *Tristan and Isolde*. After the death of her brother and the birth of her first child with Bulow, Cosima's health deteriorated. She was sent to the mountains to recover. Wagner visited her while she was there.

Cosima was by no means a beautiful woman. She had inherited her father's tall, lean physique, as well as his long, horsy face and prominent nose. Nonetheless, her playfulness and adventurous spirit captivated Wagner. Away from her depressive husband, Cosima's vitality returned. Wagner found her full of good humor and "wild ways." It was probably at this time that he began to fall in love with his future wife.

For years Wagner had been trapped in an unhappy marriage with a very conventional woman who could not understand his artistic genius. He had remained in the marriage because, even though he was a very unconventional man, he treasured the notion of a stable home. He saw in Cosima a woman who cared little about what other people thought of her but, at the same time, was capable of the most complete devotion. The fact that, at the moment, she was giving that devotion to another man was hardly an impediment to an egotist like Wagner. When Cosima was twenty-six, she and Wagner chanced to be alone together again when Bulow succumbed to one of his black moods. Soon Cosima was pregnant with Wagner's child.

Cosima's marriage to Bulow continued, even after Bulow became aware of the affair. The child of a broken love affair, Cosima did not want to subject her own children to that misfortune. Although she lived with Bulow, she continued to visit and have sex with Wagner. Over the next five years she gave birth to two more children, all sired and acknowledged by Richard Wagner.

At this point Cosima and Wagner dropped the pretenses and decided to marry. Bulow, who was apparently still waiting for his wife to come to her senses, fought the decision to no avail. When she was thirty-two, Cosima divorced Hans Bulow and married the forty-six-year-old Wagner.

For Cosima, marrying Wagner was the same as finding a career. At last she had a genius to manage. She did so deftly and with no objection from the composer since her unquestioning respect for his ability was assumed. She worked quietly behind the scenes, but her intellectual energy, diplomacy, and support were all evident in the composer's subsequent rise to legendary status. As she grew older, Wagner had affairs but these mattered little to Cosima. She had a warm fondness for the man, but it was the artistic excellence he represented that really held her passion.

Cosima's calculated disregard for convention early in her relationship with Wagner was typically overlooked even by the most prudish of Wagner's fans. Her ardent support of her husband and almost angelic forbearance of his faults earned her general admiration. Though she outlived Wagner by many years (he died when she was forty-eight), Cosima seemed more than pleased with her role as widow of the world-renowned composer and primary advocate of his work. She died at ninety-three.

Other Examples

Marlene Dietrich (German-born movie star who was as sexy in a tuxedo as she was in an evening gown). Born December 27, 1901 (Celebrity Birthday Guide).

Sharon Stone (American actress). Born March 10, 1958 (Celebrity Birthday Guide).

If you have Mars in Capricorn with Venus in Pisces you are . . . the Succulent Slave of Love

You are a romantic dreamer who is practical and persistent enough to make your dreams into realities and your erotic fantasies into concrete experiences. Perhaps more importantly, you have the sexiness and persuasive power to get other people to join you in your sexual dreamland. Of course, whether that's good news or bad news depends entirely on the nature of those fantasies.

You are typically less concerned with controlling other people in your life than you are with controlling your dream. In many instances that erotic dream can become so expansive and all-consuming that it becomes the dominating feature both of your life and the lives of those who love you. You are the most open-hearted and lovable of all the Mars in Capricorn Lovers, but when it comes to your dreams, you can be cold, calculating, and relentless.

Case History

Leopold von Sacher-Masoch (Austrian author of Venus in Furs for whom the term "masochism" was coined). Born January 27, 1836, in Lemberg, Galicia (Cleugh 1967).

Sacher-Masoch was the son of an ennobled Austrian official. He was brought up in a normal, though privileged, environment. There are various theories about how he acquired his strange sexual tastes. His own had to do with a beautiful aunt who spanked him after she caught him spying on her and her adulterous lover. This sounds too much like one of

Sacher-Masoch's later fictions. Another notion is that the political turmoil that took place in central Europe and the bloody atrocities that accompanied these troubles influenced him during his youth.

Sacher-Masoch was a brilliant pupil. He was a doctor of law before he was twenty and then became a lecturer in history at the University of Prague. He published his first book, a somewhat scholarly work on an ancient rebellion, when he was twenty-one. He followed this with a successful novel. Around this time he also began an affair with Anna von Kottowitz, the sensual wife of an apparently unappreciative doctor. Her husband, who was noted for his own philandering, attempted to blackmail Sacher-Masoch when he found out about the affair. The physically unimpressive writer responded by challenging the doctor to a duel. The doctor backed down. Anna left him to live with Sacher-Masoch.

By this time Sacher-Masoch's sexual tastes were firmly established. He enjoyed sex only when it was mixed with pain and humiliation. He wanted Anna to terrorize him, to beat him with whips and birch rods, and verbally abuse him without mercy. After these rituals Sacher-Masoch would make passionate love to his beautiful torturer. Anna apparently enjoyed the rituals herself. For a time the couple seemed happy. But after a while, Sacher-Masoch began to find fault with his lover. Anna, liberated as she was, cared more for pretty clothes and jewelry than she did for his erotic fantasies. In order to really make her angry, he had to goad her by complaining about the price of some bauble she had purchased, and this grew tiresome.

Sacher-Masoch's relationship with Anna ended after four years when he found that she was unfaithful to him with a Polish count. The infidelity didn't upset Sacher-Masoch (in fact, he found it rather exciting), but the fact that Anna contracted syphilis did. He challenged the Pole to a duel and sent Anna to a clinic. A short time later the count was revealed to be an imposter, and Sacher-Masoch's relationship with Anna was over.

It took a while for Sacher-Masoch to find another woman regal and cruel enough to fit his special erotic schemes. When he did, he immediately made her sign a contract. The contract, made when he was thirty-three with a young woman named Fanny Pistor (Baroness Bogdanoff), allowed this woman to treat Sacher-Masoch like a slave and punish him accordingly for eighteen hours each day over a period of six months. Sacher-Masoch reserved six hours daily to pursue his profession as writer. He also prohibited the party of the second part from reading his mail. Otherwise, Fanny was contractually obligated to make him miserable.

In accordance with this agreement, Sacher-Masoch traveled with Fanny as her servant. After a while the writer suggested that Fanny take another lover. Fanny, who was a practiced adventuress, began looking for the right man. Sacher-Masoch had requested a duke but they settled for an actor. Sacher-Masoch's plan was to spy on the couple as they were making love, thus adding to his humiliation, but the actor discovered him and became upset. To Sacher-Masoch's delight, Fanny suggested the other man beat her impudent servant, and he did.

Despite these sterling moments, Fanny also fell short of Sacher-Masoch's cruel ideal. She became bored with the ritual of fur and whips. The contract was not renewed. Meanwhile, Sacher-Masoch completed his most famous work, *Venus in Furs*. It was a summation of his sexual philosophy and his relationships with both Anna von Kottowitz and Fanny Pistor—only better. The heroine of *Venus in Furs*, called Wanda, is Sacher-Masoch's perfect virago: a large, imposing woman who finds pleasure in hurting and humiliating her man. The "other man" in the story is also perfect: a snarling Greek lout who gloats as the hero suffers.

Sacher-Masoch already had a literary reputation because of his scholarly books on history and several novels. *Venus in Furs* brought him a very different kind of notoriety. He began to get "fan mail." Among these letters he found a message from a woman who described herself as being very like the heroine of *Venus in Furs*. She even signed the letter "Wanda."

The correspondent's real name was Aurora von Dunayev. She was an uneducated commoner who had approached the writer with hope of luring him into marriage. By the time Sacher-Masoch found out, he had already built such a fantasy around this "Wanda" that there was no turning back. Even when the woman confessed her plot and admitted that she in no way shared his sexual tastes, Sacher-Masoch remained determined. They were married when he was thirty-six.

Sacher-Masoch had a good reason for rushing to marry his "Wanda," that went beyond her large, shapely physique and natural ferocity. From the very beginning of the relationship, he saw that she was a woman who could rule over him in sex, yet allow him to dominate the relationship. It was Sacher-Masoch who directed their activities outside the bedroom. It was his career and sexual obsession that dictated where they lived, what they did, and with whom they consorted.

The problem that Sacher-Masoch faced now was finding the third element of his fantasy: the "Greek." His fervent search for the right man to make him a cuckold became something of a comedy. Wanda, particularly after the birth of their three sons, often wavered in her enthusiasm for this part of the ritual, but Sacher-Masoch was obsessed. After several years they found a student who was naive enough to be duped into the role. Wanda played it according to plan. She whipped her husband and ordered him to wait outside the door while she had sex with the student. Sacher-Masoch was allowed to peek at them through the keyhole. Later, Sacher-Masoch was delirious with happiness. The student, dazed and confused, fled the premises.

After this incident the relationship between Wanda and Sacher-Masoch deteriorated. By the time the writer was forty-six, Wanda was openly sleeping with another man and not for her husband's pleasure. Sacher-Masoch was looking for her replacement when he found a mousy, Prussian woman who was employed as a translator. Physically, Hulda Meister was totally miscast as the "Venus in Furs," and she lacked the "tigerish" instincts of Wanda. Yet the ex-governess was young and enough in love with Sacher-Masoch to learn how to please him. When the writer was forty-seven he divorced Wanda and married Hulda Meister.

Sacher-Masoch's second marriage was apparently more successful than his first, even though his last years lacked the creative fecundity that had characterized his time with Wanda. He and Hulda had three children and lived quietly in the country; however, Sacher-Masoch's sexual preferences had not changed. His home was still full of furs and implements of torture. A Galician maid was employed to tie him up and whip him when Hulda was too busy. Toward the end of his life, Sacher-Masoch's obsession with pain became pathological. He had seizures that could only be relieved by burning or piercing his flesh. He died of a heart attack at fifty-nine.

Other Examples

Mabel Dodge Luhan (*American socialite and avant-gardist noted for her sponsorship of talented people ranging from D. H. Lawrence to Georgia O'Keeffe). Born February 26, 1879 (Hahn 1971).*

Marvin Gaye (*American singer noted for his troubled relationships with women). Born April 2, 1939 (Celebrity Birthday Guide).*

Drew Barrymore (*child star who survived a troubled youth to become a successful actress). Born February 22, 1975 (Celebrity Birthday Guide).*

Chapter 11

Mars in Aquarius
The Sexual Liberator

General Characteristics

Mars in Aquarius Lovers are the least physical of all the Mars types. Of course, these Lovers have the same sexual energy, physical needs, and desires as all of us. With Mars in Aquarius, these needs are processed in such an intellectual, objective fashion that sex seldom has the same pressing, corporal reality that makes it so problematic for the rest of us. For these Lovers everything important about sex happens in their heads. In one sense this gives them extraordinary freedom. They can use sex the way a mathematician uses calculus or an artist uses perspective—to achieve a specific goal. These goals can vary a great deal. They may choose to use it as a source of inspiration and spiritual revitalization; as a means of charming or persuading others; or, for its shock value, as a way of getting the attention of those who are more physical than they are.

This abstracted approach to sex means that Mars in Aquarius Lovers naturally feel free to experiment with their sexuality. The emotional conditions and social restrictions most people place on the sex act mean little to these thoroughly rational and unconventional Lovers. The only restrictions they recognize are those of time and space. At their best, the

351

absolute freedom with which these Lovers approach both sex and love is inspirational. Time spent with them can be a true liberation for us "less adventurous" souls.

It shouldn't be assumed that Mars in Aquarius Lovers break the rules just for the fun of it. This daring, experimental approach to sex is always secondary to the notion these Lovers have that sex has to be tied to some larger purpose. This is one of the most idealistic placements of Mars—meaning that for these Lovers, love is understood in terms of ideas—usually big ideas. It is not so much that these people think they can change the world by making love. It's more that the sex act, as well as their partner, must in some way fit into an overall idealism—into a system of ideas, hopes, and dreams that makes this otherwise simple, biological function significant.

Their extreme idealism with regard to sex means that Mars in Aquarius Lovers often have an easier time loving "causes" or humanity as a whole than they do loving one individual. Kindness, self-sacrifice, and service come easily to these people, but intimacy is always a problem. It is not unusual for those who love Mars in Aquarius individuals to feel distant and out of touch. No matter how much a Mars in Aquarius Lover may profess to love someone, there is always a sense that he or she could get along just as well alone.

This might not be such a problem if it weren't for the incredible charismatic charm that these Lovers often possess. They are so cool-headed and unique, and so full of idealism and purpose that it's hard not to notice them. Of course, the allure of a Mars in Aquarius Lover is not sex appeal. This allure tends to be more compelling from a distance than up close. Loving a Mars in Aquarius individual can certainly have its corporal rewards, but it is primarily an intellectual exercise.

The bottom line here is that the Mars in Aquarius Lover is always inferior to the Mars in Aquarius Friend. These people will always choose the ease and camaraderie of friendship over the intensity and passion of love. This in no way limits their sex lives. As far as these folks are concerned, friendship is a wonderful basis for a sexual relationship. There is warmth and camaraderie but none of that nasty emotional stuff that often makes love and sex so irrational and dangerous. The Mars in Aquarius Friend is capable of compassion, gentleness, and loyalty. They seek to teach, reform, and help the people they care about and they stand by these folks through every kind of trial. In fact, the Mars in Aquarius Friend is so terrific that after a while any partner of a Mars in Aquarius individual starts wondering why they ever wanted a Lover!

If you have Mars in Aquarius with Venus in Aries you are . . . the Zealous Liberator

You are a sexual zealot—a wild-eyed revolutionary in the arena of love. Your far-reaching enthusiasm and irrepressible optimism give you a charm that is undeniable, as well as an enormous capacity for making a mess of your love life. It's not that you don't think things out. All your escapades start as part of a grand plan—an exuberant dream of meaningful sex and larger-than-life love. You have a way of pushing your fascinations to the farthest and most unrealistic extremes. This invariably leads to problems.

Fortunately, you are gifted with enough erotic energy to weather almost any of the crash-and-burn scenarios that come your way. You have a wonderful capacity for recovering from your own folly and reinventing your desire. Still, you will always do best when you are paired with a partner who is smart enough to know when you are reaching too far, and strong enough to make you stop and reconsider.

Case History

William Morris (*English poet, painter, designer, and social activist who combined medieval craftsmanship with socialism). Born March 24, 1834, in Walthamstow, Essex, England (Lindsay 1975; Daly 1989).*

Morris was born into a large, middle-class family with Welsh roots and a deep sense of family history. A sickly child, he grew into an exceptionally strong, clumsy youth noted for his fiery temper and impulsive energy.

Morris attended various schools away from home throughout his teens. During this time he developed a strong relationship with his younger sister, Emma. Emma shared his idealism and interest in poetry. In return, he sided with her when she adhered to the Church of England, in opposition to the more radical evangelical beliefs of their parents. The closeness of these two siblings became obvious when Emma decided to marry. Morris wrote a poem in which a young woman is loved by two men and has to choose one over the other (a theme to which he often returned as his work progressed).

Morris was sent to Oxford where he discovered the ideas of John Ruskin. Ruskin inspired his students to love the arts and architecture of the Middle Ages and to hate the inequities of modern capitalism. Ruskin found a responsive pupil in Morris. At twenty-one Morris shocked his mother, who had expected her oldest son to pursue a career in the church, when he announced he was going to be an architect. A year later he shocked her again when he told her he was also going to be a painter.

The man who had inspired Morris to take up painting was Dante Gabriel Rossetti, who was a charismatic young poet and painter, and the leader of a group of artists called the Pre-Raphaelite Brotherhood. The Pre-Raphaelites, like Morris, had a reverence for the art of the Middle Ages. They believed in a realistic representation of natural objects (Morris was also a fervent naturalist), and high degree of spirituality. Under the tutelage of Rossetti and the rest of the Brotherhood, Morris advanced quickly as a draftsman and a painter. But it was his efforts at design and pattern that were most promising.

Even in this high-minded company, the unworldly Morris was often chided for his shyness around women. He cared only for his work and he applied himself to it with unreserved ferocity. Then when he was twenty-four and working on a mural project in Oxford with the rest of the Brotherhood, Morris met the girl of his dreams: Jane Burden. He said nothing to her at first. Instead he allowed Rossetti, who was as persuasive with women as he was with men, to ask her to model for the group. Fortunately for Morris, Rossetti was soon called away from the project because of the illness of his mistress, Lizzie Siddal. Morris was given the opportunity to woo Jane on his own.

Jane Burden was the daughter of a stablehand and had little, if any, formal education. Yet she carried herself like a lady and had exceptional physical beauty. She was tall, slender, with large eyes, and strong, perfectly proportioned features. For the Pre-Raphaelites, who had an almost mystical reverence for feminine beauty, she was an untouchable goddess. She must have felt more than a little overwhelmed by their attention, but was sensible enough to keep her mouth shut and allow her looks to speak for her. She made no objections when the impetuous Morris, with his dreamy notions and sizable income, began to pay her court.

Morris' courtship of Jane consisted mostly of reading books to her. Later, after she had accepted his proposal, he continued to augment her education. Already he saw Jane as part of a larger plan. He began construction of a house he called "Red House" in which all his ideals were to be brought together. The architecture was medieval, the decoration and furnishing all of his design, and the queen of that house was to be a great beauty of unquestioned purity and refinement.

When Morris was twenty-five he and Jane Burden were married. Jane proved to be an apt student and quickly acclimated to her exalted new role. Meanwhile, Morris turned his energy toward other projects. He was beginning to make headway as a poet, and he continued his interest in design and craftsmanship. He and other artists formed a company for the production and sale of furniture and household objects, which were all designed and manufactured according to Morris' ideas.

For six years the marriage was almost idyllic, at least from Morris' point of view. He was deeply involved in work that he loved. He was married to a beautiful, compliant wife who made exquisite embroidery, and gave him two beloved daughters. Then the dream fell apart. Financial and business concerns forced Morris and his family to abandon Red House, which was never completed, and move to London so he could be close to his production company. Jane was unhappy in London. She was often ill and withdrew from Morris after the birth of their second child. It is speculated that her illnesses may have been a ruse to avoid sex with her husband.

By the time Morris was thirty-four his wife was having an affair with his good friend Rossetti. Rossetti had become a rather tragic character. His great love, Lizzie Siddal, had committed suicide, leaving him a broken, guilt-ridden man. Jane had the same ethereal beauty as Siddal, and he was now drawn to her by an irresistible combination of guilt and lust.

Morris believed that marriage should not be a property arrangement and that a married couple had to be free to pursue their individual happiness. Now that belief was put to the ultimate test. Jane confessed to Morris that she had never really loved him and that now she loved Rossetti. Morris loved Rossetti, too, as a mentor and as a man who shared his ideals. The only thing he could do was let his wife have her way. He even rented a country house so that Rossetti and Jane could be together without raising too much gossip.

This singular arrangement continued for four years until Rossetti suffered a breakdown and attempted suicide. Jane returned to her husband, but this apparently made little difference in his sex life. When he was thirty-eight Morris confessed in a letter to a friend that he was impotent.

Morris continued to have many women friends and confidants. The closest of these was Georgiana, the wife of his good friend Edward Burne-Jones. Georgiana's husband had fallen in love with one of his models and she had much in common with the jilted Morris. Moreover, she shared his fiery idealism and desire to work for good causes; however, it appears that their relationship, as intense and affectionate as it was, never became sexual.

Meanwhile Morris' advocacy for beauty in common everyday objects led him to an advocacy for the "common" man. In his later years he became an active supporter of workers' rights and socialism. Jane was still with him, even though she rather disapproved of her husband's preference for living like a common worker. Morris continued to fight for his ideals until his death at the age of sixty-two.

Other Examples

Louis XV (*king of France noted for his unusual alliance with Madam Pompadour who began as his mistress and later became his closest friend and advisor). Born February 15, 1710 (Encyclopedia Britannica, Vol. 7).*

Ted Kennedy *(United States senator from Massachusetts). Born February 22, 1932 (Celebrity Birthday Guide).*

If you have Mars in Aquarius with Venus in Taurus you are … the Lascivious Liberator

You are constantly torn between sex of the body and sex of the mind and it doesn't help a bit that you are so good at both. The sensuality of your erotic nature makes it necessary for you to bring your ideals into the real world and express them in physical terms. This makes you a particularly adept Lover for whom the mind becomes just another artful appendage that is useful in the gathering of earthly delight.

The most difficult choice you have is not between the mind and the body but between rebellion and conformity. You are far too conservative to be a good sexual adventurer. You prefer to do your experimenting behind closed doors and are drawn to stable, enduring relationships. Yet the thirst for variety in your sex life and your intolerance of even the most benign restrictions on your behavior often make this kind of discreet stability difficult to attain. You are a Lover who clearly sees all the advantages of settling down but often postpones doing so indefinitely.

Case History

Tennessee Williams *(Thomas Lanier Williams—American playwright noted for his prizewinning dramas* A Streetcar Named Desire, *and* Cat on a Hot Tin Roof*). Born March 26, 1911, in Columbus, Mississippi (Spoto 1985).*

Note: Date differs from other published data.

The son of a Southern belle and a hard-drinking businessman, Williams' early life was characterized by instability and family strife. During his earliest years his father was seldom present. Even after the family was united in St. Louis, they moved constantly. It was Williams' mother and his genteel grandfather who most influenced his childhood. They attempted to give the family at least the aura of Southern aristocracy. Williams was delicate and overprotected. He had minimal contact with boys his own age. His chief playmate was his older sister, Rose, who was as delicate and high-strung as he was.

Williams dated girls in high school and college. Some were attracted to him because of his interest in poetry and literature. Others had to be procured for him by more aggressive male friends. Williams' attachments to these women were never sexual. Recalling this period, he claimed he had been a puritan—too shy and reserved to bring up the subject of sex. He also recalled having sexual feelings for some of his male friends but he was never quite sure what to do about them.

Even before Williams left high school, he had already published poems and short stories. His interest in writing often detracted from his schoolwork, and his grades were lackluster. When he was twenty-three his father became so disgusted with Williams' performance that he pulled him out of college. He put him to work as a clerk in the shoe factory where the elder Williams was an executive. Williams soon suffered a nervous breakdown. Once again he was allowed to pursue his desultory academic career.

Williams' first sexual experience occurred when he was twenty-six with one of his more forward girl friends. But his real sexual awakening did not occur until the next year when he was living in New Orleans and became a full-fledged bohemian. It was an atmosphere in which casual homosexual encounters were not considered out of the ordinary. Williams soon developed a fondness for quick, anonymous sex that would never leave him.

Williams' belatedly activated libido became one of the two driving forces of his life for the next several years—the other was his single-minded ambition to become a successful writer. Williams was constantly on the move, forming strong and influential friendships, but no permanent sexual relationships. His preference for "pickups" continued. Even men with whom his contact was more sustained were shut out by his intense involvement in work and constant search for sexual variety. He was particularly in his element during World War II. Williams was working as a screenwriter in California. He lived near a wooded area that was a meeting place for homosexuals and lonely sailors. His friend Christopher Isherwood, who was also homosexual but much more conservative than Williams, was amazed at the other man's appetite for these faceless encounters in the dark.

In some ways Williams never completely escaped his early puritanism. Some of his friends felt he was unhappy as a homosexual, and that his inability to form strong emotional bonds with his male lovers was proof of this. Williams continued to court women. He considered his homosexuality a temporary condition long after he became an active homosexual. Williams often talked about his rampant libido as if it were a curse. He once confessed that he hoped age would someday free him from his obsession with sex; however, neither age nor copious applications of booze and barbiturates curbed his desire.

When Williams was thirty-seven he began what was perhaps his only enduring love affair with a man named Frank Merlo. Merlo was a practical fellow with a gift for making Williams' life easy. He took care of mundane affairs that the writer found onerous. Williams' friends, who considered Merlo a man of integrity and a stabilizing influence on Williams, universally liked him. But his task was not an easy one, particularly after Williams became famous and decided he was entitled to anything he wanted.

As Williams grew older, alcohol and drugs competed with work and sex for a place in his life. His addictions often made him capricious and wildly paranoid. It was Merlo who suffered the brunt of these deficiencies. To make matters worse, the writer's fascination for cheap sex was unabated. Merlo wanted a solid, monogamous relationship, but Williams was repulsed by the very idea of monogamy. He was unfaithful to Merlo at every opportunity.

The first break between Williams and Merlo occurred seven years into the relationship when Merlo declared he would not be Williams' "yes" man. They were later reunited but, even though he found him indispensable, Williams was often uncomfortable when his friend was around. The final break occurred when Williams was fifty. He had many affairs after this but he typically treated these men more as employees than lovers. None of the relationships endured. In the end, he was left alone. He died at the age of seventy-two.

Another Example

Leonardo da Vinci *(Italian Renaissance artist). Born April 15, 1452 (Celebrity Birthday Guide).*

If you have Mars in Aquarius with Venus in Gemini you are . . . the Liberator of the Mind

You are perhaps the least physical of all the Mars types. This can be either a blessing or a curse, depending upon your point of view. It is a blessing because it allows you to play with sex without being burned by desire. You can be a very exhilarating Lover—free-spirited, inventive, and kind. You will rarely be driven by the physical need for sex to do anything contrary to your own well-being. You treat sex like a toy and never let it assume too much importance in your life.

When it comes to expressing intimacy, this intellectual approach to sex can have significant drawbacks. You are always more comfortable when you are talking about sex or flitting around the edges of desire than you are in the clinch. The visceral immediacy of other people's physical passion is likely to leave you feeling out of place and even a bit intimidated. Some people will consider your attitude cold and clinical. But even though your adventurous spirit, technical skill, and witty conversation may not be enough to satisfy every partner, it will certainly be enough to fascinate many.

Case History

Anthony Trollope (English novelist noted for his artful observations of Victorian life and his independent female characters). Born April 24, 1815, in London, England (Hall 1991).

Trollope's father was a lawyer with ambitions toward becoming a gentleman farmer. His failure at both professions brought much hardship to both himself and his children. The elder Trollope moved his family to a farm near Harrow, the prestigious English public school. There he hoped that his four sons could gain a good education inexpensively. But "day boys" (local boys who attended the school) were looked down upon and bullied by other students, who were often wealthy and titled. Anthony Trollope, whose elder brothers had already graduated by the time he started school, was forced to pass through this gauntlet of pain and humiliation alone.

Trollope was a natural target. He was a large, clumsy boy who was often dirty and ill-clothed, and, by all appearances, none too bright. Trollope suffered greatly, having neither the physical aggressiveness nor the charm to fend off his tormentors. Even his teachers couldn't resist making fun of him. The situation deteriorated further when Trollope was taken out of Harrow by his father and placed in a private school. There he was punished, along with three other boys, for an unnamed offense that could only have been homosexuality. Trollope claimed he had nothing to do with these other boys—"curled darlings" he called them—and that he had only been accused because he was fresh from Harrow where such offenses were rumored to be commonplace. Whatever the truth, Trollope recalled the incident with a mixture of deep shame and moral outrage for the rest of his life.

Meanwhile, the fortunes of the Trollope family continued to wither and his father showed signs of mental illness. Trollope's mother, Francis, took two of her children and left for the United States. Her plan was to work in a utopian community that one of her high-minded friends had started. Instead she spent three years wandering around the country. Her observations of America, most of them unfavorable, were published in a book. This book became very popular and saved the family from complete bankruptcy.

The remarkable Mrs. Trollope obviously had a decided influence on her youngest son, who already had secret ambitions to become a writer. But Trollope had little contact with his mother during this period. After her long trip to America, Francis Trollope became occupied with nursing her sick husband and another son who had contracted consumption. They lived apart from Trollope who, at nineteen, started a career in the post office in London.

Trollope was free in London. When he recalled this period later in life it was with a certain degree of chagrin. He experimented with many of the vices, including prostitutes and flirtations with barmaids and the like, but he saw no glory in these activities. Once a working-class girl with whom he had dallied took the notion that Trollope was going to marry her. He lacked the nerve to refuse her outright. He simply put it off until the girl's mother appeared at his office and demanded that the trembling clerk make his intentions clear.

At this point Frances Trollope returned to London. She still had little time for her younger son. Instead she encouraged Trollope's older brother who had become an author of travel books. But her "salon" attracted many young women, and flirting with these clever but untouchable beauties diverted Trollope from less intellectual encounters with girls of the lower classes.

During this time Trollope was less than a model postal clerk. He was often late for work and inattentive when he got there. When he was twenty-six Trollope asked for a new position in Ireland. This job paid better and it also gave him a new start. The shy and fumbling adolescent became a mature and responsible employee in Ireland who impressed his boss and was well liked by the other men. He began to hunt, dance, and go to parties. Most importantly, he began seriously looking for a wife. A year after arriving in Ireland, Trollope was engaged to Rose Heseltine.

Trollope's wife came from a middle-class background similar to his own. She was a quiet woman who often went nearly unnoticed, even by people who knew the author quite well. Trollope allowed her, and no other person, to read his manuscripts before they were presented to the publisher. This may have been only to gain her input in matters relating to fashion and domestic craft. All in all she was a very conventional and exceptionally loyal wife. She presented her husband with two sons and otherwise remained in the background of his life. She had two outstanding qualities that made her a natural match for Trollope: She enjoyed traveling and was unperturbed by her husband's flirtations with other women.

Marriage allowed Trollope to concentrate on his writing in a way he had never done before. He published his first novel soon after his wedding. It failed. A second novel did likewise. A third did better but made no great stir. Trollope finally established his reputation as a first-rate writer with his fourth novel, published when he was forty-two.

Fame brought Trollope admirers, including many young women because he showcased strong female characters in his books. Trollope took great pleasure in these "drawing room flirtations." He enjoyed the attention of independent women and he liked "pretending he was in love." One of these romances with Kate Fields, an American girl twenty-three years his junior, lasted many years. Trollope never allowed his relationship with any of these women to move past the bounds of Victorian propriety. His involvement with Fields took place mostly through correspondence and never was a love affair in any sense other than fantasy.

Anthony Trollope was hardly a rebel but he was often critical of the sexual repression of the society in which he lived. He resisted the efforts of some publishers to censor his work.

He chided readers who bemoaned his representations of such taboo subjects as adultery and prostitution. Trollope declared that the notion of keeping young women ignorant of these grim realities was senseless, "a system of perpetuating childhood." He remained a staunch moralist who found no glamour in sin. But he tended to regard the sinners, particularly prostitutes, as objects of pity who suffered greatly for a misconduct that was "slight."

Trollope was a very prolific author, producing vast numbers of novels and stories. Even as his audience diminished, he never stopped writing. Rose remained his loyal helpmate, and he continued his flirtatious correspondence with Kate Field. Many of his contemporaries, like the boys at Harrow, found him to be too loud, too dull, and too oafish. Those who knew him only through his books apparently liked him better. He died at the age of sixty-seven.

If you have Mars in Aquarius with Venus in Cancer you are . . . the Lunar Liberator

You are the most difficult Mars in Aquarius Lover to understand. You alternate between self-possessed coolness and abject submission, and between sexual adventurism and extreme emotional vulnerability. You cry for security one minute and long to break free and be on your own the next. Even those who love you the most are never sure whether it's freedom or cuddling you require. That's because you need both so desperately.

On the positive side, this combination of intellectual aloofness and emotional need gives you a sexual allure that is very (almost wickedly) effective. When you want to, you can seduce, charm, and manipulate other people with a devilish ease. But this is seldom your pleasure. What you're really looking for is a relationship in which dependence will seem like independence and love becomes a transcendent cause. When you find such a magical arrangement, you use every bit of your seductive coolness to make it work.

Case History

Djuna Barnes (*American journalist and writer most noted for her novel* Nightwood *and her unabashed bisexuality). Born June 12, 1892, in Cornwall-on-Hudson, New York (Herring 1995).*

Barnes' father was a high-energy wastrel. He was remarkably talented in many areas but was never able to hold a job. Shortly after Djuna was born, he brought his mistress to live with his family. He had children by both his mistress and wife over the next several years. This large, polygamous family was supported, for the most part, by the labors of Barnes' grandmother, Zadel Barnes, who was a writer and social activist. But Zadel's efforts were only barely sufficient to make ends meet. Barnes grew up knowing both intellectual excellence and dire poverty.

Barnes' relationship with this odd family unit was complex. Her father and his ideas about free love remained an important part of her life for many years, but she felt a great deal of anger toward him. Her mother, who divorced her father when Barnes was twenty, was simply a beloved victim. The only member of her family that Barnes felt truly close to was her grandmother. Letters exchanged between Zadel Barnes and her teenage granddaughter reveal a sexual intimacy that is rather shocking. The letters allude joyfully to a time when the two shared a bed. These letters include endless jokes based on the nicknames they had given their breasts (Barnes' were "cuddlers" and grandma's were "pint tops").

Barnes told different stories about how she lost her virginity. In one story her father, in accordance with his free-love theories, asked a neighbor to introduce his sixteen-year-old daughter to the joys of sex. In another it was her father himself who raped her. Regardless how she told the story, it was always with an emphasis on the pain and humiliation she suffered.

When Barnes was eighteen she entered into an unofficial marriage with a man in his fifties, but the marriage only lasted a few months. One reason for the breakup may have been the fact that she was not a virgin. Barnes apparently had little feeling for her husband and probably entered the marriage to escape from her unusual and stressful domestic situation.

Barnes first major love affair began when she was twenty-two and working as a journalist in New York City. Her lover was Ernst Hanfstaengl, a tall, sophisticated German art dealer who had lived in the United States for many years. For two years the couple was very close. Then Hanfstaengl told Barnes that for dynastic reasons he could only marry a German. Barnes was deeply hurt by this rejection, though later she said that Hanfstaengl had probably saved her life by refusing to marry her.

Barnes had some passing sexual encounters with women even before her affair with the German. In letters written during this period, her father kidded Barnes about her attachments to her own sex. But it was only after her break with Hanfstaengl that Barnes sought a more serious love affair with a woman. Her lover was a fellow journalist named Mary Pyne. Barnes wrote little about her relationship with Pyne, but it was obviously an intense commitment. Barnes was nursing Pyne when she died of tuberculosis about a year after the beginning of their affair.

After these two unfortunate love affairs, Barnes allowed herself to sink into the carefree bed hopping typical of her Greenwich Village milieu. Then at twenty-five she made another stab at a committed relationship with the brilliant but unstable writer and socialist, Courtenay Lemon. Lemon was a man of great intellectual passion who was working on a book that he felt would certainly change the world—a book that would never be finished. He was also an alcoholic. Barnes' infatuation with this difficult man lasted two years. Then she moved to Paris.

It was in Paris that the twenty-nine-year-old Barnes met the love of her life: Thelma Wood. Wood was a tall, striking, nineteen-year-old American who was worldly beyond her years. Barnes was completely taken with her. Her passion for Wood reduced the free-loving Barnes to monogamy. During their eight-year relationship, and even for a period of time afterward, Barnes could not entertain the thought of another lover. Unfortunately, Wood was not an easy person to love. She flirted with other women, including her previous sponsor who was still competing with Barnes for her favors. And like Lemon, Wood was an alcoholic. It was probably during this unruly relationship that Barnes developed her own alcohol addiction. The end of her relationship with Wood inspired Barnes' most notable literary work, *Nightwood*.

During the period of her emotional recuperation from Wood, Barnes became increasingly dependent upon the financial and emotional support of wealthy friends, particularly Peggy Guggenheim and Natalie Barney. After a hiatus from love, she began an affair with a pretty young bisexual named Charles Henri Ford, but she was no longer striving for monogamy or continuity in her relationships. She told a friend, "I have had my great love, there will never by another" (Herring, 166).

Despite her unfettered lifestyle, Barnes could be highly critical of promiscuity. Her review of Ford's novel about male homosexuals deplored the kind of casual, mechanical sex he portrayed. Earlier, when she was still living with Wood, Barnes wrote a satirical novel about the lesbian community of Paris in which she skewered this same kind of sexual irresponsibility among that group.

Barnes closed out her last major love affair when she was forty-seven. Immediately afterward she attempted suicide. Alcoholism and poverty were the outstanding themes for the next several years of Barnes' life. Remarkably, she was able to stop her dangerous downward spiral and get control of her alcoholism at fifty-eight.

Sober and renewed, Barnes returned to her writing with remarkable vindictiveness. When she was sixty-six her play, *The Antiphon*, was published. In this dramatic work, a mixture of confession and biting satire, Barnes took scathing revenge on her friends and family. The play was her second and last great literary success.

Always a private person, Barnes spent the second half of her life living like a recluse in her tiny Greenwich Village apartment. Although she never disavowed the free-love philosophy of her grandmother and father, her ideas about sex became surprisingly conservative. In particular, she resisted the attempts by many in literary circles and in the feminist movement to label her a "lesbian" writer. She died, still defiantly independent and cantankerous, at the age of ninety.

Another Example

William Powell (actor noted for his suave, cool-headed screen persona and his affection for tough-talking, blond bombshells). He was married to Carole Lombard and later engaged to Jean Harlow. Born July 29, 1892 (Celebrity Birthday Guide).

If you have Mars in Aquarius with Venus in Leo you are . . . the Grand Liberator

You are a flamboyant Lover who feels that there is no joy in breaking the rules unless everyone notices. Your charm, warmth, and generosity make you a very desirable partner. You are capable of flashes of the most intense passion; however, it is always the intellectual side of love that is most likely to hold you. For you, sex is a great way to get attention, particularly from the people you really like, but it's sincere and lasting friendship that really gets you off.

You are one of the most controlling of the Mars in Aquarius Lovers, but this isn't saying a lot. Although you can be a bully at times, you typically seek to charm and persuade people into letting you be the boss. You are happiest when you are dominating an equal and you are not necessarily going to be turned off when the equation is reversed. Often your efforts toward control will seem halfhearted or ineffectual. Yet the partner who thinks he or she can seriously threaten your primacy is in for a very rude awakening.

Case History

Truman Capote (American writer who scored his big success as a young man and afterward became a professional celebrity). Born September 30, 1924, in New Orleans, Louisiana (Clarke 1988).

Capote's mother was a beautiful, restless woman who sought to escape her small-town existence by marrying a wealthy man. After her first attempt failed (with Capote's father), she left her infant son to be raised by her relatives in Alabama and fled to New York City. Capote spent his early years pampered by a selection of eccentric aunts, but he never forgot the trauma of being deserted by his mother.

When Capote was ten his mother remarried. He went to live with her and her new husband in New York City. She was not pleased with his willful and effeminate behavior. Since her new husband had plenty of money, she opted to send her son to a military academy to toughen him up. Capote had already had his first homosexual experience with a teacher when he was in the sixth grade and he felt no shame about his sexual nature. But at the academy, the tiny, girlishly pretty youngster suffered many more such experiences, only under duress. Capote was quite miserable at this school, though it was there that he developed a taste for lovers who were overtly masculine.

Despite his mother's objections and his military academy experiences, Capote became quite proud of his distinctive look and manner. His charm was such that even people who found him repulsive at first glance could be won over as friends or even lovers. In high school he decided to seduce the most handsome boy in his class. When he succeeded, he bragged about it to all his friends.

When he was twenty-one and making his first inroads into the literary community, Capote began an affair with a tall, handsome scholar named Howard Doughty. Doughty happily introduced Capote to Newton Arvin, another homosexual academic with whom Doughty had long had a sexual relationship. Somewhat to Doughty's surprise, Capote fell immediately in love with the bald, schoolmarmish Arvin and quickly switched lovers.

Over the next three years Capote and Arvin saw each other as often as their careers allowed. Both had other casual contacts, but remained emotional true to each other. Arvin was a neurotic man in his forties, consumed by his work and intensely private. Capote brought wild parties, eccentric friends, and the fresh breeze of youth into his world. Both seemed happier for it. But among the liberties Capote felt were his to take was the reading of his lover's secret diary. There he learned that Arvin had had sex with a young man whom Capote considered his best friend. It is unclear whether Capote took this as an insult or as evidence that the older man was growing tired of him. In any case the affair ended soon afterward.

When he was twenty-four Capote began the most significant and prolonged relationship of his life. This was with a writer and ex-dancer named Jack Dunphy. Dunphy was everything Capote was not. He was masculine, pugnacious, quiet, and unsociable. He was also divorced and had only recently begun to experiment with homosexuality. Capote preferred lovers who looked and acted straight and was intrigued by Dunphy's moodiness and independence. The relationship lasted, in one form or another, for the rest of Capote's life.

Inevitably, considering the differences in their personalities, this love affair had its rough moments. Dunphy, who had some success as a writer, was never comfortable with the fact that it was Capote's talent and fame that paid their exorbitant bills. Capote had wormed his way into the hearts and onto the yachts of many of the world's wealthiest people. His high-powered social life did not always appeal to Dunphy. But what upset Dunphy most about his lover was Capote's increasing dependency on alcohol and pills.

When Capote was twenty-five he began to write a book about a murder in Kansas that would eventually be called *In Cold Blood*. The research and writing took him nearly five years, mostly because he couldn't finish the book until the death sentence had been carried out on the two killers. During this time Capote became personally involved with the two men. Their deaths left him deeply disturbed. After *In Cold Blood* was published, he confessed to a friend that he might well never write another word. For all practical purposes, he was speaking the truth.

For nearly twenty years Capote's relationship with Dunphy was relatively exclusive. Although he occasionally liked to experiment and had a weakness for sex with celebrities, Capote was infinitely more interested in sexual gossip than he was in sexual acts. When he was forty-five, at his initiative, the sexual side of his relationship with Dunphy stopped. At this point, Capote, who had thus far watched the sexual revolution from the sidelines, decided to make up for lost time.

A series of relatively undistinguished lovers followed Dunphy. All were in Dunphy's image—married men who looked "normal" and came from poor backgrounds. None of these lovers had Dunphy's independence or integrity. It was obvious to everyone (including Capote) that it was Capote's money that held them to him. Capote allowed himself to be used by these men to a point, but he could also be very controlling and spiteful. He considered hiring a "hit man" to take care of one lover who left him (he was eventually satisfied with having someone put sugar in the man's gas tank), and he "outed" another to his unsuspecting wife.

Throughout these affairs Capote maintained his close, platonic relationship with Dunphy. But when it came to Capote's most pressing problem—his drinking and pill-taking—Dunphy was strangely unsympathetic. A tough man himself, he expected Capote to fight his way through his troubles by returning to his writing. But Capote was never able to retrieve his elusive muse. He died of an overdose at the age of fifty-nine.

Another Example

Marcello Mastroianni (Italian actor). Born September 28, 1924 (Celebrity Birthday Guide).

If you have Mars in Aquarius with Venus in Virgo you are . . . the Friendly Liberator

You are an easygoing rebel who takes a more pragmatic approach to sex than most Mars in Aquarius Lovers. Your attitude toward the erotic is still extremely rational and nonjudgmental. You are likely to experiment and, once you find something that feels good, you won't hesitate to do it as much as you can. It is your senses and not your ideals that will guide your sexual choices and you will not seek controversy for its own sake. As far as you are concerned, using sex to make a point is a waste of sex.

You are one of the most agreeable Lovers of this type, always ready to compromise and anxious to please. This does not make you the easiest to love. The fact is, you are more apt than any Mars in Aquarius Lover to shut out those you love from your emotional life. Your self-sufficiency means that even people who want to be close to you find themselves loving you from afar. You are a warm, witty, and exceptionally sexy Lover, but you can't expect people to truly care about you if they can't really know you.

Case History

Ed Wood, Jr. (producer, director, and screenwriter who has the dubious honor of being known as the worst filmmaker of all time). Born October 10, 1924, in Poughkeepsie, New York (Grey 1992).

Wood's childhood appears to have been quite conventional, except for his mother dressing him as a girl when he was little. Wood later considered this anomaly as the source for his fondness for cross-dressing as an adult. He wore women's clothing for fun as a teenager. He continued to wear women's underwear under his uniform even after he joined the Marines during World War II.

Wood was very casual about this preference, particularly after he moved to Hollywood following the war and became involved in the movie business. All of his friends were aware of it. Most of them saw him in drag at one time or another. Throughout his life he dressed in woman's clothing both to relax and for inspiration when he was working. He and his girl friend dressed alike around the house when he was young. When he was older he would sit in his office cranking out pulp fiction dressed in a frilly nightie. He had a particular fetish for angora sweaters and even sent a photo of himself dressed in white angora home to his mom. His friends claimed Wood would pick up a girl just because she happened to be wearing an angora sweater and, after sex, try and talk her into leaving her sweater with him. In this way he accumulated a trunk full of angora.

Wood claimed he never had a homosexual experience. His friends concurred that he always appeared to be straight and never behaved in a feminine manner, even when he was dressed in women's clothing. Wood did enjoy decking himself out in full drag and going to transvestite bars. On such occasions he called himself "Shirley" and he did pass for a woman, at least until he became too drunk to maintain the pretense. Even though he may not have been gay, Wood counted homosexuals and transvestites among his many friends. He later wrote graphically and knowledgeably about homosexuality in his X-rated pulp novels.

When Wood was in his early twenties and trying to make a start as a producer, he began living with Deloris Fuller, an attractive actress and model who was somewhat older. Wood was full of grand schemes, but it was Fuller who paid the bills.

Fuller starred with Wood in his first motion picture, *Glen or Glenda*, in which the lifestyle of cross-dressing males is "scientifically" examined. In some ways Wood used this movie to "explain" himself to the world. But the director's primary goal was to use the unusual subject matter to attract an audience. At the end of the movie, Fuller's character demonstrates her acceptance of her boy friend's preference by taking off her angora sweater and handing it to him. In real life, however, Fuller was never comfortable with Wood's exotic tastes. She left him after the completion of his next movie, *Plan 9 from Outer Space*.

When he was thirty-two, Wood married Kathy O'Hara Everett. She proved more indulgent, both of his clothing fetish and his alcoholism. The marriage lasted until the end of Wood's life, but it was often unhappy. Wood was never able to establish himself as a legitimate filmmaker. Soon he and Kathy were reduced to living in cheap apartments, while he tried to support them by writing pornography. Meanwhile, Wood became more and more addicted to alcohol. His fights with his wife fit into a common pattern. They were loud and vulgar, sometimes violent, and often centered on money or his drinking. Wood often threatened to leave Kathy, but he never got far.

After multiple failures in the horror genre, Wood went on to make both soft- and hard-core sex films. Wood acted in small roles in these films, sometimes in drag. After this he wrote "adult only" novels. Though directed toward a "straight" male audience, Wood's sex films and books frequently explored unconventional sexual practices, reflecting both Wood's taste for the macabre and his experiences as a transvestite. He was an amazingly prolific writer (at least when he was sober enough to find the typewriter), but the trashy novels he cranked out made him little money. Neighborhood toughs often stole what money he did make. Slowly the inveterate optimism that had always been Wood's trademark wore away. He died from the effects of alcoholism and failure at the age of fifty-four.

If you have Mars in Aquarius with Venus in Libra you are ... the Loving Liberator

Yours is a delicate sexuality that thrives in an atmosphere of ideal beauty and withers quickly when exposed to the rough realities of life. You can be an extremely smooth, adventurous, and satisfying Lover, but only if you are allowed to take an oblique approach to the dirty deed. Sex that comes to you too directly, too much "in the raw," and not sugarcoated with your own brand of intellectual prettiness will almost certainly put you out of the mood.

You value relationships more than most Mars in Aquarius Lovers. This gives you a sense of loyalty that sometimes passes for passion. You need a partner—a special friend who shares your ideas and ideals, and who is as worthy of you as your are of him or her. Your expectations of what a relationship should be are pretty high and you are not shy about experimenting with different combinations. The partners who meet your standards will find you a charming and affectionate Lover. The ones who don't will probably consider you cold and unreachable.

Case History

Ignacy Paderewski (Polish pianist considered one of the most electrifying performers of his time). Born November 6, 1860, near Zhitomir (present-day Ukraine)(Zamoyski 1982).

Paderewski's father was an impoverished member of the Polish gentry. His mother died shortly after his birth, and his father was a political prisoner for a period during Ignacy's childhood. Nonetheless, Paderewski's musical skills were duly noted, and his family arranged for him to have music lessons despite their poverty.

When he was eleven the young prodigy was taken to Warsaw where he gained entrance into the Institute of Music. He obtained a degree there, even though some disapproved of his technique. He began giving lessons to support himself. When he was eighteen he came to the attention of a young patrician named Helene Gorska. Her interest in the pianist was not romantic at this point, but she became his advocate and gave him emotional and material support.

Meanwhile, Paderewski had fallen in love with one of his students, a woman four years his senior. Even though his financial prospects were dim, they married when he was twenty. Ten months later Paderewski's wife died giving birth to their first child.

After the death of his wife, Paderewski traveled to Berlin to continue his education. Gorska continued her support but now their arrangement was more intimate. Despite the fact that she was married, Paderewski and his sponsor became lovers. At the same time, another female benefactor, Helena Modrzejewska, entered Paderewski's life. The forty-four-year-old actress gave the pianist money to study in Vienna.

In Vienna the twenty-four-year-old Paderewski willingly submitted himself to an instructor noted for his high standards and rigorous, even brutal, teaching methods. Paderewski did well. He succeeded in adding both the elderly teacher and the teacher's pretty young wife to his growing list of admirers.

The turning point in Paderewski's career came when he was twenty-seven and gave his first concert in Paris. The audience went wild. When the pianist finished his performance, he was literally dragged back to the piano by his admirers to play encore after encore. From this point on Paderewski was known as the performer who drove his listeners, particularly young women, mad with delight.

Paderewski was a skillful pianist, but it was his appearance that was the key to his popular success. Tall and lean, he seemed born to wear a tuxedo. At the same time his massive shock of wild, reddish hair and narrow, Tartar eyes bespoke of a primitive, animalistic passion. Early in his career Paderewski was shy and uncomfortable when performing for the public. But he soon became a practiced showman who made the most of the worshipful admiration of his fans.

After his triumph in Paris, Paderewski reunited with Gorska after a separation of three years. Although there were many other wealthy, high-born women clamoring for his attention, his secret attachment to Gorska remained his primary sexual involvement. His loyalty to her is uncertain. He was, after all, Europe's newest "sex symbol." He turned heads in drawing rooms and at parties in every capital. Women pursued him when he left his concerts in the same way that fans pursue modern rock musicians. Yet there is no evidence that Paderewski took advantage of all this feminine adoration.

When he was twenty-nine Paderewski began an affair with Princess Rachel de Brancovan, a wealthy French woman who introduced the pianist to the most elite levels of European society. Paderewski was attracted to her physically, but it was the glamour and refinement of her world that held him. Never forgetting his impoverished background and never sure of his talents, Paderewski worked feverishly to make enough money to live a princely lifestyle.

For several years Paderewski managed to conduct his secret affairs with the Princess and Gorska simultaneously. Constantly on the move, he spent time with each woman when it was convenient for him. Neither suspected the existence of the other. However, by the time he was thirty-five, the affair with the princess had apparently run its course. Paderewski had become somewhat disenchanted with the lifestyle she symbolized and thought about settling down. Meanwhile, Gorska's husband finally became wise to the affair that had been raging between his wife and the pianist. An amicable annulment was arranged. When Paderewski was thirty-nine, he and Helena were married.

Helena and Paderewski enjoyed a close relationship after their marriage. She accompanied her husband on his tours and they were seldom apart. Paderewski never lost the Polish patriotism he had learned from his father. He devoted more of his attention to politics, and Helena continued to be supportive. In fact, her protective mothering of Paderewski and thoughtless interference with government business for the sake of her husband's comfort, which continued even after he was elected premier of Poland, caused many of his colleagues to dislike her. Paderewski bristled at any criticism of his wife and defended her against all comers.

When he was sixty Paderewski became disillusioned with politics and resigned as premier. He returned to his career as a pianist and remained a notable musician and public figure for the rest of his life. Helena's health deteriorated sharply and she died when he was seventy-four. Paderewski died at the age of eighty-one.

If you have Mars in Aquarius with Venus in Scorpio you are . . . the Sexy Liberator

Sex often brings out the worst in you. It's not that you're an inept Lover. On the contrary, you take sex so seriously and approach it with such intensity and imagination that you are always in demand. What holds you back, however, is your inability to compromise on issues of desire. Your ideas are fixed and your needs a bit overwhelming. You tend to be a difficult and demanding partner even when your intention is to be gentle and loving.

You are so hard to deal with because you are always pulled between an intellectual aware-ness of sex as a simple, unromantic transaction and your deep, emotional ties to the sexual experience. You are a Lover who is equally capable of white-hot passion and icy cruelty, or touching loyalty and callous wanderlust. You can overcome this inconsistency because, above all else, you are still an idealist who wants love to be true and sex to be meaningful. But it's not going to be easy.

Case History

Erskine Caldwell (American writer who wrote novels about the South filled with grotesque humor and biting social criticism). Born December 17, 1903, in White Oak, Georgia (Klevar 1993).

Caldwell's father was a surprisingly open-minded Presbyterian minister who possessed an overriding conviction that the purpose of Christianity was to ease human suffering. Caldwell's mother, however, was a stiffer, more dominating personality. She dressed her only child in feminine-looking outfits and let his curly hair grow long. Caldwell's father finally took his son to a barber and bought him boy's clothes when he was about six, but he could do nothing about his wife's determination to teach her son at home. Because of this, and the fact that the family often moved, Caldwell grew up with few playmates.

There is no definite information about Caldwell's earliest sexual experiences. Several inci-dents of adolescent sex play occur in his writings but it cannot be assumed that these accounts are autobiographical. What is evident is that, from an early age, Caldwell was an extremely curious youngster and that this curiosity most definitely extended to sex. He made an unsuccessful attempt to seduce his mother's mulatto maid when he was a teen and he quickly acquired girl friends when he was finally allowed to attend public school.

Even though he published some newspaper articles while he was still in high school, young Caldwell had no sense of vocation. He left high school without a diploma but still managed to enter a local Presbyterian college. After an undistinguished year there, he bolted for the big city and ended up in New Orleans. Here, at eighteen, he secretely shared a bed in a warehouse with a prostitute. This prostitute became his ideal of what a woman should be—naturally sexual and totally at his service.

Caldwell ended his Louisiana adventure jailed as a vagrant. After his parents fetched him back to Georgia, he managed to get a scholarship to the University of Virginia. He proved to be a lackluster student, still more interested in real-life experiences rather than books. At twenty-two, he met a brilliant graduate student named Helen Lannigan. Rejecting the incremental niceties that were so much a part of both his Southern background and hers, Caldwell began the relationship by asking Lannigan point-blank to go to bed with him. Fortunately, Lannigan was plainspoken enough to appreciate this directness. She took a rain check.

Caldwell and Lannigan married soon after they started having sex. Helen reported that she married Caldwell because he was good in bed and he was so passionate about his desire to be a writer. Interestingly enough, there is no evidence that Caldwell expressed this ambition to anyone previous to his involvement with Helen. Her presence in his life suddenly focused his diffuse experiences and talents toward the ultimate goal of writing fiction.

Caldwell's new wife proved to be the perfect partner for this risky venture. Better educated than Caldwell and in some ways much wiser, Helen was an invaluable editor and advisor. Over the next few years Caldwell struggled to learn his craft, always with Helen's optimistic support. They formed what seemed to be a perfect partnership. Not only was Helen his editor, but he also maintained an unwavering sexual fascination for her.

Despite his great emotional and intellectual dependence on Helen, Caldwell was frequently unfaithful to her. His infidelities began less than two years into the marriage and continued throughout. After sleeping with another woman, Caldwell would often confess his sin to his wife, usually in detail that was totally unwarranted by the situation. But before and during his affairs the writer was deliberately and almost compulsively deceptive. He lied to Helen without compunction, and begged for her love even when he actively pursued other women.

Caldwell attempted to be a controlling husband. He badgered Helen about her handling of the household accounts, the way she raised their three children, and even dictated what he felt was her perfect weight. It is unclear how effective Caldwell was in his domination. In many ways Helen remained an independent woman, despite her very conscious decision to overlook Caldwell's extramarital affairs.

After seven years of desperate struggle, Caldwell made it big as a writer. Two of his novels, *Tobacco Road* and *God's Little Acre*, did well. He was given a contract to write screenplays for Hollywood. Over the next few years, sales of his books, theater productions of his stories, and movie rights made him a rich man. Unfortunately, this success would contribute to the end of his marriage.

When he was thirty-two, Caldwell became involved in a project that resulted in the book, *You Have Seen Their Faces*, in which photographs of rural Southerners are accompanied by life narratives. Caldwell was to write the narrative, and a well-known magazine photographer named Margaret Bourke-White was to take the photos. At first Caldwell didn't like Bourke-White. She was a manipulative and brazen "Yankee" who understood nothing about the people they were interviewing, though she knew precisely how to take their pictures. Caldwell threatened to call it quits five days into the project, but Bourke-White found a way to change his mind.

Caldwell later claimed that Bourke-White "raped" him, but his proven susceptibility to women makes this unlikely. Caldwell was seduced by the opportunity he saw to join art and social purpose to sex. In a sense, it was a renewal of the creative and sexual partnership he had enjoyed with Helen during his struggle to become a writer. At first Helen treated this affair like his others and waited for Bourke-White to go away; however, she soon had to concede that the crafty photographer had stolen her husband.

When Caldwell was thirty-four he divorced Helen and married Bourke-White. He continued to travel with his new wife and work with her when he could, but her career was in high gear and her restlessness was even greater than his own. After four years of waiting for her to settle down, Caldwell began to feel neglected and he sought the solace of a younger lover. At thirty-nine he divorced Bourke-White and married June Johnson, a pretty and vivacious college senior.

Caldwell continued to write, but his work never again achieved the vigor and raw humanity of his early novels. Instead, he concentrated on business deals and investments. Meanwhile, he remained a difficult husband, as moody and emotionally closed with his latest wife as he had been with Helen and Bourke-White. She sought help in psychoanalysis and then began to sleep separately from Caldwell. She finally divorced him when he was fifty.

At fifty-three Caldwell married for a fourth time to a divorcée in her thirties named Virginia Moffet Fletcher. This woman seemed capable of giving the aging writer the kind of selfless adoration that he obviously needed. His marriage to her lasted until his death at eighty-three.

Other Examples

Willa Cather (American writer). *Nothing is really known about Cather's sex life, though it is widely believed she was a lesbian. She dressed like a boy until her first year in college and kept her hair cut short. She also took male parts in theater productions and signed her name "William." She never married, and most of her closest friendships were with other women. Some of these friendships were suspiciously intimate. But before her death, Cather gathered all of her correspondence from her various friends and destroyed it. Despite her unusual lifestyle and dynamic personality, Cather was a conservative person who held close to the Midwestern values that were part of her upbringing. Born December 7, 1873, in Back Creek Valley, Virginia (Woodress 1987).*

Winona Ryder (American actress). *Born October 29, 1971 (Celebrity Birthday Guide).*

If you have Mars in Aquarius with Venus in Sagittarius you are ... the Liberator on the Loose

You don't like to confront the question of sex too directly. It's more your style to veil your approach with idealism or high-toned intellectual purpose. At times you can be a rather timid Lover. You attempt to hold sex at an intellectual distance. Yet, you are equally capable of bursts of sexual daring and lightning raids into the erotic jungle. The truth of the matter is that it is not sex that you fear. It's commitment.

This is not to say that you have no desire to settle down. The ideal of a singular, transcendent love is quite appealing to you; however, your own sexual passions are so quickly spent and so easily diverted that it can seem an impossible goal. For you, this kind of special relationship is more likely to grow out of friendship rather than lust.

Case History

Rainer Maria Rilke (Rene Maria Rilke—Austrian-born poet whose work fuses lyric romanticism with existential angst). *Born December 4, 1875, shortly after midnight in Prague (present-day Czech Republic) (Freedman 1996; Prater 1986).*

Rilke's mother was a domineering woman who thought she was marrying for money. She was shocked to learn that, despite his impressive family background, her husband's earning power was meager. She never forgave her spouse for this misrepresentation. Much of her subsequent frustration and spite was taken out on their only child. She treated her son like a girl during his childhood. She dressed him in girl's clothes, gave him feminine playthings, and encouraged the imaginative youngster to develop a female alter ego. At the same time, she left him in the care of servants while she visited her boy friend after she and her husband had separated.

Rilke's father enrolled him in a military academy when the child was ten years old. The goal was for the youngster to develop into an officer in the Austrian army, which was a decent profession for a boy with no other prospects. Even though he was at first excited by the notion of military grandeur, Rilke proved to be a poor soldier. His weak body and feminine mannerisms earned him a great deal of taunting and some severe beatings from the other boys. Rilke accepted these trials with stoic, almost masochistic, silence. He embraced martyrdom with romantic zeal.

Despite his problems, Rilke graduated at fourteen to the next level of military academies. Here, at fifteen, he developed an infatuation with a fellow student. It is unlikely anything physical occurred between the boys, but Rilke's odd behavior was enough to alarm the men in charge. Rilke's friend was warned to keep his distance. Rilke abandoned his military career soon afterward.

At this point a rich uncle decided that Rilke could be trained for a position in his company. Rilke was sent to a business school. He almost immediately began an affair with a working-class girl. When his parents expressed outrage because of the relationship, Rilke and the girl fled. They hid together in a rented room until the police found them and they were forcibly parted.

Rilke quickly found a new love, a girl from his own class who was both clever and artistically inclined. The girl later recalled that she was not physically attracted to Rilke. His thick lips and large, heavy-lidded eyes seemed grotesque to her, an impression furthered by bad acne and severe halitosis. But she became his fiancée despite these drawbacks. For a time Rilke thought he had found his muse; however, two years later the perpetually restless Rilke had broken with the girl and moved to a new city.

Rilke's ambition to become a writer had been established during his early teens. Despite the career plans imposed upon him by his family, he never wavered from it. By the time he was twenty-one he had published a book of poetry and much prose work. Some of his writings caught the interest of a woman named Lou Andreas-Salome. Salome was also a writer. She found Rilke's advanced ideas and fervent idealism compatible with her own. Rilke agreed and began an ardent courtship. Soon they were lovers.

Salome was fourteen years older than Rilke. She was by all accounts an impressive thinker and a remarkably independent woman. She was married to a Russian academic but never had sex with her husband. Instead she cultivated affairs with young intellectuals who were picked for their ideas as much as for their bodies. She thrived in an atmosphere in which high culture and effete intellectualism mixed freely with love and sex. She became Rilke's teacher as well as his lover. Rilke apparently considered himself extremely fortunate on both counts.

After a while Salome's husband joined the couple, but this placed no great impediment on their affair. This situation changed two years into their relationship when the odd threesome moved to Russia. In St. Petersburg, where Salome and her husband were well known, precautions were necessary in order to protect the couple's reputation. Rilke was forced to live apart from his lover. Rilke reacted to this by beginning a flirtation with another woman. Meanwhile, the now forty-ish Salome recognized that her sexual hold on the twenty-something Rilke was not going to last forever. She decided the only thing to do was to give him his freedom.

After leaving Salome in Russia, Rilke settled for a time in an artists' colony in northern Germany. There he met two young artists—a sculptor named Clara Westhoff and a painter named Paula Becker. Rilke was drawn to both women. For a time he enjoyed a double-sided flirtation, which was all the sweeter because of the idealism and sense of purity that flourished in the artists' community. After a few blissful weeks he was forced to make a choice. Becker was already engaged, so he decided to propose to Westhoff. The two were married when he was twenty-five.

Marriage brought the real world crashing in on Rilke. He and Westhoff moved into a house in the country. They had notions of supporting themselves on their earnings as artists (plus a small stipend Rilke still received from his family), but their means fell far short of their ideals. The birth of a daughter did nothing to help the situation. After a year the couple abandoned their love nest, and Rilke abandoned his marriage.

Rilke received an offer to go to Paris to write about the great sculptor Auguste Rodin. Trying to survive there on almost no income, he experienced dire poverty for the first time. Living in the slums, he had daily contact with the underground world of crime and prostitution. He was at once repelled and attracted by the grotesque things he saw, and these experiences later enriched his poetry.

Rilke's own sex life at this point is a matter of mystery. Even when his wife joined him in Paris, they slept in separate beds. He was often away from her, moving restlessly from country to country. Sexual images permeate the poetry he wrote during this time, but his sex life may have been limited to lusting from a distance (for prostitutes on the streets of Paris, for young virgins strolling on an Italian beach, and for farm-bred maidens frolicking in the grass).

As he neared his thirties, Rilke developed a penchant for lightning-quick seduction and short, passionate love affairs. Often the women he seduced were wealthy and shared his love of art and beauty. They were part of a delicate web of friendship and support that had become essential to the poet's survival. Even though his poetry was widely read, his earnings were still meager. It was the generosity of the very rich that provided his livelihood.

Although the sexual part of these romances was typically short-lived, the relationships often continued for years through correspondence. Rilke's acute sensibilities and poetic charms were such that women were happy to support him even when he wasn't sleeping with them. Salome was one of these "sexless" lovers. She continued to be Rilke's advisor and confessor long after their affair had officially ended. In fact, Rilke told one of his few male friends that he believed the differences between the sexes would diminish in the future. He stated that men and women would relate more easily as "siblings and neighbors" than as sex partners. Rilke died at fifty-one.

Other Examples

Cecil Beaton (bisexual English photographer noted for his long and frustrating pursuit of Greta Garbo). Born January 14, 1904 (Celebrity Birthday Guide).

Thomas Merton (writer who gave up sex and life in the material world to become a monk). Born January 31, 1915 (Encyclopedia Britannica, Vol. 8).

Cary Grant (British-born film star). Born January 18, 1904 (Celebrity Birthday Guide).

If you have Mars in Aquarius with Venus in Capricorn you are ... the Down-to-Earth Liberator

Your sexuality is driven by your intellect. Your ability to enjoy erotic stimulation is always more dependent on what you think than what you feel. But there is also an earthiness about your sexual nature, an old-fashioned horniness that weighs you down and often makes your idealistic flights of erotic fancy seem silly and unsubstantial. You may pine after the airy notion of pure, loving companionship, but you also have to face the cold reality of lust.

This conflict between your strong physical need for sex and your essential idealism can make you a very confused Lover. But you are also a very practical Lover, and there is a clarity to your vision of sexual happiness that can't be denied. The only thing that can keep you from breaking through the confusion and finding the relationship you need is a lack of nerve, or perhaps a taste for misery.

Case History

Sinclair Lewis (American Nobel prize-winning author noted for his searing criticism of the American scene). Born February 7, 1885, in Sauk Centre, Minnesota (Schorer 1961).

Lewis was born in a small, Midwestern town very much like the ones he later depicted in his novels. He claimed he had an active, outdoorsy upbringing but, in fact, he was an awkward daydreamer who preferred reading to hunting and fishing. He was regarded as an oddity by his neighbors and had almost no friends. His father was a doctor and he encouraged his son toward higher learning. Lewis' mother died when he was six, but his strong-willed step-mother was particularly attentive to him.

Lewis was an unattractive youth who grew into a conspicuously ugly man. He was tall and thin with long, spindly legs and an unruly head of red hair. His face was long, freckled, and pitted by acne, and he was hollow-cheeked with bulging blue eyes. The girls in his hometown typically rejected him, though he crowed to his diary whenever he succeeded in getting a kiss or a hug from one of them. When he traveled east to attend Yale University, his countrified manner made him even more undesirable. He was reduced to long-distance infatuations and falling in love with fictional characters in the books he read.

Despite these rejections, Lewis never lost his intense interest in the opposite sex. There was hardly a time during his youth that he was not actively flirting or completely infatuated with some female. He usually approached these women with poetry and highbrow banter. At other times, when he was with his male friends, Lewis revealed a thoroughly earthy appreci-ation of coarse humor. He noted in the diary that he kept while at Yale that he and a friend had made arrangements to visit a prostitute. He failed to record the result of this meeting, or even if he went through with it.

When Lewis was twenty-one, he and his best friend left Yale to live in a commune set up by the muckraking author, Upton Sinclair. Lewis didn't last long in the commune, which required that its members contribute manual labor to the venture. But he was there long enough to fall in love with Upton Sinclair's secretary, Edith Summers. A few months later Lewis, who was attempting to support himself through free-lance writing, proposed to Summers. Unfortunately for him, his friend had also fallen for Summers. She accepted his proposal instead of the one from Lewis.

Lewis eventually returned to Yale and completed his degree. He dealt with his sexual frus-tration by masturbating and continued to pursue women who would not have him. At twenty-seven, he finally met a girl who would. Her name was Grace Hegger. Like him, she was making a living writing for magazines in New York City. They were married after a long engagement when Lewis was twenty-nine.

Grace was a pretty young woman who wrote articles about fashion and style. She quickly made major changes in her rangy husband's wardrobe and encouraged him to work at diminishing his strong Midwestern accent. Lewis willingly submitted to his wife's instruction on these matters. Early in the marriage his attachment to her was unquestioned and cement-ed by a collection of silly pet names and juvenile rituals.

Lewis began to sell fiction to prestigious magazines for large sums by the time he was thirty. Several unsuccessful novels followed until he was thirty-five and he published *Main Street*. *Main Street* was not only good, it was controversial. Lewis satirized the complacency and the conventionality of American small-town life. His pointed criticism struck a nerve in the reading public. Before long, Lewis was one of the most famous authors in America.

Success changed Lewis. The more famous he became, the more he drank. He had become a raging alcoholic by the time he reached the peak of his accomplishments. Always an outsider, he was never quite comfortable rubbing elbows with the rich and powerful or even his fellow famous authors, though he avidly sought their company. He was widely considered a "hick" and a bore. Even though he possessed the ability to charm, he could also be unforgivably rude and egocentric.

Grace took the worst of this change. The high-spirited playmate with whom she had shared baby talk and a love of writing had become an abusive drunk with an explosive temper and a compulsive need to seduce younger women. Lewis discovered that fame is the ultimate antidote for ugliness; he surrounded himself with young female admirers and took full advantage of their adulation. Grace broke with Lewis several times during the next few years, only to be lured back by his heartfelt contrition. When Lewis was forty-three, they divorced.

Lewis was a high-energy individual. Among some of his friends, his frenetic womanizing seemed only a product of this nervous energy. At one point, when some of his companions came to rescue Lewis from a drunken stupor, a bag of patent medicine was found in his possession. It was a drug designed to restore virility to undersexed males. Apparently, Lewis' confidence in his sexual prowess was as fragile as his confidence in his literary worth.

Immediately after divorcing Grace, Lewis proposed to the noted journalist Dorothy Thompson. Thompson was an accomplished woman in her thirties. She was charmed by Lewis and found him to be a good companion, full of good humor, and ready for adventure. These were traits she appreciated and, with some reservations (she was never able to convince herself he was good-looking), she accepted Lewis' proposal. For a time the two worked together. They shared a liberal political agenda and a burning interest in current affairs. But soon Lewis' drinking and infidelity began to destroy their blissful partnership. Thompson's career, which required her to be away from home much of the time, was probably the only reason the marriage survived ten years.

In the end, it was Lewis who begged Thompson for a divorce. He claimed that his violent alcoholic binges were a threat to her and their son. It is likely the writer already had a new wife in mind. A few years before, Lewis had turned his attention to the stage as a playwright and as an actor in summer stock. This activity brought him in contact with many young women. He had become particularly smitten with one of these impressionable youngsters—a lovely eighteen-year-old actress named Marcella Powers.

Lewis' relationship with Powers was the stuff of comedy. At fifty-five Lewis looked old for his years. He seemed a most unlikely boy friend despite his impressive energy and intellectual facility. For a year prior to his divorce Lewis had acted in plays with Powers and showed her off to his friends. After his divorce the relationship seemed to wind down. Lewis remained attached to Powers and at one point he hired her mother as a housekeeper just to remind him of the absent girl. Powers eventually became engaged to younger man. Lewis withdrew into crusty bachelorhood. He died at the age of sixty-five.

Another Example

John Belushi (Saturday Night Live comic). Born January 24, 1949 (Celebrity Birthday Guide).

If you have Mars in Aquarius with Venus in Aquarius you are . . . the Unlimited Liberator

You are the coolest of the cool—a detached and unemotional Lover for whom sex is seldom a problem. Your approach to physical pleasure is uncomplicated and thoroughly rational. Your adventurous spirit and disregard for convention make you a thrilling, if somewhat clinical, partner. Physical sex has little meaning to you unless it somehow also engages your mind. No matter how numerous and varied your sexual experiences, true passion will always remain a function of your intellect.

Because of your intellectual approach to love and sex, loyalty can become a touchy issue. Your romantic interests tend to change as you mentally grow and adapt. This can make you seem unreliable and faithless. The truth is that you would like nothing better than to find a partner with whom you can establish an intellectual link that is so solid and fundamental that it lasts forever. If you are fortunate enough to find a connection like this, your loyalty will astound all who doubted you.

Case History

Nancy Cunard (English poet, publisher, and social activist most remembered for her flamboyant lifestyle). Born March 10, 1896, in Leichestershire, England (Chrisholm 1979).

Cunard's father was an English lord and her mother an American heiress. She was assured great wealth and social position as their only child, but she received little in the way of personal attention from her parents. Both felt that the chores of childrearing were best left to the lower classes. Cunard was looked after by servants while her parents devoted themselves to work and pleasure.

Cunard's mother was regarded as one of the most notable and influential hostesses of her time. Endowed with good taste and a passionate interest in the arts, she made her home a gathering place for the best and brightest of European culture. Some of the writers and artists she entertained became her lovers, but she was always very discreet. Lady Cunard continued to consider herself a happily married woman, even when she moved out of her home and took up residence with one of her lovers.

Cunard was fifteen when this move occurred. She deeply resented it. She was already showing the independence of mind that would later be her trademark. She developed into a tall, slender lady with striking beauty and a unique style that readily attracted the attention of men. World War I interrupted her official entrance into society. She saw many of the young men who had admired her go off to fight. One of them, Sydney Fairbairn, was wounded and brought back to England. When Cunard was twenty she married him.

Why Cunard entered into this marriage is something of a mystery. She said later it was only to escape the control of her mother, but she couldn't have picked a less likely route of escape. While she was extremely liberal in her beliefs and writing poetry, Fairbairn was a proud Philistine. It is possible she was caught up in the spirit of the war effort and the lure of a hero in uniform. In any case, by the time Fairbairn returned to active service a few months after the wedding, Cunard considered her marriage over.

When she was twenty-two Cunard had an affair with Peter Broughton Adderley. He was another upper-class soldier, but shared her idealism and sensitivity. Some felt that this was her only true love affair. It ended after a few months when Adderley was killed in battle.

When the war was over, Cunard separated from her husband and moved to Paris. There she met and had an affair with an Armenian novelist who called himself Michael Arlen. Arlen used Cunard as the model for a character in one of his novels. He depicted her as a sexually adventurous, but dangerously cold woman who used men as playthings and laughed at their protestations of eternal love. The novel became wildly popular. It established Cunard as the prime example of the joys and evils of the "flaming youth," as Britain's postwar generation was called.

During her relationship with Arlen, Cunard had surgery for a gynecological complaint (possibly an abortion). The resulting complications made it necessary for her doctors to perform a hysterectomy. What psychological affect this misfortune had on Cunard is unclear, but it did free her from the possibility of an accidental pregnancy.

After her affair with Arlen ended, Cunard had a brief fling with another novelist, Aldous Huxley. Huxley was a member of her own class and had long been an acquaintance. She refused to take him seriously as a lover, even when he followed her from nightclub to nightclub and paced the street beneath her bedroom window all night long. She found Huxley's adoration and jealousy rather pathetic. She was quite glad when the writer's wife finally jerked him back into line. Huxley used Cunard as a model in three different novels he wrote during the 1920s, always portraying her as a cold-hearted, free-loving vamp.

Cunard showed little concern about how these and other writers depicted her in their books. She was too busy living the life about which they could only write. Throughout her adulthood (or at least after the failure of her marriage), Cunard had sex with any man who chanced to interest her. If this behavior disturbed the man who considered himself her boy friend at the moment, that was his problem. Even though she could be a warm and charming woman, she never formed any close attachments to her bedmates. It many cases, her independence only inspired the men to be more demonstrative in their attempts to win her heart. At least one of her lovers attempted suicide. But no act of love or violence was capable of piercing Cunard's essential aloofness.

Even though she was very interested in sex, several of her lovers testified to the fact that Cunard was hardly a sensualist. She had great difficulty achieving orgasms, either because of her hysterectomy or for other reasons and she considered oral sex degrading. As experimental as she could be with regard to her sex partners, she apparently was much less daring when it came to sex play. She used sex as a means to shock people and avoid boredom, but she never found much depth in the experience itself.

Cunard's most enduring relationships were always those in which sex was not a great concern. One of her closest friends was the Irish writer, George Moore, who had once been her mother's lover. Moore asked to see Cunard naked, but otherwise served as an avuncular advisor and companion. Another close friend was Norman Douglas, who was totally devoted to young boys by the time he met Cunard. Cunard was extremely loyal to her friends. These relationships tended to be as sustained as her sexual contacts were fleeting.

Despite her sexual coldness, Cunard was noted for her flights of passion and terrible temper. She was passionate about her poetry and about literature in general. When she was thirty-two she purchased a printing press. She published small editions of books by unknown authors she admired. She was also deeply interested in music, and expressed a particular taste for American jazz while still in her teens.

It was her enjoyment of this kind of music that led Cunard to what was to become her most notorious love affair. When she was thirty-two Cunard began patronizing a band that featured an African-American piano player named Henry Crowder. Crowder was older than Cunard, and a relatively conservative man. He was surprised when she picked him, and not one of his younger and more virile compatriots, to invite to her apartment. Despite his reservations, the stylish Cunard and her jangling armful of African bracelets soon had Crowder entranced.

Cunard's affair with Crowder lasted over six years, but she was never faithful to him. She slept with many other men during that period. The significance of her relationship with Crowder was that it introduced Cunard to a new cause. Her involvement with a black American sensitized her to racial discrimination. She began a vociferous campaign to protest and combat the oppression of blacks. Her efforts culminated in the publication of an anthology of black culture and history called *Negro*.

Cunard showed remarkable courage in her fight for civil rights for American blacks. She received death threats from the Ku Klux Klan and risked losing the financial support of her mother. But it is also evident that she never really comprehended how truly deadly racial hate could be. Crowder often felt exposed to physical danger because of his white girl friend's determination to do battle with the forces of oppression. Cunard's apparent disregard for his safety and his misgivings about being turned into one of her causes finally put an end to the relationship.

Other men and other causes followed. Always a fervent, if somewhat naive Communist, Cunard supported the leftists during the Spanish Civil War and became interested in Latin culture and literature. But her great run was nearing its end. World War II destroyed the Europe in which she had romped during the 1920s and 1930s. The generation that followed saw her as an aging, drunken throwback. When she was sixty Cunard was placed in an institution after she suffered a mental collapse. She died six days after her sixty-ninth birthday.

Another Example

Robert Wagner (American TV and film star). Born February 10, 1930 (Celebrity Birthday Guide).

If you have Mars in Aquarius with Venus in Pisces you are . . . the Lyrical Liberator

You are the most subjective Mars in Aquarius Lover. You get emotionally involved with your ideals and fall in love with abstractions. You are apt to be more shy than most Lovers of this type and are not so ready to leap into the unknown. But when you do decide to take the plunge and get radical about sex, you do so with an emotional intensity and an all-out openness that can be absolutely breathtaking.

The problem with your sexuality is that you're not always what you appear to be. People respond to your emotional vulnerability and sweet sexual allure. They automatically assume you are ready to accept them into your gentle and sensual fantasy of love, but yours is a fantasy without forgiveness. You measure every prospective partner against the clinically precise standards of excellence that rules both your mind and heart. Only those who meet these specifications get the privilege of stepping inside your sexual dreamland.

Case History

Hugh Hefner (American magazine publisher whose magazine and lifestyle became part of the sexual revolution). Born April 9, 1926, in Chicago, Illinois (Brady 1974; Chidley 1994; Talese 1980).

Hefner's parents were farm-bred Midwesterners who went to the big city in search of the American dream. They found it and worked hard during the Depression to hold on to it. While his father devoted long hours to his job, it was Hefner's staunchly religious mother who dominated his upbringing. He developed into an inhibited teenager with a genius IQ.

Despite her strong religious convictions, Mrs. Hefner had a relatively open attitude toward sex education. She brought home books on human sexuality for her young sons to read and she didn't flinch when her eldest boy showed a marked interest in racy magazines like *Esquire*. Her apparently reasonable attitude only caused Hefner to rebel more openly against what he saw as the repression and hypocrisy of the values of her generation. By the time he entered college, Hefner was not only extremely well-read on the subject of sex, but also held some fairly unconventional opinions for the time.

When Hefner was eighteen he met a bright woman in his high school class. They embarked on a very conventional courtship, with a lot of handholding but no sexual intercourse. Despite all his reading on the subject, Hefner had little personal knowledge of sex. He considered his new girl friend's reserve to be only proper. After he returned from a two-year stint in the army, Hefner found he was no longer able to deny his physical needs. When they were twenty-two, Hefner begged his young love to perform fellatio on him while they were riding in a bus late at night. To his surprise and everlasting delight, she complied.

Over the next few months, Hefner discovered that his pure, fresh-faced girl friend could also be a wanton woman. They continued to experiment with oral sex, both fellatio and cunnilingus, and Hefner persuaded her to pose in the nude while he photographed her. She seemed to enjoy sex and breaking the rules of propriety as much as Hefner did. She proved this when she had an affair with another man. She confessed this to Hefner, expecting him to dump her. Hefner remained true to his ideals and overlooked her infidelity. They were married when Hefner was twenty-three.

Hefner's determination to publish his own magazine began early in life. He started humor magazines in high school, in the army, and in college—usually featuring his own cartoons.

At first he had little luck at getting a job in publications. This changed after he published a moderately successful book of cartoons when he was twenty-four. After this, he landed a job with *Esquire*, a magazine he had admired since his childhood. Unfortunately, it proved far less glamorous than Hefner expected. When he was twenty-five he left *Esquire* for another job and began preparing to produce his own magazine for men.

His wife quietly supported Hefner through his incessant job-hopping and his early efforts to put together the magazine that would become *Playboy*; however, marriage had apparently taken much of the excitement out of their sex life. No amount of experimentation seemed capable of renewing it. Hefner already had a mistress—a nurse with whom he made his first attempt at filming himself having sex.

Hefner was twenty-seven when the first issue of *Playboy* was published. The success of the venture was obvious by the time the second issue was produced. What was also obvious, at least to his wife, was that Hefner had a new bride. When the operation moved out of their kitchen and into an office, Hefner moved with it. From this point on, he ate, drank, and slept with his dream, rarely seeing either his wife or his daughter. The marriage lasted several more years, and even produced one more child, but it finally ended in a divorce.

It was probably little comfort to Hefner's wife that through the magazine her husband was reliving the astounding discovery he had made with her—that the all-American "girl next door" could also be sexual. *Playboy* was not the first magazine to publish nude pictures of women. But by presenting his models as women from the reader's own world, and not as jaded prostitutes or eccentric nudists, Hefner added a new dynamic to the voyeuristic experience. In concert with these images, Hefner offered a rational and well-researched defense of hedonism. It was a philosophy that taught the reader that he too could aspire to both the women and the lifestyle described in the magazine.

Hefner did not begin as America's primary hedonist. Early in the life of the magazine he worked hard. Sex, like food and sleep, was a secondary issue. He had affairs with women on his staff, and with some of his "playmates," but remained a rumpled and compulsive workaholic. Then, as his prosperity grew, Hefner began to act and dress like the playboy he had created in his magazine. His sex life evolved accordingly. His high-tech bedroom and huge, round bed became legendary, as did the orgies he conducted there. At these orgies he was rubbed with oil and masturbated by a half-dozen beautiful women, while a closed-circuit TV camera recorded it all.

Most of the hundreds of women Hefner slept with during this period were simply representations of his ideal, and the ideal expressed by his magazine. A few achieved individuality. He became particularly enamored with a young woman on his staff who was the first real "amateur" to pose for the "centerfold." Much later, when he was in his forties, Hefner began a much-publicized relationship with a young actress name Barbara Benton and, at the same time, he courted a buxom Texan named Karen Christy.

Hefner's affairs with Benton and Christy, and his quixotic attempt to hold on to both relationships, revealed the publisher's hidden vulnerability. He saw Benton in California while Christy was hidden away in his Chicago mansion. Christy fled when she found it impossible to endure Hefner's unfaithfulness. Hefner roamed the streets in his limousine searching for her. His tearful apologies finally lured Christy back to the round bed, but not for long. In the end, both Benton and Christy abandoned Hefner.

Relationships with other playmates followed, as Hefner seemed intent on settling into a more permanent relationship. Then Hefner suffered a stroke when he was fifty-nine. After he recovered he began a relationship with yet another centerfold, Kimberley Conrad. To the amazement of many, they were married when he was sixty-three.

The marriage quickly produced two children. The aging Hefner seemed to be settling into a blissful domesticity with tricycles in the driveway and a whole new attitude toward monogamy, but the joys of bachelorhood were still calling him and after ten years he bolted from his marriage to take his place as the aging high priest of hedonism. Meanwhile, the management of his various businesses passed to his eldest child, Christie Hefner, although Hefner still maintains control of the magazine and the images of women that appear there.

Another Example

Alice Neel (American painter noted for her expressive portraits). Neel was married to a Cuban aristocrat when she was twenty-five. The marriage ended when she was thirty and her husband took their two children back to Havana. Neel was hospitalized when she suffered a nervous breakdown. After this she attempted suicide and was kept in restraints until she recovered. She moved to Greenwich Village where she immersed herself in left-wing politics and art. Her career as a painter remained stagnant, but her love life was enormously active. She had many love affairs: some of them quite pleasant, others quite dangerous. One of her lovers, a jealous sailor, slashed several of her paintings with a knife. She bore two sons to different lovers and raised them on her own in what she called a "normal" household. As she entered what for many people would be considered old age, Neel found herself suddenly a famous painter, sought after by the wealthy for portraits. The most unique feature of her portrait work was the ability she had as a plump, charming grandmother to convince her often staid, middle-class sitters to undress. Her greatest joy was painting ordinary people in the nude. Born January 28, 1900 (Nemser 1975).

Chapter 12

Mars in Pisces
The Love Addict

General Characteristics

For the Mars in Pisces Lover, to love and be loved is a compulsion—an all-consuming drive that affects every part of their lives. It is their demon, their madness, and the monkey that won't ever leave their backs even when they are old and gray. Obviously, this compulsion to love makes these people very vulnerable. But their vulnerability—this acute sensitivity to feelings and emotional situations—just becomes one more aspect of their sexual attractiveness. With Mars in Pisces we confront the essence of sex appeal, an endlessly open heart-of-hearts that no amount of desire can completely fill.

If you think that this passive approach to sex puts these Lovers at a disadvantage, think again. Even though sometimes they appear to be helpless victims of love, Mars in Pisces Lovers typically dominate relationships simply through the power of their emotions. A relationship with a Mars in Pisces Lover can seem like a headlong plunge into an emotional and sexual abyss. No end in sight, but who cares? They demand a lot from the people who love them and guided by an almost mystical sensitivity to the feelings of other people, they have little trouble finding partners who are up to the challenge.

The real strength of this type, however, is not in their ability to lure the rest of us into mad affairs. It is in their ability to survive them. Their emotional flexibility and their pliant, ever optimistic approach to sex allow Mars in Pisces Lovers to walk away from emotional crack-ups that would leave more sturdy souls in a straitjacket. In fact, these Lovers often thrive in circumstances of emotional upheaval. They typically do all they can to keep their romantic situations fluid.

Deception and subterfuge often play large roles in the love lives of Mars in Pisces Lovers. Their needs and desires are so diffuse and prone to change with circumstance that even they are often surprised at the directions they take. Emotional security means a great deal to them, but they also thrive in a state of emotional flux. They sometimes appear weak and vulnerable, yet they are capable of the most amazing acts of emotional will. They can be very loyal, but they can also be infuriatingly susceptible to romantic diversions. No wonder it's so hard to get a straight story from these sexy and slightly delirious Lovers. They rarely have a clear idea of what it is they want.

The sexual response of Mars in Pisces Lovers is always keyed to their emotional state. In some instances, physical sex can mean very little to them despite their essentially sensuous natures. At other times, it can mean everything. Promiscuity is not always a problem here, but there is probably no other Mars type that is so prone to use sex as an emotional crutch. Their capacity for finding a replacement for emotional security in the momentary comfort and release of meaningless sex is probably the most dangerous and certainly the most heart-breaking quality of this type. It not only disrupts their lives, but also the lives of the people who love them. Yet they are so lovable, desirable, and romantic that it's always easy to forgive even the most misguided of Mars in Pisces Lovers. Perhaps that is the most problematic quality of this type. It's just too easy to forgive them.

If you have Mars in Pisces with Venus in Aries you are . . . the Emphatic Love Addict

You are a pushy Mars in Pisces Lover who believes that the best emotional defense is to always be on the offense. You hide your vulnerability behind a facade of daring and sexual bluster. You compensate for your own tendency to fall in love too quickly and too often by making everyone fall in love with you first. This aggressive stance makes you one of the most visible and dynamic Lovers of this type, but it also leaves you open to emotional injury.

Since it is you who takes the initiative in relationships, it is very likely that you will find the warmth and emotional support you so desperately need. It's making it last that's the problem.

What you lack is patience. When hard times hit a relationship, or you feel less than totally adored, you immediately begin looking for an exit. It always seems easier to make a new start than to ride out an emotional storm. Until you learn to deal with this restlessness (some might call it cowardice), you will never find the secure bond you desire.

Case History

Marilyn Monroe (Norma Jean Mortensen—perhaps the most enduring and enigmatic sex symbol of the twentieth century). Born June 1, 1926, in Los Angeles, California (Spoto 1993).

Monroe's father was unknown to her. Her mother, who was eventually diagnosed as schizophrenic, was unable to provide a secure home. During her childhood Monroe was shuttled between relatives, orphanages, and various foster homes. In the process, older males twice subjected her to sexual advances. Eventually, her mother's best friend, an assertive and utterly star-struck woman, took charge of the neglected child. It was she who first encouraged Monroe to become a movie star.

As an adolescent Monroe quickly became aware of her physical attributes and the impact they had on men. But at this point what Monroe wanted more than anything was a stable home. When she was sixteen and a young man with a good job and five years her senior asked her to marry him, she leaped at the chance.

To some extent Jim Dougherty's marriage to Monroe was an act of charity. Her foster mother was leaving town and it looked like Norma Jean would have to be put back into an orphanage. It is also likely that the strong, confident Dougherty was enticed by Monroe's youth and apparent passivity. He probably assumed he would dominate the marriage and mold his bride into the perfect housewife and bedmate. This would have been a completely erroneous assumption.

The marriage was beset by problems from the very beginning. The young Monroe proved to be as domestically inept as she was emotionally insecure and flighty. Doughterty claimed he had a great time sexually and that his teenage bride was insatiable. Monroe's account of the marriage stressed her ignorance about sex, and her husband's inability to satisfy her. It's possible, of course, that with time the young couple would have overcome these problems; however, World War II arrived before this could be achieved. Doughterty went off to sea as a merchant marine, while Monroe worked in a factory where she had her first taste of independence.

By the time she was eighteen Monroe had been transformed from a shy, schoolgirl bride to an ambitious young model. In the process she had discovered the one lover who would never desert her: the camera. Accounts of Monroe's performances in bed vary greatly. It appears that often she was a passive, lackluster sex partner, more concerned with her own emotional pain than the pleasure of the moment. But Monroe became the confident aggressor once she was in front of a camera. She projected a soft, yet vibrant, sensuality that made men stop in their tracks. Photographers were quick to notice this natural sex appeal. Her future as a model was assured.

Monroe had greater ambitions. At twenty she signed a one-year contract with Twentieth Century Fox. From the very beginning Monroe understood that her overriding desire to succeed in motion pictures meant that she had to make herself sexually available to the right people. Although she didn't exclusively sleep with men who could help her career, most of her sexual attachments were in some way related to her ambition, or at least to her need to survive until that ambition could be realized. She made the mistake of falling in love with one of her early sponsors, who was handsome and marriageable. After this affair ended badly, Monroe concentrated on men who were much older, and either physically weak or ugly, so as to avoid such emotional entanglements. Since she was always more hungry for a father figure than she was for a lover, these arrangements were generally quite rewarding for her. Not only did they give her the film roles and the attention she needed, but they also gave her a provisional sense of security.

Monroe was on the way to becoming a major star by the time she reached her mid-twenties. At this point a recently retired baseball hero named Joe DiMaggio began to court her. DiMaggio was everything that Monroe had denied herself during her struggle for recognition. He was young, athletic, and eminently marriageable. He was the epitome of the strong, silent American male. She saw the promise of sexual happiness and emotional security in his calm, confident masculinity.

There was a problem, however. DiMaggio was old-fashioned and didn't approve of working wives, particularly when that work included being ogled by other men. As much as the athlete's strength and values attracted Monroe, she was still determined to hang on to the career for which she had labored so long. While they were dating, the couple was able to gloss over these differences, but it became impossible for either of them to ignore the problems once they were married. They were separated after only a few months, though DiMaggio may have pined for Monroe for the rest of his life.

Monroe had always been attracted to intellectuals (she had fantasies about marrying Einstein). Despite her poor education, she had an eclectic fascination for books and ideas. Even before she was properly divorced from DiMaggio, Monroe revealed to a friend that she had her eye on Arthur Miller, a highly respected writer of socially conscious plays. While studying acting in New York City after her break with DiMaggio, Monroe renewed her acquaintance with Miller. When she was thirty, they were married.

At first Monroe was content with the aloof and controlling playwright. Her apparent happiness was, in reality, fortified by barbiturates. She suffered two miscarriages during her marriage to Miller. Her withdrawal from the Hollywood treadmill only left her with too much time to stand in front of the mirror and contemplate her aging body. As her emotional instability became apparent, Miller's attitude toward his actress wife became distantly paternal. He was supposed to be working on a screenplay in which he and Monroe hoped to join their creative forces, but the project was frequently postponed. By the time it was ready to begin production as *The Misfits*, a handsome French singer named Yves Montand had already distracted Monroe.

In the end, Monroe's affair with Montand accomplished nothing more than to bring her marriage to Miller to a sad, whimpering conclusion. Without a strong male presence, the thirty-five-year-old sex symbol deteriorated at an alarming rate. She became tragically dependent upon the doctor who was her primary source of barbiturates. Her ability to work as an actress was seriously in doubt. She attempted one last fling with the man who might well have represented to her the ultimate father figure: the president of the United States, John F. Kennedy. Biographers differ as to the number of times she and Kennedy had sex (author Donald Spoto maintains their schedules would have only allowed for one possible assignation), but this probably made little difference to Monroe. Her fascination with Kennedy was a central feature of the last months of her life. Some feel it was at least a contributing cause of her death at the age of thirty-six.

Other Examples

Elizabeth Taylor *(film star). Born February 27, 1932 (Celebrity Birthday Guide).*

Steve McQueen *(film star). Born March 24, 1930 (Celebrity Birthday Guide).*

Michelangelo *(Michelangelo Buonarroti—Italian Renaissance painter and sculptor). Born March 6, 1475 (Encyclopedia Britannica, Vol. 8).*

If you have Mars in Pisces with Venus in Taurus you are . . . the Cautious Love Addict

You are one of the luckier Mars in Pisces Lovers. Not only do you possess a doubly sensuous nature, capable of making sex both physically pleasurable and emotionally fulfilling, but you are also a sexual conservative. This conservatism gives you the ability to protect your feelings while still having a good time. It makes you a careful Lover—one who reveals the true depth of his or her sensuality to only a chosen few and only in an atmosphere of trust and control.

The problems in your sexual nature are rooted less from your emotional vulnerability than from your inherent selfishness. Your sexual impulses are so immediate, so intense, and so deeply rooted in your psyche that they tend to absorb you completely. Even though you are very sensitive to the emotional needs of others, it is nearly impossible for you to think of anyone but yourself when your own sexuality is engaged. At your worst, this sensuous singularity can make you appear almost infantile. But as with all Mars in Pisces Lovers, it's all too easy to forgive you for even the most childish of behavior.

Case History

Spencer Tracy (American actor noted for his skill and range as a thespian, and for his self-destructive alcoholism). Born April 5, 1900, in Milwaukee, Wisconsin (Davidson 1987; Swindell 1969).

Tracy's father was a successful Irish businessman and his mother was a Protestant from an old New England family. Tracy mingled well with the toughs from the local Irish ghetto despite his thoroughly middle-class beginnings. He developed into a pugnacious but well-liked youngster whose attention to his schoolwork was spotty. Early on he talked of several careers: business, the navy, medicine, and even the priesthood. It wasn't until he reached college at the age of twenty-one that Tracy discovered his natural ability as an actor.

Accounts of Tracy's early sexual development are sparse and contradictory. Some recalled that he was charming when it came to the opposite sex, while others said that he was painfully shy and preferred the company of his male friends. Tracy himself rarely talked about his youth or early sex life. It's likely that his erotic experiences before marriage were not extensive.

At twenty-two Tracy went to New York City where he hoped to find work as an actor, while he continued his education at the American Academy of Dramatic Arts. Although many noted his talent, success did not come easily. After a year of struggle he found a job as a bit player with an out-of-town production. There he instantly fell in love with the leading lady, a young actress named Louise Treadwell. Tracy advanced quickly in the company and was soon playing opposite her. They were married when he was twenty-three.

Tracy had previously worked hard at acting in order to impress his family. Now he worked even harder to support his wife and the son that arrived soon after the marriage. His devotion to his work was intensified by the fact that the boy was born deaf. Louise withdrew from acting in order to devote all her time to her child. Tracy's only recourse was his work and drinking.

It is unclear exactly when Tracy's drinking left the bounds of male camaraderie and became an addiction, but the discovery that his son was deaf was an important turning point. Many observers felt Tracy drank out of a sense of guilt over his child's condition, as if it were divine retribution for some unspecified sin he had committed. It is also possible that, as Louise devoted herself wholeheartedly to educating their handicapped son, Tracy felt neglected and unloved. The guilt he expressed could well have been caused by the painful recognition that he was jealous of his own child.

As Tracy's alcoholism increased, so did his need for extramarital sex. One friend recalled that during this period Tracy approached him for help. The actor was too shy to approach prostitutes in bars. His friend took him to a high-class bordello. After this, whoring became an integral part of Tracy's alcoholic binges. At one point, he was banned from a house of prostitution because he became violent with one of the women. Louise was apparently aware that her husband was becoming restless. At the time Tracy had a part in a long-running light comedy in New York City. Louise pushed him to leave this role to play more serious parts out of town. To some extent her motive was to steer him toward drama, which was always Tracy's strength, but she may have also wanted to separate her weak-willed husband from the temptations of the big city.

This turned out to be a shrewd career move. It was in such a dramatic role, at the age of thirty, that Tracy was spotted on Broadway by scouts from Hollywood. With a degree of reluctance, Tracy accepted their offer to make a prison movie called *Up the River*. Once he arrived in the film capital, the accomplished theater actor never looked back. He had found his medium.

The anything-goes atmosphere of Hollywood did little to curb Tracy's self-destructive habits. He became notorious for his binge drinking and for taking liberties with pretty girls on the sets of his movies. In addition to entertaining actresses and extras in his dressing room, Tracy continued to patronize prostitutes. As a result, he was once arrested for being drunk and disorderly near one of the more noted houses of ill-fame in Hollywood.

When Tracy was thirty-three he became involved in a much different kind of love affair with film star Loretta Young. Their relationship was steamy enough to get into the gossip columns. Louise and Tracy separated for a time, but after a year Tracy returned to his wife and children. From this point on Tracy was very careful to keep his weaknesses for booze and women out of the public eye.

He was helped in these efforts by the fact that his wife was widely regarded in Hollywood as something of a saint. Her efforts to give her own son a better life had evolved into a highly visible advocacy for deaf children in general. Eventually, she started a clinic for the education of deaf children. Even the most hardened of Hollywood's gossipmongers were reluctant to embarrass such a paragon. Tracy himself, despite his Irish temper and history of destroying property and slugging stagehands, was highly regarded both by his fellow actors and the press. Even though Tracy's drinking and womanizing continued, he remained free from scandal.

When Tracy was forty he began a relationship with a young actress named Katharine Hepburn. Hepburn was a strong-willed and sophisticated woman who, like Tracy, was often singled out both because of her talent and her eccentricity. At first a love affair between these two seemed highly unlikely. Hepburn was a liberal feminist and the conservative Tracy disapproved of both her opinions and the trousers she typically wore, but despite all appearances, Katharine Hepburn was a woman who needed a man she could take care of and Tracy was a man badly in need of care.

In order to facilitate their secret love affair, Tracy and Hepburn arranged to work together on several pictures. Oddly enough, this made the natural chemistry that existed between them obvious to millions and caused them to be forever paired in the minds of the moviegoing public, even while they struggled to conceal their real-life liaison. As the years went by, Tracy's emotional dependence on Hepburn increased. When work forced her to be away from him, he dropped out of sight and surrendered totally to his addiction to alcohol. Despite the fact that it was Hepburn who rescued him from these binges and put him back to work, Tracy refused to entertain the notion of divorcing Louise and marrying Hepburn. Tracy still considered himself a family man and a good Catholic.

The relationship between Tracy and Hepburn continued for twenty-seven years. It was hardly a secret to Hollywood insiders but, even after all that time, it was not discussed. After several aborted retirements, Tracy was persuaded to make one last film with Hepburn called *Guess Who's Coming to Dinner*. He died soon afterward at the age of sixty-seven.

Other Examples

Violet Trefusis (*English heiress noted for her tempestuous affair with Vita Sackville-West*). *Born June 6, 1894 (Jullian 1976).*

Anton LaVey (*American showman and cultist who became the world's most visible Satanist*). *Born April 11, 1930 (Lyons 1988).*

If you have Mars in Pisces with Venus in Gemini you are . . . the Artful Love Addict

You are a sweetly duplicitous Mars in Pisces Lover, who uses a charming smile and a rational explanation to conceal seething emotions and desperate sexual needs. Often you are trying to escape the extreme feelings that sweep through your sexual nature, or at least to avoid looking at them too closely. For this reason you may appear calm and aloof with regard to sex when, in fact, you're just befuddled and fearful of what the next wave of sexual madness might bring you.

You are even more reluctant than most Mars in Pisces Lovers to commit yourself to relationships. Instead of using your keen sensitivity to guide you to the perfect partner, you often use it to manipulate the feelings of others and dance around the issue of love. Of course, sooner or later your need for emotional security forces you to stop playing games and find a serious relationship. Once this happens and your secret is out, you will find that being a hopeless love addict is really not so bad.

Case History

Benny Goodman (American jazz musician who was dubbed the "King of Swing"). Born May 30, 1909, in Chicago, Illinois (Collier 1989; Firestone 1993).

Goodman's parents were Jewish immigrants who arrived in Chicago in search of work. His father was a skilled tailor, but the only work he could find in America was in a sweatshop. Later, he was even denied this job and had to work in the stockyards where he shoveled hog guts. Goodman grew up feeling a deep indebtedness to his father as well as a sadness that stayed with him into adulthood. When he was forced to recall his father's sacrifices the stoic Goodman would be reduced to tears.

Goodman was the ninth of twelve children born in one of the worst slums in America. However, from a very early age it was obvious that young Benny did not plan to stay in the slum. At six he got his start with the clarinet through a charity organization called Hull House. By thirteen he was already earning a living as a musician. At sixteen he traveled with a popular dance band and made enough money to support his entire family. His hard-working father retired. Unfortunately, the old man's leisure was short-lived. He was hit by a car and died when Goodman was twenty.

Goodman, who spent his adolescence playing in saloons and rubbing elbows (and who knows what else) with prostitutes, developed an easy familiarity with sex. He never spoke of his early sexual adventures. Even though he was not particularly handsome, the young musician apparently had a way with women. At fourteen he was the steady boy friend of a dancer named "Thelma." His later conquests included some of the most attractive singers in the business.

None of these love affairs deterred Goodman from his determination to escape from the poverty of his youth. It was not enough for Benny Goodman to be a brilliant sideman in someone else's band, where his paycheck was dependent upon the fortunes and ego of the band leader. He needed to be in control of his own destiny. When he was twenty Goodman broke with the Benny Pollack band, in which he served a long and fruitful apprenticeship, and went out on his own.

Goodman's defection from the Pollack band came at the beginning of the Depression, but this did not stop the ambitious musician from making money. To a large degree, his success in these hard times was a testament to Goodman's talent. But his businesslike attitude toward music was also an important factor. Goodman was reliable, punctual, and versatile. When Goodman began to put together a band of his own, he continued to be just as businesslike. He haggled with his musicians over money like a hardened capitalist.

Goodman's new band featured a seventeen-year-old female singer named Helen Ward. Ward had a schoolgirl look and a sexy yet natural singing style. At some point she and the bandleader became lovers but, as reliable as he was as a musician, Goodman proved a perfectly unpredictable boy friend. He dated Ward sporadically for two years, breaking with her several times to pursue other women. Then he suddenly asked her to marry him. Almost immediately afterward he reneged on the proposal, claiming he needed to devote himself to his career. When Ward responded to this betrayal by leaving the band, Goodman completely failed to see the point.

By the time Goodman reached his thirties, his hard work and diligence won him all the success he could hope for. He was the leader of one of the most popular big bands of the era and a very rich man. Along the way he made friends with a blue-blooded musical amateur named John Hammond, who supported Goodman's style of playing and Goodman in particular. Through this friendship he met Hammond's sister, Alice. At the time Alice was married to an English aristocrat, but the marriage was failing. To the absolute shock of many, when Goodman was thirty-three he became Alice Hammond Duckworth's second husband.

The contrast between Alice's privileged lineage (she was related to the Vanderbilts) and Goodman's impoverished origin was in itself enough to bring the marriage into question. Despite her affection for her brother and his "bohemian" friends, it hardly seemed likely that this regal and strong-willed woman would ever fit into the lifestyle of a musician. As it turned out, she didn't. Goodman fit himself into her lifestyle instead. He changed the way he dressed, the way he lived, even the way he talked. He developed an eye for painting and an appreciation for the finer elements of culture. After years of fleeing from the poverty and degradation that had ruined his father, Goodman seemed happy to take on the airs of an aristocrat.

Goodman's marriage became a model of devotion and mutual respect between two very different personalities. Goodman continued to work, but he never lost the strong emotional connection he had with his wife and their two children. A tough, uncompromising perfectionist as a bandleader, he became a warm and indulgent family man.

The marriage lasted almost thirty-six years before Alice died of a heart attack. In his seventies Goodman met Carol Phillips, an attractive businesswoman who had been a fan of his from her girlhood. The two began an affair that lasted the rest of Goodman's life. Phillips recalled that the aging musician was still a remarkably sensual lover. Goodman died at seventy-seven.

Another Example

Tammy Wynette (country singer). Born May 5, 1942.

If you have Mars in Pisces with Venus in Cancer you are . . . the Erratic Love Addict

Emotionally, you are one of the great Lovers of all-time—a virtual font of warmth, affection, and loyalty. Sexually, you can also be pretty terrific, but not without first tackling some very sticky issues. Your sexual responses are so powerful and laden with deep, uncontrollable compulsions that you can never predict where they are going to take you. Sex for you is always a mixture of ecstasy, joy, and massive destruction. For this reason you often are more comfortable in relationships in which sex is not a major issue. It's not that you lack erotic desires. It's just that you don't always trust yourself.

You are a person who deeply craves commitment and stability in relationships. You are also a person who has a great deal of difficulty finding and sustaining such arrangements. One reason for this is the incessant ebb and flow of your emotional life. You also have a problem with focus, particularly in the area of sex. You are so full of love, and the world is so full of distractions, that you often find it impossible to limit yourself to one partner.

Case History

James Baldwin (*African-American novelist, essayist, playwright, and poet noted for his literate expressions of black anger and protest*). *Born August 2, 1924, in New York City, New York* (*Leeming 1994*).

Baldwin was an illegitimate child. His mother married a poor preacher, somewhat older than herself, two years after Baldwin's birth. Initially, the relationship between Baldwin and his stepfather was affectionate. It became strained as Baldwin grew older and his stepfather's paranoia became more apparent. A particularly hot issue between them was Baldwin's friendship with the whites and the white patrons that Baldwin attracted. The elder Baldwin had an almost pathological mistrust of white people.

At fourteen Baldwin was still a small, sickly youngster with an effeminate manner and a distinctive face. One day a man slipped his hand up Baldwin's short pants and fondled his genitals. The combination of fear and pleasure that resulted from this encounter sent Baldwin running into the arms of the church, where he underwent a cathartic rebirth and became a "boy-preacher." But his faith was not strong enough to hold down the lust that burned inside him. By the age of sixteen he was involved in a homosexual relationship with a local thug. Baldwin left the church. At the age of eighteen, he was living in Greenwich Village among bohemians.

Baldwin took a job as a waiter in a "hip" cafe. His intellect and impassioned talk soon brought him into the center of the group of artists and writers who gathered there. Baldwin was a flamboyant character who could be both an intellectual and a tough boy from the streets. He often challenged his white friends about their attitudes toward African-Americans. He also showed an eagerness to learn from these individuals, and had a deep respect for literature and art.

At this point in his life Baldwin was still trying to have relationships with women. He lived with a woman for a time when he was twenty-two, but most of his sexual contacts were fleeting homosexual encounters. Baldwin's sustained infatuations tended to be with men who were not homosexual. Even though these men were fond of Baldwin and considered him a close friend, they were not going to have sex with him. In many ways these sexless relationships affected him more deeply than his more carnal associations with either women or men. When one of these untouchable men committed suicide, Baldwin made the painful decision to desert his very needy family and flee to Paris.

Baldwin was twenty-four when he arrived in France. He had no money, but the essays he had published in New York had earned him a small literary reputation. His circle of Greenwich Village friends had extended to include writers already living in Paris. Baldwin quickly fell into a comfortable, though financially strapped, crowd of like-minded folks. For a time he seemed quite happy. But after a brush with the law landed Baldwin in jail, he came to the sobering conclusion that no matter how far he moved from American racism, he could never escape his origins.

When he was twenty-five Baldwin met Lucien Happersberger, the man who would become the love of his life. Happersberger was a seventeen-year-old who had escaped from his middle-class Swiss family to try his luck on the streets of Paris. Some of Baldwin's other friends considered him an opportunist, but he gave the writer love and support at a particularly low point in his life when he had little to offer in return. Baldwin never forgot this. Even though the sexual relationship between the two men ended, more or less, after a couple of years and Happersberger later married three times, Baldwin's enduring passion for the wayward Swiss was one of the recurring themes of his life.

There were other passions, of course. Primary among them was writing. Baldwin's first novel, *Go Tell It on the Mountain*, was published when he was twenty-seven. Other novels and books of essays followed. Another overriding passion was the American civil rights movement. Even though he continued to maintain a home base in various places in Europe, Baldwin often traveled to the United States and was an active participant in the struggle. He became familiar with black leaders ranging from Martin Luther King Jr. to Malcolm X. He used his position as a black writer accepted by the white establishment to bring their message to a wider audience.

There were also other romantic passions. Baldwin's emotional ties to Happersberger did not stop him from seeking other sexual partners once that relationship had grown distant. Baldwin often seemed to be very much in love with these young men. He expressed a longing for a loving and stable domestic arrangement. But his rootless lifestyle and the character of the men he chose made this impossible. As always, the men and women he was not sleeping with were often much more important to him emotionally than his bedmates.

As he grew older and more affluent, Baldwin became more maternal in his attitude toward his young lovers. He worried about their health, he went home with them to meet their parents, and encouraged them in various careers. Despite his affectionate concern, these relationships were often stormy. Baldwin was still drawn to men who were bisexual. Jealousy was often a problem. His lovers also felt threatened by Baldwin's continuing fascination with Happersberger and by the encroachments of his constantly changing, constantly growing entourage of old friends, curious intellectuals, and literary groupies.

Toward the end of his life as his health failed, this entourage became much more important to Baldwin than any lover. He purchased a farmhouse in southern France and settled there with a loosely grouped "family" of friends and associates. The group was diverse: white, black, homosexual, bisexual, and heterosexual. Servants were also brought into the circle and old friends arrived to nurse the ailing Baldwin. Despite his poor health, and to some degree because of it, Baldwin held emotional sway over the household, causing strong personalities to find a way to get along. Baldwin died at sixty-three in this warm atmosphere of love and diversity.

Other Examples

Errol Flynn (*Australian-born film star noted for his on-screen daring and his off-screen sexual high jinks*). *Born June 20, 1909 (Celebrity Birthday Guide*).

Hermann Hesse (*German writer, author of* Steppenwolf *and* Siddhartha). *Born July 2, 1877 (Celebrity Birthday Guide*).

If you have Mars in Pisces with Venus in Leo you are . . . the Autocratic Love Addict

You are a very passionate person, but one who cares deeply about appearances. You want love with dignity. For a Mars in Pisces Lover, that's an awful lot to ask. For this reason you always look for ways to keep your sexual and emotional passions under control. At times your approach to sex is almost dictatorial. You have to have it your way or no way. Because of this, only those closest to you ever know how warm and pliant your sexuality really is.

The biggest problem in your sex life is how to deal with change. You love it and you hate it. You love the notion of new sensations and new beginnings. Too much consistency, even loving consistency, is bound to leave you bored and understimulated. But you also see change as a threat to your sense of control and to the emotional security that you value so highly. Because of this duality in your thinking, your reaction to changes in your sex life is likely to be abrupt, contradictory, and (horror of horrors) a little undignified.

Case History

Debby Boone (*popular singer who scored a big hit very early in her career and then retired to marry and raise a family*). *Born September 22, 1956, in Teaneck, New Jersey (Boone 1981*).

Boone is the daughter of pop singer Pat Boone. She was brought up in a home that mixed "born-again" Christian doctrine with regular appearances on TV. Her father, determined to shelter his daughters from the immoral influence of show business and the rebellion of the 1960s and 1970s, ruled the household with an iron hand. Of all his daughters, however,

Debby was the one most apt to resist his authority and experiment. This tendency led to much conflict between the two during her mid-teens. She received her last spanking from her father when she was nineteen.

A particularly dangerous moment in her teenage rebellion came when she was seventeen. A handsome thirty-one-year-old hairdresser began taking her out. Not only did Boone's parents object to the age difference between the two, but they were also upset because he was not a Christian. For Boone, the fact that this man seemed so mature and apart from the lifestyle in which she had grown up added to his allure. She admitted she felt a very strong sexual attraction for this man, even though their relationship remained quite innocent.

In their efforts to persuade Boone to break with this boy friend, her parents brought in her minister and members from her church to talk to her. Despite her rebellion, Boone remained true to her faith. She finally concluded that God had another man waiting for her somewhere. She broke off the relationship. A short time later the hairdresser died.

When Boone was eighteen she began to see Gabri Ferrer. Ferrer was near Boone's own age and also the child of celebrities (Jose Ferrer and Rosemary Clooney.) He was also a born-again Christian. The two youngsters shared Bible study and a fervent interest in religious issues. Despite their obvious emotional affinity, sex was not an issue between them. It was six months before Ferrer attempted to kiss Boone for the first time. She never felt any pressure from him to go any further. In fact, Boone claimed that the couple's intense commitment to their mutual spiritual development seemed to preclude sexual desire.

Suddenly, Boone came to the conclusion that God was telling her to separate from Ferrer. She was not sure why, but after much soul-searching, she confessed to Ferrer that she felt uneasy in the relationship and that God was calling her to do something else. Ferrer understood and agreed to let her go.

At first Boone wanted to pursue a singing career, but her parents talked her into going to a bible college instead. Ferrer continued to write to her while she was in school. Boone felt she needed to work on spiritual issues and did not answer his letters.

After a year in bible school, at the age of twenty, Boone got an offer to record a song called *You Light up My Life*. Boone was still performing in her father's show and was unsure about going off on her own, but she agreed. The song was a major hit. It led to a concert tour, TV appearances, and Boone won a Grammy for best new artist. Boone, whose fresh face and Christian lifestyle appealed to many, became a star.

At the same time, she renewed her relationship with Ferrer. Ferrer told her that God had told him that he was meant to marry Boone. Boone's parents approved of Ferrer and encouraged the relationship. They even allowed Boone, who was twenty-two at the time, to travel alone with Ferrer to Hawaii. The two stayed in separate rooms. By mutual agreement, they did not have sex.

Boone was still uncertain about their relationship. She felt that Ferrer lacked ambition. Moreover, as a performer she was constantly exposed to handsome, sexy men and often felt tempted. She finally decided that the only solution was to marry Ferrer and abandon her skyrocketing career. Ferrer complied by proposing. They were married shortly before her twenty-third birthday, and had their first child the next year. Boone returned to performing some years later but with only limited success.

If you have Mars in Pisces with Venus in Virgo you are . . . the Pragmatic Love Addict

You can't be fooled by your own lust, unlike most Mars in Pisces Lovers. You don't romanticize your physical desire for sex, and you have a clear awareness of how emotionally vulnerable this desire makes you. The excesses of your sexual nature never take you by surprise and you are very practical and matter-of-fact in dealing with the problems caused by these excesses. Some might think that your capacity for cool analysis makes you a more careful, even reasonable, Mars in Pisces Lover, but it rarely does.

Commitment comes easily for you but so does disengagement. Even though you can love with unmitigated intensity for a while, you often lack staying power. No Mars in Pisces Lover is more susceptible to distraction. At your best, you can be the most pliant and physically affectionate Lover of this type—someone who can make the most mundane act of kindness a token of deepest love. At your worst, you are simply not "there."

Case History

Martina Navratilova (Czech-born tennis player who defected to the United States and became a sports star). Born October 18, 1956, in Prague, Czechoslovakia (Navratilova).

Navratilova inherited her athletic gifts from her mother, but it was her stepfather who provided the encouragement and direction that made her a star player. Her vocation was established very early and overshadowed everything else in her life, including sex. By the time she was seventeen she had a boy friend and had experimented sexually, but was not happy with the results. One concern was the effect that a pregnancy would have on her tennis career. She continued to have sex with men over the next couple of years, but only occasionally. At the same time, she was also becoming aware of her attraction to women.

At eighteen Navratilova made the decision to defect to the West. It was a painful decision that restructured her life in many ways, but it had one immediate benefit. In Czechoslovakia, homosexuality (especially lesbianism) was looked upon as a mental illness. In the United States, on the other hand, Navratilova felt free to experiment.

Her first homosexual affair was with an older woman who took the initiative. Navratilova was heartbroken when this woman broke off the relationship. She continued to have lesbian relationships, but none were important until she met a self-declared lesbian writer named Rita Mae Brown when she was twenty-two.

Brown wrote about homosexuality, and was also active in various homosexual causes. Navratilova's relationship with her was emotionally intense in itself, but it also represented a public announcement of her sexual preference. Navratilova had good reason to be concerned about public opinion. Being "outed" could cost her millions in product endorsements and jeopardize her attempt to become an American citizen. Navratilova remained remarkably levelheaded and courageous in the face of these problems. Although she never flaunted her lesbianism, Navratilova became an outspoken advocate of gay issues.

Brown's relationship was remarkable in Navratilova's life because she was one of the few people close to the tennis player who was not involved in sports. Brown did not find sports important and pushed Navratilova to expand her interests. But Navratilova was still devoted to tennis. Her determination to improve her game, which had suffered since her defection, led her to become friends with a woman basketball star when she was twenty-five.

Navratilova maintained in her book that her relationship with this woman was not sexual. She went to live with her only because the basketball player offered to help her gain control of her diet and physical conditioning. Brown thought otherwise. She and Navratilova fought bitterly and broke off their relationship. Despite Navratilova's objections, Brown claimed that her lover had left her for another woman.

By the time Navratilova was thirty she was back on top of her game and unquestionably the best female tennis player in the world. She also had a new relationship with a former beauty queen named Judy Nelson. Nelson left her husband and gave up custody of her two sons in order to live with Navratilova. This affair lasted six years. It ended in a palimony suit filed by Nelson, who claimed that Navratilova had promised her half of the $10 million earnings for the period of their relationship. Navratilova felt deeply wronged by this turn of events and remarked upon it with bitterness years later.

If you have Mars in Pisces with Venus in Libra you are . . . the Faithful Love Addict

You are the Mars in Pisces Lover with the highest standards with regard to sex. The sexual experience has to be perfect for you—an effortless meshing of physical pleasure, emotional fulfillment, and intellectual understanding. It might be presumed that these stratospheric standards would limit your choice of partners, but this isn't true at all. It's your ability to believe, and not the quality of your partner, that really makes the difference. Once you've made that initial leap of faith, your partner will become your special superhuman Beloved, whether he or she wants to or not.

Your attachment to the person you love is always intense and singular. It is likely that your love relationship will be the most important factor in your life. This places you in a very vulnerable position. A bad relationship with the wrong person can do you irreparable harm. On the other hand, a good relationship with the right person can be nothing short of your personal salvation and more than worth the risk.

Case History

Bo Derek (Mary Cathleen Collins—California girl who became the number one sex symbol of the 1980s). Born November 20, 1956, in Torrance, California (Broeske 1993; Brower 1984; Gittelson 1981; McGuigan 1979; Katz 1994).

At sixteen Derek was the kind of girl everyone associates with California. She lived for the sun and the sand and had little thought about her future. Her parents were divorced. She lived with her mother who was a hairdresser. She was ten pounds overweight and not much inclined toward self-discipline. Then an agent spotted her and introduced her to independent filmmaker and photographer John Derek.

John Derek had been a matinee idol in his youth, but his later years had been devoted to directing the careers of his wives. He had already guided one wife, Ursula Andress, to a successful film career. He was working on a second, Linda Evans, when he was introduced to Cathleen Collins. According the Derek, her romance with the forty-six-year-old director developed naturally. John immediately notified his current wife that he had found a new love interest. After some initial recriminations, Evans gracefully accepted the transfer.

The relationship between John and Bo Derek was a source of much conjecture. John took control of every aspect of his new wife's life. He changed her name and her diet, and consciously molded her into a sex symbol. His authoritative style, and Derek's unquestioning acceptance of it, caused many to see the young actress as merely the instrument of her husband's ambition. John Derek was called a "Svengali" who held women under a spell and exploited their beauty. Derek adamantly denied these accusations. Yet she never denied her absolute devotion to her husband or the fact that his discipline and critical eye provided the structure of her life.

Derek's big break came when she was twenty-three with the movie *10*. She was cast as the embodiment of an older man's sexual fantasy, a role that made the maximum use of her remarkable physique and undeniable sex appeal. Even though she did little real acting in the film and was not its star, *10* made Derek a household word. She became America's newest model of feminine beauty.

John Derek's involvement with *10* was minimal. He more than made up for this lapse by photographing the poster and the *Playboy* pictorial that accompanied the movie's release. These images promoted his wife as a robust and outdoorsy sex symbol whose allure was brisk, natural, and absolutely untouched by puritan shame.

Once *10* made Bo Derek a star, she and her husband became one of the most desirable, and, in some cases, dreaded teams in Hollywood. They turned down many lucrative offers in favor of a project in which they were guaranteed a large budget and total artistic control: *Tarzan, the Ape Man*. This film featured Derek as both the producer and star. She played Jane, whose role in the story had been expanded and modernized. Critics panned the movie but, because of Derek's box office appeal, it still managed to make a nice profit.

Their next project was *Bolero*. It was written and directed by John and produced by Bo. The film was controversial even before it was released because of its graphic sex scenes that stopped just short of being X-rated. Some observers even accused the Dereks of infusing the film with their own moral agenda, which included opening mainstream movies to X-rated erotica. Others preferred to remark on the oddity of a husband directing his beautiful young wife as she made love to another man. All this controversy was not enough to make *Bolero* a successful film. It was universally condemned by critics and its failure to conform to an "R" rating limited the film's distribution and its earnings.

After *Bolero*, the Dereks began to fade from public view. The Hollywood power brokers that had clamored for their attention a few years before now wanted nothing to do with the troublesome couple. Bo and John took this downward slide with remarkable grace. Bo Derek was still a marketable sex symbol and could have continued to make movies, but she refused to work without her husband. The couple settled on a forty-acre ranch and proceeded to live a quiet, healthy life together.

By her late thirties, Derek was working again in films. John Derek stayed at home but the actress insisted that her return to the public eye represented no breach in their relationship. She had become the aging impresario's oldest wife. (He had divorced his previous wives shortly after they reached thirty.) Their marriage continued until John's death in 1998.

If you have Mars in Pisces with Venus in Scorpio you are . . . the Awesome Love Addict

You are a formidable Lover who takes all aspects of sex and love to the extreme. You are passionate, demanding, devoted, and vengeful. There are no halfhearted feelings in your arsenal. You tend to be a very loyal Lover because you value security above everything; however, your strong emotional reactions and your unceasing thirst for love often lead you into some rather ambiguous romantic situations. No matter how secure you may seem, someone who feels as deeply as you do can never be predictable.

Even though you may be emotionally explosive, you are also one of the strongest Lovers of this type. You have a way of not only surviving your emotional extremism but of coming out a winner. You control situations by simply wanting things more than anyone else in the room. No matter how crazy in love you appear, you always have a cunning awareness of what is truly to your advantage and what is not. When it comes to love, you are one tough customer.

Case History

Rebecca West (Cicily Fairfield—British author and feminist often most remembered because of her love affair with H. G. Wells). Born December 21, 1892, in London, England (Glendinning 1987).

West's father was a restless man. He had already traveled around the world by the time he married West's mother but he never really settled down. Although he lacked a real profession, her father made an uncertain living through journalism, art, and various business ventures. He set a high intellectual standard for his three daughters. West thought him glamorous and exciting but he never provided her or any other member of his family with anything close to security. When West was eight, her adored father abandoned his family for a job in Africa. He died when West was in her teens.

West's feelings for her father were mixed. His distant but compelling masculinity greatly influenced her sexual development, and his failure as a journalist did much to inspire her subsequent successes. She also deeply resented his desertion of the family, and his mistreatment of her mother helped galvanize West's feminist viewpoint.

After making an attempt to become an actress, West began publishing criticism and essays at the age of eighteen. By nineteen she was already one of the most talked-about young writers in London. Her acerbic satire, literate feminism, and tendency to take on established male authors made her widely read and socially sought after. One article she published concerned the then-internationally famous H. G. Wells. She called the author of *The Time Machine* a sexually obsessed "old maid." When Wells read the article he was far from upset. Instead, he sought out the brilliant and beautiful journalist and eventually made her his lover.

Wells was in his forties by this time. He was the veteran of many love affairs and several notorious public scandals, none of which had weakened the emotional and intellectual connection he had with his remarkable wife, Jane. It would have been impossible for West not to be aware of the history and circumstance of her lover. She must have also realized that he was an unabashed egotist. But despite these facts, and her own ambitions, the twenty-year-old West was unable to resist the older writer's charm.

It was soon evident that Wells and West were not involved in a passing romance. During one of their first hasty meetings, West became pregnant with Wells' son. Even though she did not welcome the pregnancy, West bravely undertook to raise the child on her own. Wells paid for a home for his new mistress and child, hired servants, and established a dual residence that seems to have pleased him greatly. It was less pleasant for West. She reacted to this ambiguous domestic situation with various nervous and physical ailments. She fought with the servants, spent too much of Wells' money on clothes, and spent too little time with her child.

West's salvation during this emotionally trying time was the fact that she was still able to write. She continued to publish criticism and brought out her first novel, effectively establishing her own literary career quite separate from Wells. Even though her literary success gave her a modicum of financial and intellectual independence, West was still unable to end her emotional dependence upon her lover. There is no indication that West had any illusions about Wells' relationship with his wife. Yet she still held on to a faint, irrational hope that the writer would change the pattern he had set with his earlier affairs and find a way to marry her.

Finally, after ten years, the intense sexual passion that had fueled the union and led the two writers to refer to each other as "panther" and "jaguar" began to wear away. Wells grew less tolerant of West's nervous complaints. West began to rebel at his selfish egotism and senseless jealousy. West got an offer to lecture in the United States. She used this as an excuse to take the upper hand in the relationship and give Wells an ultimatum: marry me or else. The result was the end of the affair.

Several men had attempted to seduce West throughout her long relationship with Wells, but she had remained steadfast in her sexual loyalty. Her inhibitions gave way toward the end of the affair. She slept with powerful Canadian publisher Max Aitken (Lord Beaverbrook). When she finally left Wells, West assumed that Beaverbrook would soon take his place. She arranged to meet him in the United States. To her surprise, the expected transfer did not occur. The circumstances surrounding this event are not clear. By some means,

West was left thinking that her new lover found her physically unexciting. Throughout her life West was haunted by this and by the feeling that men were put off by her erudition and "masculine" mind.

West had other affairs after her break with Wells but she always felt she was essentially a monogamous being. By the time she was in her mid-thirties, she made a decision to find a husband. She settled on Henry Andrews, a businessman with intellectual aspirations who was two years younger than her. Andrews was an agreeable man, who looked upon his wife's literary accomplishments with pride. He tried to make her happy. Despite the calculated manner in which they entered into marriage (West proposed the marriage as a way of dealing with Andrew's dire financial situation), they quickly grew to love one another.

The first five years of the marriage were happy ones for West. Then Andrews suddenly stopped having sex with her. West was never sure why, though she later learned he had several extramarital affairs during their marriage. She assumed he had sought other women because he could not deal with her success. She had her own affairs through her forties and fifties, but never got over this rejection by her husband. Even though the marriage remained an important source of emotional stability for her over the next thirty years, West often regarded it as an inconvenience.

West was fond of pointing out the many failings of the male sex in her feminist writings. Her son reported that her attitudes were so pro-woman when he was growing up that he often felt ashamed of being born a male. She proposed that there was no real reason any woman should marry who could keep herself financially stable. At the same time West confessed to a friend that, as bad as men were, she always needed to have one around. She had many dear female friends and even theorized that she would have been better off as a lesbian, but it was only with a man that West could find emotional security.

West's passion was very evident in her writing. Her two most famous books, *Black Lamb and Grey Falcon* and *The New Meaning of Treason* were about love and hate. The first expressed her deep emotional identification with the Serbian people and the strange new nation called Yugoslavia. It was written in the midst of an unconsummated love affair with her Serbian interpreter and guide. The second, which was based on her work as a reporter at the Nuremberg trials, savagely expressed her hatred of the British Nazis who betrayed England, a hatred which she later extended to include Communist traitors.

West's long career as a journalist, novelist, and social critic spanned the greater part of the century. Throughout it she was constantly brought back to her early affair with H. G. Wells, partially because of her strained relationship with their son, and partially because many people still regarded this as one of her most memorable achievements. West came to view this affair as nothing more than a youthful indiscretion and a painful lesson in love. Rebecca West died at the age of ninety.

Other Examples

J. Paul Getty (*American millionaire who became so fearful of lawsuits that he made the women he picked up sign a contract before he slept with them). Born December 15, 1892 (Celebrity Birthday Guide).*

Ava Gardner (*American movie star). Born December 24, 1922 (Celebrity Birthday Guide).*

If you have Mars in Pisces with Venus in Sagittarius you are . . . the Adventurous Love Addict

You are one of the most exciting Mars in Pisces Lovers but also one of the most unstable. You have an almost visceral need for emotional security. In the absence of a loving relationship, you are prone to desperate, uncontrollable behavior. You also need a sense of freedom, fluidity, and change in your sex life. You are an inherently restless Lover for whom the thought of being tied down is almost as frightening as the thought of being alone.

As confused and extreme as your reactions may be, you are still a very desirable partner. Your openness, your great sense of fun and adventure, and your incomparable Mars in Pisces sexual allure are always sure to please. However, because sex is so troublesome for you, and it provides such an overload for your supersensitive emotional nature, you might be well advised to take a vacation from it once in a while. You usually find that the most meaningful and consistently happy relationships of your life are those outside the sexual sphere.

Case History

Francis Bacon (*British painter noted for his extreme, tortured representations of the human figure). Born October 28, 1909, in Dublin, Ireland (Feaver 1992; Sinclair 1993).*

Bacon had an arduous childhood. His father was an erratic and dictatorial man born into the lower fringes of nobility. He had a passion for horses and for discipline. He used both to make his son miserable. Bacon was a sickly, fearful child. He received no sympathy from his father who insisted the boy ride horseback, even though horsehair aggravated the boy's asthma to the point that he couldn't breathe. When young Bacon failed to meet his father's expectations, he was put across a saddle and whipped by the grooms who worked in his father's stables. Later these same grooms gave the teenage Bacon his introduction to homosexual intercourse.

Bacon was clearly at odds with his family by the time he was sixteen. He later claimed it was because of his sexual encounters with the grooms that his father kicked him out of the house. In fact, young Bacon was asked to leave when his father caught him wearing his mother's clothing. Bacon had little contact with his family after this. His inability to win the affection of his brutal father haunted Bacon the rest of his life.

Despite his youth, Bacon had no difficulty making a life for himself on the streets of London. A friend of his father's who was a homosexual stepped forward to become his patron. This man took Bacon on jaunts to Berlin shortly after World War I. The youngster saw homosexual nightlife at its boldest and most decadent.

By the time he was eighteen, Bacon found another older lover who helped him get started as a furniture designer. Despite some early successes, Bacon never pursued this career with much fervor. He preferred living in the slums, moving frequently, and stealing to feed himself, when necessary. He shared his home with the elderly woman who had been his nanny. Even though Bacon had male lovers during this period, it was his deep affection for this woman that remained one of the few constants in his unsettled life.

Bacon looked for older men in his youth, typically conventional and "straight" in their bearing, who reminded him of his father. He admitted that he had a reluctant sexual attraction for the cruel, distant figure his father represented. By winning the love of such men, even temporarily, he felt somehow less abandoned. When he grew too old to attract such lovers, Bacon switched to younger men who often had a rough, uncivilized edge.

One of his early sponsors had left him with some connections with the art world, but Bacon's sexual choices were not driven by his career goals. In fact, even after he gave up design and turned to painting, Bacon was never a proper careerist. He painted in dim, unbelievably cluttered studios, often while he was drunk, using dog-eared photographs as his models. He destroyed most of the work produced during the first ten years of his career. Many of his later paintings are presently in poor condition because of his haphazard technique. Despite all this, by the time he was thirty-five, Bacon was acknowledged as one of greatest figurative painters in the world.

Bacon's paintings are graphic expressions of his emotional turmoil. The images have the lurid attraction of an automobile accident or a murder scene, showing human nature at its worst. He painted twisted, naked figures acting out grisly personal dramas before a flat, optimistically-colored backdrop. They are often screaming, sometimes fornicating, and always disturbed, desperate, and tragically alone.

During his forties, Bacon had a long-term affair with a young piano player named Peter Lacy. Bacon was extremely emotionally attached to Lacy. Their relationship was so volatile that he had difficulty painting when the young man was near. They were often at odds. Many of Bacon's friends considered Lacy a sadist. He was certainly an alcoholic. It was from alcoholism that he died when Bacon was fifty-four. Bacon learned of his lover's death during the opening of a triumphant retrospective exhibit of his paintings in London.

Bacon began to keep company with George Dyer shortly after Lacy's death. Bacon claimed that he met Dyer when the young man attempted to burglarize his studio. This was said in jest, but Dyer did have a criminal past. Bacon's relationship with Dyer was just as troubled as his affair with Lacy had been, though now it was Bacon's turn to be cruel. Dyer was always out of place among Bacon's intellectual friends. Bacon and his friends never tired of reminding him of this fact. Bacon sarcastically referred to his lover as "she" and laughed at Dyer's repeated suicide attempts. Despite this abuse, Dyer remained with Bacon for nearly ten years, and served as the model for many of his most famous and disturbing paintings. One of these works shows Dyer in his underwear throwing up in a bathroom sink and then sitting lifeless on a toilet. This was exactly the way Dyer ended his life eight years after the painting was made. As with Lacy, Bacon was attending a large exhibit of his work, this time in Paris, when he learned of Dyer's suicide. The distraught artist said that he was torn between laughing and crying, and finally screamed.

Bacon's next lover was a young man from the working class whom he found tending bar in London. This youngster and his family became the beneficiaries of Bacon's financial largess. Bacon had gambled away his money as quickly as he made it earlier in his career, but by the end of his life his income was such that even his compulsive gambling couldn't make it disappear. So he simply gave it away. Bacon remained sexually active and surprisingly youthful, considering his dissolute lifestyle, into his old age. He began a new love affair at eighty with a man who lived in Madrid. He died in that city at the age of eighty-two.

If you have Mars in Pisces with Venus in Capricorn you are ... the Organized Love Addict

Yours is a lush and earthy sexuality. You never let your strong emotional needs interfere with your constant and clear awareness of the physical. Unlike most Mars in Pisces Lovers, you have an uncanny knack for managing your feelings. You know how to use your volatility to intimidate and gain sympathy and how to direct your devastating sexual allure. This allows you to not only pick your targets, but also control relationships, thus guaranteeing that you always get exactly what you need from them.

This tendency to take control of relationships and to calculate your emotions does not always serve you well. It deprives you of the incomparable experience of truly letting your feelings take charge of your life. It can also make you seem hard and stilted when, in fact, you are brimming over with passion that you can never properly express. In terms of material expressions of affection, you can be outstandingly generous and reliable. When it comes to love, you are often so cagey that you end up cheating everyone, including yourself.

Case History

Aristotle Onassis (Greek shipping tycoon who accumulated one of the largest fortunes of his time). Born January 20, 1906, in Smyrna, Turkey (Fraser 1977).

Onassis was the son of a successful Greek businessman who lived in a Greek enclave on the coast of Turkey. Thanks to his father's prosperity, his childhood was relatively happy and privileged, disturbed only by young Onassis' irrepressible penchant for mischief. When he was sixteen, a dispute between Greece and Turkey brought this happy period to a terrifying end. Onassis' father was imprisoned, and Onassis himself barely escaped to the Greek mainland. By default, he found himself in charge of what was left of the family fortune. He attempted to use this money to win the release of his father and other relatives. When the older men of the family were released, they took a dim view of Onassis' efforts. Stung by their rejection and ingratitude, the restless teenager immigrated to Argentina.

Onassis arrived in Argentina with few resources beyond his charm and capacity for hard work. He took a night job as an electrician with the telephone company and used his days to make deals and extra money. After a few years of frenetic efforts, he had enough capital to import tobacco from Greece for Argentinean customers. He branched out into cigarette manufacturing and developed markets in other Latin American countries. At twenty-six, he took the small fortune he had made in the tobacco business and began to buy ships.

Onassis was every bit as precocious as a lover as he was as a businessman. At twelve he attempted to seduce his mother's maid. A short time later he began an affair with his French tutor, who was in her twenties. Even as a young foreigner on the make in Argentina, working long hours and seemingly obsessed with making money, Onassis still found time for women and never had trouble gaining their interest. Long before he was rich, Onassis had established a reputation as a ladies' man. His appetite for sexual pleasure only increased as he grew more affluent. He had mistresses and enjoyed the decadent nightlife of Buenos Aires. For Onassis, making money and making love were equally strong compulsions.

As he grew older, Onassis looked for ways to combine his favorite pastimes. About the time that he was starting his shipping company, Onassis began a love affair with a tall, slinky Norwegian divorcée named Ingse Dedichen. The affair was extremely passionate on all levels. Even though her friends found it odd she would pair off with this short, paunchy Greek, Dedichen considered Onassis the most sensual man she had ever known. He made love with slow dedication and showed a particular appreciation for his mistress's feet.

Even while he was developing a very close and loving relationship with Dedichen, Onassis was also using her international web of social contacts for his own advancement. Under his influence, she drew away from her friends in the arts and other areas that were of no interest to Onassis. They concentrated their efforts on relatives in the shipping business and other powerful friends who could be useful to her charming boy friend.

Dedichen came to see the darker side of Onassis' passion as the relationship began to wind down. He was extremely jealous and prone to physical violence. He beat Dedichen. On at least one occasion, he seriously injured her. Despite his promises of marriage, Dedichen could see that he had no real desire to formalize their arrangement. After six years she began to withdraw from the relationship though Onassis, either because he was slow to see the change or just didn't care, continued to seek her out.

Even though he had no intention of marrying Dedichen, Onassis was thinking of marriage. However, he was more interested in dynastic concerns than good sex. In a manner that was surprisingly conventional for Onassis, he courted the seventeen-year-old daughter of the greatest of the Greek shipping magnates. Her name was Tina Livanos. She was beautiful and very used to being rich. They were married when Onassis was forty.

Early in the marriage, Onassis' bride was overwhelmed by the high profile, jet-set lifestyle he offered her, but after a few years the couple began to grow apart. Tina was a cool, stylish woman who apparently had little taste for her husband's rapturous but lowbrow sensuality. Her unresponsiveness acerbated Onassis' insecurity and caused him to worry about impotence and the difference in their ages.

Of course, Onassis had other women, but Tina was willing to overlook this kind of behavior as long as he was discreet. For several years the couple covered their differences with a happy front for the sake of the children and the press—until Onassis met Maria Callas.

At the time, Callas was regarded as the greatest female voice in opera. She also was a strong-willed, independent Greek who had been forced to struggle during her early years. Onassis felt an immediate emotional and sexual bond to her. Their mutual attraction was so obvious that both Tina and Callas' husband were alerted, but to no avail. Soon Callas told her husband that she was in love with Onassis. Tina fled to America with her children and filed for divorce.

Even though Callas remained Onassis' "secret" lover, he was never shy about being photographed with her, nor was he bothered when their names were linked in the press. In fact, some felt this notoriety was the millionaire's favorite part of their relationship. It is also true that Onassis found in Callas both a kindred spirit and someone who was willing to submit herself utterly to his will. Noted for her temper tantrums as a performer, Callas turned out to be an extremely passive mistress. Not only did Onassis dominate her sex life but he also took charge of her financial affairs, all the while claiming they were just good friends.

Callas was anxious to marry her wealthy patron after she secured her divorce, but Onassis continually backed away from this idea. As with Dedichen before her, the fact that Onassis could be sexually content with Callas seemed to disqualify her as a bride. Sex was for fun. Matrimony was a matter of ambition.

When he was sixty-two Onassis shocked the world by marrying Jacqueline Bouvier Kennedy. From Onassis' point of view, this marriage to one of the most famous women in the world was the perfect validation of his position and power. His feelings toward Jacqueline are unclear, but there seems to have been little sentiment in his approach to marriage. It is not surprising, therefore, that Onassis found little pleasure in his new bride once the sense of personal triumph had worn away. Divorce was considered but this would have represented a defeat and Onassis had never publicly admitted to defeat. The marriage "lasted" until his death at the age of sixty-nine.

Other Examples

W. Somerset Maugham (*English author*). *Born January 25, 1874 (Celebrity Birthday Guide).*

Cindy Crawford (*American model*). *Born February 20, 1966 (Celebrity Birthday Guide).*

If you have Mars in Pisces with Venus in Aquarius you are . . . the Radical Love Addict

You are the Mars in Pisces Lover who never closes his or her eyes, no matter how emotionally intense the moment. You are a very sensitive, vulnerable person, but you also have the ability to view your feelings with a cool, intellectual distance. This essential objectivity in the midst of the most rapturous emotional episodes doesn't necessarily save you from painful errors. It does give you the ability to judge your behavior objectively and learn from your mistakes.

You are an idealistic person with a strong sense of fair play and high moral standards all your own. You are also a very single-minded Lover and are willing to do whatever it takes to secure the kind of warm, emotionally-sustaining relationship you need. In some ways this uncompromising attitude toward love is your most positive trait. It enables you to overcome many obstacles and fight for what you need. At times it can also make you seem selfish, high-handed, and even dictatorial.

Case History

Simone de Beauvoir (*French author noted for her novels, left-wing politics, and articulation of modern feminism*). *Born January 9, 1908, in Paris, France.*

De Beauvoir was a passionate child, even though she tended to keep her passions secret from her conservative, middle-class parents. She read of the sufferings of the saints as a youngster and sought to imitate them by imagining herself burning at the stake. She even whipped herself with an improvised lash until she bled. She developed into a rather bookish adolescent, and preferred doing her reading in the forest where she could also masturbate in secret.

At twenty de Beauvoir had distinguished herself intellectually enough to be allowed to study in Paris. On her own in the city, she went to bars, not to drink, but to observe the side of life from which her middle-class parents had so long struggled to protect her. Sometimes she claimed to be an artist's model or even a prostitute. She relished rubbing elbows with thugs and dope dealers. Surprisingly, despite some dangerous moments, she managed to pursue this research and hold on to her virginity at the same time. Fascinated as she was by the world of sin, de Beauvoir was still philosophically committed to the idea that sexual feelings were best sublimated. Neither her early boy friends nor her more adventurous girl friends could persuade her to do more than look.

When de Beauvoir was twenty-one, a student a few years older whose wild antics and intellectual fireworks she had been watching from afar suddenly took notice of her. His name was Jean Paul Sartre. Almost immediately, a bond formed between these two that transcended everything else in either of their lives. De Beauvoir was alarmed at the changes brought about in her consciousness by her emotional and sexual relationship with Sartre. Suddenly her sexual desires were so strong that they caused her endless anxiety. Even though Sartre was neither a particularly attractive man nor a stellar lover, she could not stand to be apart from him. Unfortunately, their ambitions made frequent separations a necessity.

It was Sartre who proposed that he and de Beauvoir have an "open" relationship. De Beauvoir agreed, perhaps because she recognized that to be monogamously bound to a man of Sartre's brilliance would tend to diminish her own reputation in many circles at that time. Her agreement did not stop her from feeling jealous when Sartre slept with other women. This jealousy deeply disturbed the analytical de Beauvoir, and she struggled to control it. It didn't help that Sartre had placed a "transparency" clause in their agreement. He vowed to tell her everything about his "secondary" relationships, never realizing that his confessions only added to the pain de Beauvoir felt.

De Beauvoir was thirty before she took lovers of her own. The first was a student of Sartre's. Later she had affairs with men who were quite separate from her "main" lover. They were also more physical men with fewer intellectual pretensions who were quite different from Sartre. In her forties, de Beauvoir lived with a man seventeen years her junior. She used her experiences with these men in her novels, transcribing them so directly that at least one of her lovers was deeply offended.

Meanwhile, she and Sartre established themselves as leaders of the intellectual scene of France. They coedited an influential journal. They published philosophical books and novels that espoused an individualistic point of view called existentialism. De Beauvoir was also a vocal advocate of equality for women, particularly in the intellectual sphere. Her book, *The Second Sex,* became a milestone of modern feminism.

Throughout her life, de Beauvoir had intense relationships with women. She even wrote that bisexuality was probably an advantage for women, though she maintained she had not had an erotic experience with a female. De Beauvoir began a relationship in her fifties with a student. This girl became her constant companion and, toward the end of her life, de Beauvoir adopted her. When asked to define her relationship with this girl, de Beauvoir was intentionally ambiguous.

Sartre remained the one constant in her life. Their relationship was undisturbed by the other men or women in de Beauvoir's life, possibly because she had decided to spare Sartre the full force of "transparency." He was aware of her secondary affairs but heard little about them from de Beauvoir. Although their sex life probably ended early in the relationship, Sartre and de Beauvoir remained the staunchest of intellectual allies and were emotionally inseparable regardless of their separate lives. Sartre died first, when de Beauvoir was seventy-two. She died six years later and was buried next to him.

Other Examples

Gertrude Stein (American-born poet and avant-gardist). Born February 3, 1874 (Wallace 1981).

Jack London (American author of adventure stories). January 12, 1876 (Wallace 1981).

If you have Mars in Pisces with Venus in Pisces you are . . . the Fantastic Love Addict

You are in pursuit of a dream, and by no means is it a peaceful dream. You fantasize about extraordinary passions, extreme emotions, and romantic insanity. The search for this dream often makes you agitated and restless. You blow through people's lives like a hurricane, leaving a path of shattered hearts and broken promises. You long for stability and commitment, but only the relationship of your dreams will satisfy you. All other relationships are expendable.

If you are lucky enough to find your dream early in life, then you have a wonderful capacity for living happily ever after. If you don't, then the situation can get out of control. Physical sex is always less important to you than emotional security, but your emotional needs are so intense that you often don't take time to notice the difference. Any kind of emotional release—even the most casual or callous—can sustain you for a while. When your dream seems distant and unattainable, you are all too willing to settle for these short-term fixes.

Case History

Giacomo Casanova (*Italian con man and writer who billed himself as the greatest lover who ever lived). Born April 2, 1725, in Venice, Italy (Masters 1969).*

Casanova's mother was the daughter of a shoemaker who had married an actor. His real father was probably a member of one of the patrician families that controlled Venice. By means of this ambiguous connection to wealth and power, Casanova acquired an education and developed a taste for high living and privilege.

Casanova boarded with another family as a boy so that his mother could pursue a career on the stage. He resented this for the rest of his life. It was during this period that he was introduced to sex. An older girl, who was supposed to be giving him a bath, fondled his genitals. Casanova was uncertain how he should respond. It seemed impossible to him that this girl could be feeling the same animal lust that he felt. It is also likely, however, that at this point in his life he found sex intimidating.

Fittingly enough, Casanova had his first complete sexual experience with not one, but two girls—sisters who shared a bed. He made love to one and then the other while they pretended to sleep. Early in life Casanova developed a knack for knowing which women would respond to his advances and how best to approach them. Not only did he understand women and their feelings, but he also genuinely enjoyed their company.

Despite his charm, Casanova's reputation as a lover hinged more on pure stamina than skill or sensitivity. He aroused quickly, could sustain an erection in almost any circumstance, and achieved orgasm repeatedly. Many of his encounters read more like rapes than seductions. He lived in a time when men of the upper class looked upon almost any woman of a lesser station as available for sexual intercourse. Casanova took full advantage of this masculine privilege. Any innkeeper's daughter or servant girl who bent over in his presence was apt to be attacked.

Casanova was not just an unfeeling hedonist. He was an extremely emotional man who fell in love many times and was capable of long and heartrending courtships. Casanova behaved quite differently when he was in love. Sometimes he was willing to forget about sex, at least for a while. Other times he was so blinded by his passion that he allowed himself to be manipulated in the most scurrilous fashion. He was always generous with the women he loved. With these lovers he showed tenderness and a nobility of spirit that was totally miss-ing in most of his relations with men. One of his great loves referred to Casanova as "the nicest man" she had ever met.

The women he loved were typically outsiders like him. They were actresses or concubines, who lived on the fringes of the upper crust and depended upon their beauty, their wits, and the indulgence of wealthy men to survive. When Casanova was in his twenties these women were often older than he was, though he always described them as being younger in his mem-oirs. All of these women shared Casanova's uninhibited approach to sex. Many were lesbians. One of his more intense courtships was with a "castrato," a male singer who had supposedly been castrated at birth. It was only in the "clinch" that Casanova was able to prove what he claimed he had suspected all along—that the boy was actually a girl in disguise.

None of these intense relationships ended in marriage. The reasons for this were as var-ied as were the relationships, but the deciding factor was usually Casanova's reluctance. He typically ended the affairs before they could acquire any kind of domestic finality. Casanova needed sex and he needed love, but he never showed any desire to settle down.

Not all of Casanova's lovers were women. He was never as forthcoming about his homo-sexual affairs, but they obviously existed. As a young man he was "adopted" by a wealthy, Venetian bachelor. This older man acted as his adviser and protector. Casanova developed a deep emotional attachment to him that lasted long after the old man ceased to be his bene-factor. Casanova never admitted to having sex with this protector but he did confess to homosexual encounters in Turkey (where such things were taken for granted). Much later in his life, he quite frankly described his infatuation with a homosexual army officer in Russia. It is likely that Casanova had other affairs with men during his long life, both for fun and for profit, but they never interfered with his basic fascination for women.

By the time Casanova was in his late thirties he was on a downward slide, both in terms of his material circumstance and his sex life. The frequency and the quality of his love affairs slowly decreased. It was during this period that he became infatuated with the youthful con-cubine of an elderly statesman. Before he could have sex with the girl, her mother interced-ed. The mother turned out to be one of Casanova's old lovers. She informed him that the girl he was lusting after was his own daughter. He had sex with the girl anyway. A few years later, when the girl was married and anxious to produce a child for her ninety-year-old husband, it was Casanova who got her pregnant.

Casanova had no real profession. He was essentially a benign swindler who lived from one scheme to the next, often at odds with the law. In his fifties he was reduced to spying on other libertines and criminals for the Inquisition and living on a government stipend. He finally acquired what might be called a "regular" job in his sixties as a librarian on the isolated estate of a German nobleman. It was here that he wrote his autobiography that would immortalize his name. *The Story of My Life* was not published until long after his death at the age of seventy-three.

Other Examples

Billie Holiday *(blues singer noted for her turbulent lifestyle). Born April 7, 1915 (Celebrity Birthday Guide).*

Vincent Van Gogh *(Dutch-born painter who cut off his earlobe and sent it to a prostitute). Born March 30, 1853 (Celebrity Birthday Guide).*

Elizabeth Barrett Browning *(English poet noted for her romantic bond to Robert Browning). Born March 6, 1806 (Encyclopedia Britannica, Vol. 2).*

Appendix

The Mars/Venus Chart

How To Find Your Mars And Venus Signs

In order to find the placement of your Mars and Venus signs, consult the Mars/Venus chart on the following pages. The chart is divided into two sides within a column: the left side of the column contains the Mars placement during a given year; the right side of the column contains the Venus placement during the same year. So to find your placement, do the following:

1. Find the year in which you were born within the chart. (Let's use October 1, 1968, as an example.) Read down the chart until you reach 1968 in the left side of the column. Look for the approximate "placement" of October 1.

   We've listed the dates each planet "changed" signs during that year. You can see in the left side of the column that in 1968 Mars passed from Leo to Virgo on September 21, and from Virgo to Libra on November 9. If you were born on October 1 of that year, you have Mars in Virgo. (October 1 falls between September 21 and November 9 in this example.)

To the right of that column, you will see the changes for Venus. You see that Venus moved from Libra to Scorpio on September 26 and from Scorpio to Sagittarius on October 21. With your October 1 birth date this means you have Venus in Scorpio.

Note: The chart covers dates ranging from 1920 to 2010.

2. Turn to the corresponding chapter and page number for your Mars/Venus combination listed in the table of contents at the front of the book.

3. Read the information under "General Characteristics" in the chapter associated with your Mars sign. This gives you an overall general description of Mars in that sign.

4. Find your Venus placement within that same chapter and read its description. You'll find the Venus placements under headings like this:

   If you have Mars in Virgo with Venus in Scorpio you are . . .
   the Basically Scandalous Lover

5. Read the case history that follows your particular Mars/Venus combination. A case history is a brief sexual biography of an individual having that same combination of Mars/Venus.

   Note: Some Mars/Venus combinations list an additional celebrity having that same Mars/Venus combination, although not all of the combinations contain this information.

6. Have some additional fun and look up and read the Mars/Venus combinations for your lover, friends, parents, children, and future offspring!

What do you do if you were born on the actual day either Mars or Venus changed signs? You can do one of two things. You can read both the signs involved to determine which one you think fits you best, or you can have a horoscope charted for yourself. A professional horoscope is drawn for your specific time and place of birth and it will tell you where all your planets are, including Mars and Venus. This is not nearly as difficult an option as it might sound. In this wonderful age of computers, it takes only a few minutes to make an accurate chart and there are many astrologers ready to provide this service.

Mars	Venus	Mars	Venus
1920		Sept. 13–in Capricorn	Oct. 10–in Sagittarius
Jan. 31–in Scorpio	Jan. 4–in Sagittarius	Oct. 30–in Aquarius	Nov. 28–in Scorpio
	Jan. 29–in Capricorn	Dec. 11–in Pisces	
	Feb. 23–in Aquarius		
	Mar. 18–in Pisces	**1923**	
	Apr. 12–in Aries	Jan. 21–in Aries	Jan. 2–in Sagittarius
Apr. 23–in Libra	May 6–in Taurus		Feb. 6–in Capricorn
	May 30–in Gemini	Mar. 4–in Taurus	Mar. 6–in Aquarius
	June 24–in Cancer		Apr. 1–in Pisces
July 10–in Scorpio	July 18–in Leo	Apr. 16–in Gemini	Apr. 26–in Aries
	Aug. 12–in Virgo		May 21–in Taurus
Sept. 4–in Sagittarius	Sept. 5–in Libra	May 30–in Cancer	June 15–in Gemini
	Sept. 29–in Scorpio		July 10–in Cancer
Oct. 18–in Capricorn	Oct. 24–in Sagittarius	July 16–in Leo	Aug. 3–in Leo
	Nov. 17–in Capricorn		Aug. 27–in Virgo
Nov. 27–in Aquarius	Dec. 12–in Aquarius	Sept. 1–in Virgo	Sept. 21–in Libra
			Oct. 15–in Scorpio
1921		Oct. 18–in Libra	Nov. 8–in Sagittarius
Jan. 5–in Pisces	Jan. 6–in Pisces		Dec. 2–in Capricorn
	Feb. 2–in Aries	Dec. 4–in Scorpio	Dec. 26–in Aquarius
Feb. 13–in Aries	Mar. 7–in Taurus		
Mar. 25–in Taurus	Apr. 25–in Aries	**1924**	
May 6–in Gemini	June 2–in Taurus	Jan. 19–in Sagittarius	Jan. 19–in Pisces
June 18–in Cancer	July 8–in Gemini		Feb. 13–in Aries
Aug. 3–in Leo	Aug. 5–in Cancer	Mar. 6–in Capricorn	Mar. 9–in Taurus
	Aug. 31–in Leo		Apr. 5–in Gemini
Sept. 19–in Virgo	Sept. 26–in Virgo	Apr. 24–in Aquarius	May 6–in Cancer
	Oct. 20–in Libra	June 24–in Pisces	
Nov. 6–in Libra	Nov. 13–in Scorpio	Aug. 24–in Aquarius	Sept. 8–in Leo
	Dec. 7–in Sagittarius		Oct. 7–in Virgo
Dec. 26–in Scorpio	Dec. 31–in Capricorn	Oct. 19–in Pisces	Nov. 2–in Libra
			Nov. 27–in Scorpio
1922		Dec. 19–in Aries	Dec. 21–in Sagittarius
Feb. 18–in Sagittarius	Jan. 24–in Aquarius		
	Feb. 17–in Pisces	**1925**	
	Mar. 13–in Aries	Feb. 5–in Taurus	Jan. 14–in Capricorn
	Apr. 6–in Taurus		Feb. 7–in Aquarius
	May 1–in Gemini		Mar. 4–in Pisces
	May 25–in Cancer	Mar. 24–in Gemini	Mar. 28–in Aries
	June 19–in Leo		Apr. 21–in Taurus
	July 15–in Virgo	May 9–in Cancer	May 15–in Gemini
	Aug. 10–in Libra		June 9–in Cancer
	Sept. 7–in Scorpio	June 26–in Leo	July 3–in Leo
			July 28–in Virgo

Mars

1925
Aug. 12–in Virgo

Sept. 28–in Libra

Nov. 13–in Scorpio
Dec. 28–in Sagittarius

1926
Feb. 9–in Capricorn

Mar. 23–in Aquarius

May 3–in Pisces

June 15–in Aries

Aug. 1–in Taurus

1927
Feb. 22–in Gemini

Apr. 17–in Cancer

June 6–in Leo

July 25–in Virgo

Sept. 10–in Libra

Oct. 26–in Scorpio

Dec. 8–in Sagittarius

1928
Jan. 19–in Capricorn

Feb. 28–in Aquarius

Apr. 7–in Pisces

May 16–in Aries

Venus

Aug. 22–in Libra
Sept. 16–in Scorpio

Oct. 11–in Sagittarius
Nov. 6–in Capricorn

Dec. 5–in Aquarius

Apr. 6–in Pisces

May 6–in Aries
June 2–in Taurus

June 28–in Gemini
July 24–in Cancer

Aug. 18–in Leo
Sept. 11–in Virgo
Oct. 5–in Libra
Oct. 29–in Scorpio
Nov. 22–in Sagittarius
Dec. 16–in Capricorn

Jan. 9–in Aquarius
Feb. 2–in Pisces
Feb. 26–in Aries
Mar. 22–in Taurus

Apr. 16–in Gemini
May 12–in Cancer

June 8–in Leo
July 7–in Virgo

Nov. 9–in Libra

Dec. 8–in Scorpio

Jan. 3–in Sagittarius
Jan. 29–in Capricorn
Feb. 22–in Aquarius

Mar. 18–in Pisces

Apr. 11–in Aries
May 5–in Taurus

May 30–in Gemini
June 23–in Cancer

Mars

June 26–in Taurus

Aug. 9–in Gemini

Oct. 3–in Cancer

Dec. 20–in Gemini

1929

Mar. 10–Cancer

May 13–in Leo

July 4–in Virgo

Aug. 21–in Libra

Oct. 6–in Scorpio

Nov. 18–in Sagittarius

Dec. 29–in Capricorn

1930
Feb. 6–in Aquarius

Mar. 17–in Pisces

Apr. 24–in Aries

June 3–in Taurus

July 14—in Gemini

Aug. 28–in Cancer

Oct. 20–in Leo

1931
Feb. 16–in Cancer

Mar. 30–in Leo

Venus

July 18–in Leo

Aug. 11–in Virgo
Sept. 4–in Libra
Sept. 29–in Scorpio

Oct. 23–in Sagittarius
Nov. 17–in Capricorn
Dec. 12–in Aquarius

Jan. 6–in Pisces
Feb. 2–in Aries
Mar. 8–in Taurus

Apr. 19–in Aries

June 3–in Taurus

July 8–in Gemini
Aug. 5–in Cancer

Aug. 31–in Leo
Sept. 25–in Virgo

Oct. 20–in Libra
Nov. 13–in Scorpio

Dec. 7–in Sagittarius

Dec. 31–in Capricorn

Jan. 24–in Aquarius
Feb. 16–in Pisces
Mar. 12–in Aries

Apr. 6–in Taurus

Apr. 30–in Gemini
May 25–in Cancer

June 19–in Leo

July 14–in Virgo
Aug. 10–in Libra

Sept. 7–in Scorpio
Oct. 12–in Sagittarius

Nov. 22–in Scorpio

Jan. 3–in Sagittarius
Feb. 6–in Capricorn
Mar. 5–in Aquarius

Mar. 31–in Pisces

Mars	Venus	Mars	Venus
1931		**1934**	
	Apr. 26–in Aries	Feb. 4–in Pisces	
	May 21–in Taurus	Mar. 14–in Aries	Apr. 6–in Pisces
June 10–in Virgo	June 14–in Gemini	Apr. 22–in Taurus	May 6–in Aries
	July 9–in Cancer	June 2–in Gemini	June 2–Taurus
Aug. 1–in Libra	Aug. 3–in Leo		June 28–in Gemini
	Aug. 27–in Virgo	July 16–in Cancer	July 23–in Cancer
Sept. 17–in Scorpio	Sept. 20–in Libra		Aug. 17–in Leo
	Oct. 14–in Scorpio	Aug. 30–in Leo	Sept. 11–in Virgo
Oct. 30–in Sagittarius	Nov. 7–in Sagittarius		Oct. 5–in Libra
	Dec. 1–in Capricorn	Oct. 18–in Virgo	Oct. 29–in Scorpio
Dec. 10–in Capricorn	Dec. 25–in Aquarius		Nov. 22–in Sagittarius
1932		Dec. 11–in Libra	Dec. 16–in Capricorn
Jan. 18–in Aquarius	Jan. 19–in Pisces	**1935**	
	Feb. 12–in Aries		
Feb. 25–in Pisces	Mar. 9–in Taurus		Jan. 8–in Aquarius
Apr. 3–in Aries	Apr. 4–in Gemini		Feb. 1–in Pisces
	May 6–in Cancer		Feb. 26–in Aries
May 12–in Taurus			Mar. 22–in Taurus
June 22–in Gemini	July 13–in Gemini		Apr. 16–in Gemini
	July 28–in Cancer		May 11–in Cancer
Aug. 4–in Cancer	Sept. 8–in Leo		June 7–in Leo
Sept. 20–in Leo	Oct. 7–in Virgo		July 7–in Virgo
	November 2–in Libra	July 29–in Scorpio	
Nov. 13–in Virgo	Nov. 26–in Scorpio	Sept. 16–in Sagittarius	
	Dec. 21–in Sagittarius	Oct. 28–in Capricorn	Nov. 9–in Libra
1933		Dec. 7–in Aquarius	Dec. 8–in Scorpio
	Jan. 14–in Capricorn	**1936**	
	Feb. 7–in Aquarius	Jan. 14–in Pisces	Jan. 3–in Sagittarius
	Mar. 3–in Pisces		Jan. 28–in Capricorn
	Mar. 27–in Aries	Feb. 22–in Aries	Feb. 22–in Aquarius
	Apr. 20–in Taurus		Mar. 17–in Pisces
	May 15–in Gemini	Apr. 1–in Taurus	Apr. 11–in Aries
	June 8–in Cancer		May 5–in Taurus
	July 3–in Leo	May 13–in Gemini	May 29–in Gemini
July 6–in Libra	July 27–in Virgo		June 23–in Cancer
	Aug. 21–in Libra	June 25–in Cancer	July 17–in Leo
Aug. 26–in Scorpio	Sept. 15–in Scorpio	Aug. 10–in Leo	Aug. 11–in Virgo
Oct. 9–in Sagittarius	Oct. 11–in Sagittarius		Sept. 4–in Libra
	Nov. 6–in Capricorn	Sept. 26–in Virgo	Sept. 28–in Scorpio
Nov. 19–in Capricorn	Dec. 5–in Aquarius		Oct. 23–in Sagittarius
Dec. 28–in Aquarius		Nov. 14–in Libra	Nov. 16–in Capricorn
			Dec. 11–in Aquarius

Mars	Venus	Mars	Venus
1937		Nov. 19–in Pisces	Dec. 1–in Capricorn
Jan. 5–in Scorpio	Jan. 6–in Pisces		Dec. 25–in Aquarius
	Feb. 2–in Aries		
	Mar. 9–in Taurus	**1940**	
Mar. 13–in Sagittarius	Apr. 14–in Aries	Jan. 3–in Aries	Jan. 18–in Pisces
May 14–in Scorpio	June 4–in Taurus		Feb. 12–in Aries
	July 7–in Gemini	Feb. 17–in Taurus	Mar. 8–in Taurus
	Aug. 4–in Cancer	Apr. 1–in Gemini	Apr. 4–in Gemini
	Aug. 30–in Leo		May 6–in Cancer
Aug. 8–in Sagittarius	Sept. 25–in Virgo	May 17–in Cancer	
Sept. 30–in Capricorn	Oct. 19–in Libra	July 3–in Leo	July 5–in Gemini
Nov. 11–in Aquarius	Nov. 12–in Scorpio		Aug. 1–in Cancer
	Dec. 6–in Sagittarius	Aug. 19–in Virgo	Sept. 8–in Leo
Dec. 21–in Pisces	Dec. 30–in Capricorn	Oct. 5–in Libra	Oct. 6–in Virgo
			Nov. 1–in Libra
1938		Nov. 20–in Scorpio	Nov. 26–in Scorpio
Jan. 30–in Aries	Jan. 23–in Aquarius		Dec. 20–in Sagittarius
	Feb. 16–in Pisces		
Mar. 12–in Taurus	Mar. 12–in Aries	**1941**	
	Apr. 5–in Taurus	Jan. 4–in Sagittarius	Jan. 13–in Capricorn
Apr. 23–in Gemini	Apr. 29–in Gemini		Feb. 6–in Aquarius
	May 24–in Cancer	Feb. 17–in Capricorn	Mar. 2–in Pisces
June 7–in Cancer	June 18–in Leo		Mar. 27–in Aries
	July 14–in Virgo	Apr. 2–in Aquarius	Apr. 20–in Taurus
July 22–in Leo	Aug. 9–in Libra		May 14–in Gemini
Sept. 7–in Virgo	Sept. 7–in Scorpio	May 16–in Pisces	June 7–in Cancer
	Oct. 13–in Sagittarius	July 2–in Aries	July 2–in Leo
Oct. 25–in Libra	Nov. 15–in Scorpio		July 27–in Virgo
Dec. 11–in Scorpio			Aug. 21–in Libra
			Sept. 15–in Scorpio
1939			Oct. 10–in Sagittarius
Jan. 29–in Sagittarius	Jan. 4–in Sagittarius		Nov. 6–in Capricorn
	Feb. 6–in Capricorn		Dec. 5–in Aquarius
	March 5–in Aquarius		
Mar. 21–in Capricorn	Mar. 31–in Pisces	**1942**	
	Apr. 25–in Aries	Jan. 11–in Taurus	
	May 20–in Taurus	Mar. 7–in Gemini	Apr. 6–in Pisces
May 24–in Aquarius	June 14–in Gemini	Apr. 26–in Cancer	May 6–in Aries
	July 9–in Cancer		June 2–in Taurus
July 21–in Capricorn	Aug. 2–in Leo	June 14–in Leo	June 27–in Gemini
	Aug. 26–in Virgo		July 23–in Cancer
	Sept. 20–in Libra	Aug. 1–in Virgo	Aug. 17–in Leo
Sept. 24–in Aquarius	Oct. 14–in Scorpio		Sept. 10–in Virgo
	Nov. 7–in Sagittarius	Sept. 17–in Libra	Oct. 4–in Libra
			Oct. 28–in Scorpio

Mars	Venus	Mars	Venus
1942		Nov. 11–in Leo	Nov. 12–in Scorpio
Nov. 1–in Scorpio	Nov. 21–in Sagittarius		Dec. 6–in Sagittarius
Dec. 15–in Sagittarius	Dec. 15–in Capricorn	Dec. 26–in Cancer	Dec. 30–in Capricorn
1943		**1946**	
Jan. 26–in Capricorn	Jan. 8–in Aquarius		Jan. 22–in Aquarius
	Feb. 1–in Pisces		Feb. 15–in Pisces
	Feb. 25–in Aries		Mar. 11–in Aries
Mar. 8–in Aquarius	Mar. 21–in Taurus		Apr. 5–in Taurus
	Apr. 15–in Gemini	Apr. 22–in Leo	Apr. 29–in Gemini
Apr. 17–in Pisces	May 11–in Cancer		May 24–in Cancer
May 27–in Aries	June 7–in Leo		June 18–in Leo
July 7–in Taurus	July 7–in Virgo	June 20–in Virgo	July 13–in Virgo
Aug. 23–in Gemini	Nov. 9–in Libra	Aug. 9–in Libra	Aug. 9–in Libra
	Dec. 8–in Scorpio		Sept. 7–in Scorpio
		Sept. 24–in Scorpio	Oct. 16–in Sagittarius
1944		Nov. 6–in Sagittarius	Nov. 8–in Scorpio
	Jan. 3–in Sagittarius	Dec. 17–in Capricorn	
	Jan. 28–in Capricorn	**1947**	
	Feb. 21–in Aquarius	Jan. 25–in Aquarius	Jan. 5–in Sagittarius
	Mar. 17–in Pisces		Feb. 6–in Capricorn
Mar. 28–in Cancer	Apr. 10–in Aries	Mar. 4–in Pisces	Mar. 5–in Aquarius
	May 4–in Taurus		Mar. 30–in Pisces
May 22–in Leo	May 29–in Gemini	Apr. 11–in Aries	Apr. 25–in Aries
	June 22–in Cancer		May 20–in Taurus
July 12–in Virgo	July 17–in Leo	May 21–in Taurus	June 13–in Gemini
	Aug. 10–in Virgo	July 1–in Gemini	July 8–in Cancer
Aug. 29–in Libra	Sept. 3–in Libra		
	Sept. 28–in Scorpio	Aug. 13–in Cancer	Aug. 26–in Virgo
Oct. 13–in Scorpio	Oct. 22–in Sagittarius		Sept. 19–in Libra
	Nov. 16–in Capricorn	Oct. 1–in Leo	Oct. 13–in Scorpio
Nov. 25–Sagittarius	Dec. 11–in Aquarius		Nov. 6–in Sagittarius
			Nov. 30–in Capricorn
1945		Dec. 1–in Virgo	Dec. 24–in Aquarius
Jan. 5–in Capricorn	Jan. 5–in Pisces	**1948**	
	Feb. 2–in Aries	Feb. 12–in Leo	Jan. 18–in Pisces
Feb. 14–in Aquarius	Mar. 11–in Taurus		Feb. 11–in Aries
Mar. 25–in Pisces	Apr. 7–in Aries		Mar. 8–in Taurus
May 2–in Aries	June 4–in Taurus		Apr. 4–in Gemini
June 11–in Taurus	July 7–in Gemini		May 7–in Cancer
July 23–in Gemini	Aug. 4–in Cancer	May 18–in Virgo	June 29–in Gemini
	Aug. 30–in Leo	July 17–in Libra	Aug. 3–in Cancer
Sept. 7–in Cancer	Sept. 24–in Virgo	Sept. 3–in Scorpio	Sept. 8–in Leo
	Oct. 19–in Libra		Oct. 6–in Virgo

Mars	Venus	Mars	Venus
1948		Aug. 18–in Leo	
Oct. 17–in Sagittarius	Nov. 1–in Libra	Oct. 5–in Virgo	Nov. 9–in Libra
	Nov. 26–in Scorpio	Nov. 24–in Libra	Dec. 8–in Scorpio
Nov. 26–in Scorpio	Dec. 20–in Sagittarius		
		1952	
1949		Jan. 20–in Scorpio	Jan. 2–in Sagittarius
Jan. 4–in Aquarius	Jan. 13–in Capricorn		Jan. 27–in Capricorn
	Feb. 6–in Aquarius		Feb. 21–in Aquarius
Feb. 11–in Pisces	Mar. 2–in Pisces		Mar. 16–in Pisces
Mar. 21–in Aries	Mar. 26–in Aries		Apr. 9–in Aries
	Apr. 19–in Taurus		May 4–in Taurus
Apr. 30–in Taurus	May 14–in Gemini		May 28–in Gemini
	June 7–in Cancer		June 22–in Cancer
June 10–in Gemini	July 1–in Leo		July 16–in Leo
July 23–in Cancer	July 26–in Virgo		Aug. 9–in Virgo
	Aug. 20–in Libra	Aug. 27–in Sagittarius	Sept. 3–in Libra
Sept. 7–in Leo	Sept. 14–in Scorpio		Sept. 27–in Scorpio
	Oct. 10–in Sagittarius	Oct. 12–in Capricorn	Oct. 22–in Sagittarius
Oct. 27–in Virgo	Nov. 6–in Capricorn		Nov. 15–in Capricorn
	Dec. 6–in Aquarius	Nov. 21–in Aquarius	Dec. 10–in Aquarius
Dec. 26–in Libra		Dec. 30–in Pisces	
1950		**1953**	
Mar. 28–in Virgo	Apr. 6–in Pisces	Feb. 8–in Aries	Jan. 5–in Pisces
	May 5–in Aries		Feb. 2–in Aries
	June 1–in Taurus		Mar. 14–in Taurus
June 11–in Libra	June 27–in Gemini	Mar. 20–in Taurus	Mar. 31–in Aries
	July 22–in Cancer	May 1–in Gemini	June 5–in Taurus
Aug. 10–in Scorpio	Aug. 16–in Leo	June 14–in Cancer	July 7–in Gemini
	Sept. 10–in Virgo	July 29–in Leo	Aug. 4–in Cancer
Sept. 25–in Sagittarius	Oct. 4–in Libra		Aug. 30–in Leo
	Oct. 28–in Scorpio	Sept. 14–in Virgo	Sept. 24–in Virgo
Nov. 6–in Capricorn	Nov. 21–in Sagittarius		Oct. 18–in Libra
Dec. 15–in Aquarius	Dec. 14–in Capricorn	Nov. 1–in Libra	Nov. 11–in Scorpio
1951			Dec. 5–in Sagittarius
Jan. 22–in Pisces	Jan. 7–in Aquarius	Dec. 20–in Scorpio	Dec. 29–in Capricorn
	Jan. 31–in Pisces		
	Feb. 24–in Aries	**1954**	
Mar. 1–in Aries	Mar. 21–in Taurus	Feb. 9–in Sagittarius	Jan. 22–in Aquarius
Apr. 10–in Taurus	Apr. 15–in Gemini		Feb. 15–in Pisces
	May 11–in Cancer		Mar. 11–in Aries
May 21–in Gemini	June 7–in Leo		Apr. 4–in Taurus
July 3–in Cancer	July 8–in Virgo	Apr. 12–in Capricorn	Apr. 28–in Gemini
			May 23–in Cancer

Mars

Venus

1954
July 3–in Sagittarius

June 17–in Leo
July 13–in Virgo
Aug. 9–in Libra

Aug. 24–in Capricorn

Sept. 6–in Scorpio

Oct. 21–in Aquarius

Oct. 23–in Sagittarius
Oct. 27–in Scorpio

Dec. 4–in Pisces

1955
Jan. 15–in Aries

Jan. 6–in Sagittarius
Feb. 6–in Capricorn

Feb. 26–in Taurus

Mar. 4–in Aquarius
Mar. 30–in Pisces

Apr. 10–in Gemini

Apr. 24–in Aries
May 19–in Taurus

May 26–in Cancer

June 13–in Gemini
July 8–in Cancer

July 11–in Leo

Aug. 1–in Leo
Aug. 25–in Virgo

Aug. 27–in Virgo

Sept. 18–in Libra

Oct. 13–in Libra

Oct. 13–in Scorpio
Nov. 6–in Sagittarius

Nov. 29–in Scorpio

Nov. 30–in Capricorn
Dec. 24–in Aquarius

1956
Jan. 14–in Sagittarius

Jan. 17–in Pisces
Feb. 11–in Aries

Feb. 28–in Capricorn

Mar. 7–in Taurus
Apr. 4–in Gemini

Apr. 14–in Aquarius

May 8–in Cancer

June 3–in Pisces

June 23–in Gemini
Aug. 4–in Cancer
Sept. 8–in Leo
Oct. 6–in Virgo
Oct. 31–in Libra
Nov. 25–in Scorpio

Dec. 6–in Aries

Dec. 19–in Sagittarius

1957
Jan. 28–in Taurus

Jan. 12–in Capricorn
Feb. 5–in Aquarius
Mar. 1–in Pisces

Mars

Venus

Mar. 17–in Gemini

Mar. 25–in Aries
Apr. 19–in Taurus

May 4–in Cancer

May 13–in Gemini
June 6–in Cancer

June 21–in Leo

July 1–in Leo
July 26–in Virgo

Aug. 8–in Virgo

Aug. 20–in Libra
Sept. 14–in Scorpio

Sept. 24–in Libra

Oct. 10–in Sagittarius
Nov. 5–in Capricorn

Nov. 8–in Scorpio

Dec. 6–in Aquarius

Dec. 23–in Sagittarius

1958
Feb. 3–in Capricorn

Mar. 17–in Aquarius
Apr. 27–in Pisces

Apr. 6–in Pisces
May 5–in Aries
June 1–in Taurus

June 7–in Aries

June 26–in Gemini

July 21–in Taurus

July 22–in Cancer
Aug. 16–in Leo
Sept. 9–in Virgo

Sept. 21–in Gemini

Oct. 3–in Libra

Oct. 29–in Taurus

Oct. 27–in Scorpio
Nov. 20–in Sagittarius
Dec. 14–in Capricorn

1959
Feb. 10–in Gemini

Jan. 7–in Aquarius
Jan. 31–in Pisces
Feb. 24–in Aries
Mar. 20–in Taurus

Apr. 10–in Cancer

Apr. 14–in Gemini
May 10–in Cancer

June 1–in Leo

June 6–in Leo
July 8–in Virgo

July 20–in Virgo

Sept. 5–in Libra

Sept. 20–in Leo
Sept. 25–in Virgo

Oct. 21–in Scorpio

Nov. 9–in Libra

Dec. 3–in Sagittarius

Dec. 7–in Scorpio

Mars	Venus	Mars	Venus
1960		**1963**	
Jan. 14–Capricorn	Jan. 2–in Sagittarius		Jan. 6–in Sagittarius
	Jan. 27–in Capricorn		Feb. 5–in Capricorn
Feb. 23–in Aquarius	Feb. 20–in Aquarius		Mar. 4–in Aquarius
	Mar. 16–in Pisces		Mar. 30–in Pisces
Apr. 2–in Pisces	Apr. 9–in Aries		Apr. 24–in Aries
	May 3–in Taurus		May 19–in Taurus
May 11–in Aries	May 28–in Gemini	June 3–in Virgo	June 12–in Gemini
			July 7–in Cancer
June 20–in Taurus	June 21–in Cancer	July 27–in Libra	July 31–in Leo
	July 16–in Leo		Aug. 25–in Virgo
Aug. 2–in Gemini	Aug. 9–in Virgo	Sept. 12–in Scorpio	Sept. 18–in Libra
	Sept. 2–in Libra		Oct. 12–in Scorpio
Sept. 21–in Cancer	Sept. 27–in Scorpio	Oct. 25–in Sagittarius	Nov. 5–in Sagittarius
	Oct. 21–in Sagittarius		Nov. 29–in Capricorn
	Nov. 15–in Capricorn	Dec. 4–in Capricorn	Dec. 23–in Aquarius
	Dec. 10–in Aquarius		
1961		**1964**	
Feb. 4–in Gemini	Jan. 5–in Pisces	Jan. 13–in Aquarius	Jan. 17–in Pisces
	Feb. 2–in Aries		Feb. 10–in Aries
Feb. 7–in Cancer		Feb. 20–in Pisces	Mar. 7–in Taurus
May 6–in Leo	June 5–in Taurus	Mar. 29–in Aries	Apr. 4–in Gemini
June 28–in Virgo	July 7–in Gemini	May 7–in Taurus	May 9–in Cancer
	Aug. 3–in Cancer	June 17–in Gemini	June 17–in Gemini
Aug. 17–in Libra	Aug. 29–in Leo	July 30–in Cancer	Aug. 5–in Cancer
	Sept. 23–in Virgo		Sept. 8–in Leo
Oct. 1–in Scorpio	Oct. 18–in Libra	Sept. 15–in Leo	Oct. 5–in Virgo
	Nov. 11–in Scorpio		Oct. 31–in Libra
Nov. 13–in Sagittarius	Dec. 5–in Sagittarius	Nov. 6–in Virgo	Nov. 25–in Scorpio
Dec. 24–in Capricorn	Dec. 28–in Capricorn		Dec. 19–in Sagittarius
1962		**1965**	
	Jan. 21–in Aquarius		Jan. 12–in Capricorn
Feb. 1–in Aquarius	Feb. 14–in Pisces		Feb. 5–in Aquarius
	Mar. 10–in Aries		Mar. 1–in Pisces
Mar. 12–in Pisces	Apr. 3–in Taurus		Mar. 25–in Aries
Apr. 19–in Aries	Apr. 28–in Gemini		Apr. 18–in Taurus
	May 23–in Cancer		May 12–in Gemini
May 28–in Taurus	June 17–in Leo		June 6–in Cancer
July 9–in Gemini	July 12–in Virgo	June 29–in Libra	June 30–in Leo
	Aug. 8–in Libra		July 25–in Virgo
Aug. 22–in Cancer	Sept. 7–in Scorpio	Aug. 20–in Scorpio	Aug. 20–in Libra
Oct. 11–in Leo			Sept. 13–in Scorpio
		Oct. 4–in Sagittarius	Oct. 9–in Sagittarius
			Nov. 5–in Capricorn

Mars	Venus	Mars	Venus
1965		Sept. 21–in Virgo	Sept. 26–in Scorpio
Nov. 14–in Capricorn	Dec. 7–in Aquarius		Oct. 21–in Sagittarius
Dec. 23–in Aquarius		Nov. 9–in Libra	Nov. 14–in Capricorn
			Dec. 9–in Aquarius
1966		Dec. 29–in Scorpio	
Jan. 30–in Pisces	Feb. 6–in Capricorn		
	Feb. 25–in Aquarius	**1969**	
Mar. 9–in Aries	Apr. 6–in Pisces	Feb. 25–in Sagittarius	Jan. 4–in Pisces
Apr. 17–in Taurus	May 5–in Aries		Feb. 2–in Aries
May 28–in Gemini	May 31–in Taurus		June 6–in Taurus
	June 26–in Gemini		July 6–in Gemini
			Aug. 3–in Cancer
July 11–in Cancer	July 21–in Cancer		Aug. 29–in Leo
	Aug. 15–in Leo		
Aug. 25–in Leo	Sept. 8–in Virgo	Sept. 21–in Capricorn	Sept. 23–in Virgo
	Oct. 3–in Libra		Oct. 17–in Libra
Oct. 12–in Virgo	Oct. 27–in Scorpio	Nov. 4–in Aquarius	Nov. 10–in Scorpio
	Nov. 20–in Sagittarius		Dec. 4–in Sagittarius
Dec. 4–in Libra	Dec. 13–in Capricorn	Dec. 15–in Pisces	Dec. 28–in Capricorn
		1970	
1967		Jan. 24–in Aries	Jan. 21–in Aquarius
Feb. 12–in Scorpio	Jan. 6–in Aquarius		Feb. 14–in Pisces
	Jan. 30–in Pisces	Mar. 7–in Taurus	Mar. 10–in Aries
	Feb. 23–in Aries		Apr. 3–in Taurus
	Mar. 20–in Taurus	Apr. 18–in Gemini	Apr. 27–in Gemini
Mar. 31–in Libra	Apr. 14–in Gemini		May 22–in Cancer
	May 10–in Cancer	June 2–in Cancer	June 16–in Leo
	June 6–in Leo		July 12–in Virgo
	July 8–in Virgo	July 18–in Leo	Aug. 8–in Libra
July 19–in Scorpio		Sept. 3–in Virgo	Sept. 7–in Scorpio
Sept. 10–in Sagittarius	Sept. 9–in Leo	Oct. 20–in Libra	
	Oct. 1–in Virgo	Dec. 6–in Scorpio	
Oct. 23–in Capricorn	Nov. 9–in Libra		
Dec. 1–in Aquarius	Dec. 7–in Scorpio	**1971**	
		Jan. 23–in Sagittarius	Jan. 7–in Sagittarius
1968			Feb. 5–in Capricorn
Jan. 9–in Pisces	Jan. 1–in Sagittarius		Mar. 4–in Aquarius
	Jan. 26–in Capricorn	Mar. 12–in Capricorn	Mar. 29–in Pisces
Feb. 17–in Aries	Feb. 20–in Aquarius		Apr. 23–in Aries
	Mar. 15–in Pisces	May 3–in Aquarius	May 18–in Taurus
	Apr. 8–in Aries		June 12–in Gemini
Mar. 27–in Taurus	May 3–in Taurus		July 6–in Cancer
			July 31–in Leo
May 8–in Gemini	May 27–in Gemini		Aug. 24–in Virgo
June 21–in Cancer	June 21–in Cancer		Sept. 17–in Libra
	July 15–in Leo		Oct. 11–in Scorpio
Aug. 5–in Leo	Aug. 8–in Virgo		
	Sept. 2–in Libra		

Mars	Venus	Mars	Venus
1971		July 27–in Virgo	Aug. 14–in Leo
Nov. 6–in Pisces	Nov. 5–in Sagittarius		Sept. 8–in Virgo
	Nov. 29–in Capricorn	Sept. 12–in Libra	Oct. 2–in Libra
Dec. 26–in Aries	Dec. 23–in Aquarius		Oct. 26–in Scorpio
1972		Oct. 28–in Scorpio	Nov. 19–in Sagittarius
Feb. 10–in Taurus	Jan. 16–in Pisces	Dec. 10–in Sagittarius	Dec. 13–in Capricorn
	Feb. 10–in Aries	**1975**	
	Mar. 7–in Taurus	Jan. 21–in Capricorn	Jan. 6–in Aquarius
Mar. 27–in Gemini	Apr. 3–in Gemini		Jan. 30–in Pisces
	May 10–in Cancer		Feb. 23–in Aries
May 12–in Cancer	June 11–in Gemini	Mar. 3–in Aquarius	Mar. 19–in Taurus
June 28–in Leo	Aug. 6–in Cancer	Apr. 11–in Pisces	Apr. 13–in Gemini
Aug. 15–in Virgo	Sept. 7–in Leo		May 9–in Cancer
Sept. 30–in Libra	Oct. 5–in Virgo	May 21–in Aries	June 6–in Leo
	Oct. 30–in Libra	July 1–in Taurus	July 9–in Virgo
Nov. 15–in Scorpio	Nov. 24–in Scorpio	Aug. 14–in Gemini	Sept. 2–in Leo
	Dec. 18–in Sagittarius		Oct. 4–in Virgo
Dec. 30–in Sagittarius		Oct. 17–in Cancer	Nov. 9–in Libra
1973		Nov. 25–in Gemini	Dec. 7–in Scorpio
Feb. 12–in Capricorn	Jan. 11–in Capricorn	**1976**	
	Feb. 4–in Aquarius	Mar. 18–in Cancer	Jan. 1–in Sagittarius
	Feb. 28–in Pisces		Jan. 26–in Capricorn
Mar. 26–in Aquarius	Mar. 24–in Aries		Feb. 19–in Aquarius
	Apr. 18–in Taurus		Mar. 15–in Pisces
May 8–in Pisces	May 12–in Gemini		Apr. 8–in Aries
	June 5–in Cancer		May 2–in Taurus
June 20–in Aries	June 30–in Leo	May 16–in Leo	May 27–in Gemini
	July 25–in Virgo		June 20–in Cancer
Aug. 12–in Taurus	Aug. 19–in Libra	July 6–in Virgo	July 14–in Leo
	Sept. 13–in Scorpio		Aug. 8–in Virgo
	Oct. 9–in Sagittarius	Aug. 24–in Libra	Sept. 1–in Libra
Oct. 29–in Aries	Nov. 5–in Capricorn		Sept. 26–in Scorpio
	Dec. 7–in Aquarius	Oct. 8–in Scorpio	Oct. 20–in Sagittarius
Dec. 24–in Taurus			Nov. 14–in Capricorn
1974		Nov. 20–in Sagittarius	Dec. 9–in Aquarius
Feb. 27–in Gemini	Jan. 29–Capricorn	**1977**	
	Feb. 28–in Aquarius	Jan. 1–in Capricorn	Jan. 4–in Pisces
	Apr. 6–in Pisces		Feb. 2–in Aries
Apr. 20–in Cancer	May 4–in Aries	Feb. 9–in Aquarius	
	May 31–in Taurus	Mar. 20–in Pisces	
June 9–in Leo	June 25–in Gemini	Apr. 27–in Aries	
	July 21–in Cancer		

Mars	Venus	Mars	Venus
1977		**1980**	
June 6–in Taurus	June 6–in Taurus	Mar. 11–in Leo	Jan. 16–in Pisces
	July 6–in Gemini		Feb. 9–in Aries
July 17–in Gemini	Aug. 2–in Cancer		Mar. 6–in Taurus
	Aug. 28–in Leo		Apr. 3–in Gemini
Sept. 1–in Cancer	Sept. 22–in Virgo	May 4–in Virgo	May 12–in Cancer
	Oct. 17–in Libra		June 5–in Gemini
Oct. 26–in Leo	Nov. 10–in Scorpio	July 10–in Libra	Aug. 6–in Cancer
	Dec. 4–in Sagittarius	Aug. 29–in Scorpio	Sept. 7–in Leo
	Dec. 27–in Capricorn		Oct. 4–in Virgo
		Oct. 12–in Sagittarius	Oct. 30–in Libra
1978		Nov. 22–in Capricorn	Nov. 24–in Scorpio
Jan. 26–in Cancer	Jan. 20–in Aquarius		Dec. 18–in Sagittarius
	Feb. 13–in Pisces	Dec. 30–in Aquarius	
	Mar. 9–in Aries		
	Apr. 2–in Taurus	**1981**	
Apr. 10–in Leo	Apr. 27–in Gemini	Feb. 6–in Pisces	Jan. 11–in Capricorn
	May 22–in Cancer		Feb. 4–in Aquarius
June 14–in Virgo	June 16–in Leo		Feb. 28–in Pisces
	July 12–in Virgo	Mar. 17–in Aries	Mar. 24–in Aries
Aug. 4–in Libra	Aug. 8–in Libra		Apr. 17–in Taurus
	Sept. 7–in Scorpio	Apr. 25–in Taurus	May 11–in Gemini
Sept. 19–in Scorpio		June 5–in Gemini	June 5–in Cancer
Nov. 2–in Sagittarius			June 29–in Leo
Dec. 12–in Capricorn		July 18–in Cancer	July 24–in Virgo
			Aug. 18–in Libra
1979		Sept. 2–in Leo	Sept. 12–in Scorpio
Jan. 20–in Aquarius	Jan. 7–in Sagittarius		Oct. 9–in Sagittarius
	Feb. 5–in Capricorn	Oct. 21–in Virgo	Nov. 5–in Capricorn
Feb. 27–in Pisces	Mar. 3–in Aquarius		Dec. 8–in Aquarius
	Mar. 29–in Pisces	Dec. 16–in Libra	
Apr. 7–in Aries	Apr. 23–in Aries		
May 16–in Taurus	May 18–in Taurus	**1982**	
	June 11–in Gemini	Aug. 3–in Scorpio	Jan. 23–in Capricorn
June 26–in Gemini	July 6–in Cancer		Mar. 2–in Aquarius
	July 30–in Leo		Apr. 6–in Pisces
Aug. 8–in Cancer	Aug. 24–in Virgo		May 4–in Aries
	Sept. 17–in Libra		May 30–in Taurus
Sept. 24–in Leo	Oct. 11–in Scorpio		June 25–in Gemini
	Nov. 4–in Sagittarius		July 20–in Cancer
Nov. 19–in Virgo	Nov. 28–in Capricorn		Aug. 14–in Leo
	Dec. 22–in Aquarius		Sept. 7–in Virgo
		Sept. 20–in Sagittarius	Oct. 2–in Libra
			Oct. 26–in Scorpio
		Oct. 31–in Capricorn	Nov. 18–in Sagittarius
		Dec. 10–in Aquarius	Dec. 12–in Capricorn

Mars	Venus	Mars	Venus

1983
Jan. 17–in Pisces

Jan. 5–in Aquarius
Jan. 29–in Pisces
Feb. 22–in Aries

Feb. 24–in Aries — Mar. 19–in Taurus

Apr. 5–in Taurus — Apr. 13–in Gemini
May 9–in Cancer

May 16–in Gemini — June 6–in Leo

June 29–in Cancer — July 10–in Virgo

Aug. 13–in Leo — Aug. 27–in Leo

Sept. 29–in Virgo — Oct. 5–in Virgo
Nov. 9–in Libra

Nov. 18–in Libra — Dec. 6–in Scorpio

1984
Jan. 11–in Scorpio

Jan. 1–in Sagittarius
Jan. 25–in Capricorn
Feb. 19–in Aquarius
Mar. 14–in Pisces
Apr. 7–in Aries
May 2–in Taurus
May 28–in Gemini
June 20–in Cancer
July 14–in Leo
Aug. 7–in Virgo

Aug. 17–in Sagittarius — Sept. 1–in Libra
Sept. 25–in Scorpio

Oct. 5–in Capricorn — Oct. 20–in Sagittarius
Nov. 13–in Capricorn

Nov. 15–in Aquarius — Dec. 9–in Aquarius

Dec. 25–in Pisces

1985
Feb. 2–in Aries

Jan. 4–in Pisces
Feb. 2–in Aries

Mar. 15–in Taurus

Apr. 26–in Gemini — June 6–in Taurus

June 9–in Cancer — July 6–in Gemini

July 25–in Leo — Aug. 2–in Cancer
Aug. 28–in Leo

Sept. 10–in Virgo — Sept. 22–in Virgo
Oct. 16–in Libra

Oct. 27–in Libra — Nov. 9–in Scorpio
Dec. 3–in Sagittarius

Dec. 14–in Scorpio — Dec. 27–in Capricorn

1986
Feb. 2–in Sagittarius

Jan. 20–in Aquarius
Feb. 13–in Pisces
Mar. 9–in Aries

Mar. 28–in Capricorn — Apr. 2–in Taurus
Apr. 26–in Gemini
May 21–in Cancer
June 15–in Leo
July 11–in Virgo
Aug. 7–in Libra
Sept. 7–in Scorpio

Oct. 9–in Aquarius
Nov. 26–in Pisces

1987
Jan. 8–in Aries

Jan. 7–in Sagittarius
Feb. 5–in Capricorn

Feb. 20–in Taurus — Mar. 3–in Aquarius
Mar. 28–in Pisces

Apr. 5–in Gemini — Apr. 22–in Aries
May 17–in Taurus

May 21–in Cancer — June 11–in Gemini

July 6–in Leo — July 5–in Cancer
July 30–in Leo

Aug. 22–in Virgo — Aug. 23–in Virgo
Sept. 16–in Libra

Oct. 8–in Libra — Oct. 10–in Scorpio
Nov. 3–in Sagittarius

Nov. 24–in Scorpio — Nov. 28–in Capricorn
Dec. 22–in Aquarius

1988
Jan. 8–in Sagittarius

Jan. 15–in Pisces
Feb. 9–in Aries

Feb. 22–in Capricorn — Mar. 6–in Taurus
Apr. 3–in Gemini

Apr. 6–in Aquarius — May 17–in Cancer

May 22–in Pisces — May 27–in Gemini

Mars	Venus	Mars	Venus
1988		Apr. 3–in Cancer	Apr. 13–in Gemini
July 13–in Aries	Aug. 6–in Cancer		May 9–in Cancer
	Sept. 7–in Leo	May 26–in Leo	June 6–in Leo
	Oct. 4–in Virgo		July 11–in Virgo
Oct. 23–in Pisces	Oct. 29–in Libra	July 15–in Virgo	Aug. 21–in Leo
Nov. 1–in Aries	Nov. 23–in Scorpio	Sept. 1–in Libra	Oct. 6–in Virgo
	Dec. 17–in Sagittarius	Oct. 16–in Scorpio	Nov. 9–in Libra
1989		Nov. 29–in Sagittarius	Dec. 6–in Scorpio
Jan. 19–in Taurus	Jan. 10–in Capricorn		Dec. 31–in Sagittarius
	Feb. 3–in Aquarius	**1992**	
	Feb. 27–in Pisces	Jan. 9–in Capricorn	Jan. 25–in Capricorn
Mar. 11–in Gemini	Mar. 23–in Aries	Feb. 15–in Aquarius	Feb. 18–in Aquarius
	Apr. 16–in Taurus		Mar. 13–in Pisces
Apr. 29–in Cancer	May 1–in Gemini	Mar. 28–in Pisces	Apr. 7–in Aries
	June 4–in Cancer		May 1–in Taurus
June 16–in Leo	June 29–in Leo	May 5–in Aries	May 26–in Gemini
	July 24–in Virgo	June 14–in Taurus	June 19–in Cancer
Aug. 3–in Virgo	Aug. 18–in Libra		July 13–in Leo
	Sept. 12–in Scorpio	July 26–in Gemini	Aug. 7–in Virgo
Sept. 19–in Libra	Oct. 8–in Sagittarius		Aug. 31–in Libra
Nov. 4–in Scorpio	Nov. 5–in Capricorn	Sept. 12–in Cancer	Sept. 25–in Scorpio
	Dec. 10–in Aquarius		Oct. 19–in Sagittarius
Dec. 18–in Sagittarius			Nov. 13–in Capricorn
1990			Dec. 8–in Aquarius
Jan. 29–in Capricorn	Jan. 16–in Capricorn	**1993**	
	Mar. 3–in Aquarius		Jan. 3–in Pisces
Mar. 11–in Aquarius	Apr. 6–in Pisces		Feb. 2–in Aries
Apr. 20–in Pisces	May 4–in Aries	Apr. 27–in Leo	June 6–in Taurus
May 31–in Aries	May 30–in Taurus	June 23–in Virgo	July 6–in Gemini
	June 25–in Gemini		Aug. 1–in Cancer
July 12–in Taurus	July 20–in Cancer	Aug. 12–in Libra	Aug. 27–in Leo
	Aug. 13–in Leo		Sept. 21–in Virgo
Aug. 31–in Gemini	Sept. 7–in Virgo	Sept. 27–in Scorpio	Oct. 16–in Libra
	Oct. 1–in Libra	Nov. 9–in Sagittarius	Nov. 9–in Scorpio
	Oct. 25–in Scorpio		Dec. 2–in Sagittarius
Dec. 14–in Taurus	Nov. 18–in Sagittarius	Dec. 20–in Capricorn	Dec. 26–in Capricorn
	Dec. 12–in Capricorn	**1994**	
1991		Jan. 28–Aquarius	Jan. 19–in Aquarius
Jan. 21–in Gemini	Jan. 5–in Aquarius		Feb. 12–in Pisces
	Jan. 29–in Pisces	Mar. 7–in Pisces	Mar. 8–in Aries
	Feb. 22–in Aries		Apr. 1–in Taurus
	Mar. 18–in Taurus		

Mars	Venus	Mars	Venus
1994		**1997**	
Apr. 14–in Aries	Apr. 26–in Gemini	Jan. 3–in Libra	Jan. 10–in Capricorn
	May 21–in Cancer		Feb. 3–in Aquarius
May 23–in Taurus	June 15–in Leo		Feb. 27–in Pisces
July 3–in Gemini	July 11–in Virgo	Mar. 8–in Virgo	Mar. 23–in Aries
	Aug. 7–in Libra		Apr. 16–in Taurus
Aug. 16–in Cancer	Sept. 7–in Scorpio		May 10–in Gemini
Oct. 4–in Leo			June 4–in Cancer
Dec. 12–in Virgo		June 19–in Libra	June 28–in Leo
			July 23–in Virgo
1995		Aug. 14–in Scorpio	Aug. 17–in Libra
Jan. 22–in Leo	Jan. 7–in Sagittarius		Sept. 12–in Scorpio
	Feb. 4–in Capricorn	Sept. 28–in Sagittarius	Oct. 8–in Sagittarius
	Mar. 2–in Aquarius		Nov. 5–in Capricorn
	Mar. 28–in Pisces	Nov. 9–in Capricorn	Dec. 12–in Aquarius
	Apr. 22–in Aries	Dec. 18–in Aquarius	
	May 16–in Taurus		
May 25–in Virgo	June 10–in Gemini	**1998**	
	July 5–in Cancer	Jan. 25–in Pisces	Jan. 9–in Capricorn
July 21–in Libra	July 29–in Leo	Mar. 4–in Aries	Mar. 4–in Aquarius
	Aug. 23–in Virgo		Apr. 6–in Pisces
Sept. 7–in Scorpio	Sept. 16–in Libra	Apr. 13–in Taurus	May 3–in Aries
	Oct. 10–in Scorpio	May 24–in Gemini	May 29–in Taurus
Oct. 20–in Sagittarius	Nov. 3–in Sagittarius		June 24–in Gemini
	Nov. 27–in Capricorn	July 6–in Cancer	July 19–in Cancer
Nov. 30–in Capricorn	Dec. 21–in Aquarius		Aug. 13–in Leo
		Aug. 20–in Leo	Sept. 6–in Virgo
1996			Sept. 30–in Libra
Jan. 8–in Aquarius	Jan. 15–in Pisces	Oct. 7–in Virgo	Oct. 24–in Scorpio
	Feb. 9–in Aries		Nov. 17–in Sagittarius
Feb. 16–in Pisces	Mar. 6–in Taurus	Nov. 27–in Libra	Dec. 11–in Capricorn
Mar. 24–in Aries	Apr. 3–in Gemini		
May 2–in Taurus		**1999**	
June 12–in Gemini		Jan. 26–in Scorpio	Jan. 4–in Aquarius
July 25–in Cancer	Aug. 7–in Cancer		Jan. 28–in Pisces
	Sept. 7–in Leo		Feb. 21–in Aries
Sept. 9–in Leo	Oct. 4–in Virgo		Mar. 18–in Taurus
Oct. 30–in Virgo	Oct. 29–in Libra		Apr. 12–in Gemini
	Nov. 23–in Scorpio	May 5–in Libra	May 8–in Cancer
	Dec. 17–in Sagittarius		June 5–in Leo
		July 5–in Scorpio	July 12–in Virgo
			Aug. 15–in Leo
		Sept. 2–in Sagittarius	Oct. 7–in Virgo

Mars	Venus	Mars	Venus
1999		Aug. 29–in Virgo	Sept. 8–in Scorpio
Oct. 17–in Capricorn	Nov. 9–in Libra	Oct. 15–in Libra	
Nov. 26–in Aquarius	Dec. 5–in Scorpio	Dec. 1–in Scorpio	
	Dec. 31–in Sagittarius		
		2003	
2000		Jan. 17–in Sagittarius	Jan. 7–in Sagittarius
Jan. 4–in Pisces	Jan. 24–in Capricorn		Feb. 4–in Capricorn
Feb. 12–in Aries	Feb. 18–in Aquarius		Mar. 2–in Aquarius
	Mar. 13–in Pisces	Mar. 4–in Capricorn	Mar. 27–in Pisces
Mar. 23–in Taurus	Apr. 6–in Aries	Apr. 21–in Aquarius	Apr. 21–in Aries
	May 1–in Taurus		May 16–in Taurus
May 3–in Gemini	May 25–in Gemini		June 10–in Gemini
June 16–in Cancer	June 18–in Cancer	June 17–in Pisces	July 4–in Cancer
	July 13–in Leo		July 29–in Leo
Aug. 1–in Leo	Aug. 6–in Virgo		Aug. 22–in Virgo
	Aug. 31–in Libra		Sept. 15–in Libra
Sept. 17–in Virgo	Sept. 24–in Scorpio		Oct. 9–in Scorpio
	Oct. 19–in Sagittarius		Nov. 2–in Sagittarius
Nov. 4–in Libra	Nov. 13–in Capricorn		Nov. 27–in Capricorn
	Dec. 8–in Aquarius	Dec. 16–in Aries	Dec. 21–in Aquarius
Dec. 23–in Scorpio		**2004**	
2001		Feb. 3–in Taurus	Jan. 14–in Pisces
Feb. 14–in Sagittarius	Jan. 3–in Pisces		Feb. 8–in Aries
	Feb. 2–in Aries		Mar. 5–in Taurus
	June 6–in Taurus	Mar. 21–in Gemini	Apr. 3–in Gemini
	July 5–in Gemini	May 7–in Cancer	
	Aug. 1–in Cancer	June 23–in Leo	Aug. 7–in Cancer
	Aug. 27–in Leo	Aug. 10–in Virgo	Sept. 6–in Leo
Sept. 8–in Capricorn	Sept. 21–in Virgo	Sept. 26–in Libra	Oct. 3–in Virgo
	Oct. 15–in Libra		Oct. 29–in Libra
Oct. 27–in Aquarius	Nov. 8–in Scorpio	Nov. 11–in Scorpio	Nov. 22–in Scorpio
	Dec. 2–in Sagittarius		Dec. 16–in Sagittarius
Dec. 8–in Pisces	Dec. 26–in Capricorn	Dec. 25–in Sagittarius	
2002		**2005**	
Jan. 18–in Aries	Jan. 19–in Aquarius	Feb. 6–in Capricorn	Jan. 9–in Capricorn
	Feb. 12–in Pisces		Feb. 2–in Aquarius
Mar. 1–in Taurus	Mar. 8–in Aries		Feb. 26–in Pisces
	Apr. 1–in Taurus	Mar. 20–in Aquarius	Mar. 22–in Aries
Apr. 13–in Gemini	Apr. 25–in Gemini		Apr. 15–in Taurus
	May 20–in Cancer	May 1–in Pisces	May 10–in Gemini
May 28–in Cancer	June 14–in Leo		June 3–in Cancer
	July 10–in Virgo	June 11–in Aries	June 28–in Leo
July 13–in Leo	Aug. 7–in Libra		July 23–in Virgo

Mars	Venus	Mars	Venus
2005		July 1–in Virgo	July 12–in Leo
July 28–in Taurus	Aug. 17–in Libra		Aug. 6–in Virgo
	Sept. 11–in Scorpio	Aug. 19–in Libra	Aug. 29–in Libra
	Oct. 8–in Sagittarius		Sept. 24–in Scorpio
	Nov. 5–in Capricorn	Oct. 4–in Scorpio	Oct. 18–in Sagittarius
	Dec. 15–in Aquarius		Nov. 12–in Capricorn
		Nov. 16–in Sagittarius	Dec. 7–in Aquarius
2006		Dec. 27–in Capricorn	
Feb. 17–in Gemini	Jan. 1–in Capricorn		
	Mar. 5–in Aquarius	**2009**	
	Apr. 6–in Pisces	Feb. 4–in Aquarius	Jan. 3–in Pisces
Apr. 14–in Cancer	May 3–in Aries		Feb. 3–in Aries
	May 29–in Taurus	Mar. 15–in Pisces	Apr. 11–in Pisces
June 3–in Leo	June 24–in Gemini	Apr. 22–in Aries	Apr. 24–in Aries
	July 19–in Cancer	May 31–in Taurus	June 6–in Taurus
July 22–in Virgo	Aug. 12–in Leo		July 5–in Gemini
	Sept. 6–in Virgo	July 12–in Gemini	Aug. 1–in Cancer
Sept. 8–in Libra		Aug. 25–in Cancer	Aug. 26–in Leo
Oct. 23–in Scorpio	Oct. 24–in Scorpio		Sept. 20–in Virgo
	Nov. 17–in Sagittarius		Oct. 14–in Libra
Dec. 6–in Sagittarius	Dec. 11–in Capricorn		
		Oct. 16–in Leo	Nov. 8–in Scorpio
2007			Dec. 1–in Sagittarius
Jan. 16–in Capricorn	Jan. 4–in Aquarius		Dec. 25–in Capricorn
	Jan. 28–in Pisces		
	Feb. 21–in Aries	**2010**	
Feb. 25–in Aquarius	Mar. 17–in Taurus		Jan. 18–in Aquarius
Apr. 6–in Pisces	Apr. 12–in Gemini		Feb. 11–in Pisces
	May 8–in Cancer		Mar. 7–in Aries
May 15–in Aries	June 5–in Leo		Mar. 31–in Taurus
June 24–in Taurus	July 14–in Virgo		Apr. 25–in Gemini
Aug. 7–in Gemini	Aug. 9–in Leo		May 20–in Cancer
Sept. 29–in Cancer	Oct. 8–in Virgo	June 7–in Virgo	June 14–in Leo
	Nov. 8–in Libra		July 10–in Virgo
	Dec. 5–in Scorpio	July 29–in Libra	Aug. 7–in Libra
Dec. 31–in Gemini	Dec. 30–in Sagittarius		Sept. 8–in Scorpio
		Sept. 14–in Scorpio	
2008		Oct. 28–in Sagittarius	Nov. 8–in Libra
Mar. 4–in Cancer	Jan. 24–in Capricorn		Nov. 30–in Scorpio
	Feb. 17–in Aquarius	Dec. 8–in Capricorn	
	Mar. 12–in Pisces		
	Apr. 6–in Aries		
	Apr. 30–in Taurus		
May 9–in Leo	May 24–in Gemini		
	June 18–in Cancer		

Bibliography

Akbar, M. J. *Nehru: the Making of India*. New York, Viking, 1988.

Ackroyd, Peter. *Dickens*. New York: HarperCollins, 1990.

Ahern, Brian. *A Dreadful Man*. New York: Simon & Schuster, 1979.

Alpers, Antony. *The Life of Katherine Mansfield*. New York: Viking Press, 1980.

Alpert, Hollis. *Fellini: A Life*. New York: Atheneum, 1986.

Amburn, Ellis. *Pearl: The Obsessions and Passions of Janis Joplin: A Biorgraphy*. New York: Warner Books, 1992.

Anderson, Wayne, with Barbara Klein. *Gauguin's Paradise Lost*. New York: Viking Press, 1971.

Bair, Deirdre. *Anaïs Nin: A Biography*. New York: Putnam's Sons, 1995.

Barry, Joseph. *Infamous Woman: The Life of George Sand*. New York: Doubleday, 1976.

Batty, Peter. *The House of Krupp*. New York: Stein & Day, 1966.

Bedford, Sybille. *Aldous Huxley: A Biography*. New York: Knopf, 1974.

Benfey, Christopher. *The Double Life of Stephen Crane*. New York: Knopf, 1992.

Bergreen, Laurence. *James Agee: A Life*. New York: E. P. Dutton, 1984.

Bertin, Celia. *Marie Bonaparte: A Life*. New York: Harcourt Brace Jovanovich, 1982.

Binion, Rudolph. *Frau Lou: Nietzche's Wayward Disciple.* Princeton, N.J.: Princeton University Press, 1968.

Block, Maxine editor, "Pavel Tchelitchew." *Current Biography: Who's News and Why, 1943.* New York: The H. W. Wilson Co., 1942.

Boone, Debby, with Dennis Baker. *Debby Boone, So Far.* Nashville: Thomas Nelson Publishers, 1981.

Booth, Stanley. *Keith: Standing in the Shadows.* New York: St. Martin's Press, 1995.

Bosworth, Patricia. *Diane Arbus: A Biography.* New York: Knopf, 1984.

Bradshaw, Jon. *Dreams That Money Can Buy: The Tragic Life of Libby Holman.* New York: Morrow, 1985.

Bradford, Sarah. *Disraeli.* New York: Stein & Day, 1982.

Brady, Frank. *Hefner.* New York: Macmillan, 1974.

Branden, Barbara. *The Passion of Ayn Rand.* New York: Doubleday, 1986.

Broeske, Pat H. "A Comeback? Just Say Bo." *Entertainment Weekly* (July 9, 1993).

Brower, Monty, "A Bareback '10' Rides Again." *People Weekly* vol. 21, no. 8 (February 27, 1984): 21–23.

Brown, Judith M. *Gandhi: Prisoner of Hope.* New Haven: Yale University Press, 1989.

Bugliosi, Vincent and Curt Gentry. *Helter Skelter, The True Story of the Manson Murders.* New York: W. W. Norton and Co. Inc., 1974.

Callow, Simon. *Charles Laughton: A Difficult Actor.* New York: Grove Press, 1987.

Carpenter, Margaret Haley. *Sara Teasdale: A Biography.* Norfolk, Virginia: Pentelic Press, 1979.

Celebrity Birthday Guide. Ann Arbor, Michigan: Axiom Information Resources, 1997.

Chandler, Charlotte. *I, Fellini.* New York: Random House, 1995.

Chester, Ellen. *Margaret Sanger: Woman of Valor.* New York: Doubleday: Anchor Books, 1992.

Chidley, Joe. "Hef at Home: The Suavest Bachelor Turns Family Man." *MacLeans* vol. 107, no. 3 (August 15, 1994): 40–41.

Chrisholm, Anne. *Nancy Cunard: A Biography.* New York: Knopf, 1979.

Clarke, Gerald. *Capote: A Biography.* New York: Simon & Schuster, 1988.

Cleugh, James. *The First Masochist: A Biography of Leopold von Sacher-Masoch.* New York: Stein & Day, 1967.

Collier, James Lincoln. *Benny Goodman and the Swing Era.* New York: Oxford University Press, 1989.

Comini, Alessandra. *Egon Schiele's Portraits.* Berkeley: University of California Press, 1974.

Cowie, Peter. *Ingmar Bergman: A Critical Biography*. New York: Charles Scribner's Sons, 1982.

Crocker, Lester G. *Jean-Jacques Rousseau: The Quest (1712–1758)* and *Jean-Jacques Rousseau: The Prophetic Voice (1758–1778)*. London: Collier-Macmillan, 1973.

Crosby, David, with Carl Gottlieb. *Long Time Gone: The Autobiography of David Crosby*. New York: Doubleday, 1988.

Crosland, Margaret. *Piaf*. New York: Putnam's Sons, 1985.

Daly, Gay. *Pre-Raphaelites in Love*. New York: Ticknor & Fields, 1989.

Davidson, Bill. *Spencer Tracy: Tragic Idol*. New York: E. P. Dutton, 1987.

De Courcel, Martine. *Tolstoy: The Ultimate Reconciliation*. Translated by Peter Levi. New York: Charles Scribner's Sons, 1988.

de Jonge, Alex. *Baudelaire: Prince of Clouds*. New York: Paddington Press, 1976.

Demaris, Ovid. *The Director: An Oral Biography of J. Edgar Hoover*. New York: Harper's Magazine Press, 1975.

DeSalvo, Louise. *Virginia Woolf: The Impact of Childhood Sexual Abuse on Her Life and Work*. Boston: Beacon Press, 1989.

Di San Lazzaro, G. *Klee: A Study of His Life and Work*. Translated by Stuart Hood. New York: Praeger Pubs., 1957.

Drake, William. *Sara Teasdale: Woman & Poet*. New York: Harper and Row Publishers, 1977.

Du Cann, Charles Garfield Lott. *The Loves of George Bernard Shaw*. New York: Funk and Wagnalls Co. Inc. 1963.

Dunaway, David King. *Huxley in Hollywood*. New York: Harper & Row, 1989.

Eells, George, and Stanley Musgrove. *Mae West, A Biography*. New York: Morrow, 1982.

Ellison, Katherine. *Imelda: Steel Butterfly of the Phillippines*. New York: McGraw-Hill Book Co., 1988.

Ellmann, Richard. *James Joyce: New and Revised Edition*. New York: Oxford University Press, 1982.

———. *Oscar Wilde*. New York: Alfred A. Knopf, 1988.

Erickson, Carolly. *Great Harry: The Extravagant Life of Henry VIII*. New York: Summit Books, 1980.

Eyman, Scott. *Mary Pickford: America's Sweetheart*. New York: Donald I. Fine, Inc. 1990.

Feaver, William. "Francis Bacon: An Old Master of the Elusive." *Art News* vol. 91, no. 6 (Summer 1992): 48–50.

Ferguson, Robert. *Henry Miller: A Life*. New York: W. W. Norton, 1991.

Fermigier, Andre. *Toulouse-Lautrec*. Translated by Paul Stevenson. New York: Praeger Pubs., 1969.

Field, Andrew. *VN: The Life and Art of Vladimir Nabokov*. New York: Crown, 1972.

Finney, Brian. *Christopher Isherwood: A Critical Biography*. New York: Oxford University Press, 1979.

Firestone, Ross. *Swing, Swing, Swing: The Life and Times of Benny Goodman*. New York: W. W. Norton, 1993.

Flowers, Gennifer, and Jacquelyn Dapper. *Gennifer Flowers: Passion and Betrayal*. Del Mar, California: Emery Dalton Books, 1995.

Forster, Margaret. *Memoirs of a Victorian Gentleman: William Makepeace Thackeray*. New York: Morrow, 1979.

Francis, Claude, and Fernande Gontier. *Simone de Beauvoir: A Life . . . A Love Story*. Translated by Lis Nesselson. New York: St. Martin's Press, 1987.

Fraser, Nicholas, Philip Jacobson, and Mark Ottaway. *Aristotle Onassis*. Philadelphia: Lippincott, 1977.

Freedman, Ralph. *Life of a Poet: Rainer Maria Rilke*. New York: Farrar, Straus & Giroux, 1996.

Frey, Julia. *Toulouse-Lautrec: A Life*. New York: Viking Press, 1994.

Friedenthal, Richard. *Goethe: His Life and Times*. Cleveland: World Publishing, 1963.

Frischauer, Willi. *The Aga Khans*. New York: Hawthorne Books, 1971.

Fritscher, Jack. *Mapplethorpe: Assault with a Deadly Camera*. Mamaroneck, N.Y.: Hastings House, 1994.

Fuller, Jean Overton. *Swinburne: A Critical Biography*. New York: Schocken Books, 1971.

Funicello, Annette, with Patricia Romanowski. *A Dream Is a Wish Your Heart Makes: My Story*. New York: Hyperion, 1994.

Fusero, Clemente. *The Borgias*. Translated by Peter Green. New York: Praeger Pubs., 1972.

Gado, Frank. *The Passion of Ingmar Bergman*. Durham: Duke University Press, 1986.

Gattegno, Jean. *Fragments of a Looking-Glass*. Translated by Rosemary Sheed and Lewis Carrol. New York: Thomas Y. Crowell Co. 1974.

Gay, Peter. *Freud: A Life for Our Time*. New York: W. W. Norton, 1988.

Gerson, Noel Bertram. *The Prodigal Genius: The Life and Times of Honoré de Balzac*. New York: Doubleday, 1972.

Gittelson, Natalie. "Bo Derek: The Even '10' Takes an Odd Turn." *McCalls* vol. 108, no. 4 (January 1981): 96, 133–135.

Givner, Joan. *Katherine Anne Porter: A Life*. New York: Simon & Schuster, 1982.

Glendinning, Victoria. *Edith Sitwell: A Unicorn Among Lions*. New York: Knopf, 1981.

———. *Rebecca West: A Life*. New York: Knopf, 1987.

———. *Vita: The Life of V. Sackville-West.* New York: Knopf, 1983.

Golden, Eve. *Platinum Girl: The Life and Legends of Jean Harlow.* New York: Abbeville Press, 1991.

Goldman, Albert Harry. *Elvis.* New York: Macgraw-Hill, 1981.

———. *The Lives of John Lennon.* New York: Morrow, 1988.

Goldstein, Malcolm. *George S. Kaufman: His Life, His Theater.* New York: Oxford University Press, 1979.

Gollis, John Stewart. *Havelock Ellis: An Artist of Life: A Study of the Life and Work of Havelock Ellis.* New York: William Sloane, 1959.

Graham, Judith. *Current Biography Yearbook, 1996.* New York: H.W. Wilson 1996.

Grey, Rudoph. *Nightmare of Ecstasy: The Life of Edward D. Wood, Jr.* Los Angeles: Feral House, 1992.

Grunfeld, Frederic V. *Rodin: A Biography.* New York: Henry Holt & Co., 1987.

Guest, Barbara. *Herself Defined: the Poet H. D. and her World.* Garden City, New York: Doubleday and Co. Inc., 1984.

Hahn, Emily. *Mabel: A Biography of Mabel Dodge Luhan.* Boston: Houghton Mifflin, 1971.

Hall, Lee. *Elaine and Bill: Portrait of a Marriage: The Lives of Willem and Elaine de Kooning.* New York: HarperCollins, 1993.

Hall, N. John. *Trollope: A Biography.* Oxford: Clarendon Press, 1991.

Hamilton, Marybeth. *"When I'm Bad, I'm Better": Mae West, Sex and American Popular Entertainment.* New York: HarperCollins, 1995.

Haney, Lynn. *Naked at the Feast: A Biography of Josephine Baker.* New York: Dodd, Mead & Co., 1981.

Hanson, Lawrence, and Elisabeth Hanson. *Noble Savage: The Life of Paul Gauguin.* New York: Random House, 1954.

Heiberg, Hans. *Ibsen: A Portrait of the Artist.* Translated by Joan Tate. Coral Gables, Fla.: University of Miami Press, 1967.

Herrera, Hayden. *Frida: A Biography of Frida Kahlo.* New York: Harper and Row, 1983.

Herring, Phillip. *Djuna: The Life and Work of Djuna Barnes.* New York: Viking Press, 1995.

Higham, Charles. *The Duchess of Windsor: The Secret Life.* New York: McGraw-Hill, 1988.

Hodin, J. P. *OK: Oskar Kokoschka, The Artist and His Time: A Biographical Study.* Greenwich, Conn.: New York Graphic Society, 1966.

Hofman, Paul. *The Viennese: Splendor, Twilight and Exile.* New York: Anchor Press, 1988.

Hogrefe, Jeffrey. *O'Keeffe: The Life of an American Legend*. New York: Bantam Books, 1992.

Holloway, Mark. *Norman Douglas: A Biography*. London: Secker & Warburg, 1976.

Hooks, Margaret. *Tina Modotti: Photographer and Revolutionary*. New York: HarperCollins, 1993.

Howe, Russell Warren. *Mata Hari: The True Story*. New York: Dodd, Mead & Co., 1986.

Hubner, John. *Bottom Feeders: From Love to Hard Core, The Rise and Fall of Counterculture Gurus Jim and Artie Mitchell*. New York: Doubleday, 1992.

Hunt, John Dixon, *The Wider Sea: A Life of John Ruskin*. New York: Viking Press, 1982.

Irving, David. *Goring: A Biography*. New York: Morrow, 1989.

Jackson, Stanley. *Caruso*. New York: Stein & Day, 1972.

James, Lawrence. *The Golden Warrior: The Life and Legend of Lawrence of Arabia*. New York: Paragon House, 1993.

Jullian, Philippe, and John Phillips. *The Other Woman: The Life of Violet Trefusis*. Boston, Massachusetts: Houghton Mifflin Co., 1976.

Katz, Ephraim. *The Film Encyclopedia*. New York: Harper Collins, 1994.

Keegan, Susanne. *Bride of the Wind: The Life and Times of Alma Mahler-Werfel*. New York: Viking Penguin, 1991.

Kennedy, Richard S. *Dreams in the Mirror: A Biography of e. e. cummings*. New York: Liveright Publishing, 1979.

Kirstein, Lincoln. *Paul Cadmus*. New York: Chameleon Books, Imago Imprint, 1984.

Kitchen, Paddy. *Gerard Manley Hopkins*. New York: Atheneum, 1979.

Klee, Felix, ed. *The Diaries of Paul Klee 1898–1918*. Berkeley: University of California Press, 1964.

Klevar, Harvey L. *Erskine Caldwell: A Biography*. Knoxville: University of Tennessee Press, 1993.

Lacey, Robert. *Grace*. New York: Putnam's Sons, 1994.

Leamer, Laurence. *As Time Goes By: The Life of Ingrid Bergman*. London: Hamish Hamilton, 1986.

Leaming, Barbara. *If This Was Happiness:. A Biography of Rita Hayworth*. New York: Viking Press, 1989.

Leeming, David. *James Baldwin: A Biography*. New York: Knopf, 1994.

Lever, Maurice. *Sade: A Biography*. Translated by Arthur Goldhammer. New York: Farrar, 1993.

Lewis, Richard Warrington Baldwin. *Edith Wharton: A Biography*. New York: Harper & Row, 1975.

Lindsay, Jack. *William Morris: His Life and Work*. New York: Taplinger, 1975.

Lovell, Mary. *Cast No Shadow: The Life of Betty Pack, The American Spy Who Changed the Course of World War II.* New York: Pantheon, 1992.

Lucas, Robert. *Frieda Lawrence: The Story of Frieda von Richthofen and D. H. Lawrence.* Translated by Geoffrey Skelton. New York: Viking Press, 1973.

Lyons, Arthur. *Satan Wants You: The Cult of Devil Worship in America.* New York: Mysterious Press, 1988.

MacCarthy, Fiona. *Eric Gill: A Lover's Quest for Art and God.* New York: William Abrahams Books, E. P. Dutton, 1989.

MacKenzie, Norman, and Jeanne MacKenzie. *Dickens: A Life.* New York: Oxford University Press, 1979.

Maddox, Brenda. *Nora: The Real Life of Molly Bloom.* Boston: Houghton Miffflin Co., 1988.

McCumber, David. *X-Rated: The Mitchell Brothers: A True Story of Sex, Money, and Death.* New York: Simon & Schuster, 1992.

McGuigan, C. "The Making of a Goddess." *Newsweek* vol. 94, no. 24 (December 10, 1979): 139.

Maddox, Brenda. *D. H. Lawrence: The Story of a Marriage.* New York: Simon & Schuster, 1994.

Manchester, William. *The Arms of Krupp, 1587–1968.* Boston: Little, Brown & Co., 1968.

Manvell, Roger. *Chaplin.* Boston: Little, Brown and Co., 1974.

Martin, Ralph G. *Golda Meir: The Romantic Years.* New York: Charles Scribner's Sons, 1988.

Masters, John. *Casanova.* New York: Bernard Geis, 1969.

Masters, William H., and Virginia E. Johnson. *Human Sexual Response.* Boston: Little, Brown & Co., 1966.

Maurois, Andre. *Byron.* New York: D. Appleton & Co., 1957.

Mellen, Joan. *Hellman and Hammett: The Legendary Passion of Lillian Hellman and Dashiell Hammett.* New York: HarperCollins, 1996.

Meredith, Scott. *George S. Kaufman and His Friends.* New York: Doubleday, 1974.

Meissner, Hans Otto. *Magda Goebbels: The First Lady of the Third Reich.* New York: Dial Press, 1980.

Meyers, Jeffery. *Scott Fitzgerald, A Biography.* New York: HarperCollins, 1994.

Milford, Nancy. *Zelda: A Biography.* New York: Harper & Row, 1970.

Milton, Joyce. *Tramp: The Life of Charlie Chaplin.* New York: HarperCollins, 1996.

Mondadori, Arnoldo. *The Life, Times and Art of Rembrandt.* New York: Crescent Books, 1977.

Monsarrat, Ann. *An Uneasy Victorian: Thackeray the Man: 1811-1863*. New York: Dodd, Mead and Co., 1980.

Morgan, Ted. *Literary Outlaw, The Life and Times of William S. Burroughs*. New York: Avon Books, 1988.

Moritz, Charles, ed. "William H. Masters." In *Current Biography Yearbook 1968*. New York: H. W. Wilson, 1968.

———. "O. J. Simpson." *Current Biography Yearbook 1969*. New York: H.W. Wilson. 1968.

Morris, Michael. *Madam Valentino: The Many Lives of Natacha Rambova*. New York: Abbeville Press, 1991.

Morrisroe, Patricia. *Mapplethorpe: A Biography*. New York: Random House, 1995.

Mosley, Nicholas. *Rules of the Game/Beyond the Pale: Memoirs of Sir Oswald Mosley and Family*. Elmwood Park, Ill.: Dalkey Archive Press, 1991.

Muggeridge, Kitty, and Ruth Adam. *Beatrice Webb: A Life, 1858-1943*. New York: Alfred A. Knopf, 1968.

Naifeh, Steven, and Gregory White Smith. *Jackson Pollock: An American Saga*. New York: Clarkston N. Potter, 1989.

Navratilova, Martina, with George Vecsey. *Martina*. New York: Knopf, 1985.

Nemser, Cindy. "Alice Neel: Teller of Truth." In *Alice Neel: The Woman and Her Work, Sept. 7–Oct 19, 1975*. Athens: Georgia Museum of Art, University of Georgia, 1975.

Nicolson, Nigel. *Portrait of a Marriage*. New York: Atheneum, 1987.

Painter, George D. *Andre Gide: A Critical Biography*. New York: Atheneum, 1968.

Paris, Barry. *Garbo: A Biography*. New York: Knopf, 1995.

Parker, John. *King of Fools*. New York: St. Martin's Press, 1988.

Pawel, Ernst. *The Nightmare of Reason: A Life of Franz Kafka*. New York: Random House, Vintage Books, 1985.

Peters, Margot. *Bernard Shaw and the Actresses*. New York.: Doubleday, 1980.

Pierson, Ransdell. *The Queen of Mean: The Unauthorized Biography of Leona Helmsley*: New York: Bantam, 1989.

Powers, Richard Gid. *Secrecy and Power: The Life of J. Edgar Hoover*. New York: Free Press, 1987.

Prater, Donald. *A Ringing Glass: The Life of Rainer Maria Rilke*. Oxford: Clarendon Press, 1986.

Priminger, Frank Lee. *Gypsy & Me: At Home and on the Road with Gypsy Rose Lee*. Boston: Little, Brown & Co., 1984.

Quinn, Edward, ed. *Max Ernst*. Translated by Kenneth Lyons. Boston: New York Graphic Society, 1976.

Reed, Susan, Ann Maier, and Vickie Bane. "Love Match No More." *People Weekly* vol. 35, no. 26 (July 8, 1991): 28–31.

Reich, Ilse Ollendorff. *Wilhelm Reich: A Personal Biography.* New York: St. Martinís Press, 1969.

Robinson, Roxanna. *Georgia O'Keeffe: A Life.* New York: Harper and Row Publishers, 1989.

Rodden, Lois. "Chart of People in the News: The Roles We Play." *The Mountain Astrologer* vol. 10, No 1 (April–May 1997): 48.

———. *The American Book of Charts.* San Diego: Astro Computing Services, 1980.

Rose, June. *Modigliani; The Pure Bohemian.* New York: St. Martin's Press, 1991.

Safra, Jacob. *The New Encyclopaedia Brittannica.* Chicago: 1997.

Salisbury, Harrison E. *The New Emperors: China in the Era of Mao and Deng.* Boston: Little, Brown & Co., 1992.

Saxton, Martha. *Jayne Mansfield and the American Fifties.* Boston: Houghton Mifflin, 1975.

Schmidt, Margaret Fox. *Passion's Child: The Extraordinary Life of Jane Digby.* New York: Harper & Row, 1976.

Schneider, Il'ia Il'ich. *Isadora Duncan: The Russian Years.* New York: Harcourt, Brace & World, 1969.

Schopp, Claude. *Alexandre Dumas: Genius of Life.* Tranlated by A. J. Koch. New York: Franklin Watts, 1988.

Schorer, Mark. *Sinclair Lewis: An American Life.* New York: McGraw-Hill, 1961.

Seaman, Barbara. *Lovely Me: The Life of Jacqueline Susann.* New York: Morrow, 1987.

Seroff, Victor Ilyitch. *The Real Isadora.* London: Dial Press, 1971.

Seymour, Miranda. *Ottoline Morrell: Life on the Grand Scale.* New York: Farrar, Straus & Giroux, 1992.

Shelton, Suzanne. *Divine Dancer: A Biography of Ruth St. Denis.* New York: Doubleday, 1981.

Shipman, David. *Judy Garland: The Secret Life of an American Legend.* New York: Hyperion, 1993.

Shirer, William L. *Love and Hatred: The Troubled Marriage of Leo and Sonya Tolstoy.* New York: Simon & Schuster, 1994.

Shulman, Irving. *Valentino.* New York: Trident Press, 1967.

Sinclair, Andrew. *Francis Bacon: His Life and Violent Times.* New York: Crown Publishing, 1993.

Skelton, Geoffrey. *Richard and Cosima Wagner: Biography of a Marriage.* Boston: Houghton Mifflin, 1982.

Slater, Robert. *Golda: The Uncrowned Queen of Israel, A Pictorial Biography.* New York: Jonathan David, 1981.

Smith, David C. *H. G. Wells: Desperately Mortal.* New Haven: Yale University Press, 1986.

Sokoloff, Alice. *Cosima Wagner: Extraordinary Daughter of Franz Liszt.* New York: Dodd, Mead & Co., 1969.

Spoto, Donald. *Lenya: A Life.* Boston: Little, Brown & Co., 1989.

———. *Marilyn Monroe: The Biography.* New York: HarperCollins, 1993.

———. *The Kindness of Strangers, The Life of Tennessee Williams.* Boston: Little, Brown & Co., 1985.

Stassinopoulos, Arianna. *Maria Callas: The Woman Behind the Legend.* New York: Simon & Schuster, 1981.

Steegmuller, Francis. *Cocteau: A Biography.* Boston: Little, Brown & Co., Atlantic Monthly Press Book, 1970.

Stenn, David. *Bombshell: The Life and Death of Jean Harlow.* New York: Doubleday, 1993.

Stirling, Monica. *The Wild Swan: The Life and Times of Hans Christian Andersen.* New York: Harcourt, Brace & World, 1965.

Summers, Anthony. *Official and Confidential: The Secret Life of J. Edgar Hoover.* New York: Putnam's Sons, 1993.

Swindell, Larry. *The Last Hero: A Biography of Gary Cooper.* New York: Doubleday, 1980.

———. *Spencer Tracy: A Biography.* New York: World Publishing, NAL Book, 1969.

Symonds, John. *The Great Beast: The Life of Aleister Crowley.* London: Rider & Co., 1951.

Talese, Gay. *Thy Neighbor's Wife.* New York: Doubleday, 1980.

Tarriktar, Tem, Maya del Mar, Bruce Scofield, and David Solte. "Bill Clinton's Tangled Web." *The Mountain Astrologer* no. 78, (April–May 1998): 12.

Terrill, Ross. *Mao: A Biography.* New York: Harper & Row, 1980.

Thomas, Bob. *Golden Boy: The Untold Story of William Holden.* New York: St. Martin's Press, 1983.

———. *Liberace: The True Story.* New York: St. Martin's Press, 1988.

Thomas, Robert David. *With Bleeding Footsteps: Mary Baker Eddy's Path to Religious Leadership.* New York: Knopf, 1994.

Thorson, Scott, with Alex Thorleifson. *Behind the Candelabra: My Life with Liberace.* New York: E. P. Dutton, 1988.

Todd, Michael. *A Valuable Property: The Life Story of Michael Todd.* New York: Arbor House, 1983.

Tomalin, Claire. *Katherine Mansfield: A Secret Life.* New York: Knopf, 1988.

Tornabene, Lyn. *Long Live the King: A Biography of Clark Gable.* New York: Putnam's Sons, 1976.

Van Abbe, Derek Maurice. *Goethe: New Perspectives on a Writer and His Time.* London: Allen & Unwin, 1972.

VanDerBeets, Richard. *George Sanders: An Exhausted Life.* New York: Madison Books, 1990.

Vickers, Hugo. *Loving Garbo: The Story of Greta Garbo, Cecil Beaton and Mercedes de Acosta.* New York: Random House, 1994.

Wallace, Irving, Amy Wallace, David Wallechinsky, and Sylvia Wallace. *The Intimate Sex Lives of Famous People.* New York: Delacorte Press, 1981.

Walling, William A. *Mary Shelley.* New York: Twayne Publisher Inc., 1972.

Wayne, Jane Ellen. *Cooper's Women.* New York: Prentice Hall Press, 1988.

Wayne, Pilar, with Alex Thorleifson. *John Wayne: My Life with the Duke.* New York: McGraw-Hill, 1987.

Weaver, William. *Duse: A Biography.* San Diego: Harcourt Brace Jovanovich, 1984.

Weinberg, Jonathan. "Cruising with Paul Cadmus." *Art in America* vol. 80, no. 11 (November 1992): 102–108.

Weisstein, Ulrich. *Gerhart Hauptman.* New Haven: Yale University Press, 1954.

Weld, Jacqueline Bograd. *Peggy: the Wayward Guggenheim.* New York: E. P. Dutton, 1986.

Weller, Sheila. *Raging Heart: The Intimate Story of the Tragic Marriage of O. J. Simpson and Nicole Brown Simpson.* New York: Pocket Books, 1995.

Whitford, Frank. *Egon Schiele.* New York: Oxford University Press, 1981.

———. *Oskar Kokoschka: A Life.* New York: Atheneum, 1986.

Wilson, Colin. *The Misfits: A Study of Sexual Outsiders.* New York: Carroll & Graf, 1988.

Winegarten, Renee. *The Double Life of George Sand: Woman and Writer: A Critical Biography.* New York: Basic Books, 1978.

Winwar, Frances. *Wingless Victory: A Biography of Gabriele d'Annunzio and Eleonora Duse.* New York: Harper & Brothers, 1956.

Woodress, James Leslie. *Willa Cather: A Literary Life.* Lincoln: University of Nebraska Press, 1987.

Wright, William. *All the Pain That Money Can Buy: The Life of Cristina Onassis.* New York: Simon & Schuster, 1991.

———. *Lillian Hellman: The Image, the Woman.* New York: Simon & Schuster, 1986.

Zamoyski, Adam. *Paderewski.* New York: Atheneum, 1982.

Zehme, Bill. "The Man Who Loved Women." *Esquire* vol. 30, no. 2 (August 1998): 58.

Zeigler, Philip. *King Edward VIII: A Biography.* New York: Knopf, 1991.

Zolotow, Maurice. *Shooting Star: A Biography of John Wayne.* New York: Simon & Schuster, 1974.

Index